DATE DUE

DE 23 '94			
86. 8			

A World Fit for People

A World Fit for People

Edited by
Üner Kırdar and Leonard Silk

Thinkers from many countries address the political,
economic, and social problems of our time.

NEW YORK UNIVERSITY PRESS
New York and London

Copyright ©UNDP 1994
All rights reserved
Manufactured in the United States of America

Library of Congress Cataloging-in-Publication Data

A World fit for people : thinkers from many countries address the
  political, economic, and social problems of our time —/ Üner Kırdar
  and Leonard Silk.
     p. cm.
  "United Nations Development Programme Publications, UN sales no.
  E.93.III.B.2"—T.p. verso.
   ISBN 0-8147-4648-9
   1. Democracy. 2. Economic development. 3. Environmental policy.
  4. Social problems. I. Kırdar, Üner, 1933   . II. Silk, Leonard
  Solomon, 1918-
  JC423.W64 1993
  909.82'9—dc20   93-8945
                                                                CIP

The content of this book does not necessarily reflect the views of the United Nations
Development Programme. The papers in this volume were contributed by the authors in
their personal capacities and they are solely responsible for their views.

New York University Press books are printed on acid-free paper,
and their binding materials are chosen for their strength and durability.

This book is dedicated to the memory of three eminent contributors, G. Arthur Brown, Saburo Okita, and Turgut Özal, all of whom passed away during the editing and printing period. Throughout their lives, each of them was committed to improving the human condition, and also served the international community as true global citizens.

Contents

Foreword

The end of the Cold War and the collapse of bipolarity have transformed the international scene. Ideological barriers have come down, and the risk of nuclear conflagration has greatly diminished. These are remarkable developments, and there is a sense that this is a time of promise and hope in international relations. There are great opportunities for a new start in international cooperation. For the first time since the United Nations Charter was signed nearly half a century ago, the UN has the potential to become what it was always intended to be: an instrument designed to maintain international peace and security, to advance justice and human rights, and to achieve "social progress and better standards of life in larger freedom."

Alongside these aspirations for a better world, and the clear prospect of a hitherto unimagined unanimity among states about the way forward in international relations, we must set the magnitude of the tasks faced by the international community. Enormous tasks of economic restructuring and political institution-building face the newly independent states of the former Soviet Union. Many developing countries in Africa, Asia, and Latin America face huge difficulties as they struggle to provide decent standards of living for their people. Hunger, malnutrition, disease, homelessness, and illiteracy affect millions; pressure on resources—including natural resources such as land and water—is causing environmental degradation in many parts of the world. The burden of debt, and low export earnings caused in part by a sluggish international economy, inhibit remedial action by member states. In many developing countries, as well as in the countries in transition, investment levels are disappointing.

To move forward to tackle these issues will require a new, integrated approach. The promotion of peace and security, of economic and social development, and of democracy, are now seen as one and the same. The ending of the Cold War has revealed the indivisibility of the tasks of the UN.

Some of the tasks are organizational; some involve attitudes and policies. I am already pursuing a restructuring of the UN machinery in the economic and social sector. But a new, integrated approach of peace, development, human rights, and democracy requires a profound rethinking of many conventional ways of looking at these issues. It requires detailed study and reflection.

A World Fit for People contains contributions by more than 50 global thinkers on some of the most important issues of our time. There is a great deal of food for thought in this volume. It will provide a stimulating source of ideas and analysis on current trends in international political, social, and economic life. Studies of this type are an indispensable prerequisite if we are to rise to the conceptual and political challenges the world now faces. The UNDP Development Study Programme is to be congratulated on this initiative.

August 1993

Boutros Boutros-Ghali
Secretary-General
United Nations

Introduction

The world is now passing through an era of shocks and transformations that are unprecedented in the opportunities and risks they present. At the end of the 1980s, the easing of East-West tensions and the end of the Cold War hastened the collapse of totalitarian regimes and the demise of ideological rivalries in many parts of the world. This historic phenomenon has promoted political democracy, market forces, and private enterprises as the fundamental institutions likely to shape the world's development in the 1990s and the century to come. These changes have opened new horizons for people to achieve their aspirations for a better life, free from tyranny and oppression.

Unfortunately, however, the people striving to build a new and freer way of life, whether in East or Central Europe, the former Soviet Union, or parts of Asia and Africa, are facing enormous hardships and mounting disappointments. For many, living standards are falling, jobs have been wiped out, hunger and starvation are widespread, and violence and threats of even greater violence are on the rise. Radical nationalism, religious and ethnic separatism, autocracy, corruption, and genocidal tyranny have turned newborn hope into fear. The United Nations already has a long agenda of peacekeeping and peacemaking assignments, from the Balkans to Somalia, from Cambodia to Cyprus, from Iraq to Kuwait to Angola and El Salvador. Other countries and regions confronted by nationalist or ethnic violence, anarchy, and starvation may get onto the UN agenda in the years ahead.

Economic breakdown and the heritage of totalitarian rule exacerbate all these problems and more. The worst environmental degradation in the world has been found in those countries where dictatorial governments suppressed freedom of speech, and (a controlled) press failed to deal with threats of nuclear, chemical and other industrial pollution. Nowadays, in the midst of the difficulties faced by Russia and the other transition countries, some politicians and political theorists argue that the development of a market economy is inconsistent with democracy, at least in its early stages. But one must be wary of seeking to separate economic from political freedom. The crimes against humanity, the genocide and mass starvation of the twentieth century, stemmed from totalitarianism. In our view, political and economic freedom are indivisible. Democracy and political stability cannot be ensured without economic and social progress. There cannot be development without democracy, nor can there be democracy without development.

The revolutions in Eastern Europe and the former Soviet Union were triggered by economic failures and aggravated by the arms race with the West, but they gained irresistible strength from national and popular demands for personal freedoms and democratic rights. The new nations of Eastern and Central Europe and the Commonwealth of Independent States will be gravely weakened if their governing systems have dubious legitimacy; and if their economies fail, dangers will grow that democracy will perish—and the threat of war will increase.

Likewise, in parts of Asia and Africa, economies may fail and famines and warfare erupt or worsen, as a consequence of dictatorial or corrupt governments, anarchy, or warlord rivalry. The members of the United Nations cannot turn aside from such threats to humanity; peacekeeping must clear the way for peacebuilding, which will involve economic, social, and political reconstruction. In the absence of responsible and competent national government, international peacekeeping and peacemaking efforts will be crucial to prevent new tragedies.

In 1992, the presidential election campaign in the United States promoted liberal use of the word "change" and the need for change gained key importance and prominence in that country's domestic politics. In an increasingly inter-dependent world, there is little distinction between domestic and international issues, and the need for change is as important at the international as at the national level. Recognizing this, the UNDP Development Study Programme, in September 1990, launched the series, Round Table Conferences on Global Change, with the first taking place in Antalya, Turkey. Its proceedings were published in a five-volume set entitled, *Change: Threat or Opportunity?*

The second Round Table in the series was held in Bucharest, Romania, from September 4 to 6, 1992. This time the title was *Change: Systems and People.* The present volume reflects different views expressed at that conference on the many aspects of ongoing systemic changes. They offer specific proposals for making this "a world fit for people"—an allusion to Lloyd George's speech at the end of World War I, when he uttered the once-celebrated remark: "What is our task? To make Britain a fit country for heroes to live in."

Our title, we hope, is humbler and more realistic than that. We want to make the world fit for ordinary people hoping for a better life for themselves and their children. The heroes are, as always, in short supply and there now appears to be an oversupply of villains, many of them veterans of the secret police, amateur and professional spy networks, and underground economies of the old order.

Nor do we suffer from the illusions of how easy it would be to achieve peace and prosperity that flowered after World War I, again after World War II, and, once again, very briefly, immediately after the Cold War. We are aware of the difficulties of the tasks that lie ahead; it is virtually impossible not to be cog-nizant of those difficulties in this turbulent time.

Nevertheless, we consider it crucial to try, and so, in the four major parts of this book, we have considered and put forth policy proposals for political reconstruction, economic development, strengthening human and ecological values, and helping the countries in transition to achieve freer and more effective economies and governing systems.

The contributors and editors of this book share the view that all over the world people should have the right to freely choose their own systems of gov-ernance. Societies can no longer operate through systems which our shrinking planet has made obsolete. The revolutionary changes now taking place provide the countries of East and West, North and South, with the unique challenge of meeting the demands of their people for more rapid economic and social advan-cement and equality of opportunity. This challenge involves charting a safer, saner, and more rewarding future in which human capabilities can grow and individual initiatives and aspirations run free. This message is the framework within which the findings and views of the authors are set.

We cannot conclude this introduction without expressing our thanks to our host country, Romania, and to all the participants in the Bucharest Round Table and the contributors to this book. The authors have given their personal views, which should not necessarily be attributed to the institutions with which they are affiliated. We are deeply indebted to the statesmen, people of practical affairs, and scholars who joined in this collaborative international effort. Final responsibility for the selection and editing of the papers rests with the editors.

August 1993   Üner Kırdar
                                                               Leonard Silk

Contributors

B.O. Abu Affan, Vice President, African Development Bank, Abidjan.

Yaman Baskut, Ambassador of Turkey to Romania, Bucharest.

Benjamin Bassin, Director of the Finnish International Development Agency (FINNIDA), Ministry of Foreign Affairs, Helsinki.

Joseph S. Berliner, Professor of Political Sciences, Brandeis University and Harvard Russian Research Center, Massachusetts.

Keith Bezanson, President, International Development Research Centre, Ottawa.

Oleg T. Bogomolov, Member, Academy of Sciences of Russia, Moscow.

Jozef M. van Brabant, Principal Economic Affairs Officer, Department of Economic and Social Development of the United Nations Secretariat, New York.

John Brademas, President Emeritus, New York University; and former member, U.S. Congress.

G. Arthur Brown, Late Governor, the Central Bank of Jamaica.

David Bryer, Director, OXFAM, United Kingdom and Ireland, Oxford.

Nicholaa Malet de Carteret, Journalist and Management Consultant and Representative, Brahma Kumaris World, Spiritual University, Kenya.

Mary Chinery-Hesse, Deputy Director-General, International Labour Office, Geneva.

Daniel Daianu, State Secretary, Ministry of Economy and Finance, Bucharest.

Persephone Economou, Associate Transnational Corporation Affairs Officer, United Nations, New York.

Louis Emmerij, Senior Advisor to the President, Inter-American Development Bank, Washington, D.C.; and former President, Development Centre, Organization for Economic Cooperation and Development (OECD), Paris.

Sveneld Evteev, Assistant Executive Director, United Nations Environment Programme, Nairobi.

John S. Flemming, Chief Economist, the European Bank for Reconstruction and Development, London.

Nicholas Georgescu-Roegen, Distinguished Professor of Economics Emeritus, Vanderbilt University, Nashville, Tennessee.

David Gold, Chief, Global Issues Unit, United Nations, New York.

Neva Goodwin, Senior Environmental Research Analyst, Tufts University, Medford, Massachusetts.

Ravi Gulhati, Former Director, Department of Development Economics, World Bank, Washington, D.C.

Andreas Gummich, Assistant Vice President, Deutsche Bank Research, Frankfurt am Main.

Talat Sait Halman, Professor, Department of Near Eastern Languages and Literatures, New York University; Member, Executive Board of UNESCO, New York; and former Minister of Culture of Turkey.

Mahbub ul Haq, Former Minister of Finance and Planning, Pakistan; and Special Adviser to the Administrator of the United Nations Development Programme, New York.

Holland Hunter, Professor of Economics Emeritus, Haverford College, Haverford, Pennsylvania.

Shafiqul Islam, Senior Fellow, Council on Foreign Relations, New York.

Peter Jankowitsch, Former Minister of Foreign Affairs and Development Cooperation, Vienna.

Lord Judd of Portsea, Former Minister of Overseas Development and Former Director of OXFAM UK, London.

Nemir A. Kirdar, President and Chief Executive Officer, Investcorp Bank, Manama.

Lawrence R. Klein, Nobel Laureate and Professor of Economics and Finance, University of Pennsylvania, Philadelphia.

Volkmar Köhler, Member, German Bundestag, Bonn.

Flora Lewis, Senior Columnist, *The New York Times,* Paris.

Alexander Love, Chairman, Development Assistance Committee, Organization of Economic Cooperation and Development (OECD), Paris.

Kishore Mahbubani, Deputy Secretary General, Ministry of Foreign Affairs, Singapore.

Charles William Maynes, Editor, *Foreign Policy,* Washington, D.C.

Adrian Nastase, President, National Assembly of the Republic of Romania, Bucharest.

Göran Ohlin, Former Assistant Secretary-General, United Nations, New York.

Saburo Okita, Late Minister for Foreign Affairs, Japan; and Chairman, Japanese Institute for Domestic and International Policy Studies.

Christian Ossa, Director, General Analysis and Policy Division, Department of Economic and Social Affairs, United Nations, New York.

Turgut Özal, Late President of Turkey.

Jozef Pajestka, Member, Polish Academy of Social Studies, Warsaw.

I.G. Patel, Former Governor, the Reserve Bank of India; and former President, London School of Economics.

Dankwart A. Rustow, Distinguished Professor of Political Science and Sociology, City University of New York; and Editor, *Comparative Politics,* New York.

Masahiro Sakamoto, Professor, International Relations, Kobe City University, Japan.

Andrew Schotter, Professor of Economics and Chairman, Department of Economics, New York University, New York.

Norman Scott, Chief, Trade Division, Economic Commission for Europe, Geneva.

Paul Streeten, Professor Emeritus, Boston University, Massachusetts.

Gedaliahu G. Stroumsa, Martin Buber Professor of Comparative Religion, The Hebrew University of Jerusalem.

Princess Basma Bint Talal, Chairperson, Queen Alia Jordan Social Welfare Fund; and Jordan National Committee for Woman's Affairs, Amman.

Makoto Taniguchi, Deputy Secretary-General, Organization for Economic Cooperation and Development (OECD), Paris.

Carl Tham, Director General, Swedish International Development Agency (SIDA), Stockholm.

Joseph C. Wheeler, Former Chairman, the Development Assistance Committee (DAC), Organization for Economic Cooperation and Development (OECD); and Director, UNCED Conference.

John Williamson, Senior Fellow, Institute for International Economics, Washington, D.C.

Salvatore Zecchini, Assistant Secretary General of the Organization for Economic Cooperation and Development (OECD); and Director, Centre for Co-operation with European Economies in Transition, Paris.

Anatoli Zlenko, Foreign Minister of Ukraine, Kiev.

Part 1 · Political Reconstruction

Overview
Louis Emmerij, Üner Kırdar, and Leonard Silk

The startling political upheavals through which we are passing are generating intense hopes and fears. The most important change, unparalleled in modern history, is that the world now has the potential of becoming a far safer and better place. The end of the Cold War, in breaking down ideological barriers and superpower rivalries, has diminished the threat of nuclear war. There are greater hopes of enhancing international cooperation and of channeling the dividends of peace to uses that will improve human lives all over the world and reduce the inequities among nations. Prospects have improved that people may be able to achieve their aspirations of fulfilling their personal and social goals in an environment of greater freedom.

But, with all these exciting promises, the world remains a dangerous place. As the major nuclear powers are negotiating arms reductions, the proliferation of both conventional weapons and weapons of mass destruction continues. Unemployment and the existence of excess capacity for producing arms—at a time of general stagnation in the world economy—hampers nations' willingness to cut military production and even intensifies the foreign sale of weapons, increasing threats of war and terrorism in many parts of the world. Racism, nationalism, and religious and ethnic antagonisms have become the most destructive forces against peace and security, within countries and between countries. Devastating economic and social problems result from the widening gap between rich and poor. Mental and physical disease, famine, drug trafficking, and crime undermine societies, aggravate oppression by the powerful, and spread despair among working people, the jobless, the poor, and the homeless. Barriers to trade, unchecked population growth, and economic stagnation are producing millions of new refugees and displaced persons, migrating within and beyond national boundaries.

The collapse of the Soviet Union and the revolutions in Eastern and Central Europe, as well as those in the new Central Asian republics, have altered the world balance of power, with consequences that cannot yet be fully assessed. Despite the efforts to make the transition to more democratic political structures and market-oriented economies, dangers of failure persist. It is hard to believe that the people will voluntarily choose to return to the totalitarian regimes from which they have fled, but if economic breakdown cannot be halted and reversed, dictatorship, with all its cruelty and repression of human rights, could emerge as the alternative to chaos.

The struggle for democracy and ethnic identity has led to the creation of a number of new sovereign states. However, the long-term economic viability of some of these new states is doubtful in a world of increasing regionalism and globalism. And, in different parts of Europe and Asia, aggressive movements of nationalism and ethnic, religious, and racial hostility are provoking armed conflicts, "ethnic cleansing," murder and rape, and aggressions for territorial expansion, hegemonic domination, political oppression, and genocidal tyranny. Grim memories of the wars and oppression that took place earlier in this century have been awakened. Thousands of innocent lives have been sacrificed, homes destroyed, and cultural heritages damaged in some of the worst tragedies since World War II.

There are many examples of the alarming political threats. One of the most heralded peace efforts of the post-Cold War era—the 1991 accord reached in Angola—is now faltering, and rebel forces are contesting the outcome of free elections by reverting to armed struggle. Other international efforts to heal the wounds of regional, national, and civil conflicts are also faltering, as the cases of Afghanistan, El Salvador, Somalia, South Africa, and Cambodia reveal. In all of these countries some hope existed at the beginning of the 1990s for a peaceful solution to existing differences. More alarming, in the case of Bosnia and Herzegovina, the world sits and watches ineffectually as hundreds of thousands of innocent people are killed or ousted from their homes, and more than 20,000 women are brutally raped, as part of a comprehensive policy of "ethnic cleansing."

Democracy and Market Orientation

The fall of totalitarian regimes has opened the way for democracy as the supreme and only viable system for political, economic, and social life. Democracy brings with it hope of political pluralism, personal freedom, and free and fair elections, as well as a growing convergence of views on effective approaches to economic and social development. In this new quest, the market economy and private enterprise are becoming prime ingredients for economic recovery in most parts of the world.

No doubt there is a close linkage between political freedom and the efficient operation of a market economic system. Similarly, in our view, achieving world security is inseparable from progress toward building democratic societies and open economies. Political stability depends on economic, social, and ecological sustainability. As said earlier, there cannot be development without democracy, nor can there be democracy without development.

Free Choice and Better Understanding

Certainly, each country must determine freely the socioeconomic governing system most likely to ensure its own development. But we have learned that this choice should not be as categorical as it used to be—between the extreme alternatives of public and private sectors, planned or market economies, efficiency- or equity-oriented systems.

To build true democratic and pluralistic societies, we must reject all types of racial, religious, and ethnic bigotry, discrimination, and aggression. We must learn and practice freedom and tolerance where diversity is fully respected and protected. Genuine democracy requires full respect of fundamental freedoms, human rights, deeper understanding, and equal treatment of minorities and vulnerable groups in every society.

We urgently need to understand what provoked the causes that led to present changes. We must consider how we can respond to existing and mounting disappointments and divergences, and concentrate on the real issues of how to improve people's lives.

In searching for a better future, people of countries in transition are confronted with enormous economic, social, and employment problems. They need the full support of the international community. To maintain global peace and security, the iron curtain which has been lifted between East and West should not be replaced by a curtain of poverty and social ills, dividing Europe again into two camps. Support for the East must not displace North-South cooperation.

In this post-Cold War period, there is no single model of transition to be prescribed for all countries or for post-Communist societies as a whole. Each country must take into account its own special needs, traditions, cultural heritage, and values.

In the following chapters of Part I of this book, the reader will find different but generally convergent views on questions such as: What is the nature of the new world we have entered? What shape or shapes will the transition from one world to another take and what will be their impact on people? What relationship, if any, exists between political freedom and economic efficiency? What kind of capitalism or mixed economy would be best for East and South? In this context, could we design a type of "capitalism with a human face" and what are the various models that can be developed from the lessons of experience?

Shaping a "New World Order"

Three years ago, a wave of optimism invaded the West and indeed the world in general. A hope was held for a better world with more freedom and more efficient economies. Central and Eastern Europe, as well as the countries of the former Soviet Union, were to return to "normality." To quote the poet, "Bliss was it in that dawn to be alive." Today, the situation in many Eastern European countries has deteriorated; the transition road is very bumpy, and the outcome uncertain.

There is a view that the "new order" may be defined as "the West and the Rest." Some feel that the "rest" of the world has to adjust to and accommodate the ways of the "West" and that the West has no need to make adjustments of its own. This is, of course, untrue.

The trend towards globalization in the world economy is not truly global. While the East makes a desperate attempt to link to the main thrust of the world economy, parts of the South are being de-linked. This is particularly the case for Africa, which is gradually drifting away. Nevertheless, dynamic changes are taking place both in East and South. This is true with respect to political institutions and the trend towards democracy as well as to economic and financial polities stressing liberalization, privatization, and deregulation. East and South are now trying to practice what the West has preached for so long. But as these countries move to restructure their economies, the West seems to be struck by a strange immobility. The West does not practice what it preaches, as illustrated by, for instance, its agricultural policies, the Multifibre Agreement, budgetary deficits, and other policies that hamper the readjustment of "the rest."

Thus, there is a growing discrepancy between the changes in national governance in East and South and the immobility of the level of international governance, which is largely in the hands of the major industrial countries. There is a lack of vision in the Western democracies and a confusion on governance, between *less* governance and *good* governance. Instead of long-term perspectives, short-term interests and inward-looking politics prevail.

Links between Political Freedom and Economic Efficiency

Many countries in the South and the East are trying to achieve market economies and political democracies simultaneously. But the relationship between political freedom and economic efficiency is more complex than is commonly assumed.

Some of us feel that if one looks at what has actually been happening, the relationship has often been the other way around: from economic efficiency to political freedom. This was the case in Spain, in Chile, and, even more dramatically, in East Asia, including Japan and South Korea. One should, therefore, be careful in assuming that political democracy is a prerequisite for economic growth and development. However true that maybe in the long run, there can be no sustained economic development without an incentives system that gives more initiative and freedom to the individual. In a period of transition, a delicate balance must be struck between political democracy and economic development. In order to be able to establish a long-lasting true democratic system, development needs to take priority—the reason being that through economic progress a working and middle class with a vested interest in a free and stable political system will emerge.

Development is about far more than economic performance alone; it is about the whole of social and cultural life. Ethical and moral values are fundamental to all human endeavor. Freedom and the safeguarding of human rights are essential to the improvement of the human condition.

So is responsible government—that is, government that is responsive to the will and the needs of the people. The people are lost and betrayed if social and economic discipline and order break down. The term "democracy" must be understood more profoundly; there needs to be sensitivity to the diverse forms democracy can take. But its invariable principle is accountability of power, and if government leaders lose the trust and support of a nation, the people must have the right to change their government in peaceful and open elections.

Both public and private power, in a free society, must be accountable. There is no rigid or absolute line that divides public and private, yet the distinction between the two remains vital to a healthy society. The public sector seeks to protect and promote the common good of the society; the private sector is the domain within which individuals and groups pursue their own interests, under law, in the expectation that they will thereby serve wider interests as well. A free and democratic society is one in which all people are safeguarded from the arbitrary, brutal, or corrupt use of power, whether wielded by politicians, bureaucrats, or private owners and controllers of wealth.

Chapter 1 · In Search of a Saner World

Section 1 · The West and the Rest[1]

Kishore Mahbubani

The West won the Cold War, the conventional wisdom holds, not because of its military superiority, but because of the strength of its social, economic, and political institutions. Hence, it is not surprising that a new consensus has quickly developed that the West merely has to hold a steady course in the post-Cold War era. Francis Fukuyama, with his celebration of the triumph of Western values, captured the spirit of the moment. The rest of the world, if it is to free itself from the "mire" of history, will have to adjust and accommodate to the ways of the West. Having already got things basically right and facing no imminent threat, the West has no need to made major adjustments of its own.

This essay will challenge these widely held assumptions. It will argue that "steady as she goes" is not a viable option for the West; that while it may not face any immediate military threat, the West faces serious and growing dangers of other kinds; that it cannot afford to turn its back on the Third World because the Cold War is over; that in a shrinking and increasingly overcrowded world, in which the population of the West constitutes an ever smaller percentage, a comprehensive new strategy is needed; and that an aggressive effort to export Western values to non-Western countries does not constitute such a strategy, and will only serve to aggravate already serious problems.

Arriving at a sound strategy, a difficult enough task in the best of circumstances, will be harder because of the deeply ingrained habits acquired during the long years of the Cold War. There is a real danger that problems will be wrongly identified and defined, and that consequently the West's strategic sights will be pointed the wrong way. For someone of my background, this danger recalls the famous British guns of Singapore in December 1941. The guns of that supposedly impregnable fortress were confidently pointed seaward as the Japanese came quietly over land on bicycles and on foot to conquer the island with embarrassing ease. This analogy is particularly apt because one of the most serious challenges that will confront the West in the new era will also arrive on bicycles and on foot, or their equivalents: the challenge posed by mass immigration from Third World countries. Superior Western military technology will be useless against these invading armies because they will arrive as poor and defenseless individuals and families, moving without commanders or orders, and seeping slowly through porous borders. If and when this happens, it will be only one dimension of a multiple crisis, a crisis resulting from the combination of a fundamentally changed Western attitude toward the Third World, and some well-known but inadequately understood secular trends.

The Retreat of the West

For the four decades of the Cold War, both sides attached great importance to the Third World. Seeing themselves as engaged in a global struggle for the highest stakes, neither felt able to treat any country, however small, poor, or distant, as unimportant. Everything counted, nothing was irrelevant. Even as the West shed its colonial empires, the Third World successor states became more rather than less strategically relevant, especially for the United States. Because everyone else was already committed to one camp or the other, these countries constituted the main arena of competition, the contested hearts and minds and territories of the Cold War.

Although most Third World countries belonged at least nominally to the Non-Aligned Movement, that organization was incapable of providing them with effective security. For that, most felt they had only two effective choices: to identify to a greater or lesser degree with either the Western or Soviet camp. Thus a system of patrons and clients, one with an elaborate if mostly tacit set of rules, spread over the globe. Third World states were by no means always the passive objects of superpower manipulation in these arrangements, and many became very skillful at exploiting the Cold War for their own ends. It was, however, a dangerous game, requiring precise calculation. Those playing it observed carefully what happened to countries like Cambodia and Ethiopia—two vivid symbols of twentieth-century tragedy—when they got things wrong. They also noticed that if the Soviets kept Mengistu in power in Ethiopia, the West kept Mobutu in Zaire. This was a time when strategic imperatives did not allow for exquisite moral scrupulousness.

With the end of the Cold War, this state of affairs no longer pertains. Following the disappearance of the Soviet Union, Soviet proxies have either already fallen (like Mengistu) or been left exposed, without protection or subsidies, at the end of a long limb. The West, too, has reordered its priorities. No longer is there the same compulsion to prop up unsavory allies, in the name of national security. More stringent tests of human rights and democratic rectitude can be applied, and the inability of such allies to transform themselves at short notice to comply with these higher standards has been used as justification for abandoning some of them without feeling much in the way of guilt.

Whatever the ethical merits of thus using and then ditching allies, this sudden joint Soviet and Western abandonment of their erstwhile Third World friends has sent a powerful message to most nations of the Third World. The rules of the game have definitely changed; indeed, the game itself has changed. Third World regimes have begun to realize that their previous "usefulness" has come to an end, and the West now sees little value in taking any real interest in their fate.

The results of this are not all bad. The end of superpower competition has created the conditions for ending many conflicts that were kept well-stoked by the Cold War, ranging from El Salvador through Namibia and Afghanistan to

Cambodia. Many dictatorial regimes have disappeared. This is to be welcomed. But the removal of Cold War pressures also means that forces that have been bottled-up in these societies can now erupt.

To understand the epochal significance of this new Western tendency to withdraw and leave most of the Third World societies alone (observe, for example, how many Western embassies are closing down throughout Africa; the British have in recent years closed their missions in Burundi, Congo, Gabon, Liberia, and Somalia), consider that these societies have been subjected to heavy Western involvement in their affairs since the colonial era started in the sixteenth century. The current Western tendency to disentangle itself from the Third World should therefore be seen as the end not merely of a four-decades-old involvement, but of one that is four centuries old. All the indigenous processes that were smothered and subdued for centuries, either because of metropolitan pressures or because global forces were raging above them, can finally surface. To hold these historically pent-up forces in place, the Western world has left behind in the Third World a thin veneer of Western concepts of national sovereignty, the nation-state, sometimes Western parliamentary institutions, and some principles of international law.

True, these forces were not totally bottled-up during the Cold War. But the end of that struggle has seen such an acceleration and intensification of these phenomena that it amounts to a qualitative change. Tribal warfare in Africa, ethnic strife in Pakistan, Hindu-Muslim strife in India, and Islamic fundamentalism in Algeria: all can surface now with greater strength. The disintegration in 1991 of Somalia (one of the more ethnically homogeneous states in Africa) would not have been viewed with indifference—would not have been allowed to happen—ten years ago. During the Cold War, the main political fault lines in South Asia were *between* India and Pakistan, fault lines accentuated by their superpower patrons. Today, the main fault lines are *inside* India and Pakistan.

The Shrinking Globe

In short, the reversal of centuries-old Western processes of intervention in the Third World is probably going to lead to the emergence of a cauldron of instability in most of the Third World. In previous centuries, geographic distance would have insulated the West from this cauldron. Ironically, it was during the Cold War that Western technology shrunk the world into a global village, destroying the insulation provided by distance and time.

Global communication networks that give the West a ringside seat when a Tiananmen Square explodes or a Persian Gulf War breaks out have an equally spectacular reverse effect. Increasingly, once-remote villages in China, Central Asia, and the heart of Africa now have clear pictures of the comfortable and affluent lives of ordinary citizens in the West. Clausewitz once observed that "once barriers—which in a sense consist only in man's ignorance of the possible—are torn down, they are not easily set-up again." It is a remark worth bearing in mind in this context.

The simple practical effects of all this is that a single mental universe and a single global society are in the process of being created. All through the early and middle decades of the twentieth century, Western societies struggled to eliminate the gross inequalities that resulted from the early years of industrialization. This they essentially did. Now they are faced with a much, much larger proletariat on their doorsteps—one drawn irresistibly by an awareness of Western affluence and opportunity.

Western Europeans are beginning to understand this. If something goes wrong in, say Algeria or Tunisia, the problems will impact on France. In the eyes of the North African population, the Mediterranean, which once divided civilizations, has become a mere pond. What human being would not cross a pond in order to improve his or her livelihood? Through all previous centuries, men and women have crossed oceans and mountains to seek a better life, often suffering terrible hardship in the process. Indeed, it is this drive that explains the wide geographic span of "Western" societies outside their origins in continental Europe, stretching from North America through South Africa to Australia and New Zealand. Today, many more people feel that they can make similar journeys. So far Western Europeans have only seen the beginnings of such mass movements, and already they are deeply troubled.

In 1990, the ratio of Europe's population to that of Africa was 498 million to 642 million; according to UN projections, the ratio will be 486 million (a decrease, be it noted) to 2.265 billion—that is, a ratio akin to the white-black ratio in today's South Africa. Two nations, currently of the same population size, demonstrate the meaning of this trend. In the past few years, despite net immigration, Italy's population has been declining. Egypt's is growing by a million every eight months. Italy reacted very harshly to the Albanian boat people. How much more harshly would it react if the boat people were not fellow Europeans? Or consider this: In 1960 the combined population of Morocco and Algeria amounted to half that of France. Today it is about equal; in another thirty years it will be double that of France.

To put it simply, within a few decades, when Western Europe will be confronted with teeming impoverished masses on its borders and when increasing numbers will be slipping in to join the millions already there, Europeans will find themselves in essentially the same strategic plight as the affluent but vastly outnumbered white population of South Africa today.

Even the United States, separated from the fast-growing population centers of Asia and Africa by two mighty oceans, is not immune. As Ivan Head observes, "North America is home to one of the fastest growing of all national populations. The population of Mexico in 1950 was 25 million. Before this decade concludes, it will be 100 million." Despite the magnetic power of American popular culture (which once made even the French feel threatened), some of the southwestern states of the United States are effectively becoming bilingual societies, reflecting the great population influx from the South. At what point will the nature and fabric of U.S. society and culture change irreversibly because of this?

The term "population explosion" is disarmingly familiar, a cliché. But like many clichés it expresses a vital truth. From 1750 to 1950, there was a dramatic surge of population growth in the Third World, largely resulting from the spread of Western methods of hygiene and basic health care. The population balance between Europe and North America and the rest of the world has been irretrievably altered. In the year 2000 (a mere seven years away), out of a projected global population of 6.25 billion, 5 billion will live in the Third World. Ninety-seven percent of the world's population increase will take place in Third World countries.

Population numbers do matter. With extreme differences, they create security dilemmas that, in different ways, nations like Israel, Mongolia, Nepal, and white South Africa face. Even in the absence of such conventional security threats, this imbalance, which is aggravated by the enormous disparity in living standards, will be the fundamental underlying cause of the new threats facing the Western world, ranging from migrations of the poor and dispossessed to environmental damage and increased drug use, disease, and terrorism.

The Impact of East Asia

The stark picture of an affluent West and a poor Third World is complicated and confused by the increasing importance of the East Asians, the only non-Westerners already in, or poised to enter, the world of developed nations. Although their economic success, especially that of Japan, is seen as a serious problem by some observers in the West, in the larger context of relations between the West and the rest it should surely be seen as part of the solution. For Japan and the other East Asian success stories are setting off ripples of development in the Third World in a way that no Western society has ever succeeded in doing.

Consider this great historical oddity: Why is it that decades of proximity to and contacts with North America and Western Europe did not inspire any of the neighboring societies in Latin America, the Middle East, or Africa to plunge into the free-market universe, despite the obvious economic benefits of doing so? Why is Japan the only developed nation to simulate such emulation?

The answer will inevitable be complex, but one critical factor, largely overlooked, has been the psychological. In 1905, when Japan, an Asian nation, defeated Russia, a white power, it unintentionally provided a tremendous psychological boost to anticolonialism. If not the vast majority, then at least the emerging educated elites of non-European countries could for the first time conceive of the possibility that colonial subjugation was not necessarily a permanent condition, a state of nature. The generation of Jawaharlal Nehru, a boy of fourteen at the time of the war, was greatly stirred.

Today, Japan's economic success is having a similar psychological impact on developing societies all over the world, gradually convincing them that they too can make it into the developed universe. This psychological leap is crucial. Until recently, most Third World nations believed subconsciously that developed status was out of their reach. Today, after looking at Japan and its neighbors, many believe otherwise.

Japan did not intend this. Global benevolence has not yet infused the Japanese character. But its success convinced its neighbors, from Korea to Taiwan to Singapore, that they too could do it. Their success, in turn, significantly affected China, where the economic take-off in the coastal provinces has reduced Beijing's ability to reverse course from economic liberalization and has helped convince Indonesia, the world's fifth most populous nation, to deregulate faster, suggesting that a new economic synergy is developing in East Asia.

The effect is not restricted to that region, however. Largely unnoticed, pilgrims from all other parts of the world have been coming to East Asia to observe and learn. Turks, Mexicans, Iranians, and Chileans are fascinated by East Asia's success. If the East Asians can do it, why not they? So far no Islamic nation has successfully modernized. But if Malaysia and Indonesia, two Muslim countries far from the birthplace of Islam, can be swept along by the rising Asia-Pacific economic tide—and the process is well under way—the winds in the Islamic world will no longer move from West to East Asia, but in the reverse direction. This would be a major historic change. Over time, countries like Algeria and Tunisia may also be drawn in to this process.

Looked at in this way, Europe and North America, which are increasingly feeling threatened by Japan's economic advance, may indeed have a vested interest in its progress. If the belief and expectation of economic development can be planted in to minds of billions of people, massive migrations may be averted. Those Western Europeans who are already fearful of such migrations from North Africa should do some fundamental strategic rethinking and begin viewing the challenge from East Asia in a different light. What is a short-term challenge could bring long-term strategic redemption.

Economic Horses, Democratic Carts

As the numbers mount and the prospect of ever-worsening poverty and massive immigration looms, most of those Westerners who have not become entirely indifferent to the Third World seem to be determined that first priority must be given to the promotion of human rights and democracy. For the first time since decolonization, many countries have been told that development aid, even from multilateral institutions like the UN Development Programme, will be conditioned upon moves toward democratization. This campaign for democracy and human rights in the Third World could backfire badly and undermine Western security in the post-Cold War era.

The collapse of Communism in the face of challenges from democracies has given a powerful new burst of confidence in democratic values. These values strengthen the social and political fabric of Western societies because they involve all citizens in national affairs and hence develop in citizens a commitment to their society. In addition, democratic systems lead to constant circulation within the ruling elites, thereby ensuring the infusion of new blood and new ideas in critical councils. As well as the moral strength of these values, their functional strengths will enhance the global trend toward democratization and increasing respect for human rights. Those that fail to adapt to this trend are likely to suffer in the long-term Darwinian contest between societies. Japan, for example, could remain far ahead of China for centuries if China fails to create a system that will enable it to extract and use its human talent as effectively as Japan.

The question remains, however. How does one successfully transplant democracies into societies that historically have had very different social and political systems? The conventional wisdom in some U.S. political and intellectual circles today is that any society, including China, can make this transition virtually immediately. Yet most Western societies (including the most recent cases, like Spain and Portugal) did not make the leap overnight from traditional or semi-feudal systems. Economic development came first, creating both working and middle classes that had a vested interest in stability and would therefore not be pulled apart by demagogic democratic politicians trying to capitalize on ethnic and other sectional differences. That has also been the path taken by those who have made the successful transition to democracy in East Asia.

Today the West is encouraging, and sometimes demanding, the opposite approach in the Third World. It is promoting democracy before economic development. It assumes that democracy can be successfully transplanted into societies that are at low levels of economic development and that are deeply divided socially across many lines—tribal, ethnic, and religious, among others. In a developed and industrialized society, a democratic system draws in the established middle class that has a vested interest in stability. In many Asian and African cases, without such middle classes, the national polity breaks down into ethnic and tribal loyalties. If this in turn leads to internecine warfare, can one argue that democracy will always bring beneficial consequences?

As far back as 1861, John Stuart Mill said democracy is "next to impossible in a country made up of different nationalities." Even earlier, John Jay, writing in *The Federalist Papers*, stressed that Americans were "descended from the same ancestors, speaking the same language, profess the same religion, attached to the same principles of government, very similar in their manners and customs." He added that they were surely "a band of brethren" and "should never be split into a number of unsocial, jealous and alien sovereignties." Earlier theorists of democracy would be surprised by the twentieth-century conceit that democracy can be applied to any society, regardless of its stage of development or its internal social divisions.

To avoid misunderstanding, let me stress that I am not arguing that democratic systems are necessarily antithetical to development in contemporary Third World societies. Theoretically, it is possible to have both. In some cases, it may even work. But a calm and dispassionate look at Third World conditions suggest that a period of strong and firm government, one that is committed to radical reform, may be necessary to break out of the vicious circle of poverty sustained by social structures that contain vested interests opposed to any real changes. Japan was able to go into high growth after World War II in part because of the wide-ranging socioeconomic reforms that General Douglas MacArthur imposed. No democratically elected Japanese government could have done what he did. By contrast, the failure of the United States to carry out similar socioeconomic reforms in the Philippines is one reason why the economy of that country has not developed well in the postwar years.

Of course, the Filipino case demonstrates that authoritarian governments can be antithetical to development. However, it is equally true that some authoritarian governments have been good for development, as is shown by the dramatic economic growth of South Korea and Taiwan in the early years. The point here is simple: the crucial variable in determining whether a Third World society will progress is not whether its government is democratic but whether, to put it simply, it has "good government."

"Good government" is hard to define, especially in the U.S. context, where the term is almost an oxymoron. In the United States, good government often means the least government. In Third World societies, burdened with huge development demands, the common characteristics found in the successful East Asian societies may help to provide a useful definition of "good government." These would include: (1) political stability, (2) sound bureaucracies based on meritocracy, (3) economic growth with equality, (4) fiscal prudence, and (5) relative lack of corruption. With these criteria in mind, it should be possible for multilateral institutions like the World Bank to work out an operational definition that would determine eligibility for foreign aid.

The effect of such a reorientation of Western policies toward the Third World would be that less attention would be paid to the *process* by which Third World governments come into being and more attention would be paid to their *performance*. If their performance leads to serious and consistent improvement in the living conditions of the population, both the humanitarian and pragmatic considerations that underlie Western policies would be satisfied: the humanitarian, because there would be less starvation and suffering, and the pragmatic, because improving conditions would mean less migration to the West.

While human rights campaigns are often portrayed as an absolute moral good to be implemented without any qualifications, in practice Western governments are prudent and selective. For example, given their powerful vested interest in secure and stable oil supplies from Saudi Arabia, Western governments have not tried to export their standards of human rights or democracy to that country, for they know that any alternative to the stable rule of Saudi government would very likely be bad for the West.

The recent Algerian experience introduces another complication for Western advocates on immediate democratization. Democracies work all to well in bringing out the true social and cultural face of a society. In Algeria the centuries-old Islamic heritage had been suppressed by the secular and modern values introduced by the postcolonial elite. That Islamic heritage is now surfacing, and it will probably surface in other Islamic societies that hold democratic elections. If these governments elected by popular mandate impose strict Islamic laws which restrict some human rights (as Iran has), should we respect their right to decide their own values and practices? There are no easy answers.

The reaction of the West to the military coup in Algeria illustrates the moral and political ambiguities. Nominally, most Western governments have condemned the coup. However, in reaction to the questions posed by the citizens of France, Italy, and Spain as to whether democracy in Algeria is good for their own countries, most Western governments have quietly welcomed the coup, a sensible pragmatic decision based on Western interests. In the eyes of many Third World observers this pragmatic application of moral values leads to a cynical belief that the West will only advance democracy when it suits its own interests. The same cynicism can develop over human rights campaigns. Would the West be as tough on the Chinese regime in Beijing if China were located where either Turkey or Mexico is today? Would the West then be as sanguine about the prospects of millions of boat people emerging from China if the regime broke down and chaos prevailed?

Take the case of Peru. In Peru, as in Algeria, there was a spectacular reversal in the trend toward democratization. But Peru was punished with sanctions, while Algeria was not. The Europeans wisely calculated that sanctions on Algeria would further destabilized the volatile socioeconomic situation and exacerbate the flow of Algerian refugees. Hence nothing was done. Peru was further away from any Western society. So even though sanctions would be equally destabilizing in an equally volatile socioeconomic environment, they were imposed.

Westerners should surely have asked: What kind of authoritarian government was Fujimori imposing? Was he going to become a Marcos and enrich his personal coffers, or was he desperately trying to reverse course for a society on the verge of serious breakdown? Curiously, few have noticed that if *current* Western policies had been in force in the 1950s and 1960s, the spectacular economic growth of Taiwan and South Korea could have been cut off at its very inception by the demand that the governments then in place be dismantled.

In Peru, one additional cause for concern is that if the sanctions succeed in their purpose of unseating the Fujimori government, the possible alternatives of chaos or a Latin American version of Pol Potism could be much worse for the Peruvian people. Those who firmly advocate sanctions on Peru should be prepared to accept moral responsibility for the consequences of those sanctions, good or bad. If they do so, the world may avoid a repetition of the Cambodian experience, where all those who advocated the removal of the Lon Nol regime refused to accept moral responsibility for the genocide that followed. If the West chooses to be prudent in targeting human rights abuses where its own interests are involved, does it not have an obligation to exercise the same prudence when others may be affected by these campaigns?

In the face of these moral and political complexities, Western governments may determine that it is in their best interest to explain to their citizens that prudence may have to be a crucial consideration in the promotion of human rights and democracy. Unfortunately, while Western governments are prudent in practice, they find it almost impossible to speak honestly to their own citizens about the subject. Philosophically, it is difficult to discuss prudence in promoting democratization; it is not an uplifting, inspirational virtue, particularly in this context. Yet both honesty and self-interest suggest that Western governments should begin do so.

No Western government has publicly confessed that in determining its particular human rights and democracy policies, it weighs them against other vital national interests. Yet every government does so. The Germans, for example, take a strong stand on Kurdish rights; the United States does not. The United States and the United Kingdom come down hard on Qaddafi; Italy does not. This pattern of inconsistencies in turn devalues the merit of these human rights policies in the eyes of the ostensible beneficiaries, the Third World societies, because instead of being impressed by the moral courage of Western governments, they notice the pragmatic and calculated application of moral principles.

The human rights campaigns launched by Western governments and nongovernmental organizations have done much good. They have, for example, created a new global consensus that militates against the return of gross and egregious violators of human rights like Pol Pot, Idi Amin, and Boukassa. The victims of such regimes can breath a sigh of relief. Similarly, the strong global consensus against the gross forms of torture which prevailed in many parts of the world is recognized as a great advance in human history.

But from the viewpoint of many Third World citizens, human rights campaigns often have a bizarre quality. For many of them it looks something like this: They are like hungry and diseased passengers on a leaky, overcrowded boat that is about to drift into treacherous waters, in which many of them will perish. The captain of the boat is often harsh, sometimes fairly and sometimes not. On the river banks stand a group of affluent, well-fed, and well-intentioned onlookers. As soon as those onlookers witness a passenger being flogged or imprisoned or even deprived of his or her right to speak, they board the ship to intervene, protecting the passengers from the captain. But those passengers remain hungry and diseased. As soon as they try to swim to the banks into the arms of their benefactors, they are firmly returned to the boat their primary sufferings unabated. This is no abstract analogy. It is exactly how the Haitians feel.

In the long run, it may be wiser for the West to encourage a more viable process of transition in developing societies—one that puts the horse before the cart and promotes economic development through good government before it promotes democracy. This is not to argue that the international community should tolerate vicious dictators like Pol Pot or Idi Amin as long as they promote economic development in their nations. Rather, Third World governments should be treated with the same degree of pragmatic realism as is already applied to the governments of Algeria, Morocco, and Tunisia by European governments.

Implementing this apparently simple reversal would be very difficult for most Western governments. Promoting democracy in most cases involves little in the way of costs or sacrifices. But promoting economic development has significant costs, direct or indirect. What may be good for the Third World in the long-run (promoting economic development first) could prove painful for Western societies in the short run. The EC would, for example, need to abandon its massive subsidies to inefficient European farmers. If the West persists in taking the easy road in the short run, by promoting democracy first, it will ultimately prove painful and costly, because the effects of massive Third World poverty and instability will appear on its doorstep. Unfortunately, when there is a conflict between the short term and the long term in democratic politics, it is usually safer to bet that short-term considerations will prevail.

Western Democracy vs. Western Interests

The record of Western democracies in overcoming the various challenges they have faced is impressive. Unlike Athens, they have so far triumphed in both peace and war. The resilience of these societies should never be underestimated. Yet it is dangerous to assume that they have no institutional defects.

In the absence of a clear and imminent threat, most Western governments find it difficult to convince their populations that given the seriousness of the post-Cold War challenges, they must be prepared to accept some painful changes and sacrifices. The problem is not lack of leadership in these societies, but institutional arrangements. The global effects of these institutional defects of democracy can be demonstrated with two examples, both of which have harmed the non-Western world a great deal: the U.S. budget deficit and the EC Common Agricultural Policy (CAP).

Despite a wide consensus in the United States that budget deficits have to be stopped, the budget has effectively become a monster that no government institution can effectively tame. Gramm-Rudman failed miserably. The problem arises out of institutional defects in the democratic system. The interlocking network of votes by the various lobbies means that they have a stranglehold on the budget process, thereby guaranteeing the perpetuation of the enormous deficits.

Private lobbies distort the economic competitiveness of the United States in other ways, with ramifications that extend beyond U.S. borders. For example, as far back as the early 1980s, the U.S. auto industry asked for and, through the intervention of the U.S. government, received respite from Japanese competition in the form of voluntary restraints. In the decade that followed, the industry, instead of trying to learn from Japan and investing in competitiveness, continued to pay both the shareholders and management rich dividends. No effort was made to check whether this public intervention was being used for public or private good. This is not true in Japan, where the government's intervention in the economy carries with it the clear understanding that long-term Japanese national interest lie in enhancing, not undermining, the international competitiveness of Japanese industries. This is not so in the United States, where government institutions respond to ad hoc pressures from many private interests.

The CAP is another monster that has been created out of the institutional defects of Western democracies. In private, virtually no EC leader can defend the CAP. In public, no French or Spanish or Italian leader would criticize it for fear of loss of support and votes. By absorbing more than two thirds of the EC budget, the CAP draws funding away from those industries that could enhance the EC's competitiveness in the marketplace.

It has also crippled the General Agreement on Tariffs and Trade (GATT) discussions, because the non-EC nations see no reason why they should accept painful changes when the affluent EC nations will not do so. Why, for example, should Indonesia, Brazil, and Zaire—three nations that could form an "oxygen cartel"—curb their lucrative deforestation activities when the affluent EC societies will not agree to make any sacrifices? Only the lack of awareness of such problems can explain why the crippling of the Uruguay Round of GATT talks in December 1990 was allowed to happen by the West. This crippling has seriously aggravated the new threats that the West is facing in the post-Cold War era.

To present massive migrations from the poor to the affluent societies, a significant burst of economic development would be needed around the globe. One crucial global instrument that is needed to trigger such widespread economic development is GATT. If all societies abide by its rules, it creates a single and massive global marketplace which all societies, rich and poor, can plug into. GATT has already demonstrated its power by carrying a significant portion of people—those living in the West—to the highest levels of comfort and affluence enjoyed in history. It does this quite simply by creating a "level playing field" in which each society can exploit its comparative economic advantage. The impact on global productivity has been enormous.

There were few protests when the Uruguay Round was crippled in December 1990. Perhaps it was seen as merely a "trade" issue. The Brussels meeting failed because the EC wanted to protect certain industries from global competition. This will eventually prove futile, because capitalism is fundamentally a dynamic process. In trying to protect their industries from new competition, the West is trying to freeze an unfreezable process.

Given the historical impact it has already had and its relevance to the central problems of the immediate future, it is puzzling that more strategic thinkers have not focused on the GATT. It is definitely a mistake not to do so. By denying the vast masses of people an opportunity to improve their livelihood, a retreat from the GATT toward protectionism will force them to pound on the doors of the West.

Conclusion

Reorienting Western strategy in the post-Cold War era is a major task, requiring the sort of leadership that the United States so handsomely provided after World War II. Unfortunately, at the end of the Cold War, the leadership of the West had been fractured among the United States, Europe, and Japan. Unfortunately, too, Western societies are under strong pressure to turn inward when they should be looking outward. Having created a technology which has brought the world, with all of its attendant problems and promises, to it very doorstep, the West now has a strong impulse to shut the doors, a futile impulse. Futile because it has created a universe in which "interconnectedness" is the order of the day.

The real danger is that the West will realize too late that—like the defenders of Singapore—it has been preoccupied with old challenges while new ones have been assuming massive proportions.

Notes

1. This section is reprinted with permission, copyright *The National Interest*, No. 28, Washington, D.C.

Section 2 · Changing Northern Policies and Disparate Southern Responses

Shafiqul Islam

This paper examines the changing relations among major capitalist powers and their influence on the policy choices and development outcomes of the Third World. An adequate analysis, however, must be embedded in a broader context.

Central Global Changes

The End of the Cold War

This seminal event in fact involves three interrelated developments: the end of the East-West rivalry and the bipolar world; the collapse of Communism as an ideology; and the breakup of the Eastern Bloc and the Soviet Union. In broad economic terms, the world is now composed of three groups of capitalist countries: the advanced and industrialized (the North), the industrializing and developing (the South), and the post-Communist transitional (the former East).

The Decline of the United States and the Ascendance of Japan and Germany

The relative economic decline of the United States, which was accompanied by the relative economic rise of Germany and (especially) Japan, began in the late 1960s. This economic shift accelerated in the 1980s, as Japan became the world's largest creditor country and increasingly challenged U.S. supremacy in high finance and high technology. If the units of analysis are the major capitalist *nation-states* (powers), the relevant capitalist power across the Atlantic is Germany, not Europe. The European Community (EC) is not yet a single economic entity, let alone a unified political power. It is not a nation with a single, unified economic or security policy. If the focus of analysis falls on the major *economically integrated areas*, which may or may not be politically unified, the EC can be viewed as an economic pole as it stumbles toward one market and one currency.

Globalization of Production, Technology, and Markets

Globalization is not a new phenomenon, but its dramatic acceleration since the 1980s is. The transnational corporations are increasingly establishing production chains across national boundaries, setting up enormous joint ventures, and cooperating in joint research, development, and production. Accelerating globalization of production, trade, technology, and finance makes it increasingly difficult for governments to implement national trade, regulatory, financial, and monetary policies. The forces of globalization erode the power of the nation-state from above. In this context, it is worth mentioning that growing ethnic conflicts undermine the nation-state from below. This double squeeze on the nation-state may well represent part of an overall explanation of disparate development outcomes across and within regions of the South.

Regionalization, Regionalism, and the Decline of Multilateralism

It is crucial to distinguish *regionalism* from *regionalization*. The former is regional integration created by intergovernmental agreements; the latter is largely driven by market forces. Regionalism within the South is not a novel development. What is new is the aggressive pursuit of regionalism by the United States—the brain and the brawn behind postwar economic multilateralism. Another new development is North-South regionalism and regionalization. The North American Free Trade Agreement (NAFTA) is an example of U.S.-led North-South regionalism, whereas the increasing trade and investment linkages in East Asia are largely an outcome of North-South regionalization with Japan as the regional economic pole.[1] The 1992 free trade agreement (AFTA) among the Association of Southeast Asian Nations (ASEAN) is a case of South-South regionalism within a broader process of North-South regionalization.

Paradoxically, as globalization intensifies, the reactive forces of Northern economic nationalism and exclusionary regionalism are eroding the postwar paradigm of economic multilateralism. Thus we are living in an increasingly integrated and interdependent world where the Northern governments are taking the lead in undermining the spirit of multilateralism.

Unbalanced Multipolarity, Economic Tripolarity, and Global Governance

The relations between the advanced capitalist nations during the 1990s (as well as the role of the new international forces in shaping the policy choices and development outcomes of the developing countries) cannot be adequately analyzed without explicitly taking into account the interplay of economics and security. It is first necessary to challenge the conventional wisdom that economic power now matters more than military power. Economic power has always mattered more and has always been the source of military power. It so happens U.S. postwar economic power was unparalleled and was thus taken for granted. Now that the United States feels its economic primacy is being challenged, the underlying significance of economic power in sustaining military power is increasingly appreciated. The collapse of the Soviet Union as the primary military threat has only reinforced this view. But as Japan's payments to the United States for the Persian Gulf War showed that economic power matters, the U.S. decision to wage war against Iraq and the quick victory showed that military power matters just as much, if not more. This is a critical point in light of the fact that the global Cold War may be over, but certainly there are plenty of regional hot wars going on around the world.

The second point is that *geopolitically* the world now is neither tripolar nor unipolar. These characterizations are legacies of the old bipolar thinking. The world is not tripolar because Japan and Germany are not full global superpowers even though they are economic superpowers. In today's world, a global superpower must meet three conditions: economic might, military muscle (including nuclear power), and the capacity to provide global leadership guided by a broadly accepted global mission and ideology. Capacity to lead requires not only economic and military power, but also political power, diplomatic skills, and the confidence of those being led. More critically, leadership is indivisible.

Therefore, neither Japan nor Germany are yet ready to provide global leadership. Also, Japan and Germany are both non-nuclear powers, constrained from playing a global military role, and are not yet permanent members of the UN Security Council. The EC cannot be viewed as a major power—it is more than a customs union and political alliance, but is less than a federation, let alone a nation-state. Thus, the EC cannot be a member of the Security Council or the Bretton Woods institutions. Its failure to provide any leadership in the Yugoslavian crisis only reinforces this point. Indeed, German support for the independence of Croatia and Slovenia and French sympathy for Serbia show that they are the major powers of Europe, but the EC is not a Northern power with a single European foreign and security policy. Even the 1992 Single Market Act (SMA) allows the individual EC member nations to pursue certain policies different from those agreed upon at Brussels.

Thus the United States is now the world's only military and economic superpower. In that sense, the world is unipolar. But America's "tin cup diplomacy" during the Persian Gulf War also demonstrates the imbalance between this nation's military muscle and monetary might. If joint leadership or collective security means that one partner makes decisions and provides the military machine, and then forces the other to pay for it, then the outcome is resentment on both sides, as the Gulf War has demonstrated. With domestic economic and financial crisis continuing and the costs of high-tech war rising, it is hard to see the United States waging a similar war using the UN fig leaf. In broad geopolitical terms, therefore, the world can be viewed as one characterized by *nonpolarity* or *unbalanced multipolarity*.

In narrow economic terms, however, there are three major clusters of nations, each centered around an "economic pole." North America (with the United States as the pole), Europe (with Germany as the pole), and East Asia (with Japan as the pole). Thus, the world can be seen as characterized by *economic tripolarity*.

The unbalanced multipolarity has created a gap in the capacity for global leadership. The gap is between politicomilitary capacity and economic-financial capacity. The United States has the former, but not enough of the latter. Japan and Germany have the latter, but suffer from a shortage of the former. Russia and China rank above Japan and Germany in the former category, but they are severely diminished in their economic capacity. However, as nuclear super-powers and members of the Security Council, both possess the ability to block any global initiative in the security arena.

The military-monetary gap led a striking disparity between the economic and security dimensions of global governance. The major decisions involving global economic matters are made in the G-7 (with the G-3 as the core), the two Bretton Woods institutions, and the General Agreement on Tariffs and Trade (GATT). Here the major powers are Japan and Germany (on trade matters, increasingly the European Commission) with the United States still on top. Russia and China are recipient countries influencing decisions only so far as they can use their enormous leverage to destabilize security.

On matters of war and peace, the UN, with the Security Council at its core, seems to be the only game in town. NATO is still important, and some other regional European institutions on the margin are also important. The Security Council appears to be the premier organization for addressing security issues in the post-Gulf War world order. Here again the United States is first among equals. Japan and Germany—the world's second and the third largest economies—are still not major players, but Russia and China are. Britain and France are important actors here, not because of their current economic and military power, but because of the legacy of their past prowess and primacy.

The United States, again, is the only power that dominates both types of institutions and provides a linkage between economic and security issues. Indeed, the world is suffering from a shortage of superpowers. The risk is a loss of the old balance in the security arena. The argument that the United States uses the Bretton Woods institutions to promote its foreign policy is an old one. The new argument, increasingly heard, about the increased importance of the UN in promoting global peace is a sham. The United States is now using the Security Council as an effective instrument for promoting its own unilateralist goals and ambitions under the cover of multilateralism.

Finally, Russia and China are major powers, well on their ways to becoming capitalist poles with their own spheres of influence. While both are now aid-receiving nations, Russia is certainly not part of the Third World, and China is a separate category unto itself. China will overtake the United States in absolute GNP by the end of the 1990s (no country has done achieved this goal in the twentieth century) if it can sustain the last decade's growth rate. The long-awaited awakening of the sleeping giant is rapidly becoming the most destabilizing force in the security and economic balance of East Asia.

Globalization, Regionalism, and Nationalism: Fusion and Fission

Three seemingly contradictory trends are taking place at the same time: globalization of markets, technology, and production; regionalization of the world economy into economic/trade blocs driven by market forces and discriminatory intergovernmental agreements; and a three-way bilateral economic conflict among the three Northern economic poles: the United States, Japan, and the EC.

Trade wars are not likely between trade blocs—a trade war between the United States and Japan is much more likely than between the NAFTA and the EC. More interesting are the trade conflicts within a bloc. Within weeks of Clinton's inauguration, his administration imposed a dumping duty on steel to which Canada immediately retaliated. Britain, France, and Germany continue to fight bitterly over trade issues. In fact, in many cases, a member of a bloc sides with a member of another bloc in opposition to a fellow bloc member. For example, in 1992, Canada defended Japan when the United States government accused Honda in Canada of violating local content rules of the U.S.-Canada free trade agreement.

The New International Context of Development and North-South Relations

Development Model

The collapse of Communism has heightened the recognition of the differences between models of capitalism practiced in the United States, Japan, and Europe. The differences are perceived to be the sharpest between the U.S. and Japanese models. Canada and the major members of the EC are viewed as representing mixed models. The main differences between the U.S. and Japanese models are the relationship between the state and the market, the role of the bureaucracy, worker-management-company relations, the relationship between finance and production, industrial organization, the time horizon of corporate managers, the relative importance between individuals and groups, public opinion on income equity, social security, and the provision of public investment in human capital such as health and education.[2] With the socialist model dead, such differences are influencing the development strategies of the countries of the South. These differences are also gradually influencing the thinking and the policy conditionality of the international financial institutions.

Domestic Factors

The central goal of this paper is to examine how the changing international environment will influence the South's economic development in the 1990s, but that exercise must be grounded on the premise that domestic forces have played and will continue to play the primary role. Ultimately, policy choices are determined by the response of the state (and the ruling elite) to external influences, interests, risks, and opportunities, as well as its role in the policy-making and resource-allocation process. The postwar experience has amply demonstrated that if the local leadership is not committed to development of a country, no amount of external financial assistance and policy advice from the multilateral development agencies can make a major difference.[3] By the same token, a committed and competent government can sustain the country's development process in the face of a hostile international economic environment, and can often turn external risks into national opportunities.

The Divided South

There is no monolithic "South" or "Third World," but there is a group of developing countries with highly divergent per capita income, degrees of industrialization, and stages of economic and social development. The 1990 per capita income of the five regions of the Third World ranged from a paltry $350 to almost $7,000. At a level of further disaggregation, while the 1990 per capita income of Mozambique was $80, it was over $11,000 for Singapore and Hong Kong. By 1990, Taiwan had achieved a higher standard of living than some EC members of the Organization for Economic Cooperation and Development (OECD), such as Ireland, Spain, Portugal, and Greece. In terms of overall economic development, Southerners like Singapore and South Korea are now closer to these European members of the North than such middle-income developing countries as the Philippines (1990 per capita income of $750), Turkey (a NATO and OECD member with a per capita income of $1,650), Chile (the Latin American star with a per capita income of $1,950) and Mexico (a free trade area partner of the United States with a per capita income of $2,500). Hong Kong and Taiwan cannot formally join the North because they are ultimately provinces and outposts of China (per capita income of $370); but South Korea (per capita income of $5,400) may shortly join the OECD.

The regions are also divided in terms of income and stage of development. For example, in Latin America Peru's 1990 per capita income was $1,160, and Venezuela's $2,560. Haiti is also part of the same region with a 1990 income of $370. The South is also divided in terms of the future trend of development. For example, while Thailand and Colombia have about the same level of income today, their development prospects are very different. By the end of the 1990s, with a much higher anticipated average annual growth raise, Thailand is likely to be far more developed by the dawn of the twenty-first century than Colombia.

The South is also divided by economic relations that cut across the traditional North-South divide. For example, Malaysia appears to feel less economic and political solidarity with India than it does with Japan. Mexico, in joining its fate and fortune to those of the United States and Canada, may be further eroding its economic integration and political solidarity with its Southern neighbors.

Institutional and Regime Shifts

Most of the institutions and mechanisms through which the major Northern powers exert their influence on the South have existed for long. Some are new, but even the old channels are going through a relative shift of importance. The old official mechanisms involve direct bilateral dealings. These dealings include exclusive clubs such as the G-7 (with the G-3 at its core), the Bretton Woods institutions, the World Bank Group and the International Monetary Fund (IMF), GATT, regional development banks (most importantly, the Inter-American Development Bank, the Asian Development Bank, and the African Development Bank), the UN Economic and Social Council (ECOSOC), and other UN development agencies, such as the United Nations Development Programme (UNDP).

Although bilateralism and multilateralism remain the most important conduits of Northern influence, the balance of power among the major actors is undergoing a gradual shift. More specifically, Japan has now replaced the United States as the largest donor country.[4] And yet, in the Bretton Woods institutions, the United States has so far succeeded in maintaining its veto power and overall political dominance. Japan has been increasingly advancing new initiatives—for example, the 1988 Miyazawa proposal for resolving the Third World debt crisis. Japan is also challenging U.S. ideological hegemony that has until now shaped these institutions, their development philosophy, lending strategy, as well as the principles and practice of policy conditionality. Notwithstanding its anachronistic and imperialist veto power, the dominant influence of the United States appears to be gradually eroding on the Bretton Woods twins' development strategy, as well as day-to-day concrete decisions.

The multilateral trading system and the GATT has already been weakened by the growing unilateralism, bilateralism, and regionalism increasingly practiced by the United States and the EC. The trade prospects of the developing countries now hang in uneasy limbo as the Uruguay Round talks remain stalled with the United States and the EC (more specifically, France) caught in a gridlock on agricultural subsidies and trade. The Uruguay Round impasse has further undermined the GATT's effectiveness and weakened the multilateral mechanisms of promoting international trade and resolving disputes. The GATT, weak as it is, is more democratic than many other multilateral institution where developing countries exercise some bargaining power.

The picture is mixed when it comes to the importance of the regional development banks relative to their big two relations in Washington, D.C. Despite resistance from the United States and some European members, Japan has succeeded in enhancing the financial and intellectual clout of the Asian Development Bank. With a dynamic and savvy Latin American president at the helm, the Inter-American Development Bank is also strengthening its role in the region. But this may be a temporary phenomenon. The financial role of the African Development Bank has also increased over the years, and the trend is likely to continue. Yet the African Bank's leadership in the policy area remains marginal given the dominant influence of the Bretton Woods institutions in the region.

In a paradoxical shift, security considerations are gaining primacy over economic issues. The UN developmental agencies are shrinking and disintegrating under the pressure of budget cuts, donor disenchantment, and chaotic restructuring. By contrast, decisions made in the Security Council are having profound developmental impacts. The Security-Council-sponsored Persian Gulf War devastated the economies of Iraq, Jordan, and others in the region. It also had serious adverse economic effects on South Asia, the Philippines, and other developing countries that supply the bulk of the region's work force. Furthermore, the oil price swings had major distributional and disruptive effects on the developing world. With ethnic conflicts and civil wars spreading around the globe, decisions made in the Security Council are likely to shape the global environment for development more than those made in the Economic and Social Council (ECOSOC), United Nations Conference on Trade and Development (UNCTAD), UNDP, and so on.

The new mechanisms and institutions for exerting Northern influence over the South include the restructuring of the EC under the Single Market Act (SMA), the building of the Economic and Monetary Union (EMU) under the Maastricht Treaty, and new types of unilateralist trade policy, such as the U.S. Super 301. The further Europeanization of the major European capitalist nations with decisions made jointly at the EC level will affect the geographical and sectoral distribution of development aid, change the pattern of trade and investment with various Southern regions, and benefit some countries while hurting others.

Two-Way Leverage

The influence does not flow only from the North to the South. It has always been a two-way process, but the Northern powers, with their economic and military supremacy have, of course, always possessed greater bargaining power. The nature of the leverage, however, has changed in the North and in the South. With regard to the North, the political/security conditionality for development aid is not new—the distribution of development aid by the United States and the international financial institutions during the Cold War period was always guided by political/security conditionality. What has changed is the global context, and the nature of the conditionality of the donors.

For example, the United States is returning to the promotion of democracy and human rights rather than fighting Communism as the key principles around which to anchor its foreign policy. Japan has also declared the state of democracy and human rights as well as production and exports of weapons of mass destruction as criteria it would consider in allocating ODA. The Development Assistance Committee (DAC) and the Bretton Woods institutions have also adopted these guidelines for political, military, and social conditions in their lending programs. For example, on 10 May 1992, the World Bank announced that it would take into account "nonproductive" military spending in its lending decisions to 85 Third World members.[5] Three days later, the Paris Club group of donors told Malawi that it would get $75 million of development assistance only if it improves its human rights record.[6]

Unilateral use of new types of protectionist trade weapons is another mechanism with significant development implications. These Northern unilateralist tools were invented to protect domestic producers against trading partners from the South and the North. But given the Southern countries' weak bargaining power and potential for using trade as the engine of economic growth, the protectionist weapons may inflict greater long-term welfare loss on them.

With the end of the Cold War and the disintegration of the Soviet Union, instruments of the developing countries' leverage have changed as well. In the days of the Cold War, the developing countries obtained financial assistance, trade preferences, and military weapons by playing the U.S. fear of Communism and Soviet expansion against the Soviet Union's desire to increase its sphere of influence. The South feared that the end of the superpower rivalry would leave them without this bargaining power. Happily, a host of transnational phenomena are gradually replacing the Soviet Union and Communism as the common enemy. These new enemies include environmental degradation, global warming, ozone depletion, terrorism, drugs, disease, production and exports of weapons of mass destruction, nuclear proliferation, ethnic violence, regional conflicts, and mass migration to the North. The decimation of the rainforests, nuclear proliferation, and increasing migration are the post-Cold-War "immoral equivalents" of the Soviet Union and Communism.

It is ironic that in an age when the free flow of goods, services, and capital are much praised and promoted, the free flow of people (mass migration) is yet a "threat" that the Third World countries can use as an effective weapon of leverage in negotiating with the Northern free traders. Another irony is that the recipient countries can turn the new conditionalities into leverage against the North. For example, the North may end up bribing a developing country with aid money to have the recipient halt its nuclear program. Or, countries such as Malawi can hold "violation of human rights" as a hostage to extract more money from the Northern donors.

Changes in the North and Their Impact on the South

How will the changing relations among the advanced capitalist countries influence the process of economic development of the Third World in the 1990s? To what extent can they explain highly disparate policy choices and development outcomes across regions?

The influence of the North on a particular developing country or region emerges out of dynamic interactions among global trends, regional relations, and the changing bilateral relations of the global economic superpowers or superblocs with individual developing countries. For example, the influence of the North on the Philippines results from dynamic interactions between global forces such as globalization of production and markets, the trend and the level of ODA, and other official flows. Also influential are such regional developments as its participation in the ASEAN free trade agreement and recent jumps in inflows of Taiwanese direct investment and Japanese ODA, not to mention shifting bilateral relations with the global economic superpowers. Within this overall dynamic context, it is difficult to ascertain how the shifting relations within the North are influencing the policy choices or the development outcomes of the Philippines.

The economic influence of the North—and its internal conflicts and cooperation—are transmitted to the South through several broad categories of transfers: ideas and ideology (development model) and three types of capital—financial, human, and technological. One may say the transfer involves four M's: mind, (wo)men, money, and machine. These transfers go through three types of channels: bilateral and multilateral official development assistance (aid) and other official financial flows; direct investment; and other private financial flows (portfolio equity, bonds, and bank loans). None of these transfers are one-way phenomena: the official transfers are spurred by national security and economic considerations, and the private flows are driven by the profit-motive. The most obvious two-way interaction is the North-South trade mechanism of promoting global productivity and growth by exchanging market access and exploiting the existing (static) and potential (dynamic) comparative advantage of the trading partners.

With this prelude, three consequences may be highlighted of the conflicts and cooperation within the North on the development outcomes within the South during the 1990s. First, the Northern economic powers and blocs are becoming increasingly protectionist against agricultural exports of developing countries, and manufacturing exports of those which have succeeded in putting into practice the Northern advice of creating an outward-looking competitive economy. For example, the share of trade with the developing countries restricted by rigid nontariff measures (quotas, voluntary export restraints, etc.) in 1986 was 17 percent in Japan, 19 percent in the United States, and 23 percent in the EC. These shares were higher than those applied against other industrial countries in two out of three cases—16 percent in the United States and 14 percent in the EC.[7] By 1990, nontariff protection against the South had risen further in the United States and the EC, but had declined slightly in Japan.[8]

Second, the impasse on the Uruguay Round continues to delay the process of lowering trade barriers against the developing countries, and threatens future hikes in the Northern protection against the South. The final agreement will probably achieve modest results. But that outcome is far better than a total collapse which is sure to push the trading partners into a vicious cycle of retaliations and regionalism of the worst kind heralding an end of the postwar liberal trade regime perhaps preparing grounds for a new global depression.

Finally, while closed regionalism (North-North or North-South) is likely to further divide the South and regions within the South, open regionalization may globalize the Japanese "flying geese model" where the head goose is not a nation-state but a region. As already noted, Mexico trades little with its Southern neighbors. By joining NAFTA, Mexico will become an "insider" of a largely Northern bloc. Unless it makes a conscious effort to seriously integrate with the "southern outsiders," it will fragment further away from the rest of the region. Open regional integration does not create the insider-outsider problem, where individual countries benefit from new interregional trade and investment linkages. If a particular region prospers through increased regional as well as global linkages in trade and investment, it can then promote growth in other open regions.

The second, and perhaps the central question is, to what extent can the influence of the three economic poles and their regional semihegemonic roles explain the diverse policy choices and development outcomes across regions in the South? Much of the explanation lies in interactions among three key factors: regional differences in the choice of a capitalist development model and the capacity to effectively implement it; the economic dynamism, as well as the region-wide development strategy and linkages of the regional economic pole; and the depth and breadth of each region's overall linkages with all three global economic poles.

The thesis that regional disparity partly depends on the choice of the development model is valid, but a great deal of confusion and controversy surrounds how to exactly specify that model. The view that the development model adopted by most, if not all, countries in the region is the one preached, if not practiced, by the regional economic hegemony appears to be somewhat off the mark. This view apparently rests on the fact that, out of the five regions, two—Northeast Asia and Southeast Asia—appear to be following some version of the "Japanese model," while one—Latin America and the Caribbean—seems to be following the "American or Anglo-Saxon model." The notion that South Asia and sub-Saharan Africa are practicing the Anglo-Saxon model is hard to substantiate. Although there is plenty of disagreement on what the central differences between these two models are, more disturbing is the fact that there are simply too many countries in the three regions that do not appear to emulate the "regional prototype development model." For example, two out of three countries in Northeast Asia—Hong Kong and Taiwan—did not seem to follow the Japanese model in the 1970s, let alone during the 1980s. Indeed, if there is one economy in the world that practices the "American model of laissez-faire," it is not the United States but Hong Kong. The differences in the development strategy pursued over the last three decades among the three Northeast Asian NIEs are quite significant; only South Korea appears to have emulated a version of the Japanese model.

In Southeast Asia, two (Singapore and the Philippines) out of the five countries did not pursue the Japanese model during the 1980s and are not emulating it now. Evidence does not support the argument that trade and industrial policy; worker-management relations, social views on employment security and distribution of income and wealth, and attitudes toward the developmental role of foreign capital and direct investment in these countries resemble the Japanese model more than the U.S. paradigm. Many Latin America and Caribbean countries do not seem to be practicing the U.S. model either. Examples are Brazil, Venezuela, Colombia, Peru, Jamaica, and quite a few Caribbean islands. On trade policy, the "regional model hypothesis" creates a cognitive dissonance as empirical evidence challenges the conventional wisdom that the Japanese paradigm is neoconservative and that the U.S. counterpart is neoliberal. It appears that East Asia is indeed following the Japanese model and Latin America the Anglo-American model; the only problem is the specification of the model have gotten switched!

This brings us to the final point. The two models are often misspecified, and the major regional disparities in the development strategy and policy choices on the whole depend on differences between one or two key elements of the Japanese model and the ideology preached—if not always practiced—by the United States.

In fact, there is a growing international consensus on what constitutes an effective development strategy. The 1989 report of the Development Assistance Committee (DAC) describes the central elements of this consensus strategy as promoting broad-based economic growth "with careful prioritized infrastructure investment and the build-up or rehabilitation of productive capacity in agriculture, industry, and other sectors; stimulating productive energies through investing in people and through participatory development with a more equitable sharing of benefits; and ensuring environmental sustainability and slower population growth."

The 1991 World Bank Development Report offers a variation of this consensus, which it calls a "market-friendly approach." The strategy consists of five dynamically interactive central components: investing in people; making markets work (providing infrastructure, deregulation of industrial markets, developing financial markets, and clarifying property rights); integrating with the global economy through trade and foreign direct investment; fostering and maintaining macroeconomic stability; and implementing effective environmental policies. What distinguishes the development strategy of East Asia from that of Latin America is a few key elements of this consensus strategy.

The successful East Asian countries appear to have been pursuing macroeconomic stability, outward orientation, and a trade and industrial policy where infant industries with perceived future potential are developed with protection and state subsidies. If the infant succeeds in becoming an adult, initial protection is replaced by gradual liberalization. If the infant fails to grow up, the state ultimately pulls the plug, although vested interests often keep the infant alive for long. The success of this policy, however, depends a great deal on a strong state with politicians committed to economic development and a competent bureaucracy able to carry out the necessary policies.

Since the U.S. model and the Bretton Woods institutions also emphasize the importance of macroeconomic stability and outward orientation, the "Japanese" contribution turns out to be simply "dynamic manufacturism" carried out by a competent state bureaucracy.

Furthermore, the dynamism of East Asia does not emanate from Japan alone; other special factors are also playing a critical role. Indeed, as far as trade and investments are concerned, some East Asian countries are more closely linked with the United States than with Japan. Similarly, in terms of trade and investment linkages, the United States is not the sole economic pole of Latin America and the Caribbean. Many countries from this region, such as Argentina, are more closely linked with the EC. Japan has also become an important Northern economic partner of this region.

In 1991, Chile's total trade was higher with Japan than with the United States. Compared to East Asia, this region suffers from the fact that the two economic poles it is most closely linked with do not have an effective strategy for regional development. South Asia is similar to an orphan with no strong linkage with any of the three Northern poles. Sub-Saharan Africa is still closely associated with the individual member countries of the EC through their former colonial ties, but with the EC preoccupied with implementation of its one market, one money process of integration, sub-Saharan Africa is also becoming "orphanized." The collapse of the Soviet Union only accelerated the marginalization of some of Africa's former Soviet orient states.

Finally, in terms of the depth and the breadth of overall global linkages, Northeast and Southeast Asia are also way ahead of other regions. Latin America and the Caribbean ranks second. South Asia and sub-Saharan Africa once again occupy the bottom of the totem pole.

Thus, all three factors—the choice of the development model and the state capacity to implement it; the development strategy and linkages or the lack thereof of the principal economic pole(s); and the extent of overall linkages with all three global economic centers—appear to be playing a role in explaining the relative success of East Asia. These factors also seem to account for the diversity of development outcomes within a region.

Conclusion

Three central conclusions emerge from the above analysis. First, while the United States is the only economic and military superpower in the post-Cold War world, the world is suffering from a global leadership capacity gap. The United States is maintaining its military-political supremacy but not its economic might, while Japan and Germany are only half-powers with primacy in the economic domain but lacking power in the military sphere. So geopolitically, the world is characterized by an unbalanced multipolarity. Economically, the post-Cold War world is characterized by tripolarity, with the EC being the third pole along with the United States and Japan.

Second, with the collapse of the Soviet Union, the common enemy uniting the major capitalist powers is gone. This, plus the relative decline of the United States, has resulted in economic insecurity within the United States and conflicts among the global economic poles. The outcome is exclusionary regionalism led by the United States—the erstwhile champion of a multilateral and liberal trade regime: increased Northern protectionism against the relative successful Southern countries (mostly from East Asia) and the continued impasse in the multilateral trade talks. All these developments have adverse effects on the developing countries, especially those using trade as the main engine of growth.

Finally, three factors seem to account for most of the regional diversity in development outcomes. The first is the state capacity to effectively implement a developmental strategy based on macroeconomic stability and outward-orientation, with a state-led strategy of "dynamic manufacturism." The second is the region's close economic linkages with the regional economic pole, but within a well-defined framework such as the "flying geese model." The diffusion of entrepreneurship and the human and financial capital of "the overseas Chinese network" have also accelerated the dynamic development of East Asia. The third element is the depth and the breadth of a region's overall linkages with all three global economic poles. Once again, East Asia has done much better on this score than the other three regions. South Asia and sub-Saharan Africa are the worst performers, while Latin America and the Caribbean fall somewhere in between.

Notes

1. There is little evidence to support the view that Tokyo bureaucrats are creating a new coprosperity sphere in East Asia.

2. See Lawrence B. Krause, "Japanese Capitalism: A Model for Others?" *International Economic Insights* (November/December 1991): 6-10; and Richard Evans "May the Best Capitalism Win," *Global Finance* (October 1992): 12-20.

3. Shafiqul Islam, ed., *Yen for Development: Japanese Foreign Aid and the Politics of Burdensharing* (New York: Council on Foreign Relations Press, 1991).

4. See Uma Lele and Ijaz Nabi, eds., *Transition in Development: The Role of Aid and Commercial Flows* (San Francisco: International Center for Economic Growth, 1990).

5. World Bank Plans to Watch Aid Seekers' Arms Budgets," *New York Times*, 11 May 1992, D7.

6. "Malawi Aid Tied to Human Rights," *Financial Times*, 14 May 1992, 4.

7. World Bank, *World Development Report 1991* (New York: Oxford University Press, 1991).

8. International Monetary Fund, *Issues and Development in International Trade Policy*, Washington, D.C., 1992, 116.

Section 3 · A Cry for Global Strategy

Lord Judd of Portsea

There is today an ever increasing gap between the rapidly advancing science and technology which benefits the few and the slow advance of social progress for the majority of humankind. This gap creates both thematic and geopolitical global stress. Why should this be a source of concern? The basic reality of life is interdependence. Whether we like it or not, we live *in* society. Pollution or fallout will affect even the desert island. Life itself must surely be about fulfillment in the context of handling this reality. We need to look to the "holistic" dimensions of the social sciences, their interrelationship with each other and with the arts—economics, psychology, sociology, ethics, philosophy, history, geography, literature, music, art, etc.—and also their interrelationship with the physical sciences. There is a real danger that expertise has become a matter of knowing more and more about less and less, and that this is central to an impending and potentially overwhelming crisis. Perhaps it will be helpful to summarize briefly some of the social realities and the implication of a number of interrelated inequalities. We dug the Channel Tunnel, probed outer space, built Trident, developed the ability largely to destroy the human species, but statistically worldwide, a small child still dies every 2.4 seconds of every day from poverty, one in five families still lives on less than £175 per annum, average life expectancy is still 12 years shorter in the South than in the North, 1.5 billion people still live without adequate sanitation, the South's maternal mortality rate is still 12 times higher than in the North, and 1.2 billion people still live in absolute poverty. Even in the North's own city centers the homeless in their cardboard boxes accumulate. Despite the solemn pledges from rich nations, aid flows falter. In the United Kingdom we are down to 0.32 percent of GNP against the 0.7 percent UN target. Too often the aid that is provided is wasted or even proves counterproductive.

As has yet again become clear at the General Agreement on Tariffs and Trade (GATT), the world's trading system is still operated in the interests of the industrialized world. The CAP continues to play havoc with agricultural production in the South. The terms of trade for primary commodities have seriously deteriorated.

Debt remains a massive problem. Even the minimal Trinidad Terms have not been fully applied and have not yet secured endorsement by the United States. The World Bank estimates that net flows of wealth from South to North will persist until the mid-1990s and possibly beyond. Structural adjustment programs, too often devoid of rigorous prior assessment of their social consequences, have frequently accentuated poverty.

Eminent scientists at the U.S. National Academy of Science and the Royal Society in the United Kingdom have forecast that there are no more than thirty years within which effective action must be taken to prevent a potentially terminal environmental catastrophe. The price of correcting the world's environmental problems is said to be in the region of $625 billion per annum of which $125 billion needs to be transferred from North to South. But in 1990 the 21 Development Assistance Committee members of the Organization for Economic Cooperation and Development (OECD) provided little more than $54 billion in official aid to the South.

Meanwhile the protective ozone layer in heavily populated latitudes of the northern hemisphere is thinning twice as fast as scientists until recently believed; 35 percent of the earth's land surface, accommodating one fifth of the world's population, is in danger of becoming desert; forests are rapidly disappearing: some 7.5 million hectares of tropical forest and some 3.8 million hectares of open dry forest each year, with a further 4.3 million hectares degraded. Quite apart from the climatic impact, this deforestation spells dire consequences for forest dwellers, like those of Amazonia or the Pygmies of Zaire, leading to still more environmental degradation; the number of "food insecure" people has risen to 100 million in Africa alone. Global warming, with consequently rising seas, already threatens the poor in low-lying places like Bangladesh, Egypt, and the Nigerian River States. At the same time effective stewardship of marine life and the seas remains minimal.

Sustainable development alone will either usher in an era of unprecedented tyranny, as the minority hold on to what they have perhaps maximizing it and keeping the majority at bay, or will begin an era of unprecedented anarchy as the excluded stand up and demand their share. Commitment to sustainable development has immense implications for equity and justice. UNCED at Rio will be judged in history by what subsequently transpires. What was sadly absent from the outcome of the conference itself was both additionality of resources and convincing marching orders to the international financial institutions and GATT to make their agendas relevant.

The population explosion continues. Effective population strategies related to functional literacy, primary health, and community work with women are few and far between. At the same time the rich industrialized countries of the North, with only 25 percent of the world's population, still take an 80 percent share of the resources consumed by the world.

Infant and maternal mortality, short life expectancy, waterborne diseases, malnutrition, and general ill health affecting millions have now been compounded by AIDS, which is attacking the present and future productive generations of both the South and the North. Drugs also affect all social classes, though paradoxically they produce incomes for the rural poor as well as for the drug barons and their agents.

Is Peace Achieved?

The extraordinary Eurocentric view of "peace since 1945" is cruelly belied by the 150 wars, mainly in the South, that have disrupted and destroyed agricultural production, rural and urban communities, development programs, and entire economies. The arms trade feeds the war monster and has accentuated widespread damaging instability, even where no formal conflict exists. Has the horse bolted? The disintegration of the former Soviet Union, adjacent as it is to the Gulf and the Middle East, underlines the dangers. But already Iraq, Israel, India, South Africa, and others have developed or are developing nuclear capability. Biological and chemical capabilities are also multiplying. Terrorism has challenged all the traditional "mind set" concepts of security. Nuclear, chemical, and biological capabilities indicate nightmare scenarios. The weapon of mass destruction in a container ship, a civilian airliner, or brought into a city in bits by hand luggage, is a prospect we or our children may very well have to face.

Nationalism, vulnerability of ethnic minorities, cultural intolerance, racism, and isolationism are now well-established worldwide phenomena. Migration, whether caused by harsh economic factors, conflict, or environmental crisis, is insistently spreading and will not go away. There are 17 million refugees in the world. In addition, there are at least 24 million people displaced within the borders of their home countries, who are without the status or protection of refugees.

How much longer can the sacrosanct principle of the sovereignty of the nation-state still be accepted (how far and by what objective criteria has it already been set aside) against the principle of the integrity of the people? Must we not face up to the case of "external" humanitarian intervention, especially when such sovereignty is claimed by governments with no democratic or popular legitimacy? Has the information technology explosion improved either the quantity or the digestion and evaluation of information? Are we drowning in information? Are we losing the ability to precis and prioritize? What is happening to original, creative thought? Has decision making improved? Is action inhibited? What is the overall historical cost to humanity?

The Context

In considering how to meet these realities, the context is important. With the revolution in the former Soviet Union against 75 years of Communism and 300 years of imperialism, we have an unrivaled opportunity to move from a bipolar, disastrously ideological world in which values and pragmatism apply, to a new age of common sense and reason. Will we have the guts to challenge the omnipotence of liberal economies and the market, appreciating that whatever the undeniable relevance of their disciplines they alone will never ensure the survival of humanity? Or is it to be an era of unquestioned unipolar ideological power with all the sinister implications that might entail? In a multipolar world how will a political equilibrium be established? In place of the old "threats" and "common dangers," what is to underpin this equilibrium? Will this be the new threats and dangers as listed? Can we identify common tasks to meet them? Is that one way in which the negative thematic and geopolitical elements of social reality can be turned to positive effect? Can we combine in such positive endeavors? For example, is it possible to generate a strategic approach to migration that builds on dealing with the interplay of conflict, defense policy, the arms trade, labor needs in proportionately aging populations, Common Agricultural Policy, aid, international finance, environment, and the rest, which recognizes the inherent challenge to sovereignty and which takes on board the grim gap between the status of refugees and the status of the displaced? More generally, is it possible to generate a strategic approach to global economic development, bringing together trade, aid, finance, conflict resolution, education, health, environment, and more?

A Possible Approach

If we accept the underlying theme of international interdependence, it is sensible to start at the international level. Effective global governance is no longer an idealistic option. It is an imperative. That brings us to the multiplicity of conflicting institutions. Ideally we need a strengthened UN Security Council with responsibility for strategic direction—an international cabinet. To have credibility this new Council would need revised membership. This should include Germany and Japan, although there might eventually be a place for the EEC as such.

The secretary-general would need something similar to the EEC Commission working committedly with him to keep the dynamism and strategic direction alive. The international finance institutions would then work with the Security Council through the secretary-general and his/her team as would the other UN agencies, rationalized, reduced in number, and cooperating together on well-defined tasks. Minds must concentrate on the pressing imperative to drag the UN system out of its institutional politicking and ensure that it becomes task orientated. There would, as originally envisaged, have to be a highly professional Chiefs of Staff Committee, responsible for collective security operations and serviced by high quality international intelligence outputs. This Committee would work with the Security Council through the secretary-general. Criteria should be established whereby the UN on the authority of the Security Council could challenge sovereignty if this was warranted on humanitarian, political, and strategic grounds. In this context, before throwing up our hands in horror, we should remember that conditionality, a very real infringement of sovereignty, is already applied by the International Monetary Fund (IMF) and the World Bank, and that the procedures for citizens to appeal over their governments on human rights matters are in place.

As happens in the EEC it would be essential to have different political manifestations of the Security Council working on different sectors of global policy, but all accountable to *the* Security Council in its most senior form. Foreign ministers would frequently attend the Council. At other times the latest communications and information technology could be applied in a disciplined way to facilitate their deliberations and decision making. High on the agenda of the Council would be the world economy, environmental policy and its implementation (follow up to UNCED), migration, conflict and its resolution, peacekeeping, and humanitarian emergencies.

To those who ask "But why *Security* Council?," the answer is surely that lasting peace and security depends upon the fulfillment of human, economic, and social rights and upon the accountability of power, and that the imminent environmental catastrophe is every bit as much a "threat" to humanity as those envisaged by the founders of the UN in 1945.

All this will not happen immediately, but in the short term the authority of the secretary-general must be increased both in terms of the seriousness given to the appointment itself and in terms of the resources at his/her disposal. At a time when the virtues of good governance and democracy, in other words accountable government, are preached to the South, it is incredible that the same disciplines are not accepted globally. The IFIs must be brought into line with a cohesive strategy. They should play a critical role in deciding what economic and social policies are *economically possible*, but beyond that they are there to service economic and social priorities, not to dictate them. By the same token GATT is overdue for reform, perhaps combining with the United Nations Conference on Trade and Development (UNCTAD), but taking more firmly into its remit environment, food security, poverty, and accountability of the transnational companies.

Groupings like G-7 or the Commonwealth will continue to have a useful role to play but never as an alternative to a revamped UN system. Rather they will always serve as catalysts assisting its strategic success.

Within the global system there remains a potentially vital contribution to be made by such natural regional groupings as the European Economic Community (EEC), the Organization of African Unity (OAU), the Association of Southeast Asian Nations (ASEAN), the Organization of American States (OAS) and perhaps the Commonwealth of Independent States (CIS), to economic and social organization. But the challenge is to keep such groupings geared to the global system and not to permit a centrifugal process, or even worse. This suggests that eventually the Security Council should be made up of regional rather than national representatives. In the meantime, this process could begin in the IMF, the World Bank, UNCTAD, and the other key agencies. Rationalization of the military within regional groupings may well make sense, but always with a developing demonstrable commitment to global collective security.

Enlargement of the EEC should almost certainly be limited to East and Central Europe, the Baltic and Nordic states, and perhaps Cyprus. Even this could tend to detract from the dynamic of the Commission that has driven the ministers: the Commission could become a conference; things could begin to run into the sand. Within the EEC the development of collective political, economic, and social foreign policy towards global responsibility must become a priority. This will necessitate a radical revision both of the CAP and Lome, extending the concerns of the latter to Asia, South America, and non-ACP nations. There can be little doubt that it is the Commission which has provided the core strength of the EEC's development. With its identifiable political objectives it has contrasted starkly with the amorphous pudding the UN system has sadly become.

Conclusion

The tension is between the excitement of intellectualism—living—and the pitfall of self-indulgence; between the search for truth and the imminence of disaster. The 1980s have certainly been the quantitative decade, and there is consequently a huge qualitative vacuum to be filled. It is, I suggest, by a massive reassertion of qualitative concern about values that the awareness and discipline for the urgently essential strategic approach will be generated. But in the end it is will that matters. Unless there is a will to avoid catastrophe, it cannot be avoided. Many of us must share an acute sense of foreboding lest we are fiddling while hurtling towards the apocalypse, lest tactics are indeed in process of becoming the fatal enemy of strategy.

Section 4 · Impacts of a Changing World

Turgut Özal

The topic of "change" deeply occupies all countries and will no doubt be the subject of intensive discussion in the years to come. Change is inherent in the history of human societies, and in this sense, we are accustomed to it. But the magnitude of the change occurring now involves no less than the breakdown of post-World War II international systems, the disintegration of many countries and regions, and the collapse of a dominant ideology, together with its socioeconomic system and values. The need for countries in transition to adapt to such change can only be qualified as metamorphoses.

Risks and Opportunities

A process of change, while presenting opportunities, always embodies a certain level of risk. Accordingly, the process under way is laden with risks commensurate to its magnitude. The greatest risk arises out of the euphoria and hope that the sudden fall of authoritarian structures tends to unleash. Public frustration, accumulated over the years, may threaten the new and fragile basis of the societies in convalescence. Nevertheless, we must recognize that there is no easy way to fulfil these hopes in a reasonably short period of time. The sudden change, which swept like a hurricane across the countries of East and Central Europe and the former Soviet Union, while not physically devastating the economic structures, has wreaked havoc on the sociopolitical fabric of the area. As a result, in addition to the colossal problems of developing countries, the international community now faces the equally important problems of multifaceted adjustments in Central and Eastern European countries and the building of nationhood and statehood in the newly independent countries.

The precondition of socioeconomic progress is the existence of a political order. It is of vital importance for individual countries and the international community that this order be based on democracy, respect of human rights, and economic and social equity. Change in existing frontiers on ethnic lines in one country risks unraveling the international order based on nation-state. Therefore, tragedies in countries like Bosnia-Herzegovina need to be stopped if new ones are to be avoided in the future.

The Role of the Individual

On the threshold of the twenty-first century, we can see that the 1990s witnessed the culmination of the struggle against the omnipotent state. As a by-product, the age of the masses as the driving force of history came to an end. Technological revolution spurred by microinformation and biotechnology is now eliminating the need for people to be concentrated in huge industrial complexes and metropolitan cities.

As a result, the individual is becoming the centerpiece of the society, indeed of the world, legally as the inviolable subject of human rights, politically as the irreducibly independent unit of the sovereign state, and economically as a self-contained production force. Hence, he or she is restoring full independence in self-identity. The conviction that the individual was subordinate to the society and subservient to the state is fast becoming obsolete. In fact, the role of the state is being reduced to providing people with services to facilitate human development. Thus, the tension stemming from the competition between the state and the individual is being diffused.

The developments just outlined caused drastic changes in the capitalist world and were instrumental in the collapse of Communism. They are now obliging the restructuring of the transition countries of East and Central Europe and the former Soviet Union. The reason is quite simple—people are becoming more creative, productive, and civilized as compared to their predecessors, who were squeezed between the state and the society.

The twenty-first century will be dominated by the force of information. The services sector, comprising such economic activities as telecommunications, computers, modern transport, construction, and leisure, will be employing more than 80 percent of the total labor force. This sector, which will shape the destiny of the next century requires more talented and better educated and trained manpower. In other words, the transformation will begin with the individual. The top priorities of the restructuring efforts must, therefore, be made in the areas of education and high technology.

The Three Freedoms

It is impossible for a society to develop and reach the targets of this process unless there is full respect for the freedom of thought and expression. Even national unity depends in the final analysis on respect for the views of individuals and institutions. After all, "civilization is progress from an indefinite, incoherent homogeneity towards a definite, coherent heterogeneity." The second principle is the freedom of religion and belief in its nonsectarian and universal sense. The third is freedom of initiative. In order to trigger the creative forces of the individual, conditions should foster a civilized form of competition which, in turn, calls for a smaller state and less state interventions.

Conclusion

Developments in the world, particularly in Europe during the last few years, oblige us to look ahead. Our responsibility is to make this world a better place, based on respect for human rights, freedom, and economic and social equity throughout the world. History has entered the right path. Nothing will reverse the process, because its source is the will and the determination of the people.

Section 5 · Towards a More Democratic World

Volkmar Köhler

Now, at the end of the twentieth century, the antagonism between East and West, between socialism and free democracy, between economic planning and social market economies, which determined the course of events during the last 40 years, has been overcome. As a result, the relationship between North and South has also changed: North-South issues are no longer overshadowed by the East-West conflict, and bipolar thinking is being superseded by the recognition that we live in a multipolar world. The Group of 77, set up in 1967 as a cartel of developing countries to extract political and economic concessions from industrialized countries, has had its day. Increasing regional differences and the ever-wider gulf between the poorest of the poor, the least developed countries, and the newly industrialized countries have severed the thin bond that used to link the now 125 members of the Group of 77. Given this fragmentation of the South, there is a danger of the Third World's plight being forgotten. This is disastrous for the 47 least-developed countries, 28 of which are located in Africa. In the new interplay of forces they are threatened with marginalization. To put it in a nutshell: The old world order that emerged after World War II no longer exists, but a new order still has to take shape. This change is accompanied by much anxiety and uncertainty and prompts us to ask:

> What principles should guide us in framing the order of this changing world? Does the constant change actually allow any kind of formative policy? I believe it does, but only if we heed some fundamental precepts. . . . Freedom of the individual must be recognized as the bedrock of human life. It is the basis for all other parameters. Thus I count on freedom of the individual as the link between development, democracy, and a social market economy.

Development and Democracy

In the debate on development, the latter is only gradually undergoing a decisive change. Old development theories were based on a static conception of development—static in the sense that industrialized countries were described as developed, and Third World countries as underdeveloped. Yet the development of industrialized countries, too, is constantly advancing, and their existing level of development is not predetermined by any plan. The global ecological problems now confronting us, for example, did not feature in our plans and ideas for the future. If we are to shape the future responsibly, our static notion of development must first of all be replaced by a dynamic one. It has to be dynamic precisely because development is not a final state of affairs, but a continuous, open-ended process. This basic open-endedness of the development process derives from the freedom of the individual, who has to be at the center of our efforts. Development aims at human beings in their entirety and cannot therefore be measured in purely economic terms. Though economic growth is a necessary condition of human development, it is not sufficient on its own.[1] An adequate income is but one of many aspects: a long life; good health; education; political, economic, and social liberties; personal security; and guaranteed human rights—these are factors constituting a person's quality of life. A more extensive development goal is the opportunity freely to foster one's own creativity and productivity.

Did Development Aid Succeed?

Despite major efforts in the past—from 1950 to 1990 the Federal Republic of Germany alone spent DM 355 billion, including DM 147 billion in the form of official development aid—it cannot be claimed that these development goals are even beginning to be attained worldwide.

Worse still, the chasm between North and South, between the rich and the poor, is widening at an alarming rate: Since 1980 the population of the world's 25 richest countries has dropped by 6 percent, while their share of world income has risen by the same percentage. In the same period the population of the 25 poorest countries increased by 14 percent, but their share of world income fell by 2 percent. Thus today one fifth of the planet—the population of industrial nations—disposes of over four fifths of world income. This means that four fifths of the world, the inhabitants of developing countries, have to make do with just under one fifth of world income.

When seeking to identify the reasons for these negative trends one must avoid monocausal explanations because they do not do justice to the extremely complex nature of the problem. Both economic, social, and political factors within developing countries themselves and the global economic and political environment have to be taken into consideration when analyzing the obstacles to development. The international division of labor and increasing integration into world markets mean that developing countries, too, are susceptible to global economic fluctuations. This applies less to newly industrialized countries like Hong Kong, Singapore, Taiwan, and South Korea, which thoroughly benefit from this integration and have achieved double-digit export growth rates (22.5 percent in 1987, 15.7 percent in 1988). As exporters of manufactures—those countries account for two thirds of developing countries' exports of manufactures—they are affected far less by decreases in demand and changes in terms of trade than are commodity-exporting countries. Exporters of commodities—most of the poor sub-Saharan countries belong to this category—suffered a drop in exports and a grave deterioration of their terms of trade in the 1980s (by over 20 percent in 1986). This development is all the more serious as population growth in those countries averaged 3.1 percent in that period. In short, more and more people had to survive on less and less food.

Commodities make up over 70 percent of the exports of no fewer than 64 countries in the world, including 33 in Africa. Seventeen countries (11 of them in Africa) export exclusively commodities. This problem is further exacerbated by the fact that their exports often consist of very few commodities.

Attempts at reversing price trends by means of international commodity agreements or export cartels failed completely. Examples of this are OPEC, which was highly successful in the 1970s but which has largely lost its influence on world market prices, and the abortive International Tin Agreement.

Both the free play of forces on the world market and regulatory intervention can therefore give rise to problems. Agricultural protectionism shows very clearly that more freedom on the world market would certainly help developing countries. According to recent studies, even a relatively modest liberalization of international agricultural trade leading to a 10 percent rise in world market prices would raise the income of developing countries by $26 billion. The World Bank has calculated that the welfare losses of developing countries caused by industrial nations' protectionism are twice the amount of the official development aid received. The negotiations of the more than five-year-old Uruguay Round on the further liberalization of world markets must stop and reverse the tendency towards more protectionism.

Market Economies and Democracy

What basic concepts should underlie world politics and the world economy in the future so that developing countries can be integrated and liberated from their scandalous poverty? Of course, solidarity demands that we support poor countries with public aid—and even in the long run I can hardly imagine us being relieved of this duty. But at the same time the principle of subsidarity requires that developing countries be given the chance to participate increasingly in international trade by dint of their own potential. "Help through trade" is the motto.

However, merely demanding justice and using purely morally based judgments in the field in question pose exceptional risks, in my view. I would claim that employing moral judgments without regard for the laws of economics leads to irresponsible results. The application of morals to economic phenomena without considering economic laws results in moralism—and hence the opposite of morals.

Is a world order geared towards just distribution at all reconcilable with our understanding of democracy? Does such a mentality of just distribution not mean that developing countries are permanently dependent on us because they have no incentive to take the initiative? Does it not ultimately lead Third World countries into a new form of tutelage?

Particularly after the revolutionary political upheavals of the late 1980s in Central, Eastern, and Southeastern Europe the topics of national self-determination, democratization, and a social market economy have been taken up and discussed to an increased extent by the world public. These developments have given rise to the restructuring of international relations, with the collapse of the Berlin Wall vividly symbolizing the disintegration of socialism, and have triggered processes of reform in many Third World countries, notably in Africa. The disintegration of socialism means that humankind has not just lost a hope, but has simultaneously gained another. The events in Central and Eastern

Europe activated democratic principles in countries of the Third World; the close interaction of democracy and economic stability again became clear.

On all continents there are increasing signs that only growing democratic support by the people lastingly guarantees the process of economic restructuring in countries. This insight has prompted a debate on whether development assistance should not in future promote market economies and democracy more consistently. The criteria cited for this are personal development, reliable policies, certainty of the law, respect for human rights and domestic harmony. There is indeed a close link between democracy and development. Development strategies imposed on a population can at most have temporary success. The highly complicated process of genuine development, which extends far beyond economic growth, requires active participation by the people concerned if it is to prove successful.

However, the implementation of democratic principles will remain difficult, because in many Third World countries the actual shape that democracy takes depends on highly different factors. In this context democracy must be construed in a wide sense as broad participation and mobilization of the population.

Now that the Organization for Economic Cooperation and Development (OECD) has specified in its aid programs for Eastern European countries such basic conditions as the establishment of the rule of law, respect for human rights, free elections, multiparty systems, and market-orientated economic systems, developing countries must also accept such conditionality. The linkage of human rights and democracy with market economies is not an arbitrary act on the part of the OECD, but results from the experience that the two are directly interconnected. In our own history we Germans have become all too aware of this interdependence. The recent past of the eastern half of Germany, of the GDR, has taught us that under autocratic and centralistic regimes an economy cannot flourish and lags behind the needs of the people. In contrast, the end of the Weimar Republic showed that democracy can hardly prosper in an economic crisis. Thus democracy and a market economy are closely interrelated and can stabilize each other.

Freedom of the individual and the basically open-ended nature of development processes call for a free and open economic system. The notion of a definitive political and economic order runs counter to the very essence of human existence. Freedom is a fundamental anthropological category. It is characterized by flexibility and the possibility of choosing. We have to realize that definitive orders are per se inimical to democracy. A market economy does not seek a definitive order in this sense—for this reason it does not fit in with the constantly propagated "new international economic order," but is itself an open-ended process. It provides a regulatory framework. The freedom and rights of the individual always have to be limited by the freedom and rights of one's fellow beings. A social market economy does justice to this moral demand by seeking a synthesis of market essentials and social progress. Thus a social market economy is not a purely economic model, but assigns clearly supportive functions to the economy. It can be described as an irenic formula aimed at achieving a sensible balance of justice, freedom, and economic growth. It has proved its worth as a real economic order; it is not just the latest *World Development Report* which refers to a market-orientated economic order as the prerequisite of social and economic development. But as an open system a social market economy must be constantly advanced, refined, and critically appraised. In addition, the balance sought for every country must be determined and adapted on a case-by-case basis.

Conclusion

Now that the old antagonisms are obsolete, one might get the impression that everyone agrees on the aims and methods of global development. However, things look different in reality, and even where agreement exists, there are still many complicated details to sort out. Moreover, the calls for a "new international economic order" have become quieter but have not yet disappeared completely. Let me make this clear once more. Since the development of many countries is already restricted by internal obstacles to personal initiative, the worst possible reaction to existing problems would be to organize a world order in such an inefficient manner.

Instead, both national and international orders must be geared towards the following criteria, which are ideals in a Kantian sense: freedom (which includes respect for human rights), democracy, and a market economy aimed at social justice. We must not harbor the illusion of a just and perfect world order. We can merely move in the direction of such an order, but never actually attain it. If we heed these precepts, we can—despite all problems—confidently embark on the road leading into the third millennium.

Notes

1. The *1990 Human Development Report* impressively bears this out, citing Sri Lanka and Saudi Arabia as examples. In Sri Lanka the average life expectancy is 71 years and the rate of adult literacy is 87 percent at an average per capita income of merely $400, while in Saudi Arabia the per capita income is $6,200, but life expectancy is 64 years and the literacy rate is estimated to be only 55 percent.

Section 6 · Unleashing the Energy to Be Normal

Flora Lewis

There were no plans, no precedents, not even established theories to guide the transformation of societies emerging from Communism. The collapse of the old system came about because so many people were convinced that change was essential. But in the days of dissidence, of gathering demands for reform, people answered the question of what they wanted instead with only a notion. "A normal society," they said, not because they did not have more specific ideas, but because they were chary of "isms," of blueprints and engineered designs, of artificial utopias.

Quick Choices

Still, when the time came to replace opposition politics with new construction, something more than vague "normality" had to be proposed. The available options were democracy for political life and the market for economic life. These are very general methods, however, not even systems, for organizing power and production. There is a wide diversity of available models, each developed in the particular circumstances of history, geography, and culture of the societies concerned. Yet decisions had to be made urgently if chaos and utter ruin were not to follow the destruction of the failed system. Democracy and the market economy were, in various adaptations, the central theses of the countries which had succeeded in delivering what may be considered at this period of history "a normal society," with living standards and an acceptable range of individual liberties beyond the achievement of any other experiment. Therefore, they have become the new goals.

But even if the will were just to copy the way other countries implemented and practiced these precepts, the material and human means were simply not available. The choices were limited, risks unavoidable. There was no revolutionary map, and change had to be sought by groping, adapting, daring to unleash unguided energies. Some intellectuals thought they could evoke a "third way" between Communism and capitalism, a careful synthesis of the benefits of each.

This was particularly evident in East Germany, and bitter disappointment remains there as these people discovered that West Germans were not willing to wait for them to piece and patch, that the momentum of events overwhelmed their capacity to stay in the lead. After all, the dilemma of whether to apply an existing model or to invent a new one was illusory. Neither is possible. The decisions have to be an excruciating combination of inspiring confidence to leap into the unknown and insisting on what is practical and rapidly effective.

Impacts

The transition and its strains are giving rise to conflict, too often I think attributed to a natural eruption of ethnic hostility once the lid of repression is removed. There are historical roots, of course, but the evil flowers of violent hatred were not foreordained to bloom again. They have been encouraged by the void left by the breakdown of old forms of authority without the establishment of new institutions. Since Communism can no longer be the base for authority, some are turning to nationalism to take its compelling place. This tends to be a substitute for democracy, an easier way to lash people together than appealing to their reason and better instincts which they had so long been denied the right to use. In my view, that is what both Slobodan Milosevic and Franjo Tudjman have done in what was Yugoslavia, it is the difference between Vladimir Meciar and Vaclav Havel in what has ceased to be Czechoslovakia, and it is happening in various parts of the countries that used to form the republics of the Soviet Union.

This is regression. Europe has known too many tribal wars. They can no longer be attributed to ignorance, lack of exposure to people who are different, and lack of social intercourse. Bosnia's diverse groups lived together without hostility, but now murderous confrontation has been deliberately inflamed there to provide power to new demagogues. Self-determination does not deserve the unquestioning, almost sanctified aura with which it was endowed in the Wilsonian approach to smashing empires after World War I, nor in the Western propaganda jargon in the Cold War. It is a prescription to be taken in a well-considered dose if the effects of its supposed cure is not to be worse than the disease. How big must a "self" be to determine its right to statehood? What constitutes a "self"? How appropriate is statehood to the human and material needs of a specific group of people? Even such a large, democratic, and well-off country as Canada is torn by these questions, the answers to which are not self-evident.

The Changing Role of the State

What is evident is that the role of the nation-state is gradually and subtly changing. The economic world is now postnational, with less and less respect for borders and less and less independent command by state capitals. The political world is still mostly, though no longer entirely, national, and the ethnic world is prenational. The European Community's existence reflects these facts and the enlightened decision that they must be accommodated. So does the CSCE's provision for minority's rights, which all member states have endorsed but by no means yet enforced. These basic shifts in the facts of world life are creating disputes and tension everywhere, but they are particularly acute in the former Communist states. The resulting conflicts will not be solved by "the parties concerned," as the powers piously suggested at the outset of the foreseeable Yugoslav wars. They require acceptance by all parties of what the phrase "international community" implies, that is a responsibility to insist on democratic order. In these situations, politics and economics often pull in opposite directions, to the deterioration of both, and the constraints of a broader, agreed framework are required.

Democracy and Market

The link between democracy and the market is far more complex than conventional rhetoric suggests. When the market hurts too many people, through unemployment for example, democracy enables them to demand limits and subsidies which can undermine transition to the market. When democracy disperses and consumes too many resources to permit fruitful investment, the market managers seek to restrain the functioning of democracy.

The Asian "tigers," even Japan with its formal but very docile democracy, are favorite case of histories for those who argue that economic reform must be imposed within tight political limits, or all control would be lost. But they are not really applicable examples, partly for cultural and societal reasons, partly because of recent history. The "tigers" built from scratch, on the ruins of war, so every step was visible progress, and they were sustained by the Confucian ethic of duty. The authorities in China shudder—and smirk—at what happened in the Soviet Union, proclaiming that it occurred because Moscow failed to keep the Party strong while it opened economic pockets within the country to world markets. Pekin's mandarins forget that they came to economic reform after the Cultural Revolution had devastated the Party, forcing far-reaching renewal, and terrorized the population into silence. Moscow came to reform after stagnation, which petrified the Party so that it had to be blasted out of the way of change and left the people cynical and demoralized.

The well-known quip that "I pretend to work and they pretend to pay me" was the attitude reform had to face in Europe and the Soviet Union. Since "they" still could not pay to promote economic reform, something else had to be offered to induce people to work differently. That had to be political reform. Further, people were well aware that their mismanaged economies were the result of ideology and tyranny, the effect of the political cause which therefore required change. There is no more striking example of how badly lack of democracy damaged Eastern economies that the environmental devastation which has now come to light. Even the most untamed capitalism could not long get away with such irresponsibility where democracy ruled. And not only the people's health and surroundings were left to suffer, their economies are that much more degraded by the cost of pollution and its discouragement of investment.

In the long run, democracy and the market must go together, both for the way they sustain each other by freeing initiative, innovation, and individual responsibility and for the way they check each other to limit excess. That means some conflict, which is healthy so long as both democracy and the market attend to the mutual interest of keeping it in moderate bounds.

A New Gap in the West

Western societies are experiencing a new gap between the two, a disconnection as the broad public finds politics too distant, too unresponsive to its immediate concerns, and too closely entwined with the market in the sense of focusing the power of money. This is an unresolved problem, aggravated by the newly dominant communications. Former German Chancellor Helmut Schmidt makes a distinction between what he calls "TV democracy" and "print democracy," and he has a point. Television, which touches more people but in brief spurts privileging imagery and emotion over reasoned argument and adequate information, also greatly multiplies the role of money in politics. There is room for reform here, a need to restore the balance that the dual reign of democracy and market implies.

Democracy is primarily about government, what it should and should not do, so the role of government in regulating, correcting, and compensating for the market is for democratic definition. There are no panaceas that can permanently settle these issues. The issues themselves necessarily change with the times. The important point is to assure the capacity and will of government to respond to the democratic expression of need, including protection of the minority which is quintessential to the democratic method. This is not just rule by the majority but assurance to the minority that it can survive, flourish, and grow to be majority if it presents a convincing cause.

But not all social maladies are susceptible to government or even democratic cure, particularly the pathologies of crime, drugs, ethnic hatred, moral decay. There must be other institutions to provide the moral aesthetic and spiritual guidance and satisfaction which all societies need to remain cohesive and productive. This may come from the church, the family, a sense of immediate community, the many groups and links which form that elusive but important entity called civil society. There are some things government can do; provide policing, education, and rehabilitation in the case of drugs, for example. But it cannot answer the question of why some people are so driven to despair and defiance, of what is lacking in the social fabric to make them so self-destructive and destructive. The cause and the likely remedy lie deeper in the social consciousness. Here is an area where the West is falling down, where neither democracy nor the market is proving effective.

Conclusion

We do not really know why, nor whether either democracy or the market themselves are to blame or whether it has to do with some philosophical tide which has to be turned after too much worship of materialism and science. We are sure that tyranny is not the answer, nor fanaticism, which tends to violence and oppression.

History has not ended. We are not even sure of what makes "the good society," let alone how to get there, though we are indeed sure that it ought to be a good deal better than what we know. Perhaps there will never be an answer, only a need for new contributions, new concepts, new forms of change. It will take immense resources, also of energy and imagination, and it should be possible to draw on them constructively now that we are spared the foolishness of wasting them on rival arguments about systems and superiority.

Section 7 · Global Role of Transition Countries

Peter Jankowitsch

The grave economic situation confronting most transition countries has been exacerbated by a whole series of ethnic and regional conflicts. Some of them have been manifested in civil strife or interstate warfare. In other cases, some of them are trying to influence events in neighboring countries, thereby raising the stakes of other regional powers for counterinterventions. These are indeed most disturbing developments, affecting the peace and security of the region. These issues certainly require urgent attention. In a broader context, however, it is important to determine what the future role of the countries in transition could (or should) be in an increasingly global system.

The Old Order

Before even attempting to find an answer to this difficult question, one must reflect upon the current state of the global society. Arguably, the most important feature of the international system at the end of this century is the emergence of new guiding principles governing the new world system. In Western Europe and in some other parts of the world the principle of integration is guiding the policies of state actors. Yet, if one looks at developments in Central and Eastern Europe and the former Soviet Union, as well as in the developing countries of the South, the principle of the "nation-state" is exerting strong influences, and thus is helping either to maintain or replace the older structures. At present, one can therefore observe the coexistence of opposing guiding principles in an emerging global system.

During most of the nineteenth century, the international system had been shaped by the balance of powers and maintained among a limited number of influential states. In contrast, the breakdown of this old order after World War II not only cleared the way for the emergence of two new superpowers, but also ended the colonial supremacy of Western Europe over large parts of the Southern Hemisphere. This breakdown of the colonial order created a certain power vacuum that both superpowers competed to fill.

Although the international system clearly was shaped by U.S.-USSR politicomilitary competition during most of the post-World War II era, their domination certainly did not encompass all aspects of the system. While the bipolar system was guided by the principle of hierarchical control of the respective alliances, other countries repeatedly challenged this by insisting on national self-determination and democratic decision making, within the United Nations and other international fora. This competition between guiding principles certainly contributed to the current state of global affairs, in which the principles contained in the Charter of the United Nations—ranging from collective security to respect for human rights and fundamental freedoms—have not been widely accepted nor universally implemented.

The Shaping of a "New World Order"

The end of the Cold War and the changes in Eastern Europe have dramatically altered the parameters for global action in the political and military fields. However, while this opens up new possibilities and potentials for truly collective security arrangements on a global and/or a regional basis, the prospects for similar arrangements appear to be much dimmer when it comes to the economic sphere of international cooperation. In this domain, a more complex system has emerged in the aftermath of World War II. There too, however, rivalries existed between the two economic systems—market and centrally planned economies. The true economic competition took place among the Western industrialized economies. The reemergence of Japan and Germany as major economic powers, the increasing importance of regional economic integration in Western Europe and the Far East, and the rise of several newly industrializing economies in the South, gradually reduced the previously dominant position of the United States within the West. Major imbalances within the U.S. economy further accelerated this trend to a point where we can already speak of a multipolar world in the economic sphere.

It can be argued that the technological change contributing to the economic multipolarity has been another key factor which provoked dramatic changes that have swept away the old regimes in the East. The relative strength of each of these economic poles towards the others is largely determined by the ability to master the new technologies of what has been labeled the "third industrial revolution." Yet, while in previous periods comparative advantages, caused by technological advances, could be compensated for many national economies to reproduce them. The complex nature of these new advances technologies necessitates a highly developed infrastructure in terms of education and research and development. They require sometimes prohibitive capital investments and a much longer lead period to develop.

The New Regionalism

It has recently become fashionable to argue that competition among the three major economic poles—the United States, Japan, and the European Community (EC)—might or will eventually extend also to the politics of the politico-military sphere. Some observers even use the term "continentalism" to describe a potential situation where peripheral nations—voluntarily or involuntarily—will be attached to the center geographically adjacent to them. Thus, they argue, looming ahead is the threat of several continents vying for global supremacy.

Rather than pursuing such speculative thoughts, any serious observer of international relations needs first to take a closer look at the currents driving regionalism. Fishlow and Haggard recently distinguished between explanations describing regionalization alternatively either as an economic process or as the formation of political groupings.[1] In the former case, natural economic forces (e.g., proximity, income and policy convergence, etc.) lead intraregional trade and investment to grow more rapidly than that with other regions. Regionalism defined as political cooperation, in contrast, sees the growth of intrabloc trade primarily as a consequence of explicit policy decisions (e.g., caused by extraregional competitive pressures, intraregional hegemonic power relations, etc.).[2]

While the relationship between the two phenomena is far from clear, one can nevertheless observe that at least in the case of the EC, both economic and political factors have been causal in the formation of this most successful regional integration scheme. The founding fathers of European integration were consciously trying to set in motion a process that would make renewed warfare in Western Europe unthinkable. The complimentary structure of the Western European economies facilitated their task of, first, accelerating and expanding on the natural economic forces already at work, while, secondly, preparing the ground for regional political cooperation.

Lessons to Be Learned

The development of the European Community into one of the most powerful actors in the world economy has become a model for integration schemes in other regions. However, one should be very cautious in using the EC as a blueprint for either economic or political regional integration. In the case of Western Europe, favorable structural and policy conditions prevailed. More importantly, the EC has never restricted itself to remain a regional player. Partly because its past colonial linkages, but also due to a widely shared feeling of global responsibility, the EC has continuously helped and supported the disadvantaged regions around the world, first in the South, and today in Eastern Europe. It is the large share of exports and imports from and to the developing countries which truly makes the European Community a global player.

What might nevertheless be instructive for the transition countries is the continuous need to reconcile national and regional interests with global requirements. Regardless, whether these countries may wish to develop their own regional or subregional identity, or whether they may wish to become part of some larger integration scheme, they should know that in either case they will be called upon to contribute towards the attainment of some regional "public good."[3] For this, it will foremost be necessary to redefine the concept of "security." Items such as human rights, basic needs, a sound environment, etc., should be included in any agenda for strengthened cooperation within the region. For any long-lasting resolution there is the need to address these types of issues. Otherwise, there will be a constant source of new instabilities.

Conclusion

In finding solutions to highly pressing regional problems, one should not ignore the existence of interregional issues that often call for global solutions (e.g., global arms control, drug control, migration, global environmental problems, and particularly the need for development assistance). Admittedly, it is sometimes very difficult for policy makers to pay equal attention to national and global problems simultaneously. Yet they should keep in mind that in a truly interdependent world no one region can isolate itself from global developments. Furthermore, no one region can remain unaffected by developments taking place in other regions. Regional conflict resolution and regional security therefore needs to become part and parcel of a truly global collective security system, as originally envisaged by the founders of the United Nations.

Notes

1. See Albert Fishlow and Stephen Haggard, *The United States and the Regionalization of the World Economy* (Paris: OECD Development Centre, 1992), 12-13.

2. Fishlow and Haggard.

3. Integration schemes usually founder when gains are unequally distributed amongst members. Of course, members are also expected to contribute (at least) proportionally to their ability.

Chapter 2 · Changing Systems

Section 1 · Dictatorship to Democracy

Dankwart A. Rustow

Events in the former Soviet Union and East-Central Europe since the late 1980s have been truly startling. Mikhail Gorbachev proclaimed *glasnost* and *perestroika* (openness and restructuring), called for "tolerance" and "independent solutions to national problems," and condemned Moscow's military interventions in Hungary in 1956 and Czechoslovakia in 1968. Soon, Communist dictatorships toppled in countries from Poland and East Germany to Bulgaria and Albania. Late in 1989, Romania's repressive leader Nicolae Ceaucescu was sentenced to death by a rebellious crowd; as the Berlin Wall opened, East and West Germans proceeded toward their democratic reunification; and in Poland in December 1990, Solidarity leader Lech Walesa succeeded General Wojciech Jaruzelski as the country's democratically elected president. Back in Moscow in August 1991, a coup by Communist hardliners failed, and, in its wake, power shifted from the hesitant Gorbachev to the reformist Boris Yeltsin. The Soviet Communist party dissolved, statues of Lenin toppled, and Leningrad reverted to its original name of St. Petersburg. By the end of 1991, the Soviet Union was dissolved, as 11 of its 15 member republics adopted the name Commonwealth of Independent States.

Dramatic as events have been in the former Communist bloc, they are only the latest wave in a global tide toward democracy that began a decade earlier.[1] In the mid-1970s, Europe's oldest dictatorships in Portugal and Spain were transformed into democracies that soon joined the European Community. In the 1980s, Third World military dictators were replaced by elected civilians in countries from the Philippines, South Korea, and Turkey to Brazil and Argentina; and civil wars were ended by elections or peaceful negotiations from Nicaragua to Ethiopia and Cambodia. With Haiti's unprecedented democratic election in December 1990, all of Latin America, except for Fidel Castro's Cuba, is free of dictators for the first time in memory.

In the previous two centuries, democracy had been struggling against absolute or constitutional monarchy, against populist dictatorships from Bonaparte to Mussolini and Hitler, and against the global challenge of Communism. Now, for the first time in history, democracy appears to stand unopposed as the world's dominant political ideology. Even major non-democratic regimes proceed toward basic reforms: South Africa's deKlerk promises to phase out *apartheid*; in Iran, Khomeini's successors are providing a more liberal interpretation of his "Islamic revolution;" and China's octogenarian Communist leaders, while maintaining stern political control, proceed toward decentralization and liberalization of the economy—and they certainly do not advocate Leninism or Maoism as a worldwide program of revolution. Remarkably, by the 1990s, even exiled monarchs, such as King Michael of Romania, presented themselves as advocates of democracy. Presumably they did so because democratic monarchies such as Great Britain and the Scandinavian and Benelux countries offered the best model for a monarchic future in Europe, and particularly, because of the shining example of King Juan Carlos's return from exile in 1975 to preside over Spain's transition to democracy after Franco's death.

Still, there have been notable setbacks in the global movement toward democracy. In 1991, Haiti's elected president was ousted by followers of the old dictatorship. In 1989, the prodemocracy demonstrations in Beijing's Tiananmen Square were brutally repressed. In Algeria in 1992 military intervention annulled the democratic election victory of an Islamic party. And in a number of Central European or post-Soviet countries, the old Communist establishment reasserted itself in new guises. The former Yugoslavia was deeply mired in ferocious warfare, and ethnic conflict threatened the post-Communist order from the Trans-Caucasus to Moldova. Israel, the Middle East's only well-established democracy, continues its repressive military occupation over Palestinians. And in South Africa, negotiations between the white minority government and the African National Congress broke off amidst continuing violence.

Such setbacks raise a very basic question: Do the dramatic changes since the 1970s from Madrid and Manila to Moscow and Montevideo mean that humankind by the year 2000 will be headed for a "New World Order" of global democracy—or will all these events add up to no more than a brief moment of deceptive hope?

The Future of Democracy

To help find the answer to this question of the global democratic future, this paper will examine the political essentials of democracy. First among these is the need for a clear sense of *national identity,* whether based on a common language or some powerful set of common historic experiences. For, in the absence of such an unquestioned sense of identity, the economic and political crises of transition to democracy might lead to internecine warfare, as in Yugoslavia or in some parts of the former Soviet Union.

The second of these essentials is what I call "Democracy's Multi-Organizational Imperative." It requires a politically neutral, *well-established state* as well as two or more well-organized, nationwide *political parties*—and all this in a setting that provides freedom of expression and association. For, in the absence of a well-established government or of freely competing parties, the organizational vacuum of newly proclaimed democracies might be filled by military coups, as it was in much of the Third World in the 1960s and 1970s,[2] or by populist or quasifascist movements, as it might be in some of the post-Communist states of Central and Eastern Europe.

A Prerequisite of Democracy: Sense of Identity

"Democracy" is the Greek word for "people's government," and if "We the People" are to rule, we must have a secure sense of collective identity, typically rooted in common historic experiences. No matter how serious the dividing issues, there must be a feeling that "we are in this together" and that there are no plausible alternatives—a feeling that transforms even the most serious feud into a bitter family quarrel. Since democracy is government by discussion, by talking—or shouting, but not shooting—it out, a common language can be a major asset for the development of such a democratic consciousness of self.

Yet while a majority of established democracies did grow in a setting of a single language, there are a number of old and recent democracies (notably Switzerland, Belgium, Canada, and India) which have established a sense of common identity across linguistic divisions. Conversely, there are number of nations with a single language (notably the East Asian countries of China, South Korea, Vietnam, and Thailand) where democracy has not yet, or only recently, developed. All of which is to say that linguistic unity should be seen as a favorable but not an essential condition for democracy.

Most nations of Western and Northern Europe (Britain, France, the Scandinavian countries) inherited their linguistic unity and a sense of collective identity from their pre-democratic past. The unified language of France, for example, is largely due to centuries of monarchic rule. By 1589, France's kings from their residence in Paris began to organize a centralized bureaucracy, drawn from all parts of the realm, schooled in Paris, and sent back as the king's administrators—thus making Parisian French the standard idiom. And once "we the people" challenged royal authority, there was little doubt as to the identity of their "we."

In immigrant countries, such as the United States, Australia, New Zealand, and Israel, linguistic unity is the result of voluntary assimilation. A third group of democracies have established careful patterns of tolerant diversity, most notably Switzerland and the Netherlands. Both live in difficult natural habitats, the Swiss amid steep mountains and the Dutch behind fragile dykes on the North Sea. These terrains gave each an advantage in fighting for political independence from Austrian or Spanish foreign rule, the Swiss after 1291 and the Dutch after 1568. Both peoples developed their scientific and commercial skills; the Dutch inventing the telescope, and the Swiss becoming the world's watchmakers. And in their internal politics, there emerged a system of decentralization and toleran- ce—in both countries between Protestants and Catholics, and in Switzerland among speakers of German, French, Italian, and Romansch.

Close parallels to this tolerant cooperation among linguistic or religious groups can be found in the struggle against foreign domination that drew together Flemings and Walloons in Belgium, and Finnish- and Swedish-speaking inhabitants of Finland; or in the struggle against adversities of nature that unites the many linguistic groups of arid Botswana in southern Africa and mountainous Papua New Guinea in Southeast Asia.

A more complex pattern developed in India, its tradition of government by civil service throughout the subcontinent going back to centuries of British colonial rule, and its sense of identity to Gandhi's peaceful resistance in the 1920s and 1930s. Still when independence was attained in 1947, Muslim Pakistan split away. Also, the continued use of English in national politics introduces an elitist element into Indian democracy—and the country has only recently begun to grapple with its problems of ethnic-pluralist integration.

Elsewhere, there have been conflicts between political and national identity that have defeated or delayed democracy. Italy and Germany were the last European countries to be nationally unified by military action in the nineteenth century—and the first to succumb to fascism in the twentieth.

In the twentieth century, political boundaries among Arab countries offer a close analogy to those within Italy and Germany in the nineteenth. Most of the Arab region came under European domination (c.1880-1950) only after the spread of nationalism—and after Westerners themselves had grown apologetic about their imperial mission. Aside from Egypt, most Arab countries also were faced with an organizational vacuum—almost the entire governmental establishment of the Ottoman-Turkish empire having been inherited by Turkey, and foreign rule over Arab countries (as in the French and British Mandates over Syria, Lebanon, Iraq, and Transjordan) not lasting long enough to build up any alternative civil service tradition. Whereas Turkey thus was able to assert its sovereignty in a war of independence (1919-23) and move from benevolent one-party rule (1923-50) toward democracy (with some brief relapses into military rule in 1960-61 and 1980-83), the vacuum in the Arab countries from Iraq to Algeria typically was filled by military dictatorships.

Similarly, Pan-Arab dreams typically involved visions of violent unification under leaders from Egypt's Gamal Abdul Nasser to Libya's Muammar al-Qaddafi and Iraq's Saddam Hussein—as opposed to commitment to a score of separate states from Mauritania to Oman. By contrast, Nasser's successor Anwar al-Sadat shifted from Pan-Arab dreams to a firm course of Egyptian national interest and peace with Israel; yet, significantly, he entitled his autobiography *In Search of Identity*.

Many Arabs still feel ambivalent between commitment to an Arab nation or to their own state; yet inter-Arab boundaries, artificial as many of them are, have proved durable. The "United Arab Republic" of Egypt and Syria lasted a mere three years (1958-61) and was dissolved just when it was to have been economically implemented. Th unification of North and South Yemen in 1990 remains the only successful merger. Thus the trend in most Arab countries would seem to be an increasing acceptance of existing boundaries—perhaps on the pattern of Spanish South America after the failure of Simon Bolivar's experiment of "Gran Colombia" (1819-30). As the Iraq-Kuwait crisis of 1990-91 indicated, border revisions can have some popular appeal in the name of anti-imperial Arab nationalism, but they threaten virtually *all* existing political establishments. Thus Saddam Hussein faced a coalition led by the United States and including Arab countries as diverse as Saudi Arabia, Egypt, and Syria.

Most African countries south of the Sahara are faced with the opposite problem. They have many linguistic groups within the same postcolonial boundaries. Few, other than Botswana, took any early steps toward democracy. But here, too, the irresistible trend is to accept inherited boundaries—because one forced revision could provoke countless others. And even in sub-Saharan Africa there have been many indications in recent years of a movement from authoritarianism to democracy.

One major unresolved question of territorial-national identity is that between Israelis and Palestinians within the borders established in 1967, which by the 1980s mired Israel's democratic institutions in the violence of the *Intifadah* and repressive martial law. But even here there is hope of progress toward peaceful resolution since the negotiations in Madrid in October 1991, when resident Palestinians for the first time represented themselves, and the Israeli election of June 1992, which gave a firm majority to parties committed to negotiation.

Nonetheless, even within countries with well-established boundaries, ethnic or linguistic divisions can become sharply drawn in times of transition and uncertainty—when human beings instinctively rally to those they can *understand*. As Spain slid into its crisis of the 1930s, the civil war battles raged along the ancient borders of Castille and Aragon—united by royal marriage in the fifteenth century, but still marked by distinctive linguistic and cultural traditions. Similarly, the civil wars in the 1980s in Peru and Nicaragua (the latter after half a century of repressive dictatorship by the Somoza family) were aggravated by Cold War tensions and arms supplies—yet the original lines of division were in large part based on ethnic differences between Spanish Americans and indigenous Indians or mestizos.

The collapse of Communism in the former Soviet Union and in East Central Europe in recent years has produced a number of similar conflicts. Most of these countries are successor states of the Habsburg, Ottoman, and Czarist-Soviet multinational empires. Most of the East-Central Europeans from Czechoslovakia to Bulgaria and Albania gained their national independence only in the nineteenth or early twentieth centuries, and their borders typically were drawn not as a result of their own struggle for independence but by the victors in great power wars from 1815 to 1918 and from 1940 to 1945. All this means that they have had much less experience than Western Europeans of living together as "we the people"—and most of the post-Soviet republics have had no such experience at all.

Thus, in Czechoslovakia, tensions flared up between Slovaks and Czechs—linguistically close, but divided by historic memories and major differences in economic development between the prosperous Czech republic and the less developed Slovakia, largely agrarian and heir to an obsolete arms industry. By mid-1992, Slovakia insisted on dissolving the federation. To the south, what was once Yugoslavia moved into bitter political and military conflict—the linguistic and religious differences (e.g., between Orthodox Serbs, Catholic Croats, and Muslim Bosnians and Albanians) aggravated by the post-Communist economic crisis and by the massive store of weapons retained by the post-Communist Serbian leadership.

Similar problems arose in various parts of the former Soviet Union—which, as successor to the Czarist realm, was the one European colonial empire to have survived the decolonization of the 1950s and 1960s. The collapse of the party dictatorship and its command economy brought to the fore latent ethnic tensions—aggravated by the massive (voluntary or forced) relocation of populations under Soviet imperial rule. Some of these ethnic frictions—e.g., between Azerbaijanis and Armenians and between Moldovans and Russians—were also aggravated by former Communist *apparatchiks* eager to perpetuate their own grip on power and to sabotage *perestroika* or democracy.

Looking toward the future, it seems clear that no democracy is possible in a multiethnic country unless the union among the ethnic elements is truly voluntary. This, of course, presupposes, at a minimum, that all major linguistic groups have the right to speak and print their own language in public and to have their children schooled in it. It also implies that a secession movement should be allowed to proceed. Thus Gorbachev early in 1991 tried to repress Baltic independence by military force, but soon the demand for independence spread to the Ukraine and the Transcaucasian republics, leading to the demise both of Gorbachev and the Soviet Union. Still, it just might turn out that the overpowering economic problems that all post-Soviet republics face in the wake of the collapse of more than half a century of centralized planning might give them enough of a sense of "being in this together" to work out a peaceful and voluntary economic integration in their newly-proclaimed "Commonwealth of Independent States."

By contrast, China (aside from Tibet, which was militarily reannexed in 1950) is heir to a long tradition of governmental centralization and common identity from imperial to republican to Communist days. Hence, whenever a future generation of leaders decides to move toward economic liberalism and political democracy, it can do so without threatening the cultural identity or geographic cohesion of the Chinese realm.

The Multi-Organizational Imperative

Dictatorships, notably of the National Socialist and Leninist-Stalinist variety, have tried to centralize all of politics, economics, and society into a single organization commanded from the top—and, typically find themselves in deep crisis upon the death of the supreme dictator. By contrast, democracies need at least *three* organizations. There must be a neutral government, preferably based on broad merit recruitment, that collects taxes, gives civilians control over the armed forces, and provides those services that are government-supplied in even the most liberal economies, such as police protection, courts of law, schools from elementary to college level, and "infrastructure" facilities such as roads and airports. And there must be two or more well-organized political parties with a broad popular base throughout the nation.

There are many variations upon these essential democratic themes. The governmental organization can be unitary (as in most of Western and Northern

Europe) or it can be federal (as in Canada, the United States, and Switzerland), providing much room for regional or ethnic diversity but also creating a more delicate balance of unity. The governmental structure can be presidential (as in the United States and most Latin American countries), providing for the possibility of strong leadership, but also inviting the dangers of demagoguery and succession crisis, or it can be parliamentary (as in Britain and many other established democracies), providing for natural recruitment of leadership in government and opposition parties, but requiring a well-respected and neutral head of state.

A very crucial feature of any democracy is the electoral system by which party candidates are voted into public office. One alternative is the single-member-plurality system (as in Great Britain and the United States), which tends to consolidate political rivalries into a two-party system. Another is proportional representation, which provides for greater diversity of parties in parliament, but also can lead to recurrent deadlocks (as in Israel in the 1980s, Turkey in the 1970s, and Germany in the 1920s). Whatever the particular party pattern, democratic diversity in politics, of course, is naturally reinforced by the decentralization of economic power in a liberal system of private enterprise, and even more by the wide variety of expression under a democratic system of free press and assembly.

In sum, it could be argued that democracy makes for much unnecessary effort in political campaigning and organizational rivalry, but that it provides for essential alternatives. Thus dictatorships of the Leninist-Stalinist variety undergo major succession crises as the leader dies or becomes incapacitated. By contrast, a democratic party can resolve its leadership problem while it goes into opposition. In matters of policy, whereas dictatorships commit themselves to a single mistaken or disastrous policy, democratic parties give their electorates a choice between at least *two* sets of mistakes. And the large variety of presidential and parliamentary, unitary and federal, and other democratic procedures gives the competing leaders in each new democracy an opportunity to develop forms of organization which their constituents, after trial and error, will consider most properly suited to the country's particular historic heritage and present and future problems.

In the older Western democracies, a complex pattern of organization was gradually developed over centuries of transition from monarchy to aristocracy and democracy (as in Britain from 1640/88 to 1832/1918) or (as in the United States) in an victorious war of independence. There were, of course, severe crises along the way, such as the civil wars in Britain (1640-49) and the United States (1861-65) and the French revolutions of 1789, 1830, and 1848 (and in Paris in 1870).

The difficulty for many newly proclaimed democracies in the late twentieth century is that they find themselves in an organizational vacuum. Yet they are under tremendous international pressure to achieve this process of democratic organization almost instantly. Colonial regimes in Asia and Africa, for example, gained their freedom (with the partial exception of Algeria, Vietnam, and

Indonesia) not in wars of independence, but because of the exhaustion of the colonial powers after World War II. The East Central European countries had independence fall into their laps even more unexpectedly as a result of Gorbachev's *perestroika*.

Generally, nascent democracies must cope with the crises that brought down the preceding regimes. Military dictatorships often collapse after a lost war and civilian dictatorships after economic crisis. Thus the Argentinean generals were forced to surrender power after losing the Falklands/Malvinas war of 1982 and the Greek colonels after the Cyprus crisis of 1974. In the Soviet Union itself, Gorbachev's policy of *glasnost* and *perestroika* was prompted above all by the recognition that the Soviet economy could not carry the triple burden of maintaining the country as a space-age superpower, supporting Communist regimes or wars from Cuba and Nicaragua to Angola and Afghanistan, *and* providing a minimally acceptable standard of living for Soviet citizens at home. But, of course, Gorbachev's hesitant policies of *glasnost* and *perestroika* had the inevitable effect of aggravating the crisis of the economy—a situation where the command economy functions no longer and a liberal economy functions not yet. And to this economic chaos, the demise of the Communist party and of the Soviet Union adds a political vacuum.

Just as every newly democratic country has to find its own particular formula of unitary or federal, presidential, or parliamentary government, so each one of them must fill the postdictatorial vacuum by whatever means are available. Thus Poland is lucky to have had a Solidarity trade union that survived a decade of Communist and martial law repression, although recent elections show that, with the disappearance of the Communist antagonist, there is little incentive for continuing unity in the movement. And Hungary is lucky to have had several decades of economic decentralization preceding its transition from Communism to democracy.

Still, there are at least as many economic choices to be made in a transition to a free market as there are political choices in a transition to democracy. Should it be done by "shock treatment" as attempted in Poland, or by a more gradual transition? How should inflation be controlled? How should state property be decentralized? Should it be by entitlements for every citizen, as attempted in Czechoslovakia; by recognition of property claims before Communist expropriation, as in East Germany; by transformation into workers' cooperatives; or by de facto independence of former state managers, as seems to be happening in much of the former Soviet Union?

The Need for a New Marshall Plan

The end of the twentieth century provides a unique international setting for democracy. Earlier, there were major international efforts to spread democracy, but their successes remained very limited. Although World War I was started by traditional monarchies and World War II by a totalitarian dictatorship, both were eventually won by democratic coalitions. Nonetheless, Woodrow Wilson's postwar hopes for a "world . . . made safe for democracy"[3] went unfulfilled. Most of the newly proclaimed national republics from Finland to Yugoslavia soon turned into dictatorships; and the conversion of former German colonies and Arab parts of the Ottoman Empire into "League of Nations mandates" continued colonialism under a euphemistic label. The outcome of World War II allowed for the development under Allied occupation of democracies and of strong liberal economies in both West Germany and Japan; the Marshall Plan provided crucial economic aid for what became the European Economic Community. But soon the global scene changed into an escalating "Cold War," with the Soviet Union imposing dictatorships in Eastern Europe. Both Washington and Moscow supported dictatorial or militarist regimes from Latin America to Africa and Southeast Asia.

The recent collapse of Communism is the only historic occasion when major regime changes have occurred peacefully. And the change came after decades of the Leninists' own propaganda had convinced the citizenry of their countries that capitalism and bourgeois democracy were the only available alternative to their own "proletarian socialism." But neither democracy nor capitalism can be achieved overnight—creating the danger that high expectations will soon yield to a deep sense of frustration.

Nonetheless, in contrast to the Marshall Plan of the late 1940s, there have only been hesitant efforts by the leading liberal democracies to provide systematic and large scale aid to the post-Communist countries of East-Central Europe and the emerging Commonwealth of Independent States. The United States finds itself in an unprecedented debt crisis, and after a decade of foreign adventures under Reagan and Bush into Lebanon, the Persian Gulf, and Central America, is likely to turn its attention to long-neglected domestic problems. Germany faces the immense economic cost of unification—and perhaps the mounting frustration of East Germans with a "unification" that turned out to be more of an outright annexation by the West. The countries of the European Community are deeply immersed in their plans for more complete economic and perhaps political integration, and possible membership applications by former EFTA members from Norway and Finland to Switzerland and Austria. And Japan, for the first time in decades, is facing a recession at home—and its deep-seated ambivalence about becoming involved in major foreign policy ventures.

Also, the Marshall Plan and later programs of U.S. aid to the Third World were formulated at a time of mounting Cold War competition between Washington and Moscow. Now, with the collapse of the Soviet bloc, such compelling "national security" incentives seem to be absent. Still, as President Yeltsin of Russia has hinted and former U.S. President Richard Nixon has explicitly warned, a failure of the post-Soviet experiments in liberal democracy might produce a situation of political and military chaos far worse than the present transition crisis—and far more difficult to resolve than the former Cold War.

One therefore may hope that the domestic crises in the three leading industrial nations might abate soon enough to allow the formulation, perhaps under leadership by the International Monetary Fund, the recently founded Bank for

European Development, or the United Nations, of a bold program of foreign aid and encouragement of regional integration that would do for the post-Soviet bloc what the Marshall Plan of 1947 did for the economic recovery and integration of Western Europe. Yet, whatever much-needed plans for economic and technical assistance are offered to the post-Communist countries, it must be remembered that the crucial choices of economic policy and political organization must be made by the leaders and voters of those countries themselves.

The Prospects for Regional Integration

One of the key features of the Marshall Plan was that it asked Western Europeans to agree among themselves about the details of distribution of U.S. aid throughout the region, thereby providing a major stimulus for later regional integration. And the Western European example, in turn, shows how important regional cooperation can be in building up successful liberal democracies after the collapse of previous regimes.

Specifically, the European example also illustrates the logical sequence of integration from economics to politics. Its first phase was the removal of tariff barriers, allowing each country to maximize its "comparative advantage" in a rapidly growing regional economy. Then came other steps of regional economic and political coordination, such as reducing nontariff barriers and opening frontiers to free migration. A decade after its inception in 1957, the European Economic Community was such an unquestionable success that Great Britain gave up its initial opposition and, along with other EFTA members, joined the Community in 1972. By this time the EC also made it clear that only democracies would be admitted as new members, And it turned out that this requirement had major effects in accelerating the movement toward democracy in Greece, in Portugal and Spain (admitted in 1981 and 1986), and even in Turkey, which became an associate member in 1964 and applied for full membership in 1987, at a time when its democracy was fully restored.

This European example might well be followed in Latin America, where Brazil, Argentina, and Chile decided on closer economic relations after emerging from military rule in the 1980s. Perhaps the next steps could be the dismantling of tariff barriers, along with a phasing out of the many economic subsidies provided over decades of protectionism, and expansion of membership in such an economic community to all of South and Central America. Such regional economic liberalism would let Latin Americans develop their economy on the pattern of the South Korean and Taiwanese economic miracles, and support many of its fragile democracies. The final step might be a strengthening of the political ties among the Latin member states of the Organization of American States.

The same pattern of step-by-step economic integration might accelerate economic development in sub-Saharan Africa. Similarly, it might help members of the Arab League overcome their pattern of military competition and Saudi Arabia's unsuccessful policy of winning Arab friends by dishing out subsidies, and instead help move members toward liberalizing their political systems, as

Egypt has done under President Hosni Mubarak, and Kuwait and Saudi Arabia briefly contemplated doing during the Iraq-Kuwait war.

For post-Communist countries from Estonia to Albania and Bulgaria the obvious choice would seem to be between developing economic integration within East-Central Europe or applying for association and ultimate membership in the EC, with Hungary, Poland, and the Czech Republic presumably the candidates most likely to be accepted. Perhaps there is, in the long run, an even better chance for a post-Soviet "Commonwealth" from Kiev to Vladivostok, since the newly independent republics soon will find that, willy-nilly, they have become economically interdependent after 70 years of Communist rule and central economic planning and after years of post-Communist political and economic crisis.

A Farewell to Arms?

In considering the recent movement toward global democracy and its future prospects, we should recall that the post-World War II economic miracles of Germany and Japan were in large part made possible by their disarmament and the consequent transfer of their industrial energies from military to civilian production. Perhaps the lingering economic crisis in the United States could also be overcome by shifting productive energies in a post-Cold War era from the overgrown military-industrial complex to the rebuilding of U.S. railroads and other decaying infrastructure and to the revival of the global competitiveness of its automobile and electronics industries.

Above all, we must remember that the greatest threat to newly proclaimed democracies in the Third World in the 1960s and 1970s turned out to be an epidemic of military coups, based on a growing arms trade encouraged by Cold War competition between Soviets and Western powers, and, in the Middle East, by the massive inflow of oil money since the 1970s.[4] Similarly, the single severest threat to the emergence of democracy in post-Communist countries has been interethnic warfare as between Azerbaijan and Armenia or, worst of all, in Bosnia and other parts of the former Yugoslavia.

One possible scenario of overcoming such conflicts is suggested by the experience of Costa Rica. After a decade of a devastating civil war that neither side could win, the leader of the temporary victors, José Figueres, proposed a bold program of disarmament on both sides that reduced the country's armed forces to a civilian police. This voluntary disarmament helped transform Costa Rica into a prosperous democracy, while other Central American countries (Cuba, Panama, Nicaragua, El Salvador) continued to succumb to dictatorship or civil wars, that were soon aggravated by U.S.-Soviet rivalry in the Cold War. It is also noteworthy that, by 1987, President Oscar Arias Sanchez of Costa Rica won the Nobel Peace Prize for mediating a democratic resolution for the bitterest of those civil wars in neighboring Nicaragua.

A far broader and more effective solution—now that the Cold War competition is over—would be to phase out the massive arms export trade from developed countries that has made those antidemocratic military regimes and destructive civil wars possible. A logical first step would be for the United States and its major European allies (Britain, France, and Germany) to agree on a schedule of drastic reduction and eventual elimination of their exports of conventional weapons and the conversion of most of their arms factories to civilian industrial purposes at home and perhaps to Marshall-Plan exports to help rebuild the industrial infrastructure of Central and Eastern Europe. Other arms exporters, such as Israel, China, North Korea (and perhaps Russia and Slovakia) and weapons importers anywhere in the world should be induced to join this same plan for global arms reduction by being denied foreign aid or being suspended from the International Monetary Fund (IMF) and World Bank privileges until they do.

The ultimate aim would be to reduce world armament levels to police protection at home and to participation in peacekeeping missions abroad that are sponsored by the United Nations or regional organizations such as the European Community or the Organization of American States. The net effect would be to phase out civil wars and military coups through gun control at the source, and thus to realize, one century later, Woodrow Wilson's dream of a "world safe for democracy." Ultimately, such a program of arms control would let the world's leading industrial powers establish a "New World Order," peaceful and democratic, and centered around a set of truly "united" nations.

Conclusion

It would be a major mistake to interpret the collapse of Communism as a mere Western victory in the Cold War. Rather it is a victory for those forces of change which, since the mid-twentieth century, have been transforming the world into a "global village": the escalating flows of international trade, from which dictatorial regimes exclude themselves at their own peril; the public concern about human rights developed by the Carter and Reagan administrations and by members of the European Community; and, above all, the ever more intensive network of global communications. Thus, one of the major factors undermining the East German dictatorial regime was the fact that its citizens could not be stopped from receiving West German television; and the dominant elites of even the most traditional Arab monarchies show little hesitation in spending their newly acquired oil wealth on the latest products of international technology.

Indeed, the current democratic revolution fulfills in part the prediction that Marx and Engels made in their *Communist Manifesto* as far back as 1848—a document that did not anticipate any "proletarian" or "socialist" revolution in countries such as Russia or China, but rather a proletarian revolution preceded by global victory of the bourgeoisie:

> The bourgeoisie, by the rapid improvement of all instruments of production, by the immensely facilitated means of communication,

> draws all . . . nations into civilization. The cheap prices of its com-
> modities are the heavy artillery with which it batters down all Chinese
> walls. . . . It compels all nations, on pain of extinction, to adopt the
> bourgeois mode of production . . . [and] to become bourgeois them-
> selves. In one word, it creates a world after its own image.

And indeed, a century and a half after that historic *Manifesto,* such global economic and political unification through the bourgeoisie is exactly what we seem
to be witnessing. Even the ultimate reduction of exploitation of people by other
people and a "withering away" of the traditional nation-state are no longer
inconceivable; but, contrary to Marx and Engels, a global proletarian revolution
is not in the offing. Indeed, the more likely outcome is a classless global
bourgeoisie—but only if, in the world of the future, worldwide industrial development, global disarmament, and free migration can gradually reduce the historic pattern of crass exploitation.

Above all, the future is not predetermined—and indeed it is the chief virtue
of political democracy and economic liberalism that they multiply the choices
available to humankind.

Notes

1. See Samuel P. Huntington, *The Third Wave: Democratization in the Late
Twentieth Century* (Norman: University of Oklahoma Press, 1991); and Dankwart A.
Rustow, "Democracy: A Global Revolution?" *Foreign Affairs,* 69 (Fall 1990): 74-91.

2. On the postcolonial problems of dictatorship and democracy in the Third World,
see my book *A World of Nations: Problems of Political Modernization* (Washington:
Brookings, 1967). On the basic problem of transition see my essay "Transitions to Democracy: Toward a Dynamic Model," *Comparative Politics,* 2 (April 1970): 337-363.

3. "The world must be made safe for democracy" was Wilson's crucial plea in
proposing to Congress, on 2 April 1917, that the United States declare war on the Central Powers.

4. For details of oil income and arms trade see my book *Oil and Turmoil: America
Faces OPEC and the Middle East* (New York: Norton, 1982), 282ff and on the
prevalence of military coups, my earlier book *A World of Nations,* 170-206.

Section 2 · Transition to a Market Economy

Saburo Okita

The world has been experiencing a period of rapid change since the late 1980s. Most dramatic were the revolutionary changes in the former Soviet Union and Eastern Europe—especially the calls for democratization and the moves for economic reforms including the desire to switch to market economies. Such moves were unimaginable not long ago. Generally speaking, the world trend today is that, while economy and technology push globalism, culture and social factors work for preserving local or regional identity. As the globe is getting smaller and smaller because of the advancement of communication and transportation technology, the world economy is distinctly moving toward globalism. When I was invited to the Soviet Union in 1986 to exchange views with experts there, Academician Yevgeniy Primakov, that time head of IMEMO (Institute for World Economy and International Relations) gave me three reasons for the need of the Soviet Union to introduce *perestroika*: the intolerable time lag of technological progress will be caused by lack of contact with the outside world; isolation in the world economy will result in economic inefficiency; and nuclear weapons are unusable in the world today and tomorrow.

The Market and the Government's Role

While it is often argued in the West that this shift to market mechanisms is proof positive that market-oriented economies are superior to centrally controlled economies, it should be remembered that market mechanisms are not infallible. Given the environmental, resource, energy, and other constraints that exist, it is, I would argue, important to reconcile the two systems and to find an effective way of combining market mechanisms and government planning. This is especially important as the developing economies and formerly planned economies seek to define new relations and divisions of responsibility between the public and private sectors. Unlike the industrial countries, these countries can be said to still need government intervention not only to offset market failures, but also because their private sector economies are less mature and their markets underdeveloped compared to those in the industrial countries. Whether or not government intervention is effective depends not on the extent but on the quality of the intervention. What, then, is entailed in the concept of policy quality? Basically, policy quality is determined by the mix of four factors: the enhancement of administrative capabilities and policy guidance for market function complementarity; the role of government in the field of social and physical infrastructure; long-term policy consistency and compatibility; and consideration for cultural factors.

Looking at the first of these four factors, since development must take place in a situation of continuously changing parameters beyond government control, it is necessary to appreciate the market's coordinating functions, to take fullest possible advantage of the market mechanisms' ability to work through the inter-action among individual economic entities to create a general equilibrium with conditions conducive to the attainment of overall balance. By so doing, it should be possible to avoid excessive administrative bloating, the emergence of vested interests and corruption that make it difficult to effect policy changes with government intervention, massive fiscal deficits, and other failures of govern-ment. Instead it should be possible both to enhance administrative capabilities and to approach a situation in which entities concerned are able to conduct market-based economic behavior—to approach what might be called economic democracy.

Japan's Experience

Looking specifically at the Japanese example by way of explanation, the govern-ment of Japan announced a national income-doubling plan in 1960. This plan was drawn up in full awareness of the Japanese economy's growth trends in an effort to eliminate the barriers to growth, to rectify the various imbalances that existed, and to lessen social and economic inequalities.

Under this plan, Japan hoped to double its national income within the decade. In fact, this goal was achieved in only seven years. With this success, Japan entered upon a period of very rapid growth, with the per annum growth rate averaging 10 percent a year for 15 years. As such, this plan played an important role in consolidating the foundation for Japan's postwar economic development.

In 1982, Professor Lester Thurow coordinated at symposium on Japan's postwar economic performance at the Massachusetts Institute of Technology, the results of the symposium later published by MIT as *The Management Challenge: Japanese Views*. Commenting on the five priorities that Japan had set in the 1960 national income-doubling plan, professor Thurow wrote:

> Considering the five elements in the Japanese economic strategy at the beginning of the income-doubling decade: strengthen social over-head capital, push growth industries, promote exports, develop human ability and technology, and secure social stability by mitigat-ing the dual structure of the economy. This list could easily serve as strategic objectives for the American economy by the year 2000.

Once one accepts that the economy works through the free activity of corpo-rations and market mechanisms, it is clear that the private sector must be the driving force for the attainment of any goals or targets for industry in general. When people in the private sector realize how economic development is achieved, their creativity, efforts, and entrepreneurship make it possible to solve numerous problems and to achieve society's goals. The role of the government is to create a climate in which the private sector can act, to remove any barriers that may arise, and to indicate general directions. Although the government may want to assist these corporate efforts, to offer stimulation, encourage industry to work toward set goals, its economic role can only be complementary.

There are some aspects of the Japanese model that have been seen overseas as indicative of strong government intervention. However, it would be more accurate to attribute Japan's growth not to government intervention, but to fierce competition among private-sector companies and to the vigorous workings of market mechanisms. In fact, Japanese public-sector corporations have not been active investors in consumer goods or services. The relations between the public and private sectors and privatization has been revived in an effort to streamline the government sector.

Recently, the railways and telecommunication were privatized in Japan, but ownership is still in large measure in the hand of the government. However, a distinction needs to be made between the privatization of management and the privatization of ownership. For small enterprise, this separation is unrealistic. For large enterprise—as opposed to small enterprise—the privatization of management should be promoted through a policy of avoiding excessive intervention by government and encouraging the entrepreneurial skill and ability of the manager. In case of privatization of ownership, however, it should not be promoted too hastily because there is some possibility that it could bring about social and political difficulties and it would be desirable to take a step-by-step approach. Mere transfer of ownership from public to private will not guarantee the improvement in the management efficiency. There must be competition among enterprises.

Infrastructure Development

However, the government can take a central role in field of social and physical infrastructure development. This is the second factor whereby the quality of policy is determined. In particular, it is essential that development planners and strategists realize how very important the government's role is in the development of human resources, namely investing in people. Although elementary education, health and hygiene, nutrition, and the other basic human needs generally yield low short-term financial returns, it should be noted that they can yield a very high economic return if they are effectively planned and implemented. Equally important is the role of government to construct necessary infrastructure such as road, port, communications, power, and so forth, keeping balance with the development of private sector.

Role of Planning

The third aspect, long-term policy consistency and compatibility, highlights the importance of planning based upon the assumptions of liberal economic structures. The significance of medium- and long-term planning is that most governmental and corporate policy planning tends to be too caught up in short-term issues and objectives, and planning—part forecast and part persuasion—should stimulate governmental and corporate policy makers to take the longer term perspective.

The following three points define the role of economic plans in Japan. First is the educational role of economic forecasting. The outlook for the overall economy as stated in the plan is not simply a list of objective forecasts, but also serves as a statement of government policy goals. The various sectors of the private economy then have this government outlook before them and can take it into account in setting their own production and investment plans and policies aimed at maximizing profits. Second is that Japanese planning communicates the long-term commitments of government economic policy. Japanese government economic plans formulated during 1960s and 1970s all had a section on the distribution of investment in the public sector and a section detailing upcoming government policy programs. Third is that the planning process functions as a means of accommodating and reconciling diverse interests. Planning in Japan is not the exclusive work of government economists, but includes participation by a broad spectrum of people, including representatives from industry, labor, the media, and academia.

The Role of Culture

In the fourth aspect of the government's role in the cultural field, the South Commission stated in its 1990 report *Challenge to the South* that culture must be a central component of development strategies in a dual sense. On the one hand, the strategies must be sensitive to the cultural roots of the society, and on the other hand, they must include the development of the culture itself as a goal. Because the traditional culture functions to preserve the existing social features, it is essential that development be compatible with the basic social and cultural characteristics.

In this regard, for countries like China and India with a large population and cultural diversity, a sweeping and across the board liberalization would be very risky in terms of political stability and the sustainability of economic restructuring. While giving priority for the reform in areas which contribute to the foreign exchange earnings are necessary, a step-by-step approach might be desirable for other areas.

A New Pass for Development

Premised upon these four factors mentioned above and depending upon their stages and processes of development and their levels of introduction of market mechanisms, the developing economies and the formerly planned economies can adopt patterns of behavior different from the industrialized countries, even within the capitalist paradigm. This realization was also important for Japan as a later-developing industrialized country in a number of respects. First is the fact that, while it is important to liberalize microeconomic areas, it is essential to articulate broad guidelines governing the formulation and establishment of macroeconomic policies. Second, it appears that those countries that are attempting to catch up with more industrialized countries need stronger government leadership that the front-running industrial countries do. The third dimension is the requirement that planners read the market signals carefully and incorporate them in their planning. This means planning *with* market forces rather than planning *against* market forces. Actually, there are many rooms in capitalism's house. Professor Chalmers Johnson of the University of California at San Diego has called Japan a "capitalist developmental state." Emphasizing its dynamic process of development, it could just as well be called "catch-up capitalism" or the "capitalism of the latecomer."

I think there are two additional points which have to be considered in the current state of the world, which can be seen as a time of transition. One is the accelerating global interdependence in environmental concerns, security arrangements, economic relations, development cooperation, and every other field. In particular, the multipolarization of the world economy has created an enhanced need for macroeconomic policy coordination and systemic harmonization. While the advances in transportation, telecommunications, and information processing are fueling the drive to the creation of borderless economies, there is bound to be national friction as long as there are nations. This means that the countries that choose to fully participate in the world economy would inevitably face a far-reaching adjustment of their external and internal policies through such negotiations as the General Agreement on Tariffs and Trade (GATT), Uruguay Round, and Structural Impediments Initiatives between Japan and the United States in 1990 and 1991.

The second point is the global environment. Humankind is today limited by environmental considerations and finite resources. It is essential that we mobilize our full technological and financial resources in a global response to these constraints. The environment is the very basis for continued survival, and it is impossible to believe that the human race will prosper unless we use the environment wisely so that future generations can also enjoy its blessings. At the same time, given that development is imperative if the developing economies are to eradicate poverty and we are to enable all peoples everywhere to live in a more civilized fashion, it is essential that we approach this with a view to reconciling the dual imperatives of environmental conservation and economic development. This in turn demands the concept of sustainable development. Some degree of material affluence is essential to the attainment of market economies and democratic government, and the pursuit of material affluence necessarily entails energy consumption. Thus the attainment and maintenance of market economies and democratic government demands some measure of development and growth, as well as expanded energy consumption. Yet measures must also be taken at the same time to alleviate the environmental impact.

The question of the role of the government and market in the context of the global environmental protection is represented by the axiomatic corollaries that no ecological policy can be pursued efficiently without respecting fundamental economic principles and that no economic policy can be pursued successfully without regard to the ecological consequences.

Conclusion

With rapidly changing world economic conditions, the Asia-Pacific region is becoming increasingly important not only in GNP or trade terms, but also in terms of the economic policies followed by the economies of the region. There are success stories of increasing savings rates, export-oriented growth policies, business-government cooperation, and more. The experiences of development in the Asian-Pacific economies, particularly the East Asian economies, should have relevance for other developing economies and for the socialist economies undergoing the transition from a centrally controlled economy to a more market-oriented economy.

Section 3 · The Mixed Economy: A Practical Target

Lawrence R. Klein

What kind of model economic system should serve as a target for restructuring areas of the world? Economics will naturally figure importantly in answering this topical question of the moment, but cultural, political, social, and engineering considerations will also shape the answer. As an economist, I shall pay more attention to the economic aspects of the issue, but I fully realize that the end result must be acceptable on a broader base than just economics.

The question is being put before the citizens of former Warsaw Treaty Organization countries (WTO) and also before numerous developing countries that are trying to restructure their economic systems. It is relevant to the economy of China, the largest in numbers in the entire world. China, like the WTO countries, is in the process of restructuring a socialist system that was formerly like those in Eastern Europe and the Soviet Union, but China's targets and processes are quite different from those of the WTO countries. China, however, is also a developing country as well as a socialist country, so the structural reforms are related to those being considered at the moment in the developing world.

There is also considerable restructuring taking place in many industrial countries, and these, too, must take decisions about targets and such.

Two Opposing Systems

Before the world set out on courses of massive reform, there were two dominant systems—one of strict and rigid socialist planning and the other of unfettered free markets, functioning in a private mode of decision making. There are countries that were closely associated with one or the other of these two extremes, but nothing is pure in practice. Perfect socialism or perfectly competitive free markets existed in economists' minds but not in practice. Soviet Russia exemplified the rigid centrally planned system, while Hong Kong was probably the best example of the free enterprise extreme. The Soviet Union has fallen apart, and Hong Kong will soon be integrated into China, so other examples will have to be sought. Perhaps they do not exist.

The Soviet Union tried at one time to be a closed, self-sufficient system, but by the 1960s it fully recognized that its operations had to be opened, at least to foreign trade, but probably to even more nonsocialist modes of operation. Many aspects of Soviet foreign trade were already "contaminated" by capitalist practices. That was natural, given Soviet objectives. Not only in the course of international trade, but also in international finance, there was a nonsocialist infiltration of the Soviet Union and the Eastern bloc countries. For example, Poland, a WTO country, became heavily indebted to Western financial institutions, much to the worrisome chagrin of socialist theoreticians in the Soviet Union, and was the first in the massive wave of borrowing countries who could not service debt, in the late 1970s and 1980s. This occurred even before Mexico succumbed in 1982.

In addition to Poland's debt entanglements, Hungary introduced reforms along the lines of the market mechanism at an early stage. This was another step among WTO countries in moving away from rigid central planning. Chinese economic reform began in 1987 and moved along some lines that have been inspired by Hungary's experience as well as along lines that were peculiarly Chinese. In any event, rigid, socialist planning did not prove to be a sustainable extreme position. The polar extreme at the socialist end did not remain pure.

The successful working of the market mechanism in a private enterprise environment requires many restrictive features if it is to be theoretically sound for the economist; that is, if it is to be deemed "optimal." There must be complete competition, availability of market information, free entry in areas of production, free movement of workers, and absence of monopoly power. Nothing must interfere with competitive market clearing.

The formal proofs that a competitive equilibrium exists at the capitalist polar extreme and is "optimal" in the sense of Pareto, generally refers to a static system in which production is carried out under conditions of decreasing or constant returns to scale, without explicit allowance for the dynamics of technical change. The full competitive equilibrium implies the existence of full employment, while the law of the business cycle clearly refutes the full employment criterion. Even, if on average, over the course of the business cycle, employment is not full for a variety of reasons, this does not mean that capitalism has failed. It simply means that the optimality conditions have not been met in a dynamic context.

The problems generally associated with the present form of free-market capitalism are fluctuations, volatility, and inequality; those associated with rigid central planning are misalignment of prices, too little economic innovation, a high degree of corruption, and economic inequality. Although the intent is for an egalitarian society, just as free-market capitalism may be for economic stability, this aim is not realized. Perhaps it cannot be realized, by the very nature of the economic system, but inequality, although not on the extreme scale found in the manner of the market economies, does persist under rigid central planning.

The extreme cases, given human organizational and institutional fallibilities are not likely to exist anywhere in the pure state that their advocates envisage. This is the rational for the mixed system. It is not only a theoretical rationale; it is a practical outcome that is likely to prevail. Try as they may, the leaders at either extreme will not be able to cope with exceptions and imperfections; therefore we turn our attention to the mixed system of socialized market economy or market-oriented socialism. Call it what one will; it is a mixed system.

Some Successful Cases of Intervention

The advocates of competitive free markets with private ownership argue that economic activity is invariably better in the private than in the public sector.

This argument goes beyond ownership and management; it also precludes regulation and activist economic policy. It argues against regulation, guidance, and almost any economic intervention on the part of public authorities, except possibly control of the money supply, which ought to be set by a rule.

There are, nevertheless, some striking examples of state intervention that have been successful. Distinct from rigid central planning, we can find, in the industrial democracies, some good—even excellent—examples of successful state economic activities or initiative. One of the most spectacular achievements of the era since the end of World War II, let us say the second half of the twentieth century, has been the economic ascendancy of Japan.

The Japanese System

Although the point has been debated by economists, there is ample evidence to show that Japanese authorities intervened through the medium of *industrial policy*. Such policy is far different from central planning as it was implemented in the Soviet Union, China, or other tightly controlled socialist countries. The name for this kind of planning is *indicative planning*, which suggests that authorities simply show private industry how to develop and leave it to private industrial managers to carry out the directives.

Certain key industries become targeted for public sector help in expanding, acquiring the latest technology, and in finding markets. Some of the public sector support takes the form of encouragement through the use of financial benefits, some from the formation of information and some through the provision of supportive services or facilities in the economy's infrastructure. It is generally thought that Japan aided, encouraged, and pushed activities in modern textiles, steel, electronics, optics, cars, and other lines. By the latter part of the 1950s it had become apparent that Japan had made a basic recovery (to their old trend lines). For the 1960s, the government launched the income-doubling decade, requiring real growth of at least 7.2 percent per annum. This target was exceeded for the decade but was not sustainable after the first oil shock in 1973. Even though rapid progress was not sustainable, Japan continued to expand with a new industrial strategy, and moved from strength to strength to become one of the leading industrial nations of the world. It was poor and backward in many modern lines of activity in 1950. Many quantitative indicators were then at the relative position of some current developing countries.

Indicative planning, or industrial policy, is based on suggestion, allocations, or favoritism in specific sectors of the economy. Macroeconomic policy is needed to support an expansion like Japan's, but the choices of individual sectors involves far more specific detail. In a sense, it involves microeconomic policy, not down to the level of the individual form but to the industry or similar sector. Not only were certain sectors targeted, but their products were marketed round the world, partly through governmental initiatives.

Although Japan developed the automobile industry by a very large multiple of its position just after the war, it was not purely for export. In 1960 drivers were largely professional—chauffeurs, taxi operators, truck operators, etc. The car was then made accessible to the individual driver, but this needed a substantial infrastructure of streets, roads, highways, parking areas, traffic control, licensing, and other things—both physical capital and services—that made car ownership feasible on a broad scale in a short time period.

Government and business in Japan were not basically confrontational. They cooperated well with one another. In this case, intervention was a tremendous success. Of course, the entire success was not due to industrial policy alone. Many factors came together. The defense burden was very small, at about 1.0 percent of GDP; productivity rose markedly. People were willing to work for the joint good of the firm and the country. The United States helped Japan get a start after the war. Many things came together at once, but industrial policy was at the forefront of the effort; intervention was very successful.

The English expression, "industrial policy," is widely used and understood, but it should not be surprising that the French had their own word for it, namely *dirigisme*. They directed the economy, and did not *force* it on any path. The public sector, however, provided excellent support.

The French System

The rebuilding of the French economy after the devastation of World War II was achieved under the Plan Monnet (named after Jean Monnet). This form of planning was special because it was based on reconstruction, but the French style indicative planning can be clearly seen through citation of unusual projects. Two such projects of high profile are the nuclear power facilities of Electricté de France and the high speed train of SNCF.

France has the highest share of electricity generated through nuclear power facilities of any leading industrial country. The facilities are generally efficient and safe. These large-scale public sector investment projects have fared far better than those in the United States (built and maintained in the private sector) and in the Soviet Union (built and maintained in the state sector). France has had no Three Mile Island breakdown and no Chernobyl disaster. There are good and bad examples in both sectors, but the French have shown how care and meticulous planning in the public sector can work in the case of nuclear power generation and distribution.

France has also succeeded in building and operating and efficient rail system over many decades. It is not so much the successful running of a state rail system that needs citation and emphasis; it is rather the ability to demonstrate to the world that the public sector can innovate, in this instance by delivering the world's fastest train service.

The Japanese system, with fast trains at an early stage, showed how well a public office could operate a rail system. The high-speed trains on the Tokyo-Osaka line were renowned for their fast and accurate times, but the system was not profitable. It was intensively used and served society well, but has been privatized. It continues to deliver a good transportation service.

The main point is not that public enterprise is either superior or inferior to private enterprise. Both can function well in the appropriate economic environment, and the various public sector success stories cited here illustrate that a mixed system, with certain things done by the public sector, can work well—even to the point of doing some outstanding things.

These examples in transportation and electric power (generation and distribution) both involve heavy capital outlays for construction and equipment, but one economic activity that is attracting a great deal of attention now is the provision of health services, covering medical facilities, public health, physician services, clinics, and whatever else is needed for people to have complete treatment, examination, and disease prevention. One of the most ambitious was the National Health Service of Great Britain, established after World War II under the persistent prodding of Lord Beveridge. Although there has been much dispute and controversy over aspects of the system from all sides, the overwhelming attitude of the British people is that this service, which is a fixed part of their lives, has been a success. Most advanced industrial countries, and even some that are much poorer, too, have adopted some form of comprehensive socialized medicine. This has been, of course, one well-publicized feature of public service in the socialist countries. It is mainly in the United States, where public medical plans have never been implemented on a comprehensive scale, that the cost of medical services are extremely expensive and access to high-quality services is unequal.

The U.S. System

The U.S. system is fundamentally private and the top quality is excellent. The total amount spent, either in absolute terms or as a fraction of GDP, is high, but the availability of service across the population is extremely uneven. Some people have the world's best care, while many are priced out of the market. Medical personnel have good incomes. The main problem is that the excellent facilities available are not well distributed.

It can be said that a private health system can provide the highest quality care. The system can produce well, on that basis of consideration. It is both a success and failure. Great Britain has a fully comprehensive system so that nearly everyone is provided with public treatment, but some people elect to pay very high fees for the most superior service. Other countries in Europe, the Far East, and North America have developed comprehensive public systems that are well established and reach the entire population. Public provision of medical/health care can be done on a very acceptable plane; only the United States remains as an outsider, with an expensive private system that is not well accepted by its people. Future political changes may be triggered by the way the U.S. system functions.

Other successes that have been mentioned are based to a large extent on technical considerations. There are many technical aspects of a health care system, but the public-private issue is not primarily decided at the technical level; it is a fundamental humanitarian issue. The economic side is very important, but the weight of the decision whether to place this system in the private or public sector is heavily influenced by humanitarian considerations.

Some Unsuccessful Cases of Intervention

The massive failure of the Soviet and other WTO economies is not decisive in the debate being considered in this paper. The China story is quite different from the Soviet story. To a large extent, the Soviet mismanagement of its system represents a failure to use the right tools and processes to guide the economy. Also the Soviets had some excellent successes—in space, in science, in cultural presentations, all done in the public sector.

The main issue to be considered here is the identification of failed public sector projects in the industrial economy, which is basically private. A case in point is public housing in the United States. Some of these projects, which seemed to be so politically appealing at first, have turned out to be dismal slums ridden with poor security and poorly functioning equipment. In some cases, public housing projects in the United States had to be demolished because they deteriorated so much. All public housing either in the United States or elsewhere has not been a failure, but some very large projects have failed. At least one can say that public housing has not proved to be a solution to the housing problem. It is one significant part of the entire poverty problem. Poverty has not been abolished. As standards rise at the minimum level, which is appropriate for an advancing society, we find in the United States an increase in the numbers (absolute or relative) of people living below the poverty line. It does not necessarily mean that public investment in housing is a failed approach; it simply means that it has not been done right.

Since 1950, we have been full of hope that such things as the Beveridge Plan for Britain and Sweden's "middle way" would show the way for development of caring societies that could eradicate major ills of our system. Many aspects of Lord Beveridge's great vision did not cure social ills, especially in a fluctuating economy that did not systematically maintain full employment as a norm. But many things did improve, and the Tory government could dismantle some features of socialism, through privatization, but such major features as the National Health System and many aspects of social insurance have survived. The Tories would not even want to try to scrap the system as a whole.

In the case of Sweden, the social system ceased to serve as a model for the world to copy. As in Britain, difficult economic times provided a poor environment for complete maintenance of the system of broad-based social services. A new government, recently elected, has set out to dismantle some of Sweden's vast network of social services. It is as if to say that the social experiment failed, or went too far in an egalitarian direction. The end result will probably be a scaling back of social services in an overall weakening of the "middle way."

It is too early to say whether scaling back, as in Sweden and with Britain's privatization, will prove to be correct and sustainable policy decisions. The large scale privatizations in developing countries, as in Chile, Mexico, and Argentina are just beginning to function on a regular basis. Many economists are firmly convinced that these changes represent transformations that will not be reversed, but those countries have also witnessed nationalizations in the not too distant past, and the volatility of those countries does not lead one to think that the latest change is certain to be permanent. Also, some of the privatizations in industrial countries have yet to show their profitability and strength against institutional reversals, British Telecom, NTT (Japan), Japan Railways, and other are thus far disappointing for the very optimistic purchasers of their shares.

There are, however, some particular programs in the private sector or some that involve market clearing that do look attractive. It is said, for example, that the U.S. education system has problems in the K-12 grades, but that higher education in the United States is truly outstanding on a world scale. There are exceptions in U.S. higher education, but the prime institutions are privately endowed and operated without heavy public sector influence or guidance. It is true that some public institutions, such as the University of California, are ranked with the leading private institutions of higher education, but, by and large, the preeminence of U.S. higher education owes much to private governance.

Military service provides another interesting example. As an alternative to conscription, or the compulsory draft, we can consider the volunteer military (army, navy, air force, and marines) services. Under the best of circumstances, the draft has been less than fully popular. During the Vietnam War it became a ridiculed and despised institution. Market-clearing economists proposed basing the U.S. military on volunteer forces. This meant paying a sufficiently high wage and generous fringe benefits to attract young recruits. Is has been argued that volunteer forces will be more professional and more efficient.

The idea of a market oriented military establishment was suggested by economists during World War II. A.P. Lerner circulated a memorandum which proposed the setting of initial prices for individual items and the allocating of expenditures sums among theaters of war. Generals were then allowed to bid against each other and allow prices to be set by world supplies and demands. Fantastic as this may have seemed, some seasoned military commanders were intrigued by the idea (one being one of my tutees in Oxford after the war). It is also a technique used by large private corporations in allocating activities among many departments.

These ideas were reflected in the shift from compulsory military service by draft to the concept of a volunteer army (plus navy plus marine corps plus air force). In this case the market bidding takes place between the labor market in the private sector and military jobs in the public sector. While there may have been many questions raised initially when the volunteer force technique went into operation, it seems to have worked well for the United States during the Persian Gulf War. The young American recruits seem to have taken the attitude that they signed up in order to do a job for pay and that they were ready to fulfill their commitments when the military engagement became real.

The volunteer army concept has functioned according to market principles after the Gulf War and after the ending of the Cold War in the sense that world conditions strongly supported a phase of arms reductions, with employment layoffs of many volunteers. This process has been taking place by means of the adjustments that would be expected in private markets.

In managing the macroeconomy through public works projects that support the working of the economy's infrastructure, we find an interesting mixture of public and private investment. The decisions about the size and timing of the infrastructure investment is largely in public hands, but the implications are both public and private. Individual citizens derive direct benefit from transport, educational, sanitary, and other infrastructure services that are produced by public investment, but the private producing sector is enabled to operate more efficiently by virtue of having access to these facilities that move goods, communicate, train people, remove waste, etc. There are clear grounds for beneficial economic cooperation between the two sectors. That is the essence of the mixed economy.

Socialist Planning: Theory

Strict planning by a command system did not work well after decades in the Soviet Union and WTO countries in the sense that economic improvement eventually became slow. Prices, as signals for economic substitution, were not allowed to do their intended job. They became rigidly outdated. In this respect, China began to make fundamental changes as early as 1978, after only 3 decades of command planning. In a sense, one can say that China is trying to implement a modernized socialism that contains a mixture of private and public activities.

The theoretical basis for market (modern) socialism was intensively discussed during the 1930s and 1940s, particularly by A.P. Lerner (the same economist who proposed market-system warfare) and O. Lange. They built on earlier papers by E. Barone and Fred Taylor. At an abstract theoretical level, it was argued by F.A. von Hayek and L. van Mises that a logical price system was not compatible with socialist or public sector ownership of the means of production. Barone and many general-equilibrium theorists have shown that rational prices can, in fact, be determined in a mathematical model of a socialist economy. Lange and Lerner showed in a practical sense how such prices should be determined, in fact, by market clearing. Their ideas become known as "market socialism" or "Lange-Lerner socialism." In many respects, their ideas lie at the base of the mixed economy. It becomes a question of the degree of mixture: basically private, with a few public economic activities, or vice versa? The major industrial countries are mixed in the sense that productive capital, except in the infrastructure, is privately owned. There are accompanying pubic activities to serve and operate the infrastructure as well as to provide humanitarian service.

When the Soviet Union introduced *perestroika*, there were some hesitant questions asked whether the aim was to establish market socialism of the Lange-

Lerner type, but the policy makers undoubtedly did not understand the subtleties of this approach, although there were many mathematical economists in the Soviet Union who could appreciate the relevant issues.

In an exchange meeting, organized by the Committee for Exchange with the USSR of the American Economic Association, held at Princeton, New Jersey, December, 1990, the theoretical issues were spelled out in a paper prepared by Herbert Scarf of Yale, "Economic Equilibrium and Soviet Economic Reform." His paper demonstrated the mathematics of the determination of prices in a theoretical model. This prompted Soviet theorists to prepare some preliminary models for the next meeting in the exchange series, held in Moscow, March 1992. One of the intents of the Soviet Exercise was to develop models for estimation of shadow prices that could be used in wealth evaluation, but the effort has obviously been transformed by the political shifts leading to the breakup of the Soviet Union.

The Chinese economic reforms are intended to modernize the economy and to make it function more efficiently under socialist institutions. It could be said that China is experimenting with something resembling Lange-Lerner socialism. It is not, however, guided by an abstract economic theory, but rather by practical economic policy. It is heading toward a mixed system, in which the predominant mode of organization is socialist, while Western industrial democracies function in a mixed system in which the predominant mode of organization is private capitalism.

The immediate reactions in former WTO countries, where economic reform on a broad scale started in 1989-90, favored maximum change for the prevailing system. The economies now are in states of transition, but their targets are to develop as much private capitalism as possible. The mixed nature of their economies are due to inertial obstacles in reform, but in the end, they will probably be mixed with some significant degree of social service—health, retirement, infrastructural planning, education, environmental protection, and other activities under state guidance, control, or regulation.

The former WTO countries are experiencing the pains of transition in varying degrees, which depend on the speed of the restructuring program. The gains from restructuring are yet to be experienced. The restructuring processes initiated recessions in all Eastern European countries and the republics of the former Soviet Union. The remarkable aspect of the gradualist Chinese reform program is that widespread recession has been avoided and inflation never got out of control by rising above low two-digit levels. It has been successfully restrained in recent years, without generating a recession. It is my opinion that gradualism, towards a mixed economy target, is to be preferred to so-called shock therapy.

Conclusion

There are two issues for operating a mixed economy. One deals with micro-economies and the other with macroeconomics. At the micro level in small industries the mixture should lean towards non intervention, except for regulation in the social interest. Small enterprises and agriculture should be entirely private. For large-scale enterprises, industrial policy or indicative planning can be very helpful. The objective should not be to minimize the number of regulations, but to maximize economic well being for the country. Too often, zealous advocates of free-market capitalism merely count the number of regulations that have been abolished or avoided.

At the macro level, a great deal of guidance through policy intervention—fiscal policy, social welfare policy, monetary policy, and commercial policy—are needed in order to achieve dynamic stability, with growth, at an aggregate level of performance. Social welfare policy should guarantee some basic human rights in this process.

Unfettered free markets for the determination of relative prices with minimal intervention at the macro level, relying mainly on strict monetary control, generally do not work. Policy intervention must be flexible and well rounded. Economies, at all levels of their development, which rely purely on delicate monetary intervention are presently finding that this minimalist approach does not bring quick correction for departures from full employment. The overall level of activity cannot simply be assumed to be steady at full capacity levels. That is a serious mistake that is made by those who have no tolerance for a mixed economy.

Section 4 · How to Improve Capitalism

Andrew Schotter

The history of the Soviet Union presents us with a controlled experiment in institutional design. Its rise, fall, and its current transition to capitalism have been seen as proof that economic institutions, which do not harness the basic instincts of human beings and provide incentives for them to exercise their creative talents, are doomed to fail. The contrast in economic well-being between East and West Germany is, perhaps, an even better case in point. In that case, the experiment even controlled for cultural influences. The only difference between the two Germanys was the institutions governing their economic affairs, and capitalism clearly won.

The general assessment of events in Eastern Europe is that the major beneficiaries of the fall of Communism are the Eastern European countries themselves. As a result, they will now be allowed to make a peaceful transition from their old and inefficient economic institutions to the economic institutions of capitalism. It is my contention here, however, that the West might ultimately end up being even a greater beneficiary, since it will now be free to take an even closer look at its own economies, examining them critically without fear that such a scrutiny will be called socialist. Socialism has been a distraction to the West in its main task of making capitalism, which is the most productive system, a more humane economic system.

In this essay I will outline exactly why I feel that the West will be the major beneficiary of the events of the past five years in Eastern Europe. Then I will offer some words of caution for Eastern European countries that are currently rushing to embrace capitalist institutions in a less than cautious manner.

Why the West Will Benefit

There are many problems that capitalist countries face. A walk through any major U.S. city makes them clear. Many of them are technological, however, and not unique to capitalism. For example, while our rivers and the air we breathe are polluted and acid rain is killing our forests, the polluted rivers of East Germany and the acid rain of Eastern Europe are of no less magnitude. When countries produce they pollute. A clean environment depends on the amount of goods and services decision makers are willing to give up to eliminate pollution and maintain the environment. Nothing in the theories of socialism or capitalism states that socialist air will be cleaner than capitalist air. Nothing in the theory stipulates socialist tastes or the trade offs socialists will face.

But there are problems that are uniquely capitalistic. In a capitalistic system people are paid their "marginal product" which measures, in some sense, how much society would lose if their services were eliminated. Hence, if a famous brain surgeon stopped performing operations, we would lose the services of all those people who would have been saved by his operations, if he had continued to work. When a famous baseball player retires, society loses all of the enjoyment derived from his talents. His compensation is measured by how much people are willing to spend to see him play. In capitalism, if you are capable of doing something that other people value, you get paid for it.

American society has produced a group of people who, for whatever reason, have almost zero marginal product. An illiterate seventeen-year-old ghetto dweller, who lacks the discipline to work and is dependent on drugs, has a zero marginal product in honest employment. Take one of them away and our GNP either stays the same or may even go up (if this person is engaged in activities that harm others). Therefore, free-market capitalism would award such a person a zero wage—there is no place for him or her. The theory of free markets is incomplete here, however, since it does not specify what such people should do. If one reads conventional texts, where such a problem is never mentioned, one would assume that such people are expected to sit in their rooms and peacefully stare at the walls. But such a solution is contradictory to the essence of capitalist society. What we can expect is that these people will rationally respond to the incentives they face, allocating their efforts in the direction that will maximize their earnings. In short, they will weigh the benefits of working honestly (at an almost zero wage) or engaging in criminal activities which, even after adjustment for the risk of being jailed, will bring them a better return. (Free-market policies like eliminating the minimum wage only makes the problem worse.)

The choice is clear and we see it every day when we travel to work or read our newspapers. The price that capitalism pays for its incentives is seen in the precise incentive system that it creates for its underclass. You cannot have it both ways. You cannot rely on the incentive system to bring you the Apple Computer without understanding that it will also bring you your local crack dealer. You cannot rely on the incentive system to bring you fifty channels on you cable television box without also having your windshield washed by an army of irate homeless workers every time you drive across town or without having your car window broken six times a year in search of your car radio that was stolen two years ago and never replaced. In the past the response would be: "well this is bad but would you rather live in Russia?" Now at least it is commonly agreed that we certainly would not want to live in Russia, but that fact does not make it any easier to live in the United States. The time for introspection has arrived and hopefully it can be done without the distraction of a socialist competitor or free-market ideologues.

It could be easier if we reexamine the defects of capitalism without contaminating the analytic process by importing into it our hostility toward socialism. Inevitably, we would conclude that if the underclass has improper incentives, they must be changed. But changing them may involve measures that to some smack of socialism. Take a poor woman who heads a household with four children and has no high school degree. Whose incentives are we worried about? Clearly not hers; the economic battle for her is, unfortunately, probably lost. What we must care about is offering the right incentives to her children by creating an environment where honest work is preferable to dishonest work.

This means educating and otherwise preparing them to respond effectively to new incentives.

This may also entail a dole to the mother—welfare not workfare. Although there is national hostility toward welfare, enlightened selfishness suggests that, despite the weak economy, in the long term it would be wise to subsidize her in order to allow her to provide for her children.

A Caution to the East

Before one embraces a new economic institution it would be prudent to examine exactly what the benefits of this new institution promise to be. It has always struck me as odd that Adam Smith's exact promise in his *Wealth of Nations* is often confused with a utopian vision of life in a perfectly competitive economy. Knee-jerk conservatives seem never to question the fact that a move in the director of free markets must be welfare improving, yet the limits of such claims are never examined. This raises the question of exactly what is the nature of the carrot being held out by capitalist institutions for the countries of Eastern Europe. An examination of economic theory answers this question quite simply. Free-market institutions are efficient; they eliminate waste. More precisely, the exact benefits of free-market organization are summarized by what economists call the Fundamental Theorems of Welfare Economics, which indicate that if you leave economic agents alone to truck, barter, and trade, they will determine outcomes that are optimal in a particular sense of the word—they are Pareto optimal. This term means that the equilibrium of perfectly competitive economies is a state of the world so efficient that no rearrangement of resources could make some one person in the economy better off without making another person worse off.

In short, the way free markets allocate resources everyone cannot be simultaneously better off. What is not generally known to the public, however, is that this is the only sense in which free-market economies determine optimal outcomes. The problem is that Pareto optimal states may be dismal places in which to live. For example, an economy that produces efficiently, but distributes all of its income to the top two percent of its population, might very well be Pareto optimal. But this redistribution of wealth from the top to the bottom, while making the bottom better off, will make the top worse off and hence will violate the precepts of Pareto optimality. Such inequitable states are consistent with the outcomes of free markets and yet they might not strike any of us as "optimal," especially if the bottom 98 percent of the population does not accept its poverty graciously.

In addition, the mix of goods we observe being provided in a free-market economy is similarly determined by the distribution of income generated by the free market. If high-quality medical care is allocated to wealthy urban areas leaving poor rural towns unattended, such an allocation is still Pareto optimal, since any reallocation will hurt the urban residents while benefiting the rural inhabitants. The point then is that before Eastern Europe signs on the bottom line, the nations should take a close look at exactly what it is that they are buying. While I would not suggest that they buy a difference product, I think that they might very well demand some changes in the model they are buying.

Some Problems with Changing Institutions

Even if Eastern Europe buys the free-market model without alteration, it is not clear that these same institutions will work identically when transported to Eastern Europe. The institutions of capitalism which work so well in the West are supported by a whole host of norms of behavior that have developed over the past 200 years and which form a behavioral infrastructure upon which free markets are supported. Without these norms and behavioral attitudes it is not clear that free markets will function appropriately. Further, it is not clear that these norms have been developed so far in Eastern Europe. For example, since individual work has not been supported by incentives, there has been no norm of hard work developed by the work force. Shirking is the norm and hard work by any individual is seen as rate busting and worthy of punishment, not admiration. Unemployment as a natural corollary to the free-market system is something that people is Eastern Europe have little experience with. Hence its allocative and disciplinary effects are lost on the population. The entrepreneurial spirit, so often touted as the driving force of capitalism, is likewise missing or sometimes frowned upon in Eastern Europe.

To illustrate exactly what I mean here, let me quickly summarize some laboratory experiments I have conducted at New York University with a colleague of mine, Haig Nalbantian. In these experiments, undergraduates perform a stylized version of a group work task under two different group incentive systems. One of these systems replicates a stereotypic socialist incentive system, in which subjects share the group output equally no matter how much effort they expend individually. The second system is closer to a capitalist incentive program, where the group as a whole is given a target output. If surpassed, it generates income for the group; if not met, it generates either zero or minimal payoffs. Such group incentive plans are becoming more and more common in Western corporations. Different groups performed these experiments in different orders; some did the socialist system first and then the capitalist system, while others did the capitalist system first and then the socialist. We call the socialist incentive system Revenue Sharing and the Capitalistic system Profit Sharing.

We found that the performance of the capitalistic Profit Sharing Scheme is very sensitive to whether it was performed before or after the Socialists Revenue Sharing Scheme. When Revenue Sharing is performed first, a norm of shirking is established among the subjects, since it becomes apparent to them that the system is vulnerable to free riding. Therefore, when the experimenter introduces the new profit sharing-scheme in the second part of the experiment, it becomes hard for the laboratory subjects to break the shirking norm established earlier in the Revenue Sharing experiment. Group output is therefore lower than when the profit-sharing experiment was performed first—that is, when no previous shirking norm was established. The analogy should be obvious. Since workers in

Eastern Europe have an established norm of shirking, the introduction of a new incentive system will be heavily influenced by this previous history. Consequently, Western incentive programs are likely to function in a totally different manner when transplanted to Eastern Europe and the rejection possibility must be understood before they are instituted.

Conclusion

The fear of socialist taint (even from Western socialisms) and the effect of that fear on social policy debate have long distracted us from our main task of making capitalism, the most productive economic system in the world, more humane.

That fact has been evident in the conservatives' equating a large and active U.S. government with socialism. This equation paved the way for the government's abdication of its responsibilities in education, housing, poverty, health care, and care for the homeless.

Similarly, by arguing that Communism's spectacular failure after 70 years proves capitalism's success, U.S. ideology has fallen into a trap of faulty logic. When Communism failed in Eastern Europe, the number of people living in poverty in the United States did not change. Our rivers did not become cleaner, nor did the drug problem become less threatening.

The collapse of Communism (or socialism, as its leaders called it) can benefit our economy if we consider it an opportunity to examine our system critically without fear that the process and outcome of such scrutiny will be stigmatized as socialist. When all government actions in the West were judged by their distance from socialist doctrine, many potentially beneficial government interventions were considered dangerous and consequently not worth consideration. Now that socialism is dead, such rational intervention may be considered on their merits and not their ideological implications. This is how people in the West will benefit from the events in Eastern Europe.

Section 5 · Transformation as Transplantation

Joseph S. Berliner

A few months ago there occurred an event that made medical history. A team of surgeons at the University of Pittsburgh performed the first interspecies organ transplant operation. They replaced the liver of a man dying of hepatitis B with the liver of a baboon.

Reading the article at the time I was ruminating about the global changes now occurring in the former Communist world, I was astonished by the similarities between the medical operation and those social transformations. For what do such transformations consist of but the grand transplantation of institutional organs from one species of society into another.

Analogies abound. Both transplantation and transformation are undertaken only when a system has been functioning so badly that extreme measures may finally be contemplated. The greatest danger is that of rejection; that is, the receiving system is unable to incorporate the alien organ successfully, and the patient emerges from the operation with neither the diseased old organ nor a functioning new one. Under the best of circumstances the receiving system suffers an extreme shock; the patient's condition deteriorates rapidly during the transition, after which he may recover very rapidly, or perhaps slowly, or he may never recover at all. On reflection, however, it is not these intriguing similarities that are most relevant. It is rather one large difference between the two types of operations; in particular, the difference in their order of complexity.

To the layperson, the medical operation appears to be phenomenally complex. Our minds can scarcely fathom the number of physiological details that medical doctors must have under their control in order to coax a human body to accept so complicated an organ from another biological species. If there existed a scale by which to rank the complexity of contemporary human endeavors, surely this operation must rank near the very top.

There is a sense, however, in which this transplant operation is of a lesser order of complexity than the transformations now under way in the post-Communist world. What those countries have undertaken is the transplantation not of a single institutional organ, but of an entire complex of social institutions. The operation entails the transplantation of new legislative forms, new government executive organs, new legal and judicial systems, new property forms, new economic mechanisms, new banking and financial institutions, and many other institutions of social organization.

The proper medical analogy would be an operation that required the transplantation not only of the baboon's liver, but of his kidney as well, and perhaps also his heart, and maybe half of the lung, with a portion of the brain possibly thrown in as well. Your first giddy reaction would be to wonder whether the patient, if he survived at all, would still be human being, or rather a baboon, or perhaps an entirely new hybrid species, no doubt to be called a "huboon."

A Megaoperation

I have no doubt that medical doctors will never ever entertain the idea of an operation of such unimaginable complexity. Yet this is precisely the kind of megaoperation that Boris Yeltsin and the reform leaders of the former Communist countries are now performing. The political doctors are all engaged where the medical doctors fear to tread.

I have belabored the point for a particular reason. Commentators and analysts do often allude to the extensive and historic changes under way in the former Communist lands, but I have felt that the full extent of their complexity has not really been incorporated into the thinking of many of the people who are concerned with the process. The International Monetary Fund (IMF), for example, routinely refers to the historic nature of the transformations in process. But the way in which they deal with the countries struggling to carry them out differs little from the way in which they might deal with the naughty government of a Third World country that simply needs more backbone in order to run its affairs properly. All you have do, runs the advice, is to balance your government budget and your international financial problems will be over. If Bolivia or Nigeria can be made to produce a balanced budget when their backs are to the wall, so can Russia and the other former Communist countries. If Argentina and Great Britain can successfully privatize their state-owned enterprises in the course of a few years, Russia and the others should be able to do so as well, though it may take a bit longer.

Turning to the economic system in particular, the transplantation involves principally two sets of institutions. One is the implantation of a market mechanism, taken from the capitalist baboon, to replace the diseased Soviet-type central planning mechanism of the socialist species. The other is the replacement of state ownership by the institution of private ownership. The transplantation of an ownership structure is a much more complex operation than that of a market mechanism, and it is with that I wish to deal.

Economy Privatization and Enterprise Privatization

The term "privatization" is used to refer to two rather different processes. One process is the conversion of an individual state-owned enterprise into a privately owned enterprise. The second is the transformation of an entire economy from one based on state ownership to one based on private ownership. I shall refer to the first as "enterprise privatization" and to the second as "economy privatization."

Enterprise privatization is one way of accomplishing the objective of economy privatization, but it is not the only way. There is a second process that can contribute to economy privatization. That is the process of entry of newly founded private enterprises.

All the transforming countries are encouraging the entry of private enterprises, although with differing degrees of political enthusiasm. These enterprises tend to be concentrated in certain branches, such as retail trade, food catering, commerce, consumer services, construction, farming, and handicrafts. Some countries had a substantial lawful private sector even during their Communist period, such as the farm sector in Poland and the consumer services sector in Hungary.

The country in which the entry of newly founded enterprises has proceeded most rapidly, interestingly enough, is China. To be sure, most of these new entrants are not strictly privately owned. These so-called "town and village enterprises," or TVEs, have been founded by local governments, but they behave very much like private enterprises insofar as they are profit oriented and they receive no subsidies, production directives, or other instructions from the state. The TVE sector has expanded at a remarkable rate, rising from 22 percent of total industrial output in 1978 to 45 percent in 1990. The rapid growth of this nonstate sector has attracted the attention of experts and is increasingly cited as evidence of the possibility of very rapid economy privatization through the entry of new private enterprises.

Shock Therapy or Gradual Approach

Full economy privatization, however, cannot be based on entry alone, for as long as the state-owned enterprises carried over from the Communist period endure in that form, there will remain a substantial state sector. The major controversy is over the question of how to privatize these enterprises.

Everyone agrees that the state should divest itself of all of its small-scale property. This includes small stores, workshops, restaurants and catering establishments, repair and other consumer services, and construction organizations; productive property like trucks and taxis; and residential apartments. This process of so-called "small privatization" is now fairly well along in some countries and on the drawing boards in others. Together with the newly founded private enterprises, they now form a substantial private sector. The remaining issue is the controversial one of the privatization of the large state-owned enterprises, upon which I shall concentrate.

The central issue is whether enterprise privatization should be carried out as rapidly as possible, or whether it should be done gradually, in an evolutionary manner. The economic case for rapid privatization is that the gains in efficiency will be so large that they should be secured as quickly as possible in order to offset the high costs of the transition to a market economy. The economic case for evolutionary privatization is that time is needed in order for a true entrepreneurial class to evolve, with sufficient wealth to buy out the state's interest in its enterprises and to manage the privatized property efficiently.

My own view is that those who urge rapid privatization do not sufficiently appreciate the complexity of the operation required to transplant an ownership structure from one economic species to another. The lesson to be learned from viewing institutional transformation as a form of megatransplantation is that gradual evolutionary development is the best guarantee against the danger of rejection.

Micro- and Macroprivatization

The term "privatization" is itself a transplant from the economic lexicon of capitalist countries. In that context it refers to the sale to private owners of property that had formerly been owned by the state. The term came into particular prominence under the government of Margaret Thatcher, who launched the extensive privatization of state-owned property in the United Kingdom. Enterprise privatization is now the fashion in a great many capitalist countries, both underdeveloped and overdeveloped.

The task that confronts the former Communist countries, however, is not simply to slip a handful of state-owned enterprises into a sea of private enterprises. It is rather to convert all the country's large enterprises from state ownership to private ownership, in an economy in which there had been no large private enterprises at all before the transformation began.

It is unfortunate, again, that the same expression, "enterprise privatization," has to be used to describe both of those processes, because it gives the impression that they are much the same thing. For example, when the IMF exerts pressure on the Russian government to speed up "privatization," it seems to be asking no more than it might of the United Kingdom, or of Argentina, or Zimbabwe; and the IMF itself seems to believe that it is asking no more than that. Similarly the World Bank has a great deal of experience in assisting countries to "privatize" their state enterprises, and it seems to believe that experience gives it a certain authority in urging the Russians to "privatize" rapidly.

I have elsewhere proposed that the two processes be distinguished linguistically by referring to them as "microprivatization" and "macroprivatization." The microprivatization of one or a few enterprises affects so small a part of the economy that its impact on the rest of the economy is negligibly small. The macroprivatization of all or most of the enterprises in an economy is so massive a process that its impact on the rest of the economy cannot be ignored.

The fundamental insight of modern macroeconomics derives from the writings of John Maynard Keynes. Analyzing the rate of saving, Keynes showed that an increase in a single household's savings will cause national income to rise, but if every household decides to increase its savings, the national income might fall. More generally, you can create a lot of mischief if you think that your experience and knowledge of microprocesses gives you the wisdom to pronounce on macroprocesses. With respect to the subject at hand, experience and knowledge about how to carry out the microprivatization of individual enterprises confers very little wisdom about how to carry out the macroprivatization of an entire economy, and no wisdom at all about how to do it rapidly.

The unfortunate fact is that nobody has the knowledge or experience required to understand the full range of consequences of rapid macroprivatization because no country has ever undertaken it before. That is the significance of the oft-repeated observation that this kind of transformation is historically unique. Nor is there anything resembling a theory of transformation, for before Mikhail Gorbachev came along nobody thought it worth spending time mulling over an event as improbable as a Communist society deciding to transform all of its state property into private property. Rapid privatization is a true "leap in the dark," in the words of Peter Murrell, informed by no more than some crude guesswork about some of the outcomes that might be expected.

If one focuses on the implications of the fact that the transformation involves not microprivatization of the familiar kind but a historically unprecedented form of macroprivatization, a number of implications follow about how the process should be conducted. In my view they all favor the case for evolutionary rather than rapid privatization.

Private Wealth

Of the many differences between the capitalist and socialist economic species, one is the relationship between the volume of private wealth and the total value of the state-owned assets. In a capitalist country like the United Kingdom there are few state enterprises to be sold and a great many people with the wealth to buy them. In the post-Communist countries there is a huge number of enterprises to be privatized but few people with the private wealth to buy them.

The strategies of rapid privatization and evolutionary privatization deal with the problem of the paucity of private wealth in different ways. The first would divest the state of the ownership of these enterprises as rapidly as possible by simply giving the property away to the population, or by selling it for a nominal price. The case for rapid privatization is that the gains in efficiency would be very large, which would help to cushion the transitional costs of transformation.

Under the evolutionary strategy, the highest item on the government's agenda is maximal support for the entry of new private enterprises and for small privatization, as a way of encouraging the rapid accumulation of private wealth. As wealth accumulates in this rapidly growing private sector, the property of the state-owned enterprises would be gradually sold off, at their full market value, to both foreign and domestic buyers. The case for evolutionary privatization is that the property will be transferred in the course of time to competent persons, who will have demonstrated their ability to function successfully in a market economy and to accumulate private capital from their business activity.

The chief weakness of evolutionary privatization is that it will take a longer time for the economy to be privatized. The chief weakness of rapid privatization, on the other hand, is that in the interest of equity, each individual receives initially no more than a small portion of all the shares in any enterprise. To preserve effective shareholder control over the managers under these conditions, the shares are to be held, though not owned, by newly organized mutual stock funds, holding companies, insurance companies, investment banks, and other enterprises. Control over management will therefore be exerted entirely by people who are not themselves principal owners but serve as fiduciary agents of the mass of small individual citizen owners.

The evolutionary approach will produce a form of owner control much like that in capitalist countries, where one or more stockholder groups own blocs of stock sufficiently large to restrain the self-interested activities of management. Even where these arrangements have been long established, however, the preservation of owner control continues to be a serious problem. In some countries, for example, managers have succeeded in securing such large compensation packages for themselves that many stockholders and the public are beginning to seek redress.

Under rapid privatization, however, the managers will not even have to contend with the power of large blocs of private stockholders of their enterprises. They will be responsible only to the directors of the mutual funds or pension funds that hold their shares. It remains to be seen whether those directors will have the knowledge and self-interest to perform the job of control that large private stockholders do.

It is true that in capitalist countries a large and growing proportion of all stocks are held by institutions like pension funds, mutual funds, and insurance companies. Institutional investors, however, have generally avoided taking responsibility for the control of management, leaving that to the private stockholder groups.

It may turn out that the directors of these stockholding institutions will control the managers of the production enterprises at least as well as the private stockholders in an established capitalist economy. My guess is that they will not. In the absence of experienced private stockholders with a very large personal stake in the profitability and the capital gains of the enterprise, the managers will be much freer of genuine control than they would be under the more gradual evolutionary strategy. Enterprise managers, sometimes in collusion with the workers, and perhaps also with the collusion of the mutual fund managers, will end up managing the enterprises in their own interest rather than in the interest of the mass of small stockholders as economic efficiency requires.

Under the evolutionary approach, on the other hand, the property will eventually pass into pure private ownership of a kind scarcely distinguishable from that in capitalist countries. In the long run there will be virtually no scars remaining from the transplant operation, whereas the countries that have rushed into rapid macroprivatization will always bear the marks of a hasty and botched operation.

Social Infrastructure

The second implication of the macroeconomic nature of privatization in the former Communist countries is that the economy lacks the social infrastructure required for a private-enterprise economy to function efficiently. The production enterprises of an established market economy operate in an environment that includes a great many other institutions with which they interact. These include the institutions of banking, finance, insurance, accounting, market research, advertising, law firms and the courts of law, and many others. The people who run those institutions have long years of experience in servicing the needs of the production sector, and the efficiency with which business is conducted depends on their ability to deliver their services effectively.

With microprivatization of the British sort, there is sufficient slack in this social infrastructure that the services required by a few newly privatized enterprises barely make a ripple. The newly privatized firms can count on litigating a legal claim or floating a bond or commissioning a certified audit with no less ease than any other firm. Microprivatization is thus like the transplant of a baboon's liver into a human organism, all the other organs of which continue to function normally.

Soviet-type central planning, however, did not need financial intermediation or certified auditing, and the legal institutions were organized to deal with problems entirely different from those that arise under private property. Therefore if an economy-wide privatization is undertaken before the Soviet-type infrastructure is replaced by a market-type infrastructure, the private property transplant will probably be rejected by the economic organism. Macroprivatization must be a megaoperation, requiring the transplant not only of the baboon's liver, but of his kidney and his brain and who knows how many of his other organs.

Viewed from this perspective, rapid privatization is an operation fraught with danger. Under evolutionary privatization, on the other hand, the infrastructure has the time to evolve organically with the increasing demand for its services by the expanding private sector. Increasing litigation over fraud or breach of contract will increase the demand for lawyers and for courts of law, and the political and educational systems will have time to respond by producing more of the specialists who provide those services.

Conclusion

In this paper, I have not considered the differences among the various transforming economies. The advantage of evolutionary over rapid privatization is smaller in some countries than in others, depending upon such considerations as cultural traditions and the length of time the society had lived under Soviet-type socialist conditions. The relative disadvantages of rapid macroprivatization are likely to be smaller in Czechoslovakia and Hungary than in the countries of the former USSR, for example.

Each country will have to choose its own approach, and while we outsiders should feel free to offer advice, it would be irresponsible to exert any pressure in favor of one or the other approach. Foreign governments and international agencies in particular should understand that their experience with microprivatization in various countries conveys no special knowledge about how macroprivatization should be carried out. Some social transplants are more complex than others, and none in history has rivaled that of the social transformations now proceeding in the countries of Eastern Europe and the former Soviet Union.

Section 6 · Rising Regionalism

Masahiro Sakamoto

A wave of regionalism has been rising worldwide since the 1980s. The integration of the European Community (EC) has taken the lead in such movement, and there have been some reactions to it in North America which affect Asia. Theoretically, regional integration has the effect of increasing intraregional trade and accelerating regional growth. However, since it has discriminatory effects outside the region, a concern exists that such integration also represents a step towards blockism. Nevertheless, if the trade expansion effect is large and confers certain benefits on the growth of outside regions, a claim can be made that such integration is a first step toward globalism.

Regionalism, however, has political influence on the world system. In terms of military leadership, the world has become a unipolar system managed by the United States. However, the EC has become noticeably influential in terms of politics, and the role of Japan has also been increasing. World politics has begun to search for a new framework in relation to regionalism.

What course should Asia take in such movement? This is the question posed in the East Asian Economic Grouping. Asia is not in a position to bring about regional integration as rapidly as the EC. In the postwar period, regional security has been achieved by the participation of the United States in the Pacific area. Thus regionalism across the Pacific Ocean has remained an important factor in Asia. In this development, APEC, an intragovernmental organization, was established in 1989. The role of the enlarged ASEAN Foreign Minister Conference has also been expanding as a security mechanism in the Pacific area.

Japan, as a G-7 member and an Asian country, could have a considerable influence on the world's framework and the system of Asia. Japan has played the leading role in Asia's industrialization and has become one of the few countries in the world which currently has surplus funds. It is also true, however, that Japan has internal and external constraints on its international cooperation.

The Rise in Regionalism in the 1980s

The rise in regionalism during these years was heavily dependent on the state of affairs in Europe. The integration of the EC, which forms the center of such progress, has a long history. Under the bipolar system of the United States and the Soviet Union in the postwar period, the European Common Market was formed in 1957 with an aim of settling years of antagonism between Germany and France and securing the independence of Western Europe.

The collapse of the bipolar system brought new factors to bear on EC integration. First, the dissolution of the Soviet Union restored the "independence" of Europe from the two superpowers. Second, it created a trend toward the reorganization of an "enhanced Europe" surrounding the EC that includes the neighboring European nations as well as countries of the former Soviet Union.

Further, the unification of Germany has substantially strengthened the position of Germany in Europe and changed the relationship between Germany and France within the EC, which had previously been lead by France, thereby greatly affecting the process of integration. Currently, the EC is reinforcing its internal unity and showing a "deepening" tendency towards monetary and political integration. At the same time, it is showing a tendency towards "widening" the integration with the members of the EFTA and Eastern European countries.

There have also been substantial changes in the area of security. Europe used to be the center of global antagonism between the East and the West, and the situation in Europe could have possibly ignited global military hostilities. With the end of the Cold War, the relationship between the United States and Europe has changed. Reorganization of NATO, expansion of the Security Council of Europe, and a greater role for the Western European Union have been proceeding in response to the "independence" of Western Europe.

This movement in Europe has affected North America. When President Reagan proposed the North America Free Trade Area in the early 1980s, the reaction was quite limited. But after the meeting between Reagan and Prime Minister Mulroney of Canada in 1985, negotiations made remarkable progress and an agreement on the U.S.-Canada Free Trade Area was concluded in 1988. There was a change in the traditional anti-United States sentiment of Mexico after President Salinas came to power. A large increase in regional trade between these three North American countries has been backing such movement.

Current U.S. trade policies follow three directions: promotion of the Uruguay Round, with regard to globalization; increase of bilateral free trade agreements; and promotion of exports though reciprocity under Super 301. The United States tends to put more weight on bilateral agreements, under which circumstance the Uruguay Round makes poor progress. Following agreements with Israel and Canada, the United States has regarded the North America Free Trade Area as the first step towards liberalization in a more global sense.

This movement also affects Asia. Southeast Asia has rapidly increased regional communication in recent years and is a new area of economic growth, but the degree of its regional integration is considerably low. Prime Minister Mahathir of Malaysia made a proposal at the end of 1990 for an East Asia cooperative plan that excludes the United States. This plan, he reasoned, was made to deal with the creation of EC92 and the North America Free Trade Area under conditions that do not allow East Asian countries, though they account for a considerable portion of world trade, the opportunity of expressing their views, while the Uruguay Round was deadlocked at the end of 1990 because of the confrontation between the United States and Europe. Establishment of an ASEAN Free Trade Area (AFTA) was agreed upon at the ASEAN summit conference, and political movements, such as enhancement of the ASEAN Foreign Minister Conference, have drawn much attention. The Pacific region, which includes East Asia, founded PECC and APEC in 1980 and 1989, respectively, establishing the first agents of discussion in the Pacific. It has been vigorously carrying out activities that can be characterized as "open" regionalism.

The Logic of Postwar Regionalism

The movements of regionalism mentioned above have attracted some concern that they might lead to blockism. Regional integration has the effect of both creating trade within a region and shifting trade from outside regions. It is clearly blockism if discrimination by one country leads to retaliation by another region, which in turn draws retaliation from the discriminating country or region. This is what happened in the 1930s. Therefore, the reaction of the United States and the response of Asia to the movement in Europe in the 1980s can be said to include a reaction to a discriminatory tendency.

However, such discrimination against outside regions can be evaluated differently from a medium-term viewpoint. When the effect of creating regional trade is large, it accelerates the economic growth of the region. This growth could be further accelerated by other factors caused by an expansion of the regional market, stabilization of market prices, increased investment in production facilities, and stimulation of consumption. When taking into consideration the economic effects brought about through the reorganization of regional division of labor, the demand occurring in countries outside the region would more than offset the short-term losses caused by the trade shift. This is a vital effect of regional integration. Nevertheless, it should be noted that such vital advantages could possibly be enjoyed only by strong, competitive countries.

Regional integration becomes stronger according to a ladder of integration: from a free trade area to a tariff union, common market, economic union, currency union, and political alliance. Regional ties become stronger and discrimination against outside regions is greater. Reinforcement of regional ties, however, increases the necessity to solve problems within the region, including industrial adjustment, regional gaps, and maintenance of the income of different nation. That is to say, the functions similar to those of a nation-state, such as welfare schemes and redistribution of income, will be of increasing necessity as regional integration proceeds. The EC currently is supporting agriculture and providing financial support on the basis of these requirements.

A problem arises when competition within the region becomes restricted and barriers against outside regions are raised, resulting in negative effects on the economic vitality of the regional integration. The General Agreement on Tariffs and Trade (GATT), in Section 24, requests that a free trade area or a tariff union not raise barriers against countries outside the region, as this would be a policy causing poverty in neighboring regions.

Increasing horizontal division of labor characterizes the postwar world economy. This is mainly due to the technology and the affluent social model of the United States spreading throughout the world, but the activities of multinational corporations have served as the driving force. The advances made by the U.S. multinational corporations into the Western world was noticeable in the postwar period, and the goods and corporate strategies which supported the affluent society in the United States rapidly spread throughout the world. The overseas advancement of Japanese and European companies gradually became stronger. These corporations employed a strategy of international logistics that mobilized resources of different countries and incorporated them while reducing costs. Thus intracorporation trade developed regionally. Progress in information technology and financial integration in the 1980s boosted the overseas activities of corporations, leading to establishment of global corporations. These corporations have opened regional headquarters on a tripolar regional basis and, moreover, maintain their existence through utilization of global resources, supporting regional integration by their corporate activities.

Regional integration naturally has a political aspect. The postwar regional integration of Western Europe, which was more political than economic, had three purposes. The first was to maintain the peace and economic prosperity of Europe through the reconciliation of France and Germany, as observed in the Shuman Plan and the Common Market of the European Economic Community (EEC). The second was the solidarity of Western Europe, which aimed at the improvement of its position in the chasm created by the conflict between the United States and the Soviet Union, as characteristically advocated by France, which did not participate in the formation of the Yalta System. Third, regional integration was formulated to deal with the East as a step in the formation of the Atlantic alliance of NATO. Europe was the central area of the conflict in the nuclear Cold War at the peak of the military confrontation between East and West and was incorporated into the system led by the United States.

The collapse of the bipolar system at the end of the 1980s greatly affected the framework of world politics. The independence of Europe occurred first, the centripetal force of the fear of the East was eliminated, and Germany, gaining increasing power, changed the political map of Europe. However, the political and economic integration of the nearly half century of the postwar period maintains its initial force and the impetus for integration in dealing with the economic challenge of Japan, the United States, and the Pacific countries still remains. However, the feeling of nationalism is still strong in Europe, as demonstrated by the result of Denmark's direct vote on EC integration, and there may be a delay or modification of the plan for currency integration, while the possibility of the occurrence of political antagonism and discord among Western European countries is becoming lower. Rather, there will be more instances where Europe has to deal regionally with problems in Eastern Europe and the countries of the former Soviet Union.

Regionalism and the International System

The conflict between East and West was an ideological one, and the leadership of the United States has been so strong that cooperation on economic policies in the West under the free trade system has become extremely intense. This system, in place for as long as half a century, has brought about a strong interdependence based on democracy and the market economy in the West and established an integral and cooperative system beyond the framework of the nation-state in Western Europe. Similar conditions, though to a different extent, are found also in North America and the Pacific region.

The collapse of the bipolar system especially restored the "independence" of Europe, and the three poles, while improving their independence, have been strengthening dimensional integration systems in each region. Europe has enhanced integration, while North America reviews cooperation in the Western hemisphere, and Asia and the Pacific region have had the interdependence of the United States and Japan and reinforced cooperation among East Asian countries. The blockism system in the 1930s was centered around regional major powers and had the structure of colonial empires with strong social strata. However, in the current structure, of which the EC is typical, many sovereign nations are forming equal dimensional ties. Moreover, international cooperation centering on the G-7 Economic Summit, which connects the three core poles is still intensive, while a new framework in world politics is being sought.

Second, behind regionalism are corporate strategies that pursue scale merits and international division of labor. Strong political integration and close cooperation on economic policies under the bipolar system created a very favorable environment for the international activities of corporations. Following the positive overseas advancement of multinational corporations of the United States, the internationalization of European and Japanese corporations proceeded rapidly. Overseas investment grew considerably, and intracorporation trade became a backing for world trade and caused a rapid expansion of regional trade in the Western Pacific region, North America, Europe, etc. Progress in information technology and financial integration in the 1980s have formed global business activities. Global corporations establish regional headquarters with increasing independence at the three poles in order to maintain their survived worldwide, but this concurrently connects these poles. Internationalization of corporate activities further proceeded even after the collapse of the bipolar system, thereby boosting international trade and investment and linking local economies, and has become an influential factor in international society.

Third, the movement of regionalism has created regional public goods and supporting the global cooperative system. Under the bipolar system, disputes in various regions were related to the conflict between East and West, and security literally required global response. Since low-intensity disputes require regional response, the necessity of dealing regionally with security problems has been rising. This is typically seen in the peacekeeping operations of the UN.

Fourth, regionalism poses important problems in relationships with outside region. The first is an adjustment of the competitive relationship among the three poles. For example, there will be no know-how regarding maintenance and operation of the global monetary system upon the realization of a common European currency as one of the key currencies. In addition, preferential measures limited to a region are one type of discrimination.

Fifth, regionalism has an extremely different structure in each region. Asia has not yet formed a structure which could be called regionalism. In the postwar structure, the strong participation of the United States fostered stability and growth in Asia, and something rather like Pacific regionalism has been strongly maintained. But how will this fare in the future? If the participation of the United States remains strong, it may affect regionalism in North America. But if it becomes weak, will it create a demand for a new order in Asia? The future of Japan will thus be greatly influenced by these circumstances. At the same time, Japan's choices will have a considerable effect on these circumstances. The world will see great influence from Japan in Asia. This situation, to the contrary, will have a great deal of effect on the international system.

Regional Cooperation in Asia and the Pacific

Viewing the situation in Asia and the Pacific, it is clear that the international system in East Asia varies greatly from that in Europe. Historically, Asia's international relationships were for a long time based on China's unipolarity. However, beginning in the nineteenth century Asia was ravaged by the imperialism of Europe and Japan. For many years, it was divided up geographically. The aftereffects of colonialism remained strong after the war and has been demonstrated in the mutual relationships among the Asian countries.

East Asia progressed rapidly in the 1980s. The growth of the semi-advanced countries and the ASEAN members was remarkable. Such development was supported by a high motivation in each country and flexibility in policy selection. Restoration of fiscal discipline, development of monetary systems, a considerable rise in savings rates, stabilization of commodity prices, and expansion of exports were achieved in the 1980s. Although this development was largely helped by the demand for industrial goods in the United States, it is also clear that trade has rapidly shifted to the Western Pacific region since the latter half of the 1980s. Investment and trade were furthered by Japan, Taiwan, and Korea; in the Pacific region the pace of both grew rapidly. Trade and investment quickly diversified and increased. As a result, although the trade of the countries of East Asia, including Japan, is largely dependent on outside regions, such as the United States, its ratio within the region has become far greater than the ratio of the trade of America and Europe with East Asian nations. Backed by these circumstances, the breakdown of the structure of the Cold War has created further necessity for more regional cooperation. The case of Cambodia is expected to trigger an interest in regional security.

Second, corporate activities in the Western Pacific region are so vigorous that there is already a clear assertion of Asian capitalism. Regional business development by Japan, the semi-advanced nations, and the capital of overseas Chinese merchants have promoted regional integration, such as local economies that reach out beyond national boundaries. Furthermore, the ratio of trade and investment within the region has become increasingly higher. Third, electrification in Asia will increase coal-based thermoelectric power generation, which in turn will necessitate a regional solution to environmental problems, including acid rain and energy problems. Fourth, regional cooperation has been rapidly increasing in developing human resources in the Pacific region.

The Role of Japan

What is the role of Japan in the situation mentioned above? Japan's position has several aspects. The first is its participation, in cooperation with the United States and Europe, in solving global problems. Greater expectations have begun to be placed on Japan as a financially and technologically advanced country to promote global cooperation on macroeconomic policies, to provide economic aid to the former Soviet Union, to foster growth in developing countries, and to suggest solutions to global environmental problems.

Furthermore, Japan must not forget that it is a member of the Pacific as well as Asia. On one hand, in Asia there will be more instances of security, environmental, and economic problems requiring regional solutions; on the other hand, it is necessary to offer solutions from the viewpoint of Pacific regionalism. The aftereffects of the bipolar system remain serious, especially in Asia, and the settlement of security problems through Pacific regionalism is essential.

Finally, there are large constraints on Japan, both domestically and internationally, on playing a more positive international role. These constraints are deeply related to World War II. It seems inevitable that Japan will have to review its constitution in order to make a greater contribution to the peacekeeping operations of the UN.

Conclusion

In relation to other countries, it will be of great importance for Japan to deepen mutual understanding with Asia. The key here is for Japan to confront its history since the beginning of the Meiji era, then to discuss the future. Japan, on one hand, is a leading country in the industrialization of Asia, and it is clear that the Japanese model has become the foundation for the economic development of Asia, as in the case of Korea. Most of the elite in Korea study in the United States, but Japan has had a large influence on the economic laws, financial structure, and organization of the governmental agencies of Korea. On the other hand, however, the recent "comfort women" problem shows that Japan has not yet settled all its problems related to World War II. Japan's understanding of and confrontation with its past are the premise for its discussion of the future and will be the starting point for its promotion of open regionalism in Asia and the Pacific.

Chapter 3 · Linkages between Democracy and the Market

Section 1 · The Relationship Between Political Freedom and Economic Efficiency

Louis Emmerij

Renewed emphasis has been placed on the importance of political democracy since November 1989, that is since the fall of the Berlin Wall. The difficulties experienced by Eastern European countries and the Soviet Union were seen as proof that economic efficiency was allergic to autocratic types of government. Even for the casual observer, however, it is obvious that the relationship between political freedom and economic efficiency is far more complex than it is now made out to be. It is perfectly legitimate to have economic efficiency as a priority objective; it is equally legitimate to set as a policy target the attainment of political freedom in the form of political democracy. But the causal relationship between the two cannot be considered as straightforward.

Long definitions of democracy and democratic systems are not necessary here. Suffice it to say that any genuinely democratic system must be characterized by political freedom, the supremacy of law, and the protection of individual rights. Although the relationship between political democracy and economic development is usually discussed mainly at the national level, I would like to look at this issue at both the national and international levels.

At the National Level

The exceptional combination of political freedom and economic efficiency has been achieved in very few countries. More frequently, a simple and unidirectional relationship has been established between democracy and development. Thus one can read in a publication from an otherwise pragmatic country that "democracy is one of the prerequisites for making advances in development."[1]

Many, if not all, OECD countries are enrolling development aid as a way of pressuring countries to adopt the Westminster model of parliamentary democracy.[2] One of the central hypotheses of liberal democratic theory indeed associates rapid economic development with political democracy. However, it can be shown empirically that there are several possibilities:

1. the coexistence of political freedom and economic efficiency;
2. economic efficiency leading to political freedom;
3. economic efficiency leading to bureaucratic authoritarianism; and
4. autocratic rule of the Stalinist variety leading to economic inefficiency.

The first possibility—the coexistence of political freedom and economic efficiency—is a rare bird indeed. It can mainly be found in the OECD area, but even here in many countries there have been lapses into authoritarianism of different types. Only a handful of countries, literally, can pride themselves in having combined these two objectives all along. The Netherlands would be a case in point here. Outside the OECD area, one can identify, for example, India, which has combined political democracy and economic growth since Independence.

The second possibility—economic efficiency leading to political freedom—can be observed on all continents. In Spain, for instance, the "economic miracle" started in the early 1960s, leading only 15 years later to the onset of political democracy. The same phenomenon can be observed in Chile where, under Pinochet, the economic conditions were set that have led to the political freedom prevailing today. South Korea is a particularly interesting case. All the industrialized countries gathered within the OECD are busy congratulating that country for its economic achievements and would gladly welcome it into the OECD "club." This club is composed of the very countries that today are not only so enthused by political democracy, but are also adepts of the simple and unidirectional relationship between political democracy and economic development. But political democracy is not yet widespread in South Korea! However, over the past few years, there have been definite signs of a clear movement towards a change in political institutions. Increased income of the people almost unavoidably leads to pressure being exercised on the political institutions of a country in the direction of greater freedom and flexibility.

The third possibility—economic efficiency leading to bureaucratic authoritarianism—is typical of Latin America. G.A. O'Donnell has shown that in the Latin America of the 1960s and 1970s, high rates of economic growth produced what he calls "bureaucratic authoritarianism."[3] These were omber years of military rule from which Latin America has only recently emerged.

Finally, the fourth possibility—autocratic rule leading to economic inefficiency—is, of course, most dramatically demonstrated in Eastern Europe and in the former Soviet Union. It is this fourth "model" that has led to the present fashion of the simple and unidirectional relationship.

Those pushing for the generalization of the Westminster model must answer a whole series of questions. For example, it must be recalled that the authoritarian character of the colonial economy prevented the growth of liberal democracy. Moreover, how can Western values like tolerance, moderation, and loyal opposition be developed in societies marked by intolerance, violence, and polarization? Furthermore, in old and well-established cultures, such as those of Java or China, imposing a foreign body of habits can do more harm than good. There are more ways between heaven and earth to reach the same objectives.

These brief examples show that the relationship between political democracy and economic development is indeed more complex than is sometimes thought. However, *in the longer run*, economic development is only sustainable if incentives are introduced to stimulate the individual. Such an incentives system would probably be a cross between political democracy and what I call economic democracy, as well as, of course, human rights.

One must be careful that today's emphasis on political democracy does not result in the introduction of mere *formal* democracies. It is not enough to have 26 political parties, one must have a say in the day-to-day economic decision-making process. People must be able not only to vote once every two or four years, but also to exercise an influence in their villages, in the informal sector, and in their enterprises. This is what I call "economic democracy." It is more generally known as the concept of participatory economic development. I could imagine that, at a given level of economic development, economic democracy may take priority over political democracy.

Indeed, an obvious link exists between democracy and material well-being. There can be no meaningful exercise of political democracy or human rights in a country where economic resources are scarce and the bulk of the population lives below the poverty line. In other words, a stable and sustainable democracy requires a certain level of economic development, and a viable social contract.

We need to review some of the thinking of the 1970s on the subject of basic needs development strategies, as updated in the South Commission report.[4] This document asserts that development is the process of self-reliant growth, achieved through the participation of the people acting in their own interests under their own control. Its first objectives must be to end poverty, provide productive employment, and satisfy the basic needs of all the people.

At the International Level

The just-cited South Report can be seen as a commitment by the developing countries to democratic values, respect for fundamental rights, fair treatment for minorities, concern for the poor and underprivileged, probity in public life, and willingness to settle disputes without recourse to war. But it associates this with a plea for justice, equity, and democracy in the global society.

In the *new world* we have entered, important changes are taking place in the South and in the East. New political generations are coming to the fore, new political institutions are being established, and new, different economic and financial policies are being introduced. If one defines good governance, as the term is now used, in its political and institutional meanings, as well as in its economic and financial ones, there are tremendous changes taking place in national governance in both South and East. We are in the presence of great movement and dynamism. I do not say that the policies adopted are necessarily the right ones, but I do maintain that both East and South are practicing more and more what the West, namely the OECD countries, has been preaching.

But the West seems strangely immobile. If one looks at international governance (that is, the way the world economy and polity is being governed), which is, of course, largely under the control of the G-7 and other minor gods in the OECD universe, one gets a definite impression of inertia. Examples abound. There are the agricultural policies of the OECD countries which are not only very expensive for the OECD taxpayers and consumers, but are also becoming an embarrassment worldwide. There is the Multifibre Agreement, renewed again until the end of 1992. For 30 years now the OECD countries and certain others have been trying to restructure their textile and clothing industries. What we want others to do in five years, we ourselves cannot do in a generation. And then, of course, there is the Uruguay Round which is three years behind schedule.

Thus there is a growing discrepancy between the changes and dynamism in East and South on the one hand, and the immobility at the level of international governance on the other. As the former Chief Economist of the OECD has said: "For the first time in international economic history, the pressure of trade liberalization now comes from the South and the East and no longer from the countries that traditionally have been pushing for it."

The bottom line is that the very countries that are pressing for political democracy within the developing countries are not practicing what they preach at the global level. A better system of *international* governance must be introduced, and this lies largely in the hands of the G-7 countries which continue to liberally distribute praise and blame at their annual Summit meetings. Hence there is an urgent need to restructure international organizations in general, and the United Nations system in particular. In a world where global markets and global enterprises are becoming generalized, international good governance must increasingly become of even greater importance than national governance.

Globalization implies a need for global economic management. There is a danger that as the process of globalization proceeds, the existing set of international institutions will become increasingly ineffective and obsolete. We may soon reach a situation where no governmental organization, be it national or international, is in effective control of global economic affairs and where no one can be held accountable for events in the global sphere. This is another reason why the issue of international governance must be high on the agenda in coming years. In this connection, the so-called Stockholm Initiative on Global Security and Governance has important things to say about the restructuring of the United Nations.[5]

Conclusion

First, just as development assistance was successful in maintaining the status quo during the Cold War years, it could very well be successful today in pressuring for political democracy. But whether this will lead to the satisfaction of basic needs and to economic democracy remains an open question. Yet these are inseparable objectives.

Second, the industrialized countries are putting heavy pressure on the developing countries to introduce better governance: more political democracy, multipartism, less military expenditure and corruption, etc. But better international and global governance must lead the way to better internal governance. It is clear that the G-7, which meets regularly, is hardly an example of transparent and democratic international governance. The need for new concepts and institutions to face the challenges of tomorrow is therefore even more urgent.

Notes

1. Ministry for Foreign Affairs, *Swedish Policy for International Co-operation, Budget 1991-1992*, Stockholm, 1991.

2. There is a growing literature on this topic. See Overseas Development Council, *Encouraging Democracy: What Role for Conditioned Aid?*, Policy Essay No. 4, Washington, 1992.

3. G.A. O'Donnell, *Modernisation and Bureaucratic Authoritarianisation: Studies in South American Policies* (Berkeley and Los Angeles: University of California Press, 1973).

4. South Commission, *The Challenge to the South* (Oxford: Oxford University Press, 1990).

5. *Common Responsibility in the 1990s: The Stockholm Initiative on Global Security and Governance*, Stockholm, Prime Minister's Office, 1991.

Section 2 · Democracy at Bay

Carl Tham

Today the idea of democracy is triumphant; the model is in principle embraced in almost all of the countries of the world. You may say that the very word democracy has been hailed and misused earlier in history. The most repressing and totalitarian regimes have tried to mask themselves as "real" or "peoples" democracies. What has happened, however, is a historical demasking of these false pretenses.

Democracy

What do we mean by democracy? There is now a general agreement that democracy cannot be defined by purpose or policy or levels of mass mobilization. It must be defined as a political system where different parties or individuals compete for power through regular free elections in which all adult citizens have a vote. Moreover, a democracy must uphold certain basic human rights and well-defined freedoms that make the free political process possible and must respect the opinion and integrity of the individual. No other definitions hold, and we should be careful when we talk about "real" democracy versus "formal" democracy. A society in which real life upholds the constitutional or formal democratic principles and which in practice applies the rights these principles imply, is by definition a democracy. A society with a beautiful-sounding constitution but where none or few of these rights are respected is certainly not a democracy.

Governance

It is important to understand that democratic government does not necessarily mean good government in the sense that those in power make wise or well-considered decisions. Nor does it mean that conflicts inherent in the society are reduced to a minimum. Demands for democracy, social justice, and a better life have historically gone hand in hand, but this does not mean that the establishment of a democratic system actually does lead to an improvement in social conditions or equality.

It is also quite clear that some societies have a sort of outer shell of democracy, but in reality exclude large groups of people from having any political influence whatsoever. The actual differences in living conditions are so enormous and so entrenched that these people can have no confidence at all in the political system even if it is democratic according to the definition I have used. In these cases—for example in some Latin American countries—one can talk of a "masked hegemony with competing elites," where the outcome of struggles for power has little relevance for the masses. It is a sort of social and political half-authoritarian system—but disguised as a democracy—where the military often has a significant influence.

Market Economy and Democracy

In the rhetoric of the day, the terms market economy and democracy are used as if they were synonymous, or at least naturally emerging at the same time. But this is wrong—or at least misleading. When the market economy or capitalism finally established itself in the 1800s and came to characterize modern industrial civilization, democracy was at best in its infancy. In fact, one could argue that democracy grew out of the contradictions and social dynamism inherent in the market economy or capitalistic system.

In this century we have a long list of terrifying and repressive regimes which have nevertheless upheld the virtues of a market economy. That some of these regimes have for ideological and security reasons been hailed as bastions against Communism and so dignified members of the so-called free world does not transform them into democracies. In this company it is perhaps unnecessary to remind ourselves that the colonial system was assuredly not democratic, but was certainly based on capitalistic or market economy principles. It is the sad but irrefutable historical coupling of Western democracy, colonialism, and the plundering of resources in the name of the market economy, which for understandable reasons, meant that many of the leaders of national liberation movements looked for alternative models to follow for the development of their young nations.

In this connection it can be worth remembering what Nelson Mandela said soon after his release from 26 years of prison in the market economic but racist state of South Africa; "When we in the ANC during 40 years struggled for democracy we were put in prison by the same people who are now telling us how we should behave to promote the democracy we have been rejected by all these years." While we can see that a market economy does not automatically lead to democracy, a functioning democracy—as we have defined it—does seem to require some form of free economic system.

Theoretically, a political democracy could be combined with an economy totally controlled by the government, but experience has shown this is very difficult. One could even argue that it is impossible, since democracy implies a certain freedom of economic choice and independent economic actors. A functioning democratic system presupposes a civil society—in practice, independent institutions, companies, organizations, the media, and so on, regulated by law but not subject to or controlled by those in power.

Is There a Global Model?

We must also see that there are no unambiguous relations between economic growth, development, and democracy. Democratic governments are never very successful when it comes to structural reforms that may be to the disadvantage of important interests in the society, nor when it comes to welfare. The developing countries that have achieved the greatest success economically and socially over the last 20 years are the East Asian nations, which have all had various kinds of more or less authoritarian systems.

However, that does not mean that you can use these countries as models for the rest of the world. There is no globally valid link between an authoritarian form of regime and economic development, not even when development is defined only in terms of autocentric growth. Many political scientists—not to mention the legions of political philosophers—have tried to find some systematic connection between what we call development or modernization on the one hand, and the political system on the other, but all have failed. One of them, Professor Jorgensson, recently made a fascinating comparative study, stressing "that the abstract distinction between democracy and authoritarianism does not provide sufficient guidance for deciding about the effects on economic development or welfare."

A Prerequisite

What is obvious, however, is that one of several prerequisites for economic growth and development is legitimate and reasonably well-functioning government and governance. If the free market is to be a motor for development and improved welfare, and not just a meeting place for robber barons, the Mafia, and speculators, you must have a regulating and supportive state. If economic history teaches us anything, it is just this. Consider the astounding development in Germany after the war, or in Japan and the other East Asian countries some years later. There are many differences, but what they have in common is a well-functioning government apparatus with a long tradition. To quote the UN *World Economic Survey*: "Both historical and contemporary experience suggest that the State has indispensable functions in defining legal frameworks, providing infrastructure, establishing monetary and financial stability, ensuring education and health, maintaining an acceptable distribution of income and social justice, safeguarding the environment and providing a vision of the future role of the country in the world economy." And the World Bank says the same.

That brings us to some very awkward questions. Is democracy only possible when a country has first attained a certain economic and social standard? Can an established democracy survive if it does not provide economic progress and improved social standards?

Democracy in Crisis

Today we find ourselves in a historical situation where a large number of countries in the former Communist states of Europe, in Africa, Asia, and Latin America, are at one and the same time trying to establish new democratic systems and new economic mechanisms. The situation is unique, and the intrinsic problems are unprecedented. Democracy as an idea has triumphed, but in its practice it is in profound trouble. It is no exaggeration to talk of the crisis of democracy.

The former Communist countries are certainly in crisis. As a by-product, there is an intense suspicion of the political institutions, of the state, and the parties. In this way the legitimacy of democracy and the ability of the politicians to deal with the fundamental problems of society has been undermined. The lack of a democratic tradition is not overcome from one day to the next.

Many of the developing countries that are attracted to the democratic system of government have similar difficulties. The introduction of a multiparty system does not in itself mean that one can manage the conflicts and social problems in a democratic way. Both in the East and the South countries are trying, at one and the same time, to change the political and economic system. When the whole society is convulsed by economic changes, and where people's living conditions fundamentally change, it is not easy to develop and maintain a political system based on compromise and respect, including respect for minorities.

As in previous history the deep crises in legitimacy and general frustration fosters national and ethnic conflicts. These conflicts establish themselves in a society where the authoritarian system, economic crises, and the breakdown of traditional values rob people of any other kind of kinship than ethnic.

We cannot avoid seeing disturbing signs of this crisis also in the "established democracies" of the wealthy nations. Opinion polls from a large number of countries indicate a growing suspicion, not of democracy as such, but of its institutions, politics, parties, and politicians.

In the United States the political system has congealed in an extremely commercial form. Distrust and dissatisfaction seem massive. The system creates its own logic of self-destruction. Politicians who seek to be elected try to make themselves popular by depicting themselves as nonpoliticians, as "true" representatives of the people. This is a classic trick that has always been used by the enemies of democracy. Enormous sums of money are spent on political propaganda that is less and less informative. The political system is not capable of managing or even seriously discussing the problems of society.

Opinion polls, the participation in elections, and election results show the same tendency in Europe as in the United States. The advance of extreme right-wing and populist parties in Germany, France, and Italy speaks for itself. The feeling in many countries is characterized by a belief in democracy as a concept, but at the same time by distrust of and hostility towards its institutions. The politics and the politicians are not acknowledged as morally motivated. Politicians are forced into a pattern which confirms the voter's suspicion. It is obvious that the state of democracy varies from country to country, as do the reasons for a feeling of dejection. But there are some similarities too.

The continuing and the noticeable internationalization limits the national freedom of political choice, available alternatives, and makes it more difficult for people to see the connection between "politics" and their actual living conditions. The governments are restrained by international economic events. The reaction of the stock exchange may be more important than that of the voters. The election results determine the stock exchange prices—but is it perhaps not the case that the stock exchange, indirectly, also governs the election results? People feel themselves to be the victims of major economic changes, but no one seems to be responsible and they themselves feel they have little chance of influencing the outcome. The absence of clearly identifiable alternatives between the larger political parties provides opportunities for the populists and the extremists.

Lessons from the Past

There is indeed reason to reflect on the lessons of the history of our turbulent and cruel century. After World War I, the first apocalyptical catastrophe, there was the time when the world should be safe for democracy. What we actually got was the impotence of the democracies to address the economic and social problems of the day, and the establishment of totalitarian regimes in the Soviet Union, Italy, Spain, Germany, and in the new democracies of Central and Eastern Europe. In the other democracies there was a profound crisis of values. A world of mass unemployment, deliberate destruction of food when people were starving, of passive government fixed in their fanatical belief in the free forces of the market and social fatalism—all of this almost destroyed the democracies from the inside. After World War II, there was a strong consensus in all the victorious democracies that everything must be done to avoid anything similar to the social and political collapse that occurred between the wars. That was the end of social fatalism and the emerging of the welfare society. Professor Herbert Tingsten, a noted Swedish political scientist, wrote in 1957: "We may be conservatives, liberals, or socialists; none of us accept the kind of chaos that some decades ago was called economic freedom. Citizens of a democratic society should not live in poverty or unemployment—that position is today as indisputable as the universal suffrage or the political freedom." According to Tingsten the welfare democracies had now reached a kind of mature political position, with a proper balance between the public and private, between the political realm and the economic. He was not alone in his belief; it was generally upheld in many countries and political scientists like Tingsten and Dell announced the end of ideologies.

The Dangers of Going Back

But during the last 10 or 15 years the memory of this history lesson has faded. The ideological clock was put back. The welfare society was now out of fashion: poverty, beggars, and people sleeping in the street were again a part of daily life. As late as the 1970s, it was argued that modern democracy could not stand mass unemployment, as it then was defined at about 5 to 7 percent. But unemployment continued to increase. It passed the 10 percent limit, and the conservative governments in power noticed that the feared revolt did not materialize. They learned that social and ideological rollback was after all possible. As a result, growth, social welfare, and employment are no longer the first objectives of the industrial countries. The key objective is to drive down inflation, more or less irrespective of the tremendous social costs and based on the rather gratuitous belief that this policy "at the end" should promote growth. But the process of contraction tends in itself to discourage rather than encourage investment.

We are now reaping the bitter harvest of that policy in the industrial world as well as in transition economies and developing countries. That is not to say that we are back in the 1930s, but we are experiencing an unnecessary recession based on a deliberate policy of contraction. The impact on the rich countries is global. The social failures start to hurt people and affect their attitude towards society. The decent politicians seem unable to change the situation; extremists, racists, and populists are given new opportunities. To quote the recent UN *World Economic Survey*:

> It was becoming increasingly clear that the high unemployment—and the non-employment due the disenchanted withdrawal from the labor force—in industrial countries is directly related to widespread frustration, homelessness, drug trafficking and abuse, crime, and ethnic tensions. In developing countries on every continent, poverty, economic chaos, and fear of the future promotes fanaticism, terrorism, uncontrollable migration, or civil war, compounding the problem of getting development onto its tracks. The optimistic mood of the collapse of the Cold War has disappeared. The peace dividend has not materialized. Conflicts and civic unrest are emerging. The rich societies are still very affluent but also frustrated, uncertain, and afraid of what the future may bring. The newly-born democracies are at bay. But the advice about how this process should proceed, delivered mainly by Western economists and conservative politicians, have in actual fact an extremely fragile theoretical and empirical basis. Generally, the advice bears the stamp of the prevailing ideological atmosphere in the West, with its mixture of neoliberalism, opportunism, and right-wing policy. This applies to the economic transformation as well as to the political.

Conclusion

The establishment of a legitimate democracy is a long and painful process and, needless to say, embedded in the domestic social and political traditions and forces. Other countries can do a lot to destroy such a process—there are legions of examples—but it is much more difficult to strengthen and promote it. The most important factor today is, in my opinion, to embark on a global growth-oriented policy. It would be healthy for the rich countries themselves and it would be crucial for many economies in transition. The governments of the rich world have to get out of their self-imposed straitjacket of contraction. Moreover, they should make important structural changes in policy towards the developing world concerning assistance, trade, and debt relief. For example, it is a scandal—nothing less—that the West has not yet made a radical reform of debt relief to the least developed countries, many of which try to embark on a new course of democracy and economic reform.

To quote once more the *World Economic Survey*:

> There is today much concern about the lack of resources for such urgent needs as the reconstruction of the East, a concerted attack on poverty and human development in the poorest countries, and environmental investments of all kinds. If the growth of world output returns to the level of the 1980s, total output would grow by about one trillion dollars a year. There is, in fact, no other way to resolve the economic and political crises multiplying in the world community than to give priority to the restoration of growth.

We are certainly not at the end of history. We are rather at a dramatic turning point, a moment of many possibilities and many dangers. What we do now, for a few years ahead, may direct the future for several decades—like the dramatic and fateful years immediately after World War II. All nations, all governments, have a responsibility. The rich world has a special responsibility, not just moral, but because of its enormous economic and political power.

Section 3 · Development and Democracy in the Aid Relationship

Benjamin Bassin

In 1980 Gunnar Myrdal, the grand old man of development research in Nordic countries and winner of the Nobel Prize, published an angry attack on the development cooperation policies of countries of the Organization for Economic Cooperation and Development (OECD) generally and on the policy of his country, Sweden, in particular.[1] In arguing for a tougher line in dealings with the corrupt and dictatorial regimes of some recipient countries, he wrote (my translation from the original Swedish):

> The truth is that to achieve the kind of development we must wish for, what is required is not distributive reforms, carried out through financial transfers via taxes and contributions, of the kind which can be effective in developed countries, but profound institutional reforms.

Although this article aroused quite a debate, the donor bureaucracies tended to dismiss it with a shrug of the shoulders and a shake of the head, deploring the fact that such an eminent scientist could have so thoroughly misunderstood the development cooperation relationship.

A decade later the OECD Development Assistance Committee, meeting at the level of Aid Ministers and Heads of Aid Agencies, had this to say: "There is a vital connection, now more widely appreciated, between open, democratic and accountable political systems, individual rights and the effective and equitable operation of economic systems."[2]

Myrdal had been vindicated at the highest level of the aid bureaucracies of the most important donor country group. And the OECD Ministers are not alone. The British, French, Japanese, German, Nordic, and other governments have at high political levels proclaimed their faith in the universality of democracy and human rights, in their importance to development of the developing countries and, therefore, to the aid effort undertaken by the developing and developed countries together. Interestingly enough, a number of recipient countries have endorsed these thoughts, such as the South Commission under the chairmanship of former president of Tanzania Julius Nyerere and the Commonwealth in its Harare Declaration in 1991. What was heresy in 1980 had become orthodoxy in 1992.

The affirmations of the new faith have been so frequent and so fervent that one is tempted to exclaim with St. Augustine: "Extra ecclesiam nulla salus," meaning, "There is no salvation outside the church." The purpose of this paper is to examine closer some of the tenets of the faith. The starting points of this astonishing change are essentially two, the wave of democratization in the world since the mid-1970s and the end of the Cold War.

It has been calculated that between 1974 and 1990 more than 30 countries in Southern Europe, Latin America, East Asia, and Eastern Europe have shifted from authoritarian to democratic systems of government.[3] It is the third wave of democratization in the modern era—the two previous ones having occurred between the early nineteenth century and the end of World War I and the second between the end of World War II and the beginning of decolonization in the early 1960s—and probably the most important political trend of the late twentieth century. If we accept this chronology, it is worth noting that the democratic trend predates the end of the Cold War by a decade and a half and its causes, although far from established yet, seem not to be entirely connected with great power politics. This puts the recent proclamations of donor countries on democracy and development in an interesting perspective.

That the end of the Cold War has drastically changed the aid scene is obvious to the well-informed observer. The effects have, on balance, been salutary. A host of issues overshadowed and obscured by security objectives have emerged more clearly to view and can now be debated free of the passions of great power rivalry.[4] Since the motives of many donor countries' aid programs were as much if not more to be found in the ideological confrontation as in economic development, aid seems to have lost an essential source of inspiration and, indeed, of legitimacy. It is not inconceivable that the rather sudden interest of the donor community in democracy, human rights, and the benefits of the market economy is linked to the search of a new legitimacy for aid programs. It has been pointed out that "aid constituency is gradually being reduced to businessmen who see foreign aid programs as a way to increase sales"[5] and that might be too narrow a power base for the aid bureaucracies which operate in a democratic setting.

Promoting democracy and human rights through the aid programs gives rise to a vast number of questions. The problems of methodology alone will demand years of planning and experimenting, not to speak of meetings, seminars, and colloquia where the instruments are honed. In this section, we will not grapple with these issues, but will examine briefly only three questions which seem rather fundamental and problematic:

1. What is the nature of the linkage between the political system of a country and its economic development?
2. What kind of democracy do the donors wish to support?
3. What is involved in political conditionality of aid?

Linkage between Democracy and Development

Always implicitly and often explicitly, the pronouncements issuing from the donor community assume a positive correlation between democracy and development. A recent policy document of the Dutch government offers a succinct formulation; ". . . a society that is not free leads to power being vested in the hands of a few, and this power is inevitably used to deny others access to welfare."[6]

Other donors have offered variations of this basic theme. The view is supported by a large number of well-founded arguments. The free markets, which are a hallmark of a democratic society, are seen as creating a countervailing power to that of the government which ultimately guarantees the existence of democracy. The growth of an indigenous middle class is deemed by many to be an essential component in democratization. The general mutually reinforcing effect of economic and political liberalization is seen as a potent force in development.

The degree of conviction of these policy documents is, unfortunately not matched by research results in this area. It is perhaps fair to say that authoritarian or totalitarian regimes do not, on the whole, reach any higher economic growth rates that pluralistic, democratically oriented states. A recent international symposium reached the follow conclusion:

> Some countries have developed with strong technocratic bureaucracies relatively uninfluenced by public opinion. But there appeared to be no correlation between development and either democratic or authoritarian rule. At the same time, most participants accepted that there was a mutually conducive relationship, even if not a simple and straightforward one, between markets and development.[7]

The World Bank's *World Development Report* of 1991 contains an excellent discussion of the role of the state in development, which deserves to become a classic in the field. The best it can say in this respect is, however, cautious enough, ". . . there is suggestive evidence that links features of democratic systems positively with overall aspect of development and welfare."[8] Not exactly a rousing battle cry for democratic reform.

In my knowledge the most comprehensive up-to-date survey of research in this field is an article by two American political scientists, Larry Sirowy and Alex Inkeles.[9] They review thirteen cross-national, quantitative studies evaluating the economic consequences of differences in the democratic character of national regimes and twelve similar studies on the effect on democracy on societal inequality. These studies were conducted in the period from 1967 to 1968. For the sake of brevity, the interesting substance of the rather voluminous article is omitted here. The conclusions speak for themselves:

> . . . political democracy does not widely and directly facilitate more rapid economic growth. . . . Beyond this, however, very little else seems clear. . . . The evidence appears to allow us to conclude that political democracy does not widely exacerbate inequality, net of other factors.[10]

It may be shocking for someone raised in the democratic tradition and in a market economy to realize that the empirical evidence in support of the linkage between democracy and development is tenuous, at best. The only fairly certain aspect of the problem is that the linkage is more complicated and less direct than is implied in the policy declarations of the donor community. On the other hand, the arguments for authoritarianism are not entirely convincing, either. They fall mainly in two categories.

The first set of arguments for the development-promoting qualities of authoritarian rule concerns the level of development. Authoritarian rule is seen as being the preferable form of government in the early stages of economic and social development, when tough and unpleasant decisions have be to taken. The birth and stabilization of a middle class is often seen as the stage where democratic feature can "safely" by introduced into the national life. The former prime minister of Singapore, Lee Kwan Yew, is a articulate defender of this point of view, on the strength of his own experience.[11] He sees a higher level of education and new working habits arising out of industrial production among the managerial class as a necessary precondition for introducing democracy. It has on the other hand been pointed out that in Japan, the development of the middle class and the economic rise of the country started simultaneously. This contradicts the idea that democratization can come only after a certain level of affluence has been achieved.[12]

It is perhaps not without interest to note in this context that the "democratic centralism" which was the official doctrine related to the functioning of democracy in the Soviet Union and the socialist states of Eastern Europe, was based on an argument akin to the one supporting authoritarian rule at early stages of economic and social development. The avant-garde of the proletariat, the Party, had to take decisions on behalf of the masses as the latter still had the "false consciousness" of pre-Revolution days. As long as the decisions were in the interest of the masses, they were by definition democratic.

The argument that democracy can prevail and human rights respected only after a certain level of development has been achieved reflects a double standard—differentiation between the North and the South—which negates the essence of human rights, namely their universality.[13] Although it is beyond doubt that each nation must develop its own particular version of democracy which reflects its history and socioeconomic situation, the basis of any system that can be recognized as democratic must be rule of law, equality before the law, fundamental rights and freedoms. To maintain that a group of people—in fact, the vast majority of the planet's inhabitants—must raise their level of affluence to be accorded democratic rights, contradicts the basic principles of liberal democracy. (In this perspective it is surprising to observe that Article I of the UN Declaration on the Right to Development of 1986 is open to the interpretation that "human rights and fundamental freedoms can be fully realized" only after development has taken place).

The other set of arguments, closely linked to the former, center around the thesis of "development dictatorship," ascribed to the German political scientist Richard Löwenthal, who in 1962 wrote: "Every step towards freedom is paid with the slowing down of economic development."[14]Authoritarian governments are thought to be less vulnerable against powerful interest groups and popular pressures and more decisive in difficult times, for instance in carrying out painful structural reforms. More specifically, authoritarian regimes are like to create higher domestic savings by forcing public savings or promoting inegalitarian polices conductive to private savings.[15] Commenting on a speech by the International Monetary Fund's (IMF) managing director Camdessus extolling the virtues of democratization, *The Economist* states the case laconically and bluntly, "Governments that follow Mr. Camdessus's advice may well be booted out of office before their policies have borne fruit."[16]

As evidence for the "development dictatorship" thesis the cases of the Far Eastern "tigers" are often introduced. It is much too facile to lay aside these examples with a reference to special circumstances due to the tradition of Confucianism and favorable external influence.[17] It is amusing to note that until after the economic rise of Japan in the 1950s Western observers were mostly in agreement about the development-retarding effect of Confucianism's adherence to tradition, ritual, and to a strictly hierarchic view of the world. Its development-promoting effects are a recent discovery which might have surprised the rather conservative Master Kung himself.

A recent study of the Taiwanese and South Korean experience ascribed the "leap to sustained growth" to the ability of the authoritarian regimes to resist pressures of special interest groups.[18] The less than satisfactory economic performance of the world's largest democracy, India, over the last four decades, may be explainable precisely by this factor, the marriage of elected politicians to special interest fed by an antiquated economic system.

To refute the "development dictatorship" argument one can only refer to the inconclusive nature of the research as described above. Were the authoritarians in a position of advantage to promote development, it would certainly show in empirical data. It does not and thus the jury is still out. One can also theorize about the time perspective and construct a fairly believable case for democracy as a long term force for development while the authoritarians might have an advantage in the short term. But, as Lord Keynes pointed out "In the long run we'll all be dead. . . ."

While waiting for the scholars to produce something more definitive, one can console oneself with recent research results indicating that the crucial ingredient differentiating, for example, South Korea and India is not democracy per se, but rather the openness of the economy.[19] Allowing new ideas, techniques, and products to enter has given investment the extra push that was needed to spur development. This observation may stimulate new thinking about development, not only among planners in developing countries, but in the donor community as well.

Another train of thought, which may not offer consolation to friends of democracy, but may help lay a ground for development, is that democracy is only one possible source of a regime's legitimacy, that is, only one of the reasons people feel that their government is entitled to be obeyed. If you have legitimacy and consensus, you may be able to constitute the basis for sustainable development.[20] Many developing country governments may have used up the legitimacy they gained from the struggle against colonialism a generation ago but they may—theoretically, at least—be able to gain new legitimacy from ideology or national tradition, with or without democracy. And ultimately, the oldest and most fundamental way for a regime to achieve legitimacy is to govern well and in the interest of those governed. Democracy is not a means to this end.

From a donor's point of view, the inescapable conclusion is that the case for democracy as an economic force for development is far from clear. An exception is to be made for emergencies of various kinds, which are far easier to deal with through an open, accountable system of government.[21] In these circumstances, the only intellectually acceptable solution is to divorce the argumentation for democracy from that of economic development. In other words, democracy must be "sold" to its "consumers" by other arguments than economic ones, preferably on its own, idealistic merits. A serious disservice to democracy in countries entirely lacking in democratic traditions would be to raise expectations that aid flows will be maintained or even increased if the forms of democracy—multitude of political parties, elections, parliaments—will be instituted.

What Kind of Democracy?

As we have seen above, the universality of the principle of democracy and human rights plays no small part in the argumentation for the donors' case. If it could be demonstrated that democracy is suitable for one nation or tribe or village but not for another, the dictators of this world would not fail to play that card to their advantage. Therefore the question of definitions, of standards, and of indicator assumes major importance.

Regrettably, it is an issue of enormous complexity. As democracy is not a ready-to-wear doctrine imported by kind foreigners but ideally a tradition growing organically from the history and culture of a population group, the product of decades or centuries of experience, it is understandably hard to standardize and equip with handy markers to allow measurement of progress. Sirowy and Inkeles discuss the problem of measurements in the conclusions of the study,[22] pointing out that of the numerous measurement problems to be addressed, none is more central than valid and reliable measurement of democracy.

By the same token, it is clearly unfair to apply the same standard to all recipients of aid. To judge African, Latin American or Asian nations by the standards of democracy and human rights, of say, Finland, would clearly make little sense. It would provide an excellent justification to those in the recipient countries who maintain that these are in any case alien, Western ideas, inherently unsuitable for African/Latin American/Asian situations and contrary to their traditions and folkways.

The absence of standards leads, of course, to prevalence of subjective judgments. In practical terms, international media, which contribute a lot to the perception of faraway countries among the decision makers and opinion-leaders in the industrialized world, have a major impact in formulating donor views regarding democracy, human rights, and related questions in recipient countries. It is not unthinkable that a recipient country is judged more severely for breaches of human rights or of democratic rule simply because the donors had higher expectations of that country than of a neighboring one.

And yet, applying different standards to different countries also goes against the grain of our ideas of the sovereign equality of states as enshrined in the Charter of the United Nations and in modern international law. Unless we accept *de jure,* and not only *de facto* that there are first and second class "citizens" in the international community, the standards applied by a donor country in assessing the degree of democracy in a recipient country should be as uniform as possible. Governments also prefer that their foreign policy stance is seem as a logical and principled one. No government likes to find itself in a position of having to explain why it did not live up to its principles in a given instance.

The fact that precedents are virtually nonexistent does not make the situation any easier. To my knowledge no study has been conducted correlating the aid received by developing countries to their presumed degree of democracy, but I entertain some doubts as to whether a positive correlation really exists. Democracy has so far not been visibly rewarded by aid donors, nor has the lack of democracy been punished, with the exception for the last few years. Thus no methodology has been developed for the kind of operation now facing the donor countries, not least those of the OECD.

This leads one to contemplate the option of directing the aid effort to support democracy by relative rather than absolute indicators, that is, by the direction of change rather than its magnitude. To take a suitably remote example, if a country moves from military dictatorship to a system resembling Ayub Khan's "directed democracy" of the 1960s, does this constitute a step towards the desired direction large enough to warrant a favorable change of aid policy? Were this principle followed, it would allow a basically authoritarian regime to prolong the aid relationship by making a long series of small concessions, a situation which would be difficult to explain satisfactorily to media and decision makers in the donor country.

As we know, liberal democracy—which seems to be the ideal to strive for in the light of the policy declarations of the donors—stands on two pillars. One of them is majority rule, the other a set of values which includes the rule of law, equality before the law, human rights and freedoms, and other central features of liberal political culture. There is an inherent logical gap in liberal democracy since there is not a priori reason to assume that the majority would wish to uphold these values. To see that this is not empty theorizing we need only to think of the instances in recent political history which have brought to power majorities inimical to democracy, sometimes even setting the abolition of democracy on the program in their election campaign. It may be futile to speculate how the donor community would react to supporting democracy in destroying itself but the dilemma is real, albeit extreme.

Where does all this leave the donors? One hears the argument that since democracy is likely to improve the efficiency of aid, one must find ways of supporting democracy. It is doubtful whether this contention is sustainable. The same problem of measurement must apply to the efficiency of aid as is applied to economic growth more generally. Its positive correlation to democracy is difficult to prove. Moreover, seeing efficiency of aid as the objective and democracy as the means might not strike the right political note in donor countries.

Perhaps the key lies in the recognizing the "organic" nature of the growth of democracy, its roots in the history, economy, and social situation of each nation. First of all, it helps the donors to put their efforts in a proper time perspective—one speaks of decades and generations rather than years. Secondly (and more importantly, perhaps) it helps to direct the external assistance to the foundations of democracy instead of the machinery itself. A proper balance between the public and private sectors, a more efficient administration, less corruption, more freedom of expression are these foundations from which a party system, constitution, parliamentary tradition etc. can spring up.

The Case for Political Conditionality

Political conditionality has always been a part of the aid scene as aid programs have from their inception been intimately linked with the political aspirations of both donors and recipients, not least in the context of the Cold War. Of late, conditions have been extended to concern explicitly human rights performance, environmental and social policies, as well as structures of political systems such as accountability, openness, and transparency of decision making. To a degree, this represents a novelty in international politics and must be examined both from the legal and practical point of view.

The principle of nonintervention in the internal affairs of another state was probably first inscribed in international law in the Treaty of Westphalia in 1648, where the faith to be practiced by each of the constituent parts of the German Empire was left to the ruling prince. It is to be noted that the principle of nonintervention was a bulwark of the weaker against the stronger, in this case the princes against the Emperor, from the outset. It has remained so throughout the following three and a half centuries.

The duty to abstain from such intervention is contained in the UN Charter (Art. II, in particular paragraph 7). At the same time, the Charter enshrines the obligation of all Members to seek realization of respect for the principles of human rights and for the self-determination of peoples. A standard interpretation of scholars of international law has been until now that the duty to abstain from intervention is firmly grounded in rules of customary law as well as in numerous treaties whereas the obligations relating to human rights and self-determination still lack true acceptance by the international community.

If we accept the above interpretation, the next question must logically be; has the acceptance of human rights and self-determination appreciably increased in recent years? The wave of democratization referred to in the introductory section above would point to an affirmative answer. The shift from a bipolar to a multipolar system of international relations which is taking place at present may result in the not too distant future in a less universal acceptance of such values. The honest answer must be that we do not know yet. In this time of upsets and transitions donor countries must beware of confusing their own wishful thinking with the consensus of opinion in the international community, in spite of encouraging signs in the direction they hope to move. In any case it is doubtful to state, as some writers have done, that the ratification of the 1966 UN Conventions by a large number of UN member states could be interpreted as invalidating the principle contain in the Art. II, para. 7 of the Charter.[23] On the contrary, had that interpretation been possible, that is, had the ratification of the Conventions implied the abrogation or watering-down of the principle of nonintervention, it is highly questionable whether ratifications would have been forthcoming in such numbers.

Were one to attempt to construe a legal justification for intervention, one might attempt to find an analogy in the so-called humanitarian intervention, the legality of which has been considered by scholars since Hugo Grotius. This refers to situations where a state treats its people in a way as to "shock the conscience of mankind," to use the word of Lauterpacht. Although the legality of such an intervention is by no means established some scholars[24] are willing to consider it "providing an absence of selfish aims could be demonstrated." From such a starting point one could begin the search of legal justifications for intervention more generally.

A rapid development in international relations in this respect has taken place in recent years. The world has seen a number of political and military developments which cannot but reflect a new interpretation of the principle of nonintervention. The culmination of this new trend so far has been UN Security Council Resolution 688 (5 April 1991) on the situation in Iraq. It might well remain a milestone in the development of this vitally important part of international law.

The practical implication of this new state of affairs has been concern on the part of developing countries in particular that the international community will be divided to those with a right to intervene and those without. This seems to have found expression in a communique from the OAU heads of state in July 1990, in a joint Chinese-Indian pronouncement in December 1991 and in statements at the Commonwealth Summit in Harare in October 1991.[25] In this perspective and in view of what was said above about the rule of nonintervention being the bulwark of the weak against the strong, other than recipient countries would seem to have a long-term interest in upholding traditional standards of international law.

The mechanism for use of political power are understandably the most sensitive part of a nation-state's everyday life. Outside interference with them could perhaps be compared to interference with the life of an individual through means of modern psychiatry. In view of this donors would be well to consider carefully the extent of intervention necessary to achieve all the aims they have set out to achieve. It nears repeating that democratic rule in itself does not necessarily ensure the protection of human rights and fundamental freedoms. Democracy has to be nondiscriminating and combined with an independent judiciary as well as with social and economic policies rooted in principles of social justice.[26] Two questions for the donors arise out of this:

1. Are the donors ready to shoulder the responsibility of an intervention of such dimensions?
2. Do the donors run the risk of inserting themselves in functions of the recipient government?

In the latter case the donor would create the famous "governance gap" so eloquently described by Faaland and Parkinson.[27] They distinguish four categories of influence, which they discuss in a general manner but each of which could come into question in the specific instance of promoting democracy, good governance, and respect for human rights and fundamental freedoms:

1. Setting objectives which determine the priorities of development.
2. Attempts to intervene in general policy issues.
3. Influence in implementation of assisted development programs.
4. Attempts to realize donors' objectives or ambitions in accepting programs.

The consideration of these aspects should ideally result in improved coordination between donors. The alternative of each donor promoting its own views of desirable political progress might result in unspeakable confusion. In the longer run donors should develop a set of unified criteria for responses to recipient country situations and improve the coherence of promoting democracy and human rights.[28]

Conclusion

Above, we have questioned some rather basic assumptions which are animating the international development debate. Having quoted one Father of the Church, St. Augustine, at the outset, one might conclude by quoting another, St. Tertullian who said, "Credo quia impossibile est," which means, "I believe because it is impossible."

Out of the skepticism, some programmatic elements emerge. First of all, donors should accept the possibility that there may not exist a systemic relationship between democracy and growth, unless, of course, later research manages to conclusively demonstrate the opposite. Democracy should be seen as the best way of safeguarding the interests of the governed against those of the governing. That is justification enough to promote it worldwide.

Second, donors should recognize what above has been called the "organic" character of democracy, that it must grow out of a society as a plant grows out of soil. Outsiders can water and fertilize the soil, but should interfere with the growth of the plant as little as possible.

Third, political conditionality has severe limitations. Donors erode the principle of nonintervention in internal affairs of other states at their own peril. As international understanding is needed on the extent and substance of aid to chance political processes in developing countries.

Notes

1. Gunnar Myrdal, "Nödhjälp i stället för utvecklingsbistånd," *Ekonomisk debatt* 8 (1980): 565-569.

2. OECD, *Policy Statement on Development Co-operation in the 1990s*, 1989.

3. Samuel P. Huntington, "How Countries Democratize," *Political Science Quarterly* 106, no. 4 (1991-92): 579-616.

4. Keith Griffin, "Foreign Aid After the Cold War," *Development and Change* 22 (1991): 645-685.

5. Griffin, 677.

6. Ministry of Foreign Affairs, "A World of Difference," The Hague, 1991, 57.

7. Ministry of Foreign Affairs, "Democratization and Development," International Symposium, Tokyo, October 1991.

8. Larry Sirowy and Alex Inkeles, "The Effects of Democracy on Economic Growth and Inequality: a Review," *Studies in Comparative International Development* 25, no. 1 (Spring 1990): 126-157.

9. World Bank, "The Challenge of Development," *The World Development Report 1991* (Oxford: Oxford University Press) 134.

10. Sirowy and Inkeles, 150, 151.

11. *The Economist*, 29 June 1991, 18-19.

12. Yasunori Sone. "Democracy and Foreign Aid: Political Systems and Economic Development." Paper prepared for International Symposium on Democracy and Development, Tokyo, Oct. 1991.

13. Katarina Tomashevski, "A Critique of the UNDP Political Freedom Index 1991," *Human Rights in Developing Countries, Yearbook 1991*, Oslo, 1991, 8-9.

14. Peter P. Waller, "Hilfe für Demokratie und Menschenrechte," *E + Z* 8 (1992).

15. Overseas Development Institute, "Aid and Political Reform," briefing paper, January 1992.

16. *The Economist*, 28 February 1992.

17. See Waller.

18. Robert Wade, "Goberning the Market," quoted in *The Economist*, 29 June 1991, 18.

19. *The Economist*, 4 January 1992, 20.

20. World Bank, "Sub-Saharan Africa: From Crisis to Development," 1989, 60.

21. Jean Dreze and Amartya Sen, *Hunger and Public Action* (Oxford: Oxford University Press, 1989).

22. Sirowy and Inkeles, 151.

23. See Waller.

24. Gerhard von Glahn, *Law Among Nations* (London: Macmillan, 1969), 163.

25. Overseas Development Institute, 4.

26. Bård-Anders Andreassen and Teresa Swinehart, "Promoting Human Rights in Developing Countries: The New Political Conditionality of Aid Policies" in *Human Rights in Developing Countries, Yearbook 1990* (Kehl am Rhein, 1991), x-xi.

27. Just Faaland and Jack Parkinson, "The Governance Gap," in *Trade, Planning and Rural Development: Essays in Honour of Nurul Islam* (London, 1990), 53-75.

28. Andreassen and Swinehart, xi.

Section 4 · Lessons for Africa

B. O. Abu Affan

The theme of this book, *A World Fit for People*, reflects an appreciation of the extraordinary flux in political and economic relations that has occurred, and is occurring, on the global scene. The end of the Cold War, which defined international relations in the postwar era, has unleashed movements and forces that are daily giving shape to an emergent world order.

As of now, the countries of the nascent world order are as yet indistinct; they will only become clear with the passage of time. Nonetheless, the global political and economic forces that are giving it shape are already apparent. Among the most important banners heralding the "New World Order" are those of "democracy" and the "market economy." The calls for democracy and respect for fundamental human rights, are today heard in all corners of the globe: from Eastern Europe and the former republics of the Soviet Union, to Asia, Africa, and Latin America. And with the manifest failure of the long and arduous experiment with command and state-controlled economies, calls for a the reform of economies, and the adoption of "market friendly" policies, have become commonplace.[1]

Political freedom, as guaranteed by democratic forms of governance, and economic freedom, as secured by market economies, are seen by many as interlinked and inseparable. It is often argued that political freedom can only be ultimately secured by economic freedom; and that economic freedom, in turn, can exist and flourish only in conditions of political freedom and democracy.[2]

Against the background of this international debate, in this chapter we seek to address the issue of the linkages between democracy and the market economy, as they, in particular, relate to Africa. These are clearly issues of vital importance for all those countries on the continent that are in transition towards democratic forms of governance. They are also central issues for the many countries that have opted for major structural economic reforms, with a view to establishing the institutions of the market economy.

Democracy and the Market Economy: Concepts and Linkages

The questions of what constitutes democratic forms of governance and what are the essential institutions of the market economy are issues that are subject to considerable debate and discussion. While there may be agreement on some of the essential features of democracy and the market economy, there is no facile agreement as to what should be included or, alternatively, what should be left out, in defining these two terms.

In Western liberal thought, democracy is identified with two essential attributes: popular sovereignty and individual liberty. An essential property of democracy is the notion that legitimate power ultimately rests with the people; and that the people have the right to choose, as well as dismiss, their government. Complementing this fundamental axiom of popular sovereignty is the inalienability of such basic human and political rights as the right of free speech and political assembly.[3]

While there may be broad agreement on these basic properties of democracy, contemporary discourse is marked by debate on whether rights, other than the purely political, should also be included in the notion of democracy. Many would argue, for example, that the right to basic needs, such as a minimum supply of food and acceptable shelter, as well as the right to work, should be included in the notion of democratic rights. Similarly, others would argue that, in the context of the developing world, the specific values and cultures of a people should be reflected in the structures of governance.[4]

While we may disagree on what basic rights and values should be encompassed in the notion of democracy, we should, however, note that, historically, the notion of democracy has progressively expanded over the centuries. It is important to recall that when proponents of democracy argued passionately for the "rights of man" in the seventeenth and eighteenth century, they did not include the rights of women, not the rights of people of color. Further, we should note that it is only in this century, and particularly in the Cold War period, that the notion of "economic rights" has gained some ground.

There may be less disagreement, if not total accord, as to what elements constitute the market economy. Following classical economic doctrine, we could postulate that the market economy is constituted by the following features: private ownership of the means of production; free competition among economic agents; the right to freely enter and exit any line of production or employment; and the determination of prices, and the allocation of resources, through the free play of market forces.[5]

This definition of the market economy is, however, an abstract concept, with few economies fully conforming to it in practice. While the economies of the Western industrialized countries, and those of the newly industrialized developing countries, may approximate in important respects these feature of the market economy, few fully comply with it. All the means of production are not privately owned; significant segments are owned and controlled by governments. In many sectors, competition has increasingly taken the form of oligopolistic competition rather than the free competition that exists when there are many buyers and sellers. And many important prices, such as those of agricultural commodities, are not determined by the interplay of market forces alone, but may be influenced by government interventions or monopolistic forces.

But despite these deficiencies, the generally acknowledged "market economies" do exhibit many of the fundamental traits ascribed to market economies proper. It is perhaps in comparison with the centralized command economies that used to exits in Eastern Europe and the former Soviet Union, and that are still found in the few remaining socialist countries, that these features clearly stand out. In the latter types of economies, private ownership of the means of production is severely restricted, the state has preeminence over all economic issues, and the role of markets is highly circumscribed.

Taking these concepts of democracy and the market economy as a starting point, we can now address the following basic questions regarding the linkages between democracy and the market economy. First, in what ways are the institutions that make for the existence of democracy related to those of the market economy? Second, is the existence of democracy an essential prerequisite for the functioning of the market economy and for its development and sustainability? Does political freedom imply economic freedom? Or conversely, is the market economy a necessary and sufficient condition for the emergence of democracy? In other words, is economic freedom a prerequisite for political freedom?

When examining the historical record, or the contemporary experience, what becomes immediately apparent is that the relation between democracy and the market economy is neither simple nor straightforward but, as can be expected, quite complex. It is indeed impossible to establish a simple one-to-one relation between the two. Thus, it is difficult to argue, for example, that the market economy always implies democracy, as numerous historical counterexamples for such a proposition can easily be found.

But having said this, it is also clear that there are certain economic conditions, namely boundary conditions, that have to be respected if democratic conditions are to prevail, and conversely, there are certain political and legal conditions that need to be fulfilled if the market economy is to exist and develop. While these conditions may not allow us to posit a clear and unambiguous relationship between democracy and the market economy, they, nonetheless help us to elucidate the complex and necessary linkages that exist between the two.

In examining the historical experience of those countries that have succeeded in establishing both democratic forms of governance and market economies, a number of interesting "observational truths" emerge. In almost all cases, the institutions of the market economy proceeded the structures of what could justifiably be called democratic forms of governance. In Europe, the seeds of the market economy were sown in the emerging urban centers and towns that served as hubs for trade and industry during the era of feudalism. And Europe was still under Absolutism when these centers began expanding and establishing the institutions of the modern market economy.[6]

What the European experience also clearly shows is that it took two to three centuries for the institutions of democratic forms of governance to evolve and be firmly established and take root. Even then, serious setbacks have periodically occurred; Nazism in Germany, Fascism in Italy, and Communism in Eastern Europe being prime examples in this century.

The European experience also shows that the notion of democracy has progressively expanded over the centuries to encompass an increasing number of rights. Segments of the population who were to be considered entitled to such rights has also been enlarged, often following bitter social and political conflicts. The right of suffrage was, for example, initially limited to a handful of property owners, but was gradually extended to all adult males, and finally to women. Similarly, the right of political association was for a long time circumscribed to a few acceptable political parties.

For countries that are in the throes of the transition to democracy and the formation of market economies, a number of useful lessons, regarding the linkages between democracy and the market economy, can be gleaned from the European experience. The first is that the market economy, in its evolution over the last few centuries, has coexisted with various forms of political systems, both democratic and nondemocratic. But, the second, and perhaps the more important, is that with the firm establishment of market economies, political systems in Europe have, over time, converged to democratic forms of governance. Thus, although political systems in individual European countries necessarily bear their own individual historical imprints, the similarities in fundamental traits of democratic governance outweigh the individual peculiarities. A first conclusion that we could draw would thus be that while democracy may not be a necessary condition for the existence of the market economy, democratic forms of governance do in fact thrive and take root in societies where market economies exist.

A review of the historical experience of developing countries would also appear to confirm these observations. Market economies in the developing world have coexisted with various forms of governance, ranging from authoritarian and repressive political systems to fairly open democratic political orders. The most successful market economies of the developing world, those in East Asia, did develop and thrive under authoritarian political systems, although, of late, movements towards democratic forms of rule have taken hold in some of these countries. And in Latin America, the celebrated "economic miracle" of Brazil in the 1970s, and the major restructuring of the Chilean economy along free-market principles, took place under military rule.

It is, however, interesting to note that it is virtually impossible to find in either past or contemporary experience, cases of democratic systems of governance coexisting with economic systems other than those of the market economy. In Europe, as noted earlier, there are no historic examples of democratic systems being established before the emergence of the market economy (with the possible exception of classical antiquity). And in the developing world, although the nature of individual market economies may differ, there have hardly been any cases of established democracies coexisting with economic systems other than those of market economies. The riddle of market economies coexisting with different political systems, but democracy coexisting, by and large, with only market economies can be explained when we consider, first, what political and legal conditions need to exist to enable the market economy to function, and, second, what economic conditions need to be fulfilled for democratic rule to be firmly established.

The minimum political and legal conditions necessary for a market economy to function adequately are a system of property rights that is transparent and nondiscriminatory; an efficient legal system for the enforcement of contracts and legal undertakings; a framework that allows competition, entry, and exit; and equality before the law for all *economic* agents.

Now it is clear that these political an legal conditions for the workings of the market economy do not necessarily imply the existence of a democratic system of governance. Authoritarian and nondemocratic governments can also provide them. Among developing countries, a number of nondemocratic governments have met the political and legal conditions necessary for the efficient functioning of market economies. They have even gone further in implementing specific "social projects" to strengthen both the market economy and individual economic agents. The various interventions of the East Asian states, which some authors have called a policy of "governing the market," are prime examples of such actions.[7]

Democratic systems of rule could, of course, enhance the transparency of laws and regulations, and also ensure a level playing field for all economic agents. They could also ensure that the outcomes of market systems do not unduly benefit some group at the expense of others, and that economic outcomes are socially desirable. A strong case can also be made that a social consensus, which only democratic forms of governance can make possible, is a prerequisite for stability and sustained development.[8] Nonetheless, the historical record clearly shows the market economy can function in a nondemocratic political setting, but within a frame work which meets certain specific conditions.

By contrast, a case can be made that democratic systems of governance require economic systems that broadly correspond to the institutions of the market economy. More specifically, it can be argued that for democratic systems to function, economic systems will need to exhibit the following characteristics. In the first instance, the system must result in a fairly wide dispersal of economic power, such that no group, including state functionaries, wields inordinate economic power. This would require, in turn, that individuals and groups have the right to hold private property, and that a clear and transparent system of property rights exist. Second, the system must allow free entry and exit, and a nondiscriminatory system of economic competition.[9]

These conditions are necessary if the accumulation of inordinate or excessive economic power, be it by state bureaucrats or by an oligarchy, is not to threaten or subvert popular sovereignty, as well as individual freedoms and liberty. If the levers of economic power are controlled by such small groups, the notion of popular sovereignty can, in practice, become devoid of real content. For under these conditions, economic power can easily be translated into political power, and instead of political decision making reflecting directly or indirectly the will and aspirations of the people, it can be subjected to the whims and mercy of powerful economic elites. The inordinate concentration of economic power can also undermine individual freedom and liberty, so essential for the functioning of democratic forms of governance. In the absence of countervailing powers, accumulated economic resources can be used to curb freedom of speech, assembly, and political organization of those groups and individuals that economic elites oppose.

The painful historical experiences of a large number of developing countries in which economic elites have successfully frustrated moves towards democratic forms of governance attest to the validity of these concerns. The history of developing countries in the postwar period is replete with instances of powerful oligarchies undermining existing democracies or, alternatively, blocking the transition to democracy. And in still others,the control of national economic resources by bureaucratic elites or military regimes has enabled such groups to establish authoritarian systems of rule, enabling them to frustrate popular demands for the establishment of democratic forms of governance.[10]

An essential attribute of the market economy and one that allows for democratic forms of governance to thrive is thus the dispersal of economic power. This is mainly effected through competition. Free and fair competition is essential if a society's wealth is to be augmented constantly, and if the set of claimants to economic power are to change and expand, and if claims are to continuously validated by the objective criteria of the market. As democracy in itself implies the dispersal of political power among a citizenry, and conversely, the absence of the concentration of power in an either an autocrat or an oligarchy, it would appear that such a dispersal of political power must find its echo in the dispersal of economic power, if popular sovereignty is to become a reality.

Prospects for Democracy and the Establishment of Market Economies in Africa

Now turning to Africa, the principle questions that need to be addressed concerning the prospects of the transition to democracy on the continent, the outlook for the establishment of market economies, and the linkages between the two, are the following. In the light of other historical experiences, will the establishment of market economies in Africa support the movement towards democracy? And conversely, will the establishment of democratic forms of governance promote the establishment of market economies? And, finally, what role should the international community play in support of the political and economic reforms taking place on the African continent?

During the last decade, Africa has been undergoing profound political and economic changes, which some have called a "silent revolution."[11] In the face of the severe economic difficulties of the last decade, many countries have initiated radical economic reforms to address the challenges facing them. This has, in the main, involved the jettisoning of old economic structures that relied on state control and direction, in favor of the establishment of market economies. Often such reforms have been undertaken with the cooperation and assistance of multilateral financial institutions, such as the World Bank and the African Development Bank.[12] It is interesting to note that over the last decade, some two hundred and fifty individual reform and adjustment programs have been financed by the multilateral financial institutions.[13]

In their attempt to establish market economies, African countries have undertaken a number of radical measures. Many countries have attempted to reduce the role of the state in the economy, and to limit the economic activities of the state to those essential activities that only states can perform. This has entailed the privatization of many state-owned enterprises, and the restriction of the economic role of the state. The proper role of the state is viewed increasingly as maintain a stable macroeconomic system and providing essential physical and social infrastructure, and efficient legislative and judiciary systems.

Governments have also sought to give adequate financial and legal support to the private sector. Increasingly, the private sector is viewed in many countries as a vital agent of rapid economic growth, and an indispensable partner in economic development. Accordingly, the private sector is being encouraged to assume a much more prominent role, primarily through the creation of a enabling environment for entrepreneurship, and privatization of public enterprises.[14]

The results of the economic reforms that countries have undertaken is, to date, rather mixed. In a number of countries, there are encouraging signs of economic recovery and growth; and a vigorous private sector, encouraged by the change in economic policies, is emerging. In other countries, it has become clear that development of a dynamic private sector—one capable of discharging its anticipated role—will require some time. As a consequence, the transition from state-directed economic systems to full-blown market economies is expected to take a much longer time. In general, it is increasingly becoming clear that the transformation of African economies is not a short-term undertaking, as had originally been envisaged, but one that will require sustained effort over a much longer period of time. Thus, the early optimism of a quick transformation has given way to a more realistic appreciation of the complex task at hand.[15]

In reviewing the experience with economic restructuring efforts, it has also become quite clear that the short-term social costs of adjustment are quite high. As governments seek to achieve external and internal balances through adjustments of the exchange rate, elimination of subsidies, price decontrols, and divestiture of state enterprises, a number of adverse social consequences have been observed. These include increased unemployment, due to the retrenchment of the public sector, the attenuation of social safety nets, and considerable hardships for some of the poorer segments of the society that had hitherto depended on state expenditures and price controls for their livelihoods.[16] And as the restructuring of African economies is now understood to be a medium to long-term undertaking, governments, with the assistance of multilateral institutions, have sought to implement poverty alleviation schemes. These seek to directly mitigate some of the adverse consequences that have befallen poor and vulnerable groups due to structural adjustment policies.[17]

Many of the reform efforts in Africa aimed at restructuring economies have been attempted during a decade marked by a unfavorable external economic environment. Over this period, the prices of the primary commodities that most African countries export have been depressed, with the prices of some reaching all-time lows.[18] In addition, the debt overhang of some $264.3 billion, equivalent in 1991 to 93.2 percent of GNP, has resulted in approximately one third of export receipts being used to service the debt burden. Further, external resource flows to African countries, both private and public, have declined in per capita terms, thus reducing the resources available for investment and economic recovery and growth.

Within such an adverse external economic environment, a key determinant of success in transforming economies and establishing market economies is the extent and scope of the external support that countries receive. Those that have succeeded in mobilizing considerable external resources in support of their reform efforts have managed to bring about major structural transformations. By contrast, reform efforts have flagged in those countries, which have faced difficulties in obtaining the requisite external support.[19]

The silent revolution in Africa has not been limited to restructuring economic relations, but has also involved the transformation of political systems, Partly as a response to the manifest of past authoritarian and statist political systems, and partly in solidarity with the worldwide movement towards democracy, the peoples of Africa have, over the last decade, sought to bring about democratic forms of governance.[20] They have, in a number of countries, succeeded in establishing pluralistic democratic systems, and have managed to carry out open and fair elections. In others, transitions to democratic forms of rule are well underway. And in still a large number of countries, fundamental democratic rights, such as free speech and the right of peaceful assembly, are progressively being respected.

Despite the gains made, the general progress made with respect to political reform efforts is also mixed. In some countries, firm national consensuses seem to have been reached and the nascent institutions of pluralist democratic systems are being to take root. In others, on the other hand, protracted national debates have now been going on for some time over the appropriate routes to democratic rule. While the progress a number of countries have made in the direction of democratic forms of governance is encouraging, the experience so far also indicates the possible pitfalls that may stand in the way of such transitions.

A fundamental problem that countries face in their efforts to establish democratic forms of governance is the issue of the appropriate institutional forms that democracy should take. It is generally agreed that the emerging democratic institutions should reflect the values and customs of individual nations, while at the same time respecting fundamental democratic precepts. The issue of reconciling the two, which may at times be at variance, is one of the most important challenges that the democratic movement in Africa faces.

Another critical problem is the problem of the reconciliation of seemingly contradictory basic democratic rights. As most countries in Africa are constituted by a mosaic of ethic groups, the question of how to reconcile ethnic and citizen's rights has naturally come to the fore. If the right of ethnic groups to self-determination, including secession, is viewed as a fundamental democratic right, then the threat this poses to the very existence of states in Africa is obvious. In a number of African countries, this issue has assumed added urgency as the transition to democracy has set loose powerful ethnic-based movements which argue for the primacy of ethnic rights over citizen or national rights.[21] It is interesting to note how countries have adopted very different approaches to the question of ethnicity. Nigeria, has, for example, sought to tackle the issue by allowing only two national parties that cut across ethnic and religious lines. Ethiopia, on the other hand has given primacy to the ethnic issue in the emerging state structures, arguing that ethnicity must become the basic building block for the nation.»

Now in considering the linkages between the transition to democracy and the emergence of market economies, a complex set of problems emerges. While each structural transformation by itself poses a unique set of formidable challenges and problems, each is, in turn, affected by the successes and failures of the other. In other words, economic reform efforts can be expected to be affected by the political changes that are now in progress; and, conversely, the prospects for the transition to democracy will in turn be affected by the outcomes of the economic reform efforts. What then are the most important linkages, or mutually dependent relations, that will affect the overall outcome?

There would seem to be little doubt that the establishment of market economies is, in the long run, an essential prerequisite for the institution of democratic forms of governance in Africa. This is what the historical and contemporary experiences of a number of countries make clear. Yet, the short-term social costs of the restructuring of economies, brought about, in part, by the very attempt to establish the institutions of market economies, can possibly undermine the transition to democracy. In other words, as the internal and external conditions under which economic changes in Africa are being tried are far from favorable, there exists a real danger that the concurrent attempts at political transformation may flounder.

Democratic governments are assuming power in many African countries in which major structural adjustment programs have been in operation for several years. The new governments have little recourse but to pursue these programs, if they are to set their economies on the path to economic recovery and growth, and if they are to continue to access external resources. Yet, the social costs associated with structural adjustment programs could prove fertile ground for populist and democratic movements. Such forces, supported by disaffected elites, could use the economic reform programs as a pretext for undermining or overturning the democratic process.[22] Thus, unless countries can mitigate the adverse social consequences of adjustment programs, and also gain access to sufficient resources to help them toward economic recovery and growth, the whole transition to democratic forms of governance could be jeopardized.

Democratic governments which assume power under conditions of structural adjustment may also face enormous pressures from their own constituencies to suspend the economic reform programs, and take more statist and interventionist measures.[23] Democratic governments could thus be forced to take measures that in effect arrest the transition to market economies. While this may yield some political benefits in the short-run, its long-term consequences both for economic recovery and for the very institutions of democracy would undoubtedly be harmful.

The success of the "twin transformations" that many African countries have launched is thus far from assured. Democracy can be thwarted by a reversal to statist forms of economic organization, and the formation of market economies can, in turn, be abandoned if the costs of the transition are deemed too high. Exacerbating the internal difficulties that Africa faces is the adverse external economic environment. This has led to a considerable loss in export earnings, and to declines in the international resource flows to Africa. The resources that governments can allocate in support of structural transformations is thus severely limited, further jeopardizing the success of the reform efforts.

Conclusion

It is in the light of the complex problems that African countries face in the transition to democracy and the formation of market economies that the positive role that the international community can play becomes all too apparent. Clearly, the international community should take a number of measures to help ensure that the transition to democracy is not frustrated by short-term economic difficulties. It should also assist countries in their efforts to restructure their economies, such that the economic transition is not derailed by popular pressures, which have these same economic difficulties as their root cause.

With respect to Africa the international community should, at the minimum, take the following measures to support the transition to democracy and the formation of market economies:

1. An international agreement to write down substantially the African debt, so as to provide additional resources for investment and for economic recovery and growth.[24]
2. A commitment by the donor community to increase substantially the resource flows to African countries in support of political and economic reform programs.
3. A special international program to support the fledgling institutions of the democratic state in those countries that have made the transition to democracy, as well as those that are in the process of such a transition.

These measures are essential if African countries are to succeed in their bold efforts to establish democratic forms of governance and dynamic economies. They are also in accord with the UN's "New Agenda for the Development of Africa in the 1990s." While the African continent is indeed in the throes of a profound political and economic change, it is too early to state with any confidence, that success will be achieved on both counts. The attempts to transform political and economic systems could flounder if the costs of transition appear to be too high. It is, however, well within the capacity of the international community—and also in its long-term interest—to assist Africa in overcoming its short-term transition problems, and achieve the two goals of establishing democracy and forming market economies.

Notes

1. See World Bank, *World Development Report 1991* (Oxford: Oxford University Press, 1991) for a discussion of the "market friendly" approach to development.

2. See Milton Friedman, *Capitalism and Freedom* (Chicago: University of Chicago Press, 1981), for a classic statement of the first postulate. Also, UNDP, *Human Development Report* (Oxford: Oxford University Press, 1991), 18-21, for a discussion of the relationship between human development and human freedom.

3. S. Bowles and H. Gintis, *Democracy and Capitalism* (New York: Basic Books, 1986).

4. See the discussion in "Conference on Democratization Processes in Africa: Problems and Prospects," *CODESRIA Bulletin*, nos. 1 and 2 (1992), for an interesting debate among African scholars of the issues.

5. See Mark Blaug, *Economic Theory in Retrospect* (Cambridge: Cambridge University Press, 1985), for a historical review of the concept of the market economy.

6. See Perry Anderson, *Lineages of the Absolutist State* (London: New Left Books, 1974) for a discussion of the rise of the market economy in the era of Absolutism.

7. Robert Wade, *Governing the Market: Economic Theory and the Role of Government in East Asian Industrialization* (Princeton: Princeton University Press, 1990).

8. The importance of democratic institutions for sustained development is made in Babacar Ndiaye, "Developpment economique et democratie en Afrique," *African Development Review* 2, no. 2 (December 1990): 49-57. See also the South Commission, *The Challenge to the South* (Oxford: Oxford University Press, 1990): 116-18, for a discussion of the issues.

9. See Barrington Moore, Jr., *Social Origins of Dictatorship and Democracy* (Boston: Beacon Press, 1966), for a classic discussion of the economic conditions that made way for the emergence of democratic institutions in Europe.

10. The difficulties that a number of countries in Africa, Asia, and Latin America have faced over the last few years in moving towards democratic forms of governance, because of the opposition of entrenched elites (both civilian and military), attests to the nature of the problem.

11. Fantu Cheru, *The Silent Revolution in Africa; Debt, Development, and Democracy* (Harare: Anvil Books, 1989).

12. See African Development Bank, *Annual Report, 1991* (Abidjan: African Development Bank, 1992), 40-41, for a summary account of the Bank's activities in support of policy reforms in Africa.

13. Giovanni A. Cornia, "Is Adjustment Conducive to Long-Term Development: the Case of Africa," *Innocenti Occasional Papers, Economic Policy Series, No. 21* (Florence: UNICEF International Child Development Centre, 1991).

14. See African Development Bank, *African Development Report, 1992*, 62-81, for a detailed discussion of the types of policy reforms undertaken by African countries.

15. See, for example, World Bank, *Sub-Saharan Africa: From Crisis to Sustainable Growth* (Oxford: Oxford University Press, 1979), for the change in perspectives from those held in the early and middle 1980s.

16. See G.A. Cornia, R. Jolly, and F. Stewart, eds., *Adjustment with a Human Face* (Oxford: Clarendon Press, 1987), for an early analysis of the impact of structural adjustments on the poor, and in particular on children and women.

17. See World Bank, UNDP, African Development Bank, *The Social Dimensions of Adjustment in Africa: A Policy Agenda*, Washington, 1990.

18. African Development Bank, *African Development Report 1992*, 38-41.

19. See African Development Bank, *African Development Report 1992*, 92-95.

20. Hans H. Bass, "Democracy and Popular Participation as Productive Factors or Constituent Elements of a New Development Vision," in *African Development Perspectives Yearbook, 1990/91* ed. Research Group on African Development Perspectives (Bremen: 1992).

21. It is interesting to note how countries have adopted very different approaches to the question of ethnicity. Nigeria, has, for example, sought to tackle the issue by allow-

ing only two national parties that cut across ethnic and religious lines. Ethiopia, on the other hand has given primacy to the ethnic issue in the emerging state structures, arguing that ethnicity must become the basic building block for the nation.

22. The reversal of the democratic transition in Haiti should serve as a lesson that the transition to democracy in Africa may be far from smooth.

23. The strong opposition to structural adjustment programs uttered by many an opposition leader should make it clear that this is not an idle presupposition.

24. The measures that should be taken to resolve effectively the African debt problem are elaborated in the "Abidjan Declaration of Debt Relief, Recovery and Democracy in Africa." *African Development Review* 3, no. 2 (December 1991): 1-9.

Part 2 · Economic Development

Overview

Üner Kırdar, I.G. Patel, and Leonard Silk

There was a strident mood at the beginning of the 1980s in the industrialized countries; many political leaders thought they had discovered a new formula for rapid economic progress—"the magic of the market," in the phrase of former President Ronald Reagan. Not only in the United States but in many other countries there was much talk about radically changing policies to reduce, if not eliminate, the economic role of government.

But by the beginning of the 1990s, the mood in the developed countries had grown more sober. There was a widespread realization that the problems had been oversimplified. This mood spread to the international organizations, including the World Bank and International Monetary Fund, as evidence accumulated that the high expectations of the 1980s have not been fulfilled. Rates of economic growth all over the world have been slow or negative, unemployment has been high, and, with excess capacity in many industries, protectionist pressures have been rising. After seven years of trade negotiations, the Uruguay Round under the General Agreement on Tariffs and Trade (GATT) has not been brought to a satisfactory conclusion. And recovery from the world slump remains fragile and uncertain, with policy hampered by large public debts, unbalanced trade and payments, unstable currencies, and fiscal and monetary policies dogged by anxieties of a resurgence of inflation. Economic troubles exacerbate other concerns. People want growth "with a human face," and they want social harmony. With productivity stagnating, living standards have fallen for working people and resentments toward the well-to-do and immigrants have grown. There are no simple, let alone magic, solutions for this wide range of complicated economic and social problems.

The Developing Countries

It has become conventional to lump the developing countries together. Originally, the term developing was a euphemism for undeveloped or less developed countries, and those terms were euphemisms for backward or poor. But the developing countries are not a homogeneous group. They are so many in number, so different in size and in social and cultural characteristics, and so far apart in levels of industrialization and living standards that many of the developing countries can no longer be thought of as "poor" or "backward." At the top of this group are countries like South Korea, Argentina, and Mexico, which aspire in the short term to become members of the Organization for Economic Cooperation and Development—the association of the world's richest nations. At the bottom of this group are Mozambique, Somalia, and other sub-Saharan countries, living in desperate poverty and suffering from widespread disease, malnutrition, and starvation. For many of those poor countries, one cannot simply prescribe foreign investment, because commercial capital will go there.

Technology Transfer and Dual Economies

Technological change is the fundamental basis of increasing economic growth and competitive power; for the developing countries, it is their one great hope. But in the short run, some of the poorest countries cannot get ahead by adopting new technologies because they lack human skills, resources to sustain existing populations, and capital. They are marginalized from the world economy and are rapidly falling behind. That is a danger from which they may seek to escape partially by applying modern technology, inviting foreign investment in some sectors, and forgetting about the rest. Unfortunately, that is what most of these countries are doing. In the process, they are creating dual economies, with a small area becoming rather prosperous, upcoming, and capable of exporting their products, but with the rest of the country left far behind.

Such an outcome usually creates its own tensions, within countries and toward the rest of the world. With the global spread of communications, poor people are aware of the lives people in other countries are leading, and become bitter and angry over their own lot. They cannot accept that a better life for them lies beyond the competence and strength of their countries. Foreign aid, even when it is made available in sizable amounts, which is rare in a capital-short world, is no *deus ex machina,* especially when governments, whether through incompetence or corruption, squander or steal that aid, so that it never reaches the people who need it most and does little or nothing to transform the stagnant economy. A cardinal question we are facing is how foreign aid and technical assistance can be made more effective.

Globalization and Regionalization

Though some countries have been left out, it is now generally accepted that globalization has created an economic and social interdependence among countries. Capital moves freely from place to place. However, the same freedom to move does not exist for labor, which is the greatest asset—or, when resources are lacking—the greatest burden of developing countries. Indeed, there are strict regulations and barriers to the movement of workers, although masses of "illegal aliens" get past them. If the goods they are capable of producing cannot move in world markets, the people themselves move. It seems that as soon as the developing countries learn to produce goods that are labor-intensive, such as shoes or textiles, restrictions are immediately put on those products. Even the Uruguay Round, if it were to succeed, does nothing to remove textile restrictions.

Regionalization, proposed by many policy makers as an alternative to a more open and closely integrated world economy, is really limited to North America,

Western Europe, and the Far East. Many regions are excluded, since there are no partners for most of the developing countries of the Middle East, Asia, and Africa. Pressures are growing for those countries to divide into blocs and trade increasingly among themselves. If looked upon as a hostile or aggressive strategy, regionalization could lead to disintegration of the world economy—and for those countries left out, lower living standards and economic growth.

Yet the trend toward regionalism, if accompanied by liberal and stimulative trade and investment policies, could actually further world economic development. Two critical conditions must be satisfied for regionalism to achieve a positive effect on world growth: First, that a dropping of internal barriers and a spur to investment, from both countries within as well as outside the region lead to more rapid growth in output, exports, and imports; and second, that the region be open to trade with other regions and countries. A lowering of trade and investment barriers within a region should pave the way to lower barriers with those outside.

The Role of Governments and Markets

During the process of transition from Communism, as well as in a capitalistic free-market system, the role of governments remains essential in certain areas. They are required to maintain economic stability, redistribute income to help the poor, correct market imperfections, and provide public goods, such as roads, highways, education, public health, clean air, and water. That gives a very large role to government. And yet, we must ask ourselves why we are disappointed in the role played by the public sector. Perhaps some of our assumptions about the nature of government are no longer valid. Governments, curiously, do not know all that much. They are supposed to spread information, but their information is often limited. They are not all that objective either, and do not always represent social interests, but can be vulnerable to vested interests on those of officeholders and bureaucrats. Even then their authority does not reach far. People manage to bypass governments, and government policy is often ineffective.

The same is true of markets. When our opinion of government deteriorates, we turn to the market for hope. But markets can be, and often are, manipulated by vested interests. When countries espouse privatization, the rich and vested interests that control the political machinery may be the only ones who benefit. The notion that markets cannot be cornered or compromised, as governments are, is romantic. A way must be found for governments to restrain the markets and markets to restrain the governments, and we believe it is possible. How this should be achieved is a matter for research and experiment, but what is at issue is not one or the other, but how to check one and balance the other.

Only the blindest ideology makes government either the only solution or the only enemy. Governments are not alike; some are basically honest and competent, others dishonest and incompetent. We must be clear when speaking about capabilities of governments. We should not forget that there are also civic organizations, universities, and churches which have a role to play, to augment or replace the role of government in serving the public good.

The question of how to make markets more competitive has no simple answer. Clearly, larger—usually globalized—markets are more competitive. The main reason for advocating the opening of borders and trading systems, even in the developing countries, is because that is the only way competition will really flow through the entire economy, improving the quality of goods and services, increasing their quantity, and reducing their costs and prices.

Policy-Based Conditionality

It is now well recognized that borrowing countries cannot have access to international lending unless they accept the rules of conditionality—the imposition of terms for economic policies or reforms as a requirement for the granting of loans. Conditionality serves to induce change in unwise policies of developing countries. It is always easy for governments to avoid taking action, but when money is needed, there is no easy way out. The World Bank and IMF possess a broad knowledge of economic development, which may not be the latest, or the best, or always be right, but is often better than what individual developing countries have. Therefore, dialogue between the lending institutions and the borrowers is useful, although the process could be improved by changing the style and the language. Instead of conditionality being imposed by one party on the other, a relationship could be shaped by a statement of common purpose, mutually agreed and based on trust. It should be a continuing relationship rather than an episodic affair, kept alive by periodic injections of money.

While the situation is now calm, there is danger that the question of conditionality will again cause a volatile reaction in both developing countries and countries in transition. There is a pressing need for social safety nets to protect the most vulnerable groups of society from the impact of adjustment policies and transition reforms. Severe tensions result when international institutions take money away from the poor countries; this is a trend that may worsen, given the attitude of the rich countries towards providing development assistance. This could make developing countries even more inflexible on economic policy. When you do not get any money, you are less likely to be receptive to the advice you receive.

The richer countries are now extending their areas of conditionality to cover governmental corruption, human rights, and the environment. It is no longer just a question of how much money is supplied and what is to be done to restrain inflation or safeguard the exchange rate. When there are internal pressures in developed countries to enlarge the area of conditionality but their power is reduced, the likelihood of strife between rich and poor increases, and it would be unrealistic to ignore it.

If a better functioning of the world economy is our common objective, the application of sound economic practices through policy-based conditionality by developing countries alone is not sufficient. Rules and responsibilities must also apply to the advanced economies of the industrialized world, including both those experiencing surpluses as well as those with deficits. These developed countries have, after all, a greater say in shaping the world economy. Recent turbulence in the world currency market is further proof of this necessity. The present policy confusions of developed countries are not a good example for the preindustrialized countries.

Exploring the Future

The future of the world economy cannot be accurately forecasted. Different scenarios need to be drawn and the most realistic and constructive adopted. This rarely happens, however, as most world leaders today seem to focus on the short term and lack long-term perspectives.

For instance, in Germany, riots and neo-Nazi terrorist acts take place under the pretext of anti-immigration activity. Similar breaks of nationalistic opposition to immigration is evident in many other countries. It is fair to assume that in the next century, immigration will take place, whether or not it is officially permitted. To contain or reverse the outflow of people from poor to rich countries, economic growth must take place at a greater rate in developing countries. There is no other way to prevent massive movements of people to the developed countries. But where can we find statesmen willing to raise such an issue nowadays?

In the future, more support must be given by richer countries to encourage technical change in the developing countries. This will require greater responsiveness to the needs of Eastern Europe, the former Soviet Union, and the developing countries. Among the developed countries, there will have to be better coordination of their policies. Given the global scope of the capital markets, what one country does affects other countries, developed and developing, capitalist, Communist, or in the transition between economic systems.

In looking ahead, we must ask whether the United Nations, or any other organization, can do the job of reconciling human efforts to achieve common goals. Human nature cannot easily be changed; it often seems naturally selfish and uncooperative. Yet we are also social creatures; we cannot survive without working together. Can something be done by institutional devices to provide a better basis for global governance and human progress than has been true so far? Could the present time of momentous change set the stage for strengthening international cooperation for the benefit of all? The papers that follow explore different aspects of these vital issues.

Chapter 1 · Markets and Governments

Section 1 · Change for the Better[1]

G. Arthur Brown

Change in the global order has proceeded at an increasingly rapid pace with profound effects on virtually every aspect of lives of people in the industrialized countries, developing countries, and the former socialist countries. These changes have been even more dramatic in the last five years.

In the political order, the Cold War has come to an end. A world order that was previously based on two superpowers striving for the allegiance and support of the developed and developing countries has now given place to one military superpower. Economic power has now been more evenly spread among a number of highly industrialized countries. Instead of world peace, however, we have substituted regional conflicts and civil wars that are very destructive for the participants.

The last two decades have seen an increasing movement towards regional economic groupings, with the European Community (EC) the most outstanding example. Democracy as a form of political organization, recognition of human rights, and the enlargement of individual freedoms have largely superseded the dictatorships and repressive regimes that were so widespread just over 10 years ago. In these areas, then, great satisfaction must be expressed at the accomplishments of peoples all over the world.

Economic Progress

In the economic field, however, this progress has not been replicated. The world is still being subject to periods of growth followed by periods of recession and indeed, the most important factor now affecting growth and development in developing countries has been the worldwide recession in the industrialized countries since 1990.

There have been great differences in the progress made in various regions. After a period of reasonable growth in the 1960s and 1970s, in the 1980s, the developing countries, particularly in sub-Saharan Africa and in Latin America and the Caribbean, retrogressed. Indeed, in the majority of countries in these regions, the standard of living has suffered a setback, as have the social sectors of health, education, nutrition, and infant mortality.

At the same time, growth in Asia, particularly in the developing countries of East Asia, has continued unabated from the 1960s, reaching an average of more than six percent in the 1980s. We must now determine the reasons behind this tremendous disparity in economic performance in these different regions.

Evolution of New Theories of Economic Development

From World War II to the end of the 1960s, conventional wisdom held that economic development required active government involvement in the productive sectors, the establishment of government-owned enterprises, subsidies to the private sector, and heavy protection of industries engaged in import substitution. Although these policies did result in economic growth up to the mid-1970s, the period since then has been one of stagnating growth, production failures, and very little improvement in standards of living. Information from the countries of Eastern Europe show that their highly centralized planning resulted in the same dismal record experienced by the developing countries that were relying on state-owned productive entities.

Several factors are responsible for the change in performance in the majority of developing countries from the mid-1970s. The two oil shocks of 1973 and 1979 did irreparable damage to developing countries other than those in East Asia. Not only was the price of the most important ingredient in economic development—namely energy—doubled and quadrupled, but it was the underlying factor behind the excessive borrowings to which developing countries resorted to maintain their import capacity. These borrowings, in turn, led to the serious debt problems. In the case of Jamaica, the servicing of this debt absorbs between 35 and 40 cents of each dollar of foreign exchange and similar percentages of the government's budget.

The reaction of the developed countries to these shocks further aggravated the problems of the developing countries, because the industrialized countries used tariff and nontariff barriers and deflationary policies to counteract the rise in oil prices. This, in turn, resulted in an unprecedented fall in commodity prices, in some cases to levels that had existed 20 to 30 years before.

This adverse external environment coincided with increase of serious domestic economic problems in the developing countries. Prominent in this was the failure of state-owned enterprises to operate efficiently, thereby requiring subsidies from the budget. At the same time, these enterprises were unable to supply the quality goods their countries required at an acceptable price. Governments reacted by incurring budget deficits to meet the subsidies and to maintain the government establishment.

At the same time, government sought to regulate domestic markets, maintain an overvalued exchange rate, maintain nominal interest rates below inflation rates, and generally to distort prices to the extent that resources ceased to be efficiently allocated. These results have led to radical shifts in thinking about development strategies. Empirical surveys have shown that countries that pursued open markets, an undistorted price system, and a generally liberalized regime experienced greater increases in output growth and standards of living than those countries that pursued opposite policies. The empirical results have in turn led to new thinking among economists, and the emerging consensus, simply put, is that governments should do less in those areas where markets work efficiently, but more in those areas where markets alone cannot be relied upon.

The Choice of Role Is Complex

This simple statement, however, contains the seeds of the complex problem. Where shall the lines be drawn between state activity and private activity? The simplistic view that the new paradigm requires a state that is totally "hands off" and that performs the barest of minimal functions is clearly not the answer.

Studies of the East Asian model have shown, for example, that governments in those countries have indeed actively intervened in various aspects of economic development and these interventions have been responsible to a large extent for the successful performance of these economies. Some economists have referred to this type of intervention as "market friendly," and the principles underlying this type of intervention should be reviewed to see whether they can contribute to a proper role of the state.

Another conclusion from empirical studies is that countries that have been able to take advantage of technological change have greatly improved their standards of living but, in turn, technological change can only be harnessed by a population that has been exposed to training and education. Technological change and a skilled workforce, in turn, increase productivity. Investment in physical capital produces inferior results if the technological advances are not embraced and the human infrastructure is poor. This is an important change in thinking from the 1960s and 1970s, when it was felt that massive capital injections to build factories, bridges, and electricity and generating plants were necessary for development.

The New Power of International Financial Institutions

An additional phenomenon in the new global order for developing countries is the rise in influence and power of the multilateral financial institutions, particularly the World Bank, the International Monetary Fund, and the regional Development Banks. These financial support of these institutions is conditional on the adoption of new economic models. Policy conditionalities have now become standard not only in general balance of payments loans, but also in project loans. Several bilateral aid organizations have adopted the same operating principles.

A redefined role for governments in this new environment will, therefore, be very much influenced by the need to organize and implement economic policies on the basis of these conditionalities. Indeed, for countries that are dependent on external assistance, these conditionalities could very well be the most dominant factors in the decisions concerning what governments should or should not do and how policy should be implemented.

Other Elements of Change

Other important elements of change in the global arena need to be taken into account by governments in formulating policies. Chief among these is the globalization of financial markets, which now has literally removed national boundaries to financial transfers. Unlike the past, when financial flows between countries largely reflected trade and investment flows, financial movements now exceed trade flows many times. These financial flows are influenced by interest rate differentials, exchange rate movements, and opportunities for arbitrage. In fact, they now have an existence quite independent of underlying economic factors. Developing countries lack the capacity for meeting the requirements of these markets. If they continue to put financial fences around themselves, they will cut themselves further off from the world economy. Clearly, this is an area in which market forces must be allowed to work.

With the continuing recession and with many countries turning inwards to concentrate largely on their new regional groupings, savings available in supporting assistance to the developing world have decreased. At the same time, the calls on these savings by the new democracies of Eastern Europe and to meet the cost of the reunification of Germany will further limit the amounts available for the developing world. In addition, there has developed the phenomenon of aid fatigue, which has resulted from countless reports about the misuse of aid and the inability to accurately show that aid has made a difference to those countries that have been its beneficiaries.

Finally, the adoption of a new economic program based on the supremacy of the market, with the private sector as the dominant engine of growth, requires a transition from one economic model to the other. Even though the new model will bring greater opportunities for improved standards of living, the transitional period is fraught with danger. Experience has shown that battles for economic reform have been lost in many cases before the planned goals and objectives have been met.

Since the justification for changing the model is that the present model has been inefficient, has been dependent on subsidies, has distorted prices, and has benefited preferred groups, any change will alter the status quo and result in hardships to many groups, particularly to those that are disadvantaged and unable to protect themselves.

How far can a government go in requiring sacrifices from its people for future benefit before the affected groups revolt and demand a halt to change? Evidence shows that in countries where governments have lost heart and have aborted reform policies, the last state has invariably been acutely worse than the state that existed during the transition. People who feel they can take no more will act against change, notwithstanding this evidence.

The only answer one can suggest is that no transformation can successfully occur without the explaining the policies to the people and securing their cooperation and support. The transformation will not succeed if previously privileged groups go all out to defend their position, if leaders continue to play on tribal loyalties, if there is deliberate spreading of false reports, and if there is general undermining of confidence.

In these situations, therefore, governments must bend backwards to be totally transparent in their actions and to encourage opinion leaders to provide constructive, even if critical, support. The information about "aid fatigue" shows that a transformation first has to occur at the national level. Developing countries cannot be saved by outside assistance. If the people realize that future progress rests in their own hands, then they may be galvanized into working to achieve the objective of a better quality of life for all in the society.

Other Factors Influencing the Role of Government

Any consideration of the role of government must take account of the global, national, political, economic, and social setting within which the government is expected to function. National considerations are fairly well understood. There is considerable disquiet about the failure of the economy to return to a path of robust and sustained growth; about the negative economic and social impact of current stabilization and adjustment programs; and about the intractability of social problems such as unemployment, crime, and drug abuse. All of them raise the call for improving the quality and performance of government.

The call is also accentuated by the profound political, economic, and social changes that have been occurring in many parts of the globe. The breathtaking pace at which these changes have occurred means that countries have not only to marshal their capabilities to respond and adjust speedily to these changes, but also to sharpen their preparedness to deal with developments yet to come.

Some Perceptions about the Functioning of Government

Recently, in both written and oral submissions, considerable concerns have been expressed about the poor quality of performances by governments. These largely centered around the overconcentration of decision making, which consigned the rest of the community to a largely peripheral role in the management of affairs; the low quality of the civil service; the overbureaucraticization of methods of work, which lead to a compliance rather than a service orientation. In general, the impression is conveyed of an overmanned, slow, lumbering, bureaucracy characterized by low morale, partly because of unsatisfactory salaries and other conditions of service, inadequate training, and a certain amount of political interference in the exercise of its functions.

These may well be exaggerated statements of the situation. It is also apparent that some parts of the private sector traditionally complain about problems of low productivity and inertia among government staffs. Nevertheless, there are many proponents of the view that the government should be downsized and its role minimized, largely because of inefficiency and insignificant responsiveness to the needs of the public, especially those of the business community. This is essentially a negative approach to the problem. Because of the national and global considerations outlined above, a more positive approach would be to restructure and reform the government in all of its component parts, to make it leaner, more cost effective, more facilitative, and supportive of the development process.

Government needs to be put in perspective. There is need to ensure that government and people regard themselves as different, but complementary, parts of the same whole; that government and its supporting bureaucracy are not seen as millstones around the necks of a powerless citizenry; that government is not encouraged to continue projecting itself as the sole provider and deliverer of a messianic dispensation that nurtures paroxysms of excess leading to the celebration of a savior one week and its crucifixion the next; that distrust, disintegrative tension, and cynicism do not continue to inform the relationship between the governors and the governed; and that the citizenry does not feel deliberately deprived of information critical to the understanding of economic change in the world at large and to the ability for the individual to cope with deep social forces operative in a society. The mass of the population has historically suffered economic disabilities and harbors to this day a particular sense of being deprived and wronged. This in turn leads to an endemic commitment to "beating the system" (presided over by government) or to making things not work.

Towards a Structure for Partnership and Participation

Historical factors, contemporary realities, and the wider issues of governance suggest a response in the way the government should function if it is to install not only a market economy designed to achieve economic growth, stability, and a capacity for ongoing development, but also attain a civil society based on the democratic principles of liberty, equality, social justice, the rule of law, and the empowerment of the citizenry.

"Privatization," "deregulation," and "liberalization" are indeed mere means to such ends rather than ends in themselves. To have them make sense against the background of the country's history, political culture, and current perceptions of the ends of government, they must serve the ends of "empowerment" of the mass of the population along with all others, whether by way of promoting worker share ownership, broadening the economic base of owners in the society, instituting land reform, or releasing the creative potential of a far larger number of private citizens. This last factor will enable the people to participate on a "level playing field" once dominated by the state (through state and parastatal monopoly enterprises) and a small elite group of corporate owners in the traditional private sector, despite the countervailing force of strong trade unions and other organizations advocating workers rights since 1938.

The aim is now the unleashing of entrepreneurial energy for the development of productive forces, with greater emphasis on facilitating private capital accumulation as a major instrument of economic production instead of having the state as such a prime player. The proven inadequacy of the latter's ability to deliver justifies the state's withdrawal from this sphere of economic development. But the proven tendency of a concentration of oligarchic economic power, when capital accumulation and production are left unregulated in the hands of private monopolies, advises caution and dictates the forging of appropriate, innovative, flexible, and responsive mechanisms to mitigate the excesses of greed and cynicism and to temper unbridled enthusiasms for rapid bottom-line success at any cost.

The New Role of Government

Apart from the traditional functions of law and order, defense, security, and foreign affairs, new nuances need to be envisaged with respect to the role of government in the economy. The establishment of market economies and the globalization of production do not, however, imply a shift to a system of laissez-faire. What it does imply is not necessarily less government, but different and better government.

First of all, facilitating, regulating, and monitoring—if pursued sensitively and creatively—become major functions of government in the market-driven economy of a country like Jamaica. An open economic system requires sensitivity to allay fears of bureaucratic clumsiness and oppression against citizens in their daily pursuit of practical affairs and creativity to enable the flexibile implementation of public policy that turns on the facilitative, regulatory, and monitoring functions of government. The system, however, cannot be so open that it runs amok in negating the very aspiration of empowerment because of the absence of agreed-on well-articulated regulative principles delineating the parameters of action.

Second, the government should conceive of itself as the hub of a network of social partners engaged in a process of continuing interaction for the purpose of policy formulation and implementation. Efforts should be made to reach a common understanding among political parties, the business community, trade unions, NGOs, and other bodies concerning the broad goals of economic and social development, the policy framework through which rules will be established for the management of the economy, and the respective roles of each partner in management. The government could function as strategic broker in trying to reconcile divergent interests among the partners and to facilitate their effective discharge of their respective responsibilities.

Third, the government has a catalytic (although not exclusive) role in strengthening the knowledge base of the country though improved systems of education and training and by stimulating research and development, including the development of information systems for use by the different actors in the economy. World production and trade are increasingly driven by new and emerging technologies in fields such as biotechnology, telecommunications, civil aviation, new materials sciences, and computer hardware and software. These are affecting the competitiveness of industries across all sectors of the economy and are opening up new avenues for international trade, especially in the field of services.

A large part of technological advances has been supported directly or indirectly by government funding. In both developed and newly industrializing countries, research and development are becoming significant claimants on public resources. It is evident that Jamaica has to follow this pattern, since there is a dire need to improve the technological sophistication of existing lines of production and to identify possibilities where such sophistication can be applied to new lines of production. Here again, the government and the private sector will have to work very closely together.

The science and technology policy adopted recently by the government sets out a number of research and development priorities. These include biotechnology, especially plant tissue culture, marine science, energy, environmental management, disaster control, remote sensing, and mathematical modeling. The execution of such a program will require trained people and money. The government should aim to collaborate with the private sector in development of the necessary human resources, in mobilizing the financing required, and in encouraging utilization and commercialization of the research results.

Fourth, the government has a distinct role in encouraging the growth of small business, the development and diffusion of entrepreneurial skills throughout the economy, and in supporting the participation of as many citizens as possible in the ownership of, and control over, assets. For example, in sectors such as agriculture and tourism, it should be particularly sensitive to the needs of the small operators for finance and technical assistance, where it should increasingly play the role of a broker and arranger rather than that of a direct provider.

Fifth, in the field of international trade, governments have to work continuously to improve access for their country's exports of both goods and services as international competition is intensifying across the globe. New regional groupings are emerging, which could place nonmembers of those groupings at a disadvantage.

Such catalytic work on the part of governments is not confined to the negotiation of intergovernmental trade agreements. Governments also need to work very closely with the private sector in ensuring the fullest possible flow of information on exports, technology transfer, investment, and financing opportunities. Differential information capacities is one area that separates developed from developing countries. The catalytic role that governments can play in promoting an adequate flow of economic and financial information is, therefore, of cardinal importance. However, it can be expected that as the economy becomes sophisticated, the private sector will increasingly take over more of the responsibility for that function. Nonetheless, it should be noted that even in the most advanced economies—Japan is a case in point—governments continue to act as strategic brokers in identifying international export opportunities and in supporting improvements in the overall international competitiveness of the country in trade, economic, and financial transactions.

Sixth, given the current situation in the country and its historical antecedents, the government must inevitably give direct attention to alleviating the situation of underprivileged groups. Economic development will not achieve its ultimate purpose of improving the human condition if deliberate measures are not taken to provide a social safety net for disadvantaged citizens in such areas as basic education, health, child nutrition, affordable housing, and social welfare services. Here, the government should increasingly focus on determining policy through the widest possible consultations and channeling resources in a dynamic partnership with the private sector and voluntary organizations.

Seventh, in thinking interface with the rest of the world, it has also to be borne in mind that a whole new range of social problems have emerged that require action by governments nationally, regionally, and internationally. These include the spread across national boundaries of environmental degradation, communicable diseases, drug trafficking, illegal migrants, and refugees. In one way or another, these could pose a treat to economic and social stability. Governments have to play their part in schemes of, and arrangements for, regional and international cooperation to attenuate the negative impact of these trends.

This leads to a related point. Given the transcendent nature of the changes taking place over the globe and the vitality which tends to accompany them, it would not be advisable for countries to adopt a static view of what the role of government should be. That role should be perceived in a dynamic context, as countries need to respond in an adequate and timely manner to current and emerging problems. This calls for a government that is flexible in both structure and operations, that is well-endowed with technical expertise including information systems, and that is working in harmony with both the private sector and the entire community. In other words, government should conceive of itself as constituting the nexus of a new social partnership, in which there is shared responsibility for establishing the goals of the society, for identifying the problems that have to be solved, and for tackling them.

Eighth, overall, by virtue of the leadership role that the citizenry has reposed in it, the government has a basic responsibility to help the country reach its full potential, encouraging in the process standards and values that would make everyone proud of their country and its heritage, and would endow them with the self-confidence to interact harmoniously with each other and with people in the rest of the world.

In all of this, the operation of the government should be conducted in an atmosphere of transparency so that the citizenry can be thoroughly informed, and that some of the circumstances that give rise to policy error, nepotism, and corruption could be avoided.

A well-governed country must have the elected government (at central and local levels) and its support mechanisms of civil service, local government officers, statutory boards, and advisory committees at the hub of interconnected activities involving the private sector and community-based organizations as partners. All three partners are to be engaged in a dynamic process of resource management and administration of political decision making, the exercise of accredited authority in the mobilization and allocation of resources generated for the growth and development of the entire society as well as the implementation of policies related to all this. It is axiomatic that the defense of the poor, who still form the vast majority of people, should be perceived as a major task of government in a majority-ruled democratic system.

It is expected that government should be held accountable to its electors for its actions through regular and duly constituted parliamentary meetings offering frank and open debate on all national issues conducted by parliamentarians of integrity, candor, and dedication. Meanwhile, procedures should be established to hold the government accountable for its stewardship by those who actually formulate policy (e.g., civil servants, executives of public enterprises, political heads of ministries). Finally, it is essential that a government be held accountable by a free press (print and electronic), with ease of access to information about the conduct of the nation's business and unfettered by censorship imposed by a whimsical political directorate or by any self-censorship that comes in the form of silence and/or sycophancy instilled by fear of political victimization of those who may publicly criticize or comment adversely (but fairly) on the performance of politicians and other public servants.

The Private Sector as Partner

The private sector in this partnership should regard itself as no less accountable in the performance of its functions to both people (as consumers and workers) and government (a fellow social contractee representing the citizenry at large).

In that partnership-structure the private sector should help to broaden its base following on the government's initiative to empower middle-sized businesses and microentrepreneurs, without impoverishing the established large entrepreneurs. Men and women of all ethnic backgrounds should be encouraged on to the playing field. And the workers and their trade unions already in tripartite partnership with employers and government in administering the industrial relations system have a pivotal role to play in the wider partnership, but with full understanding of their *own* rule in this parallel partnership.

The private sector partner should be capable of entrepreneurial activity that extends beyond traditional commission agency concerns to risk taking, innovation, and a willingness to face competition in an open market, both regional and international. This sector should exhibit the capacity to participate meaningfully in defining strategic objectives for growth and should use technology to help create a competitive advantage in funding new commodities for export as distinct from the exploitation of traditional natural resources (such as bauxite, bananas, and sugar). This sector should also commit itself to corporate responsibility for social development with a view to reaching a consensus or convergence with government on what is best for the country. The private sector will be a better partner in the new structure if it is willing to share governmental responsibilities in social investment for the public good, particularly the inescapable challenges of eliminating unemployment, hunger, ignorance, disease, fear for one's personal physical safety, and wider concerns for society's collective security.

The Community as Partner

The community, as partner, also has responsibilities in the participatory mode. Foremost among these is the commitment to civil society rooted in the values and maxims of prudence and supportive of the dignity, safety, and mental health of its members. It must collectively eschew violence as an instrument of conflict resolution whether between individuals or such groups as political parties, trade unions and their employers, and opposing teams in sport and so on.

The community must be committed to self-reliance in the building, shaping, and maintenance of social institutions necessary for stable, peaceful, and sound community life with or without the direct intervention of government (central or local) or the private sector. It must also exhibit a willingness to take the initiative, on however limited a scale, in the delivery of primary health care (through the practice of good personal hygiene, the vigilance over occupational health and safety at the workplace, and environmental care). It must also strive to improve education, with parents and teachers taking an active interest in the education of their children at all levels and participating in decisions affecting school life, curriculum development, and cultural orientation.

Conclusion

In brief, the new role of government is first to maximize the benefits of interaction between three major partners in participatory governance: the government, the private sector, and the community. The cutting edge of such interaction signifying the dynamics of the interrelationship is clearly the investment in human development. All three partners have a vested interest in the improvement and development of people, measurable in terms of such variables as education, productive capacity, health (and its linkage with education and productivity), housing (and its relation to social stability) and cultural certitude. Such a new strategy must emphasize the opportunities for release of individual creativity for the building of self-esteem and social confidence among the citizens who are, after all, the main producers of wealth and the real engines of growth.

Notes

1. This paper is based on the report of "The Committee on Government Structure," which studied the role and functions of government in transition to a market-driven economy. The Committee presented its findings to the prime minister of Jamaica on 26 March 1992. The late author was a member of the Committee. For the purpose of the Bucharest Roundtable, this paper was edited by Üner Kirdar.

Section 2 · Markets and States: Against Minimalism[1]

Paul Streeten

If we call the doctrine that the "correct" prices and markets have an important role to play in allocating resources efficiently and equitably, in promoting free choices, and in decentralizing power, *pricism,* and the doctrine that efficiency, equity, and liberty call for minimum state intervention *state minimalism*[2] (or laissez-faire), the currently prevailing view is that the two go together: get the government off our backs and let there be markets! The thesis of this paper is the opposite: that for the proper working of markets strong, and in many cases expanded, state intervention (of the right kind, in the right areas) is necessary. It is possible to favor a strong state, with a limited agenda. It would confine itself to ensuring that individuals, and the social groups in which they associate, can pursue their own purposes with a minimum of frustration. This is not the thesis of this paper. It argues for a strong state, with an expanded agenda, though a different one, differently implemented, from that which the state has commonly adopted in many developing countries.

The expression "getting prices right" has undergone a curious transformation. In the 1960s it was intended to point to the calculation of correct shadow or accounting prices in the face of "distorted" market or actual prices. Since market prices reflected all sorts of "distortions," including those caused by the existing and, from an ethical point of view, arbitrary income and asset distribution, it was the task of government to intervene and allocate resources according to the "correct" shadow prices. The purpose of government intervention was to correct distortions caused by the free play of market forces. Ten years later, the recommendation has been reversed. It is now that developing countries should get rid of state interventions in order to permit market prices to reflect the correct opportunity costs and benefits. Distortions are now regarded as caused mainly (or only) by governments.

State Minimalism and Pricism

The free, competitive market is a public good. Like other public goods, it calls for public or collective action to maintain it. When I worked with the Myrdal team on *Asian Drama,* we emphasized the need to use pricing policy rather than direct controls long before the current fashion for getting prices right had swept the profession. We thought it important for the government to organize markets so that they work efficiently, but we did not confuse price policy, measures to encourage competition, and the creation of previously absent markets, with the unrestrained play of market forces. *Getting* the right prices is open to two different interpretations. In the words of Michael Lipton, *setting* prices right is quite different from *letting* prices come right from state inaction. Contemporary discussions frequently confuse the question, how large should be the state in relation to total economic activity, with the quite different question, what policy instruments should the state employ and how should they be used?

There are several ways in which government intervention can contribute to a better functioning of markets. Not only should it provide a legal framework and maintain law and order, including the enforcement of contracts, property rights, etc. It must also encourage competition by antimonopoly and antirestrictive practices legislation or by setting up competitive enterprises in the public sector. There is nothing in the nature of free markets that either establishes or maintains competition. On the contrary, free markets make for conspiracies against the public, as Adam Smith knew. Yet, the virtue of markets depends on the existence of competition.

In addition to safeguarding competition, the government can intervene in the processes of price formation and production. It can encourage the introduction of markets for insurance, for example by providing or by guaranteeing the insurance of bank deposits. It can tax activities it wishes to discourage, such as pollution or traffic congestion or certain types of short-term stock exchange speculation, or the consumption of cigarettes or drugs or petrol, and subsidize those it wishes to encourage, like the use of public transport, or education and health.

It has a special role in promoting the development of human resources. By agricultural extension services it can improve the skill of farmers. By providing unemployment assistance and retraining facilities it can make workers readier to accept new labor-saving technologies; by providing information and conducting research it can help to reduce monopolistic practices. By investing in physical infrastructure (such as irrigation to raise agricultural price elasticities, roads to bring products to markets, harbors, and communications), it can provide the conditions for price incentives (such as devaluation) to work, and stimulate private investment. It has been widely documented that by raising profitability, public investment can "crowd in" private investment. By assisting in the design and strengthening of institutions (for land reform, information, credit, or marketing), it can contribute to the effectiveness of price policy. And so on. Some of these activities will be accepted by even extreme marketeers. The two questions are, whether a shift form present, often very inefficient, state activities to these efficient ones can be achieved by a minimalist state, and what the functions of the state should be after the transition, once markets are working.

Perhaps the largest area of controversy is the state's involvement in the area of social services, and in changing the income distribution brought about by free markets. The problem here is not one of the failure of markets, but of their successes, responding to the signals of unequal income and asset distributions. The neoliberals' view is that in any government's war on poverty, it is poverty that always wins. In the present context of the need for government action to strengthen both the allocative and the creative functions of markets, such involvement would have to be justified not on grounds of social justice or human needs, but on grounds of human capital formation, and of reducing barriers to income earning opportunities.

The proposition that pricism and state minimalism are incompatible is open to two interpretations. According to the strong interpretation, liberal markets require authoritarian regimes that prevent trade unions from pushing up wages, jeopardizing exports and foreign investment, and causing inflation, and special interest groups from grasping rents. "A courageous, ruthless and perhaps undemocratic government is required to ride roughshod over these newly created special interest groups" writes Deepak Lal.[3] This interpretation points to the East Asian economies (and perhaps Pinochet's Chile), cited as the great success stories. But it is questionable whether these regimes are truly liberal in the economic sphere. Their *dirigisme* is indeed market-orientated or, as they say nowadays, market-friendly. But if there is evidence of an invisible hand, it is surely guided by a strong visible arm.

According to the milder, and more realistic interpretation, democracies and free markets can go together, although the ruthless efficiency of markets will then be tempered by the compassion of social provisions, as exemplified by the Scandinavian countries. The current debate about the effects of the welfare state on incentives to work and save, on the swollen welfare bureaucracy and on inflation is, of course, provoked by this experience. But for the present purpose the focus is not on the state's welfare provisions but on its interventions in the areas of antimonopoly legislation, research and development, information, marketing, physical and social infrastructure, and human resource development, all of which are conditions for the efficient functioning of markets.

The state minimalists are prone to argue asymmetrically. They have pointed out, correctly, that market failure is not automatically an argument for state intervention, for this may produce even worse results. But they forget that government or bureaucratic or state failure is not necessarily an argument for private markets, at least not until much more empirical evidence is produced that the outcomes of government action in a particular case are necessarily worse than those of markets.

Shapiro and Taylor have pointed to a peculiar asymmetry in these models, "whereby individuals coalesce to force a political redistribution, but do not do the same in the market place. The political arena is depicted full of lobbyists and cartel builders, while the economy is presented as being more or less subject to competition."[4]

A related asymmetry is that rent-seeking has been indicted almost exclusively as resulting from public action. It is, however, equally common in the private sector. Private allocation of contracts to subcontractors gives rise to rents in exactly the same way as import quotas. Adam Smith recognized businessmen's "conspiracy against the public" and "contrivance to raise prices," and landlords' and others' love "to reap where they never sowed." We would expect these observations by the father of market economics to encourage us to design strategies of state intervention to counteract these private rent-seeking activities. Instead, we are served today with two ideas: first, that rent-seeking occurs only in the political process, and second, that the only way to reduce rent-seeking is to limit government. Both are wrong, or at least unproven without considerably more empirical evidence.

Private and public action often have to go together. Prices have their impact on demand and supply only if complementary action is taken by the government.

A factory may depend on a road, which is normally constructed by the government. Increases in agricultural output may depend on irrigation or research into new varieties. The ability to make use of high-profit opportunities may depend on the availability of information about inputs and markets, provided by the government. When the International Monetary Fund (IMF) recommended that Tanzania devalue the shilling, no attention was paid to the fact that the transport system had broken down and, however attractive the prices for farmers, their produce could not have been transported to the ports. In South Africa, the "black" taxi trade is often upheld as a splendid example of the spirit of free enterprise. And so it is, if we accept the absence of the need for an efficient and safe public transport system for the blacks. But with roads full of potholes and without public safety regulations, the accident rate is one of the highest in the world.

One example of the complementarity or symbiosis between public and private sectors is the "crowding-in" effect (in contrast to the normally assumed crowding out effect, resulting from higher interest rates), according to which public investment, often in infrastructure, stimulates private investment. The task of government is to raise the productivity of the investment in both the public and the private sector. There are many other nonprice, nonmarket measures, such as research, information, or the establishment of appropriate institutions, which the government must take in order to make the incentives of prices bite.

Some might say that, while the combination of price and nonprice measures is best, to get prices right by itself is a step in the right direction. This is, however, not so. I have shown that the right prices by themselves, without the complementary public sector action, can be ineffective or counterproductive.[5]

Anyone who has tried to go on a low-calorie diet has discovered that any low-calories food tastes good only in conjunction with a high-calorie food. Strawberries are fine, but strawberries and cream are much better. The same is true for the need to combine private and public sector action. Japan and South Korea are often cited as examples of successful private-public sector cooperation. It is sometimes said that the relation is supportive, not antagonistic. But looking more deeply into the nature of successful state interventions, we note that the state in Japan and South Korea, as Jagdish Bhagwati put it, issues prescriptions rather than proscriptions.[6] They intervene by encouraging and promoting selected activities, not by prohibiting and restricting. Of course, to be able to get credit for only one type of investment is not as clear-cut as it may seem.

Japan uses government intervention to promote industrial productivity. By export incentives, barriers to protect the domestic market, low-cost credit to selected investments, and policies that favor business and education. In addition, there are numerous more covert policies to favor companies that move into government-approved types of production, such as commercial intelligence services, nationalistic patent policies, etc. The government practices an art despised and condemned by most U.S. economists, who are minimalists, with regard to industrial policy.

The South Korean public sector Pohange Steel Company is one of the most efficient enterprises in the world, while the Steel Authority of India is a testimony to bureaucratic inefficiency. The Korean firm has financial autonomy, seeks to make profits, has clear objectives, has operating independence, and is open to potential competition from domestic rivals and imports. It is not burdened with multiple social objectives and the incentive structure encourages it to export. The Indian Authority accepts losses, has confusing and multiple objectives, its finances overlap with the budget, it is subject to close political scrutiny and interference, its prices are politicized, and it is protected from competition through tariffs, import licensing, and legal restrictions on domestic entry.

The East Asian success stories, moreover, illustrate that the same type of intervention, such as subsidized interest rates, that in Latin America have impeded growth, has been used by these governments to accelerate growth. The role of corruption and its control also contributes to explaining differential performance.[7] It is not generally acknowledged that "getting prices right" has not been the principal recipe for their success, although their government inventions have been "market-friendly."

Differences in the institutional arrangements of the relations between managers of public enterprises and the public authority are also important. Managers are given sufficient autonomy to proceed with their jobs, while remaining accountable to the public. With all the current talk about incorporating political variables in economic analysis, and endogenizing political change, there is remarkably little work being done on how specific political and economic institutions function.

The Civil Society

States and markets do not exhaust the players in this game. Frequently, although the need each other, they also weaken and undermine each other. States damage markets by regulations, licensing, and bureaucratic red tape. Markets tend to corrupt governments. Therefore there is a need for the civil society, which can contribute to more constructive relationships between the two.

Private voluntary organizations have come to play an increasing role, next to governments and profit-seeking companies. They comprise the most diverse organizations: religious, political, professional, educational, cooperative organizations, pressure groups, interest groups, lobbies, institutions that are project-oriented, give technical assistance, provide disaster-relief, or disaster-prevention, etc. Although they often claim to work without or even against governments, their contributions can sometimes best be mobilized jointly with governments. The most successful NGOs in the third World, such as the Self-Employed Women's Organization based on Ahmedabad, India, or the Grameen Bank or BRAC of Bangladesh, depend for their continuing and expanding (though not for their initial) operations on access to, and support and replication by, governments. Of course, in some situations their function is to criticize and exhort governments, or to fill gaps in government activities, or to do things at lower costs, with better results, and with more popular participation than governments. In others, when they promote their selfish interests, irrespective of the wider interests of the community, or when they reflect the dominant power of particular groups, government may be justified in trimming its influence.

The relationship between NGOs and governments can be understood as one of cooperative conflict (or creative tensions), in which the challenge of the voluntary agencies and their innovative activities can improve both government services and the working of markets, and help to resolve tensions between them.

In some situations the state plays a passive role, only responding to the pressures of interest groups. The outcomes will then be determined by the power of these groups, which in turn depends on their size, age, motivation, and enforcement mechanisms. In other cases the state is more active, imposing regulation and restrictions, which can give rise to competitive rent-seeking by private interest groups. In others again, both the private groups and the state work together for common objectives.

Functions are divided between the state and civil society. The institutions of civil society—churches, trade unions, interest groups, action groups, the media, and many others—are often quite undemocratic, in spite of their rhetoric. There is then a need for the empowerment of weak and neglected groups within them: women, the unemployed, ethnic minorities. There can be undesirable concentration not only of economic and political, but also of social power.

Though there is in the early stages of development a need to strengthen both states and markets, in fact they often tend to weaken and undermine each other. It is the institutions of the civil society that can intervene and inhibit such weakening and undermining.[8] Interactions between the state, markets, and civil society are complex. Both too weak and too strong a state can discourage the growth of civil society. And too strong private organizations can undermine the power of the state, as in Sri Lanka or in Lebanon, and lead to the dissolution of society.

The Loss of Some Distinctions

Some important distinctions, drawn in the 1950s and earlier, have been swamped by the neoclassical resurgence. There is the distinction between price policy, in which prices (including indirect taxes and subsidies) are used as instruments of policy, and laissez-faire, which is the free play of market forces without intervention to maintain competition, to supply information, research, and an infrastructure, to provide the formation of human capital, and to look after the victims of the competitive struggle.

There is the distinction between markets and the private sector. Privatization of a public enterprise without the managerial and technical personnel, without competition, and without the provision of infrastructure and information can only raise false expectations, while markets can exist where public enterprises compete with each other or with private ones, as Renault in France has done so successfully or the above-mentioned Pohange Steel Company in South Korea.

There is the important distinction between motivations in the private and in the public sector. Of course, self-seeking occurs in the public sector as it does in the private. What is so absurd is to maintain that this is the only motivation to be found there. Each of us behaves differently in different settings.

Even behavior in the market has been grossly oversimplified. All that it is necessary to assume for economic people to produce a stable equilibrium outcomes is rationality in the sense of constancy and consistency of behavior. Selfishness can manifest itself in impulsiveness, inconsistency, inconstancy, and irrationality. On the other hand, the perfect model of the rational person is the disinterested trustee, who administers funds completely unselfishly on behalf of others.

Finally, there is the distinction between centralized and decentralized government decision-making. Some of the criticisms made of a central bureaucracy do not apply to decentralized authorities (although others do apply). It can enhance participation, especially of small entrepreneurs and farmers, be more responsive to needs, gather more information, be more transparent and accountable, and improve the quality of government activities. It can also raise more resources, because the benefits are more visible. On the other hand, decentralized control can reinforce local power elites which are less responsive to the needs of the poor than central groups. Decentralization can also aggravate interregional disparities. The task is to design a structure of decision-making that combines the informational and motivational merits of decentralization and participation with central control.

The Unimportance of the Private-Public Distinction

Going one step further, it can be doubted whether the very distinction between private and public ownership or management is relevant. Much of the discussion is conducted in binary terms: central planning versus free markets. Sometimes a spectrum between these two poles is considered, but the ideological values attached vary with the position on this spectrum. For example, Soviet-type planning is bad; therefore the nearer we are to free markets the better. But an intermediate position between the two ends of the spectrum may be preferable to either. It is also possible to add dimensions to the linear spectrum, which render the value choices more complex: the degree of democratic accountability, freedom versus compulsion, centralized versus decentralized decision-making, the degree of involvement of voluntary organizations. A regime combining certain features of intervention with others of a free market may then avoid the failures of the two poles and be preferable to either extreme.

There is also the third sector briefly discussed above, which is neither private nor public, that consists of nongovernmental, nonprofit organizations that draw on the voluntary energies of their members. Churches, colleges, universities,

Oxfam, Bread for the World, orchestras, hospitals, museums, the Red Cross, Friends of the Earth, Amnesty International, charities, cooperatives, the Grameen Bank, neighborhood organizations, local action committees, and many others draw on people's voluntary efforts and contribute often highly efficiently not only to the gross national product but to a flourishing civil society, essential for a democracy. As in the case of the complementarity of private and public activities, the strength of the civil society and of NGOs in particular often lies not in opposing the public sector, but in cooperating with it, whether for finance, or for replication of successful ventures, or for support in opposition exploitative local power elites. In other circumstances, for example when faced with a predatory state, their function is to combat it.

Theories of the State

We now have a menu of theories of the state to choose from. According to the one I was taught as an undergraduate, an idealistic, competent, and well-informed government, like Platonic guardians, or perhaps more like Fabian bureaucrats, reigns above the interest conflicts and promotes the common good. It is implicit in the writings of A.C. Pigou, Abba Lerner, Jan Tinbergen, and James Meade. According to this old romantic theory the government can do no wrong.

The opposite theory, represented by the new classical Chicago economists, neoclassical political economists, the public choice school (better named the self-interest school), holds that the government can do no right. Citizens, politicians, bureaucrats, and states use the authority of government to distort economic transactions for their benefit. Citizens use political influence and pressures to get access to benefits allocated by government; politicians use government resources to increase their hold on power; public officials trade access to government benefits for personal reward; and states use their power to get access to the property of citizens.[9] The result is an inefficient and inequitable allocation of resources, general impoverishment, and reduced freedom.

A narrow interpretation of selfish political man/woman, pursuing ruthlessly his/her interests, can lead to mutual impoverishment. According to one version the predatory officials and bureaucrats or politicians promote actively their selfish quest for money or power; according to another they respond passively to powerful pressure groups so as to stay in power. "The model of government motivations" has been simplified "into a single-track form, supplying the public sector with a brain transplant straight out of the market place."[10] Any intervention by this "predatory state" with the "magic of the market place" is bound to make matters worse. Government action is not the solution (as it is in the first theory), it is the problem—"invisible feet [of rent-seeking] stomping on invisible hands."[11] As has been said, while according to the Platonic theory the government intervenes in order to correct "distortions," according to the public choice theory all distortions are the result of government interventions. But according to both these apparently opposite views the state is an optimizing agency. According to the Platonic view it optimizes the welfare of the people as a whole, according to the public choice view that of special interest groups: those on whose support the politicians relay, the bureaucrats, the army, the politicians themselves.

A third theory, propounded by Anthony Downs and applicable only to democracies, holds that politicians maximize their own welfare by selling polities for votes.[12] Since not many (though a growing number of) developing countries are democracies, this theory would not have wide application among them, even if it applied to democracies.

It is worth remembering, in the debate over market versus state, that real states fall under neither extreme. Dogmatism here leads to error even more than usual. A more commonsensical view, borne out by overwhelming evidence, holds that many governments are neither monolithic nor impervious to pressures for rational and altruistic policies. Moreover, if there is a cope for a positive-sum game, and if the government can hold on long enough to tax the sum, the possibility of rational policies is opened up, even on the narrow assumption about predatoriness of the public choice school.

The structure of government decision making consists of many departments, ministries, and agencies, and many layers from central government via provinces (or states in a federation) to village or town councils. Power in some countries is divided between the legislature, the judiciary, and the executive. Each of these pulls in a different direction. The obstacle to "correct" policy making is neither solely stupidity nor solely cupidity, neither just ignorance nor simply political constraints or monolithic selfishness. On occasion, governments, like charitable foundations, universities, or voluntary associations, do act disinterestedly and in the public interest, particularly, but not only, if there are pressure groups with some power or influence that constitutes the "trustees for the poor," and the "guardians of rationality."

At the same time, there are areas in which a better analysis and a clearer sense of direction would help, just as there are areas where it is fairly clear what should be done, but vested interests, whether those of the policy makers or of pressure groups on whose support they depend, prevent it from happening. Governments sometimes create rents and encourage rent-seeking; at other times they destroy rents and reduce wasteful competition in their pursuit. The private sector also creates and seeks rents. Some government officials act sometimes in their selfish interest; the same and others are at other times, or want to be seen as, moral agents, acting in the common interest. Some pressure groups, either individual or collective, domestic or foreign, are motivated by reason, solidarity, and morality.

According to this commonsensical theory, for which there is overwhelming evidence, the state does not optimize anything, neither public welfare nor self-interest. It compromises, attempts to resolve conflicts, manages bargaining between groups, and occasionally leads. Gunnar Myrdal's notion of the "soft state," in which declared policies are not implemented or not enforced, fits into this picture. But so does that of the hard state, which pursues successfully both growth and equity.

An Alternative Window

Some of the neoclassical theories regard the private sector as the source of wealth creation and the public sector as the domain of authority, exercised either benevolently or as a wasteful drain on resources. According to some adherents of this view, many governments in developing countries have usurped the sphere of production, which should be left to the private sector. The remedy lies in the state withdrawing from this area, and confining itself to the protection of its citizens against external and domestic threats.

But it is equally possible to look at the same situation in a different way, with a different division of responsibilities. We may regard each sector, or better each sphere, of responsibility as a means of creating different forms of wealth, and exercising different forms of authority and compulsion. According to this view, the private sector creates forms of wealth that can be sold for profit, and the public sector creates those that, while also useful, cannot, because powerful externalities and inappropriabilities exist. Public goods are goods characterized by nonrivalrous consumption, so that one person's use does not detract from another's, and occasionally, though not always, nonexcludability from the benefits whose costs are incurred by some. The classic example is a lighthouse (although its construction can, of course, be subcontracted to private firms, and although it benefits not all sailors but only ships in the region). Armed protection, monetary and employment stability, an efficient market, the administration of justice, and mass education are other examples of public goods, or rather, services. Certain types of infrastructure, such as underutilized roads, bridges, and subways, or harbors, dams, and irrigation, are nonrivalrous but not nonexcludable, for the provider can charge tolls or fees and thereby exclude nonpayers. But this means excluding some people whose benefits would exceed the costs of supplying them. When price discrimination is impossible, the alternative is for the government to provide these goods and services free, and finance them by taxation.

Not all public goods should be produced, provided, or financed by the central government. Some can be supplied by local government, or by cooperatives, clubs, or other interested private parties, such a group of farmers who jointly provide common control over common grazing rights.

On the other hand, there are other reasons for public sector production than the public nature of goods. They include natural monopolies, if their regulation is less efficient, and merit goods, to which a high value is attached by the community, but which cannot be afforded by the people who need them. Or goods and services, such as the arts or museums or theaters, which are regarded as important, but would not continue to exist if they had to rely wholly on private finance.

Production of different things can therefore occur in both the public and the private sector. And the same is true of authority. The private sector exercises authority through work discipline (and hiring and firing, giving and withholding payments), the public sector through the army and the police. And the authority of the state depends on widespread voluntary acceptance by the citizens. A worker can, of course, leave the firm and go to another, but citizens in many countries can also leave and move to another country. States are also constrained by both supernational bodies, like the European Community, and the subnational bodies, like provinces and municipalities. The question as to whether the private and the public sectors use their authority to the benefit of the public or wastefully or exploitatively remains to be answered.

Theology and Practice

The academic and political rhetoric about the virtues of the market and the vices of the state is far removed from the actual behavior of libertarian governments that profess to follow this rhetoric. While both the Reagan and the Thatcher administrations decried the role of the state, the role of public expenditure relative to GNP increased under both leaders. In 1990 the public sector in the United States spent 43 percent of the national income. It was 40 percent in 1980 and 38 percent in 1970. This represents an increase of over 13 percent over twenty years. It resulted from growing expenditure on defense, on state security, and on social security, on research and development and, above all, on growing interest payments on the rising public debt in an economy without a sense of direction. These expenditures, particularly those on research, reflect three powerful collective sentiments to which libertarians succumb just as much as interventionists: collective fear (defense and, more recently, environmental protection), collective greed (the desire to be competitive in international trade that leads to subsidies such as those to Sematech, the Pentagon-aided corporation consortium for improving the manufacture of semiconductors), and collective pride (the desire for international prestige reflected in the award of Nobel Prizes). There are two important areas in this debate. One is concerned with the problems of the transition from excessively interventionist to more market-oriented policies; the other is normative political economy.

Problems of the Transition

Much of the writing is concerned with how much state intervention is appropriate, what kind and by what means, but it is much less concerned with the important question of how to manage the transition (1) from excessive to reduced state intervention, (2) from interventions in the wrong areas to those in previously neglected important ones, and (3) from one form (say reliance on quantitative controls) to another (reliance on prices as instruments of policy). This is a problem with which many countries are faced today, not only in Eastern Europe and Russia, and for whose solution guidelines are needed. If, for example, reducing public sector employment is implemented by not replacing people who leave, the best will leave and only the deadwood will remain. If salaries in the public sector are kept too low, demoralization and added temptation to corruption and the search for additional outside jobs are created. If staff are just sacked without the provision of alternative jobs, unemployment and poverty are created, or the burden of maintaining them is thrown on others. The examples of Sri Lanka and China have shown that liberalization that raises output and average incomes has been combined with rising infant mortality rates and falling live expectancy. It may be that demobilization, the change from a wartime to a peacetime economy, has lessons to teach. In many respects the experience of the British economy in both mobilization for the war and demobilization after it, has been wrongly transferred to developing countries. But some aspects of it may be relevant. More transitional intervention may be needed in order to reduce, or, more importantly, to change the form of, past intervention.

Normative Political Economy

Much of the recent criticisms of governments and states by the state minimalists and the neoclassical political economists have been concerned with explaining why and how inefficiency, inequality, and deprivation of freedom arose; with the positive political economy, partly of government failures, and, more importantly, of government successes in pursuing its selfish interests at the expense of the public. They have been useful in explaining bad policies and the absence of reforms, and have thrown light on regimes such as those of Amin, the Duvaliers, Marcos, Somoza, Trujillo, and Mobutu. It has been truly said that in many developing countries the Invisible Hand is nowhere to be seen.

But in explaining the evils of predatory governments, and by advocating free markets, they have once again reasoned the state away, and reestablished the division between economics and politics. The task of integrating the two would consist in showing how the government, and pressures on it, can be used for the objectives of development. This would also help to explain the successes of development from Japan to South Korea, Botswana, and Costa Rica.

On the other hand, there are examples of political regimes that represent and promote the interests of the poor. In Malaysia, political power lies with the poorer Malays, while economic power with the Chinese and Indian communities. As a result, Malaysia has implemented policies that benefited the poor Malay community. In Zimbabwe, after power had shifted from a white to a black government, numerous measures were taken that favored human and social objectives. For example, the share of primary education in total educational expenditure rose from 32 percent in 1980 to 58 percent in 1984 and real expenditure per head on primary education doubled.[13] In Malaysia and Zimbabwe influence does not go with affluence.

Frequently authors from different schools attribute poor policies to "lack of political will." But it is futile (or tautological) to say that the political will is lacking. It is an expression that should be banned from political discourse. One does not have to be a behaviorist to think that behavior is the manifestation of will. If the will to action is lacking, there is no point in asking for the will to have the will to action. This only leads either to an infinite regress or to the charge of hypocrisy. It is a case of *ignotum per ignorius*. Political will itself should be subjected to analysis, and, for purposes of action, to pressures and to mobilization. It is more fruitful to think of how to create a strong political base for efficiency, equity, and liberty; how to build up pressure groups, how to mobilize the poor, how to shape reformist alliances, how to recruit coalitions for progress, how to strike bargains, achieve compromises, forge compacts, resolve conflicts, or permit their tolerance, how to use persuasion, when to offer compensation to losers when total gains exceed total losses, etc. Amartya Sen has used the expression "cooperative conflict" for the relations within a family.[14] Similar relations exist both within the state and between it and pressure groups.

It might be thought that if such a normative theory had to be built on pure self-interest, no research would be needed, for people are very good in discovering and pursuing their interest. But we know from parables such as those of the prisoners' dilemma, the isolation paradox, the tragedy of the commons, social trips, and the free rider, that the pursuit of self-interest in society can be mutually destructive, and that there are ways of cooperation, apparent sacrifice, and coercion that advance it. Moreover, there is no need to stick to the assumption of self-interested bureaucrats and politicians. Mobilizing the guardians for the poor and the trustees of rationality to put pressure on governments can produce good results even if governments were correctly analyzed by the public choice school. Governments can also themselves initiate reforms either in their enlightened self-interest or from motives of public interest.

In analyzing the sources of pressures on governments for reform directed at improving the lot of poor people, for example, six areas are worth exploring:

1. Common or shared interests between rich and poor.
2. Mutual interests and bargains between rich and poor, including the payment of compensation.
3. Interest conflicts within the ruling groups that can result in benefits for the poor.
4. Empowerment of the poor and participatory forms of organization.
5. Organization of distinct "trustees for the poor" and "guardians of rationality."
6. International pressures and support.

Donor Conditionality, Pricism, and State Minimalism

Structural adjustment loans have been given by the World Bank on the condition that recipients liberalize, decentralize, privatize, and deregulate. Pricism and market-orientation have been combined with state minimalism, both in domestic and foreign policies. The change from exclusive project lending to program lending with its macropolicy conditionality is the result of projects having gone sour because of the wrong macroeconomic policies. The policy conditionality was further supported by the belief that it would support like-minded domestic political coalitions in recipient countries.

Apart from the (superficial) double paradox that foreign donors are in a better position to know what is in the country's best interest, and that the country does not have to pay a fee for this good advice, but gets rewarded with extra funds, there are five problems associated with this type of conditionality.[15]

First, adjustment aid to mostly Latin American and Southeast Asian debtor countries is aid not to the countries, but to the banks in the United States and other advanced countries, if the creditors are private banks and the alternative is default. This, of course, may have contributed to the conversion of the multilateral banks and a Republican U.S. administration to program lending.

Second, policies, like projects, are substitutable and avoidable. The donor imposes a condition, which is met, but other policies circumvent the intended result. This is the macroeconomic equivalent of fungibility, which was an objection to project aid. In both cases, the donor's intentions are frustrated. For example, the donor imposes devaluation as a condition, but subsequent inflation renders it nugatory. This happened in several African countries.

Third, donors' embrace of political groups advocating "correct" policies can be the kiss of death. An example was the pressure for devaluation on India in 1966.[16] It may be wiser to refrain from seeking such allies and to encourage correct policies by signalling quietly approval through the unconditional support of good governments.

Fourth, in view of our ignorance of the impact of these conditions, both in the transition period and ultimately, the premature crystallization of flawed orthodoxies should be avoided. The neoclassical doctrines are not scientific truths, and the ability of governments to implement them, even if they were such truths, and even if the governments were willing, is often in doubt.

Fifth, our confidence in the ability of the developing countries to implement the required macroeconomic policy reforms has declined.

In the light of this, at least as much attention as to macropolicies should be paid to project design and implementation, to institution- and capacity-building, and to human rights in the aid dialogue.

Conclusion

The theoretical case for free, unregulated markets depends on many conditions, which rarely exist in reality. Adam Smith is often cited as the authority for advocating laissez-faire and state minimalism. "Shakespeare did not say it, but it is true that some men are born small, some achieve smallness, and some have smallness thrust upon them. Adam Smith, the father of modern economics, has had to cope with a good deal of such thrusting."[17] Adam Smith defended particular liberties, not liberty in general, and he objected to particular government interventions (especially in foreign trade), not to government intervention in general. One person's "freedom from" and "freedom to" implies restrictions on other people's freedom.

Adam Smith thought that the state should undertake three main tasks: defending its citizens from the "violence and invasion of other independent societies;" protecting every member of society from the "injustice or oppression of every other member of it;" and "providing certain public works and certain public institutions, which it can never be for the interest of any individual, or small number of individuals, to erect and maintain." Smith also discussed "the importance of social interdependence and the communal advantages of following rules of conduct,' even when they go against what he called 'self-love.'"[18]

This paper is entirely in the spirit of Adam Smith. Collective defense and the administration of justice are generally agreed goods for which the state is responsible. The provision of certain public works and public institutions permits a wide range of public interventions. Infrastructure, public education, and help for the poor were certainly in Smith's mind. Arguments from free riders and externalities are used today to justify them. Modern theory and events have added other justifications for state intervention. The theory of the second-best has shown that if one price is not competitive, intervention with all other competitively determined prices may be justified. The world of small producers has given place to one of large corporations and trade unions. Modern industry has polluted the environment. At the same time, Smith saw that market failure is not necessarily an argument for government intervention. There are, it is hardly necessary to say, also government failures. But equally, though less widely noticed, government failure is not necessarily an argument for the market. Only pragmatic experiments can show when and where intervention is the lesser evil.

Perhaps the most serious problems arise, as Michael Lipton has reminded us, not from market failure but from market success, not from government failure but from government success. If it were just a matter of correcting failures, the task would be relatively easy. But if the signals propagated by the market are based on a very unequal distribution of land, other assets, and income, it is market success in responding to these signals that causes the trouble. Amartya Sen has analyzed famines and shown that often total food supply was adequate, but that the purchasing power (or, more generally, the entitlements) of a particular group of poor people had declined. In those conditions the market is all too successful in its signals, incentives, and allocations, while people starve. Similarly, it is not government failure but government success (in pursuing the selfish objectives of its officials) that produces the destructive results rightly deplored by the self-interest school and the state minimalists. What is needed then is fundamental structural change, a redistribution of assets and of power.

Notes

1. The author is grateful to Professor Louis Putterman for helpful comments.
2. The terms are due to Michael Lipton.

3. Deepak, Lal, *The Poverty of Development Economics* (Cambridge: Harvard University Press, 1985), 33.

4. Helen Shapiro and Lance Taylor, "The State and Industrial Strategy," *World Development* 17, no. 6, (June 1990): 867.

5. Paul Streeten, *What Price Food?* (Basingstoke: Macmillan and Cornell University Press, 1987).

6. Jagdish Bhagwati, *Protectionism* (Cambridge: MIT Press, 1988), 88.

7. See Gunnar Myrdal, *Asian Drama* (Harmondsworth, England: Penguin Books, 1968), vol. 2, part 4, chapter 20; and Robert Klitgaard, *Controlling Corruption* (Berkeley and London: University of California Press, 1988).

8. Michael Lipton, "The State-Market Dilemma, Civil Society, and Structural Adjustment," *The Round Table* 317 (1991): 21-31.

9. Merilee S. Grindle and John W. Thomas, *Pubic Choices and Policy Change: The Political Economy of Reform in Developing Countries* (Baltimore: The Johns Hopkins University Press, 1991).

10. John P. Lewis, "Government and National Economic Development," in *A World to Make; Development in Perspective,* ed., Francis X. Sutton (New Brunswick and London: Transactions Publishers, 1990), 77. It should be noted that even in the marketplace individuals do not always behave selfishly.

11. David Colander (editor), *Neoclassical Political Economy.* (Cambridge, Massachusetts: Ballinger, 1985.

12. Anthony Downs, *An Economic Theory of Democracy* (New York: Harper and Row, 1957).

13. Giovanni Andrea Cornia, Richard Jolly, Frances Stewart (editors), *Adjustment with a Human Face* (New York: Clarendon Press, Oxford, 1987), 292-93.

14. Amartya Sen, "Gender and Cooperative conflicts," Working Paper No. 18, WIDER, Helsinki, 1987, and published in *Persistent Inequalities*, ed., I. Tinker (New York: Oxford University Press).

15. On several reasons why this conflict may arise, see Paul Streeten, "Structural Adjustment: A Survey of Issues and Options," *World Development,* 15 no. 2 (December 1987): 1469-82; and "A Aurvey of the Issues and Options," in *Structural Adjustment and Agriculture in Theory and Practice in Africa and Latin America,* ed., Simon Commander (London: Overseas Development Institute).

16. India did, of course, devalue, but the domestic groups that supported devaluation lost credibility. There are, of course, examples illustrating the opposite, such as Belaunde and the Alliance for Progress in the 1960s. Belaunde escaped political opposition to land reform, which he advocated, by blaming the Americans, who made essential aid conditional on it. The Peruvian congress acceded eventually.

17. Amartya Sen, "Adam Smith's Prudence," in *Theory and Reality in Development: Essays in Honour of Paul Streeten,* ed., Sanjaya Lall and Frances Stewart (Basingstoke: Macmillan, 1986), 28.

18. Amartya Sen, "Economic Methodology: Heterogeneity and Relevance," *Methodus,* 3, no. 1 (June 1991): 74.

Section 3 · Economic Freedom Based on Fairness

Nemir A. Kirdar

The collapse of the Soviet economic empire has clearly removed an important role model for many developing countries and for the East European countries themselves. The incompatibility of a single party state with true democracy must have been obvious from the beginning, but the success of Soviet technology and production in areas such as defense and space research and space travel disguised the fundamental failure of its economic system. The inefficiency of state ownership of the means of production and the failure of a centrally planned economic system manifested itself in low consumption standards of the mass of the population. Equality of income there may have been—except perhaps for the party leaders and the *apparatchiks* who got more then their share—but it was equality at a very low income level. The system boasted of its high rate of saving and capital formation but the rewards were clearly not seen by the bulk of the population—and could not be, since a more diversified system of production and distribution, operating through a market price system, necessary for a high consumption economy, would have been incompatible with the concentration of power at the center.

Alternative Models

But if socialism has failed in the USSR—and indeed it has failed wherever it has been seriously tried—what is the alternative? Is unrestrained capitalism the answer? All experience seems to show that a competitive market system is the most efficient way of allocating resources to meet the community's needs, and that such a system is more compatible with private ownership of the means of production, that is capitalism, than it is with state ownership of capital. But is capitalism compatible with an acceptable distribution of income and wealth and with harmony of interests between capitalists and workers? We can be convinced of the merits of a competitive market economy but have reservations as to whether the principles of compassion and equality of treatment, of social responsibility and of rejection of poverty can be incorporated.

Whether or not a capitalist system is compatible with an acceptable distribution of income and wealth and with harmony of interests between workers and capitalists has long been debated. Socialists influenced by Karl Marx have argued that only state ownership of capital, "the means of production," will fulfill these aims. At the other extreme, economists associated with the Austrian school have maintained that the aims could be achieved by a competitive capitalistic system if it is free from government intervention. In between, we have the "social market" economists, who predominate in most Western economies (the United States, Europe, and Japan), and who support a free-market economy of capitalist profit making enterprises, but also see the need for a significant government role in influencing the distribution of income and in regulating conditions of work, including in many cases the payment of minimum wages.

Relationship between Capital and Labor

A key issue is the economic relationship between capitalists and workers. John Stuart Mill, the famous English economist, writing in 1871, said "The form of association which if mankind continue to improve must be expected in the end to predominate is not that which can exist between capitalist as chief and work people without a voice in management, but the association of the laborers themselves on terms of equality, collectively owning the capital with which they carry on their operations and working under managers, elected and removable by themselves." Employee managed enterprises or cooperatives have been established in many countries, but experience has shown that such enterprises are seldom efficient or successful, and indeed are not compatible with an expanding economy and rising employment.

The reason why such enterprises tend to be less efficient than pure capitalist ones arises because they have strong incentive to maximize earnings per worker rather than maximize the value of the firm, and, an aspect of this, to prefer investment projects with short-run payback characteristics to projects with more distant prospective cash flows. These preferences arise from the fact that ownership of the employee managed firm is contingent upon employment (ownership goes with employment) which of course in the case of any employee manager is finite rather than infinite (employees retire or pass away, whereas firms can live forever). Investment projects with positive net present values which would be undertaken by a capitalist enterprise with infinite life, might well be rejected by an employee managed firm in favor of other projects that yield higher earnings per worker and/or pay off in shorter time. Thus, misinvestment, both temporal and inter temporal, tends to be endemic in an employee managed enterprise.

A further problem is the absence of, or at least the less efficient operation of, the monitoring function normally provided by the financial capital market in a capitalist market price system. In the case of a capitalist enterprise, its shares (i.e., ownership rights) can be bought and sold in financial capital markets. Market valuation of these shares represents constant monitoring of the performance of the firm, and imposes pressures on managers to make best use of capital and labor. Such pressures are generally absent in the case of employee managed firms since even if shares in these enterprises could be transferred to nonemployees, potential new investors would be hardly likely to buy them without some reduction in employee control, that is, a fundamental modification to the principles underlying an employee managed enterprise.

The net result of all these factors is a less efficient use of capital and labor by employee managed enterprise, and therefore slower economic growth of the economy as a whole and less employment creation.

A Suitable Partnership

But could a model based on partnership between capital and labor, working in a suitable macroeconomic and policy environment, provide the answer? The aim of the partnership would be to take advantage of self-centered enterprising behavior in the context of cooperation between individuals, whether suppliers of equity capital or labor, to produce the best possible outcome.

Of course, many enterprises in capitalist economics organize their business along these lines. Many of them encourage their employees (labor) and management to participate in the equity of the firm, and they tie a significant part of their remuneration to performance. But whether trends in that direction are sufficient to iron out natural conflicts between labor and capital in a capitalistic economy may be in doubt. A more institutional approach or model may be necessary.

The characteristics of such a model have been elaborated by Professor Meade of the University of Cambridge.[1] Leaving aside many complications, this model envisages the establishment of enterprises in which the shares of capital and labor in the distributable surplus of the enterprise are established at the beginning. This could be done by issuing shares to the providers of equity and shares to the providers of labor, in agreed proportions. Those going to the equity providers could be called "capital shares" and those going to labor, "labor shares." The division between labor and capital would not be immutable but be subject to negotiated change as developments in capital technology and in skill requirements altered the basic economic returns to labor and capital. All shares would carry the same dividend, and this dividend, which is tied to the performance of the firm, would be in place of the normal payment of wages to employees. This arrangement does not preclude the firm from obtaining capital on nonequity terms, for example a bank loan, or preclude the firm from hiring at normal fixed wages employees who do not wish to participate in the partnership. And of course, labor members of the partnership can also acquire capital shares by contributing to the equity of the firm.

There would be a significant difference between capital shares and labor shares. Capital shares can be bought and sold in the capital market in the normal way, and therefore can attract capital gains, whereas labor shares would be tied to the individual employee and be canceled if the employee left the enterprise. Special arrangements have to be made for employees made redundant or retire in the normal way.

The advantage of such a partnership lies in the fact that the reward to labor is tied *directly* to the performance of the firm, as is the case with the reward to the suppliers of capital. As the distributable surplus of the firm rises, so does the reward to labor; and because the relationship between firm performance and labor remuneration is direct and transparent, potential conflicts between labor and capital are largely removed. Economic justice or fairness is seen to result.

On the other hand, because the remuneration of labor is directly related to firm performance, labor, like the owners of capital, share in the risk attached to the firm. While having some advantages for the firm, this can be a particular problem for labor as compared with the owners of capital. Owners of capital can spread their risks by investing in a wide range of firms, whereas workers can seldom split up their working time among a number of enterprises. Against this, however, workers in capital-labor partnerships are probably less vulnerable to unemployment than members employed at fixed wages since their remuneration is more closely tied to the performance and profits of the firm: in effect the cost of labor declines as the distributable surplus of the firm declines, thus making it easier for the firm to maintain output and its labor force. Even so, it is the fact that linking labor remuneration directly to the profits of the firm exposes labor to the same risk as the capitalist which has discouraged the setting up of formalized capital labor partnerships. A way out may be found by encouraging a widespread ownership of capital in the nation at large so that the nation's citizens become capitalists as well as workers, an aim which was very much at the heart of Margaret Thatcher in the United Kingdom.

Of course, it is not suggested here that it would be easy or practicable to convert existing industrial organizations into capital-labor partnerships on any large scale. Nonetheless, in its broad outlines, the Meade model provided a useful role model for counties aiming to secure the economic benefits of a capitalist market based economy whilst preserving economic justice and fairness. We already see in certain Central and Eastern European countries, who have broken away from socialism, moves in this direction. A first step has been a wide distribution of ownership shares in the equity of privatized state enterprise.

The Role of Governments

Of course, no feasible organization of the nation's productive resources can fully succeed without good government; and indeed the achievement of greater harmony between labor, capital, and management, however arrived at, can only bear full fruit if the government pursues compatible macro and regulatory policies. If thought appropriate, these policies could embrace measures which encourage the setting up capital-labor partnerships, or their less formalized, less institutionalized analogues.

There is little dispute today that although most production should be left in the hands of the nongovernment private sector of the economy, and market forces should be allowed to determine in large part the allocation of resources and the distribution of output, there are some vital services that government must provide: defense, law and order, social infrastructure, education, and health. This does not preclude some contribution from the private sector, in particular in respect of health and education, but it is essential that, even in these areas, the government guarantees a minimum quality level to all the nation's citizens, irrespective of income and wealth. Indeed, a successful partnership between capital and labor, whether institutionalized or not, depends crucially on the existence of an educated and skilled labor force.

The role of the government goes beyond the provision of those social and public goods not sufficiently or equitably provided by the private market system. Previous sections of this book fully list the economic tasks of government, and it is difficult to add to them. Of key importance is the maintenance of macro-economic stability, particularly price stability, through appropriate fiscal and monetary policy. Governments can also help to promote economic growth through encouraging research in science and technology, and by investing in human capital (education) and physical infrastructure. They should aim at the removal of obstacles, to growth, such as unnecessary regulations and the power of entrenched interest groups. They have responsibilities for the protection of the environment, for the containment of social diseases such as crime, drugs, and violence as well as racial, ethnic, or religious bigotry. Of course, since it is a disgrace for any country which has achieved a reasonable level of production to permit extreme poverty, they must aim at mitigating this.

Greater Participation

Leaving all these responsibilities aside, there is one area which governments should encourage, namely greater participation in the productive process. This paper referred earlier to the need to promote a partnership between labor and capital, whether this is done on a formal institutionalized basis as proposed by Professor Meade, or through less formalized arrangements custom tailored by individual business enterprises. There is merit in encouraging the mass of the population to participate in the production process by being shareholders and property owners as well as the providers of skills and labor. This was Thatcher's intention in the United Kingdom, taking advantage of her government's decision to privatize substantial parts of British industry, formerly nationalized under previous governments. As indicted earlier in this paper, it is difficult to persuade ordinary laborers or workers to take a share in the risks of the enterprise in which they work, if their whole livelihood is dependent on the performance and prospects of that enterprise. A wider ownership of capital, which is invested in many enterprises—diversified risk bearing—should ease this problem. But how to achieve this? What can the government do?

The Importance of Savings

First, governments can encourage saving, particularly by people at the lower end of the income scale, since without saving, workers cannot accumulate capital and cannot reduce their dependence on earnings from a single enterprise or source. Thus governments should refrain from taxing saving, and tax consumption instead. The most efficient way to do this is by replacing taxes on income by a tax on expenditure. This is of course not a novel suggestion. The procedure would be to assess each taxpayer's income, to add to that sum the proceeds of any sales of the taxpayer's property and to subtract from that sum the cost of the acquisition of any new items of wealth. Tax would be levied on the amount resulting from that calculation. Tax would therefore have been levied on the *net* inflow of purchasing power to the individual which had been used to spend on consumption: net saving would be exempt from tax. There are administrative difficulties attached to this proposal which are greater when assessing the expenditure of richer income groups than with lower income groups; but they are not insuperable. In any case, what must also be taken into account is that a tax which falls wholly on expenditure and not on saving tends to increase the inequality of wealth distribution: the rich save more than the poor. This adds to the presumption that, even in the absence of an expenditure tax, forces operating in a free-market economy tend to make the rich richer and the poor possible poorer. Thus there is general agreement that if an expenditure tax is introduced in place of an income tax, it must be accompanied by a tax, preferably a low one, on all personal holdings of wealth above low exemption level, and also by some form of inheritance tax, that is, on the passing of large holdings of wealth from one owner to another on the occasion of death. Given these accompaniments to an expenditure tax, saving and wealth accumulation by the poorer members of society would be encouraged.

Fairness in Income Distribution

If the aim is to encourage citizens to participate more closely in the productive process and to bear part of the equity risk of the enterprise, it may also be necessary to provide them with some basic income which is unaffected by variations in remuneration from work or capital. This requirement underlies the proposal to pay every citizen a tax-free "social dividend," varying only with a citizen's age and family status. Such an unconditional social dividend has big advantages over a conditional benefit which, for example, may be withdrawn if an unemployed person finds work: if the benefit is withdrawn, there is less incentive for the unemployed to look for work. Unfortunately, a Social Dividend of this type unless paid at a very low rate places a substantial burden on the government's fiscal budget. It would almost certainly necessitate some income tax on higher income groups, in addition to both the expenditure tax and the tax on wealth. Of course, it would be a good deal easier if government had a source of income from natural resources, such as oil, which could be distributed equally across the community, providing a basic income for all.

Given existing inequalities in the distribution of physical and human capital, a redistributive tax is inevitable. Governments cannot avoid concerning themselves with the distribution of income between individuals. What is important is that they interfere as little as possible with the management of enterprises and with the basic distribution of income between labor and capital—by, for example, imposing direct control over the division between the return on capital and the earnings of labor, which would upset the efficient working of a competitive market economy. There will always be some trade off between a fairer distribution of income and wealth, promoted by a redistributive tax system, and the willingness of people to work and to undertake risk; because of this there will always be a trade off between equality and the rate of economic growth. Measures of this kind briefly sketched out in this paper should help to mitigate these trade offs, thereby promoting in the long run a higher level of income to be distributed, as well as a fairer distribution.

Conclusion

The world is seeking a new model of democratization and political opening—a model in sharp contrast to the one that was known in Eastern Europe and the former USSR. This new model necessitates that politics follows economics. The movement toward human rights and political participation can only be built on a strong foundation of economic stability. Energetic and prosperous business foundation and maximization of return on capital, technology, and human resources are absolutely essential for any democracy. However, no foundation could be lasting unless it is established on the basis of fairness of distribution of wealth and efficiency in allocating resources to meet the community's needs. Private ownership of business is a must but not without adherence to ground rules that ensure fair play.

Notes

1. J.E. Meade, *Agathotopia: The Economics of Partnership* (The David Hume Institute: Aberdeen University Press, 1989).

Section 4 · Global Change and Developing Countries

I.G. Patel

The aim of this book is to analyze dramatic ongoing worldwide changes in a variety of systems, and their possible impact on the lives of people. Clearly, the focus is on Eastern Europe and the former Soviet Union. This paper is intended to serve as a reminder that whether or not the second World is withering away, the Third World, alas, is very much alive. Not that the Third World is immune from the winds of change that cut across all nations. Nor even that it is all of one piece. "The happy families are all alike; but the unhappy ones are different—each in its own way." But change comes often to developing countries with a twist of its own; and the developing countries have some special concerns and constraints which need to be addressed, both nationally and internationally. This paper refers to only some of them which are particularly perplexing and which afflict many countries especially in Africa and Asia.

The "dramatic ongoing worldwide changes" should, I expect, include:

- the rapid pace of change, particularly of technological change;
- the shrinking of the world and the emergence of a global economy;
- the growing consensus on what economics is all about and heroic attempts to implement the same;
- the broadening of the democratic agenda and the reassertion of cultural, ethnic, and religious identities; and
- the groping towards "Global Governance" or a "New International Order."

These changes are, of course, interrelated and impact differently at different points on the globe; and there indeed is the rub.

Technological Change

Perhaps the most far-reaching changes in the world today are the product of the rapid pace of technological innovations. It is technology, rather than capital, that is the engine of growth as well as international competitive power. Matched only by the pace of technological change is its diversity and complexity. Computers, information technology, communications systems, biotechnology, and material science have wide-ranging applications and require a high degree of skill for absorption, let alone innovation. While developing countries have benefited from the new technologies, there is no doubt that the current wave of technological advance puts most of the developing countries at a serious disadvantage. It is not just that some of their traditional strengths, like commodity production and even textiles, are being undermined. They tend also to lose competitiveness steadily and over a wide range, particularly when they do not command scarce natural resources such as oil and timber. The specter of being marginalized internationally and of falling progressively behind other countries is all too real for many developing countries. The fact that many other factors, including internal strife, contribute to this outcome does not negate the role of uneven technical progress.

The travails of uneven technological progress are even greater internally. To some extent, even a poor country can absorb modern technology: particularly, by creating a hospitable climate for private foreign investment. But it is not easy to apply such technology across the whole range of production even in a given industry (e.g. textiles); and what we often witness is a "dual economy" or the existence side-by-side of "two nations"—one comparatively well-off, urban, coastal, and organized and the other poor, rural, in the interior, and unorganized. The spread of modern technology often has to be tempered to avoid mass unemployment and social unrest. But this can only be done by losing in international competitive power. The dilemma is all too real; and democratic societies, particularly fledgling democracies, find it difficult to resolve it. It is not an accident that societies that have found it possible so far to resolve this conflict—or at least to make people accept the growing chasm between them—have been by and large authoritarian (such as China or Chile in the recent past).

There is another dimension to the disadvantage that technology increasingly brings to the developing countries. The spread of communications and the impact of television and other media. Envy, social discontent, and a destructive sense of humiliation are the other by-products of our unequal world which nevertheless holds before us all strong mirrors in which everyone and everything is visible to each of us. Visibly at least, the world is already globalized. For those who are marginalized in every other way, this is a terrible fate. They cannot hide their shame even in the privacy of their own shacks and shanty towns. This sense of humiliation and alienation is at the root of the much greater violence internally in many developing countries, accompanied often by a throwback to some real or imaginary past and to fundamentalism of one kind or another. It takes political maturity and statesmanship of a very high order—qualities which, alas, are rare everywhere—to steer many developing societies from this suicidal path. While the poor cannot throw stones at the rich across national borders, they do attempt something similar through subversive activities or attempted migration or resort to illegal activities like trafficking in drugs which undermine the rich societies as well. It would, of course, be simplistic to think that extreme inequalities driven by technology are at the root of everything that is debilitating and destructive in many poor countries. But the link is strong and not easy to sever.

What can be done to alleviate the situation? The rapid spread of education—not just primary, but secondary as well—will help expedite the absorption of modern technologies even among the poorest countries. The UNDP and all institutions engaged in technical assistance can play a more imaginative role. Universities in the rich countries can spend more time on research relevant to the poor. They can certainly reverse the recent trend of looking upon higher education as something to export to the highest bidder rather than a sacred trust to be transmitted to all those who can benefit from it irrespective of their means.

Surely, the recent trend to seek to limit the access to new technology by poor countries by taking a narrow commercial view of intellectual property rights and to impose this view by unilateral sanctions is not in keeping with the true spirit of international cooperation in an unequal world. Technology for better health and agriculture at least was regarded till recently as internationally free goods to be shared as widely as possible; and scientists prided themselves on their code of behavior which insisted that the results of their research should be freely available to everyone. The case for patents is well understood. But it does not have to be pressed too far. While poor countries can be bribed or bullied into acceptance of anything, such acceptance would be grudging at best and will be circumvented sooner rather than later, creating much discord and misunderstanding. Is it then not at least in keeping with so much talk of reviving ethics in business that business itself recognizes the need to address the technological needs of the poor countries differently?

In fact, in matters of trade policy also, the need for protecting some industries, maintaining restrictions on luxury imports, imposing heavy customs duties on such imports, and restricting foreign direct investment in areas of conspicuous consumption cannot be disregarded. No single set of simple rules can be imposed on all irrespective of the differences in their needs and circumstances. Unfortunately, much of the recent arm twisting in international negotiations—with the connivance and support of the international bureaucracy—will give yet another push towards marginalization of many developing countries.

A Globalized World Economy

The propositions in the preceding section are not, of course, an argument for autarky or against growing integration of the economy of each country into the emerging world economy. The trend towards globalization in this large sense is both beneficial and irreversible. But this trend is not without contradictions and qualifications which put developing countries at some disadvantage.

The most glaring contradiction relates to migration. We pride ourselves on belonging to an era which puts men rather than things at the center of things. And yet, while natural resources, goods, and capital are supposed to have the whole world as their playground, it is people who have to be confined to their birthplace—a truly undeserved curse or privilege, if ever there is any. Even limited and time-bound migration related to trade and investment from developing countries is not agreed to by countries that wax eloquent over the virtues of free trade and about extending them to the sphere of services and investment. Why should it not be possible for the Chinese or the Indians to set up any business they like, say, in Italy with the import of labor from their own countries on terms that correspond to their realities rather than the realities of countries much richer than themselves?

There is much talk these days of multinational firms becoming truly international, getting increasingly detached from the mother country and setting up shop for spare parts or even finished products elsewhere not just for local consumption but for exports as well, and employing at least skilled staff from all over the world. This is certainly a welcome trend which has contributed to a more hospitable climate everywhere for private direct investment. But the trend needs to go much further. The developing countries welcome such investment not just as a source of capital and technology. They are interested also in the avenues such investment provide for export of services as well as goods. It is here that apart from the prejudice against import of services in the form of human beings, there are other constraints of a legal and psychological nature. The Chinese and the Indians can hold high positions in, say, Siemens or General Electric, in Nigeria or even Malaysia. But they will seldom reach the higher echelons of management in the United States or in Germany—however capable they are.

It hardly needs to be argued that the globalization of capital flows is but an empty dream for many developing countries. This may be the fault of nobody. But if it is an unsatisfactory state of affairs, one has to ask what we are prepared to do about it. Unfortunately, it has to be said that the sentiment for international cooperation—and for grants and concessional aid, in particular—has waned precisely when there has been more talk of a global economy. Indeed, the retreat from state intervention and the growing emphasis on markets and individual responsibility—valid as they are—have become excuses for neglecting national and international obligations which still remain relevant. The safety nets, to use the current jargon, have to spread not just over each nation but have to be extended across nations. Such sentiments, unfortunately, are on the retreat with an enormous cost in suffering however confined it may be.

Even in regard to trade, not all those who talk loudest of free trade are in favor in practice of even fair trade. Apart from glaring examples of protection of agriculture, textiles, leather goods, and many other labor-intensive products in developed countries, the developing countries are not well equipped to protect themselves against dumping or excessive pricing and even fraud in respect of their imports. They need much greater technical assistance in this area if they are to have a better bargaining power than most of them possess at present.

The growing attempts at regional integration across the world provide yet another qualification or contradiction in respect of a globalized world economy. Economists may well argue that such regional integration could be a step towards greater globalization and that the trade creating effects of regional integration may be greater than the trade diverting effects. But this does not negate a number of uncomfortable aspects. First of all, the drive towards regional integration is often driven by competitive considerations, thus implying and admitting that such integration can be a threat to those left out and unable to pose a similar threat. This would be all well if the whole world could be carved out into three or four regional blocs of more or less even strength. But as things are, most countries in Africa, the Middle East, and South Asia have little hope of joining any powerful bloc, thus adding to the threat of their marginalization.

If experience is any guide, successful regional cooperative efforts, such as in Europe, have not refrained from discrimination against some developing countries in favor of others—picking and choosing special friends for political rather than economic reasons. As for trade-creating effects being on par with trade-diverting effects, the assumption is surely not right when there is every likelihood that trade creation would take place within and trade diversion without. How to bring regional integration efforts under some international control and supervision and how to ensure that orphans are adopted by the strong and the powerful across the board internationally or are otherwise armed with equal bargaining power are some of the major challenges that arise from current trends or changes which have a mixed driving force.

New Economic Policies

There is now growing consensus everywhere on what economic policy is all about and what makes for economic growth or prosperity everywhere. In response to this consensus, wide-ranging structural and institutional reforms are being undertaken in the Third as well as the Second World. Although the final jury is still out, the tentative verdict is in favor of sound macroeconomic policies which include reduction in budget deficits and realistic exchange rates and interest rates; a shift from public to private ownership; a shift away from government controls and direction to markets; elimination of subsidies and administered prices and generally allowing prices to respond to supply and demand so that they allocate resources efficiently; a greater integration with world markets in goods, services, and capital; and aligning domestic tax rates and other policy instruments increasingly to norms that prevail elsewhere to eliminate distortions and provide a level playing field to domestic producers as well as a favorable climate for foreign direct investment. Of late, there is greater readiness to incorporate in the agenda concern for the weak and for others adversely affected. They should, it is agreed, be protected by "safety nets" and indeed by making equity considerations an integral part of the adjustment program itself. While this agenda is broadly accepted more or less universally, there are important qualifications that need to be made from the point of view of many developing countries—some of which have relevance even for the Second World.

Although there is broad agreement on the economic agenda, that leaves out many questions of speed, sequencing, priorities and preconditions, and indeed political feasibility which admit of no simple or universal answers. These have to be resolved as best as one can in each individual ease. The trouble, however, is that developing countries are at a disadvantage in arguing with international institutions and donors generally about what is right and what is not at any given time in their own circumstances. They lack, first of all, the complex skills required for alternative modelling so that often they can pitch only their hunches and judgments against the elaborate calculations of donor institutions. There is urgent need here again for imaginative and disinterested technical assistance. Second and no less important, the benefit of doubt generally goes to those who crack the whip rather than to those who suffer the consequences and are ultimately responsible to public opinion. When there is now so much agreement on basic issues, a little more forbearance and persistence on the part of the international community will be very rewarding. This forbearance is most needed in regard to overcrowding the agenda of conditionalities and overburdening it with sudden-death staging posts.

Again, although it is recognized that structural adjustment is a shared responsibility, external help is often halting and inadequate. The task in most countries is very difficult and it certainly can be eased by larger and better international support, for example by lowering the charges of the International Monetary Fund (IMF), enlarging the concessional windows and keeping them open for a longer period and generally urging donors towards more generous debt relief and concessional finance.

Structural adjustment without tears is also often not a practical proposition, however, desirable it may be. The safety net is often riddled with big holes or does not hold up at all. It is easy to recommend that food subsidies should be reduced and better targeted. The latter often remains a fond hope; and if taken seriously, it can become an administrative nightmare. One has only to imagine a vast army of local functionaries administering a means test for workers in the informal sector to realize this. The consequence is that lower subsidies win and targeting remains on paper and some of the poor suffer. The same is true of pious hopes of retraining those thrown out of employment. Indeed, even the hopes of increasing international competitive power as a result of more competition and deregulation can be—and often are—exaggerated. The point is not that the remedies can be avoided. But there can be harm in maintaining that the medicine will not be bitter or that it will work quite soon. Attempts at reform which fail because they take inadequate account of inherent difficulties dissipate the very scarce resource of national resolve.

Initial conditions also matter a great deal more than is commonly realized. That is one reason why China, for example, has managed the transition better than more active democracies. It is also one reason why reform in general should be easier in the Second World than in the Third. Despite all the criticism of Communist regimes that is well-deserved, it cannot be said that they delivered higher and more equal incomes than prevail in most of the Third World; and both these facts—greater initial equality and incomes well above subsistence levels, not to mention higher educational standards—put the Second World in a far more enviable position than the Third in absorbing the shocks of adjustment.

Countries of the First World do protect the incomes of some deserving classes like the unemployed and even of some not-so-deserving such as the farmers. For many poor countries, a similar framework for security is not possible without international support. But there is reluctance to extend internationally what is accepted nationally, such as greater stability in primary prices. In fact, adjustment to periodic external shocks—higher oil prices or low commodity prices—still remains a very formidable problem for many developing countries and compounds the difficulties of adjustment to correct wrong domestic policies. Here again, international action to reduce external shocks—or to limit the damage they cause—has been woefully inadequate.

Particular caution needs to be urged about the recommendation that developing countries should reform their tax structure and other policies to correspond as closely as possible with those in developed countries to eliminate distortions and to provide a level playing field to exporters and a favorable climate for foreign direct investment. Given a narrow tax base, most developing countries can hardly afford to have very low customs duties or more or less uniform internal taxes on all items of consumption. Nor is it prudent to suggest that the highest marginal rate of income tax in India, for example, should be 25 percent just because the United Kingdom aspires to it. Economic policy is never about perfection. There are always side effects and multiple objectives. All of us have to be content with the second-best and even with the third-best; and there is no ostensible reason why geese should pretend to be swans.

Of all the items on the economic agenda, sound macroeconomic policies including sensible exchange rate and interest rate policies are perhaps the least contested now. But it would be wrong to think that there can be similar agreement or policy precision when it comes to other items on the list, such as public ownership and privatization, or government intervention versus markets, or integration into the global economy versus some protection or control versus decontrol. These are not issues where either/or has much practical validity. Both often have to be well blended and the real issues are, say, about how and where to intervene rather than whether to intervene, how to make markets work rather than just make them legally free, how to create genuine accountability in large enterprises, both public and private rather than merely replace one set of bureaucrats by another. Nor can one overlook the obvious need for supervision, monitoring, transparent rules and regulations, promotional research, extension and provision of information and education, and even of a measure of guidance given, albeit, by financial incentives or advice rather than by command or prescription.

The point is that one need not oversimplify issues as if the choice is between two simple opposites. One is really concerned with a complex and multiple set in which a proper blend, willingness to change it in the light of experience, transparency and evenhandedness in judgment and decisions, and statesmanship to keep within check unavoidable conflicts between group and group are far more important than any theoretical model or half-baked assumptions or assertions about human nature or about the nature of societies, economies, and polities. Undoubtedly, there are some constants in all these. But they all come with a twist and contain conflicting elements. Even capitalism comes in many flavors so that the search for an end to history—even if property rights were the only constituent of history—is nothing short of historical ignorance of the most colossal dimensions. These days, when there is much dogmatism and fundamentalism about economic policy all around, one cannot emphasize too strongly that no ship of state in this work-a-day world can be put on any kind of automatic pilot for long. There are rules that must be known and followed. But there is no escape from being buffeted by a sea of change, which never reveals all its secrets to any one.

Dimensions of Democracy

An economist perhaps should not dabble in political philosophy. But briefly, there are some dimensions of current democratic strivings which seem to have great significance for the developing countries. We take for granted now the desirability of the democratic form of government—a government elected by the people and which can be sent packing home if the electorate so desires at least at periodic intervals. But there is tension nowadays about how far the writ of the majority should run. The concern for human rights and minority rights is an expression of this tension. At the level of fundamentals one can perhaps agree what human or individual rights and minority rights might constitute. But where does one draw the line between what the majority might legitimately want and what it should not transcend?

It is an irony of life that those most vocal about freedom in economic matters are the most authoritarian when it comes to social and other norms. Margaret Thatcher did say "there is no such thing as society." She meant, of course, that there are only individuals. But did she really? Do people of her persuasion believe in limiting the power of the politicians in social matters? This is really the crux of fundamentalism. For people of that persuasion, some things are non-negotiable and can be imposed on others if only the majority so wishes. Those who demur are permissive and aid the dissolution of society—or perhaps, they would prefer to say, the decline of the nation.

There is at least some truth in the proposition that nation-building and national effort require some common core of a national ethos. The absolutists or fundamentalists have a point when they argue that everything cannot be relative or determined by each of us. If counting of heads is not the best way of deciding, at least for the moment what might be of abiding value, what is? And yet, how certain can anyone be about their own convictions? The right balance between purpose and tolerance is a challenge few emerging countries can meet sensibly.

Do nations have a purpose other than that of each of its citizens? There is no simple answer to this question. In a world where nations went to war almost at will, it was easy to think so. Today they seem to want to go to war with every one economically if not militarily. Does that establish an overriding national purpose which can circumscribe individual rights? Are countries that favor curbs on trade unions but encourage business conglomerates necessarily on the road to a fascist dictatorship? Or are they, with a pinch of authoritarianism, sweetening the whole glass for everyone in the end?

Similar questions arise on minority rights and these have now been brought to a head in many countries where minorities insist not just on rights but on having a state of their own. In a world where there is no escape from different religions and ethnic or linguistic groups living together as best as they can, what is the justification for secession of any kind when history shows that it only spreads the strife rather than ends it? There is also the point recognized in the Helsinki declaration that the rights of self-determination of minorities must be circumscribed by the interests of the majority. But who is to judge who is reasonable in any given situation? What degree of local self-government is consistent both with minority or regional rights and national purpose? We live in a world where existing federal states are threatened with disintegration when others are trying to come together in new federations. What is one to encourage?

These conflicting dimensions of democracy are obviously not just matters of philosophical curiosity. The trouble is they are a reality largely in the Second and the Third World where they are already engulfing large sections of society into violent and suicidal conflict and are tempting the First World to be sucked in as well. While we talk so much of change—and some even of end of history—the trouble seems to be that history refuses to go away and some things simply do not seem to change. The conflict is particularly destructive for the poor and cries out for a sensible and durable solution. The $64 million question now is: Can this be resolved without external intervention? Can such intervention be truly disinterested? Or do these conflicts have to take their own awesome toll and come to a halt only out of sheer exhaustion of one party or the other?

The broadening of the democratic dimension is not con fined just to individual or minority or regional rights. There is also the demand for more active and regular participation in the affairs of the state to get over the sense of alienation that comes when democracy manifests itself concretely only in elections the results of which seldom have sufficient clarity or a sense of direction. Even minority governments claim the right to settle everything and the citizen feels helpless. Not all democratically elected governments can claim to be legitimate. This is yet another reason for the disquiet and even violence in many developing countries.

Conclusion

The end of the Cold War has not brought an end to wars and violence. In some parts, it has led to more violence and even wars. There have been other factors—including growing inequalities among and within nations—which have also unleashed new forces of conflict and violence, particularly in the developing countries. The general atmosphere of change has given a fresh lease of life to all hatreds and prejudices and revived memories of past cruelty and injustice whether real or imagined. Democracy does not necessarily dissolve these passions and conflicts. In one sense, therefore, the purely negative case for greater global governance has become stronger of late. The balance of terror between superpowers which produced peace of sorts has been replaced by the proliferation of terror which is all but peaceful. Apart from national statesmanship—and even as an aid to it—is there a role for some step forward in global governance?

In addition, there are, of course, the more positive opportunities that have been opened up by technical and other progress for fruitful and mutually rewarding international economic cooperation in trade, services, investment, and technology transfer as also in arts and culture and education. The problem here is not one of altogether new initiatives or of setting up new institutions. It is a tribute to the foresight of the generation that came to power at the end of the war that such institutions are already on the ground. The problem is to make them more effective and democratic—effective, in particular, in advancing the cause of the poorer developing countries. I have no answer except to say that every avenue for greater and more equitable global governance must be explored. The time is perhaps ripe what with the end of the Cold War, the prospect of environmental degradation and even global disasters, the wide spread fear of fundamentalism of all kinds and of terror that strikes increasingly at random everywhere and the possibilities that are opened up by technology and the consensus on economic matters. The approach of the 50th anniversary of the United Nations should act as an additional spur to introspection and concerted action.

Although I have hardly the competence to attempt any blueprint of global governance, one point that is central to this paper cannot be overemphasized. No authority—national or international—can be truly effective in an enduring way unless it can command a certain degree of legitimacy; and in this day and age, power is not the source of legitimacy anywhere. Apart from superior knowledge and persuasion, legitimacy requires a certain commonality of concern for the well-being of everyone, particularly of those on the lower rungs of fortune. This is true as much internationally as it is nationally. No global agency, whether under the umbrella of the UN or not, can focus exclusively on political or security problems to the neglect of the social and economic ones without losing the allegiance of people. The talk of a "new international order" today is not convincing because it comes essentially from people who only the other day laughed out of court the demand for a "new international economic order." But the striving and the need for a new international economic order will not go away. Short of attending to this need seriously and with sufficient will, resources, forbearance, and foresight, any move forward towards global governance would always smack of a new colonialism. A political G-7 is no less a combine than an economic G-7. It may be tolerated but never obeyed except under duress and certainly not respected. As such, it will always be under threat of being undermined. That can hardly be a good augury for any new order.

Section 5 · Is the Developed World Ceasing to Be an Engine of Growth?

Göran Ohlin

When the talk is about economic and political reform in developing countries, or more recently in Eastern Europe and the successor states of the Soviet Union, it tends to be assumed that the West, with its remarkable economic and political achievements, has the answers. With remarkable confidence, advice is dispensed throughout the world. Although warning voices always recall problems of historical tradition and cultural diversity, they are silenced by the massive *rayonnement* of the industrial countries, self-satisfied and confident in their superiority.

Weakness of Industrialized Market Economies

But are the industrial countries of today undisputed models? Obviously not. Leaving aside the esoteric debates about their cultural shortcomings, it is enough to note the weakness of their economic performance over a long period and the dramatic rise of poverty, crime, drug abuse, and ethnic tension. These fuel the domestic debate in most of these countries today, and they underlie the crisis of confidence in their political establishments which they share in varying degrees and which poses serious questions for democratic governance.

Many people in developing countries or in Eastern Europe simply do not want to hear that there are problems in the promised land and find it difficult to understand why the richest countries in the world suddenly act so poor. But there obviously have been very profound changes in the industrial world in the last decades, and they are nowhere more obvious then in their economic policies.

The commitment to full employment after World War II is gone, and so is full employment. Growth has shrivelled, and so have ambitions. Government are satisfied to have GNP keep up with population growth, and declines in GNP and living standards are met with Puritanical exhortations: present pain for future gain, a worthy sacrifice, and the like. Containing inflation is often said to be a primary objective—once achieved, it is hoped that the growth process will start up again.

This short note is not the place to discuss the reasons why economic performance and economic policy have changed to radically in the rich countries of the world. They are complex and controversial, and some of the most important ones, such as the reasons for the slow productivity growth that set in in the 1970s, are simply not well understood.

A New Objective: Pleasing the Market

The controversies between Keynesian and monetarists were entertaining a decade ago but both camps are neglected today. Thatcherism and Reaganomics may seem to have been more influential in their antigovernment and antitax thrust, and historians will have an interesting time with that. But what really changed the industrial world most was the globalization of the financial markets. that, in turn, was driven by technology rather than ideology. Direct dialing and computer technology broke down governments' attempts to maintain foreign exchange controls, as at the same time they were committed to openness in trade and travel. Remarkably little fanfare is made of the opening up of the world to direct dialing and satellite communication, but it brought globalization, for better or worse.

For governments, this has created a totally new environment. They not only have to please their voters, they have to please "the market" as well. They have to establish "credibility" to attract or retain funds. The "market" to which governments pay obeisance is a nebulous force in the world economy. In its immediate apparition it consists of some 2,000 young men in front of their Reuter screens in the principal banks around the world who make instant decisions based on the news of the day. it is my impression that they are programmed to react negatively to any suggestion of government activism and spending and that they constitute a formidable army making for continued stagnation in the world economy.

It is sometimes heard that central banks today lack the resources to compete with the enormous financial markets of today, which are often misleadingly measured in terms of their impressive turnover. This is obviously a serious delusion. If governments wished to control money markets, they alone have the unlimited resources that are needed to force markets into line, and there would not even be any of the present games of testing them. There has been some talk about the need for an "anchor" in the exchange markets and the monetary system, but without joint determination on the part of governments there obviously will not be one.

Conclusion

It is paradoxical that the opening of trade and financial markets in the last decades has been accompanied by a stagnation that so clearly marks a break in the growth of the industrial world. It will not last forever. The historical surge of the past is likely to reassert itself, but the world has changed in more ways than Kondratieff could ever imagine, and we are on our own in trying to fathom what the future may hold. What has happened once more in the economic history of the world is that economic space has outrun political boundaries, and it may be some time before they are again brought in rough congruence.

At the time when Western countries made their decisive leap into industrialization, things were very different, and so were their policies. Today their experts have little historical awareness, and it is left to Japan to point out, in the World Bank and elsewhere, that the policy confusions of postindustrial societies may not be the best guides for preindustrial countries.

Chapter 2 · Global Support for Development

Section 1 · New Environment for International Aid

Alexander Love

As we all know, the world has embarked on a remarkable transformation since the end of the Cold War. Changes have been dramatic not only in the countries of Eastern Europe and the former Soviet Union, but also in the countries that comprise what has been traditionally regarded as the developing world.

There is clearly a new environment for development assistance. There is also an urgent need for basic rethinking with respect to the world's future development agenda by donor and recipient countries alike. All development organizations—bilateral, multilateral, public, and private—have a key responsibility in this task. Today, citizens in many of the major donor countries are raising basic concerns over the desirability and effectiveness of development aid. Recent economic problems and related unemployment at home have heighten these questions.

Some Important Questions

In this context, we need to ask some basic questions:

- How will the nature of development assistance needs change in coming years?
- What are the comparative priorities between assisting Eastern Europe and the former Soviet Union and continuing assistance to the traditional developing countries in Africa, Asia, and Latin America?
- What are the global development challenges that are shared by developed and developing countries alike; the environment, migration, refugees, drugs, international health problems such as AIDS?
- How do these global priorities mesh with traditional aid objectives?
- To what extent do these global challenges demand greater resources?

Past Motivations

Motivations for supporting development assistance in the past have been driven by three primary concerns: the desire to pursue security objectives, most notably in the case of the United States program; broad programs aimed at promoting basic development and meeting related humanitarian assistance needs; and pursuit of commercial objectives. These three motivations in many cases overlapped in specific assistance programs.

With the end of the Cold War, the rationale for security assistance programs, including support for military base access, has substantially decreased, although not disappeared. Commercial concerns continue to be a major consideration in a variety of donor programs. The are likely to remain so in the foreseeable future.

New Opportunities

On balance, the changed world environment presents an opportunity for increasing support to meet basic development assistance objectives. Resources freed by the end of the Cold War and by resolution of civil conflict can be rechanneled to meet more basic development needs. Decreased defense expenditures in donor countries could allow for a shift in resources to meet the demand for assistance programs—including demands in Eastern Europe and the former Soviet Union.

Within the developing countries, there are at least three major changes taking place that are of key significance: there is a marked shift away from state planning and state-dominated economies toward the market economy; there is a growing movement toward more democratic and more open pluralistic systems, a change that is taking place in Africa, Latin America, and Asia as well as Eastern Europe; and there has been encouraging movement toward resolution of civil and regional conflicts in some of the traditional developing countries and many that were in the past encouraged by Cold War competition. Included here are Ethiopia, Angola, Indochina, Central America, and most recently Afghanistan. Progress, however, is still fragile. Hopefully we will soon see some progress in Mozambique. Unfortunately Somalia, Sudan, and Liberia continue as areas of Africa where internal strife has led to great human suffering; and events in Eastern Europe and the former Soviet Union show a propensity for civil strife.

Taken together, however, theses changes offer hope for substantial improvement in both the economic and political conditions in the developing countries.

The Role of Development Assistance

How can Development Assistance help in this new world environment? There have been some substantial achievements in developing countries since the end of World War II. Life expectancy has increased markedly, infant mortality has dropped, literacy rates are up, and a substantial group of former developing countries—especially in East Asia—have rapidly increased their per capita gross national product. Some are now actively considering joining the Organization for Economic Cooperation and Development (OECD) as member countries. Others in sub-Saharan Africa, by comparison, have stagnated and declined in many aspects since independence, although even there life expectancy, health, and educational levels have improved markedly. Ironically, these advances have helped fuel the population explosion in Africa in the process.

What are some of the lessons evident from the successes of past development, and how might they be applied to development challenges today?

Lessons from a recent conference on Asia's successes include a number of key ingredients:

1. a heavy investment in human capital, in education and literacy, in improving health conditions, and in working on the related problem of reducing family size with the help of liberal population policies;
2. emphasis on education which contributed to an educated labor force and a well-trained bureaucracy and policy makers;
3. maintaining macroeconomic stability, controlling budget deficits and inflation, and managing a predictable exchange regime;
4. recognition and support for the key role of the private sector and market forces, even in cases where a large public sector existed;
5. in countries other than the city-states—Hong Kong, Singapore, among others—a strong investment in agriculture as a leading sector, with major investment support in rural infrastructure; and
6. a long-term planning perspective and consistency in policies.

With real progress in many of the traditional developing countries, the once seemingly clear distinction between North and South is also becoming very blurred. There is now a wide variability in levels of development among "developing: countries ranging from the poorest sub-Saharan African to the dynamic Asian economies. Individual regions, such as sub-Saharan Africa, share common characteristics and differ markedly from problems and conditions in Latin America and Asia. sub-Saharan Africa will stand out as a special long-term challenge to development efforts. The emergence of the Eastern bloc and former Soviet Union countries as development assistance claimants rather than as donors has further blurred the picture.

New Environment for Development Assistance

I highlight these points to further underline the fact that the environment we will be operating in the 1990s and beyond will be substantially different from what we faced during the last 30 to 40 years. During that period, development agencies were heavily influenced by the Cold War confrontation. The Cold War has now ended. While that change brings with it new problems, we are looking at a world in which there is a welcome movement toward more open democratic systems, a concern for improved governance, by strengthening the public sector and reducing its role, and a greater desire to rely on the market economy. There is also an important opportunity to reduce the heavy level of military expenditure in the developed and developing countries.

How have the members of the Development Assistance Committee responded to these changing conditions? The DAC members contributed a level of official development assistance which reached $58 billion in 1991. This represents an increase of 2 percent in real terms from 1990. This is fairly consistent with the growth rate over the last decade of 2.5 percent in real terms. The contribution approximated 0.35 percent, half the long established UN target of 0.7 percent GNP. It is worth noting that official development assistance contributions have stayed steady at about 0.35 percent for the last two decades. In the current economic environment in DAC member countries, it is unlikely that increases in the next few years will substantially exceed past trends.

It is also important to underline that development assistance contributions from the former Soviet Union and Eastern Europe which once totaled $4 billion have essentially evaporated. In addition, the once large contributions from the Arab countries have substantially diminished and how have leveled off. The DAC member countries therefore remain the primary contributors of Official Development Assistance (ODA).

In this setting, members of the Development Assistance Committee are understandably concerned about assuring that the competition for resources in Eastern Europe and the former Soviet Union do not substantially divert resources from the traditional developing countries where the growing opportunities present increased requirement for ODA.

Diminishing Development Resources

The growing capital demands in Eastern Europe an the former Soviet Union, growing requirements for resettlement of refugees and development priorities within Indochina, Southern Africa, the Horn, and Afghanistan will all substantially increase demand on limited development resource. The environmental or "green increment" from the Rio Conference was large. Yet current prospects for increases in Official Development Assistance are dim. If anything, pressures in many countries are pushing in the opposite direction. What can be done to change the public attitude toward development assistance? What other steps can be taken to increase resource flows, that is, increase export earnings through greater market access for the developing countries, increasing the flow of private foreign investment, encourage repatriation of flight capital, and reducing military expenditures in both donor and recipient countries.

The above five themes are clearly not all of the major problems we may face. But they are key priorities currently being reviewed at the DAC and within OECD generally. As to the future prospects for Official Development Assistance flows, one needs to take into account the present pattern of around $60 billion a year. In my view the salient features for the years to come are the following:

1. I foresee only a gradual growth in official assistance levels in the next few years at a rate of roughly 2 percent in real terms.
2. There will be increased competition among the traditional developing countries for these concessional resources as new claimants join the queue and as traditional concessional resource flows from Eastern Europe and Arab countries decrease or disappear.

3. The countries of Eastern Europe and the former Soviet Union will continue to exert strong competition for all public sector resources including concessional assistance in the near future.
4. The next few years will also witness continuing rethinking of Development Assistance rationales in the post-Cold War world. This has been especially true in the United States following the November 1992 elections, but will occur in many other member countries as well.
5. Japan will continue to be a major potential source for substantial increases in the ODA in the next few years.

Conclusion

This scenario highlights the competitive scenario for the allocation of concessional resources within the developing world. Donors will increasingly have to decide which categories of countries are most deserving of concessional assistance. There will be a need to rethink sector allocations of development assistance. Greater attention to the efficiency of resource utilization will be more essential than ever.

DAC members will need to carefully coordinate their activities during the next few years. The rapidly changing world environment, the increasingly competitive nature of developing aid, and the rethinking process on aid objectives and aid rationale make coordination even more critical in the coming years.

Because concessional development assistance flows will not be adequate to meet demands, attention will have to be given to other critical areas such as trade and private flows. This will require greater attention to improving coherence of policies within the DAC member governments. Improved trade access could increase developing country earnings by an additional $55 billion per year. Together with existing ODA levels, the combined total resource flow of trade and aid would equal 0.7 percent of GNP—the long-standing UN target. Private flows in turn also approximate $55 billion per year and have great potential for future increases.

Overall, the world faces unprecedented new opportunities to help shape a future of nations that are increasingly democratic and free-market oriented—ingredients that will enhance the prospects of peace and prosperity for the future generations of *all* the world.

Section 2 · Developing Countries and Transition Countries[1]

Makoto Taniguchi

The impact of the easing of East-West tensions and the end of the Cold War on the economies of developing countries varies considerably depending on their stages of development and the economic, social, and cultural differences of each country. Therefore, global support for their development efforts may vary.

Dynamic Asian Economies

The Dynamic Asian Economies (DAEs), as OECD calls them, or the Newly Industrialized Countries of the South (NICS), include the Republic of Korea, Hong Kong, Malaysia, Singapore, Taiwan, and Thailand. The deep political changes referred to above, and the dramatic transformation from command economic systems to market economies taking place in the Central and Eastern European countries and former Soviet Union, have not inflicted any serious damage on the economies of the DAEs. On the contrary, these changes have provided a further stimulus for the strengthening of their market and privatization processes.

In the 1980s, the DAEs emerged as key players at the global level, and became the OECD countries' most important economic partners in the non-OECD area. For example: over the past two decades, GDP and exports of the DAEs have grown twice as quickly as those of the OECD, and these high growth rates are projected to continue during the next few years. As a result, percapital incomes in several DAEs have risen to OECD levels. GDP per capita in Singapore and Hong Kong is around the same level as in Ireland, New Zealand, and Spain. Taiwan and Korea are comparable to Greece and Portugal.

Lessons for Countries in Transition

The countries of Central and Eastern Europe and the former Soviet Union can draw important lessons from the positive and negative experiences of DAEs for the integration of their economies into the global market economy.

The DAEs have, in the space of a few decades, transformed themselves from agricultural-based economies into industrialized economies, albeit at different stages of development, and in the cases of Hong Kong and Singapore into increasingly service-based economies. The principal factors which ensured their remarkable achievements include:

1. sustained political and macroeconomic stability; social and political commitment to growth-oriented policies; and sound policies in the areas of human resource development and infrastructure;

2. outward orientation of policies and, over the last decade, growing liberalization in trade, investment, and other policies; a capacity of DAE exporters to exploit "product niches" in overseas markets; strong entrepreneurial skills, developed in competitive domestic markets;
3. favorable international economic environment and the open multilateral trading system
4. foreign direct investment, which played a key role through the transfer of technology and market know-how, and also through the competitive stimulus provided to local markets; a strong capacity to adapt and adjust by governments, business sector and the community more generally.

This seemingly simple concept of adaptability and adjustability calls for some elaboration because it is very important. All economies, and the world economy more generally, are in a constant state of change. This has been particularly the case of the DAEs as they have transformed themselves into dynamic exporters of manufactured products. However, in their rapid development, the DAEs have shown great strength in their capacity to adapt and adjust to this change. For example, there are many examples of where DAE governments, particularly Korea and Taiwan, have been willing and able to adjust policies in response to external shocks and to changing circumstances. Both countries succeeded in overcoming two oil shocks by changing their energy consumption patterns rapidly, while other developing countries were unable to do so. Also, Korea in particular, was able to expand its trade to the Japanese market and other markets when the Japanese Yen was revalued. This has been in sharp contrast, until more recent times, with the countries of Latin America. The majority of Latin American countries stuck to the "import substitution policy" in the 1970s and the 1980s, while many Asian countries shifted their policies from "import substitution policy" to "export based development policy" in the same period, adjusting their policies to the changing world economic conditions. As a result, Asian countries in general were able to expand their trade to the U.S. market while Latin American countries were not. DAE business sectors have been willing to adapt products to changing market circumstances and seek out new markets. With the strong advances in the DAEs, this has included the impressive upgrading of their products and the development of product niches. Just one example of this adaptability is that, over the last three years, with the opening up of the Central and Eastern European countries, DAE trade with those countries has risen from $2 billion to over $5 billion. DAE populations have also responded positively to, rather than resisted, change.

However, one must be careful in drawing prescriptions for the Central and Eastern European countries from the experience of the DAEs. While the DAEs have been very successful in their development process, not all of their economic or social policies have been rewarding. The inward-looking policies of certain

DAEs in the 1960s and 1970s have, in fact, had certain negative impacts. This is now the case for the Central and Eastern European countries as they undertake the dramatic transformation from command systems to market economies. It is also difficult to transfer their overall development strategies because of political, economic, and cultural differences, particularly when the starting points are so different. In addition, the international economic environment is now fundamentally different from when the DAEs were "taking off." Whether the economic success of the DAEs can be repeated, is debatable. In their transformation from a command system to a market economy system, the many factors mentioned earlier are clearly important for the Central and Eastern European countries. But above all, change and transformation depends on the capacity and willingness to adjust and adapt.

Developing Countries

At the end of the Cold War, there was fear on the part of some developing countries that donors' incentive to increase ODA for developing countries would be lost and that developed countries would have to transfer massive financial resources to assist the transformation of Central and Eastern European economies. Developing countries thought that this transition process could cause diversion of the flow of financial resources which could have been directed to them.

It is true that the ODA from the former Soviet Union, former East Germany, and other East European countries to developing countries, which was around $4.5 billion in 1990, was either stopped or interrupted. However, the amount of ODA of DAC countries has remained stationary at around the level of $50 billion annually for the past 10 years, and there would appear to be little incentive among DAC members to increase their ODA in the near future, irrespective of the political changes as a result of the end of the Cold War.

At the same time, some developing countries feared that there might be distortion in trade and in foreign direct investment as a result of the end of the Cold War. However, the majority of developing countries were not affected, and DAEs even began to invest in some Central and Eastern European countries.

We can therefore say that, in general terms, economic and political changes resulting from the end of the Cold War gave rather favorable incentive to the majority of developing countries to make a self-help effort. They realized that ODA from donors would not come to developing countries automatically if they themselves did not make structural adjustment efforts, and that foreign direct investments would not come if they did not create a favorable climate for them.

Also at the end of the Cold War, there was strong incentive in the majority of developing countries to move towards a modernized economy by enforcing marketization and privatization. It was clear that, as in the case of Latin America, those economies that aimed wholeheartedly at marketization showed much better economic performance than those that went about it in a half-hearted way.

The Least Developed Countries

However, the present problem is that there are countries, such as the least developed countries, which cannot marketize and privatize their economies by their own efforts. These countries are not blessed with favorable economic conditions. They have neither the adequate human nor natural resources. Their self-help efforts have their limitation and it would be difficult for them to implement policies to develop their economies by utilizing foreign private investment and to expand trade as DAEs are doing. They can contemplate these policies, but it would be really difficult for them to put their policies into practice. These countries, therefore, need more development assistance and technical cooperation than anyone else. Without such assistance, they will be marginalized and left behind the trend of world economic development.

Under the present circumstances, the widening gap in growth between countries which can utilize the market system effectively and those countries which cannot, would become even greater. In fact, there are some fortunate developing countries, such as the DAEs, whose per capita incomes have already reached the level of some developed countries. On the other hand, there are 43 countries where per capita incomes are lower than $600, and the number of countries in this category is on the increase. This is a dangerous gap widening process. If this trend continues, there would be further deterioration in the problems of poverty, environment, and population.

At present, it is quite natural that world attention is directed towards the political and economic transformation of Central and Eastern European countries. However, in the long term, the problems of the impoverished developing countries, and in particular those of the least developed countries, would become much more acute and serious for the sustained growth of the world economy and for world political stability.

Problems of Marketization

The most serious issues concerning the marketization of developing economies lie in the Least Developed Countries (LDCs). I believe that even in the more developed developing countries, like India and Pakistan, rapid marketization would not work effectively because of their social and economic systems. Therefore, what is desirable is a gradual process of marketization, taking into account various factors such as cultural, religious, and social differences. In the case of the LDCs, economic and social infrastructures which would be necessary for marketization do not normally exist, and it would not be realistic to leave everything to the market forces of the private sector.

In the early stages of development in the LDCs, the public sector should play a crucial role in establishing the necessary infrastructures. In particular, the LDCs need to focus their attention on the development of human resources. Without a trained work force, the marketization of their economies cannot be achieved effectively. Therefore, it is an utmost necessity for developed countries to provide adequate economic and technical assistance to those LDCs that are making efforts in that direction.

On the other hand, in the least developed countries there are not many enterprises to be privatized. For example, Mongolia is making efforts to privatize its agriculture and medium and small-scale enterprises, but at the same time, the government is planning to create new national key industries. Such being the case, the simple enforcement of a marketization process would not solve all the economic problems.

Conclusion

"Market economy" is an abstract concept and, in reality, there could not be a 100 percent pure market economy. As Michel Albert explained in his book *Capitalisme Contre Capitalisme,* there are various types of market economies, for example the United States type, the European type, the Nordic type, and the Japanese type, etc. Each has grown from its historical, economic, social, and cultural background. And who is to say which type is superior or inferior to the other? In the rush to establish a market economy system, I think that the developing countries would be well advised to select the one most suitable to their own needs, taking into account their own political, economic, and social heritages.

Notes

1. The paper has been edited by Üner Kirdar for inclusion in this book.

Section 3 · Imposing Conditions on Aid

Ravi Gulhati

The 1980s witnessed a major increase in policy-based conditional lending, an instrument that the International Monetary Fund has used since the 1950s when it was adopted by bilateral official aid agencies of the United States, the United Kingdom, and Canada. The Bank is playing a considerable role in helping Central and Eastern Europe carry out systemic economic reforms. Policy-based conditional lending is one of its major instruments in this reform effort. Structural adjustment loans at the macro level and sectoral adjustment loans focused on major parts of the economy, such as agriculture and industry, help governments to improve efficiency of resource use, to build viable institutions, and to mobilize resources necessary for sustained social and economic development. These loans are conditional on a policy agreement between a member government and the World Bank.

This paper will examine the theory underlying such conditionality and assess recent practice. Although the Bank has made a number of policy loans to Central and Eastern Europe (including Hungary, Poland, Yugoslavia, and Czechoslovakia), this experience is rather limited and it is far too recent to assess the practical effectiveness of conditionality. I will, therefore, rely on the much larger record of such lending to developing countries as a whole.

The Simple Theory of Conditional Lending

First, we should define the theory of conditional lending within the framework Graham Allison's calls the "Rational Actor Model."[1] In this setting, there is perfect knowledge, no uncertainty, and the preference functions of both the World Bank and governments of developing countries are unambiguous. There are no vested interests to oppose government's view of what should be done to pursue development. Government is viewed as a monolithic entity. Contracts are complete and there are no incentive, communication, or coordination problems interfering with the implementation of agreed policies. The decision rule, under the Rational Actor Model, is to optimize given the preferences and constraints.

In this simplified world, there is little scope for policy conflicts either within a country or between the government of a developing country and the World Bank. Consensus on what reforms are required is easy to reach on the basis of professional analysis of a country's economic situation and its existing policy framework. Also, implementation of the reforms is a straight forward matter and the risk of failure is minimal.

The justification for conditional lending is that the agreed policy reforms will raise the return to all investment, irrespective of whether it is financed by the Bank, by other foreign sources or by national savings. Such reforms will also augment the creditworthiness of the borrower country. By providing intellectual and financial support for the borrower government's reforms, the Bank makes it easier to carry them out. The costs of the reforms are reduced and their payoff is increased.

Conditional Lending Theory under Realistic Assumptions

The Rational Actor Model does great violence to reality, however. Accordingly, the theory of conditional lending is much more complicated than the harmonious picture drawn above. Knowledge is far from perfect. This is particularly so in the field of economic theory as it applies to policy reforms, a point to which I will return. There is considerable uncertainty, for example, with respect to world market conditions. It is difficult to predict primary commodity prices, interest rates, exchange rates, and capital flows. Both the World Bank and individual governments of developing countries operate under a number of constraints which are not recognized by the Rational Actor Model. These constraints are discussed below.

Constraints on the World Bank

The World Bank is an intergovernmental organization with a decision-making process based on weighted voting. All developing countries have a voice in board meetings of the Bank but their decision-making power varies according to their capital subscriptions and thereby on their economic size. The United States has a virtual veto on some important decisions. Although, the staff and management of the Bank pride themselves on being objective, their autonomy is questioned in some quarters. The doctrine or philosophy of the Bank is said to be unduly influenced by changing ideological currents in major industrialized countries.[2] Furthermore, the Bank has very little influence on economic policies of the rich countries, even those policies, such as trade and debt, which are critical for structural adjustment to take place on an equitable basis. The Bank depends for the mobilization of loanable resources on the rich countries. In this respect, the Bank's activities are asymmetrical as between the rich and the poor countries. These perceptions adversely affect the Bank's credibility as a source of objective policy advice.

The Bank does not have the capacity to deal with economic policy questions in an integrated manner. It is only one among many international organizations, each with its own mandate. The Bank's mandate is fairly comprehensive; it includes almost all sectors of the economy and such macroeconomic issues as planning, finance, and factors bearing on creditworthiness. As such, there is considerable overlap with the IMF's mandate in areas such as macroeconomic management, public finance, and external debt. The IMF has special competence and responsibility in relation to money, credit, and exchange rates. The extent of the overlap between the Bank and the IMF has increased over time. The two organizations have made elaborate arrangements to coordinate their activities and policy work in member countries. Furthermore, the membership of the two organizations is almost the same and the same rich countries play a dominant role in setting policy. Nevertheless, coordination has real costs and it is far from smooth. At a general level, the two organizations pursue the same objectives but there are many occasions when, in the context of individual countries, the staffs, managements, and boards of the Bank and the IMF make judgments which do not coincide in detail. These differences can be troublesome for individual countries trying to negotiate conditionality with the Bretton Wood twins.

Policy questions are intimately related to finance and particularly to external finance. Policy agreements between the Bank (or the IMF) and individual borrower governments are accompanied by a financial framework drawn up by the Bank (or the IMF) in collaboration with the borrower government which requires action by bilateral donors, export credit organizations meeting under the auspices of the Paris Club, private banks, and other sources of foreign capital. These financial flows may or may not materialize, although many suppliers of funds look to the leadership of the Bretton Wood organizations in dealing with developing countries. The link between rescheduling actions by the Paris Club and the IMF-Bank is a particularly strong one. Nevertheless, there have been instances in which borrower countries did not get relief from the Paris Club visualized in the financial framework.[3] Foreign commercial banks did not play the supportive role outlined in the 1985 Baker Plan (adopted by both the Bank and the IMF) to deal with the debt issue, thereby necessitating large net transfers out of many Latin American and other countries. These shortfalls in available resources become a source of difficulty in the implementation of agreed policy conditionalities. The Bank and the IMF have limited influence over other major actors who must play a role if reforms are to succeed.

Finally, although the staff and management of the Bank are competent and well-meaning, they are subject to bureaucratic and human pressures that detract from singleminded pursuit of reforms in borrower countries. There is considerable debate, inside and outside the Bank, about the formal and informal incentives that motivate Bank officials. Some claim that these incentives generate considerable pressure to achieve lending targets at the expense of quality. Although formal management directives insist on maintaining high-quality lending, including, particularly, policy-based lending, some staff members perceive that their career aims are better achieved by fulfilling lending targets. Furthermore, division and department heads in the Bank feel compelled to mind their turf and to expand their budgets just like managers in other organizations everywhere. These bureaucratic struggles have a negative impact on the design of policy-based loans. The Bank was reorganized in 1987 to deal with these and other problems, but no one claims that that these problems have disappeared.

Constraints on Borrower Governments

The substance of economic policy in a particular developing country is not only based on rational economic analysis; it is heavily affected by that country's policy-making process. This process depends on several political and institutional variables: the policy circle; the extent to which policy makers are autonomous; the nature of the civil service; interaction between policy makers and civil servants; interactions between government and domestic pressure groups; interactions between government and the public; interactions between government and the Bank as well as other sources of conditional finance. Although space does not permit a full discussion of all these variables, a few points are in order.

Policy Circle

Countries differ greatly in terms of which individuals decide the direction of economic policy. At one extreme, the policy circle can consist of one person—the absolute ruler. On the other end of the spectrum, the circle may be large, as in the United States, with many checks and balances in its Constitution.

If the policy circle is small, it is very important to know the preferences and working methods of each policy actor. Do they make decisions largely on the basis of intuition and ideology, or do they have some respect for technical inputs based on the methods and findings of research in the social sciences? Do they have a short or long time horizon? How much tolerance do they have for policy dissent? How much of a penchant do they have for secretiveness in these negotiations?

Policies reflect political choices, and policy makers are part and parcel of the regime. All regimes attach very high priority to ensuring their own political survival. Some try to buy the support of at least a part of the citizenry through special favors. To the extent that this is the case, technical inputs into economic policy based on the objective of promoting social good (stabilization, long-term economic growth, or better income distribution) will be subordinated to the politics of survival. Other regimes approach the survival issue not in terms of maintaining clients through extending patronage, but by bringing about sustained improvement in the living standards of all the citizens. This kind of regime is likely to be keenly interested in encouraging technical inputs into economic policy.

Autonomy of Policy Makers

The decision-making style also depends on how much autonomy policy makers enjoy. Countries differ greatly in terms of how power is distributed between the government and the various economic, ethnic, or regional pressure groups in its society. Such groups may be pursuing very narrowly defined interests or they may be loose coalitions. They may or may not have a very short time horizon. Their capacity to organize, to demonstrate, to go on a strike, and to influence public opinion will vary a great deal. At one extreme, government may be a prisoner of such groups and play a reactive role in response to their initiatives.

On the other, government may have a lot of room for maneuver and take the lead in formulating economic policy. In any event, negotiating with pressure groups in order to build a consensus on economic policy is an important part of the policy work of most governments. How governments acomplish this task can be of critical significance during the policy implementation phase.

Civil Service

Political leaders everywhere rely on the civil service to administer economic policies and in some countries it makes a serious contribution to analyzing issues and defining policy options.

The quality of the civil service and its historical traditions differ quite a lot in different parts of the world. The behavior of civil servants reflects a varying mix of self-interest, bureaucratic turf-minding, professional norms, and allegiance to the regime in power. Combining government work with business ventures is acceptable in some places and ruled out in others. In some cases, the bureaucracy acquires a strong interest in the existing policy framework and resists reform initiatives.

Political Leadership

The three variables discussed above are cast very much in a static framework. They help to explain why current policies are what they are. However, economic policies have changed dramatically in Central and Eastern Europe as well as in other countries. In searching for the source of dynamism, focus should be on how political leaders respond to exogenous shocks, to crisis conditions, and to the acquisition of new knowledge. For example, the contribution of civil servants to policy work depends not only on their professional competence and impartiality, but also on how leaders interact with them. Leaders can use the civil service to access new knowledge and adapt it to the specific circumstances of the country or they can discourage initiatives taken by even the best and most sincere civil servant.

Furthermore, proposals to improve the civil service seldom succeed without the strong support of political leaders. Dramatic policy changes of the kind now underway in Central and Eastern Europe require a renegotiation of many aspects of the social compact. To do this, leaders have to educate the general public, to strike bargains with pressure groups, and to negotiate with foreign interests, including the Bank. Crucial to handling these tasks is the capacity of leaders to learn from experience, to communicate effectively, and to negotiate skillfully.

Conditionality Theory Redefined

Given these constraints on the Bank and borrower governments, the theory of policy conditionality needs to be redefined. Recall that despite all the talk about a "Washington consensus" on the content of needed reforms, economic theory underlying policy change is neither complete nor without controversy. To draw attention to remaining points at issue, I want to summarize what Gerald Helleiner said at a World Bank symposium in September 1990.[4]

- No general agreement exists on the sequencing of reforms in a country, contrary to the latest Bank doctrine which prescribes, first, stabilization, then liberalization (attacking the most acute distortions first), and finally, increased investment and growth. One sequence may work better in one place and another in a different context. Selecting the best sequence remains an art rather than a matter for scientific analysis.
- There is no full agreement on the cost of market distortions or on the desirability of liberalization. This applies, particularly, to the trade regime and interest rates.
- Views on the role of incomes policy are not unanimous and the functioning of labor markets is imperfectly understood.
- There is no strong theory behind either "shock therapy" or gradual reforms. What works in one place may not be effective elsewhere.

The second point was that even if there was strong theoretical support for drawing up reform packages, there was no assurance that the Bank would be able to identify the optimal design. Ideological preconceptions, pressure on staff to fulfill lending targets, bureaucratic struggles within the Bank organization, difficulties in Bank-IMF coordination and inability to deliver the external finance required to implement the reform reduce the probability of the Bank's effectiveness in this area.

The third point is that governments of developing countries will only very rarely have the capacity to define and implement an optimal reform package, assuming that such a package can be derived from available economic theory. Very frequently, there will be a clash between economic rationality and political rationality and quite often, the civil service lacks the wherewithal to implement administratively complex reforms. What is optimal in the context of conventionally defined economic theory is not likely to be optimal when account is taken of political and administrative realities.

It follows from these three considerations that there is considerable scope for policy conflict. The decision rule in this realistic setting is not to optimize but to "satisfice," that is, to find a solution which is "good enough." Conditional lending emerges in this perspective as an instrument of limited value. Nevertheless, it is useful in three ways.

First of all, it provides a context in which existing macro and sectoral policies can be reexamined jointly and seriously by borrower governments and the Bank. Before the Bank started policy-based lending in 1980, policy reviews done by Bank staff did not command the attention of either the Bank's senior management or the policy makers in borrower countries. Conditional lending helped overcome this inertia.

Second, through the intermediation of the Bank, policy makers in borrower countries obtained access to the most recent policy trends and innovative programs on a worldwide basis. As an international organization with considerable operational research capacity, the Bank monitors the evolution of economic policies on a very wide front and undertakes very useful comparative analysis of the underlying issues in designing reforms. The results of this work are reported to the governments of borrowing countries. They can be useful in helping to formulate policy in each member country.

Finally, the economic diplomacy that is associated with conditional lending can often help build a consensus in favor of economic reforms in borrower countries. The Bank can take the initiative in stimulating discussion. It can contribute to the policy agenda and clarify the available options (and their respective implications) from which policy makers have to choose a course of action. In many countries, the Bank virtually becomes an integral part of the policy making circle.

Conditionality in Practice: The Historical Record

The historical record, showing the extent to which policy conditionality has worked in practice, has been analyzed by the Bank itself.[5] The sample examined consisted of 183 Structural Adjustment Loans and Sectoral Adjustment Loans to 61 countries during 1980-89. The conclusions are as follows:

- Loan agreement conditions were implemented fully to the extent of 66 percent. Only loans to Panama and Argentina were totally canceled for nonfulfillment of conditions. In two other loans, the scope of policy commitments was substantially curtailed.
- The extent of implementation varied widely across countries over time and according to the types of policies.
- A part of the failure to implement conditionality is the result of unexpected changes in world interest rates or terms of trade beyond the control of borrower countries.
- Another part of the failure to implement conditionality is the result of borrower governments' weak political commitment to reforms and their inadequate managerial skill in handling the reform process. Many governments signed loan documents because they were desperate to obtain funds, even though they were not fully convinced of the desirability of the reforms proposed by the Bank. In other instances, government officials in core economic ministries signed in good faith, but other ministry officials or pressure groups in the private sector succeeded in undermining the implementation process.

The Bank's attempt to analyze conditionality experience and to learn from it is praiseworthy. Questions can be asked, however, about the validity of the quantification of the extent to which policy conditions are implemented. The 66 percent average figure is rather high compared to analyses of the record of IMF conditionality. There is no obvious reason why implementation of Bank conditionality should have a higher score than IMF conditionality.[6] Furthermore, there are grounds for believing that the pressure on Bank staff to fulfill lending targets translates into unwitting acceptance of low standards for judging the implementation of conditionality in some cases. Many of these judgments are inherently subjective and it is difficult to apply Bank-wide standards. Staff who have very high professional scruples and who are self-confident do not hesitate to apply high standards. Other staff are reluctant to be associated with breakdowns in policy-based loans. Making new loan commitments and not standing in the way of disbursing existing loans is perceived by staff to be the easy and non-controversial route to career development. Rewards for insisting on high quality of lending are not perceived by them to be as powerful as those for fulfilling lending targets.

Where to Go from Here?

I start with the proposition that conditionality is a useful but limited instrument. Foreign aid without policy conditionality did not prove to be effective, except in countries which had satisfactory economic policies on their own initiative. Too much should not be expected from the application of conditionality but there are circumstances in which it can play a constructive role. On this basis, what can the Bank do to improve its use of the conditionality instrument?

A major conclusion reached in the Bank's 1988 Report on Adjustment Lending was that it should not make policy-based loans unless there is full agreement with the borrower government on the diagnosis and the entire reform program and not just on the first policy package. In other words, the borrower government must have ownership of the reform. It must in large part be an indigenous effort, not a foreign imposition. In the four years since this Report, the staff of the Bank has become much more sensitive to the ownership issue but the full ramifications of this point are not yet understood. Let me explain why.

The Bank should see its role in the policy process not so much as a doctor prescribing therapies to patients on the basis of a fully developed science but rather as a stimulator of policy ideas which deserve the serious consideration of national policy makers.[7] This requires a major reorientation of the board, management, and the staff.

Most of the work of the Bank must be done upstream—at the stage of economic analysis—including defining policy options and their implications and discussing the results with all concerned. The Bank should act like a think tank rather than as an old fashioned, authoritarian doctor. This would mean much more work than is now done on the estimation of lags and elasticities, alternative financial scenarios, and the consequences of policy options for politically influential groups over time. It would also mean a substantially expanded budget for organizing and sustaining a high-quality dialogue with officials and the top leadership of selected countries that are serious about economic reforms. Non-governmental policy actors (trade union leaders, business leaders, and party politicians, must participate in this dialogue in some appropriate way. The discussion must include economic, political, and public administration variables.

The Bank must pay much more attention to the analysis of the economic policy process in individual borrower countries. It should identify and support measures to improve institutional capacity in this area. A program along these lines is just beginning for sub-Saharan countries, but not for any other geographical location.

The Bank must recognize that reforms are economically and politically risky, often even uncertain. Given that the burden of possible failure will have to be carried by the government of the borrower country, the Bank must not take strong positions during loan negotiations on such details of the design as timing, sequencing, and speed of policy adjustment for which there is not much theoretical backing. The Bank should insist that such details be worked out by the government in collaboration with its own pressure groups, but it should be tolerant as to the outcome of these negotiations. Such tolerance is against the grain of many Bank officials today.

For similar reasons the Bank must not take a strong position on such issues as the role of the state in economic activity. Development theory on these topics does not provide unequivocal guidance, and what strategy should be followed in a particular country depends on specific circumstances and not on some general formula. A good example is provided by a recent critique of the Bank's approach to industrial policy.[8]

> The Bank's approach . . . may be described as "moderately neoclassical," which accepts that factor and product markets are not fully efficient in developing countries and that there is a role for government interventions. However, it strongly prefers functional to selective interventions; governments should make markets more efficient in a neutral way. . . . The risk of government failure haunts all discussion of selectivity. . . . The level and content of policy should reflect the abilities of the government and the nature of the activities concerned. The Bank should consider selective policies, where economically feasible, as an integral part of a package of policies to promote industrial development. (It should) help countries overcome or minimize the risk of government failure. . . .

The Bank must become well informed about the politics in the borrower countries to judge whether or not there is full agreement with the government on the diagnosis of problems and reforms, and whether or not the government "owns" the reforms. Today, the Bank has very little capacity in this area.

Conclusion

Let me conclude this paper by briefly summarizing the argument. The simple theory of conditionality greatly minimizes the scope for conflict regarding economic policy. Its assumptions do considerable violence to reality. The structure and scope of the World Bank tend to constrain its capacity as a policy organization. Ideological preconceptions, pressure on staff to fulfill lending targets, bureaucratic struggles within the Bank organization, difficulties in Bank-IMF coordination, and inability to deliver the external finance required to implement reforms tend to reduce effectiveness in the policy area. The capacity of borrower governments to base policy on rational economic analysis varies greatly and depends on the quality of leadership, their autonomy vis-à-vis pressure groups, and the civil service tradition. Furthermore, economic theory underlying reforms in neither complete nor beyond controversy. All these constraints notwithstanding, policy conditionality can be useful. It helps overcome the inertia that frequently characterizes the policy scene. Interaction between the Bank and the borrower government exposes the latter to the latest policy trends on a comparative basis. Economic diplomacy associated with conditionality can help build consensus in favor of reforms in developing countries. The Bank can enhance the value of policy conditionality by emphasizing much more than it has done so far its role as a think tank and as a source of support for building the institutional capacity for policy work in borrower countries. It should not take strong positions during negotiations in area in which economic theory is not conclusive. The exercise of leverage by the Bank does not yield sustained improvements in economic policies of member countries.

Notes

1. Graham Allison, *Essence of Decision: Explaining the Cuban Misile Crisis* (Boston: Little, Brown, 1971).

2. "The Bank is in danger of becoming like the IMF—pushing simplistic, standardised formulas that slight the particular history, culture, and politics of individual nations, and that are based more on preconceived ideology than on objective analysis." See R. Feinberg, "An Open Letter to the World Bank's New President," in *Between Two Worlds: The World Bank's Next Decade,* ed. R. Feinberg (Washington: Overseas Development Council, 1986), 12.

3. Jaycox, Gulhati, Lall, and Yalamanchili, "The Nature of the Debt Problem in Eastern and Southern Africa," in *African Debt and Financing,* eds. Lancaster and Williamson (Washington: Institute for International Economics, 1986), 61.

4. V. Corbo, S. Fischer, and S. Webb, eds., *Adjustment Lending Revisited: Policies to Restore Growth* (Washington, 1992), 181, 182.

5. Corbo, *Ibid.,* 69-73

6. T. Killick, *The Quest for Economic Stabilisation: The IMF and the Third World* (London, 1984); J. Spraos, *IMF Conditionality: Ineffectual, Inefficient, Mistargeted, Priceton Essays in International Finance,* no. 166, 1986.

7. Ravi Gulhati, *The Making of Economic Policy in Africa* (Washington: Economic Development Institute, 1990), 96.

8. "OED Study of Bank Support of Industrializing Countries: Case Studies of Korea, India, and Indonesia," manuscript, 1991, x-xiii.

Section 4 · Collapsing Vision of Global Development

Keith Bezanson

In less than three years, we will pause to commemorate the 50th anniversary of the defeat of Hitler and the end of World War II. During most of the past half century, while the ideological duel of the Cold War was conducted, the idea of global development has served as the engine and intellectual base of North-South relations. Yet today that idea and the forces that have nurtured and sustained it are in serious trouble. Poorer countries—particularly those in Africa—profess their alarm over what they interpret as international abandonment, if not betrayal, and development workers grow increasingly disheartened at the prospect of trying to do much, much more with much, much less.

Why is the idea of global development in such difficulty? It has, after all, endured for almost five decades as a towering and inspiring vision which stimulated international enthusiasm. In the brief commentary which follows, is an attempt to place the development idea in context and to offer an explanation as to why the idea itself is in danger of collapse.

Postwar Views of Development

There can be no doubt but that development as conceived in the postwar years was a radical departure and a revolutionary idea. It replaced the view of societies of the South as incomparable with the North and placed them on a single continuum of less or more advanced relative to the criteria of the industrial North. The idea of development held that Third World societies were poor and that international actions were required to change this. The idea was, of course, more complex than this and involved:

- an economic component which held that, with the right combination of finance, technology, and policy, all nations and peoples could achieve more or less equitable conditions;
- a political/ethical component which held that social justice on a global scale was both desirable and feasible through the cooperation of nations; and
- a technical and geophysical component which assumed that the resources of the planet were inexhaustible and that science and technology would ensure their availability for all.

For most of the past four decades, this idea of development has reinforced perceptions that poorer countries are filled with potential. And it has spawned a vocabulary which refers to them as "young" and "emerging."

That this idea stands under attack today as never before is manifestly not because the development effort has failed abysmally. True, many examples have been catalogued of efforts that were either misguided and naive or that applied "state of the art" knowledge and still ended in embarrassing failure. Equally true is the fact that the decade of the 1980s is characterized, quite correctly, as the "lost decade" in international development. Finally and more disturbing is the truth that the first two years of this decade witnessed declines in per capita income in developing countries as a whole (population weighted) and that such year-on-year average reductions had not previously been recorded during the entire period (over 25 years) for which the World Bank has recorded these data.

It is also, however, the case that during the period from 1960 to 1980 the gains in developing countries as a whole were impressive. GDP growth, for example, in developing countries exceeded that of the industrial North. The staggering gains in literacy, nutrition, life expectancy, infant mortality, and agricultural output are all part of the historical record. That same historical record testifies to the speed with which development, as measured by output per capita, can occur. According to World Bank calculations, it took the United Kingdom, beginning in 1780, 58 years to double its output per person. Starting in 1839, the United States accomplished the doubling in 47 years. Starting in the 1880s, Japan accomplished the same in 34 years. In the period following 1945, Brazil doubled its per capita output in 18 years, Indonesia in 17, Korea in 11 and China in 10.

Change in Perceptions

Thus, the extent of some conventional wisdom notwithstanding, the vision of global development is today in serious difficulty not because its application has consistently and dramatically failed, but for other reasons.

As early as 1969 (and at the height of what one might argue were the "good years" for development), the Pearson Report spoke of "aid fatigue" and the lessening of public and political will to sustain the idea of development. A decade later, in 1980, the Brandt Report worried about the same lessening of will and provided strong, analytical evidence that it was in the self-interest of the North to ensure that equitable and sustainable development take place in the South. The global and development context which Pearson examined at the close of the 1960s and which Brandt reexamined a decade later were not identical but they were characterized more by similarities than differences. It was the decade following the Brandt Report that witnessed staggering change and discontinuity in the world economy and in the geopolitics of our globe.

The tidal scope of these changes and discontinuities cannot be captured in a few words. Alvin Toffler refers to the "Third Wave," to the unleashing of revolutionary forces of a magnitude equalled only by the agrarian and industrial revolutions. It is these new forces that are challenging the ideas and concepts that have sustained us for many generations; the postwar idea of global development is but one of the hostages to these new forces.

The idea of global development finds itself today—principally as a result of changes compressed into the last decade—in a context which is light years apart from that confronted by the architects of our postwar order. Much intellectual endeavor continues, nevertheless, to be expended in an attempt to fit the changed context into the half-century old idea of global development, into the concept that the material condition of all of humanity is subject to ongoing and infinite improvement. New wine and old bottles? The changed context involves, inter alia, the following.

A dramatically changed political environment. Our political systems and our thinking about the management of economic, environmental, and social forces are based on the concept of the nation-state, but supranational and transnational entities increasingly erode the ability of the state—especially poorer and weaker states—to control such phenomena.

The explosive growth in social demands in developing regions. The world is belatedly coming to the realization that the global ecosystem has finite limits and will not be able to withstand indefinitely the various pressures of unchecked population growth and uncontrolled development.

The "globalization" of economic affairs. Nation-states are discovering that they are increasingly powerless in the distribution of social goods and in guiding the economic well-being of the citizenry. Financial markets have become increasingly independent of the production and distribution of goods and services. Although these changes may conceivably present new opportunities to some developing country, they also pose new obstacles, the removal of which will require major policy adjustments, highly trained professionals, and agile managers. Many of the world's poorer regions simply do not have the institutions, human resources, or financial flexibility to make these adjustments.

The content and direction of international trade. The content of international trade has shifted away from commodities (exported primarily by developing countries) toward high-technology services and manufactured products (typically the exports of industrialized nations). Powerful new regional trading blocs are fast emerging that are having major economic effects on both developing and industrialized nations.

Technological change and the emergence of entirely new technologies, principally in microelectronics and biotechnology and new materials, are fast changing the way in which the international marketplace has functioned since 1945. Individuals, groups, and nations actively participating in the generation and exchange of these new technologies will prosper in the emerging new order; those left behind will become increasingly marginalized. The risk of marginalization is particularly severe for the least developed countries.

Global shifts in sociocultural value systems, reflected in the emergence around the world of a Westernized-consumerized popular culture, the deterioration of collective bond of family, community, and kinship units, and the loss of traditional spiritual and ideological reference points.

In a recent article, Wolfgang Sachs examines the evolution, changes, and cultural context of the idea of global development. He concludes that "the idea of development stands today like a ruin in the intellectual landscape, its shadows obscuring our vision." Whether one agrees fully with the scathing indictment of

Sachs, there can be no doubt but that development as the 50-year-old conceptual framework of North-South relations is in serious trouble. Opinion surveys in the industrial nations of the North show that consistently declining numbers of citizens attach importance or accord priority to development as it has been conceived and applied over almost five decades.

The Need for a New Vision

It is a sad irony that support for the idea of development should decline under the very conditions in which it was supposed to thrive according to the founders of the United Nations and the Bretton Woods institutions. Those architects were inspired by a vision of a globalized marketplace where the constructive interplay of supply and demand would replace violence and threat in the competition among nations. That globalized marketplace is every day more a reality. Capital, technology, ideas, and information move about the globe at the speed of electronic impulse. The idea of development holds that all countries are moving or advancing along a common road; the consequences of globalization suggest that this is not so and that the materially poorer parts of the planet are separated by an unbreachable chasm from the internationalized supereconomies of the North.

It is nevertheless an inescapable fact that the highly technologized economies of the North function in increasing autonomy from the raw materials, cheap labor, or agricultural commodities from the South. Bluntly stated, the current economic reality is that the North simply does not need the South to nearly the extent it did 25 years ago. Our world is today divided not between Communism and capitalism, but—again to quote Alvin Toffler—between fast economies and slow economies. With but a few exceptions, the fast economies are all in the North.

Yet if poor countries tremble in the fact of the massive discontinuities of our times, including the globalization of economic affairs, so also do rich countries. Again to quote Sachs:

> The fear of falling behind in international competition has become the predominant organizing motive of politics in North and South, East and West. It drives developing countries further into self-exploitation, for the sake of boosting exports, and industrial countries further into the wasteful and destructive mania of production. Both enterprises and entire states see themselves trapped in a situation of remorseless competition. . . .

Hardly a climate conducive to the idea of development through cooperative international effort!

But something more is happening, something perhaps even more important than the globalization of the marketplace and its immediate effects on the idea of development. A foundation stone of Western thought and the dominant Western belief system since the nineteenth century has been a profound faith in progress, principally through advances in science and technology. Such advances had bestowed on the industrial nations, and particularly the United States, a high material standard of living and the architects of the postwar order believed that those advances would continue indefinitely. It is this idea of progress and its inevitability that today is rapidly fading. The Western expectation, for example, that the next generation will necessarily achieve an improved (i.e., more materially enriched) standard of living than the present one is now seriously in doubt.

The condition of our life-sustaining environment is calling further into jeopardy the Western ethos of the inevitability of material progress. There is little doubt but that the world economy has already reached and surpassed its sustainable physical limits. We are drawing down groundwater, eroding soils, cutting forests, and harvesting fish faster than they can replenish themselves, burning nonrenewable fossil fuels without developing substitutes, and overloading our ecosystem to the extent that our populations now fear the sunshine because of damage to the ozone layer. Faced with these realities, a very fundamental component of the Western ethos—the belief in a necessary link between advances in science and technology on the one hand, and the well-being of the earth and its inhabitants on the other—is being eroded. Again, under these conditions, it is small wonder that the once-towering vision of world development should find itself on shaky ground.

Symptomatic of these discontinuities and uncertainties are recent changes in the United Nations Secretariat itself where much of its capacity for global economic leadership has been either reduced or eliminated. This has been done in order to concentrate UN resources on peace and security issues, such issues being almost always relatively short-term in nature. The concept of security—defined, of course, from the viewpoint of the North—has gained attention and resources at the expense of the unifying postwar vision of an equitable world order.

Conclusion

The proverb holds that without vision people perish. The development vision which inspired international efforts for over four decades is, like an endangered species, close to extinction. This is not a temporary decline in interest or political will; it is not a consequence of a short-term economic downturn in the industrial North. Rather, the idea of development itself is fading from the international landscape as a direct consequence of the massive changes and discontinuities of our times. It is part of the larger—and also vanishing—Western ethos which held that advances in science and technology would necessarily and inevitable lead to improvements in the well-being of people and of the earth itself.

The decade of the 1990s will almost certainly involve a global transition of unprecedented proportions. According to Harvey Brooks, this will involve "a transition leading either towards catastrophe and social disintegration or towards a sustainable growing world society...with constantly declining population growth." The positive outcome cannot be taken for granted. It is no longer guaranteed by the secular faith that linked science, technology, and human advancement. Because of this, exceptional care will be required if an adequate and workable new vision of a sustainable world society is to be constructed.

Part 3 · Human and Ecological Values

Overview

Üner Kırdar, Leonard Silk, and Joseph C. Wheeler

Overcoming the threats to world order and grasping the opportunities for bettering people's lives will require not only technical solutions but shared moral values—a deep concern for others, especially the poor and suffering; respect for human rights, and tolerance of national, ethnic, and religious diversity. As John Donne said over three centuries ago, "No man is an island, entire of itself; every man is a piece of the continent, a part of the main; if a clod be washed away by the sea, Europe is the less, as well as if a promontory were, as well as if a manor of thy friends or of thine own were; any man's death diminishes me, because I am involved in mankind; and therefore never send for whom the bell tolls, it tolls for thee."

The need to learn that powerful lesson is greater than ever. The breakup of the Soviet empire has unleashed hatreds that had been largely hidden or repressed during the Cold War. But, even before the recent revolutions in Eastern Europe, many countries, under the pressures of inflation, sluggish economic growth, rising unemployment and falling living standards, had been reducing programs to help those people in greatest need.

Indeed, to justify the cuts in social spending, a political philosophy had emerged that saw government not as a cure but as the cause of worsening social and economic problems; and that philosophy enshrined "the market" as the only viable cure for poverty and the social ills it breeds.

But the cutbacks in social spending and taxes adopted in the name of that philosophy redistributed income and wealth toward the rich, arrested social development, and increased poverty in the affected societies. Less government did not turn out to be the same as good government—that is, decent and humane government. And moral values did not flourish as a consequence of less governance, but seemed to decay with the retreat of public responsibility for people in need of society's help.

Today, new political thinking and political forces are emerging in support of a philosophy to "put people first." The aim of this philosophy is to focus national and international policies on improving the education, skills, job opportunities, and personal liberties of the people and on correcting the social ills—the abuses of human rights, the racial, ethnic, and sexual discrimination, and the environmental degradation that threaten people's lives.

As we cannot depend on markets alone to deal with social ills, neither can we depend only on government officials, politicians, or bureaucrats. People must have the political freedom and economic independence to shape their own development. And they must be free to join with others to use their strength in voluntary political, economic, and charitable organizations to advance their own and society's interests.

Throughout the world, understanding has grown that people cannot take the natural environmental system for granted—and that many governments and industries have carelessly jeopardized human health and life by polluting the natural environment. As protection of the environment has moved higher on many national agendas, the developed countries have taken some important measures to reduce the output of pollutants, sometimes as the result of international agreements, sometimes exclusively as domestic policy initiatives. The less advanced countries of Latin America, Africa, and Asia, as well as of Eastern Europe and the former Soviet Union, have done less about their own serious environmental problems that contribute to the global threat. It will take greater global cooperation and more aid to help the developing countries deal with the risks to their own and the global environment.

Thus, in confronting the human and ecological threats posed by rapid change, we must examine the relationship between political governance, economic development, and social values.

Good Governance and Development

The concept of good governance began with the simple idea of honesty and efficiency in government. It has now become a much more detailed concept, dealing also with the establishment of enabling environment for economic and social progress, law and order, property rights, information, the transparency of decision making, and participation of the people in public affairs.

We now realize that there are also critical issues related to the psychology of populations. This is especially valid for countries in transition. How can a public consensus involves changing the public's behavior patterns. How can a market economy replace the theoretical but unimplemented values of a Communist system with more humane, yet more realistic, values?

Good governance is especially needed in economic relations between nations. Decisions on economic policies need to be made in a broadly representative framework that does not really exist today. Important decisions affecting the world economy with regard to trade and monetary issues, for instance, are now made in smaller forums. Aid processes often do not reflect sensible priorities. It is high time to consider how international processes can be made more broadly participatory and how to narrow the gap between rhetoric and performance. Good governance can be measured by how successful a country has been in achieving consensus on a strategy for development and to modernize.

Correcting Market Failures

Today, the new governing systems should examine how education and health care can best be managed and financed to ensure sustainable development.

Depending on local circumstances, various combinations of public/private partnership are possible. But, in the end, perhaps an even more important issue is, who benefits. In most cases, the present situation reflects power structures which favor ruling groups over the general public, or costly subsidies to the wealthy at the expense of the poor.

Some argue that the concept of public goods can often be separated entirely from government. People can band together to provide public goods, for example, farmers getting together to use a field efficiently for grazing. Nongovernmental organizations may also be tapped as a good source for public goods. Use of market systems and optimizing cost recovery are ways to promote efficiency in the provision of social services. But we have a serious concern about inequity in availability of services and imperfections in the market.

Correcting Social Ills

There is an urgent need to fight poverty by speeding up the process of demographic transition and attracting people out of fragile ecosystems. We are living in a period of an aging North and a young and angry South. The United Nations Conference on Environment and Development held in Rio de Janeiro in 1992 emphasized the linkage between such issues.

The Agenda 21 adopted by the Earth Summit urgently needs to be implemented by all countries—North and South, East and West. During the transition, the independent republics of the former USSR may suffer from a lack of environmental legislation. It is hoped that the pressure of public opinion, encouraged by burgeoning civic activities, will counter any such lack.

An important question is how to place a value on the environment. Use of economic instruments such as carbon taxes and tradable permits have been suggested, but there is a divergence of views on how practical these techniques might be. It is, however, fervently hoped that countries would look for ways of applying the "polluter pays" principle to North-South relationships, with the equivalent of tradable permits, the yardsticks being population size, not economic strength.

The Role of Nongovernmental Organizations

In a climate of change, we should be alert to the potential new roles of nongovernmental organizations. These may successfully provide goods and services, and be central players as innovators and advocates. There has been a rapid increase in such activity in developing countries where they often challenge society, sometimes with unwelcome messages, calling attention to problems of famine or persecution. In some cases, nongovernmental organizations are better able than governments to provide services, and they should benefit from improved legislative frameworks for their operations. These should be designed to fit the local situation, not simply be imports of outside models. A free and vigorous press is vital to investigate the causes of environmental damage and to dramatize the need for public or private actions to stop the damage.

The Status of Women

Systemic changes raise many questions about the status and role of the underprivileged in societies, in particular, the position of women. Narrowing the "man-woman" gap is a prerequisite for social and economic advancement.

The lower status of women in many societies, especially in developing countries, is one of the main factors delaying social and economic progress. Countries now moving to a market-oriented system will find that competitiveness is essential for success. This necessitates appropriate education, capability, and innovative skills for workers. Women in many societies, with underprivileged facilities in education and low participation in the labor force, are not equipped to complete on equal terms. This calls for a radical change in equality of opportunity for women, for their education, social status, participation in decision making, and the enhancement of their job opportunities.

The Impact of Diversity in Culture

Governing systems must pay closer attention to the cultural values and traditions of their own people. Governments, faced with pressing and desperate short-term needs, often overlook the importance of national cultural values and maintaining their integrity. Each nation should enjoy the dignity and creativity of its own cultural heritage. But we need to strike a balance between new technologies and cultural heritage. Even as we need to nourish the earth's natural renewal, we need to promote cultural renewal. Change is a process of recreating ourselves; to encourage this process, we must be open to outside ideas.

Respect for Human Rights: Ethnic and Religious Diversity

A dilemma confronting the international community is how to find a balance between the right of ethnic minorities to autonomy and the preservation of national unity.

It is hard to find a country in which everyone speaks the same language, shares the same faith and belongs to the same ethnic group. Most countries are mosaics of people, providing sources of enrichment to their culture, heritage, and values. However, we are now witnessing a rapid increase in the number of national, ethnic, and religious conflicts, which are becoming ever more violent. Former Yugoslavia is only the worst current example.

Despite their many differences, all systems of governance should promote and encourage freedom for all people, with full respect for human rights, regardless of race, sex, language, ethnic origin, or religion. There must be promotion of the fundamental human rights of all segments of the society, men, women, and children.

Respect for human rights and freedom must imply an equally important concept of obligation of people towards each other and towards their society.

How are these issues related to the development process. Aid should be cut off from countries sponsoring torture and other cruelties. But, in any particular case, the issue is usually complicated by the difficulty of assessing the facts, awaiting remedies, and deciding when and how to intervene and protect those under assault.

Outside countries approach the question cautiously. How far are they willing to go to defend the rights of the individual as opposed to the rights of society as a whole. How certain are they that their motivation in interfering in other countries is pure? Will their means of intervention accomplish their goals or lead to wider conflicts. If countries are prepared to intervene to suppress violence, how long will they be willing to stay—and what resources will they be willing to devote—to maintaining order. How long can they play that role without becoming imperialists, an outside force claiming moral supremacy while pursuing its own interests?

In the midst of efforts to deal with such searing dilemmas, the important role of moral and spiritual values is being rediscovered. There is a growing sense that progress in the transition calls for increased integration of human institutions on a global scale and that we can solve the fundamental problems afflicting so much of the world only with a spiritual reawakening, in which we regard other people as brothers and sisters on an earth where the natural endowment must be revered and nurtured for future generations.

Yet realism compels us to recognize that different religions and sects often act as an impediment to unity and peace; in various parts of the world, religious differences are becoming key elements in conflicts taking place for political dominance.

How can religion be prevented from aggravating conflicts that have no moral basis and turned instead into a unifying force among the diverse people of this small planet?

Although every religion has its own traditions, forms, and intellectual concepts, each contributes similar ethical precepts for human conduct and progress. We must find constructive ways of using both religious and secular institutions to bind people together, by weaving different elements of humanity into a single fabric while preserving the rich colors of their diversity. In the end we can find self-respect and fulfillment only by respecting the human rights and spiritual values of others.

Chapter 1 · Social and Cultural Dimensions of Change

Section 1 · Human Aspects

Mahbub ul Haq

Rapid change is the central reality of our time. The democratic transition in many of the developing countries, the collapse of former socialist regimes, and the worldwide emergence of people's organizations—these are not just isolated events; they are all part of a historic change. People today have an urge—an impatient urge—to participate in the events and processes that are shaping their lives.

This impatience brings both dangers and opportunities. It can dissolve into anarchy, ethnic violence, or social disintegration. But if properly nurtured in a responsive national and global framework, it can also become a source of tremendous vitality and innovation for the creation of new and more just societies.

The dangers arise when the irresistible urge for participation clashes with inflexible systems. Although there have been significant achievements in human development during the last three decades, the majority of the world's people still remain excluded from full participation in development as well as in the political process. One quarter of the global population still survives in absolute poverty. The poorest 20 percent of the world's people find that the wealthiest 20 percent enjoy 150 times their income level. Women still earn only half as much as men and, despite constituting over half of the vote, have great difficulty in securing even 10 percent representation in parliamentary bodies. The rural populations in developing countries still receive less than half of the income opportunities and social service available to their urban counterparts. Many ethnic minorities still live like a different nation within their own countries. And political and economic democracy is still a reluctant process in several countries. Our world is still a world of difference. Exclusion, rather than inclusion, is the prevailing reality.

At the same time, many new windows of opportunities are opening up. Global military expenditures are beginning to decline for the first time since World War II. The Cold War is over in East-West relations, and will probably be phased out in the developing world. The ideological battles of the past are being replaced today by a more pragmatic partnership between market efficiency and social compassion. The rising environmental threat is reminding humanity of its vulnerability and of its compulsions for common survival on this fragile planet. People are moving to the center of the stage in national and global dialogues. There are times in history when the human voice has spoken out with surprising force. And these past few years have marked just such a watershed. Humanity must choose between these dangers and opportunities. On that choice will depend the future of our planet.

There are at least five critical challenges that we face in the years ahead. If we meet them, the course of human history could be different.

Security for People

First, is it possible today to redefine security as not just security of land, but security for people? Security in the sense of education and health security, food security, job and economic security, environmental security, cultural security, human rights security—defense of people, not just defense of territory. Because the conflicts of the future may well be between people, rather than between nations as we are beginning to see already. And if we redefine human security in this fashion, it is possible today to take the one opportunity history has offered us to reduce military expenditures. Never before, at least in our lifetime, have we seen reduction in military spending, except in the last five years, by $250 billion cumulatively. Let nobody persuade you that this peace dividend is an illusion, that it is a mirage—that it was lost somewhere in the sands of the Middle East; it was not. This peace dividend is a reality. Military spending, after increasing year after year for the last 40 years, has decreased at the rate of 3 percent every year for the last five years. But, unfortunately, while it decreased by $250 billion, the link has not yet been made between this reduction and expenditure increase for human and social agenda. And, unfortunately, while this decrease came in many parts of the world—the United States, Russia, Eastern Europe, even in the Middle East and Latin America—it has not come yet in the poorest parts of the world—in sub-Saharan Africa and South Asia. We also have to link up the reduced military spending by developing countries with the global milieu. Developing countries cannot continue to reduce military expenditures if there is not at the same time a phase-out of military bases and military assistance, internationally supervised curbs on shipment of sophisticated military equipment, reduced subsidies to military exporters, and new alliances for peace around the globe. Therefore, our first opportunity today is that we can convert military spending into human spending, and redefine security as security for people, not just for land.

Sustainable Human Development

The second challenge is to redefine our models of development. Is it possible to bury the controversies about whether economic growth is necessary or not? Growth is not an option; it is an imperative. Basically, the debate is not over growth; the debate is about who participates in growth, who benefits from growth, and whether the growth is only for the present or also for the future—is it sustainable? We have added two elements to the growth models: people and sustainability. Growth must be woven around people, not people around growth. So it is sustainable human development that we have to talk about for the future. Can we construct these new models of development? Again, we should avoid unfortunate extremes on both sides. There are those who are so obsessed with growth that they will destroy nature in the process. There are others who are so preoccupied with preserving wild life that they will rather forget human life in the process—and the fact that human beings are the most endangered species on this planet. Developing countries today do not wish to sustain poverty; they wish to change the past. And that requires new models of development that put people at their very center, that treat people as both the agents and beneficiaries of change, that secure the present without mortgaging the future options.

Market Efficiency with Social Compassion

A third challenge is to find a more pragmatic balance between market efficiency and social compassion. We have gone through a major ideological battle around these issues of market and the state. And many myths have pervaded this field. There is a myth that markets can do it all. Of course, market efficiency is needed. But even in the most free enterprise economies—United States and the United Kingdom—the social safety nets consume 15 percent of GNP in terms of education, Medicare, food stamps, social security payments. And in Scandinavian countries, they consume 35-40 percent of GNP. Every society has found its own balance between market efficiency and social responsibility. There is a myth that public sectors are far too large in the developing countries. That is simply not true. The developing countries, on average, spend about half as much through the public sectors as the industrial nations. The issue is not the size of the public sectors, but their priorities. Governments in the developing countries often try to run everything that private sector can run more efficiently—agriculture, industry, trade—and they do not have the resources or the administrative capacity to run the social services that governments must often provide—education, health, nutrition programs, safe drinking water—or the physical infrastructure that the economy needs—roads, telecommunications, and power stations.

What is required is a new pragmatic balance between the roles of the state and the market. Markets must ensure competitive efficiency. But the state must also ensure that markets are people-friendly—they remain accessible to all the people by creating suitable enabling conditions. And the state must extend social safety nets for temporary periods for the victims of the market place.

It is sometimes claimed that the lesson of the last decade is that capitalism has triumphed and socialism is dead. These are simplistic notions which detract from professional analysis. If capitalism has triumphed, let us hope that it is not the triumph of only personal greed. If socialism is dead, let us hope that it is not the death of all social objectives. What we need today is to combine the creative energies unleashed by capitalism with the social objectives of human development. In such a pragmatic combination of efficiency and equity lies the viability of future models of development.

A New North-South Partnership

The fourth challenge is to forge a new partnership between the North and the South and to overcome the bitter divide that has existed for so long. This requires accommodations on both sides. Can the South accept that 80 to 90 percent of the development task is its own responsibility? Will it finally refuse to find external alibis for their internal problems? Nobody from outside has obliged Pakistan, Ethiopia, and Somalia to spend more than three times as much on defense as on education and health. Nobody has forced Cameroon to experience public sector losses that exceed the total oil revenues of the state or Argentina to lose twice as much of its GNP on inefficient public enterprises as it spends on social services. And nobody has obliged Brazil to earmark 82 percent of its health budget to expensive urban hospitals while spending only 18 percent on primary health care facilities. We in the South have done it all by ourselves. We must face up to this truth and take much-delayed actions on our domestic front.

At the same time, the North must carry its own responsibilities. It would be more realistic to expect that military spending levels will be lowered in the South if simultaneously the North reduced its own military spending as well as its military support to the developing countries. Corruption will be checked not only by domestic actions in the South, but also by exposing multinationals that corrupt governments and the international banks that give shelter to corrupt money. Maybe there should be an international NGO, Honesty International, to monitor corruption on a global scale. Similarly, the current efforts of the South to open up their economies and markets simply cannot succeed unless the Northern markets also open up. The basic point is that there is need for reforms on both sides. From confrontation, we must progress towards more understanding and greater accommodation.

A New Pattern of Governance

Finally, can we think of new patterns of governance for the next decade? The role of the nation-state is changing fast. On the one hand, the globalization of many issues—from capital flows to information systems—have eroded the power of the individual states. On the other hand, many states have become too inflexible to respond to the needs of specific groups within their own countries. The nation-state seems too small for the big things and too big for the small things.

National governments must find new ways of enabling their own people to participate more fully in government and to allow them much greater influence on the decisions that affect their lives. Greater participation in government must become the overriding theme of the future, including decentralization of government activity to the local levels, a greater role for NGOs, markets that are more people-friendly, and the nurturing of institutions of a civil society at all levels. But, still, it is the pattern of global governance that needs the most thorough examination.

Conclusion

Democracy is unlikely to be so obliging as to stop just at the national borders. Unfortunately, the present patterns of global governance may lay many claims but certainly not a claim to their democratic character. Is it not time that a major responsibility for global decision making in the development and environment field be vested in an Economic Security Council in the UN, a manageable forum where all nations are represented on a geographical basis without a veto power? And is it not time to convert the International Monetary Fund (IMF) again into an "international" monetary agency rather than the 10 percent money manager it has become since its monetary discipline applies only to developing countries? And is it not time to restore the original mandate of the World Bank to stand as a sympathetic intermediary between the global markets and the developing countries, to transfer real resources to them rather than to witness helplessly a growing negative resource transfer? Isn't it time to review the Bretton Woods institutions of yesterday to ensure that they begin to respond to the democratic aspirations of tomorrow?

If we respond to all these challenges—with courage and with wisdom—we can all write a new chapter in human destiny. We can finally celebrate the triumph of the human spirit in a period of fundamental changes, and have a world fit for people. It all depends on our actions. For human destiny is a choice, not a chance.

Section 2 · Social Aspects

Mary Chinery-Hesse

The past few years have marked the onset of far-reaching changes in political, economic, and social systems around the world. Among the most significant of these have been the transition of formerly centrally planned economies towards free markets and democracy, a parallel wave of economic reform marked by the ascendancy of the principles of market efficiency in many developing countries, the advent or reemergence of democracy in the Third World, and globalization of production and new patterns of trade and economic relationships. All these changes are generally viewed with optimism since they are perceived to hold out the promise of greater material prosperity and human freedom. The economic changes promise greater economic efficiency and more productive use of resources which should provide the basis for greater material well-being, while the political changes, if sustained, promise greater individual freedom and increased participation in economic and social life, which would give people the necessary elbow room to author their own destiny.

Social Justice: A Prerequisite for Change

For this promise to be realized fully, however, the process needs to be careful managed, both globally and nationally, to ensure that the process of change remains sensitive to the social problems which are likely to emerge, and also that the benefits of change are widely and equitably distributed, fully taking into consideration concerns of social justice. The processes of global change can be thwarted by social dissent arising from perceptions of inequity. Moreover, if these changes are unimpeded but result in greater social inequalities then their ultimate value would be seriously open to question. The promise of a better future would have been kept only for a few and betrayed for the many.

In contemplating the sweeping global changes before us, it would therefore be prudent to recognize the social problems that could emerge and the actions which can be taken to avert them. Foremost among the risks is the possibility that the newfound enthusiasm for free-market economies can lead to over-zealousness in the implementation of economic reforms. This can take the form of following the logic of market competition to its ultimate conclusion and over-looking the importance of noneconomic aspects and social factors. The manifestation of this would be the absence or inadequate levels of welfare provisions for the losers in the process of competitive change, as well as inadequate levels of labor protection to temper the excesses of market competition. Another, and related risk, is that of excessive appropriation of the benefits of change by a particular social group. This is a danger which is particularly acute in multinational, multiracial, and socially heterogeneous countries. Undue concentration of power in the hands of a particular group and unequal sharing of the benefits of development have invariably proved to be a spark for civil conflict.

The Free-Market and Labor Exploitation

These twin dangers have threatened economic and social progress in the past and it is important that we do not forget the lessons offered by economic and social history. The initial phase of the Industrial Revolution inflicted a heavy social cost in the West because of the resulting unfettered working of competitive economic forces. Pauperism met with social indifference, and exploitative labor practices were rampant. As to the other risk, that of unequal distribution of resources and benefits among social groups, the examples are more recent. These lie in the post-World War II development experience of socially heterogeneous countries, such as Nigeria, Pakistan, and Malaysia, where extreme intergroup inequalities led to civil conflict. Obviously, there is a need to integrate the protective role of governments with the efficient functioning of pure free-market mechanism.

One might legitimately question whether there is sufficient justification for referring to such risks at a time when most countries already subscribe to the principles of minimum protection for the destitute and abject exploitative labor practices. Recent experience, however, indicates that the risks have not entirely disappeared. For instance, many of the structural adjustment programs prescribed for heavily indebted countries in the early 1980s now appear in hindsight to have placed too much emphasis on economic efficiency and too little on the social costs of adjustment, as evidenced by the frequent terrible suffering inflicted on marginal sections of society by ill-timed, poorly sequenced, and callously placed economic policy measures. There has been a more recent moderation of views and increased concern with the social costs of adjustment, but this does not alter the fact that not all that long ago the social costs of change had indeed been overlooked. Similarly, long ago the social costs of change had indeed been overlooked. Hardline advocates of shock therapy as a recipe for transition economies seem insufficiently concerned with the social costs of what is being advocated.

The Rise in Poverty

Another indication that such concerns may not be misplaced lies in the growing signs that poverty and social exclusion have increased in some of the world's richest countries. This has been dramatized by images of growing homeless populations and urban riots, as people have been pushed beyond the normal threshold of tolerance. Other examples lie in the recent overthrow of authoritarian regimes in developing countries, where extreme concentration of economic power was often a primary cause. Furthermore, while it may be generally accepted in principle that social safety nets and equity are important means to put these principles into effect, they are often inadequate. Hence emphasizing the social risks inherent in change at least serves the purpose of drawing attention to the need to ensure that effective policies of social protection will not be overlooked.

Economic Efficiency and Social Equity

A central policy issue is that of striking the right balance between the concerns of economic efficiency and social equity. Admittedly there have been cases where the balance has swung to far to the side of social equity with non-sustainable levels of welfare payments and weakened incentives to work, resulting in slower economic growth. But corrective action has sometimes overshot, resulting in inadequate social protection and the erosion of basic labor rights. A fundamental principle which should guild the global changes which are underway should therefore be strict respect for the maintenance of basic levels of social welfare and labor standards. This principle should not be seen as a hindrance to economic efficiency but rather as the upholding of basic rights. Besides it intrinsic moral justification, there are pragmatic reasons for observing this principle: history has shown that the upholding of labor and social welfare standards is the best guarantee of the social consensus that is essential for the successful management of change. By what means can we increase the likelihood that these principles will be applied in practice? The answer lies in concerted action at both international and national levels.

Social Justice at the Global Level

At the international level it is important to ensure that changes in trade and production patterns do not exacerbate international inequalities. This requires that sufficient attention be given to the plight of the least developed countries. Some measure of international redistribution remains necessary and this should be reflected in foreign aid policies and trade preference.

In this context, issues relating to international migration require special attention. Growing pressures for international migration are a reflection of widening economic inequalities and differential rates of population growth between rich and poor nations. While more liberal immigration policies in rich countries will help to reduce international inequalities, the long-term solution lies in development policies which will create a sustained growth of economic opportunities in poorer countries. This is another powerful argument for directing trade and aid policies towards the reduction of international inequalities. In the meantime, however, international migration will remain as a manifestation of global change and it is imperative that the process is managed with full respect for human rights and the economic and social rights of migrant workers.

It is also important that international financial institutions reinforce their sensitivity to the social costs of economic reform in the policy advice and conditionality that is offered to developing countries undergoing structural adjustment and to economies in transition. Such a stance is not only a moral imperative, but is also essential for ensuring that fragile new democracies are not destabilized by extreme economic austerity. Foreign aid policies should accord priority to the provision of adequate support to new democracies embarking on major economic and social transformation.

The Role of the UN System

The United Nations system has a pivotal role to play in this process through its influence on aid and trade policies and its advocacy of appropriate international and national development strategies. The UNDP has provided a useful organizing concept of Human Development to guide the policy advice and technical assistance that is given by the United Nations system. By ensuring that development policies and programs give priority to poverty alleviation and the improvement of the health, educational, and employment status of the poor the specialized agencies will be making an important contribution to the socially acceptable management of global change.

In this connection the ILO has a special role to play. Its basic mission is to promote enlightened economic and social policies based on tripartite consultation and social consensus. A key means of action is the system of international labor standards which seeks to ensure that social and labor policies respect basic human and labor rights and are directed towards improving working conditions and social protection. These standards have a dual function in that they serve as an injunction against the violation of basic labor rights and standards while at the same time promoting constant improvement in labor and social conditions in line with economic progress. This role of the ILO assumes a special significance in the context of the major global changes that are underway. Through its supervisory role with respect to the observance of international labor standards it can exert pressure to ensure that the global changes underway do not undermine these standards. Since these standards are an important foundation of social policy in general, this role of the ILO can go a long way towards ensuring that the process of change is socially equitable.

In addition, the emphasis on tripartite participation and consultation in the formulation of economic and social policy in international labor standards and other ILO means of action is an important means of guaranteeing that social concerns will receive due attention in fashioning policies for change. It is worth noting in this regard that the principle of tripartite participation and consultation is not confined only to the formulation of policies at the national level but extends to the level of individual industries and enterprises. As such its effects are potentially far-reaching. There is also an added significance to this emphasis on tripartism within the context of the recent spread of pluralistic democracy. Respect for the rights of representative organizations such as those of employers and workers is an important foundation for viable pluralism within a democratic framework. The participation of such organizations in decision making from the grassroots to national levels is essential for the sound functioning of democratic institutions. Thus action by the ILO can promote socially equitable global change at the same time as it sustains the growth of democratic institutions.

Action at the National Level

Turning to action at the national level, an oblivious requirement is that there should be a firm commitment to the principles discussed above. Of particular importance is a commitment to tripartite participation in the formulation of structural adjustment and other programs for economic reform. This will be the best guarantee against the adoption of policies for change which either intentionally or unintentionally impose an excessive social cost. Related to this is the importance of full respect for basic labor rights and standards since this will be a safeguard against the emergence of exploitative economic relationships. In this connection it is important to ensure that economic arguments for deregulation, which often feature prominently in prescriptions for structural adjustment and economic reform, are not accepted without taking into account their social costs. It is also essential not to overlook the positive effects of adequate labor protection on worker motivation and productivity.

Guided by these basic principles, specific policies should be adopted to ensure that the social cost of change is minimized. Among the most important of these are overall economic policies which seek to ensure full employment. While some fall in output and rise in unemployment in the short run are often inevitable in the process of economic reform and restructuring, the goal of full employment should remain a central consideration. This can be attained through policies which ensure that the choice of industries and production techniques are consistent with the factor endowments of an economy. This requires trade and industrialization strategies which promote growth in line with an economy's comparative advantage, as well as competitive capital and labor markets which ensure that relative factor prices are in line with factor endowments. In the case of labor-abundant developing countries this implies a need to emphasizes a labor-intensive pattern of growth in order to ensure sufficient job creation to absorb a rapidly growing labor force. Such a strategy not only makes sense in terms of economic efficiency and growth considerations but is also the best means of alleviating poverty. This is because access to productive employment and decent incomes associated with it provides the best escape route from poverty.

Human Development

Such an employment strategy will need to be supported by sufficient investments in human development. Investments in health, basic education, and training are essential for raising the productive capacity of the poor and thereby strengthening their ability to claim a fair share of the economic opportunities created by economic reforms. Economic policies should thus ensure sufficient allocations for social expenditures, and also that these are adequately targeted on the poor. It should be noted that such social expenditure policies not only represent a worthwhile economic investment but also make a significant and immediate contribution to improving the welfare of the poor. Improved access to socially provided services such as education and health will constitute a significant means of raising their standard of living.

As mentioned earlier, some short-term fall in incomes and employment may be inevitable in the process of economic reform. This will result in retrenchment and increased poverty. These problems have to be dealt with through compensatory programs that provide retraining and redeployment assistance for retrenched workers, through public employment schemes, and through other forms of relief for the new poor. Since short-term social costs are clearly foreseeable, major programs for economic reform should make adequate advance plans for implementing such compensatory programs. These programs are valuable not only for the relief and assistance that they provide to the victims of change, but also for the insurance they provide against the disruption of reform programs by social discontent.

Such compensatory programs should be part of a wide concern with the provision of a minimum social safety net which should cover not only the immediate victims of change but also all those who are in extreme poverty. While most developing countries cannot afford a conventional social security system, there is a strong case for instituting well targeted measures to relieve extreme poverty. This could include public works or other forms of public employment creation for those able to work, as well as welfare relief for those who are unable to work.

Conclusion

Although this paper began with an apprehensive view of the social risks attendant upon the massive global changes that have begun, it ends on an optimistic note. This rests on the recognition that the means for dealing with the problems that have been raised do exist. The preceding discussion has argued that there is sufficient knowledge and experience to guide international and national policies for mitigating the social costs of change. What is now required is a firm commitment to the goals of social equity, and the political will to ensure that this is translated into action in the management of global change.

Section 3 · Paradigms for Paradise: Cultural Paradoxes in a World of Change

Talat Sait Halman

> . . . the world, which seems
> To lie before us like a land of dreams,
> So various, so beautiful, so new,
> Hath really neither joy, nor love, nor light,
> Nor certitude, nor peace, nor help for pain;
> And we are here as on a darkling plain,
> Swept with confused alarms of struggle and flight,
> Where ignorant armies clash by night.

These dramatic lines concluding Matthew Arnold's familiar "Dover Beach" strike an especially ironic chord today. Arnold's vision of a new culture that would seek perfection through the world's best resources of intellectual and artistic creativity remains unfulfilled. Since 1867, when "Dover Beach" was composed, as in earlier times, the world has continued to live its history of shame—wars, genocide, slavery, imperialism, colonialism, tyrannical ideologies, oppression, ignorance, mass starvation, torture, exploitation, the crushing of minorities.

All nations have sinned in different or identical ways. Yet, no political power, small or super, has been innocent. No faith has been without fault, no ideology free of abuse or injustice. Without falling prey to an abysmal Hobbesian animus, one could claim that civil society has yet to supplant evil society in many countries.

In this century, a lobotomy was performed on humanity by some totalitarian ideologies. Of these, the Nazi and fascist doctrines perished at the end of World War II. The death of Communism by 1990 heralded the collapse of the balance of terror known as the Cold War. My "Halman's Law," concerning the rise and fall of ideologies, states that "*Ideology* starts as an *idea*, evolves into an *ideal*, suffuses the collective *id* and the common *idiom*, becomes a shared *identity*, then stumbles into *idolatry*, and ends up as *idiocy*."

A Series of Irony

The "Iron Curtain" has crumbled. So many ironies, however, have emerged that an "Irony Curtain" has fallen on the world.

The first tragic irony is that Cold War animosities have been replaced by new enmities some of which have deep, bitter historical roots. Internal enemies are at each others' throats. Civil wars are raging in many lands. Jingoism and intolerance have reached new levels of violence. Ethnic aggression often erupts in uncontrollable ways of mercilessness. We have entered a new era of blood feud. The aggressive spirit poised in fear throughout the Cold War is beginning to be directed against close and easy targets, often against contiguous nations or ethnic minorities or immigrant communities. "Evil Empire" seems to be yielding its place to "evil empiricism," ideological blocs to mental blocks. Instead of world peace with its powerful prospects as the Cold War came to an end, we have created a fragmented, segmented, demented international structure whose dynamics rely on belligerence.

A second irony relates to the international scientific and intellectual community. Although it had at its command more knowledge and data than ever, it experienced a highly embarrassing failure to forecast the sweeping changes of the late 1980s. Research institutions, data banks, universities, individual scientists, and scholars were unable to foresee, even two years ahead of time, the collapse of the old order. It was a scientific disaster which could be referred to as "the bankruptcy of thinktanks" or, in more compressed form "think-tankruptcy." The international intellectual establishment is still smarting from this fiasco.

The third irony is due to a lacuna of great new ideas and visions in the political and economic sphere. At no point in history was there an accumulation of brainpower comparable to the present-day concentration. Yet, as dramatic changes are taking place, no major new ideologies are being formulated, no significant vision, no important economic theories. The world seems to be going through a barren age of groping. The "New World Order" is simply a return to the old capitalist order, with a few revisions that lack fresh visions.

Capitalism itself constitutes the fourth irony. Newly independent states, including those that have liberated themselves from Communism, have embraced an open market economy. As they do so gleefully, in some cases euphorically, capitalism stands stunned, even in turmoil, in some West European nations and has experienced a major crisis in the United States. Nonetheless, excessive idealization of its values and strategies continues. Among new nations, especially among the desperate ones, blind faith runs deep in its infallibility. As one leader of a new country proclaimed: "Our economy has only two alternatives: the first is capitalism, the second is capitalism." As the sole superpower, the United States—along with Japan and West European countries—is engaged in exporting the free-market economy with a missionary or crusading zeal. The world has moved in the direction of "Broadway capitalism" or "showbiz capitalism." In the absence of alternatives or new creative approaches, "Ockham's razor" slashes with its "principle of parsimony." Irrespective of whether or not the free-market system is suitable for their own economy or culture, many states are plunging into it uncritically. It is a new phenomenon of aping alien models. Many of the same nations, not in the too-distant past, failed because they made the assumption that monolithic ideologies like Communism or theocratic Islam could accommodate themselves to a wide diversity of national cultures. At the present time, the wholesale acceptance of capitalism as a be-all and end-all is more the rule than the exception. The monologues of totalitarian ideologues have given away their places to tirades for free trade. Yet, many "Third World" nations and former "Socialist states" seem inextricably entangled in the free enterprise free-for-all. It is of course conceivable that their new orientation will achieve success in bringing prosperity and stability. But it is also possible that the "Prophets of Profit" will be proven wrong because of social and cultural characteristics not compatible with the new system.

The fifth irony results from the failure to achieve substantial reduction of weapons and to mobilize peace dividends and new investment funds. The cutbacks made in recent years seem minimal if not nominal. Numerous major and minor states in different regions have actually increased their military expenditures. Perplexing double-standards continue: During the Cold War, many governments blamed lack of funds for their inability to allocate money for constructive purposes. Following that frustrating period, peace dividends were said not to have become available. When many peaceful projects were getting canceled and budgetary cutbacks effected, suddenly, when the Persian Gulf War broke out, the Allies were able to make scores of billions of dollars available for the war effort. While every minute at least 20 children died of starvation, more than a billion human beings lived in abject poverty, and funds were scarce for schools, roads, hospitals, it proved possible for many nations to generate a vast sum of money for the Gulf crisis, no less than $600 billion.

The unrelenting contrast between rich and poor, healthy and sick, privileged and victimized, erudite and illiterate, the well-fed and the starving, is the sixth irony, the most tragic of them all. During the first two years of the 1990s, several hundred thousand people starved to death although the world produced and kept in silos more foodstuffs than the amount needed to feed the world population.

The E's of a Good International Society

The new international order is still woefully deficient in creating a "culture of justice for human needs." The vital E's of a good international society are still underdeveloped: Equality, Equity, Education, Employment, Energy, Ethnic Equilibrium, Ethics, Equanimity, Ecological and Environmental Enlightenment, Ecumenism, Enterprise, and Economic Elan.

Significantly, in spite of the rapid growth of technological terminology in recent decades, no new language and few significant terms may be said to have emerged for the "New World Order." The vocabulary vacuum is nothing short of astounding. All great upheavals, all major revolutions have brought in their wake special concepts and brave new terms, as did the French, Industrial, and Communist Revolutions. When the Soviet Union was on the verge of collapse, words like *glasnost* and *perestroika* joined the international lexicon. One could say that a "glasnostalgia" might set in, partly because later cataclysmic changes have yielded hardly any new interesting vocabulary. Such currently fashionable terms as "subsidiarity," "conditionality," "transparency" and the like are weak in content and devoid of ideas. They are merely functional terms. The "trans" words now in wide use seem symptomatic of the syndrome: "transformation," "transfer of resources," "transnational corporations," "transitionals." We live in a "trance." We babble in the Tower of Babel, where "the Lord did confound the language of all the earth." Despite the range of change, we remain confined to a sterile nominalism. To paraphrase Lenin, a most effective way of inducing the collapse of any system is to bastardize the language first. Without meaning to attempt anything of that sort, one can observe that many terms in the international lexicon have deteriorated into new awkward forms of paronomasia.

Because innumerable concepts have become hollow and we have been unable to do away with the vocabulary vacuum, we stand bewildered between a thesaurus of brontosaurus and a glossary of disfigurations. Lexical degradation threatens to go beyond its own etiology in becoming an intellectual malady itself. A special syllabus of syndromes reflects much of the repertoire of problems confronting the world.

So many countries, large and small, are irretrievably in debt that a system of "debt-ocracy" with its own "debt-ishism" has evolved. Just as ghettos arise in some major cities in advanced countries, debtor nations tend to become "debt-oes" in the "New World Order."

As hallowed concepts turn hollow, liberalism deteriorates into libertinism and democracy into "demon-ocracy." Because the welfare state never fared well, the world has said farewell to it. Gross national product (GNP) is now an acronym for such distortions as "gross neglect policy" or "ghastly nincompoop planning" or "grim nihilistic pollution." A new sense of "futilitarianism" sets in as peace benefits become "peace misfits." Many a nation-state is in a state of hallucination. There are those who deride econometrics as "econofretrics" or ridicule the failures of macroeconomics as "macaroni comics." Many nations who had suffered in the hands of *apparatchiks* now have to contend with secessionists who could be called "separat-chiks."

A new class is emerging in many countries—what I tend to call the "poor-geoisie"—poverty-stricken people who are nonetheless consumerists with cars and all basic household goods as well as "well-off" people with all the amenities of life who are nevertheless functionally poor, leading a bourgeois life without joie de vivre. In many cases, the hunger for consumer goods and the intrinsic barrenness of many of them are creating a new type of psychological disquietude and cultural dislocation. In the developing world, a "Faust syndrome" is on the ascendancy whereby individuals and societies seem willing to sell their "cultural soul" in order to gain economic development.

Stumbling Roadblocks

In the universal transformation we are witnessing, some "iron curtains" are proving difficult to raise. In politics, there is a persistent inability to act responsively and responsibly to fulfill the aspirations of the constituents. Participatory democracy is still rudimentary even in democracies touted as exemplary. No meaningful as well as practicable modality has yet been devised to accommodate a truly functional participatory democracy. This deficiency is partly born of an intellectual failure, of weakness of creative imagination in the sphere of political philosophy. In part, it is an issue of leadership. "The Peter Principle," instead of petering out, has become entrenched, if not endemic. The observation that "in an organization, everyone reaches his/her level of incompetence" is virtually a banal fact now in the highest echelons of leadership in a broad spectrum of political systems. A glance at the map of the world will prove that the closing decade of the twentieth century is hardly an "age of great leaders." It could be stated that at no other point in modern history the world experienced such a shortage of global statesmanship in political leadership. By the same token, our era has yet to produce any major philosophers or world-class visionaries.

Rigid patterns of economic systems are also defying constructive change. The economics of poverty still constitutes the basis of development efforts. Political modalities of the powerful continue to prefer the dynamics of the dependency of poor nations on the wealthy. This phenomenon is reinforced by the neoimperialism of technology. Nonterritorial colonialism which reduces the human being to a unit of labor and to merely monetary worth is gaining ground. Ironically, the developing nations, in desperation, are finding no alternative to what could be called an "alms race." Although no more than 0.3 percent of the total income of the developed countries goes to the world's one billion poor, developing countries keep up their competitive solicitation of funds or credit from "potential benefactors" and often seem willing to accept the bondage that accompanies help.

Cultural "iron curtains," mainly militant varieties of so-called fundamentalist faiths and warmongering jingoism, are likely to arrest the development of an ecumenical international order. Even in societies which pride themselves on their humanistic values, tolerance is growing at a painfully slow pace. It is proving difficult to extricate from religions and national cultures those values which could be used for the purposes of a "culture of peace and harmony." Such efforts are frustrated by many negative themes inherent in the same faiths or cultures. Pluralism or multiculturalism remains a remote objective. In fact, in the present era, when sovereignty and self-determination are shaped by national cultures, we may expect "cultural clashes" to proliferate and to spread.

A Culture for World Unity

The evolution of a "culture of world unity" seems likely to require much longer than most visionaries of universalism had imagined. National cultures and monolithic faiths, when they retain their integrity, cannot easily be integrated into a well-functioning ecumenical and internationalist system. What divides them are at least as potent as what appears identical or reconcilable among them. Hence, all the obdurate discriminations, exclusions, oppression and even wars resulting from religious and cultural differences. Unless "faulty culturalism" is rectified, "multiculturalism" will turn into a fiasco. It is bewildering to ponder the cultural dimensions of the religious conflicts that are tearing many large and small nations apart. By the same token, some societies seem to be retrogressing because of their problems with minorities, immigrants, sects, and cults.

Human rights, despite the best efforts of international organizations, are likely to experience setbacks rather than progress in the foreseeable future. In the developing world, the absence or abuse of human rights is an extension of poverty. The obverse is not always true. Prosperity does not automatically strengthen these rights—and often economic difficulties that arise in advanced countries tend to bring in their wake certain dilemmas of discrimination for such groups as "guest-workers," immigrants and religious minorities. It is interesting to observe how several industrialized countries, nowadays vulnerable economically, have been faltering in the human rights area in various ways which they used to criticize vehemently in some developing countries. Such attitudes and acts include the closing of parties, denial of refugee rights, deportations, discriminatory practices against immigrants and minorities.

Unless national governments are willing to adopt enlightened policies based on altruism and lofty principles, we shall probably witness the perpetuation of exclusion, harassment, and abuse. The issue transcends the national will or the dynamics of participatory democracy. It is conceivable that, in many countries, the majority would explicitly express its preference for denial of minority rights—or that, if a referendum is held, such rights might be abrogated or refugees prohibited from entry. The overriding concern of modern governments should, especially in the case of human rights issues, be based on idealpolitik whereby the majority will could sometimes be set aside. Sadly, most societies have not yet reached a high enough level of humanistic maturity. Human rights cannot be left to the mercy of public opinion polls or the popularity contests of politicians.

Full realization of human rights will, under any circumstances, require a radical transformation of the economic systems currently in place. Virtually none provides full equality and freedom from exploitation. Some systems offer more upward mobility than others, but most of them are simply, and often inextricably, linked with and geared to oppressive exploitation which, in certain regions, borders on enslavement. The "New World Order" does not, in and of itself, guarantee amelioration in the sphere of human rights. It will take a "miracle" in economic change *and* cultural enlightenment to achieve a human rights regime freed from the shame of history.

Optimism for Progress

The end of the twentieth century cannot be expected to usher in the new "millenarian millennium." There is, however, good reason for optimism about progress, about amelioration. Certainly participatory democracy will gain strength in many countries—and its spread will stimulate a transition from a travesty of democracy to a more genuine spirit and structure of it elsewhere. Although some strides are likely to be taken towards better protection of the natural environment, cultural ecology may continue to suffer because of irresponsible planning for development or as a result of unplanned, sometimes rampant, growth.

It is reasonable to expect that, in the next century, development efforts will begin to take cognizance of the need to devise ways of reaching the most vitally important target—the individual. So far, strategies have been based on communities, nations, and regions. Development has been seen as an extended function of sovereign states or clusters of them, with the pious hope that benefits would immediately or eventually redound or seep down to individual citizens. It is conceivable that modalities might be created to "humanize" development by taking economic benefits less indirectly to private citizens.

Another crucial challenge facing the economic establishment is finding ways of transferring any and all savings effected from disarmament directly to productive investments and social services. In some political systems, the impression has been created that reduction of weapons does not generate real funds. Contrary to such a myth, it might be possible for economists to plan a method of freezing the savings from arms reductions and then deploying them for economic and social investment programs. Politically and scientifically, the world is—should be—capable of transforming its "arsenals" into "car-senals" and "art-senals." Humanity can convert its armies of defense and destruction into armies of constructive work.

Although it appears unlikely in this decade when a fragmented world is still struggling with civil wars, local conflicts, and various oppressive regimes, there is hope for a new international ideology with its own institutions—not a "supra" structure, but an "ultra-United Nations" with its standing "blue army" and a worldwide police force, its universal food distribution and health services, and a vast new international volunteer network to assist education, housing, community development, and the arts.

A "supra-mandate" will undoubtedly require a major adjustment in the entrenched concept of national sovereignty. Its inroads will have to have links with qualitative changes in government and culture, that is, freedom from totalitarianism and cacocracy; strengthening of tolerance for minorities and massive new migrations of labor and political refugees; openness to religious modernization; an ethical as well as practical sense of shared destiny based on shared resources and efforts; and reinforcement of pantisocratic ideals and humanistic/humanitarian values.

Conclusion

Most of these requisites, although richly articulated in all cultures, are elusive, often virtually impossible when it comes to implementation. Many of them may prove immutable because of taboos and mental tyrannies. Even if constructive values gain strength while impediments become weak, they probably could not constitute a paradigm for paradise. The end of the twentieth century is marked by an absence of utopias. Unlike many previous centuries which produced simple or often elaborate utopian ideas, ours has become a confirmed believer in the impossibility of achieving them. Evocations of paradise linger only in some traditional faiths, and the enlightenment notion of perfectibility seems to have died in our age. All we can do is perhaps best expressed in a line by the American poet Hart Crane: "We make our meek adjustments."

If it proves possible to make more than "meek adjustments," we can have stronger optimism for an accelerated solution for the world's devastating problems—and perhaps even share Walt Whitman's enthusiasm:

> O Libertad, turn your undying face
> To where the future, greater than all the past,
> Is swiftly, surely preparing for you.

Perhaps there are no panaceas. It might be possible, however, to set intellectual forces in motion in the direction of cultural change for a better world of welfare, equality, freedom, and human rights. "A nation", Alexis de Tocqueville had warned, "is least apt to change its cultural habits." Could some religious faiths, some political ideologies, some doctrines of governance relax the strictures of their scriptures? Do cultures open themselves to progressive improvements at the expense of losing some of their traditional values? Is it conceivable that ethical precepts and political ideals distilled from the best of all faiths, of all cultures, of all systems of thought will create a composite idealpolitik for a just international order? Can we produce a "culture of universal equity" which speaks "the language of peace and fulfillment for all" freed from the grammar of trauma?

For strides towards such a prospect, many cultures throughout the world will have to interact, interface, interfuse, and integrate without losing their integrity. This is the "elan vital" which promises to serve as the ultimate stage of the "Creative Evolution" that Henri Bergson perceived as inherent in life: "For a conscious being, to exist is to change, to change is to mature, to mature is to go on creating oneself endlessly."

Section 4 · Containing Ethnic Conflict[1]

Charles William Maynes

Since the Persian Gulf War, all the trends have been in the wrong direction. Rather than the strong protecting the weak, the news has been of cowards firing mortar shells into hospitals and breadlines as in the case of Sarajevo. Instead of people freely enjoying the fruits of their own labor and the rule of law, intolerance and ethnic hatred seem to be spreading across the face of Europe. Not only are the recently liberated peoples of Central and Eastern Europe using their new freedom to act on old hatreds, but ugly racial prejudices are disrupting the most politically stable states of Europe. Right-wing thugs have firebombed innocent foreigners in Germany and a former French prime minister has publicly sympathized with compatriots who object to the presence and smell of France's Arab migrant population.

Indeed, animosity among ethnic groups is beginning to rival the spread of nuclear weapons as the most serious threat to peace that the world faces. No doubt the stakes are high. The conflict between Armenia and Azerbaijan may have had little immediate impact on relations among the great powers, but much larger consequences could flow from the tensions rising between the Russian Republic and the Baltic states. If Russia were to move militarily to protect its co-nationals in Estonia or Latvia, where they are now being mistreated, a cold peace would develop between Moscow and its Western partners. Many of the hopes for a new, more cooperative world would dim.

Larger issues are also involved in the ethnic tension developing in the Serbian province of Kosovo and in newly independent Macedonia, both of which have large Albanian populations. Albania has already announced that it will act in the event of a conflict between the Albanian majority in Kosovo (of more than 90 percent) and Serbia. Greece and Turkey might then be drawn in. NATO would be shaken. The conflict could spread further.

In Africa the geopolitical stakes may be lower, but the level of human misery is greater. A vicious cycle of tribal rivalries and governmental collapse has made all talk of a "New World Order" or a crusade for democracy seem a cruel hoax to most Africans.

Somalia is not the only country in trouble; its neighbors are not in much better shape. In Sudan the central authorities from the north, who are Muslim, have attempted to impose *sharia,* or Muslim law, on the south, whose Christian and animist populations insist on autonomy. The civil war is being fought with such cruelty that tens of thousands of children have lost their parents and now roam the Sudanese countryside searching for food and shelter. Most will perish.

Mozambique is on the verge of collapse because of civil war. Ethiopia teeters. On the other side of Africa, from Angola to Liberia, the news is of ethnic conflict, mass misery, and dissolving authority. And the list grows.

Afghanistan is a cauldron of ethnic and religious hatred. There is little foreign interest in the future of Afghans whose fate was a Western preoccupation during the Cold War. In Haiti, a corrupt military protects a mostly mulatto elite by terrorizing a helpless majority of poor blacks. In short, the balance sheet for the "New World Order" does not look very reassuring. The world appears to be at the beginning, not of a new order, but of a new nightmare.

Using the UN

Since ethnic conflicts are already so well developed and only likely to get worse, many believe the source of the problem is the world's failure to substitute a "New World Order" based on collective security for the outdated Cold War order that rested on East-West hostility fueled by Soviet and U.S. arms. The old antagonism is gone now that Russia threatens primarily itself and Moscow and Washington no longer see one another as enemies. Why not implement the United Nations Charter as its drafters intended and construct a system of global collective security to deal with the new threats?

In response to that call, Secretary-General Boutros Boutros-Ghali in his June 1992 *Agenda for Peace* proposed an ambitious series of steps, including the creation of a small standing UN force. France and Russia have endorsed the creation of such a force, probably in the belief that they will have a larger voice in peacekeeping if it is directed through the UN than if it is organized on an ad hoc basis by Washington. The U.S. government under Bush reserved judgment on the secretary-general's proposal, but in his campaign speeches Clinton suggested the value of a UN rapid deployment force, which "could be used for purposes beyond traditional peacekeeping, such as standing guard at the borders of countries threatened by aggression; preventing more violence against civilian populations; providing humanitarian relief; and combating terrorism." (Despite the multiple tasks, he argued that it would "not be a large standing army but rather a small force that could be called up from units of national armed forces and earmarked and trained in advance.")

The demand for a reinvigorated UN peacekeeping effort is understandable given the many crises that are erupting around the world. But unless care is taken, UN or other peacekeeping forces could be involved in extremely dangerous situations, in which they might be unable to accomplish the goals that reformers have in mind. Most recent commentary fails to recognize, for example, that the UN system, though drawn up in the universal language of collective security where the common enemy appears to be aggression from any source, did in effect identify the likely opponents. They were the enemy states, Germany and Japan, covered in Articles 53 and 107 of the Charter. Discussions at the time the Charter was drafted make clear the general concern of member states over a resurgent Germany or Japan. In other words, a system providing a veto to the five victorious powers could work as long as they had a common enemy, and in 1945 they believed they did.

Is it possible to develop a similar consensus that instability per se is the enemy? It seems unlikely. Washington and Moscow have probably gone as far as possible in their cooperation in the former Yugoslavia, for example. A formal decision to target Serbia militarily would probably break the consensus. The Russian government is under attack from right-wing nationalists for abandoning its traditional ally, Serbia. Certainly, unless the veto could be set aside, the world body would be incapable of doing anything more than offer good offices in the event of a conflict between Russia and one of its neighbors. But even in more distant parts of the world, it is unrealistic to expect that the five countries with a veto on the UN Security Council, particularly China and Russia, will always be able to agree. From the beginning, therefore, in order to avoid unreasonable expectations, those in favor of UN reform must be realistic in their claims. It is highly unlikely that the Persian Gulf War will really turn out to be a model for the future.

Another common mistake in discussions of UN reform involves a confusion of peacekeeping with peace observing. In the past, UN troops were called peacekeepers when they were really peace observers. They were deployed only upon the agreement of the parties in conflict. They were lightly armed and were able to defend themselves only against isolated attacks, not against a major assault by a professional army. When one of the parties benefiting from a peacekeeping agreement decided to abrogate its terms, the UN forces were helpless. In 1967, Egypt demanded that the UN troops separating Israel from Egypt be withdrawn. Eventually, the UN had no alternative but to withdraw them. (The secretary-general should have procrastinated in the hope that the Egyptians would come to their senses, or that outside states would bring pressure to bear on Cairo to change its position, but that is another story.)

When the Israelis told the UN troops separating Israel and the Palestine Liberation Organization in southern Lebanon to get out of the way in 1982, again the UN had no alternative but to bend to Israeli wishes and look on as the Israelis invaded Lebanon. Neither in 1967 nor in 1982 was the UN in a military position to resist an army as large as Egypt's or Israel's. The peacekeepers could only stay as long as both wished them to stay.

Sometimes additional confusion develops because there is talk of using a UN peacekeeping force as a tripwire. But except in unusual circumstances UN peacekeeping troops cannot be equated with, say, the U.S. forces in West Berlin during the Cold War, which did serve a tripwire function. In the case of the U.S. troops in Berlin, Moscow knew that if they were attacked, there was a significant probability that military hostilities with the United States would ensue. In the case of UN troops in the Sinai or southern Lebanon, Cairo and Jerusalem knew that if UN troops attempted to bar the way and therefore were attacked, there was a very low probability of a UN military response. The patron of each side could be expected to use the veto.

The United States, in the hubris of the Reagan administration, forgot the fundamental nature of peacekeeping. It deployed U.S. Marines in Lebanon without understanding that it was essential for their safety that the United States not take sides in the Lebanese civil war. The Reagan administration decided to back the Christians and soon found its troops under attack by the Muslims and finally driven from Lebanon after the disastrous bombing of the marine barracks in Beirut.

Much of the confusion about peacekeeping has developed because of the unusual circumstances in which UN peacekeepers have found themselves in both Lebanon and Bosnia-Herzegovina. In both operations the UN deployments have enjoyed the formal approval of the concerned governments. But for the first time since the Congo operation in the early 1960s—a crisis that nearly destroyed the UN—the world body has found its troops regularly attacked by forces that are not under the control of central governments. Iran, Israel, or Syria may influence the various militias in Lebanon, but no outside force can control them completely. And certainly the government of Lebanon cannot. In such circumstances, whether UN troops can continue to perform their traditional functions depends on the extent of the challenge. If isolated attacks grow to where a large segment of the local population opposes the UN presence, its options are complete withdrawal or the invasion of the country with a force sufficient to compel compliance with UN mandates. The latter course of action is unacceptable to the international community because of the bloodshed and expense involved.

In Bosnia the situation is even more complicated. If Serbia is in adequate control of those forces violating the various UN-negotiated ceasefires, then the appropriate response is to persuade Serbia to end the defiance of UN mandates either by reaching an understanding with Belgrade or, if necessary, by compelling Belgrade through military force. But if the militias are assisted rather than controlled by Serbia, then the UN's options depend on the extent of the local challenge to the UN forces. If that challenge moves beyond isolated attacks to the point of civil war, then the UN must either withdraw from Bosnia-Herzegovina or prepare for the occupation of the country by a force large enough to suppress presumably fierce Serbian resistance. Because that task could involve hundreds of thousands of troops, the great powers have been understandably reluctant to act. Suggestions that air power alone could settle the issue seem specious. Serbs greatly outnumber the Muslims in the former Yugoslavia and the Serbs are better armed. Air attacks on the Serbs are likely to lead to even greater Serbian pressure on the Muslims, who now receive outside supplies only at the sufferance of the Serbs. The West would then be faced with the need to come to the rescue of the Muslims with military operations on the ground.

The best course for the international community therefore is a final effort to reach an agreement by negotiation. If that fails, then the United Nations should respect the demand of the authorities in Sarajevo that they be given the tools to defend themselves. With outside help and even air support, they still would be unlikely to win the war but they might limit the size of a new greater Serbia enough to carve out a place for the Muslim minority to retain their own state. No one should doubt, however, that such a solution would bring even more killing and ethnic cleansing.

It is important to understand the root of the problem in Bosnia-Herzegovina or Somalia. It is not ineptitude on the part of the UN or the European Community or the United States, though all three have made serious mistakes in those crises. The fundamental issue was underscored in a 1992 Brookings Institution study of cooperative security, which stated that

> as the bloodshed in Yugoslavia and Somalia reveals, the international community does not have the security mechanism that would be required to control serious civil violence. The available apparatus of diplomatic mediation backed by the imposition of economic sanctions or even by threatened military intervention requires a corresponding political structure to have any constructive effect.

But to create such a structure would require what might be called the World War II solution: the total defeat of the sanctioned country, the imposition of a new political order there, and a lengthy occupation until the international community was sure that new and more acceptable institutions had taken root. A World War II solution is what the world seems to be edging toward in Somalia because the cost to the international community seems manageable. But even there the great powers hesitate to make the commitment required: The United States has been reluctant to take action to disarm the country and wants to leave it early, several of the other governments participating in the occupation have indicated that they will withdraw their troops when the U.S. troops leave, and the UN is hesitant to confront the need to establish some form of medium-term trusteeship over Somalia until normal life can be restored.

But suppose that the international community were to take all those steps in Somalia. The problems of all the other UN members that are suffering from civil unrest would remain. Already African governments are suggesting UN or U.S. intervention in other ethnic conflicts on their continent. Clearly the UN cannot intervene in every ethnic conflict around the globe. The world must find other ways to address the problems of tribalism and group conflict before the hatred and mistrust are such that only outside military intervention is likely to succeed, yet is unavailable.

Divided Societies

In searching for those other tools, the world must recognize that, in regions like the former Yugoslavia or parts of the former Soviet Union, it is facing the kind of crisis for which it has never had a satisfactory answer. In this century, when two or more populations have been reluctant to live with one another in a single state, the options open to the international community have turned out to be either unconscionable or unpalatable: ethnic cleansing, repression, partition, or power sharing. Of the four, ethnic cleansing ironically appears the most politically effective, albeit the most morally reprehensible. Despite the human costs, Poland and the Czech Republic are more stable today because they were permitted to eject their German minorities. So are Greece and Turkey after they carried out massive exchanges of populations in the 1920s. But at the personal and community level such exchanges are exceedingly cruel and they were only tolerated because the wars they followed had set new standards of cruelty. The world today will rightly be much less tolerant of a state demanding the right to ethnic purity.

Repression has been another answer to ethnic conflict. It was the Communist answer throughout Eastern Europe and in the Soviet Union itself. It is the Syrian answer in Lebanon today. It is an answer that provides a temporary solution today but prepares the way for a political explosion tomorrow. Those repressed only await the day when they can rise up. The world tolerates Syrian repression in Lebanon today only because it seems somewhat more benign than the ethnic and religious anarchy that roiled Lebanese politics from the mid-1970s on. It is a miserable solution to an intractable problem.

Partition along with some form of ethnic cleansing was the world's solution in Palestine and South Asia. The difficulty with partition is that the line cannot be drawn with any exactitude. Significant minorities will be left behind. New ones will be exposed or develop. Partition has been impossible in Bosnia-Herzegovina because the Croatian, Muslim, and Serbian populations have been so mixed.

Power sharing is the most humane approach to the problem of ethnic conflict, but that is not to deny its unusual political difficulty. As John Stuart Mill pronounced in *Representative Government,* democracy is "next to impossible" in a country with a multi-ethnic population. The authorities in ethnically divided Bosnia-Herzegovina at first sought a unified state. The Serbs feared they would be permanently outvoted. Later, under the pressure of a civil war, all sides pretended to discuss power sharing with UN mediator Cyrus Vance and European Community representative David Owen. Power sharing in Zimbabwe took place only after years of civil war. It fell apart in Lebanon because demographic changes called into question the legitimacy of the power-sharing formula.

For power sharing to work in some of the ethnic conflicts that now trouble world peace, however, much more needs to be known about how different societies have attempted to resolve their ethnic conflicts. A 1972 study of conflict resolution in divided states by political scientist Eric Nordlinger did identify several key principles: agreed outcomes, proportionality, mutual vetoes, and "purposive depoliticization." Thus, conflicts are often reduced when party leaders make pre- or post-election deals (agreed outcomes) that accord the defeated parties a place at the table. Societies as different as Austria and Malaysia have reduced bitter ethnic or religious conflicts through a political process of negotiated outcomes. Regardless of election results, the numerically weaker party knew it would still have a voice in national politics.

Many ethnically or politically divided states have tamped down conflict by a proportional division of key offices. Examples of such states include Belgium or pre-1975 Lebanon. Each ethnic group was assured a certain number of key positions.

Frightened minorities may also be reassured by a system of mutual vetoes. Both Austria and Belgium have sought civil peace through such a system. No decision can be made without all key parties agreeing. "Purposive depoliticization" involves an agreement among all parties that certain subjects are outside politics—for example, religion. States that have followed that path include Belgium, Lebanon, and the Netherlands.

The final principle Nordlinger identifies is perhaps the most difficult of all and is rarely practiced. The history of ethnic conflicts suggests that they may be reduced if the stronger group is willing to make the major concessions. In Switzerland, for example, even though the Protestant majority won the civil war in 1847, it made major concessions to the defeated Catholics, who were offered equal representation even though some of their districts were smaller. The gesture was so successful that within a year the defeated cantons had declared that they "would offer their services to the Bund and fight in its army at the slightest sign of a threat to Switzerland from the outside."

Perhaps one reason the United States held together as a democracy after the Civil War is that Abraham Lincoln asked for "malice toward none" and "charity for all." The South, though crushed, regained from the victorious North equal representation in Congress. Indeed, through the seniority system in Congress, the South acquired disproportionate power in the federal government. More recently, white Americans, though a majority, under the pressure of the civil rights movement, accepted limitations on majority rights in the form of affirmative action and other racially directed policies. While those limitations have been extremely controversial, they have not been rejected because the national goal is civic peace. Now, through oddly shaped, gerrymandered districts, the U.S. political system, in the interests of racial harmony, is going so far as to effectively guarantee more seats in Congress for African and Hispanic Americans.

Ironically, studies of ethnic conflict suggest that some of the remedies that Americans assume can address the problem are, in fact, not effective.[2] For example, Americans tend to focus on individual rights rather than on group rights. That is a feature of what might be called Anglo-American democracy. But many European democracies practice what is known as "consociational democracy," which offers greater accommodation to group rights and more protection to those who feel vulnerable in a "winner take all" system of democracy. European practice seems much more appropriate for the ethnically or religiously driven conflicts that are now troubling the world.

The citizens of the United States are big believers in federalism. But specialists in ethnic conflict are wary of federal solutions because they tend to promote secession or partition and even greater intolerance toward the minority groups that are left behind.

Finally, a recent feature of U.S. diplomacy in several administrations has been a strong belief in the need to negotiate from strength. That position, more appropriate for a Cold War struggle, is then applied to other conflicts where it is asserted that no one should win at the negotiation table what has not already been won on the battlefield or through the ballot box. But deeply rooted ethnic, religious, or ideological struggles are not resolved that way. Not understanding that concept, Americans are puzzled when an election in Angola does not end the conflict or when the victorious party in Nicaragua deems it necessary to reach out to the defeated Sandinistas.

The international community needs to know more about what works and what does not in the handling of ethnic or religious conflict. The UN Security Council should commission a study of successful attempts to resolve such conflicts and hold a meeting at the foreign minister level to discuss the results. Leaders in the international community need to understand past successes better so that they may deal more effectively with the crises of today.

Provisions for Peace

Armed with better knowledge, what additional steps might the world community take? First, the international community needs to dramatically improve the UN's ability to practice preventive diplomacy so ethnic or religious tensions can be addressed before they erupt into violence. Member states have long denied the secretary-general the eyes and ears that would enhance his organization's ability to intervene early and effectively in crises that threaten international peace and security. He has no ambassadors or embassies. He has been discouraged from deploying fact finders to investigate crises. He has not been permitted to take advantage of new breakthroughs in satellite intelligence, although at one point intelsat did offer to reserve three channels on its satellites for the UN

To provide the UN the eyes and ears needed, the intelligence agencies of the great powers, searching for a new mission with the end of the Cold War, could provide weekly briefings of the secretary-general or senior UN officials. (There is much criticism of the UN for not alerting the world in time to the disaster in Somalia. But where were the intelligence agencies of the major powers?) The secretary-general could be authorized to buy time regularly on the French satellite surveillance service, spot, that is now available commercially. Moreover, since 1986 the French have proposed a UN satellite for gathering information and monitoring developments around the globe. That would be a more useful but a more expensive option.

There are, of course, provisions in the Charter that, if used, would enhance the world's ability to practice preventive diplomacy. Article 99 permits the secretary-general to bring to the council's attention any situation he deems a threat to peace. But he must know enough about the situation to be sure of his ground. He could draw on Article 99 to dispatch fact-finding missions on his own authority, as Dag Hammarskjöld did—to the dismay of the United States—when he visited China in January 1955; but even if it should be used more often, Article 99 must be used sparingly. Its regular use without the support of the Security Council could deprive the secretary-general of his authority. Rather, the great powers should exploit Article 34 of the Charter, which states that the Security Council "may investigate any dispute or any situation which might lead to international friction or give rise to a dispute." That provision should be used to create anticipatory fact-finding and mediation efforts in crisis spots from the Baltic states to the Horn of Africa.

Second, the international community must begin to redefine the obligations of nation-states so that minority rights receive greater protection. Moral approval must go to the civil state, which seeks to provide a decent life for all of its citizens, rather than to the ethnic state, which provides a home for a dominant nationality. Prince Bernhard von Bulow, the former German chancellor, wrote in 1914 that "in the struggle between nationalities one nation is the hammer, the other the anvil, one is the victor and one is the vanquished." That was the logic employed by Adolf Hitler in asserting the rights of German nationalism over all others. Today's German state is light-years away from the kind of Germany envisaged by either of those leaders, but it still continues a troubling tradition that makes it extremely difficult for non-Germans who have lived for decades in Germany to receive German citizenship. The law effectively brands all foreigners in Germany as not belonging there and so encourages ethnic violence. Japan is another state that has similarly tough citizenship laws. Moral approval for such an approach to citizenship must be withdrawn.

Minority Rights

In promoting the civil state, the UN could look to the League of Nations in the treatment of minorities. The peace treaties of 1919 required states such as Czechoslovakia, Greece, Poland, and Romania to assure full protection to all inhabitants without distinctions of birth and nationality, language, race, or religion. Meanwhile, the League worked out a procedure for the settlement of minority disputes. True, those treaties were flawed. They were too vague. The most powerful states, such as Germany, did not accept comparable obligations toward their minorities. There were no sanctions for those who ignored their provisions. But the treaties represented the first attempt in history to provide international legal protection to minority populations.

Unfortunately, instead of building on those treaties after World War II, UN members gave far less attention to the issue of minority rights. The Soviet Union, with its many minorities, did not want a strong UN interest in their fate. And the United States had its own concerns because of its large African-American minority, many of whom were then denied the right to vote. The UN human rights machinery remained more concerned with individual rights than with minority rights.

That attitude is changing. At the 1992 General Assembly, UN members adopted a resolution on minority rights that stated that persons belonging to such minorities have the right to enjoy their own culture, to profess and practice their own religion, and to use their own language. However, much more needs to be done. Members of the UN should have taken better advantage of the June 1993 meeting in Vienna of the World Conference on Human Rights to begin to develop the concept of the civil state over the ethnic state. An effort should be made to codify strong obligations that all member states would accept with respect to minorities.

Is Human Rights Neocolonialism?

Today, the Third World fears that the developed countries will use human rights to resurrect colonialism. The fears are so great that the Vienna meeting was in danger. To combat those fears, the major states, including the United States, should make it clear that all states, including the great states, will accept the same responsibilities with respect to minorities. At the Vienna meeting, the United States should have pressed for the creation of working groups that could publicly monitor the record of all states in that sensitive area. The UN Security Council should also develop sanctions to be applied against states that violate their international obligations—denial of access to international capital markets and international financial institutions or suspension of their membership in international institutions.

Realistically, world opinion alone cannot prevent a large state from mistreating its minorities if it is determined to do so. But criticism, ostracism, and sanctions can affect decision making. And most states are not in a position to defy the international community totally. As horrible as the events in the former Yugoslavia have been, it is instructive that in the face of vigorous international criticism, which was late to develop, the Serbs opened several concentration camps to inspections by the UN and the Red Cross and began releasing many of the prisoners. Part of the tragedy of the former Yugoslavia rests in the fact that, because the UN has no independent intelligence capability and the great powers do not share their intelligence with it, the appalling conditions in the camps were not news until so many had perished.

Role of Regional Organizations

Third, in order to reduce Third World fears of great power intervention in their internal affairs, part of any international effort to ensure minority rights must be a strengthening of regional organizations. Many developing countries are reluctant to see the Security Council, dominated by five permanent members, of which four are former colonial powers, as the chief enforcement instrument of intervention to maintain international peace and security and to protect minority rights. Indeed, although they deserve membership, making Germany and Japan permanent members of the Security Council will only compound the problem.

There is, in fact, a growing body of evidence to suggest that regional organizations can play a constructive role in sorting out seemingly intractable disputes. The Contadora Group of Latin American states was able to influence the outcome of the civil wars in Central America in a constructive direction, and West African states were able to intervene in Liberia during a cruel civil war, even if difficulties remain. The Association of Southeast Asian Nations (ASEAN) played a substantial role in facilitating the UN peace process that led to the signing of the settlement plan for Cambodia.

It will be objected that the world cannot depend on regional organizations to show the necessary courage. In July 1992, for example, the ASEAN countries remained silent on human rights abuses in Burma while the United States urged the region to take a stronger position. The Organization for African Unity remained silent about Ugandan dictator Idi Amin until he had finally lost power. The Arab League has examined Israel's human rights record with a microscope while turning a blind eye toward much worse abuses in the Arab world.

The way to change that reality is to again exploit the UN Charter. It provides that regional organizations cannot undertake enforcement action without the authorization of the Security Council. That provision of the Charter could be used to develop over time a greater degree of accountability on the part of regional organizations. To date, the Security Council has not made relationships with regional groups a priority.

The Security Council's credibility would be enhanced if its composition were changed. But a Charter amendment to grant permanent seats to countries like Germany and Japan is likely to take time. Meanwhile, the council has the right to create suborgans. For the purposes of peacekeeping missions, the council should create a subcommission for the direction and financing of peacekeeping operations on which Germany and Japan would be regular members. In addition, before the UN authorized a fact-finding or mediation or peacekeeping operation in a particular region of the world, key states from the region should become members of the subcommittee.

Conclusion

The world community should never rule out the use of force in principle. Often, when debating the use of force, the UN seems paralyzed by the prospect of a double standard: How can it intervene in one country when it refuses to do so in another? But the impossibility of intervening everywhere should not bar the UN from acting anywhere. The international community must accept the inevitability of what might be called opportunistic idealism. Thus, one would not have wanted to prevent the dispatch of troops to Somalia simply because the international community was unwilling or unable to take similar actions in other parts of the world. But it is important to understand that the world community will rarely use force to control ethnic and religious conflicts. The international community has neither the will nor the capacity to intervene militarily in such situations. It needs other tools.

The development of such tools need not stand in the way of moving toward the bolder visions outlined by Bush and Clinton in the campaign. The UN could, for example, create a standing military force composed of volunteers who would be willing to undertake dangerous operations under the UN flag. To prepare for the occasional emergency in which a much larger force might be needed, UN members, including the United States, could earmark national forces for peacekeeping tasks. Those forces could be trained to respond quickly, within a few days, to a UN request with which the host government was in agreement. Earmarked forces might train together, and governments providing troops could be invited to join a Security Council subcommittee that would oversee the training and preparation of the forces. But all should understand that the permanent UN force will be far too small to intervene in the many ethnic conflicts from which the world now suffers, and member states may be reluctant to offer earmarked troops for an enforcement action.

Some, especially those sensitive to current U.S. financial difficulties, might ask why the world should organize a UN force that would be used infrequently and would be so clearly unequal to the larger task. The answer lies in a belief that a UN effort to enhance minority rights legally and UN tools diplomatically and militarily would represent a global commitment to act that is now missing even on those occasions where multinational military involvement is both possible and likely to be effective. Help in Somalia, for example, might have been provided much earlier if UN members had already accepted the legal and financial commitments involved in the creation of new legal instruments, new institutional structures, and new military forces. Instead of procrastinating and then insisting that the UN effort be voluntary in order to save money—the initial U.S. position—major powers might have been more inclined to use instruments already in place and paid for.

In the end, of course, the primary need is not for more conflict, even under a UN flag. The need is for more diplomacy—early, persistent, and effective. If the world gains that kind of diplomacy, no one can guarantee that violence will never erupt again as it has in Bosnia or Somalia. But the number of such conflicts can be reduced, the lives of millions improved, and UN members brought closer to their Charter obligations. It would not be a "New World Order," but it would also not be an ignoble goal for a new and activist administration.

Notes

1. This contribution has also appeared as an article in the spring 1993 issue of *Foreign Policy*.

2. See Arend Lijphart, *Democracy in Plural Societies* (New Haven: Yale University Press, 1977); and Eric A. Nordlinger, *Conflict Regulation in Divided Societies* (Cambridge: Harvard Center for International Affairs, 1972).»

Section 5 · Religious Transformations and Societal Changes

Gedaliahu G. Stroumsa

The religious situation in most societies towards the end of the twentieth century is in many ways fluid and paradoxical, and correct assessments are quite difficult to make. Among the main impediments to a precise understanding of the interconnections between religion and various aspects of society lie problems of an intellectual nature. As the philosopher Isaiah Berlin has pointed out, those thinkers of the late nineteenth century who were so influential upon intellectual developments of the twentieth century (suffice here to mention Marx and Nietzsche, as well as Freud, some decades later) would never have imagined religion to remain a factor of such prominence in our own days. They perceived the modern world as reflecting the progressive erosion of religious practice and beliefs, which should lead to their eventual disappearance. For them, modernity was to a large extent defined by the weakening of religious forms of behavior. To be sure, they thought only about modernizing Western Europe. But their many epigones from so many corners of the world assumed as a matter of faith that their lessons were to be applied on other less developed societies, where the hope of modernization often meant a craving for the ways of European culture. As a result of this neglect, which is far from benign, we are now quite improperly equipped in order to understand phenomena which for better or for worse have a direct, and sometimes decisive influence upon our own lives.

Recent Impacts of Religions

The influence of religions, however, is far from being a simple phenomenon. The place and action of religion in any society is an extremely complex business. It is compounded in the modern world, precisely, by the global and powerful nature of the changes that have affected, and are still affecting, all societies. These changes are not of a single nature, and affect various societies with different levels of intensity. Since they are still in urgent need of a better understanding, I shall not attempt here a highly structured interpretation of numerous and vastly different phenomena. Rather, I shall give here only a few examples, but intend to come back to the various dimensions of religious impact on contemporary societies below.

The impact of the Iranian Islamic revolution and its aftermath is still being felt throughout the world. The Algerian president was murdered on 29 June 1992 by Muslim "fundamentalists" (this somewhat misleading term is now used widely throughout Islamic societies). Similar groups had already murdered the Egyptian president, Anwar al-Sadat. No doubt, one can point out to various elements in Iranian society and economy throughout the twentieth century which partly explain the rise of Ayatollah Khomeini to power. But it is certainly just as important to point out the impact of the societal changes caused by the Islamic revolution. Religion, indeed, is often a major factor of social, cultural, and even political change. In other societies, religious elites and pressure from the faithful are sometimes instrumental in encouraging respect for human rights.

Another example, out of many, could be the Janus face of contemporary Catholicism. No past Pope has traveled so much, asserting Catholic presence in so many countries, as well as affirming the Church's direct interest and responsibility in so many economic, social, and political areas as the John Paul II has done, and is still doing. At the same time, Catholic Church leaders are insisting on a staunchly conservative position on such issues as birth control, at the cost of serious dissent from the rank and file of probably most churchgoers, at least in Western or developed countries. Reference should also be made here to attitudes of the Church hierarchy and rank and file in various countries of South America, where the Christianity is often fighting for the rights of the poor and for a more policed society, with or without clear identification with the presuppositions, goals, and methods of the "liberation theology."

A third instance is that of the intimate links between religion and nationalism. In two cases, at least, in twentieth century history, religious identification was the obvious root or official reason for the establishment of new states. I am alluding to the creation of Pakistan and of Israel after World War II. (To be sure, the identification of religion and nationhood in the case of the Zionists complicates the matter further, while Pakistan was meant to be *a* model Islamic state). But the active part played by religion in the formation of national identity is of course far from being limited to these two cases. To take another instance of high international profile, after a generation of emphasis on secular themes in the definition of national identity, the Palestinian national movement seems more and more to emphasize Islamic themes in its self-perception (a trend followed with some anxiety, and felt to be ominous, by the no less nationalist-minded Christian Palestinian minority).

The conundrum between religion and nationalism is perhaps nowhere felt with such sadness as in the case of the fighting between the peoples of former Yugoslavia. The deep chasm between Serbs and Croats is obviously not only of an ethnic or linguistic nature. The two peoples are also separated by religious boundaries: the Serbs are Orthodox, while the Croats are Catholics. In the case of the Bosnians, Muslims in their majority; the religious roots of the traditional hatred and present fighting are even more obvious. Propaganda leaflets or even advertisement pages in Western newspapers will unabashedly emphasize these religious differences. It is clear, therefore, that the major although ambiguous role played by religion in the formation and transformation of ethnic identities in the contemporary world can be ignored or explained away only at a high cost.

The radical changes brought about by the collapse of Communist regimes and of the Communist ideology in the former Soviet Union and in the countries of Eastern Europe are too fresh, and the situation is still evolving so rapidly in most or all of these societies to be observed and analyzed clearly with a serious chance of reaching secure conclusions. This is the case, in particular, since

Communist ideology was strongly antireligious, and sought to uproot religious faith and beliefs throughout the societies it ruled. To some extent, obviously, such policies failed miserably. But to some extent, they succeeded in erasing traditional religious education and practice, as well as in using religious hierarchies become vassals of the political power for promoting their own pervert policies. For a classical example of such a ruthless manipulation of churches, one may refer to Stalin's behavior in Ukraine, pitting the three Churches (the Russian Orthodox, the Ukrainian Orthodox and the Ukrainian Uniate) one against the others. The legacy of Communist rule should explain the upheaval in which we find today the churches, as well as the personal identity of many, in the former Communist societies. What is certain, however, is that the state of economic poverty and the almost complete lack of a civil society in which many of these countries have been left with the demise of the former ideology encourage atavistic movements and reactions. The people in these societies are left today without a tradition of religious or political tolerance, and without the strong incentive of a powerful legal and political liberal system, reinforced by both constitutional rights and jurisprudence. Under such conditions, the easy way is to rely on the "instincts of the tribe"—those who are most noticeably different from the majority, be they the Armenians in Azerbaijan (and the Azeris in Armenia), the Slavs in Moldova, the Gypsies in Czechia, in Slovakia, in Poland, in Hungary or in Romania, and the Jews, or rather the memory of the Jews, almost everywhere, are bound to become the victims of a mixture of racial and religious tensions and traditional hatred heightened by the new conditions. One of the most puzzling and melancholy phenomena in Eastern Europe, from that perspective, is the rise of anti-Semitism, once again, sometimes, as in Poland, with no or very few Jews around. Everywhere in Europe, it seems, the centripete forces are striving towards the breakdown of larger, pluri-dimensional (in the religious or ethnic sense) societies, and enforce, or seek to enforce, a return to traditional boundaries and identities. Here, the case of the rather successful, although not quite radical, attempts at creating new frames of identity in the countries of Western Europe appears to be the exception rather than the rule.

Religion and Society: Some Historical Cases

Before we turn to these problems in some more detail, let us review some historical cases of the intricate relationships between religion and society. There is obviously no way to cover these relationships adequately, but some reflection on how problems have been stated in the past might help us in understanding the present predicament. What must be emphasized, however, is the fact that no single subordinatory model is convincing.

It would be as futile to claim that religion is a function of society (a superstructure, as the Marxists used to say) as it would be to argue that religion represents the essence of every society and that societal changes are all to be explained by religious transformations. Rather, I would suggest that religion should be considered as an integral part of the "ecological system" of a society. Such a view of things entails, first of all, an interactive or dialectical conception of the role of religion in the transformations of societies. We can approach this role from various viewpoints. We may focus on social and economic changes, on changes in the structure of power, on cultural changes, including on transformations of ethics and interpersonal relationships, or even the conception of the individual or of the person, including attitudes to the body, illness and healing, sexual attitudes, etc.

Religions, like societies, can evolve slowly, showing patterns of evolution of traditions with time and new influences. Hence, deep changes in religious conceptions are often the result of long-range evolutionary processes. But we also sometimes witness what might be called genuine religious revolutions, which have a logic of their own. As examples of such revolutions in the ancient world, one can mention the Amarna religion in ancient Egypt, the emergence and crystallization of Israelite monotheism, Zarathustra's radical reinterpretation of ancient Iranian religion, or the Upanishadic transformation of Vedic beliefs. In many cases, such transformations have reflected the passage from archaic religions (i.e., religions of archaic societies, closely related to the well-or ill-being of the society itself, rather than mainly to the fate of the individual) to religions of salvation. The focus moves from the community as a whole to the place of the individual within it, and reflects a strong interiorization of religious values and the emergence of new conceptions of the individual.

Throughout the first millennium B.C., but particularly around the middle of that millennium, a series of drastic religious transformations occurred in some deeply different civilizations that were not related to one another. The emergence of the prophetic movement in Israel, the writings of the first Greek philosophers, Zarathustra's radical reform of the old Iranian religion, and the preaching of the Buddha or the teachings of Confucius, all happened around the year 500. The philosopher Karl Jaspers, who first called attention to this apparently puzzling phenomenon, has spoken of an *Achsenzeit,* an axial age. My senior colleague at the Hebrew University of Jerusalem, the sociologist Shmuel Noah Eisenstadt, has proposed to study what he calls "breakthroughs" in religious attitudes of the ancient world and their relationships with transformations of societies and cultures, and the passage from the "archaic" to the "classical" societies.

With the early rise of the Christian movement and its progressive separation from its Jewish matrix, we can follow a different transformational pattern. The early centuries of the common era also reflect the deep transformation of the Israelite religion into Rabbinic Judaism with the destruction of the Temple in Jerusalem, as well as the "mutation," to use a biological metaphor, of monotheism into the radical dualist teachings of the various Gnostic sects and the Manichaeans. The fourth century and the reigns of Constantine the Great and his sons testify to the final victory of Christianity over paganism in the Roman Empire. In late antiquity, particularly with Christianity or with Gnostic trends, the correlations between religious thought, or theology, and practice and the definition of society and the individual changed in some radical ways. Traditional pagan attitudes to political power, to the state, to questions of peace and war, and even to economic behavior, were transformed, in some cases deeply, by the accession of Christianity as the new ideology of those in power, and then by the mass conversions and abandonment, either voluntary or induced by religious coercion, of traditional religious practices and inherited cultural attitudes and conceptions.

The case of Islam represents a phenomenon *sui generis,* because of its relative belatedness and because it reflects a profound reinterpretation of not one, but two religious traditions. Here too, the implications of the new theology for conceptions of political power or of the individual are obvious. The extent to which the concept, emphasized in early Christianity, of "returning to Caesar what belongs to Caesar" was in the Middle Ages, and remains today, inapplicable in the case of Islam is obvious: the religious community is here identified as the nation of Islam, the *umma,* which becomes the main social unit and criterion of identity.

At the outset of the modern times, the Christian Reform also had a radical and multiform influence on the transformation of societies. Hence Max Weber has argued in his seminal work on the *Protestant Ethic* that what he called the "innerworldly asceticism" of the New England Puritans should be seen as one of the main roots of U.S. capitalism. Here is obviously not the place to belabor this point, and the reference to a classic research is made simply in order to remind us of the importance of religious conceptions, beliefs, and behavior, also in the very structure of the modern times.

Religion and Society

We should now move to a schematic description of the various possible relationships between religion and society in the contemporary world.

Monoreligious Societies

Monoreligious societies are those in which the religious identification of all the population or of its vast majority is of one single religious denomination. Such is the case in societies as different as Poland, where the population is almost totally Catholic, and most countries of the Arab world, which identifies with Islam despite sizable Christian communities in Lebanon and especially in Egypt, where live about eight million Copts. We should also mention the special cases of small traditional societies, such as various Indian peoples in the Americas, although these societies have been submitted to intensive missions over the last five centuries, and are in any case in no way able to rule themselves.

Polyreligious Societies

The situation which obtains in Egypt, where two different religious groups claim to the same legitimacy about national identity, exists also elsewhere, sometimes even in clearer fashion. This is true for instance in Ukraine between Catholics and Orthodox who are both Ukrainian ethnics, in Sri Lanka between the Buddhist Singhalese majority and the Tamil Hindu minority, in India mainly between Hindus and Muslims, but also, particularly in the last few years, with the Sikhs, in Nigeria between Christians and Muslims, in Sudan between the Muslim majority and the Christian and animist minorities. It is also true in Western societies, such as Germany (before the unification, the former Western German Federal Republic was divided rather fairly between Catholics and Protestants) or in the United States, where the great number of religious identities is constantly evolving. Protestants from many various denominations, Catholics, Jews, now even substantial Muslim and Buddhist minorities, all form the religious mosaic of the United States. We should not leave out of this map the various "new" religions or cults, either native to the United States and already "established," such as the Mormons, or reflecting the "new age," like the Hare Krishna, the Unification Church (the "Moonies"), or the many groups that blossom on various fringes of North American society.

In all those cases except the last, religious plurality is bringing social unrest, and often violence. It is of course impossible to pinpoint in each case the origins or the first culprits of such violence. It may start with the minority, which tries to assert its identity in this way (thus the Sikhs), or with the majority power (thus the Islamic government of Sudan, enforcing coercion on non-Muslims, by conversion attempts or/and a rude behavior, including forced resettlement in the worst possible conditions, which is often equivalent to mass murder.

Polyethnic and Polyreligious Societies

Although in some of the cases above, particularly that of Sudan, the religious boundaries follow ethnic or tribal boundaries, other cases of such a double division are even clearer. In Israel, for instance, the main division of society is an ethnic one, between the Jewish majority and the Arab, or Palestinian, minority. Palestinian Arabs are overwhelmingly Muslims (approximately 85 percent), but the main religious line between Jews and Muslims (or Christians) follows ethnic boundaries. The same is true in Bulgaria, where the Turkish minority is identical with the presence of Islam in a country which identifies itself as Christian from a historical and cultural point of view. A similar situation exists in Cyprus, where the ethnic and religious boundaries between the Greek Orthodox and Turkish Muslims communities have resulted in the division of the island, for all practical purposes, between two independent societies. In a country like Romania, the Hungarian minority is also a religious one: Catholics in an Orthodox society.

Attitudes to Religion in Different Regimes

Democratic Societies

Some of the societies mentioned above have stable, democratic regimes, which provide a series of historically tested ways in order to effect peaceful transitions and to recognize change when it occurs. For instance, the recent vote on the legality of abortion in the German parliament or the reaffirmation of the principle of its legality (*Roe* v. *Wade*) in the U.S. Supreme Court are not primarily to be seen in a religious context, although it would be difficult to deny the religious dimensions or implications of these events. One could also add, in these societies, the numerous instances of public discussion (in the press for instance) of cases of religious tolerance stemming from totally new conditions, and their progressive assimilation by the jurisprudence.

In Canada, to take only one example, the new communities of Hindus and Muslims demand equal religious rights to those granted a long time ago to members of other communities, and the courts study these requests and require the new religious situation (which stems, obviously, from a new ethnic fabric of society) to be met by adequate conditions. Similar situations arise in various countries of Western Europe, such as England, France, or Germany, mainly with Muslim minorities. Islam is already the second religious denomination in France, where there are now many more Muslims than either Jews or Protestants.

These are quite new situations, and as we all know from even a most cursory reading of the newspapers, these transformations of societies do not come along without any backlash of religious bigotry and ethnic hatred. The extreme right, which is on the rise in all of these countries, builds on people's inherited fears and repulsions, and often proposes radical solutions such as expulsion (repatriation is the euphemism now most commonly used). A decade ago, I heard a macabre joke in West Germany: "The past of the Jews is the future of the Turks."

Nondemocratic Societies

Both in various countries of the developing world (the so-called Third World) and in societies emerging from decades of Communist rule, the conception of a civil society exists only at an embryonic stage. In such societies, religion and nationalism feed each other, and both are strengthened by the extremely harsh economic situation. Religion often appears not to be the main element in the syndrome, but rather is used as a fuel to raise the tensions which are more often of an essentially ethnic character. The growth of nationalism and of xenophobia is often directly related to a rise in the level and the strength of religious fanaticism, particularly, but not only, on the part of the majority. All these processes, of course, are of a dynamic nature, and hence they strengthen and transform one another.

Religious Transformations

It is of course impossible to define here the nature of the global change confronting us today. For our purposes, let us only list some major aspects of change directly related to transformations of religious systems of belief and/or practice.

The political transformations which we are witnessing throughout Eastern Europe and the former Soviet Union are most impressive. The collapse of Communist ideology and its antireligious ethos are obviously bound to have a direct effect on religion in many societies, and in some sense have already affected religious attitudes, perceptions, and identification. We should note here that these transformations are not necessarily or only of a positive nature. Too often the newly acquired freedom of religion seems to entail unpleasant connections between religious belief, practice, or even hierarchies, and some of the worst aspects of ardent nationalism and unleashed xenophobia (sometimes bursting out in pogroms of different kinds) which were kept under control under the Communist regimes. Yet, these political changes are not the only ones, nor may they be the most important ones for the long range. We should also take into account social and economic changes in many societies (including, in particular, underdeveloped societies). Even more potent for present and future developments are perhaps, to my mind, some major ethnic transformations of many societies happening right under our eyes. I am referring here, in particular, to the waves of immigration in the richer countries of Western Europe, coming either from the East or from the Near East and North Africa. These waves of immigration transform the religious structure of societies. Geneva has become a city with a Catholic majority, while Islam is growing in strength throughout Western Europe and the Americas.

Transformations Within a Specific Religious Tradition

Major transformations occur today in most or all major religious traditions. These transformations are mainly due to modernization and its after-effects, including a return to roots, understood in various ways. These returns to roots do not necessarily entail patterns of beliefs or behavior which we could call "fundamentalist." What they do share, however, is a deep mistrust of the new, "Westernized" and "uprooted" culture (i.e., bearing an international character). Dress habits, music, movies, and television, all seem to carry the same message; the traditional cultures which were the carriers of religious inherited attitudes are on the decline. It is to fight against this decline, which is not perceived as irrevocable, that the proposers of such revivalist movements fight.

Revivalism under its various garbs may be the most visible reflection of the transformations of religious traditions today. But we must remember that it is not the only one. Nor is it, necessarily, the most fundamental aspect of the contemporary transformation of the religious scene. After all, "revivalism" reflects a secondary behavior, one of reaction against a leading trend. This trend, a by-product of modernization, insists on the global, collective, shared, aspects of human existence at the end of the twentieth century. Men and women coming from all cultures and geographical areas are able to recognize, more and more, that they have much to share, and that what divides them is not always of the deepest significance for their lives. Hence, a growing recognition, in many places, of the value of other peoples' experience, even religious experience. This is often translated into syncretistic behavior, or syncretistic patterns of thought. Although such intellectual or cultic syncretism does not always reflect conscious choices, it shapes anew, sometimes in drastic ways, the traditional religions.

A final trait of the religious transformations in the modern era is the chasm often happening between religious faith and religious practice. Due to the ever broader influence of scientific ideas, as well as to the pervasive character of modern life, men and women from all traditions tend to ignore, reject, or doubt, to varying levels, some of the inherited beliefs and/or behavioral patterns. The fact that people develop skepticism as to the truth value of some fundamental or marginal beliefs of their religious traditions does not always, or even usually, mean that they distantiate themselves from those traditions. The "cognitive dissonance" developed can simply be reflected in a certain lack of practice, or seriousness in practice, and/or in a practice somewhat disconnected from some of the beliefs upon which it is in theory established. The will to belong and the strength of the traditional ties is often stronger that logic in religious life, and the "cognitive dissonance" means that the chasm will have at some point to be reinterpreted through hermeneutics. Throughout their history, religious traditions have evolved through such hermeneutics. The present changes are not quite novel in their nature, but only in their scope.

New Religious Identities

The inner transformations of religious traditions, however, are not the only ones to be observed today. We can follow, again in very different cultures, and under quite different conditions, various passages from one religious identity to another, as well as the complete, or almost complete, abandonment of religious practice, belief, and identity.

Conversion is of course the most obvious of these transformations of the religious identity of the individual. Various Christian missionary movements are still active today in many parts of the world; in Africa, in the Americas, in Asia and Oceania, but also, with renewed energy, in Eastern Europe and in the former Soviet lands. Parallel to the Christian, missions, we find in various places a strong appeal of Islam. In Western as well as in Eastern Africa, for instance, it seems that the conversion process to Islam is very active today. When dealing with tribal societies, or societies which were still tribal a short while ago, such conversions are often mass conversions. It is not unusual to see a whole village convert to Islam, for instance, with its traditional chief. Along with such "traditional" cases of conversion, we should mention conversion to Asian religions, mainly Buddhism in Western societies. Such conversions, though not always formal, remain fashionable, or at least possible for marginal, but rather sizable groups within Western societies, in particular, but not only, in the United States.

Last but not least, reference should be made to the conversion to various new religions or religious groups, often unabashedly syncretistic in their outlook and theology. Such groups, called "cults" by their detractors, include the Church of Unification, established by a Korean, who is a former Protestant minister, which seeks to mix into a universal theology various beliefs derived from Biblical myth, sometimes interpreted in Gnostic fashion, and a quite new belief in the exemplary role of the Korean people in human salvation history.

Still recently, it was possible to speculate on the consequences of mass alienation from any religious practice, knowledge, or identity, on the part of millions of people throughout the Communist lands. This is not possible anymore. We should here become quiet observers for some time, before any prognostics on future trends can be made. True, a similar, though benign, trend in abandonment of traditional religion has been observed throughout Western societies for some time. Here too, it is too early to tell whether it will ultimately lead to a disenchantment from religion or to new forms of religious identity.

Conclusion

The radical and polyvalent nature of the changes transforming whole societies in the contemporary world make it imperative to monitor religious transformations as adequately as possible. A careful understanding of religious attitudes and identity and of their significance is imperative, be it only because of the great tensions and potential dangers both for internal peace within the different societies and for peace among nations. In an era of global change and of global trends, our traditional approaches of the study of religion should be modified. It seems to me that we should, much more than ever before, focus our attention onto the milieu in which religions live, and to the varied and important functions they accomplish in the different societies. We should thus first analyze the situation according to the different geographical-cultural areas. Moreover, the religious situation should be analyzed according to the following parameters:

- Political identity: state, nation, legal system, and ethnicity.
- Cultural identity: language, polity, tradition of tolerance or intolerance, and again legal system and ethnicity, and attitudes towards personal status and behavior, including towards traditional kinship rules and legitimation of birth control methods.
- Economic and social identity: modes of production, social and economic spectrum, repartition of riches, and so on.

I wish to repeat once more: these different levels and parameters, as well as others omitted here, are irreducible to one another, and therefore must all be taken into consideration. In each society, the different religious situation can be understood only through the singular "kaleidoscope" image obtained through the dialectical interaction between these parameters.

The study of the place and function of religion in the various "ecosystems" along the lines suggested more than developed above is only in its beginning stages. But the urgency of our situation calls for action, side by side with observation. I propose here to seek by all possible means the adoption and application, in all states, of the UN Declaration on the Elimination of all Forms of Intolerance and of Discrimination based on Religion and Belief, adopted on 25 November 1981.

Section 6 · The Role and Status of Family and Women

Princess Basma Bint Talal

The past few decades of the twentieth century have been classified as the era of change, a time when human civilization has witnessed more change than in all of recorded history. On the threshold of the twenty-first century, this change is becoming more rapid than ever before. Although the magnitude and consequences of the worldwide changes, particularly in the past few years, are as yet relatively unknown, the impact will inevitably be on all facets of society, creating new challenges, aspirations, dimensions, and uncertainties.

The yearning for freedom and democracy has compelled the major change which saw the end of the Cold War. People now have a new voice, new hopes and new aspirations. We must seize the opportunity to set standards for international behavior for the humane and democratic treatment of all individuals.

The Role of Women in Change

My main concern is how women in developing countries will fare in this transformation period. As we are well aware, we are moving into competitive markets that are supposed to promote efficient allocation of resources and division of labor, but which also require educational and innovative skills. Women in developing countries, with half the schooling of men and low participation in the labor force, need to be well-equipped to compete in such a new situation. With such a gap, will women have an equal opportunity in market economies? As a group, will developing countries fare well in the "New World Order," while such a less-equipped group constitutes half of their societies?

These issues raise many questions about the status and role of women, and whether the change and its effect on systems and people will promote an advancement in the status of women. Will the narrowing in the man/woman gap in developing countries be a prerequisite for change?

The underprivileged status of women in developing countries is one of the main, if not the main, factor delaying social and correspondingly economic development. The new world economic order calls for and promotes innovation, competition, and entrepreneurship. Without the enhancement of their capabilities and improvement in their status, no real significant change will develop in these societies.

The Need for Change in the Status of Women

In the case of developing countries, which constitute more than 80 percent of the world's population, *A World Fit for People* above all, calls for the change in the status of women and eradication of their illiteracy. It also calls for their equal status in the society, equal participation in decision making, and the enhancement of their job opportunities in the labor market. Without these changes, the chance of a political and economical change for a new and better world may not take place.

Jordan has recently set an example of true democracy. A woman's rights to vote and be elected have been emphasized with no restrictions whatsoever. Women are free to voice their opinions in public and express their hopes and aspirations. The outcome may not have fully lived up to their expectations, but the democratic process is gaining more and more momentum in favor of women's effective participation in all spheres of Jordanian life.

Individualism vs. Dependency

As we move into the twenty-first century, the South is still poverty stricken, illiterate, struggling for its survival, and in a state of subservience and dependency. In contrast, the North is acquiring more affluence, compiling more knowledge, and has achieved both freedom with the right of choice and autonomy.

People, however, do not adapt easily to behavioral and social change; their cultural heritage, education, and family upbringing have conditioned them to live within a set of norms, according to their relative role expectations. Attention should be focused on how these societies can progress while at the same time preserving the advantageous aspects of their individualism.

The Role of Family and the Society

The family in my country is one of the main fabrics of society, of which we are most proud. During the last four decades, and as a result of the conflicts in the Middle East, Jordan has had to absorb three major waves of immigrants, which doubled the number of population and stretched its meager resources to the limit.

Without its strong collective society and the stabilizing political system that Jordan has maintained, I wonder whether we would have been able to absorb such human and regional upheavals, while at the same time maintaining the vigor for development and pursuit of a better future. Our collective society norms have also helped us to avoid many of the unfortunate features which accompany the process of development. All these are contained with a healthy and democratic environment.

Conclusion

In creating a "New World Order" we would have to bear in mind some fundamental issues. The narrowing of the socioeconomic disparities between the

North and South, with the benefits of technology shared by all. Women's role in all spheres of life should be enhanced and strengthened, to ensure the comprehensive development of the countries in the South. At the same time, the advantageous aspects of family structure must be preserved. The interest of people, the respect and recognition of human rights must come first if we are to achieve true democracy.

Section 7 · Self-Respect: A Key Value

Nicholaa Malet de Carteret

The main concern facing policy makers in the 1990s is the management of the planet. Until now, policies have focused on local and regional interests. For the first time, the turbulent and dramatic changes sweeping the world are forcing new decision-making structures to be introduced at a global level. Decision makers are faced with the need to consider broader contexts, instead of restricting themselves to detailed knowledge of particular issues. Why? The problems threatening the planet today—famine, illiteracy, population growth, climatic change—are all interconnected. They can no longer be viewed in isolation. Failures in one area hamper another. Changes in one part of the socioecological system can cause unexpected, even devastating, changes in other parts.

Applying a systems approach to development, within the context of planet management, is a useful step forward. A systems approach encourages both a holistic overview of any dynamic or problem, as well as an analysis of the relationship that exists between all of the parts contributing to the problem as a whole. This makes even more sense when the planet itself is viewed as one complex global system, comprised of multitudinous "organizations" of various sizes and capacities, all interacting. These organizations range from the smallest unit, called the "family," to the largest unit called a "nation." At the heart of all organizations lies the individual, sheltering, possibly the most complex system of all—the human mind. It is the human mind, interacting with other human minds, which is responsible in the final analysis, for all innovations, decisions, and actions carried out within any organization.

In 1990 the International Institute for Applied Systems Analysis (IIASA) examined some of the causes of unsustainable development using systems analysis. By applying such analysis to issues of population growth, development, and ecology, the conceptual models reveal many important interlinkages. However, systems analysis can also alert us to the less obvious linkages, which are the most crucial when managing complex systems.

For instance, the analysis reveals some less obvious linkages between value systems and education, needs, desires and aspirations, per capita demand, population growth, the use of natural resources, and the state of the ecology. Thus, value systems, education, and mass media are shown to influence needs, desires, and aspirations which in turn affect satisfaction which in turn determines the quality of life—described by the report as the ultimate goal of development.

In terms of analyzing changes within the framework of human and ecological values, the less obvious linkages are frequently overlooked in favor of the more obvious political and economic factors. Educational factors are more easily recognized as contributors to underdevelopment (for example the connection between failures in family planning and insufficient education for women), whereas the linkages between education and value systems, and their subsequent linkages to human psychology are ignored by workers in the field of development. Whilst the IIASA includes value systems within their conceptual model, they do not form a major part of the case study analysis. Nor does the conceptual model offer any indicator of which factors influence value systems and education.

This paper aims to shed some light on the relevance of value systems, and in particular the values of self-respect and respect for others, in shaping the process of change. Many decisions and actions concerning planet management result from the value systems of individuals and societies. Changes in these value systems—sometimes even the lack of change—are the root cause of so many of the problems facing the world community today.

Values: A Help or a Hindrance in Development?

What forms an individual's or society's value systems? A combination of thought processes, attitudes, beliefs, knowledge, motives, and conscience. What does a value system represent? It represents a statement of what an individual or society holds to be of value, socially or morally, based on standards of right and wrong.

From the perspective of psychological anthropology, the main difference between the social life of animals and those of humans, is that every human social order is also a moral order. Every society has standards of right and wrong, which it guards with a system of control. This moral order not only exists external to the individual in the form of socially sanctioned rules and regulations, but it also lies within the individual.

The internal moral order is mediated by individual conscience, which arises out of the human capacity for self-judgment. Thus, a prerequisite to morality and, ultimately, to value-based judgments is self-awareness. In other words, the awareness of internal thought processes. Self-awareness implies self-respect and self-esteem. When awareness is not internalized, or when it is misdirected, self-respect manifests negatively as pride or ego. That is to say self-awareness is consciousness: the knowledge of the self as a living, thinking, judging, being.

Consciousness, whether channeled positively through self-respect, or negatively through ego, influences individual conscience. As mediator of the internal moral order, the conscience determines standards of right and wrong, leading ultimately to the formation of value and belief systems.

Value systems are constantly changing because consciousness (awareness) is constantly changing. Attitudes, beliefs, patterns of behavior are altered accordingly. When for example, in the Western world, consciousness has become increasingly externalized, resulting in what one might call "consumer consciousness." Over the last few decades, society has endorsed, through a collective value system, purchasing power as a symbol of status and esteem. The more cars one has, or the bigger the house, the more regard one is accorded by society. It may be worth highlighting at this point the linkage between a lack of self-respect and the need to supplement internal deficiencies through material acquisition. The increase in demand for consumer goods has increased productivity worldwide. This may have boosted the economy temporarily, but the effect on the ecology has been devastating.

The latest UNDP *Human Development Report* states, "In 1960, the richest 20 percent of the world's population had incomes 30 times greater than the poorest 20 percent. By 1990, the richest 20 percent were getting 60 times more." In other words, the world's richest fifth now receives 82.7 percent of the total world income and the poorest fifth receives 1.4 percent of the total world income. In spite of efforts by development workers to improve the quality of life of the world's poor, the downhill slide in the last thirty years is irrefutable. This comes at a time when civilization is supposedly at the height of its progress. Conditions for the world as a whole are not getting better, they are becoming worse.

The well of natural resources is not an infinite one humanity can draw on as per its whim. Sustainable development will only become a reality when the world's richest fifth change their attitudes and lifestyles. One of the reasons President Bush didn't agree to signing the biodiversity treaty in Rio de Janeiro was because it would have meant a change of lifestyle for the American people. With a national election around the corner, the President was not prepared to introduce such dramatic reforms. In the developing world, traditional attitudes as well as cultural and religious beliefs have rendered a number of development strategies ineffective. By the same token, it could be said that policy makers have failed to consider the values of the people for whom they devise such strategies.

In the years following independence, African leaders sought to improve the material well-being of their peoples. They also attempted to find ways to better integrate their nations within the emerging global order. Their plans had both political and cultural consequences. But they could not be fully realized because the people themselves were unwilling to embrace change. Traditional beliefs in land tenure and the role of elders in decision-making processes posed a number of difficulties in the implementation of developmental strategies. From the beginning, people were left out of decisions-making processes. As a result, projects such as mechanized farming or forced resettlement of villagers to make way for urban renewal failed. Governments hadn't taken into account people's attachment to the land of their ancestors, in particular those lands where their ancestors were buried. In addition, adequate education wasn't provided to assist people in adapting to new technologies.

To tackle family planning, as one of the most pressing developmental issues, requires education of the masses and a whole psychological reorientation. Compulsory family planning, such as in the Peoples Republic of China, showed good results in the initial stages. More recently, however, loopholes in the system are being detected, revealing that laws cannot be enforced if they go against peoples belief systems. Strategists failed to consider the psychological consequences such a program would have. Perhaps they also did not realize how difficult it is to change deep-rooted values which espouse the importance of large families and a cultural bias towards male children. In many societies, creating a large progeny guarantees a good standing in the community, and helps to safeguard one's self-respect.

By transferring these examples onto a global scale, one can perceive the enormous repercussions of decisions taken by policy makers who ignore the role of value systems in influencing or hampering change. Plans which do not include insight into their possible effect on the psychology of people, are rendered ineffective. Policy makers must also be clear about their own motives in making decisions that change peoples' lives. What are the guidelines for taking decisions which, on the one hand promote development, and on the other hand serve to erode cultural values? Maybe values now have to change radically so that all the world's people can be accommodated within the emerging global order?

Self-Respect: A Key Value for the Future

Self-respect or self-esteem, as was discussed previously, arises out of a state of self-awareness. It is, in fact, a pure expression of human consciousness, when there is total contentment and feeling of fullness or fulfillment within. In such a state, the internal self—called human psyche or "soul"—is infused with a high level of spiritual power or energy. This energy upholds elevated thinking processes, keeping the conscience clear so that actions are motivated in the right way.

When awareness of the internal self is forgotten, or when consciousness is misdirected, self-respect turns to pride, ego, or anger. Spiritual energy drains away, and changes from positive to negative. To make up for the deficiency, the internal self seeks to replenish itself through external means, which may not always lead to the overall well-being of the individual or society. The wide range of social pathologies afflicting society, such as crime, drugs, violence etc. are considered deviations from normative behavior. They contravene the accepted standards of the social and moral order. Some of the latest research reveals the root causes of these problems to be a lack of self-esteem and an inability to take responsibility. People also lose confidence and a belief in themselves when they live in a society that no longer accords true respect to the individual. Society often ignores peoples' mental and spiritual needs in favor of their physical ones.

Low self-esteem leads to low motivation and inhibits the capacity of people to care for themselves. Hence, a growing number of people in society no longer have sufficient energy, power, or means to be self-reliant (mentally or physically), and have come to rely on state provisions. By the same token, a social order which does not accord proper respect to the dignity of all peoples leads to the marginalization of the poor within the developed world and the marginalisation of the poor nations within the global order. Discrimination and poverty go hand in hand. So does a lack of self-respect and a lack of respect for others.

Human beings will always act in ways to preserve their self-respect, even if it means using ego defense mechanisms. When self-respect is intact, there is no need to guard it; this positive state of awareness exists naturally.

Self-respect/self-esteem is the next motivating force. Meeting physical needs could then be viewed as part and parcel of meeting self-esteem needs. A person who is without food and shelter will find it difficult to maintain self-respect. However, even if physical needs are met, something more is required to satisfy self-esteem needs. Ultimately, when the individual is satisfied in the mind, self-respect exists naturally. When there is dissatisfaction or disturbance in the mind, due to lack of self-realization, self-respect is lost. The ego defense mechanism jumps in to preserve the loss of self-respect. Actions are then motivated not by self-esteem, but by negative personality traits such as greed, aggression, and ego.

When one's own self-respect is intact, it is possible to maintain respect for others. Infringements on the rights of others come about when the human beings use ego to guard their own respect, and make themselves feel better by dominating others and suppressing their opinions. These behavior patterns are also transferable onto the macro level. Weapons are the ultimate symbol of the ego defense mechanism. Wars are waged in the name of national security, but are often aggressive attempts to dominate or suppress others because of political, religious, or ideological beliefs.

Conclusion

We have attempted to demonstrate the impact of negative and positive value systems in shaping change. Value systems propelled by greed, or fear, or insecurity, promote consumer-oriented and aggressive societies which exploit the environment and sanction poverty and war. Some traditional value systems encourage, albeit unwittingly, population growth and prohibit modernization. At the heart of positive value systems lies the individual capacity for self-awareness and self-judgment. Decisions which bring benefit to the self and others can only be taken when mediated by a clear conscience and by a consciousness imbued with self-respect and spiritual energy.

The ultimate goal of development is to enhance the quality of peoples' lives within the framework of sustainable development. This will only be achieved when the inner development and well-being of an individual is accorded its proper place alongside meeting the material needs of all the world's people.

Chapter 2 · Ecology and Development

Section 1 · Change in a Sustainable Orbit
Joseph C. Wheeler

During a period of fast and profound changes in governing systems, the United Nations Conference on Environment and Development (known as the Rio Earth Summit) gave us at least a glimpse of what will face the world over the next half century. We now need to articulate a broad strategy for this coming period.

Of course, today's five-decade strategic outlook will need frequent adjustments based on evolving science and continuing experience. In this context, it is still worthwhile to look at the world in a perspective of past experiences, to understand what may happen in the next half century.

Four Long-Term Perspectives

In the international debate of the past decade, four global environmental issues have emerged.

First, there is the depletion of the ozone layer. Although some scientists have been seriously concerned about this issue for a quarter of a century, it is hardly more than a decade since alarming observations above Antarctica put the issue on the political agenda. It is truly amazing how fast the world community has moved. A convention was signed only in 1984 and we now expect zero consumption and zero production of relevant gases by the year 2000.[1]

Second, there is the threat of global warming. Here the consensus is less firm, with the United States so far arguing for caution. However, the United States acknowledges the seriousness of the issue. While stating that "scientists cannot yet establish that a human-induced warming has already occurred," the Americans have agreed that "best estimates indicate that increased concentrations of greenhouse gases are likely to increase atmospheric and ocean temperatures and alter their patterns."[2] The United States basically argues for more research in the next decade, while looking for mitigating measures justifiable on other ground. Profitable energy savings would be a good example. There are probably enough arguments to allow the year 2000 emission levels to be higher than the levels of 1990. The Climate Convention as it was signed in Rio by 153 countries reflects the serious concerns and commitments of the international community to keep the issue under close scrutiny.

Assuming world scientific observations continue to affirm the basic conclusions of earlier studies, the appropriate responding actions will be much more complex and far-reaching than the actions nations are now taking on the ozone layer issue. In terms of the next half century, it will probably be necessary to drastically reduce industrialized country emissions of greenhouse gases through radical changes in consumption and production patterns. For developing countries, equally radical changes will be required, including putting into place new consumption and production patterns and the completion of their demographic transitions. The point about these two sets of transitions in industrialized and developing countries is that both will have to be successfully accomplished in the interests of the ten billion great-grandchildren of today's 5.5 billion people. This is a joint intergenerational issue, where individuals in both North and South should be equally concerned about the outcome. They must work together as partners to achieve their respective transitions efficiently and successfully.

The third global issue perceived today is loss of biological diversity. Again, we have a convention. Again, it was signed in Rio by 153 countries, but in this case with the notable and critical absence of the United States. Again, the issue is intergenerational in character. It will be important to solidify over the next several years global consensus on how to deal with this important issue and to set in place the measures necessary. For land-based biological diversity the action will be largely in developing countries. Yet, with their populations bound to double and with the industrial production levels reflecting the fact that they are still on the lower rungs of the development ladder, the countervailing political and economic pressures working against preservation of biological diversity will be enormous. For ocean-based biological diversity, we are only beginning to understand the issues and the next decades will be characterized by increasing levels of information gathering and research.

This leads to the fourth global issue which is the damage occurring in our oceans commons. We are concerned about changes in ocean quality for many reasons. As mentioned above, oceans are the locale for much of our biological diversity. Oceans are related to the climate change issue. They also play key roles in economic life as sources of food, routes for transport, or places for tourism. In Rio, in chapter 17 of Agenda 21, countries agreed to work together to learn more about ocean processes. They also agreed to take into account our mutual oceans concerns in dealing with issues of land-based sources of pollution.

Other Global Issues

In a context where four global issues have found their way to the world's agenda during only the past few years, other issues are bound to achieve global status in the years ahead. Indeed, the only reason such issues as deforestation and desertification have not been put on the list so far is that interrelationships among issues have caused action on these to be considered eligible under existing processes under the four issues listed above. For example, forests as "sinks" are relevant to global climate change issues and forests contain a broad spectrum of species making them important to the biodiversity issues.[3]

When we talk of "global issues" we are really discussing symptoms of a sick planet. In some cases we can implement adaptive strategies. Examples would be changes in grain varieties to reflect rainfall changes or building bunds to protect against ocean rise. Adaptive or mitigating strategies are bound to be needed to deal with unintended damage already in train. But as we enter the age of global issues we need to concentrate even more attention on prevention through adjustments in our basic development paradigm.

While consumption will certainly be an important component of the development paradigm of the twenty-first century, the content of the consumption package and the production processes which produce the consumption package will have to change. Consumption and production must become environmentally benign.

Unsustainable Consumption

These issues were briefly covered in Chapter 4 of Agenda 21 as agreed by consensus at Rio. The concept of "unsustainable consumption" was articulated and it was agreed that consideration should be given to the "need for new concepts of wealth and prosperity which allow high standards of living through changed lifestyles and (which are) less dependent on the Earth's finite resources and more in harmony with the Earth's carrying capacity."[4] It was also recognized that the broad strategy should grow out of our assessment of the relationships among production and consumption, environment, technological adaptation and innovation, economic growth and development, and demographic factors. The relationship to poverty was underlined and it was asserted that developing countries will have to achieve sustainable consumption while at the same time guaranteeing the provision of basic needs for the poor. Basically, the consumption revolution on which we are now embarked is an aspect of the greenhouse gas-related climate change issue.

The Agenda probably understates the enormity of the challenge which must be faced during the coming half century. At present, I wonder how many political leaders in the industrial democracies will have the courage to tell voters the implications of reducing greenhouse gas emissions to 20-25 percent of current levels to end current unsustainable anthropogenic impacts on climate and to create environmental space for poor country development. Although such reductions can surely be achieved, there will be no single answer. Rather, the goal will be achieved by unnumbered small steps, none of which need cause a political storm. Industrial countries need an ambitious goal in mind—perhaps stated as a year 2050 goal—to make accelerated research on energy and transportation alternatives and the adoption of rules and regulations a high priority. These policies will prompt the gradual changes in household and industrial behavior.

Goals for Developing Countries

The situation in developing countries may be even more daunting. Consider some of the things they must achieve over the next five decades.

First, the question of demography. We now have the industrial country models clearly in view. The industrial countries have achieved the demographic transition through development. Most of them now have annual population growth below one percent and much of that results from immigration. This, in spite of a welcome ten-year increase over the past half century in average life expectancy. This demographic balance was achieved in industrial democracies through family planning, with decisions taken voluntarily at the household level. This societal change in attitudes and practice can only be welcomed since even current numbers with current consumption patterns are putting unsustainable pressure on the global environment.

In the post-World War II era, great progress has been achieved. Life expectancy in developing countries has gone up twenty years in this period. Fertility rates are down significantly. Education availability has increased. Food production, except in Africa, has more than kept up with population growth.

Yet, with all the progress, the demographic transition in developing countries must certainly be completed, with annual population growth rates coming down from nearly two percent to zero. This in turn will only be possible if developing countries achieve the conditions where voluntary family planning will work, as it has in the industrialized countries. These conditions include: universal education, reduction in poverty, changes in the status of women, availability of health services, extension of infrastructure, and adequate employment opportunities. It will also require much more in terms of the availability of family planning services.

Responding to inevitable population increases, developing countries will need to transform their agriculture. The basic strategy must be to make much more efficient use of what are called "high-potential lands." Over the last five decades, developing countries began this approach by increasing irrigation and by the seed and fertilizer strategies of the "green revolution." Now much of the potential for increasing land under irrigation has been used up. Further dramatic breakthroughs in genetic seed stock seem less likely. Groundwater buildup and resulting salination have emerged as serious issues. While the needed increases in production are theoretically possible by improved use of high-potential lands and while science will continue to help, the job yet to be done is formidable. Only if this strategy of increasing production on good lands succeeds will economic forces attract people out of low-potential fragile ecosystems where poverty-stricken and desperate people are overcultivating or where increasing numbers of animals are overgrazing, causing soil loss, desertification, and deforestation.

Time Is of the Essence

Only rapid development will complete the demographic transition, provide the needed schools, produce the needed food, build the needed infrastructure, and reduce the poverty-induced destruction of the natural resource base. Developing countries must do all of these things while achieving efficiency levels: time is of the essence.

I should like to say a further word about the idea that "time is of the essence." If developing countries continue on the present paths of only moderately paced development, there will be a number of implications. One implication is that the human family will sustain higher levels of poverty in the coming decades than would be the case under a strategy of accelerated sustainable development. With continuing poverty comes continuing pressure on the fragile ecosystems. Also, with a slow-paced development comes a slower completion of the demographic transition and a higher eventual level of world population. I do not argue that acceleration in the pace of development, as such, is the only concern. Surely the mix of policies will be critical. Accelerated development which leaves half the population in poverty and ignorance lacks moral force, fails the environment test, and delays the completion of the demographic transition.

To put the economies of developing countries in sustainable orbit we need booster rockets. In this case the booster rockets come in the form of efficient management, good economic policies, participatory and democratic societies, use of market systems, a comprehensive human development strategy, and extra help from the rich industrial countries in terms of both technology and financial resources. At Rio, Chapter 33 of Agenda 21 acknowledged the extra efforts needed by both developing countries themselves and the donors to successfully achieve what I am calling "orbit" or what the Conference called "sustainable development." If we achieve orbit in 2050 at ten billion people, surely our great grandchildren, whether from today's rich or poor countries, will have more options in life than if we continue a slower pace of development, reaching orbit only at the end of the century with population levels at fifteen or more billion.

Sustainability: The Main Global Issue

One reason industrial countries will be reluctant to call achieving sustainable development a "global issue" is its financial implications. For the four global issues so far agreed on there is the operational theory that needed extra actions in developing countries can be financed by providing extra funds through the Global Environment Facility (GEF) at a total supplementary cost of a bit more than one billion dollars annually. The basic costs would be financed by developing countries themselves or by normal aid-funding processes.

One billion dollars is less than two percent of world aid. In the case of accelerating sustainable development we are dealing with those basic costs—with the other 98 percent of aid. Getting behind a program of accelerated development implies both tough measures by developing countries themselves and more aid. While the implications are minor compared with current levels of waste in industrial country health systems or in terms of potential savings in military expenditures, they come from a sensitive part of the budget where political consensus is shallow, to say the least. Industrial country populations will need to be convinced that accelerating sustainable development is really a global issue in which they have a direct interest.

Conclusion

Rio had the merit of describing the complex interactions among the many factors affecting development. It pointed up the need for a new paradigm for development in the North. It described the need for accelerating development within a new paradigm in the South, while achieving sustainability. Rio acknowledged the special challenges of the emerging market economies of Central and Eastern Europe and of the new nations of the former Soviet Union.

Above all, Rio reminded us that we are all on this spaceship together—depending on each other's action at home and internationally. Our spaceship in these next five decades will experience frequent turbulence. Our navigators need a vision of a sustainable future and must point us in that direction. Rio has raised the questions and suggested some of the answers. Now each member state must translate Agenda 21 into its own sustainable development strategy. The development planning and aid processes must be transformed to reflect this new set of urgent concerns.

Has Rio caused a new day to dawn? We can hope so. As my fellow Concordian Henry David Thoreau argued in closing his book *Walden*: "Only that day dawns to which we are awake." Rio was our alarm clock. It is time to awaken to a new day!

Notes

1. See United Nations Environment Programme, *Saving Our Planet: The State of the Environment, 1972-1982*, 1982, chapter 2.

2. "U.S. Views on Global Climate Change," 1982.

3. There is, of course, no single authoritative list of "global issues." However, the participants in the Global Environment Facility have designated the four issues listed here as eligible for funding.

4. See Agenda 21, chapter 4, paragraph 4.11.

Section 2 · Global Transition and Sustainability

Neva Goodwin

There is growing concern for the interactions between human economic behavior and the natural world. Economic theory is called upon to explain important parts of human activity; good explanations bring understanding on which intelligent decisions can be based. At this time, however, in relation to the natural environment, practice and popular understanding appear to have run on ahead of economic theory.

For example, the feedback loops between economic behavior and environmental quality are becoming increasingly evident to lay persons; yet, in mainstream neoclassical economics, environmental impacts are modeled as externalities, and the theory has not successfully grappled with the fundamental changes required to understand the environment as a partner in—not just an input to—our economic life.

There is also growing general understanding and acceptance of the idea that economic behavior both affects and is affected by changing technologies, time horizons, and values, tastes, and preferences (including those regarding family size); yet these generally continue to be modeled as exogenous in neoclassical theory. In addition, attention to the deeply important concept of sustainable development has originated from the political arena, neoclassical economics has taken no leadership in calling for a shift to sustainable development, nor in attempting to define what would be required for such a shift to take place.

Leading Questions and Theoretical Support

It will not be a novelty in the history of economic thought if theory is developed in response to a practical and ethical sense of what is wrong with the existing system, along with a vision of what would be the preferred state of affairs; most of the seminal theorists were so motivated, and worked backward from the problems and the goals to organize a logic that could explain to others their understanding of the world. In order for us to move from such a concern and a vision to a theory that can usefully support policy and action, the next step must be to outline the questions that will define the research agenda of a new system of theory.

In this period of global transitions, is it possible for economic growth, as that concept has been understood in the past, to continue without disastrous consequences to the environment?

There are arguments on both sides. Although this debate continues (and it will not be quickly resolved), it seems reasonable to seriously consider the negative response, with concern for the potentially grave results if we do not explore early enough the consequences of a possible conclusion that the future of human civilization absolutely requires a reorientation of our economies, away from the traditional goal of economic growth.

This reasoning requires that we pose the following additional questions:

1. What different sorts of economic development could be substituted for the kind of growth which, in the past, has been assumed to be synonymous with healthy economic progress? This question requires, in effect, one or more operational definitions of "sustainable development."
2. How will we need to redefine our goals and values, individually and in society, in order to move toward such new conceptions of "development" and "progress"?
3. What should we expect to find the most stressful incongruities between a newly defined economic system of sustainable development and existing economic structures and institutions?
4. What institutional, educational, legal, and other changes will be necessary to persuade all parts of society to adopt and move towards appropriately altered economic goals, and to undertake the institutional and individual behavior changes consonant with those goals?

Sustainable Development

The answers to these questions will need to be found through an iterative process; as progress is made in answering one, each of the others can be further refined. The first round will not provide definitive answers to any, but will lay the groundwork for the next, more comprehensive iteration.

Thus, for a first cut at an operational definition of sustainable development, we may begin with the Brundtland Commission's definition:

> Sustainable development is development that meets the needs of the present without compromising the ability of future generations to meet their own needs. It contains within it two key concepts:
> 1. the concept of "needs," in particular the essential needs of the world's poor, to which overriding priority should be given; and
> 2. the idea of limitations imposed by the state of technology and social organization on the environment's ability to meet present needs.[1]

To put this another way, "To say that a development path is "sustainable" means, at least, that its patterns of production and consumption can be reproduced indefinitely without doing increasing or irreparable damage to essential natural ecosystems."[2]

These two definitions are cautious, in that they are static, they suggest holding the line on degradation of future opportunities, but do not promise any hope for improvement. In fact, if we were to project how the most hopeful realistic development path might look for the next few centuries, assuming we take all the optimal steps to move toward sustainability in time to avoid catastrophe, we would still draw the path of sustainable development in a wavy line, not a straight one (either horizontal or sloping upward). The reason behind a project is the question: "sustainable at what level?" The path of change that humanity is on right now does not seem to me to be sustainable. What that means is that we are living off our capital, not just our income; therefore, our heirs will have less capital from which to derive their income; therefore, once we have begun to feel the impact of this capital depletion, and until the healing effects of a new path can take hold, there will be a downward trend. Even after the "right" policies and technologies are in place, it will take time to build up a capital stock compatible with a new way of doing things. It seems reasonable to expect that for some time there will be a series of downs and ups in the way people feel about comparison in welfare among past, present and future styles of living. Part of what determines those feelings of relative welfare will, of course, be a result of culture; a large part of our wants, as opposed to our most basic needs, are culturally determined.[3] But we are getting ahead of our story.

Four Areas for Action

A first cut at moving toward sustainability might start with four agendas for action that are coming to be fairly widely accepted. Again, theory can follow the lead of common sense:

First, we must work toward making the transition from dependence on non-renewable energy to reliance on renewable sources. The ultimate goal, which, at best, will not be achieved for some time, is to become completely independent of the former.

Second, we need to alter our systems of materials processing. We now understand production as an essentially linear flow, wherein we take material from nature, process it, eat it, etcetera, and then turn it into something we regard as waste, which we throw away. Having discovered that "there is no away," we have to convert that linear flow to a circular one, where the output of one production process is the input to another. We must concert "throughput" to what I propose to call "circumput."

Third, we will have to recognize some conflict between the first two agendas. Reprocessing and recycling tend to be fairly energy intensive; hence, even with a transition to a circular materials flow, present consumption patterns, especially if the patterns of the rich are extended to those who are now poor, could require more renewable energy than we have, or than it is safe to employ, given the environmental impact of energy use. Therefore, we not only have to convert the flow of materials from a linear to a circular one; we also must control the total content and the composition of that flow. There is more leeway for using materials in "circumput," but in neither case can we continue on a path of endless increase of materials use.

Finally, it is coming to be increasingly accepted that the per capita levels of fuel use and of throughput or circumput which are sustainable are not only a function of technology: to identify the sustainable levels of these variables we must also know the size of the population.

The Limits of Sustainability

We may assume that, for any given combination of capital stock and technology there is a finite *total* amount of energy and materials to use which is sustainable. Also, we know that the way to derive sustainable *per capita* figures is to divide the total figures by the size of the population that must be sustained. It follows that the more people, the lower the standard of living.

The conclusion from this argument is direct: there is a size of population beyond which any increase will translate into significant human hardship. There are people who suspect that the maximum optimum size has already been surpassed. There are many more who believe that it will at least be reached, and very likely surpassed by the numbers predicted for the human population during the twenty-first century.

All of these points together suggest the need to look hard at the individual and societal goals and values that affect what and how we produce and consume. The next line of defense will be on the consumption side, with the requirement to change the composition of consumption. Just go give one example, if world food consumption where to shift, overall, away from meat and towards grains, the same total amount of calories and other nutrients could be made available to a growing population without an increase—possible even with a decrease—in the rate of degradation of agricultural lands.

Another line of defense concerns distribution. At one time, when asked to name the five major causes of environmental destruction, I suggested that they are: population, poverty, population, wealth, and population. Consumption, particularly of the kinds that have destructive environmental impacts, is more increased by wealth than it is decreased by poverty; hence a more even distribution of wealth would tend to have beneficial effects on the composition of output. More certainly, a better distribution (both among and within nations) will be needed to prevent severe hardship in most of the scenarios that eschew the traditional growth paths.

We return here to the "meta-question" cited above; can economic growth, as that concept has been understood in the past, continue without disastrous consequences to the environment. If the shifts from fossil to renewable fuels and from throughput to circumput, together with changes in patterns of consumption and distribution, do not, all together, suffice to achieve a sustainable development path, then the final line of defense—one that no society is likely to choose, but that could be forced upon by environmental realities—would be reduction, cessation, or even reversal of aggregate growth of output.

It is hard to know what meaning to give such a proposition. The idea of "aggregate output" is conventionally summarized in gross national product (GNP) figures, but there has been much discussion of the value and meaning of those figures. They blend together intangible services, which often have no direct environmental impact, and tangible products. They count some environmental and social ills (e.g., military costs, the Exxon Valdez oil spill, or increased medical costs due to air pollution) as contributing to GNP, while some benefits, such as the value of standing timber or the health created by preventative medicine, are neglected or undercounted. They also ignore the value of anything that is not bought and sold through a market transaction. Considering all this, one could imagine situations in which total GNP, as now measured, would decline while most people would feel better off, at least, if they were not depressed by the knowledge that GNP was declining!

These issues are beginning to be addressed by economists who are looking at the macro and global meaning of sustainable development from a perspective that is outside of the neoclassical economics framework. The following summary is representative of such alternative groups:

> Two realisms conflict. On the one hand, political realism rules out income redistribution and population stability as politically difficult, if not impossible; therefore the world economy has to expand "by a factor, of five or ten" in order to cure poverty. [This figure is the one given in Brundtland.] On the other hand, ecological realism accepts that the global economy has already exceeded the sustainable limits of the global ecosystem and that a five to tenfold expansion of anything remotely resembling the present economy would simply speed us from today's long run unsustainability to imminent collapse. We believe that in conflicts between biophysical realities and political realities, the latter must eventually give ground. The planet will transit to sustainability; the choice is between society planning for an orderly transition, or letting physical limits and environmental damage dictate the timing and course of the transition. . . .[4]

It is uncertain what will happen if population doubles (as it is predicted to do before there is much likelihood of its stabilizing) and we discover that growth of output beyond the present is unsustainable. As Goodland and Daly remark, assuming that we are already pushing up against such limits, "Since resources are finite, then more Northern growth inevitably means less room for Southern growth."[5]

The scenario, which is rarely confronted directly (probably because it is so morally abhorrent), is one in which limits are met and ignored; redistribution does not occur; ecological collapse hits the poor soonest and hardest, causing Third World famine and disease on a scale surpassing anything ever experienced by our species; and the wealthy countries learn enough to reform their ways—not in terms of helping the poor, but in reducing their own throughput.

That is the nightmare scenario; a world in which the poor countries, now containing more than three-quarters of the world's population, become ecological deserts—such as Haiti is fast becoming—while the rich countries stabilize their populations and their resource use, and arm their borders to keep out the floods of would-be immigrants. I note that we in the United States have already accepted a sizable militarization—much of it beyond our borders—to keep out the first wave, namely the flood of illegal drugs supplied by poor countries who see no other prospect for achieving the standard of living set by the United States. So far, force has been more effective against movements of people than against movements of illegal substances. However, it has not been entirely successful in stemming illegal immigration, either.

It is not, in fact, likely that we will first solve the macro question of total quantity of output and then turn to the issue of its composition. Instead, the macro solution will probably arise as a consequence of the shape taken by economies as they shift away from induced wants and planned obsolescence, to achieve their consumption goals through the cultures and technologies of conservation, miniaturization, maintenance, recycling, and industrial ecology.

We may turn with relief from the issue of total quantity to that of composition of output, where there are more encouraging things to be said. For example:

"GNP becomes an obsolete measure of progress in a society striving to meet people's needs as efficiently as possible and with the least damage to the environment. What counts is not growth in output, but the quality of service rendered. Bicycles and light rail, for instances, are less resource-intensive forms of transportation than automobiles are, and contribute less to GNP. But a shift to mass transit and cycling for most passenger trips would enhance urban life by eliminating traffic jams, reducing smog, and making cities safer for pedestrians. GNP would go down, but overall well-being would increase."[6]

On this view, the tradeoffs between sustainability, preserving options for a reasonable standard of living for people of the future, and the present welfare are fraught with uncertainties and with opportunities for taking tragically wrong decisions; nevertheless we may yet manage to find solutions in technology, culture, and governance such that there remains hope for a decent life for a growing proportion of the world's human population, both now and in the future.

Work and Investment

Until further iterations bring us to a more refined understanding of sustainable development we will not be able to identify all of the incompatibilities that are likely to arise from the current halting mode of development to a new one.

One of these is the area of work. The neoclassical economic model views work as something that is done in order to earn the income that will make consumption possible. Some neo-Marxists view consumption, in modern societies as a lure held out in order to persuade workers to hold jobs that have little or no intrinsic value to the worker.

If a development path that stabilized or reduced total output were to occur in the context of expanding population, it is possible that there would be a marked per capita decrease in the amount of work that could most efficiently be performed by human labor. This possibility is more evident in the industrialized than in the poor countries; yet when we look beneath the surface of the modern agricultural techniques in a Third World nation such as India we find a situation of "shared poverty" where it is estimated that the agricultural labor now being performed could without great difficulty be done by half the number of people. This step to "efficiency" is not taken because there are no jobs waiting for the workers who would thus be released.

Redefinition of our economic goals and values will surely require a reconsideration of the relationship between consumption and well-being: optimization of the latter is not a simple matter of maximizing the former. At the same time, unemployment, at least in the South, seems only to be growing, and with it the hardships attendant on joblessness in the world's increasingly jobs-oriented economies. Throughout the last two centuries the dominant economic policies and assumptions have adhered to the goal of rising wages, even with consequent labor displacement, because higher wages, for those with jobs, permit increased consumption. It may be necessary and desirable to learn from the "shared poverty" model another way, of "shared sufficiency."

The transition issues attendant on shared sufficiency will likely emphasize a retreat from the kinds of trends in labor-saving production, through heavy emphasis on technologies, that have typified industrialization up till now. Emphasis upon technologies will cause a shift towards more skilled labor; the economic importance of education will become increasingly critical; and relatively uneducated members of modern societies will become ever more of a "problem."

At this time it is unclear whether, in a world of information-inputs technology, the *overall* need for labor will increase or decline. In the latter case, we may expect, in the transition period, a dissonance between the economic and the psychological meanings of work. If the links between work and consumption—links of necessity and of manufactured wants—were to be weakened, this would raise serious questions regarding what work gets done, by whom, and what motivates them to do it; will it be necessary, or desirable, for all healthy adults in a sustainable society to hold what we now define as "jobs?"

Another likely incongruity will be between existing expectations surrounding profits—the magnitude of the returns now considered normal and necessary to induce investment—and the growing perception that environmental protection requires a lower rate of return.

An analysis of this issue, using "forests" as exemplary of all natural resources, begins by quoting Daly and Cobb:

> Any commercially valuable species that is not too expensive to capture, and whose rate of reproduction for all population sizes remains below the interest rate, will be exploited to extinction—and then expands on the problem as follows:[7] If environmental sustainability implies a predefined level of forest preservation, then it requires either an interest rate low enough to achieve that goal through the market, or nonmarket regulation to protect the forests. Therefore, to achieve a sustainable market economy it is necessary to keep the

interest rate below an environmentally determined ceiling. Theoretical analysis alone cannot determine that level; however, casual observation of the market pressure to cut U.S. old-growth forests and tropical rain forests suggests that interest rates may be well above the ceiling. What would happen if environmental goals required a permanent lowering of interest rates?[8]

These comments rest upon a perception of an underlying shift in economic reality, one with enormous potential consequences.

A number of policy conclusions arise from this chain of logic, including a cluster of observations about investment; for example, that "investment must shift from manmade capital accumulation towards natural capital preservation and restoration."[9] The prescription to "internalize the externalities" also turns up here; artificially high returns to investment have been maintained by ignoring the drawdown of complementary natural capital that has permitted them. When the costs to the environment that were previously externalized (that is, ignored by the actors incurring those costs) have been properly internalized (made part of the real costs paid by the actor who brought them about), this will provide part, or perhaps all, of the answers to Ackerman's question: "What would happen if environmental goals required a permanent lowering of interest rates?" That is, such a permanent lowering of overall returns to investment may require no special extra-market actions, except (a large exception!) those actions required to ensure that such costs are fully internalized.

New Balance of Power

On the global scale, there are some things which are evidently of the first importance for the attainment of a pattern of development which can satisfy essential human needs and sustain realistic hope for future progress in human civilization, while preserving the health of the earth's ecosystem. These obvious first requirements include:

- appropriate support for education. People must be educated in a manner that prepares them to work at the jobs that should and, realistically, will be available when they enter the workforce;
- appropriate support for health and nutrition. In poor countries, and among the poor in rich countries, the most significant health and nutrition measures prevent the damage to mental and physical functioning that comes from early nutrition or crippling disease;
- family planning measures to allow every woman choice over the number of children she bears; and
- access to the better known technology so that all processing of energy and materials can be performed with the least possible entropy and within the context of conservation, miniaturization, maintenance, recycling, and industrial ecology.

These five essentials are described here with a slant toward the needs of the poor. Under normal circumstances, except where family planning measures are against the law, the rich can and do purchase what they need and want in the way of education, health, nutrition, family planning, and technology.

The difficulty is to get the rich to pay to make these essentials universally available. For example, on the issue of "changes to industrial, agricultural, and other productive processes to make them more environmentally sound," the UNDP's *Human Development Report 1992* comments as follows:

> Developing countries would have to increase investment to achieve this—in some cases by up to 10 percent. Where is the money to come from? Since the whole world benefits from the introduction of environmentally sound technologies in each country, there is a strong case for the industrial countries to foot the bill. They could, for example, establish a special grant fund to subsidize the transfer of such technologies from industrial and other developing countries.[10]

Possible Ways to Transfer Resources

We have reason to believe such transfers might be forthcoming. First, a few notes will be offered on ways that have been suggested for their achievement.

The UNDP report summarizes some of the suggestions that have been made for international taxation for sustainable development. These included:

- *Fossil fuel consumption taxes*—a tax on oil of one dollar per barrel (about five percent) would yield about five percent) would yield about $24 billion a year. Taxing coal consumption as well would raise the revenue to about $40 billion. This rate is not likely to reduce energy consumption very significantly. If such a tax were used to encourage greater energy efficiency, rather than to mobilize revenues, the rates would be much higher. It has been estimated, for example, that the tax rate needed to reduce carbon emissions by half by the year 2000 would have to be about 89 percent. Some countries (such as Finland, the Netherlands and Sweden) already have consumption taxes on fossil fuel consumption at the national level, and the European Community is considering the introduction of a carbon tax in stages, starting in 1993.
- *Global common taxes* could reflect each country's usage of the global commons, including the oceans (for fishing, transportation or seabed mining) and Antarctica (for mining and communications satellites).
- *Taxes on international trade*—these fall on environmentally sensitive products, such as tropical hardwood.[11]

Other such taxes that are mentioned include a global income tax, pollution taxes, greenhouse gas permits, taxes on weapons, and taxes on consumer items.

What has to happen in order to make it possible for these ideas, or others like them, to be put into effect? There must, of course, be institutional mechanisms, with some kinds of power of law or persuasion. Other groups and individuals are working on the necessary details of how such institutions might be designed. What I would like to address, in concluding, is a set of issues that underlines the very possibility of such new initiatives.

The first passage cited above from the UNDP report spoke of the self-interest that might motivate the industrial countries to make grants to cover technology transfer. The problem with self-interest is that it is most forcefully felt in the local and short-term framework which has led to the "rational choice" school type of prediction: that the ideal achievement is to be a free rider while public goods are provided by others. The kind of self-interest that is involved in preserving the global commons, alleviating poverty in distant parts of the earth, and planning for the future, is often in conflict with narrow, short-term selfishness. Those who appeal to self-interest for generous acts may lose their way in the thickets of short-termism before they manage to make contact with broader self-interest which identifies the *self* and its interests with a community stretching out to encompass our whole species, or even the whole biosphere.

In fact, to move the human race toward shared sufficiency and sustainable development, what is required as a basis for new laws and institutions is an altered balance of power, above all between the rich and the poor groups and nations of the world. It is, of course, the rich who have a vastly disproportionate share of the world's power. When contemplating a transfer of power from the strong to the weak, it is normally the case that this transfer must be voluntary; if the weak were able to bring it about by compulsion, they would, almost by definition, not be weak. But why would the strong voluntarily give away power? I cannot answer that question, though it is obviously an important one that requires more examination. I will do no more here than to suggest that such transfers can and do occur.

In spite of all the discouraging things we encounter we read the newspapers or look at the world around us, nevertheless when we survey human history over the last few hundred years it is possible to see an extraordinary, and accelerating, record of voluntary transfers from the strong to the weak. Starting in the nineteenth century, and gaining momentum throughout the twentieth, we find, in roughly the order in which these trends became prominent:

1. the enfranchisement of women, with continuing progress toward equal treatment in various parts of society, in spite of the power disadvantage that women have because of (on average) less physical strength and a greater willingness to accept disadvantageous personal bargains for the sake of male assistance in child rearing;

2. recognition of the rights of minorities, and of the necessity to make special arrangements for their protection and advancement when they dwell in a hostile social environment;

3. acceptance of the obligation to make special efforts to integrate the physically handicapped into society and to give them the means for a full and satisfying life;

4. recognition that parents cannot always give adequate protection to children, even that parents may, in some cases, constitute a threat to the physical and mental well-being of their children, so that societies at large must accept a basic level of responsibility for children's protection and welfare; and

5. an animal rights movement that has grown slowly but persistently.

In addition to these trends, we may note three categories of relatively powerless human beings whose situation has improved markedly if we compare the world today with that of two hundred years ago, but where there is not much evidence that improvement is still ongoing.

1. Slavery—one of the notable triumphs of human civilization is that slavery is now everywhere illegal, though not everywhere extinct.

2. The condition of the mentally ill, who have been treated miserably throughout much of human history. A major change was made largely in the nineteenth and early twentieth centuries, when the mentally ill were, in effect, accepted as full human beings, in spite of Foucault's suggestions to the contrary. While medical and psychiatric advances continue to be made, so that it is possible for more mentally ill persons to escape from that category, it is not clear that the treatment of those who remain therein is becoming more humane.

3. With regard to convicted criminals, there has been progress in wide (although not universal) acceptance of laws against brutal treatment, but there seems to be stagnation in social understanding of what to do with prisoners.

The last comment may reflect a peculiarly U.S. perspective; there are certainly other countries where one would put convicted criminals on the list of groups to whom those in power have progressively, and constructively, offered a greater share of their society's resources. The rest of the list too—the five groups where I have cited continuing progress, and the three where there has been a major change, if not continuing progress—clearly would have different meanings in different parts of the world. Overall, however, the lists hold enough of humanity so as to offer a strong basis for hope.

Conclusion

These are some of the precedents which suggest that it is possible to look to something more than narrow self-interest in the hope that there will be a significant transfer of resources and power from the rich and strong to the poor and weak. As members of the human race, here is a record of which we can be proud, and on which we can build.

Now we must look to the institutionalization of the next round of changes, in which the rich countries, and the rich groups within countries, will act upon the knowledge that the human race can only escape a disastrous backlash from the environment by moving swiftly to a kind of development which emphasizes basic and appropriate education, health, and nutrition; which makes family planning universally available; and which includes the resource transfer necessary to ensure that environmentally friendly technology is developed and disseminated as widely and as swiftly as possible. We need a force that can mediate between this knowledge of what needs to be done and the institutional, legal, and cultural details of how to do it. the new strength of the "third sector" (nongovernmental, private, voluntary organizations) may have emerged at just the right time to play this role.

Notes

1. World Commission on Environment and Development, *Our Common Future* (Oxford: Oxford University Press, 1987).

2. Frank Ackerman, "The Natural Interest Rate of the Forest: Macroeconomic Requirements for Sustainable Development" (Unpublished manuscript).

3. See Marshall Sahlins, *Culture and Practical Reason* (Chicago: University of Chicago Press, 1976).

4. World Bank Working Paper #46, "Environmentally Sustainable Development: Building on Brundtland," eds. Robert Goodland, Herman Daly, and Salah El Serafy, 1991.

5. Robert Goodland and Herman Daly, "Ten reasons why Northern Income Growth is not the Solution to Southern Poverty," manuscript, 1992.

6. World Bank Working Paper #46.

7. UNDP, *Human Development Report 1992* (New York: Oxford University Press, 1992).

8. Frank Ackerman, "The Natural Interest Rate of the Forest: Macroeconomic Requirements for Sustainable Development," manuscript.

9. Ackerman, 22

10. *Human Development Report 1992.*

11. *Human Development Report 1992*, 84.»

Section 3 · Environment and Transition

Sveneld Evteev

Although the characteristics of the present worldwide changes differ from region to region, two important forms of change related to the environment and to development may be noticed in all regions. One is the change in positions regarding environmental issues, and the other is change in the world's socioeconomic structure.

Environmental Issues

Changes concerning environmental issues are now high on the political agenda. Over the years, we have moved from preaching a more conceptual relationship between the environment and development to the practical application of tools, that is, the ways and means of making socioeconomic development more environmentally sound and sustainable. The subject is not just an isolated issue anymore, but an integral part of the process of socioeconomic development throughout the world.

The historic "Founex Report," which was the cornerstone of the First Conference on Environment, referred to development only in the context of environmental problems arising in the process of development. The language used was still quite descriptive, defining concepts rather than establishing operational linkages.

Similarly, the 1972 Stockholm Declaration remained conceptual and descriptive. Its Principle 13 stated that: "In order to achieve a more rational management of resources and thus to improve the environment, States should adopt an integrated and coordinated approach to their development planning so as to ensure that development is compatible with the need to protect and improve the human environment for the benefit of their population." This observation is certainly correct and still valid, but nowadays we are fortunately a little further advanced, both conceptually and operationally.

It was only in the 1980s that the integration of the environment into socioeconomic development of countries began in the form of, for example, environmental accounting, studies of environmental impact, and cost benefit assessments and analyses. However, governments have only recently started using these assessment tools in their national development planning efforts and in the implementation of their programs and projects. Even now, these methods are used only on a limited scale and mainly by the more highly industrialized countries.

The Change in Structure

In regard to the world's socioeconomic structure, one may notice a clear conflict of interest among the following four major groups of countries:

1. traditional (old) industrialized countries;
2. rapidly industrializing development countries such as those in Southeast Asia;
3. Central and Eastern European countries and the former Soviet Union; and
4. developing countries.

When one speaks of environmental issues and needs, one may say, that in general, the more developed the country, the more attention and funds are devoted to environmental issues, and that the reverse is true for the less developed nations. Also, certain environmental issues are more or less restricted to one or two regions.

Environmental Issues Related to Transition Countries

Although there is a close similarity between environmental issues affecting the Central and Eastern European countries and those of the former Soviet Union, their nature and impact may vary according to subregion.

The Role of Governments

When comparing the role of governments in a market economy to socialist systems in their correction of market failures, there are two aspects of environmental degradation that deserve special attention. In an open market system there is, theoretically, a self-developing mechanism in which, for example, cleaner production technologies become competitive and profitable removing the need for governments to apply corrective measures in the form of legislation. The business community realizes that it can take actions that yield both environmental and economic benefits. In a 1992 report prepared by the Business Council entitled "Changing Course," Schmidheiny forcefully defends the idea that good environmental management is also good business.

However, on the other hand, governments may introduce legislation to create and enforce a normative framework for sustainable development.

In practice, an in-between situation usually exists. Market mechanisms can never function in isolation from a legal framework. Despite environmental legislation to comply with, it seems true that private enterprises tend to use less resources and produce less waste than state-owned companies. As stated by the 1992 *World Development Report,* one of the reasons is that the public sector is notoriously bad in policing itself: "...being both poacher and gamekeeper does not really work." No doubt the environmental problems of Central and Eastern Europe and the former Soviet Union demonstrate this case forcefully.

The present structure and existing mechanisms in the old industrial countries are the result of a long evolution of action-reaction. Where and when a socioeconomic development proves to be really problematic environmentally, society reacts and corrective action emerges as the response. At present, the rapidly industrializing developing countries are in a much better position to challenge such occurrences, because they can, from the beginning, introduce from ways and means that have already been tested and applied by industrialized countries.

However, for countries with economies in transition, mainly in Central and Eastern Europe and in the former Soviet Union, the situation is more complicated because they do not form a reasonably homogeneous group. Indeed, in the old German Democratic Republic, the transition is governed by the legislation of the former West Germany, and softer grace periods necessary during the transition period are being applied. In this situation, a strong governmental influence and control system is already in place; it needs only to be expanded to cover new ground.

By contrast, the countries of Central and Eastern Europe are in serious trouble as far as the role of governments in correcting environmental failures is concerned. Even though data are limited, the overall state of the environment in the region shows that centrally planned economies do not ensure proper environmental protection. With their economies moving rapidly to market oriented systems, the serious danger exists that market forces will only be geared to maximum profit. Currently, a vacuum exists as far as environmental legislation is concerned, and it is not clear how long this will last. With a sharp decline in the involvement of central institutions, the environmental damage could become even worse than before.

Need for Rapid Corrective Action

Compared to the rest of the world, the countries of Central and Eastern Europe and the former Soviet Union, must take their environmental problems more seriously, due to at least two main reasons. First, the present state of the ecology is very bad. Secondly, there is a real danger that this state may worsen as a result of uncontrolled market forces.

It is also worth noting that when the economy is sluggish, environmental issues do not occupy an important place on the political agenda of the government concerned. At present, in these countries, the control and reinforcing mechanisms are very weak. However, differences may be noticed with respect to the three subregions:

The Central and Eastern European countries: The countries in this group still have their former borders. They are individual entities with their own (central) economies and governments. In the new situation it is less difficult for these countries to adjust to a different system, because they are still working within the same boundaries/entities as before.

The Commonwealth of Independent States: This group consists of member countries of the former USSR, excluding the Baltic republics. The situation for these countries is most alarming. Once, they formed one big country. Now, new boundaries have come into existence, and within these new entities a whole new governing and economic structure needs to be organized. Environment is not a pressing issue either for the people or the governments.

The former Baltic Soviet republics: In this group the situation is again different. Even in the "old days" these republics were more on their own and can, therefore, be considered similar to the countries of Central and Eastern Europe. Fortunately, environmental standards and environmental protection were better developed and enforced than in the rest of the territory of the former Soviet Union, and probably even better than in the other Central and Eastern European countries.

Raising Consciousness

Among the leaders of the newly independent states, there is a clear understanding that common standards, approaches, and laws are necessary. On 8 February 1992, two important agreements were signed to this effect: one on "cooperation in the field of ecology and the protection of the environment," and one on "cooperation in the field of hydrometeorology." In Article 1 of the first agreement, it is stated that "...the parties shall develop and conduct a concerted policy in the field of ecology and the protection of the natural environment...taking into account the international agreements previously concluded by the Union of Soviet Socialist Republics;" and in Article 1 of the second agreement, that "...the parties shall prepare and conduct a single policy relating to the gathering and use of hydrometeorological information...taking into account the international agreements previously developed and conducted by the former Union of Soviet Socialist Republics." In Article 4 of the first agreement, the establishment of an "Inter-State Environmental Council and a related Inter-State Environmental Fund" is envisaged for the implementation of joint programs, while the second agreement envisages the establishment of an "Inter-State Council on Hydrometeorology" (Article 3).

It should be noted that Ukraine, one of the largest states with a very advanced level of socioeconomic development and a large population, has not yet signed the agreements. Turkmenistan signed, but requested some deletions relating to the establishment of the Inter-State Environmental Fund envisaged in Article 4 of the first agreement, and to the establishment of working bodies and their funding arrangements set out in Article 5 of the second agreement. It is also not clear whether the agreements were ratified by the independent states or how the agreements would be implemented.

Conclusion

Obviously, and unfortunately, political and economic problems and national conflicts in the transition countries still attract more attention than environmental problems. The same is seen in many developing countries, as well as in some industrialized states. Nevertheless, public awareness of environmental issues continues to grow. People know what is wrong, but systems are not yet ready to actually affect change. Although progress has been achieved in moving up environmental issues on the socioeconomic agenda, changes in social and economic matters still dominate the development process.

From all of the foregoing, readers may conclude that we are more or less back to where we started, or that we are going in circles with development superimposed on environment. I, however, am convinced that we are gradually moving upwards in a spiral, and this seems the right direction for change.

Part 4 · Countries in Transition

Overview

Leonard Silk and Üner Kırdar

The burst of optimism that greeted the downfall of Communism in Eastern and Central Europe and the former Soviet Union[1] has given way to the anxiety that it will take many years for these states to become effective market economies and democracies—and that some may not make it at all before dictatorship returns.

The end of the Cold War was expected to bring great benefits to people in many countries as resources were shifted from military to social uses. Thus far, however, the "peace dividend" is being paid in lost jobs and falling incomes. Theoretically, there is no reason this must be so; the greater prospects for peace should permit a nation to spend more on welfare—raising consumption and productivity—increasing investment, but that will happen only if workers are prepared and trained to take new jobs and if financial resources are reallocated to create those jobs.

In the absence of such shifts of human and material resources, there are strong economic pressures on arms-producing nations to maintain high levels of military spending, and to sell weapons wherever buyers can be found. Without a revival of national economies, and of the global economy, the production and proliferation of nuclear and conventional weapons will continue to endanger peace.

Experience after World War II showed that, if accompanied by wise and generous national and international policies, the conversion from war to peace economies can bring enormous benefits. After the most devastating war in history, with the help of the U.S. Marshall Plan and cooperation among victors and vanquished, the world economy enjoyed the longest and strongest period of economic growth in history.

But the situation that confronts the world today is radically different from that at the end of World War II. The United States could then deal with the external financial requirements for reconstruction without even running a budget deficit or a current account deficit in its balance of payments. Today, the United States has huge internal and external deficits, and there are doubts that even the G-7 major industrial countries could collectively provide enough capital for the ex-Communist countries together with those of the developing countries.

After World War II, the devastated economies of the industrial world were quickly revived. Virtually everyone was surprised by the speed of the transformation. The underlying knowledge and skills, the habits of thought, and the economic and industrial institutions were still there. "I always thought it was impossible for the German economy to recover," said Theodore Schultz, later a Nobel Laureate in economics, who served in the Allied occupation of Germany.

"We were dead wrong—British economists, American economists, and for that matter German economists too." They had all underestimated the real growth forces in West Germany. The plants and cities that had been destroyed, Schultz said "were really quite secondary, minor details soon to be remedied."

Overcoming the Legacy of the Old Order

By contrast, the collapse of Communist regimes and economies in Eastern Europe and the former Soviet Union poses unprecedented tasks of political and economic reconstruction that, in many ways, are even more difficult than those faced by war-devastated nations after World War II. The problem of capital shortage is only one of the obstacles the former Communist states must overcome. They must also get rid of the Stalinist economic institutions, and the habits and attitudes inculcated by years of Communism, that now stand in the way of economic advance.

The obstacles to growth also include an irrational structure of prices; an excessive focus on physical goods; a neglect of services and the knowledge industries; environmental neglect and destructiveness that may be the worst of any countries in the world; enormous budget deficits and loose monetary policies that have bred inflation; "soft" budgets of enterprises that have bred inefficiencies in production and hampered transfer of resources to better uses; obsolete plants and equipment, and a hangover of industrial "giantism"—poorly trained labor and management; public suspicions of the old Communist leaders, agents, operatives, and bureaucrats—and public suspicions and resentment toward the new capitalists, many of whom were drawn from the old order or from criminal elements in society.

Conventional economic prescriptions for reforming the ex-Communist economies have neglected the barriers to economic growth posed by the inadequate legal, moral, and institutional foundations for an effective market economy. The commitment of foreign capital and direct foreign investment depends on the strengthening of those institutional foundations of capitalism—and so does the revival of internal saving and investment. The "shock treatment" that many Western economists thought would swiftly do the job is putting the Eastern economies and their people through a harrowing experience, with falling living standards and rising joblessness, social discontent, and hostility toward foreigners or different ethnic groups.

The new situation facing the former Communist societies is more chaotic than the old. Crime is worse. The former reliability of various state agencies in meeting domestic or foreign obligations has given way to greater uncertainties and is complicated by frequent demands for bribes or other forms of "lubrication" before deals can be consummated. Also, the splitting apart of the old Council for Mutual Economic Assistance (CMEA) trading bloc is depressing economies before they have gained sufficient access to the world market and to foreign capital.

Yet the old Soviet system collapsed because of both its economic failures and its political repression and alienation of subjected peoples. It cannot, in any case, be restored without forcing people to give up hope of a more efficient and humane economic and political system, combining private, public, and communitarian elements.

The Problems of Privatization and Reform

Privatization has become a byword of the day. But neither in ex-Communist nor long-time capitalist regimes does the broad term "privatization" provide the answer to the most appropriate forms of ownership or control for all industries or functions. Nations need to consider the characteristics of those sectors of an economy that best satisfy individual or social needs, whether under private, public, or mixed ownership.

The privatization issue is particularly important and difficult for the transition countries because of the hazards of failure and mass unemployment that sudden exposure to the world market pose for uncompetitive industries in the ex-Communist countries. Finding the best way to privatize state industries will involve maintaining employment for those currently unable to move to new jobs but also resolving conflicts between the interests and values of different groups in a way that serves the difficult-to-define "public interest."

Is the public interest simply the sum of individual interests? Or, with those interests clashing, often because of differences in income and wealth, should the public interest be defined in terms of some principle, such as equality or social progress or individual rights or national independence and autonomy?

And should the resolution of conflicting interests or values be left to the "invisible hand" of the market—not because its solutions are perfectly just, but because it is likely to produce better and more efficient results than decisions by political interests or particular politicians? Or should a "good society" regulate and correct the outcomes emerging from the market to care for the needs of all, especially those worst off? But will politics, whatever its pretensions, inevitably serve the interests of the most powerful elements or class in the society?

As abstruse as such issues may seem, they are critical to the social and economic development of all nations, rich or poor, capitalist, Communist or ex-Communist. There is no "ideal" answer to such questions, given the differences in national histories, cultures, values, goals, and public preferences.

The Transition Process

An overriding issue that embraces all political, economic, and human dimensions of the transition is determining the nature of the relationship between political democracy and the market economy. Economic and political theorists differ in their answers. Some maintain that democracy and capitalism do not necessarily go together, indeed that they are "strange bedfellows;" they note that some countries, especially in Asia, have moved ahead economically without creating democracies on the American or Western European models.

But other thinkers argue that, whatever the problems of sequencing the transition to a market economy, democracy is, in the long run, crucial to achieving an effective and dynamic economy—and that, conversely, free markets are vital to political freedom and democracy.

Although history offers many examples of repressive societies utilizing market economies, there is not a single example of a democratic society that is not also a market economy. It would thus appear that a pluralistic market economy is a prerequisite for a democracy, although the converse may not be the case.

Historically, democracy is a struggle against oppressive structures of the state or the inherent conflicts and social inequalities of unfettered capitalism. The evolution of Western democracy is, to a great extent, the history of how capitalism and the interests it has served have gradually been restrained by democratic processes. A similar democratic process in restraint of state power may now be under way in the Far East, possibly even in China, despite contentions of leaders of the Chinese Communist Party.

However, one can also argue that the West should be careful when trying to force countries to accept a transplant of political systems that have no historical domestic basis. There is a risk to the West in trying to force the pace of the introduction of Western democracy, that might make economic development more difficult, rather than less so, and thereby, in practice, impede the movement toward a functioning political democracy.

Some feel that the market economy would work best, at least during the transition, when combined with a strong, even authoritarian, government. But others believe there is a "thirst" for freedom and democracy in many countries, stemming from ancient roots and fed by resistance to dictatorial governance (and by no means "imported" from the outside) that must not be repressed in the name of material gain. The revolution in Eastern Europe certainly reflected dissatisfaction with prevailing economic conditions, but it gained strength from national and political demands for freedom and democratic rights.

At the same time, the recently established democracies in the East will be weakened if their political systems and institutions have dubious legitimacy that can obstruct their economic revival—a point stressed by participants from the former Eastern bloc countries. If their economies fail, the dangers will increase that these fledgling democracies will also fail.

Unquestionably, there are problems in sequencing the transition from Communism to market economies, and the guiding hand of government will be needed for the transition to succeed. But unless governments themselves maintain respect for law, respect for human rights, and permit people to hold to their beliefs and express them freely, individuals will lack the power to protect themselves or their environment, and otherwise advance their economic and social interests.

How to Succeed

An open, stable, and growing world economy will require systems of government that are respected and respect-worthy. Such governments must safeguard the rights of their own people, not just those of foreigners or a privileged class within their society. The goals of political freedom and protection of human rights cannot be treated as secondary to, or separable from, the goal of economic freedom and progress. Ultimately, these goals are joined together.

In this spirit, we offer the following conclusions:

1. Managing the transition is a worldwide problem and is not limited to Eastern and Central Europe and the Commonwealth of Independent States. The problems of moving to market economies and political democracy are country-specific, because of different national histories, cultures, institutions, social values, and popular preferences.

2. The people of Eastern Europe and the CIS can succeed in achieving the economic and political development they seek, only if they take the initiative and rely fundamentally on themselves. But they need and deserve help from the outside as well.

3. Because of budgetary constraints and capital shortages in the industrialized countries, external help to Eastern Europe is likely to come less from governments than from private foreign investment, provided that the investment climate and means of payment are acceptable. Government assistance, however, will remain important, not only through financial aid and loans but especially through the opening of their markets to trade, technology transfer, and education and training of labor and management in the East.

4. World economic growth and open markets are vital to facilitating the transition of former Communist countries to market economies. Achieving global prosperity will depend most importantly on the coordination of fiscal and monetary policy among the principal industrial countries. Cooperation is also needed to ensure a stable exchange rate system.

5. Over-optimism can lead to unmanageable deficits, inflation, and economic breakdowns. Inflation will undermine the value of a nation's currency, will prevent it from participating in the global economy, and lead to stagnation or decline at home.

6. The prevention of unemployment was a major attraction of Communism. To facilitate the change to a productive market economy that satisfies people's consumption needs and desire to work, governments must take the responsibility of creating jobs and educating and training workers to handle those jobs, or people will grow resentful and restive for a return to the employment security of the

old regime. Governments should look to the need to improve the infrastructure as a means of job creation.

7. Outlays on pollution abatement should be built into current operating expenses as Eastern European and former Soviet production levels are restored.

8. Producers in the transition countries must recognize the need for continuous product and process innovation. Competition for markets and the opportunity to earn extraordinary profits will spur innovation. In addition, governmental aid to research and development can contribute importantly to the productivity and industrial growth of both large and small enterprises.

9. The West should not try to dictate or impose its own system on the countries in transition; rather, Western nations should be tolerant of diversity and be willing to learn from working with others. Economic and political reforms must be pragmatic and based on a correct evaluation of the background of every country and of the region as a whole.

10. Solutions to the diverse economic problems of the transition countries cannot be black and white; a combination of federal support and private enterprise should be sought. The reeducation of former officials and administrators of the former Soviet Union is essential, since the older managers were trained in Communist ways and the younger generation, despite having many diplomas, have frequently received a poor education, both professionally and politically. Technical assistance programs, from Western governments, corporations, and universities, especially schools of business, are required.

In conclusion, we urge the people of the transition countries not to lose heart. One of the more romantic participants in the Bucharest Round Table said during the meeting that the problem of the transition is like falling in love: at first, you have the ecstasy and the joy; then, after a while, disillusionment sets in. But, after the initial euphoria and before the disillusionment, one must avoid despair by going for the long run.

All beginnings are hard; we have had a very hard beginning to these revolutions. We are still in the midst of them and have a long way to go. We must not abandon hope, and we must not give up. We must take this transition to the end, and most of all the end must be a humane one.

Notes

1. "Eastern and Central Europe" include Hungary, Poland, what was the German Democratic Republic, Czechoslovakia, Bulgaria, Romania, and Yugoslavia, and the former Republics of the USSR: Armenia, Azerbaijan, Estonia, Georgia, Kazakhstan, Latvia, Lithuania, Moldova, Russia, Turkmenistan, Ukraine, and Uzbekistan.

Chapter 1 · Overcoming the Legacy of the Old Order

Section 1 · Economies in Transition

Norman Scott

Despite the great hopes and opportunities created by the revolutions of the late 1980s and early 1990s in Eastern Europe and the Soviet Union, the general mood is now quite pessimistic. The problems are considerable. It has proved fairly easy to break up the old structures but extremely difficult to build new ones. Fixed investment is still falling rapidly in the transition economies; this trend must be reversed if the reform process is to succeed and burgeoning unemployment levels to be checked. A growing fear is that the increasing economic strains will lead to disillusion and impatience with both the idea of the market and with the democratic process. If the Western governments wish to reduce the growing risks, a much greater commitment to the success of the reform process will be needed on their part.

The End of the Soviet Union

In 1991 the Soviet Union effectively broke up when the presidents of Russia, Ukraine, and Belarus declared their republics to be independent and signed the Minsk Agreement of 8 December creating the Commonwealth of Independent States (CIS). By 21 December 1991 another eight republics had joined the CIS whose aims now included the building of "democratically law-governed states."

The accelerating economic decline of the Soviet Union since the early 1990s was due essentially to massive disruptions in the supply-side of the economy as a highly specialized division of labor began to break down. With the collapse of central "planning" control and the acceleration of inflation, barter transactions among enterprises have replaced centrally determined enterprise flows settled in rubles. The breakdown of central authority and the emergence of elected local leaders, sensitive to the needs of their constituents, led to restrictions on the outflow of goods, especially consumer products, to other regions. Since the division of labor in the Soviet Union was highly differentiated in terms of geographical distribution as well as function, these developments were particularly damaging and strengthened the tendency toward republican mercantilism. Against this background of increasing barter, curbs on interrepublican transactions and the general dislocation of traditional economic arrangements, there was a large decline in output.

For 1991 as a whole, net material product in the Soviet Union/CIS fell by 15 percent and GDP by 17 percent. Although this fall in output affected all the individual republics, there were large variations among them. Consumers have suffered and possibly by more than is indicated by the estimate of a 15 percent fall in the volume of private consumption, since it is generally believed that the official consumer price index understates the true rise in prices. The compression of already relatively low living standards is continuing in the independent republics and is raising fears that the fragile political and social consensus for market reforms will be increasingly difficult to maintain without substantial help from abroad. These fears are reinforced by the prospect of rapidly rising unemployment. Statistics on unemployment in the former Soviet Union and in its successor states do not provide a reliable picture of its current extent. At the end of 1991, one million people were registered as unemployed in the labor offices of the CIS members. At the end of 1990 Goskomstat estimated the total, according to ILO definitions, at 2 million. Current unofficial estimates, which vary widely, start at around 4 million, but it is extremely difficult to judge the accuracy of such numbers. What does seem clear is that unemployment is now a serious problem and, in the light of experience in Eastern Europe, is likely to grow rapidly as soon as any real restructuring of the economy gets under way.

Although a great deal of legislation to support the transition to a market economy was passed the principal failures concern the fundamentals of privatization, price liberalization, monetary and fiscal policies, and the pursuit of currency convertibility. In the presence of such lacunas, progress in other areas will have little effect and, in a "second best" world, may be counterproductive. This can be seen clearly in the case of inflation. Open inflation in the Soviet Union first appeared in 1985 as a result of policy errors and the side-effects of partial decentralization. After 1989, and particularly in 1991, there was a marked increase in the fiscal autonomy of the republics. Given the maintenance of a single currency and a passive, accommodating monetary policy at the center, the republics were able to run up fiscal deficits knowing that the inflationary consequences would be diffused across the entire Union. In such circumstances there was little incentive for the republics to embark on a serious attempt at macroeconomic stabilization and, given the deteriorating relationship between the union and the republics, there was little chance of monetary control being established at the center.

A solution to this conflict, between the fiscal autonomy of the republics and the continued existence of a single currency and ineffective monetary control, is now the most urgent task facing the successor states of the ex-Soviet Union. Without a solution, macroeconomic stabilization will be impossible; and without stabilization the collapse of supply links between enterprises and republics will continue to the point of destruction.

Given the lack of mutual confidence among the successor states and their fears of a reassertion of control from Moscow, and not to mention the strength of national pride in newly-won independence, one possible solution would be to move towards an open trading area with separate currencies. This would require an effective currency reform and a coherent macroeconomic stabilization program in each republic. The prime institutional requirement is to find ways of establishing monetary control (the absence of effective bank regulations and credit control in the Baltic states is the main reason for their delay in introducing their own currencies). A problem here is that central banks in many of the republics, including Russia, are responsible to parliaments, which tend to be relatively tolerant of inflation. An alternative method of control might be to set up currency boards, which would effectively tie the money supply to changes in the balance of payments. The disadvantage is that the currency boards would probably require much more Western assistance than the amounts required for the stabilization funds to support the internal convertibility of the ruble and any new republican currencies; the advantage is that, assuming there is effective regulation of the commercial banks, the currency board is likely to be a more effective means of financial stabilization.

A final ingredient of a program that would establish stable economic relations among the successor states is the need for arrangements for effective payments among the different currencies. The issues involved here are much the same as those discussed in the proposal for a payments union among the former members of the Council for Mutual Economic Assitance (CMEA).[1] The essential objective of a payments union is to avoid an excessive contraction of trade during the period of transition towards current-account convertibility of the republican currencies. In the past, the warnings of a severe collapse in intra-CMEA trade were ignored and suggestions that a payment union might be useful as a transition measure were brushed aside. There are signs that the lessons of that collapse have been noted by some CIS members and that they are keen to avoid a repetition.

The above measures, if put into effect quickly, would establish a framework for macroeconomic stabilization and for stopping—and perhaps reversing—the rush toward autarky in the successor states of the former Soviet Union. However, if the measures are to be successful, substantial assistance will have to be provided by Western countries and the international institutions. This will have to include large-scale technical assistance in setting up banking and payments institutions as well as significant financial help.

The "republicanization" of monetary control will have to be supported by measures to control budget deficits, which means controlling public spending and/or maintaining or increasing tax revenue. Cuts in spending are extremely difficult when all the political pressures are for increases to soften the growing hardships arising from falling real consumption levels, rising unemployment, and dislocation in the supply of goods. Western grant aid in the form of food, medicine, and medical equipment can assist here in a wider role than a purely emergency one. On the side of revenue, technical assistance is urgently required to set up and operate effective tax collection systems.

The stabilization problem is now very urgent. Without significant help from the West, it is doubtful that domestic efforts alone can be successful. And without effective stabilization it is unlikely that the longer-run programs for privatization, market liberalization and industrial restructuring can make any progress. Nevertheless, in the absence of adequate help from abroad, the CIS members will probably try to do something on their own and in doing so they are likely to focus on the two sectors where, despite the degradations of the former economic system, their products are still internationally competitive. The first is natural resources, although their development is hampered by supply-side problems that could eventually be overcome with the help of foreign capital and technology; the second is the armaments industry, which could probably resume export growth fairly quickly. An export drive in military weapons, however, would not perhaps be the most welcome form of self-reliance from the point of view of the "New World Order."

Eastern Europe

In Eastern Europe the difficulties of transforming former Soviet-type systems into decentralized market economies became ever more apparent since 1991. Levels of output continued to fall sharply, even in the few countries where an upturn had been expected, and most people have had to bear large cuts in their standards of living. The popular enthusiasm for a new order that characterized the political revolutions has given way to widespread feelings of anxiety and disappointment—and even bitterness that the pace of economic change has been unable to match the speed of political development. The fact that the earlier hopes of rapid economic transformation—encouraged by Western advisers and politicians no less than those in the East—were unrealistic is now irrelevant. Political leaders, not only in Eastern Europe, but also in the West, now have the task of preserving and reinforcing support for economic transformation in the face of increasing current hardships and the disappointment of initial expectations. In particular, they will have to counter the populist and reactionary charge that the hardships of the transition are in fact the "inevitable" properties of a market economy. In this task they will need the practical support of the international organizations and institutions.

It is generally accepted that the revolutions in Eastern Europe and the Soviet Union were not foreseen. This was a major failure of political appreciation and of social science in both the Western countries and in the East. Yet despite this demonstration of a general lack of understanding of the dynamics of economic and social change, the revolutions were quickly followed by Western advisers explaining why there was "no alternative" to doing this or that if the transition to a market economy were to be successful, and by politicians declaring that the transition would be swift and painless. Given the failure to anticipate the upheavals of 1989, a greater amount of pragmatism might have been more appropriate, especially since one implication was that knowledge of the "initial states" from which the transition countries were departing was, at best, rudimentary. This began to be acknowledged at the beginning of 1991. In Germany, officials admitted that they had seriously underestimated the effects of "shock therapy" on the *Neue Länder,* which had been subject to forty years of

Communist rule.[2] In his 1991 New Year's address, President Vaclav Havel referred to the "unpleasant surprises" of the previous year and announced that "the reconstruction we had planned for and looked forward to will take longer and cost far more than we first thought. What a year ago appeared to be a rundown house is in fact a ruin."[3]

These errors of analysis are having serious consequences. In Germany, the unexpected escalation in the budgetary costs of supporting reconstruction in the former GDR had led to a sharp increase in inflationary pressures and, via the impact of higher German interest rates working through the exchange rate mechanism of the EMS, is having a depressing effect on the prospects for the recovery of activity throughout Western Europe. The electorates in the West (including North America) are unprepared for the scale of international assistance that will probably be required to ensure that the transition processes become self-sustaining; and those in the East are also unprepared for the likely duration of their hardships. As suggested above, the political task of keeping the transition processes on course is now much more difficult than it was at the start.

Another complication in creating realistic expectations and sustaining popular support for the transition process in Eastern Europe is that the destination is usually described in terms of a unique Western model that bears little relation to Western realities. One of the most powerful attractions of market economies and democratic systems is that they greatly enlarge the scope for choosing different arrangements for the conduct of economic and social affairs. There is no single Western model of democracy or of a market economy. Around a core set of institutions and values there is considerable variation between, for example, Western Europe and the United States and Japan and even within Western Europe alone. It is also highly misleading to represent Western market economies as being ruled solely by market forces. The great achievement of the Western democracies, especially since the depression of the 1930s, has been to combine market driven efficiency and resource allocation with a concern for equity and social justice. Moreover, the fairly widespread existence of market failure, in the form of externalities or noncompetitive behavior, has led to a variety of forms of government intervention ranging from nationalization to various forms of regulation. The workings of Western market economies have therefore been greatly modified by government intervention, the specific forms of which vary considerably among countries and have changed markedly over time. The policy debates and innovations of the 1980s have not really altered this picture; the state has handed over (or back) certain activities to the private sector in some countries and there have been important changes in the institutions and forms of regulation of competitive behavior. These changes have met with varying degrees of success, but one of the major criticisms made of them—in both the United States and the United Kingdom, for example—is that they have led to greater inequality.[4] This alone is likely to lead to a reappraisal of the policies of the 1980s and to a renewed search for ways of improving the trade off between equity and efficiency in the 1990s. To ascribe the relative success of the Western market economies *solely* to the uninhibited workings of free-market forces both simplifies and underestimates their achievement. The interactive evolution of a whole range of democratic, social, and economic institutions and practices have ensured the survival of Western "capitalism" and repeatedly falsified the Marxist prediction of its imminent collapse. This is a richer—and more inspiring—picture of "the market economy" than the "stripped-down" market efficiency model that is commonly presented to the electorates of Eastern Europe and of the successor states to the Soviet Union.

Many of the people in these countries must now be wondering whether the invisible hand of the market is really just an iron fist. In Eastern Europe the depression deepened further since 1991, with domestic output levels falling on average by about 14 percent. This follows an average fall of 10 percent in 1990 and 2 percent in 1989.

No country escaped the collapse of output, but the differences were considerable: in Bulgaria the fall was some 23 percent; in Romania and in the Czech and Slovak Republics, it ranged between 13 and 16 percent; while in Hungary and Poland it was about 8 percent.

All sectors have been hit by the recession. The fall in industrial output was particularly large; it averaged about 19 percent with declines ranging from 12 percent in Poland, the third successive year of falling output, to a reported 60 percent in Albania, the poorest and least industrialized country in Europe. Agricultural output also continued to fall successively.

Although the development of the services sector is expected to provide an important boost to economic growth in the medium run, so far this has failed to materialize. However, the decline in the output of services has been less than for output as a whole, so there has been some shift in its share of national output. There is also probably a greater diversity of trends within services than in other sectors of the economies of Eastern Europe. Transport and trade have been badly affected by the falls in agricultural and industrial output, while health, education, and other public services are being hit by the tightening of fiscal policies. However, business and financial services appear to be growing in Hungary and there has been some expansion in the communications sector in Poland.

In surveying this general picture of collapsing output in Eastern Europe, a decline that appears to be on the scale of the depression of the 1930s, a number of considerations have to be borne in mind. The first concerns the quality of the statistics on which the picture is based. Although many problems in this respect have been around for a long time, there has probably been a deterioration in the last few years as national statistical offices begin to switch to new methods of collection of, in many cases, completely new sets of statistics.[5] One consequence of this reorganization is that the private sector, particularly small enterprises, and new activities are still not being accurately reflected in the statistics. There is also a shift in reporting bias. Under the former "administered" regimes, enterprises tended to overstate their output levels in various ways in order to satisfy centrally determined targets and to boost their claims for bonuses and an increased allocation of investment funds. Now, the incentive is to understate production in order to avoid paying taxes, an incentive that is strengthened by the embryonic state of tax collection and enforcement systems. These factors probably lead to some exaggeration in the measured decline of production, but until better official figures are produced and published, no one really knows the extent of the overstatement. Anecdotal evidence and a general consideration of the various factors influencing activity suggest that it is unlikely to be so large as to alter radically the general picture of a severe decline in production. In Poland and Hungary, the private sector is relatively more important than elsewhere and it does appear to have been quite dynamic in industry, construction, and in some service sectors. This is a most encouraging development and one that is probably not fully reflected in the output figures—nevertheless, it is unlikely to have more than partially offset the collapse of the still very much larger state sectors.

The extent of the downturn in Eastern Europe is much greater than originally expected, although the disparity probably reflects the unrealism of the initial expectations as much as surprise developments. The proximate causes of the downturn were the introduction of large changes in relative price structures, which are central to price liberalization measures, and the restrictive macro-economic policies introduced to curb accelerating inflation and government budget deficits. The simultaneous introduction of such policies in several countries generated negative multiplier effects throughout the region, which in turn were greatly amplified by the collapse of trade among the members of the former CMEA. The collapse of trade with the Soviet Union had a major impact on Eastern Europe, especially in the countries of southeastern Europe where the disruption caused by shortages of energy and other supplies was exacerbated by severe foreign exchange constraints. These various domestic and exogenous factors have interacted and intensified their ultimate impact on levels of activity.

Nevertheless, in spite of all these factors it is important to emphasize that a recession in output was unavoidable. The transition from a Soviet-type economy to a market economy must involve a large relative price shock as the system moves from an administered price structure to one based essentially on competitive world market prices. This shift in relative prices will benefit some activities in the transition economy, but it will weaken the competitiveness of others and of some to the point of extinction. Thus a proportion of the capital stock is rendered economically unprofitable, virtually overnight. How large a proportion will be "knocked out" in this way will depend on a number of factors including the initial disparity between domestic and world prices and on whether there are any arrangements in place to extend the adjustment period. It seems reasonable to assume that a very large proportion of the East European capital stocks have been rendered economically obsolete in the manner described, especially in the industrial sector.[6] So far, little progress has been made in reducing pollution and other environmental costs in the transition economies. When action does get under way it will almost certainly lead to further reductions in the viable capital stocks, either through direct regulation or the internalization of external costs.

Rebuilding the productive capacity of the former centrally planned economies requires a strong recovery in fixed investment, but the preconditions for this are not yet in place. Gross fixed investment fell on average by 23 percent since 1991,[7] following declines of 2 and 15 percent in 1989 and 1990 respectively. In other words, fixed investment has fallen by more than one third since 1988. The fall in fixed investment is general and in some countries (Bulgaria, Poland, and Romania) has been under way since 1989. Over the last few years investment has fallen by about 19 percent in Poland and Hungary and by nearly 50 and 60 percent in Romania and Bulgaria.

The question of fixed investment is at the heart of the transformation process and the conditions for its recovery are largely conterminous with those required for the transition itself. Private investment—foreign and domestic—is at present held back by a multitude of uncertainties concerning not only the medium-term economic outlook but also the putting into place of the entire structure of laws and institutions that are necessary conditions for a market economy to function. The one country that appears to have made significant progress in this regard is Hungary, which attracted nearly $2 billion of foreign direct investment last year. Nevertheless, even there, total investment is still falling and there are still few signs of any restructuring in industry.

Privatization is generally proving much more difficult than expected. In the leading tier of reformers (Czech Republic, Slovakia, Hungary, and Poland) it is moving slowly and elsewhere it has hardly begun. It therefore seems likely that for some time to come there will still be a relatively large state-run sector in the Eastern European economies. This will create problems for incentives in general and for the propensity to invest in particular. Private enterprises will be faced with continued uncertainty over the structure of their domestic markets and the managers of state enterprises, in the absence of clear preprivatization programs and commercialization, will have little or no incentive to invest.

It is widely assumed that once effective stabilization policies have corrected internal and external imbalances, and with a price reform carried through and a realistic exchange rate in place, private investment will take off to complete the transformation process. However, as the above observations imply and the current situation in Poland suggests, the timing of the two processes may not be synchronized. How can this "timing" gap be overcome? There seems to be little point in urging governments to "speed up" the creation of new legal structures and market institutions. These are complicated matters and governments are already going as fast as they can. A more effective approach might be to consider more active and explicit industrial policies on the part of governments; these would include a whole range of "supply-side" measures to raise capacity and competitiveness, increase public infrastructure investment, introduce effective training programs (including for management), and establish a monitoring system to reveal bottlenecks and market failures and encourage a quick response to remove them. The suggestion of a more active role for governments may produce ideological reactions on the part of some advisers, but this is a nettle that may have to be grasped if the stabilization-structural transformation sequence does not proceed as it is assumed to do. If East European governments were to decide on such a course, it would be advisable to do so with the help and advice of one of the international organizations, such as the Organization for Economic Cooperation and Development (OECD), familiar with such policies in the Western market economies.

Controlling *inflation* is a difficult task for the transition economies. They need to introduce programs of price liberalization and secure significant changes in the structure of relative prices, while at the same time the legacy of institutions and practices from the previous regime continues to undermine the effectiveness of the traditional tools of macroeconomic policy. Thus, credit policy is frequently being attenuated by the large-scale resort to interenterprise credits; and rising unemployment may be accompanied, perversely, by rising wages. The jump in the price level following price reforms was generally much larger than expected and although inflation rates subsequently subsided they remain high. In Poland, inflation fell sharply in the first seven months of 1991, but it then accelerated again in the second half of the year, to 44 percent per year in December. So far, policy makers in the Czech and Slovak Republics have been rather successful in this respect; after the price reform of 1 January 1991, prices rose sharply in the first quarter but decelerated rapidly thereafter, a performance that partly reflects the more favorable conditions in which the reform was launched but also the very tight control of budgetary policy. However, there was a sharp acceleration again at the end of the year. In south Eastern Europe, the control of inflation is proving even more difficult. There has been a sharp acceleration in Romania since summer 1991, to annual rates of 367 percent. In Bulgaria the initial acceleration in the rate of inflation following the price reform was sharply reduced, but thereafter it rose again.

The persistence of high inflation rates in the transition economies is in many ways a consequence of their "transitional" state; the "command" economy has been abandoned but many of its microeconomic features remain, weakening or undermining the effectiveness of fiscal and monetary policy. Some improvement can probably be made to the effectiveness of anti-inflationary macroeconomic policies—improvements in tax systems, perhaps a more determined use of income policies—but a significant and sustained reduction of inflation will also need more positive supply-side responses to the new relative price structures.

Since the early 1990s, one sign that the "soft budget constraint" was still operating in the transition economies was the relatively low levels of *unemployment* that were prevailing despite the large and widespread falls in output. This has changed considerably since then; the number of persons registered as unemployed in Eastern Europe more than doubled when it stood at just under six million (excluding the former German Democratic Republic). In Yugoslavia the rate at the end of the year was nearly 20 percent. Although there are many uncertainties surrounding the precision of these figures, there seems to be little doubt that there has been a dramatic rise in joblessness in Eastern Europe.

As in the Western market economies, the burden of unemployment has tended to fall more heavily on women than on men, on the young, and on manual workers, rather than the more educated. The number of long-term unemployed (those without a job for more than a year) also appears to be rising, although, given that open unemployment is a recent phenomenon in Eastern Europe, it is still relatively small compared with the numbers prevailing in Western Europe. Since, as noted above, the restructuring of the transition economies is still in its early stages, both the levels and duration of unemployment can be expected to continue rising even beyond the point at which output begins to recover.

The Process of Democratic and Economic Transformation

Many of those arguing for the so-called "shock therapy" approach to the transformation of Eastern Europe do so, at least partly, because they fear that the forces of reaction are still strong and that incompetence and/or corruption in the bureaucracies may be holding back the transition process.[8] This may exaggerate (or misinterpret) the situation insofar as many officials and bureaucrats can adapt quickly to changed conditions. As Edward Gibbon noted, also writing about a collapse of regime, "officers of the police or revenue easily adapt themselves to any form of government.[9] Not all government officials will possess the same degree of flexibility, but the key issues obviously include, just as in other sectors of the transition economy, the questions of skills and retraining, and the structure of incentives. Also, the administrative systems themselves will require radical alteration since they were designed to serve a very different political system from the one now being established. Moreover, it is not always a simple matter to distinguish between the faults of individuals and the much larger failings of the system in which they are required to operate. However, from the perspective of building support for the transition process, let alone from that of common justice, the distinction needs to be made.[10]

Clearly if the economic reforms were to fail—or to look as if they might fail—then these same officials would be looking for the next best alternative rather than fighting for the current objectives. So the expectations of economic success are certainly crucial for gathering and maintaining both popular and bureaucratic support for the transition process. But, having said that, it might be questioned whether it is sensible to burden economic instruments with political and administrative considerations. Instead of, for example, trying to speed up the privatization process so as to remove the influence of incompetent or unqualified officials, it might be wiser to target the deficiencies in administration directly rather than risk a dangerous backlash from a flawed economic reform.

It is important to acknowledge the close interdependence between the objectives of economic reform and reconstruction, democratic institution building and security issues in the transition economies, but it is also wise to remember the macroeconomic policy advice to match targets and instruments. In broad terms, administrative instruments should be used to support institutional objectives, and economic instruments should not be overloaded with political targets. The question of privatization can be used to illustrate this point. In Western Europe, the privatization policies of the last decade or so have been essentially concerned with improving economic efficiency, although some proponents have stressed the adjustment of the border between the democratic state and civil society as a matter of principle. In Eastern Europe the matter of economic efficiency is of course very important, but privatization is also regarded as the most prominent sign of the overthrow of the entire conception of the organic state.[11] In other words, privatization in the former Communist countries is intimately connected to the creation of democratic states and the reassertion of the claims of civil society. It is not surprising therefore that there are considerable pressures for privatization to be carried out as quickly as possible. However, the speed of privatization that might satisfy democratic and political objectives could be too fast for avoiding deleterious economic outcomes. It has been persuasively argued[12] that the state monopolies of the former centrally planned economies should be broken up *before* they are privatized—otherwise, the highly concentrated production structures, characteristic of Soviet-type economies, would be maintained with a high probability of continued economic stagnation and weak incentives for improving economic efficiency. Such an outcome would not only increase the tensions noted above but would also make it easier to reverse the process at a later date—a possibility that is precisely what the proponents of rapid privatization claim to be avoiding. There are, in addition, many other technical and quasi-technical problems that must be overcome if privatization is to be economically successful. Skating over such problems in order to speed up the process could lead not only to sub-optimal outcomes but also to a backlash against the private sector as a whole.[13] There is, however, already an extensive framework[14] for providing technical expertise and assistance in the building and strengthening of democratic and administrative structures in the transition economies—and no doubt this could be strengthened further. Moreover, a number of conditions concerning respect for democracy, the rule of law, and human rights, have already been set as requirements for receiving economic assistance from the G-24 countries and from the European Bank for Reconstruction and Development.[15] There is, thus, both a both a framework for Western assistance for strengthening democratic institutions in Eastern Europe and the implicit threat of sanctions against a country that violates the preconditions for assistance. If the framework is used to the full and the threat remains credible, the fears of democrats in Eastern Europe will be reduced and the political overload removed from policies for economic restructuring.[16]

Western Economic Assistance

It is the view of most observers, in all parts of Europe, that the nascent democracies of Eastern Europe would be gravely threatened by a failure of the process of economic transformation. In order to avoid such an outcome, the governments of the Western market economy countries have launched a number of initiatives to assist the countries of Eastern Europe and the CIS in their attempts to restructure their economies according to market principles. In the past years there has been an increase in the flow of official financial resources to the transition economies, an expansion of technical assistance, and an improvement in access to Western markets for Eastern products. The established international financial institutions—the World Bank and the International Monetary Fund (IMF)—have increased their assistance to Eastern Europe and they have now been joined by the European Bank for Reconstruction and Development, which was inaugurated in April 1991.

One of the most important developments has been the improvement of *market access* to the European Community, which is the largest single Western market for Eastern goods. Quantitative restrictions on most manufactures had been abolished or suspended by the beginning of 1991 and all the East European countries received General System of Preferences treatment. Agricultural, steel, and textile products are subject to separate arrangements, but for the latter two there has been some loosening of restrictions. Important gains in access were obtained by the Czech and Slovak Republics, Hungary, and Poland as a result of their bilateral Association Agreements with the European Communities, which were signed in December 1991. These provide for a phasing in of free trade in nonagricultural goods between the parties to the Agreements over a ten year period. Again, separate provisions apply to sensitive products such as textiles and steel, although there are improvements in both areas. There was, however, little improvement for agricultural products. Nevertheless, the Agreements offer important market opportunities for the East European partners and constitute a significant step towards their full integration into the European economy. One disappointment for the three transition economies was that a date was not fixed for their eventual accession to full membership of the European Community. The setting of a date, however far away, could have had a positive effect in encouraging foreign direct investment in the three countries. Also, some policy makers would have welcomed such a date as a source of pressure in maintaining their progress towards a market economy. It would have established a succession of intermediate targets that would have had to have been met according to the predetermined timetable.

Trade liberalization is also under way to varying degrees in the other market economies. The EFTA has concluded a free trade agreement with the Czech and Slovak Republics and negotiations are continuing with Hungary and Poland; and the United States has improved access under the Trade Enhancement Initiative. It is important that this general movement to liberalize access continues and that it be extended eventually—and as quickly as possible—to all the economies in transition.

At the present time, the outcome of the Uruguay Round is still in the balance, but a successful conclusion could provide important benefits to the

Eastern countries. Apart from the gains from a general lowering of trade restrictions, an agreement to lower protection of agriculture in the developed market economies could especially benefit the export earnings of countries such as Bulgaria, Hungary, Poland, and Ukraine.

Despite the considerable publicity given to the growing number of financial commitments to the transition economies, the amount of genuine aid (grants and concessionary finance) from the West has been small. Between January 1990 and June 1991 the total commitments of assistance by the G-24 countries to Eastern Europe amounted to $32 billion. Commitments extended to the CIS between September 1990 and January 1992 amounted to nearly $79 billion. Of the pledges to Eastern Europe, however, only about 20 percent consists of grant aid, although there is in addition a certain grant element in some bilateral loans. The bulk of assistance to Eastern Europe and the Soviet Union consists of nonconcessionary finance and is, therefore, debt-creating. Virtually all loans have been made at market conditions, although there is some implicit subsidy since the Eastern countries either have little access to the international capital markets or have to pay a large premium over base interest rates.

The figures for commitments do not of course indicate the actual flows of funds into the transition economies. In the case of the CIS (ex-Soviet Union) gross disbursements in 1990-1991 were about $25 billion, less than one third of commitments. Disbursements lag behind commitments for a variety of reasons and may not occur at all if certain conditions or targets are not met by the potential recipient.

Western financial help for the countries of Eastern Europe, and for the successor states of the Soviet Union, is, so far, considerably smaller than the sums implied either in a "Marshal Plan equivalent" ($16.7 billion per year) or in the suggestion of the president of the Commission of the European Communities to provide the equivalent level of support as the Community gives to its own depressed regions ($23 billion per year).[17]

Inflows of private capital into the Eastern countries have generally been disappointing. Foreign direct investment in Hungary and Poland has been encouraging but elsewhere it is negligible. Private banks abroad have reduced their lending, including to these two countries, and in general, as noted above, private capital has tended to flow out of the region. This suggests that one of the main elements in the Western approach to helping the transition—promoting structural change with large amounts of foreign private capital—has not yet started to work.

There continues to be a problem with the overall framework for coordinating assistance to the transition economies in the Eastern countries. At the ministerial meeting of the G-24, in November 1991, ministers noted the need for more effective support for the transition process and in particular for a more rapid disbursement of resources, increased information sharing among donors to avoid duplication, and closer cooperation between the international financial institutions and the G-24.[18]

Conclusion

Many historians point to the important role of the confidence effects of Marshall Aid and the U.S. commitment to its success in the reconstruction of Western Europe after the war. Today, only the new eastern German Länder have a similar degree of commitment to the success of their transformation program.

However, this does raise the question of the strength of Western governments' practical commitment to the reconstruction of Eastern Europe and the former Soviet Union. As noted above, the amounts of genuine aid being given to them are very small and there seems little prospect of a significant increase in the immediate future. Many Western governments feel constrained by their own budgetary problems and by the deteriorating short-term prospects for their own economic growth. With rising unemployment at home, it is difficult for foreign assistance to qualify as a high priority. Some governments clearly hope that the problems of the transition economies can be left in large measure to the IMF and the World Bank. The danger is that the growing introspection of some of the leading Western countries will only be broken by the onset of a major crisis in one of the transition economies and that this could lead subsequently to hasty measures that would be less than optimal.

Notes

1. See United Nations Economic Commission for Europe, *Economic Survey of Europe in 1989-1990* (New York: United Nations, 1991), chapter 3.4.

2. See the interview with Otto Schlecht, State Secretary at the Economics Ministry, Boon, in the *Financial Times*, 29 April 1991.

3. President Havel's address was published in English in *The New York Review of Books*, 7 March 1991, 19-20.

4. See Dieter Helm, Colin Mayer, and Ken Mayhew, "Microeconomic Policy in the 1980s," *Oxford Review of Economic Policy* 7, no. 3 (Autumn 1991).

5. See United Nations Economic Commission for Europe, *Economic Bulletin for Europe*, 43, New York, 1991, 4-5.

6. Detailed studies are still in short supply, but the existence of negative value added, when measured at world prices, has been shown to exist in several manufacturing industries. See G. Hughes and P. Hare, "Competitiveness and Industrial Restructuring in Czechoslovakia, Hungary, and Poland," *European Economy*, no. 2, 57-110.

7. This figure excludes Yugoslavia.

8. See Anders Åslund, letter to the *Financial Times*, London, 6 March 1991.

9. Edward Gibbon, *The Decline and Fall of the Roman Empire* (Oxford: Oxford University Press, World's Classics Edition, 1903), 75.

10. One qualified observer has argued that the majority of personnel running the courts in the Soviet Union were honest and decent people. "But the system as a whole, the entire mechanism of law enforcement . . . led to a perversion of the law and the erosion of human rights for all—the accused, the investigators and the judges themselves." Anatoly Sobchak, *For a New Russia* (London, 1992).

11. The term is used as in T.D. Weldon, *States and Morals* (London: John Murray, 1962).

12. David M. Newberry, "Sequencing the Transition," *CEPR Discussion Paper Series*, no. 575, London, August 1991.

13. There is, for example, a lack of expertise in many areas in government and state enterprises which needs to be remedied. There are widespread hopes that privatization and restructuring can be speeded up with the help of Western private capital, but many government officials lack experience in dealing with Western companies and are unfamiliar with international management contracts and competitive bidding methods. Anthony Pellegrini, Head of the World Bank's infrastructure division, has recently expressed concern in this regard with respect to the water industry in eastern Europe, where some western firms have offered local government authorities contracts containing "dubious terms." See 14. *Financial Times*, 12 March 1992.

14. For example, contacts between parliamentarians are maintained through the Western European Union, the Council of Europe, the Inter-Parliamentary Union, and so on. Also, within the CSCE, the Office for Democratic Institutions and Human Rights will serve as an information exchange for technical assistance available for institution building in the new democracies.

15. These preconditions for economic assistance are also among the five conditions, laid down by the Foreign Affairs Council of the European Community on 16 December 1991.

16. Uncertainty and the threat of instability in eastern Europe has also been greatly increased by the disintegration of the Soviet Union. This has not only created severe economic disruption through the sudden collapse of trading links, but has also added to the fears of the east European countries for their security. A framework for cooperation on security issues *per se* is also developing and includes the CSCE and the new North Atlantic Cooperation Council which met for the first time on 20 December 1991.

17. United Nations Economic Commission for Europe, *Economic Survey of Europe in 1989-1990*, New York, 1990.

18. The coordination of emergency aid and other assistance to members of the CIS werⁿe discussed at the Washington Conference on 22-23 January 1992.

Section 2 · On Becoming a Normal Economy

Holland Hunter

This section addresses a few of the major questions posed by the current efforts of the economies of the former Soviet Union to become "normal economies." What was abnormal about the old Soviet economy? What steps are needed to correct the abnormalities? What difficulties stand in the way of a prompt, painless transition?

To counter these difficulties, what potential opportunities can motivate and sustain the peoples of the Commonwealth of Independent States (CIS) through a long and difficult period of change? Which individuals are likely to lead the transition process, and what positive and negative incentives will guide them?

Issues of monetary and fiscal stability properly dominate policy debates about the immediate future, and other sections will be analyzing these crucial problems. My observations focus instead on the "real" aspects of the economy, that is, on the structure of the economy's production, the impact of structural changes on the labor force, and the underlying factors that are likely to guide the CIS economies along the path toward a normal economy.

What Has Been Abnormal about the Soviet Economy?

The largest abnormality of the old Soviet economy was its disproportionate output structure. Perennial Soviet emphasis on producer goods as opposed to consumer goods has built a malformed economy that is deficient in many of the features of a normal developed economy. Household wants have had secondary or tertiary priority behind national defense and capital investment. Huge flows of raw materials and intermediate output have outweighed deliveries of final goods and services in what Arthur Smithies once called an "input-input system."

This structure was initially put together by Stalinists in the 1930s to prepare for World War II. The effort was clumsy and brutal, but the USSR managed, just barely, to survive invasion and emerge victorious. In a just-published study, my coauthor and I report on detailed experiments with an economy-wide model indicating that with feasible and reasonable alternative policies, a stronger and healthier economy could have been built.[1] The study also spells out several major lessons from the 1930s for the 1990s.

The Bolsheviks had promised that after an industrial base had been built, the economy structure would shift toward consumer goods and services, but during the four decades following World War II the inherited structure persisted. Output of basic raw materials, fuels, and heavy industrial products was over stressed, and the service sectors remained stunted. Outlays on national defense absorbed a large share of the GNP, diverting labor and resources away from consumption and civilian investment.

The basic Marxist prejudice in favor of material goods and against intangible services has similarly hampered the growth of a well-rounded, healthy economy.

Capital and labor engaged in producing services have been labeled "unproductive," although in modernization around the world the share of services in total output has steadily grown at the expense of agriculture and industry. In the USSR at the end of the 1920s, business-support services, wholesale trade, retail trade, and a variety of consumer services provided by small firms and private individuals were suppressed; they have never been adequately replaced. Except for the armed forces, service occupations including health care and education have low status. Despite its mostly northern latitude, the Soviet Union has a stunted, rundown, shoddy housing stock delivering shockingly deficient services. The urban infrastructure of water and sewer mains, paved streets, and urban transport is similarly rudimentary, undermaintained, and overloaded.

The most visible crippling legacy of the Stalinist past is the giant industrial works that dominate Soviet heavy industry. These sprawling coal mines, oil fields, steel works, machinery plants, chemical complexes, and similar installations generally embody obsolete technology, along with a production philosophy fifty years out of date. Large plants are designed for long production runs of a limited profile of product variants. Since small-scale suppliers disappeared long ago, these giants have had to meet repair and maintenance needs in-house at high costs. Their directors have been reluctant to accept innovation. In all these respects, the heritage of "gigantomania" remains an economic albatross for the CIS economies.

Needed Remedies

Even before the collapse of the old system, Soviet authorities were beginning to acknowledge that intangible forms of output could be considered genuinely "productive." The way has been opened, therefore, for rapid expansion of the service-sector activities that enhance the productivity of a normal economy. In particular, a wide variety of services supporting the business sector is needed to help make all sectors of CIS economies more efficient.

For many decades, lacking these services, a large corps of officials, administrators, and clerks (some very talented), dealt with chronic scarcities through using political connections and reciprocal favors to meet goals set by the Party. Now, however, the need is for Western-style purchasing agents, commission agents, and brokers to convey information from retailers who are alert to household needs back through the many stages of distribution and production to those in charge of production. Company sales representatives, merchandisers, advertisers, and others specialists are needed to transmit information about products and services from producers through the same stages forward to the retailer. Freight forwarders, warehousers, insurers, and other specialists can help to speed the efficient movement of raw materials, intermediate products, and final goods among all the stages of production. This large diverse group of skilled individuals in market economies mediates between manufacturers and final consumers, letting buyers know about product characteristics, telling sellers about customer desires, and spreading information about competing alternatives.

These highly useful skills scarcely exist in the former USSR, except in the unattractive form of the *tolkach* ("expediter") who scrounges for existing supplies and organizes semilegal exchanges. As normal business services develop, they will add to the national income both directly in their own right and indirectly by making other production more effective, especially in dealing with the outside world.

Another structural remedy will involve reducing the volume of wasteful primary production. Every year, millions of tons of coal, iron ore, and other minerals are clumsily extracted at high real costs that damage the environment and undermine ultimate recovery rates. Billions of ton-kilometers of excess freight traffic are generated carrying unwashed, unbeneficiated, and unprocessed raw materials to the next stage of production. Crude oil and natural gas are hastily extracted in ways that leave large fractions of a deposit unrecovered, and moved through pipelines that let large amounts escape. Scandalously large proportions of each harvest of grains and other field crops are lost through careless handling, and the volume and quality of livestock products suffer from similarly defective treatment. As this unnecessary and excessive activity is curtailed, the inputs withdrawn from wasteful activities can then be transferred to more fruitful work.

In spite of many practical difficulties, most plants engaged in production for the military can switch at least part of their capacity to civilian end uses, given time for adjustment. In some instances the most valuable inputs will be the highly-skilled scientists, engineers, and technicians who can change careers, even if a physical plant is too specialized for other applications. This human capital will be especially valuable in the former USSR, where the military were able to attract highly talented people.

As Soviet enterprises rearrange their production processes they can make overdue corrections to "gigantomania" by breaking up the sprawling works where 5,000-15,000 workers are currently underemployed in dozens of buildings. Following the example of New England's multi-storied factories more than a generation ago, obsolete operations can be closed down and a variety of smaller contemporary firms can be launched in the old buildings, ready to draw on high-tech equipment installed in selected parts of the old works to meet current household demands with low-cost efficiency.

As the large industrial works scattered over the territory of the former USSR are subdivided into smaller units, alert managers can take advantage of the trade barriers springing up among CIS members to replace supplies that used to come from distant giants with intrarepublic supplies traveling much shorter distances. The new producers would look for links with nearby suppliers willing to supply improved inputs, developing supply channels likely to be faster, more flexible, and less subject to political disruption. An important recent paper describes a number of such initiatives already underway.[2]

Some Major Difficulties

Moving away from the old economy involves major difficulties. Reorganizing obsolete, high-cost enterprises to make them efficient world competitors requires sharp reductions in employment that will be socially and politically painful. Downsizing cuts wages, usually the largest component of total costs. Substituting contemporary for obsolete equipment usually lowers labor requirements, while simultaneously lowering fuel and other production costs. It will raise labor productivity for those still on the payroll, but that is small comfort for the people displaced. Enterprises that have always borne large costs for workers' housing and numerous supplementary benefits (including food supplies), will be under strong pressure to divest themselves of these peripheral activities, thereby again cutting costs and improving the competitive efficiency of a leaner enterprise.

In other parts of the world, dealing with water and air pollution has not infrequently provided some additional employment as part of abatement programs, but in the former USSR an attack on major pollution sources is likely to mean substantial unemployment. Where massive pollution is directly proportional to production levels, drastic or total cuts in production may be the only effective public health remedy in the short run.

Many cities in the former USSR, especially at resource deposits in outlying areas, are one-industry "company towns," wholly dependent on a single mining or manufacturing activity. If obsolescence or environmental danger requires shutting down the activity, the people of that community will be stranded. Unless other activities are organized to employ them, they must move away.

Abandoning obsolete products and processes in favor of contemporary technology makes both human and physical capital obsolete. Men and women whose labor skills are tightly linked to the technology being jettisoned will lose their means of livelihood unless the skills can be used in another activity.

While these kinds of unemployment have been recognized at least since the days of Luddite protests against textile machinery, and long experience shows that the resulting problems are eventually resolved, the combination of structural and environmental unemployment problems in the former USSR appears unprecedented. No quick and easy remedies are in view.

Potential Opportunities

Though the road to a normal economy is marked with major difficulties, one can also see major opportunities ahead. Correcting the great errors and making up the deficiencies inherited from the past can provide employment for those displaced by change, restore output levels, and generate higher future real incomes. The central problem, of course, will be finding ways to finance all the potentially worthwhile projects. Other sections are addressing this issue; my intuition only tells me that plowed-back profits will play a role, and that numerous individual ventures can add up to substantial aggregates.

Renovation and expansion of fixed capital stocks could employ millions of people, not just in a short-lived construction boom but for many years. Renovating and expanding urban and rural housing, for example, would require a large and active construction sector, as would the renovation of every branch of industry. Agriculture's capital stock, although already very large, nevertheless requires substantial redirection. Channels of distribution (transport, transshipment and storage facilities, wholesale and retail facilities) need widening and deepening.

Infrastructural investment is needed to fill another enormous range of deficiencies. Towns and cities have major needs for renovated water mains, sewers, streets, mass transit, schools, hospitals, and cultural facilities. Rural settlements have even more primary and fundamental fixed capital needs, such as running water and indoor toilets. The ancient problem of Russian "roadlessness" is far from solved.

Among the service sectors most grievously undersupported in the old USSR has been the one providing health care. State-provided health care has been anything but tender, and in recent years it has deteriorated alarmingly. It seems an obvious assumption that the CIS public wants and deserves more and better health care, however financed. Perhaps under conditions of democracy, with governments more responsive to the public, both public and private facilities can compete for consumer attention.

Another major blemish on the Soviet record is the dismal performance of the controlled and distorted housing sector. Most urban housing is in apartment buildings owned and controlled by municipalities, factories, or state institutions, and a large fraction of rural housing is in state-controlled cottages, though privately-owned apartments and houses exist. Until very recently, no organized real-estate market was permitted, and Byzantine complexities were involved in exchanging or acquiring living quarters. An active real estate market and a vigorous housing sector would contribute substantially toward making the CIS economies more "normal." Small-scale private investment in housing might prove to be a rapid and flexible way of meeting the needs of, for example, military personnel returning from assignments abroad.

One bright spot among the services is the sector supplying education from preschool through university level, together with correspondence school and other adult education programs. Since movement along the road to a competitively successful economy will call on millions of people to abandon obsolete activities and learn new ones, several supplementary services will be needed. Employment exchanges and job information services are already springing up. Some retraining programs already exist, but more extensive efforts are needed to facilitate and effect the large-scale re-employment of displaced workers and employees.

Sources of Initiative

The most visible travelers on the road to a normal economy have been the street-level vendors and traders operating at the very end of the long chain running from primary producers through all the stages of production and distribution to meet consumers at the point of final sale. These individuals serve by fetching an article from some previous holder and bringing it to the buyer, by holding an inventory, and by bearing some risks of misjudgment and loss, perhaps paying rent at a location or paying for "protection." But these useful functions, however small, are unrecognized by the general public; street-level traders are as vulnerable to moral condemnation as speculators, "buying cheap and selling dear," although they do bring supply and demand together, and to this extent relieve shortages.

Nevertheless reliance on street-level activists, scurrying around the periphery of the production process while the core of the economy remains subject to *gos-zakazy* (state orders), clearly cannot move the economy very far along the road to a normal economy. The detailed nature of consumer needs and wants ought to be transmitted directly and indirectly back through all the intermediate stages of production to determine the structure of the economy's output. *Perestroika* has been ineffective to date precisely because the core of the economy has been too unresponsive to household demand.

Fortunately, however, there is mounting evidence that a handful of industrial managers, along with a few ex-Party officials and former ministerial executives have been taking control of state-owned assets in order to keep their shop or plant going by seizing opportunities in the situation around them.[3] Some of these "state capitalists" merely capture windfall gains, but others are looking for ways to increase production, launch new products, or develop new services. These initiatives have the potential to move the economy away from its concentration on physical quantities of traditional output and toward a normal diversified economy shaped by consumer preferences.

Perhaps most of a whole generation of bureaucrats will have to be pushed into retirement in order to clear the ground for the creation of an economy with consumer-oriented flexibility, but there is already ample evidence of entrepreneurial talent among the peoples of the several republics. These innovative individuals may be plant managers, or the heads of a division in a large works, or municipal officials trying to solve supply problems in their region. They link up with others who control needed supplies, or channels, or outlets, to coordinate and facilitate production. They may draw on the talents of former *tolkachi* ("expediters") who are experienced in obtaining scarce supplies. They may enlist the services of former staff people in state planning agencies, familiar with procedures for controlling budgets, allocating supplies, and managing funds.

The crucial procedural change here is that where formerly these individuals responded to production and allocation decisions handed down to them from above, at present they are finding it necessary (and possible) to make the decisions themselves. As yet they operate without a clear legal framework, since contending views in CIS legislatures have not been resolved in spite of a good deal of Western counseling.

Positive and Negative Incentives

What are the positive and negative incentives that are moving the people of the CIS economies to a normal economy? Probably one powerful factor is a survival mentality built into the experience of people who have gone through the rigors of war and revolution and found ways to eke out a tolerable existence in conditions of chronic scarcity. With a wider range of economic decisions and opportunities open to them, individuals have to make new choices. Young men and women are more alert and experimental than their elders, but for both groups the road ahead looks grim, and survival itself seems to require change.

Movement along this new road will now be spurred by an incentive that did not exist in the old Soviet economy. J. S. Berliner calls it "the invisible foot,"[4] augmenting Adam Smith's well-known image of an invisible hand. In a market economy, the guiding hand of competition may be invisible, but the rude foot of bankruptcy applied to the backside of the inefficient is highly visible. In the old Soviet economy, this foot was invisible. Firms did not fail. They were not subject to a "hard budget constraint." Now, as the World Bank repeatedly implies, if the CIS economies are to compete successfully in the world economy, their firms must be moved along by exposure to a "visible foot."

If the negative incentive of failure is to be a new factor in CIS economies, the positive incentive of high profits derived from expanded output is potentially another factor. Most of the peoples of the new Commonwealth harbor serious moral reservations about the role of profits. Popular disapproval of middlemen, speculators, and profiteers is understandable; can it be countered by examples of how increased output is a market economy's answer to windfall gains arising out of current scarcity? With unrestricted entry, a firm's high profits attract other entrants to the field, and enlarged industry output brings both prices and profits down. McDonald's in Moscow, for example, provides a dramatic case study of introducing a new high-quality product and bringing down its real costs. It will surely have rivals. Perhaps other examples will soon show that the excess profits reflecting a scandalous gap between artificially low state prices and current black-market prices can be squeezed out through the methods of Adam Smith.

Along the same line, I wonder if there are effective ways to educate the CIS public to the honorable role of market-economy businesspeople who obtain the respect of their community through providing a good or service embodying dependable quality at a competitive price. This ideal, however imperfectly realized in practice, has been the basis for Western economic progress. Seventy years of Soviet miseducation has hidden the ideal from the present generation of Russians. The McDonald's example is one form of education. Foreign travel by

Russians is another. Western literature is a repository of evidence. Academic and business school training conveys professional understanding. With influences coming through all these channels, it may still be many years before a normal market economy is not merely accepted but admired by the peoples of the new republics.

Conclusion

Let me conclude by citing Joseph Stiglitz's summary response to the general question of the roles of the private and public sectors in economic development:

> First, there is an important role for the government in setting rules for the private sector, including incentives, private property laws, and contract law. Second, competition is more important than the private-public division; giving a private firm a monopoly is not likely to improve efficiency as much as pitting a public enterprise against an open economy and subjecting it to competition. . . . Ownership is not as important as the environment in which a firm operates.[5]

Notes

1. Holland Hunter and Janusz M. Szymer, *Faulty Foundations: Soviet Economic Policies, 1928-1940* (Princeton: Princeton University Press, 1992).

2. Simon Johnson and Heidi Kroll, "Managerial Strategies for Spontaneous Privatization," *Soviet Economy* (October-December 1991): 281-318.

3. See, among many other references, the Johnson-Kroll paper cited above, and dispatches by John Lloyd in the London *Financial Times*, 13 May 1992, and Louis Uchitelle in *The New York Times*, 2 and 14 July 1992.

4. Joseph S. Berliner, *The Innovation Decision in Soviet Industry* (Cambridge: MIT Press, 1976), 528.

5. Joseph Stiglitz, *Proceedings of the World Bank Annual Conference on Development Economics, 1990*, IBRD, 1991, 433.

Section 3 · Dialectics of Transition from Communism to Capitalism

Shafiqul Islam

This section offers a primer on the economics of transition to a market economy. It is largely for noneconomist informed members of the policy community who are bewildered by the confusing—and sometimes incomprehensible—debates among economists. In brief, this section is meant to be an informal guide to the perplexed. I pursue a simple goal: to underscore the points on which economists agree and disagree, and to explain why. In the process, I pose a few questions more forcefully than most, argue that some catch phrases dominating the policy debate are more illusory than illuminating, and suggest that some of the building blocks of the conventional transition strategy may subvert the foundation more than support it. Finally, I offer some suggestions to make the transition strategy more effective and make the reform process more sustainable.

The Package and the Performance

There is an amazing degree of agreement among the Western economists (and their market-friendly Eastern colleagues) on the major components of the overall transitional policy package. While these economists rarely list the components in exactly the same way, they broadly agree that the vehicle to reach a private market economy should be built on four interlocking wheels:

1. Macroeconomic stabilization, including tight budget and credit policy to reverse the course of rising inflation and reduce the widening external trade and payments deficits to sustainable levels. Stabilization measures can be bolstered by incomes policy, that is, taxing enterprises for granting inflationary wage increases.
2. Liberalization, which includes freeing up prices, including interest rates; devaluing the currency to a realistic—perhaps super-competitive—level, and then manage the exchange rate under some sort of "flex-fix" regime such as pegging with periodic large devaluations, or frequent minidevaluations or managed float; making the currency largely convertible for the current account to buy and sell foreign exchange for international transactions in goods and services; eliminating barriers to cross-border movements of goods, services, capital, technology, and ideas as well as liberalizing financial and labor markets.
3. Privatization entails the development of a new private sector, privatization of existing enterprises and reform of ownership and management of existing state enterprises/commercialization, restructuring, and liquidation.

4. Market institutionalization, which includes developing an institutional infrastructure that is supportive of the market and redefining the role of the state; clarification of property rights; and constitutional, legislative, legal, accounting, regulatory, fiscal, monetary, and social insurance reforms.

The last three wheels can be grouped together under the overall label of *marketization*. There is also broad agreement on two other points. In order to move fast and maintain the momentum, the vehicle should initially be fuelled (not just lubricated) by massive foreign governmental assistance: moral, intellectual, technical, and financial. The official financial assistance may involve financing a currency stabilization fund, debt relief, cushioning of the consumption drop, import of critical raw materials and industrial inputs, building physical and institutional infrastructure, financing a social fund, and provision of humanitarian aid (food, clothing, and medicine) where necessary. Adequate external assistance can therefore be viewed as the essential start-up fuel to ignite the engine, get the wheels moving, and build up the momentum to put the economy on the turnpike to capitalism. The other central component is a social safety net. The birth pangs of capitalism can be alleviated and the reform process can be politically sustained with supplementary payments to pensioners and the impoverished, as well as compensation, retraining, and relocation for the unemployed. The consensus strategy for capitalist transformation is thus also a structure resting on four primary pillars: stabilization, marketization, social safety net, and foreign aid.

Economists also agree—although with more qualifications—on the essential features of the transitional performance of the Central and Eastern European countries (CEE) since 1990, and of the former Soviet Union (FSU) since 1991. For example, almost all agree that output has dropped more sharply than anticipated throughout the CEE including in the group of three big post-socialist economies (CEE-3), namely Poland, Hungary, and the Federation of the Czech and Slovak Republics (CSFR). Because of the faulty official data, they disagree on the depth of the decline. Views diverge even further on the magnitude of declines in per-capita consumption, living standards, and economic welfare.[1]

The divergence of opinion becomes the widest when it comes to explaining the output/consumption drop. Experts lay varying degrees of blame on four factors: stabilization policy, accompanied by what some feel is an excessive credit crunch (the demand side); microrigidity further compounded by policy instability and macrouncertainty (the supply side); the collapse of the Soviet-led Council on Mutual Economic Assistance (CMEA) trading bloc (the inside shock); and postliberalization competition from Western imports (the outside shock).

Although the consensus is far from unanimous, economists generally agree that the trade shock has been a major force behind the deep and protracted contraction of the CEE economies.[2] Elements of the trade shock include the collapse of the CMEA trade and payments arrangements; the loss of East Germany as a major trading partner; the 1990-91 shrinkage of the Middle East market due to the Gulf crisis; the additional chaos in the payments mechanism due to the Soviet decision to trade with the former CMEA partners in hard currencies at the beginning of 1990; the adverse terms-of-trade shift resulting from the Soviet move to world prices for energy exports; and the increasing center-republic conflicts and the loss of Kremlin authority culminating in the breakup of the Soviet Union.

While economists generally agree on components that should compose the core of the transformation strategy, the consensus breaks down on the sequencing, speed, and stress (i.e., the relative intensity of implementation) of these components, as well as on whether and how sectoralism (industrial policy) should shape their implementation. For example, Portes argues that if macroeconomic stabilization can be accomplished only at the expense of "unsustainable output falls," selective sectoral focus should take priority. He also cites Russia in 1992 as a case in point, advocating giving "macroeconomic-independent" sectors such as agriculture and energy greater attention than a high-stake gamble on stabilization.

Both Marer and Sachs would reject this proposition outright in the case of Russia, which is on the verge of a hyperinflationary meltdown.[3] They would agree instead with Fischer and Gelb that "for countries with severe internal or external imbalances, macroeconomic stabilization has to be the initial priority."[4]

But Sachs is likely to disagree—and Marer is likely to agree—when Fischer and Gelb conclude, "It seems doubtful that the private sector would handle restructuring of very large, weak industries, so the state will need to restructure or close them."[5] Sachs—but not Marer—would also disagree with the Portes proposition that financial restructuring and demonopolization should precede privatization of large enterprises.

An instructive start toward understanding the debate on sequencing, speed, stress, and sectoralism is to separate the semantics from the economics of such catch phrases as *shock therapy, big bang,* and *gradualism.*

Economics and Semantics

Opinion gurus often debate the issues of sequencing, speed, stress, and sectoralism with three code words: shock therapy, big bang, and gradualism. Most, however, do not define them precisely. The consequences are what one would expect: miscommunication and misunderstanding resulting in unnecessary confusion and controversy.

The conventional practice is to use the terms shock therapy and big bang interchangeably, and to contrast them with the alternative of gradualism (some call it a step-by-step or conservative approach). The shock therapy/big bang strategy typically implies a simultaneous and rapid deployment approach on all fronts. In terms of the four interlocking wheels described earlier—stabilization, liberalization, privatization, and institutionalization—the big bang approach means exactly what it says: get all four wheels moving together and quickly with minimum emphasis on sectoralism (industrial policy). By contrast, gradualism is usually understood as an approach involving a great deal of attention to appropriate sequencing of the various components and subcomponents of the overall policy package, as well as differentiation in speed and stress of these component reforms determined in light of sectoral considerations.

With this two-sentence summary of what economists usually mean by these catch phrases, three observations are in order. First, the quality of the policy debate will improve if the phrase shock therapy were simply expunged from the vocabulary of the public discourse. Economists would be better off if they return this technical term to where it belongs, the psychiatry departments of hospitals. The reason is that this metaphor involves a misleading analogy and carries a false negative connotation. Psychiatrists apply electrical shocks as a last resort to treat patients suffering from certain types of severe depression and catatonic schizophrenia. Here the electrical shock *is* the therapy. In other words, the shock is the intended means to achieve the end of relieving the symptoms, if not curing the patient. By contrast, for a postcommand economy, the shock that flows from a simultaneous and speedy implementation of a transitional strategy is an unintended and unavoidable consequence. Put succinctly, in psychiatry the shock is the intended therapy, whereas in the economics of transition, the shock is the unintended consequence of the therapy.[6]

These fine points of distinction would be little more than an exercise in pedantics if observers often did not take this metaphor literally and fall into the intellectual trap of viewing the shock as the intended therapy, while interpreting the alternative approach as a therapy without shock (the psychiatric analogy would be the painless drug therapy), and thus preferable. All the complex issues of sequencing, speed, stress, and sectoral activism are thus reduced to a choice between shock or no shock. Consequently, critics view economists who advocate "shock therapy" as mechanical technocrats with little compassion for the victims of their cruel treatment, and with little understanding of the political dynamics of the sustainability of economic reforms.

The second point is that the phrase big bang (which is simply another name for the shock therapy), imported from astrophysics and cosmology, does not suffer from shock therapy's adverse moral and political fallout. However, it also creates unnecessary confusion as it means different things to different people. One economist's big bang may be another economist's gradualism ("little whimper"). While a "Big Bang with two Big B's" ought to imply a simultaneous and speedy implementation of the transition strategy on all four fronts, most big bangers often put varying emphasis on the four components in terms of sequencing, speed, and stress. For example, *The Economist* defined gradualists as those who put a priority on creating market institutions over privatization and advocate a strong state role in ownership reform of large enterprises with a step-by-step approach.[7] According to this definition, Marer (1992) is a gradualist even though he believes "a transition economy requires 'shock therapy' if it inherits a highly distorted structure of relative prices or a large macroeconomic disequilibrium."[8] *The Economist* would also label Fischer and Gelb—along with many World Bank economists—as gradualists since they suggest, "It seems doubtful that the private sector could handle restructuring of very large, weak industries, so the state will need to restructure or close them."[9]

Interestingly, *The Economist*'s version of the "gradualist" model is precisely what many often criticize as a painful big bang involving simultaneous, forceful, and speedy implementation of stabilization and liberalization, but with little progress on privatization and institution-building. Indeed, this is the Polish big bang that many love to hate. Clearly *The Economist*'s big bang involves not only speedy implementation of stabilization and liberalization, but also rapid privatization of small and large state-owned enterprises (SOEs). In reality, we are dealing with a spectrum where the real policy question for a transitional economy at hand is how to design a strategy that can effectively coordinate the sequencing, speed, stress of implementation, and sectoral dimensions of the four core component reforms so that the overall strategy is internally consistent. The big bang/gradualism debate reduces these critical policy decisions into two conceptual pigeonholes.

Finally, the paradox of the big bang strategy is that it cannot be implemented in reality. After creating the Universe with a big bang, God appears to have designed the planet earth in a way that some things simply take longer than others. There is no conceivable way privatization of large SOEs and structural market reforms can be implemented as rapidly as liberalization and stabilization. This inherent "speed gap" means capitalism cannot be created with a big bang. Even in East Germany, where the Western German institutions were simply imposed on the East and the iron fist of the *Treuhand* has been pushing privatization with full force, the "time gap" remained large enough to allow the second coming of a true big bang. The lesson from the postindustrial revolution history of today's advanced industrial nations, as well as from experiments with "test-tube capitalism" since 1989 is clear. In the real world, there is no such thing as capitalism with a big bang, but only gradualism of different shapes, sizes, and of course, speed.

The Dynamics of Reforms

Economists escape the confining trap of the big bang/gradualism debate by conducting their analysis in terms of sequencing and speed of reforms. But the dynamics of implementation of the transition strategy in fact involve five related, yet distinct, elements: sequencing; stress (intensity with which a policy is being implemented); speed (the pace at which a policy is being implemented); sectoralism (the extent to which the state countervails market forces to pursue goals at the level of sectors, industries, and enterprises); and the duration of implementation (the time it takes to complete the implementation of various policy measures). Out of these five elements, three—sequencing, speed, and duration—involve time in one way or another. The other two involve differentiation in force (stress) and focus (sectoralism).

These distinctions can be illuminated by stressing three points. First, the authorities undertake the overall policy program with most reform measures proceeding simultaneously, and a few sequentially. Because most measures are complimentary, there is no linear sequence.

Second, it is important to distinguish between the stress (the intensity) with which a policy can be pursued, and the speed with which its implementation may proceed. A difficult and complex task, by definition, is one where you put in a lot of hard work, and make little headway. Privatization (or restructuring and liquidation) of large SOEs, especially the fat and weak ones, is one area where a lot of stress would yield little speed. The tasks that get top priority, require heavy stress (forceful application), and can be accomplished quickly are those that begin and end early. Macrostabilization and price reform are two good examples. The measures that also get top priority and require a lot of stress, but move at a slow speed are those that need preparation/implementation from day one, are completed only after many years. Examples include the restructuring and privatization of large-scale enterprises and institutional reform. It is the combined interaction of stress and speed that determine the duration of implementation.

Finally, while initial economic conditions—the degree of macroeconomic imbalance and that of allocative controls and price distortions—as well as the nature of political transition should, and do shape the overall thrust of the strategy (and with it the sequencing, stress, and speed of various measures) an element of choice still remains, especially when it comes to the details of implementing the policy package. The Polish privatization policy could have been put together faster, whereas price and trade liberalization could have been more selective, and the zloty devaluation could have been smaller. The Hungarian reform program could have moved faster and without Vaclav Klaus, the Czechoslovakian strategy would probably have been less "laissez-faire-ish." The East German big bang had little to do with its initial economic conditions, and a lot to do with Chancellor Helmut Kohl's political agenda.

The Speed Gap: The Impossibility of Quick Privatization

Economists agree that stabilization, liberalization, privatization, and institutional reforms are interlocking wheels of the same vehicle, and therefore need to move together. At the same time, they also recognize that restructuring and privatization of large-scale enterprises (and some critical institutional reforms) in the economies of CEE/FSU have been much too slow. This has delayed the transition and raised the level of misery by preventing price and trade liberalization from generating a positive supply-side response. The usual reaction to this time gap between privatization and stabilization/liberalization is to advocate an acceleration of privatization, if necessary, with "quick and dirty" methods.[10] The presumption is that intensified efforts at privatization will induce a quick birth of a substantially privatized market economy where strong and speedy "stabliberalization" measures will bear their intended fruits. This is the "Wild West" model of creating instant capitalism.

The problem with this prescription is that it ignores three aspects of the reality of the transitional economies: Privatization of large state-owned enterprises (SOEs) takes a long time; a substantial portion of these enterprises are not viable at world prices; and the governments are not politically capable of liquidating them immediately.[11] First, as emphasized earlier, privatization of large-scale monopolistic enterprises and conglomerates is an inherently slow process (privatization of small or micro enterprises especially in the trade and services sector like a retail store or a barber shop is easy and quick, and has already taken place on a massive scale in CEE-3 and Russia). Many roadblocks retard the pace of the privatization of large SOEs, including the problem of valuation, the lack of domestic capital, national security (and pride) considerations involving foreign ownership and control of the largest enterprises, concerns over social equity, and settlement of claims by former owners (the restitution problem). The CEE-3 countries want to privatize about half of their state-owned assets by 1994, but they are unlikely to reach that goal. According to the *The Economist,* "at their current pace, they will be lucky to reach that goal in 30 years, never mind three. In practice, selling state-owned firms have proved time-consuming, frustrating, and expensive."[12] Even with a creative voucher system, some degree of restructuring, demonopolization, and commercialization is needed. Thus it is difficult to accelerate privatization up to a speed high enough to significantly reduce, let alone eliminate, the "speed gap" problem.

For example, with all the penchant for fast privatization, as of June 1992, the CSFR government had been able to complete only the first round of "share sales" as part of the first wave of voucher privatization. Even that task took a year and a half since the launching of the stabilization/liberalization program, and required a lot of hard work by a lot of dedicated people. Further, in this round, only 1500 projects out of a total of 11,000 projects have been approved in the Czech Republic.[13] Only a big brother working "iron-fist-in-golden-glove," and round the clock—as is the case in East Germany—can accelerate privatization, and even that ultimate driving machine takes years. Many "fast privatizers" seem to forget that left to market forces, only the best of the "good" large-scale enterprises (accounting for a small portion of the economy's industrial output) can be privatized. The government, already crippled by stubborn fiscal deficits, ends up holding the big bag of "bad" enterprises.

Second, a substantial proportion of the large state-owned enterprises do not appear to be viable at world prices. For example, according to Hughes and Hare, the proportion of output with negative value-added at world prices (the value of intermediate inputs alone—not wages and profits—exceeds that of outputs at world prices) in manufacturing may be as high as 35 percent for Hungary and Czechoslovakia, and almost 40 percent for Poland.[14] Even if these estimates overstate the presence of "the negative value-added enterprises," there are two other factors that can make value-adding, but loss-making, enterprises nonviable at world prices. The present value of net cost of liquidation is lower than that of restructuring.

Some loss-making enterprises may be adding positive value (a flow measure), but they may have accumulated bad debts to an extent that their net worth is highly negative (a stock problem). These loans are typically liabilities to other domestic enterprises and banks. Some enterprises are also indebted to foreign official and private creditors, typically denominated in foreign currencies.[15] The debt problem, however, can be partially mitigated by state-owned banks writing off bad loans for those enterprises that are otherwise deemed to be viable at world prices over the medium term. There is, however, another type of liability that cannot be written off. Some enterprises are so burdened with environmental damage (and ecohostile technology) that it is cheaper to liquidate than to restructure them. More importantly, for some loss-making enterprises the resource requirements of restructuring (capital, managerial skills, the authorities' administrative capabilities, and so on) are so high, they may not be salvageable.

The upshot is that many large-scale enterprises accounting for a significant percentage of industrial sector cannot be privatized at all; they are not amenable to restructuring and must be liquidated. Leaving aside the point that privatization itself does not automatically improve corporate governance, efficiency, and productivity, the presumption that intense efforts at fast privatization will quickly produce a large private sector is simply not true. Faced with sweeping "stabliberalization" measures, a more likely picture is a deepening and widening of financial distress in large state companies. These observations are corroborated by many recent developments. For example, as of September 1991, the Polish Ministry of Industry classified 700 of out of 1500 state-owned enterprises as having crossed the thresholds designed to trigger liquidation proceedings. According to the authorities, "hundreds" of Hungary's two thousand state enterprises face imminent bankruptcy.[16]

Finally, for economic, political, and social reasons, the reformist governments are not able to liquidate the inviable enterprises immediately, or even within a year or two. The governments rightly fear that the public support for reforms cannot be sustained if massive liquidation and layoffs come in the wake of plunging outputs, and cause intolerable social distress. The managers and the workers of the nonviable enterprises faced with little prospect for alternative job opportunities also use all their political power to block the process of liquidation. The march toward marketization creates gaping holes in the "socialist social safety net." Furthermore, the fiscally-crippled governments, with little help from abroad, simply cannot prevent people from falling through if the proletariat are thrown onto the safety net in staggering numbers.

There are already signs of disillusionment turning into reactionary resentment and cynical apathy. Recent polls show that the army and the police are the most trusted institutions in Poland—a country under martial law only nine years ago. The voter turnout also plunged to a low of 43 percent in the October 1991 national election (which revealed the stunning fragmentation of national solidarity with the strongest party getting less than 14 percent of the vote and 29 parties gaining parliamentary seats) from the euphoric high of 63 percent in the first partially free election held only two and half years ago. Also, in June 1992, Poland's fledgling democracy suffered another jolt when the parliament voted no confidence in the prime minister, installing the fourth post-Communist government in three years. In Hungary, only a quarter of the voters participated in some parliamentary by-elections in 1991.

Neither a well-designed bankruptcy law nor market mechanism can win against these formidable political and social forces. For example, in this environment a well-intended prescription turns out to be impractical. Western advisers advocate that the budget constraint of enterprises must be hardened, that all government subsidies should be cut and banks should not lend to cover the losses of unprofitable companies. The policy can transform nonliquid companies into insolvent ones. But one need not worry—since the government cannot liquidate most nonviable companies, it can implement this policy only softly!

The failure to harden the budget constraint of potentially nonviable companies also impedes another widely-advocated step toward privatization, commercialization (or corporatization). Commercialization of a SOE involves three tasks: clarification of ownership rights by typically converting the enterprise into a joint-stock company; improvement of the corporate governance by appointing a board of directors largely consisting of outsiders; and hardening of the (thus far) soft budget constraint. Since the last task cannot be accomplished even for many potentially viable companies, often all that can be achieved is "soft commercialization." The SOEs are converted into joint-stock companies with outside directors, but they still drain the treasury of their predominant owner, the state.

A program of massive liquidation and layoffs is also difficult to justify on pure economic grounds. In an already collapsing economy with no major new capitalist sphere of economic activity large and dynamic enough to cushion "the liquidation shock" and absorb the unemployed, sweeping shutdowns may only deepen the economic contraction, and thus cannot strengthen the credibility of reforms and inspire business confidence. Eroding credibility and confidence compounded by political and social unrest threaten the viability of the government, and produce disillusioned domestic entrepreneurs desperate to take their capital out, not investors—local and foreign—flocking in with money to build markets.

These factors may explain why only a handful of loss-making enterprises have been shut down so far in CEE (again East Germany is the exception for obvious reasons). Two examples from Poland illustrate how the nonviability of enterprises has become the Achilles' heels of the reformists governments. After announcing a scheme for privatizing 400 large enterprises in June 1991, Poland withdrew 170 of them in October 1991 because the authorities later deemed them to be nonviable, bringing down the percentage of industrial activity to be privatized from 25 to about 10 percent. The second example speaks even louder.

In July 1991, then Prime Minister Bielecki of Poland put the bankrupt Orsus Tractor factory in Warsaw back on to the life-support system, and fired his industry minister along with a dozen high officials for pulling the plug and trying to let the market forces do their job. If market forces got their way, not only Europe's largest tractor producer would have perished laying off 22,000 employees, the shockwave would have also affected the work and livelihood of another 100,000 workers at 300 supplier factories.[17]

Sustaining unsustainable companies creates an increasingly dangerous side effect, namely a rapid rise in enterprise debts as bankrupt state-owned banks and solvent SOEs provide liquidity to the candidates for liquidation. While severe undercapitalization (and net negative benefits of enforcing bankruptcy) may prevent these state-owned banks from foreclosing these "too-big-to-fail" enterprises, the real driving force behind this "liquidize, not liquidate" phenomenon is the "liquidation risk" of the reformist state itself. The reluctance of the creditor banks and SOEs to foreclose the insolvent enterprises is likely to be greatly influenced by the fact that they are still owned by the state; they are not yet free to conduct economic calculations as privately-owned entities.[18]

Whatever incentives may drive this apparently perverse (but broadly rational) behavior of creditor banks and enterprises, the adverse consequences of these growing enterprise debts are the same. They compound the enterprise nonviability problem by creating additional roadblocks to privatization of enterprises, increase the difficulty in determining whether an enterprise should be restructured or liquidated, aggravate the systemic risk that the failure of one debtor enterprise will start a chain of insolvencies that further reinforce the government's reluctance to enforce foreclosures, and thereby, crowd away scarce credit from profitable SOEs and new private companies to nonviable entities. Thus, the vicious cycle of rising enterprise debts prevents the dynamics of market mechanism from working properly. It blocks the exit of inefficient and insolvent firms (as the state shies away from enforcing foreclosures), and it impedes the entry of efficient and solvent firms (as bad credit drives out good credit).

All this adds up to a central conundrum of the transition strategy. A "quick and dirty" approach to privatization in a postcommand economy shocked by rapid and comprehensive liberalization and strong and ongoing stabilization measures often yield dirty, not quick results. With the privatization process inherently too slow, and the government incapable of engaging in massive liquidation of nonviable companies, efforts to accelerate the privatization process do not correct the speed mismatch problem; instead, the sweeping stabliberalization program succeeds in forcing potentially viable enterprises into insolvency and putting the government into fiscally and politically distressing position of holding a much bigger bag of bankrupt companies, thus undermining the reform program. By ignoring and aggravating the problem of nonviable enterprises, the fast privatization approach thus may help the reformist government become nonviable! The way out of this conundrum seems to lie in standing the conventional wisdom on its head—correct the speed mismatch problem, not by speeding up privatization, but by selectively slowing down liberalization, and redesigning stabilization.

Sustaining Sweeping Stabilization and Liberalization

A paramount paradox characterizes the transition problem. In order to sustain the economic credibility and political viability of the reform program, the four policy wheels must move in tandem; but they can do so only if the state actively plans and manages the coordination of the wheels with an appropriate mix of the four S's: sequencing, stress, speed, and sectoralism. More specifically, a strong and speedy stabliberalization program out of synch with the process of enterprise reform and privatization can actually create a vicious cycle of "destabilizing" stabilization and "depflationary" (a superstagflationary situation with depression accompanied by high or hyperinflation) liberalization. Together they can accelerate the collapse of modernizing investment, retard the pace of privatization and development of a new private sector, provoke a perverse supply-side response, and ultimately derail the whole reform program.

More specifically, speed mismatch on a high-speed track can produce an internally conflicting strategy that can provoke at least four types of policy-performance contradictions that seriously undermine the credibility and the sustainability of the reform process. First, strong stabilization in the short run can destabilize even a largely privatized market economy (typically, a developing country) suffering from high inflation and unsustainably wide external deficits. Sharp budget cuts (largely accomplished by shrinking the public investment budget) and tax hikes can immediately reduce the fiscal deficits, but accompanied by tight money and credit policies, they typically throw the economy into a recession. The economic contraction causes social expenditures to jump and revenues to plunge, and in no time the budget deficit returns. The authorities may axe the deficit again, but if that succeeds in driving the economy deeper into the recession, the deficit springs back again.

This cycle on the output front can be accompanied by a concurrent cycle on the inflation front. Confronted with fiscal deficits that refuse to disappear and an economy that continues to collapse, the monetary authorities get caught between pressures to monetize the deficits and to battle the raging inflation. They end up doing both, and in the process lose credibility as they pursue the stop-go policies. Another typical component of the stabilization package also contributes to this "deflationary" process and makes the life of both the finance minister and the central bank governor difficult. This is a one-shot, massive devaluation of the currency to improve the economy's price-competitiveness and to narrow the external deficits. In the short run, the depreciation represents an adverse supply-side and demand-side shock, putting additional downward pressure on output while at the same time fuelling inflation. The surge in inflation of course quickly offsets the gains in price-competitiveness from the initial devaluation, and the currency is devalued again to correct the newly acquired overvaluation. Whether the postdevaluation exchange rate is fixed or managed with a crawling peg or some system of floating, the broad inflationary consequences are the same, except that the price dynamics could be different under different exchange rate regimes as they may affect policy credibility differently.

Furthermore, stabilization measures produce additional inflationary shocks in economies in transition. In a command economy, the main source of government revenues are the enterprise profits (surplus) that the government artificially generates by fixing prices of goods as well as labor (wages), and collecting them. During the transition, stabilization measures result in a collapsing economy with liberalized prices. The economic contraction turns the profits of the enterprises into losses—and with no tax reform in place—and effectively destroys the government's tax base and swells the budget deficit. With no banking reform, the loss-making enterprises borrow from the banking system essentially "monetizing the losses" even if the central bank acts prudently, which it often does not. To sum up, in a transitional economy with increasingly rigid inflationary expectations, stabilization measures running ahead of enterprise and other institutional (e.g., fiscal, financial, and so on) reforms can only further destabilize the economy—add to economic contraction, investment slump, inflationary spiral, and external deficits—calling for even stronger measures.

The experience of developing countries suggests that a stabilization program is likely to succeed when, among other things, the government (in particular, the head of state and his economic team) is strong, popular, committed, and credible; the lag of the economy's supply-side response (say, to a currency devaluation) is relatively short; the policy conditionality focuses on the broad goals and not on narrow mechanical ratios; and the program is well-funded and accompanied by measures to promote exports and other potential growth sectors.[19] In a typical postcommand economy, these conditions generally do not hold. In particular, the cycle can be even more vicious in a partly-privatized, nonmarket economy with greater rigidity of the monopolistic supply-side.

In the major CEE nations, stabilization measures have succeeded in containing the loss of foreign exchange reserves by controlling the balance of payments, the current account balance as well as the capital account. The current accounts of these countries have small financible deficits, and in some cases even small surpluses. This apparent success is largely the flip side of the economic depression. Imports have plunged, and the collapsing domestic demand accompanied by supercompetitive exchange rates have on average boosted export earnings in hard currencies. With little stock of hard-currency capital in the hands of individuals and enterprises and no currency convertibility for capital account transactions, capital flight has not become a major problem. In addition, foreign private capital inflows, especially in the form of direct investment, have added to the official reserves of Hungary and the Czech and Slovak Republics.

The second conflict arises from a comprehensive and rapid application of one component of liberalization measures, price reform, that typically accompanies stabilization. Price reform typically takes the form of an across-the-board lifting of price controls, except for some basic necessities and "special" goods and services (e.g., food, rents, utility charges, energy, and so on). Free prices get rid of the shortages and the queues, and they bring repressed inflation into the open—both desirable goals—but they also undermine one primary objective of the stabilization package by pouring gasoline on the inflationary fire. Ironically, stabilization measures meant to control inflation may contribute to it, and at the same time, price liberalization provide additional powerful fuel.

Trade reform is the third source of tension and another major component of the liberalization package. Sweeping trade liberalization often turns out to be a single-edged sword with the edge on the wrong side typically swinging at the wrong enemy. Accompanied by the national currency largely convertible for international transactions of goods and services, trade liberalization is intended to import the world price structure into the economy, make enterprises efficient by introducing competition, and fight inflationary price setting by monopolies by exposing them to foreign competition. In practice however, the enterprises face one of two types of consequences. If accompanied by large currency devaluation, trade liberalization may become a blunt sword against monopolistic price increases as the devalued currency provides monopolistic enterprises solid protection. They can raise prices without facing world competition. If unaccompanied by large devaluation or if the initial devaluation-induced protection from world competition is eroded by continuing inflation, an abrupt trade liberalization can begin to overkill by driving potentially viable enterprises (over the medium term) to insolvency.

So we have another paradox. Trade liberalization may not succeed initially in importing the world price structure and in forcing the domestic monopolies to face world competition, but if and when they do succeed, they may compound the financial distress of the enterprise sector, force companies to insolvency that need temporary breathing time, thus aggravating the fiscal drain and the budget deficit that the government is trying so hard to contain.

Finally, stabilization and liberalization measures can put a knife through the Achilles' heels of the reform program, which is the nonviability of state enterprises that are "too big to fail." Protracted and intensifying economic contraction caused by stabilization measures can deepen the pool of inviable enterprises by aggravating the financial distress of companies that would be insolvent even when half exposed to world prices, and widen it by forcing companies that were potentially viable at world prices to join "the club of the clearly insolvents." Also, cuts in direct government subsidies to enterprises to reduce the budget deficit (and correct price distortions) can increase the membership of "the Nonviable Unlimited."

Here the distinction between static and dynamic comparative advantage is critically relevant. For the enterprises that cannot be salvaged and are clear candidates for "bulldozer liquidation," an abrupt exposure to world prices does not make them "more nonviable"; it only undermines the stabilization program as the government—unable to liquidate those living deads—is forced to subsidize them, and thereby enlarge the budget deficit; and the banking system provides loans creating additional credit; and the suppliers sell them goods on credit aggravating the problem of the runaway enterprise debts.

For enterprises that appear viable at world prices, but need temporary protection and subsidies as they modernize and restructure, an abrupt and sweeping liberalization package can spell the difference between life and death. These enterprises are not competitive today at world prices (that is, they do not have static comparative advantage), but they could be competitive tomorrow at world prices if given a chance to slowly adapt, learn, and improve (they have dynamic comparative advantage). Although it is often difficult to clearly identify these "gray enterprises," it is also true that this is what entrepreneurs and businesses do everyday in the advanced capitalist economies. On balance, they are often right, but sometimes they are wrong. Indeed, one primary rationale for profits is nothing but compensation for the risk of failure. Sector-blind liberalization measures can kill off these risky, but potentially viable companies.

If mechanical stabliberalization policies fail to control high, unstable, and rising inflation, it can delay the prospect for the domestic currency becoming fully convertible for current account transactions, let alone for capital account transactions. The Czechoslovakian success in controlling inflation does not invalidate the argument that orthodox stabliberalization measures complicate the task of putting a permanent lid on inflation. Czechoslovakia is the only transitional economy with no historical memory of inflation. Also, there was little inflation (and macroeconomic imbalance) when the stabliberalization program was launched on 1 January 1991. With budgetary and monetary tightening policy accompanied by a strict incomes policy (tax-based wage policy leading to a sharp drop in real wages) to counteract the jump in inflation from price liberalization and currency devaluation, and no initial inertial inflation and inherited inflationary expectations, the CSFR government was able to prevent the one-shot price increases from turning into a persistent and rising inflationary spiral.

But the CSFR success in controlling inflation is not over. Liquidations and restructuring (driven by privatization) reinforce declining output, employment, and enterprise profits. The budget deficit is widened. As the expectations of a turnaround in the declining living standards continue to be frustrated, the Czech Republic (and even more so Slovakia) may experience workers' efforts to reverse the real wage decline and the initiation of a wage price spiral.

Supply-Friendly Liberalization and Inflation-Hostile Stabilization

With depflation ravaging the economies of the CEE/FSU and threatening the sustainability of the reform process, the overarching policy question is: Can the transition strategy be redesigned so that it can bring inflation down to low levels, jumpstart economic recovery, maintain the low-inflationary growth, sustain the reform process, and accomplish all this without significantly slowing down the march toward marketization? The short answer is that this is a tall order and there exists no perfect and single response to this challenge. The longer answer is that yes, superior ways exist for reorganizing and coordinating the four core components of the conventional strategy. But although a few general principles can guide the alternative strategy, the policy package must be tailored to the specific economic and political conditions of each economy. For example, the unique and complex conditions of Russia and other states of the former Soviet Union call for modifications and extensions of the alternative strategy, especially when formulating and implementing them.

The strategy rests on four major premises. First, the road to capitalism cannot be built on a "valley of tears." While the state enterprise sector should continue to shrink, overall economic growth must be restored soon. You cannot marketize an economy when the existing "market" is shrinking fast. It is also instructive to stand Milton Friedman's dictum that "inflation causes recession" on its head and say that recession causes inflation, especially in a postcommand economy. Second, as mentioned earlier, a more productive way to correct "the speed mismatch problem" is to soften and selectively slow down liberalization measures rather than trying to do the impossible, that is, significantly accelerate privatization of large SOEs.

Third, the weight of the collective wisdom of most Western economists notwithstanding, sector blindness can be hazardous to the healthy capitalist development of a postcommand economy. At a very aggregate level, it is useful to categorize the enterprises (I am ignoring the agriculture sector as I have done throughout) into three major groups: controlled, liberalized, and newly emerging private.[20] The controlled sector is entirely state owned, and this is where, along with natural monopolies, the bulk of the nonviable enterprises should belong. The liberalized sector consists of state-owned enterprises, as well as those that have already been privatized. State-owned liberalized enterprises should include largely viable enterprises and candidates for privatization. And then, there is the emerging private sector, which is made up of largely newly established small enterprises in the form of limited liability companies, joint ventures, fully foreign-owned companies, partnerships, and single-owner firms. The privatized former SOEs and the newly established private firms are the two components of the productive (output-producing) private sector (privatization of the existing housing stock creates private wealth, but not output-producing enterprises).

The final premise is that we need to add one more critical dimension to the analysis of sequencing, stress, speed, and sectoralism. In the first few years of change, value-producing activities, preferably those with strong economy-wide, demand-expanding spillover effects, should get greater priority and governmental support than demand-depressing liberalization, restructuring, and liquidation. Once economic recovery is underway, with the private sector increasingly able to compensate for the decline in output and employment, the focus can shift the other way. A sweeping decontrolling of the command economy and an abrupt

exposure to world prices can lead to a suicidal waves of "destructive competition" rather than the Schumpetarian gales of "creative destruction."

Conclusion

Without trying to outline a full policy package, I shall highlight some of the
main features of the alternative strategy by illustrating how it alters the design
and the implementation of the four components of the conventional strategy. I
begin with liberalization because more than any other, this critical element of the
conventional strategy intended to accelerate the transition to a market economy
appears to be accomplishing the opposite by ultimately jeopardizing the
sustainability of the reform process. Three points are worth noting. First, while
a strong overall reform program—to be carried out immediately and
later—should be announced on day one to signal a credible regime change, the
actual implementation of liberalization measures should be phased in over a
period of years, and it should be flexible and sector sensitive. For example,
while some prices should be decontrolled immediately, others (such as energy
prices in Russia) should be freed up gradually in steps. An abrupt sharp increase
in an input price constitutes an adverse supply and demand shock, and in an
inflationary environment, can make the anti-inflation task of stabilization
measures much tougher to accomplish. The OPEC shock's stagflationary effects
on market economies is a lesson that should not be lost when it comes to reforming the command economies.

Second, regarding trade liberalization, all quotas should be transformed into
equivalent tariffs, but there is a case for a gradual elimination of tariffs for sectors that need breathing time for restructuring, as well as for those enterprises
that cannot be liquidated soon. While these tariffs should not be eliminated
immediately, a time table for phasing them out should be announced. This is
standard practice in the market economies. Trade liberalizations undertaken in
various free trade agreements including past rounds of the General Agreement on
Tariffs and Trade (GATT) talks and the recently signed North American Free
Trade Agreement (NAFTA) have taken this form. In the developing world, the
widely cited case of rapid trade liberalization took place in Chile during the
1970s. In 1973, the government replaced quantitative restrictions (QRs or
quotas) with average tariffs of about 100 percent with the highest tariff rate set
over 500 percent, and it took six years to bring them down to a uniform rate of
10 percent.[21] The argument that you need a sledgehammer approach to create a
market economy out of a centrally planned economy infested with huge monopolies and a plan-friendly *apparatchik* is a faulty one; as mentioned earlier, the
consequences could in fact be counterproductive by raising the social costs of
transition beyond the level of popular tolerance.

The third point involves the role of the liberalization policy in promoting
economic recovery, and modernizing and restructuring the industrial sector to
make it increasingly competitive in the world market. The temporary protective
walls of tariffs as well as direct budgetary subsidies (not explicit or implicit

input subsidies) can be used to support the potential pockets of growth in the emerging private sector, as well as the existing SOEs that appear viable with necessary restructuring. An outward-looking approach based on the principle of dynamic comparative advantage should be pursued. Vigorous domestic competition should be encouraged by breaking up monopolies into several firms supplying the same product, while temporarily protecting these fledgling firms from global competition. The philosophy of "the survival of the fittest" should be pursued first at the national level, and the survivors should then be gradually exposed to foreign competition as they increasingly become "fitter." This two-step economic Darwinism is the model that Japan and the Asian NIEs pursued so successfully in their industrialization and overall economic development.[22] Incredibly, in 1991 the average tariff rate and the spread of nontariff barriers in manufacturing were higher in South Korea than in Poland.

But there is a problem in that Poland is no South Korea, and Russia is certainly no Japan. In other words, How do we deal with the dilemma that if these decisions are left to the post-Communist bureaucrats used to running a command economy they will instinctively pursue an anticompetitive and antimarket industrial policy? Two responses are in order. First, the transitional economies are already running and will continue to run a de facto industrial policy. It is better to recognize this reality and try to make it as promarket and procompetition as possible.

Second, one possible way to impose "an industrial policy conditionality" is to form a "Foreign Economic Advisory Committee" (FEAC) for each country. This is especially critical for Russia; if this approach is successful, other countries can follow the same path. The advisory committee should consist of a top government official and a top businessman from the G-3 countries, South Korea and one high official each from the World Bank and the International Monetary Fund (IMF). So the committee will consist of ten individuals supported by a staff of economists, industry specialists, and bureaucrats from the ministries of the participating countries. This committee can judiciously guide the industrial policy of the transitional economy with the carrot and the stick of official funds.

With regard to stabilization measures, the top priority must be inflation control. If sector-specific protection through tariffs and subsidies as well as state support for investment by the private sector and the restructuring SOEs can generate an economic recovery, or at least halt the persistent decline in demand and output, most of the deficit problem is likely to disappear. Tax reform to replace the old implicit taxation through appropriation of enterprise surplus accompanied by vigorous efforts at collection can also help. The growth of money and credit would be a lot easier to control if loss-making and apparently nonviable state-controlled SOEs receive direct budgetary subsidies, but no credit from the banking system or other enterprises. With these reforms in place, and with liberalization measures and currency devaluations sensitive to the inflationary consequences, tight monetary policy has a much better chance to succeed in controlling inflation.

Finally, to improve the supply-side response and to get a better handle on monetary control, the growing problem of enterprise debts must be addressed immediately. State-owned banks should be recapitalized by replacing their bad loans with the government securities. These recapitalized banks should be allowed to lend to only *creditworthy* private and liberalized state-owned enterprises. The government can get rid of these bad debts over time as it liquidates, restructures, and privatizes the debtor enterprises.

This growth-oriented and sector-sensitive approach may do better in controlling inflation, promoting recovery, and putting the transitional economies on a sustainable path towards capitalism. This "evolutionary model" seems to be superior to a "creationist model" being tried currently in some transitional economies.

Notes

1. See, for example, Richard Portes, "Overview: From Central Planning to a Market Economy," in *Making Markets: Economic Transformation in Eastern Europe and the Post-Soviet States*, eds., Shafiqul Islam and Michael Mandelbaum (Council on Foreign Relations Press, 1993); Andrew Berg and Jeffrey Sachs, "Structural Adjustment and International Trade in Eastern Europe: The Case of Poland," *Economic Policy: Eastern Europe*, 14 (April 1992); Andrew Berg, "A Critique of Official Data," paper presented at the IMF/World Bank Conference on The Macroeconomic Situation in Eastern Europe, Washington, D.C., 1992; and Branko Milanovic, "Social Costs of Transition to Capitalism: Poland 1990," CECSE research paper, June 1992.

2. Rodrik (1992) estimates that the trade shock caused the GDP to decline by 3-4 percent in Poland and 7 to 8 percent in Hungary and Czechoslovakia.

3. Marer, "Economic Transformation in Central and Eastern Europe," and Jeffrey Sachs, "Western Financial Assistance and Russia's Reforms," in *Making Markets*.

4. Stanley Fischer and Alan Gelb, "The Process of Socialist Economic Transformation," *Journal of Economic Perspectives* 5, no. 4 (1991): 101.

5. Fischer and Gelb, 100.

6. James Kornai, an expert on the subject, made the same point in an interview: "I hate the phrase 'shock therapy.' We don't apply the therapy for the sake of the shock. The shock is an inevitable side effect." See Robert Kuttner, "The Dustbin of Economics," *The New Republic*, 25 February 1991.

7. *The Economist*, 16 May 1992, 13-14.

8. Fischer and Gelb, 78.

9. Fischer and Gelb, 101-104.

10. Jeffrey Sachs, "Accelerating Privatization in Eastern Europe," paper prepared for the World Bank's annual Conference on Development Economies, April 1991.

11. This section draws heavily on material in Sanjay Dhar, "Enterprise Viability and the Transition to a Market Economy," Internal Discussion Paper, Report no. IDP-0113, World Bank (February 1992). See also Ronald McKinnon, *The Order of Economic Liberalization: Financial Control in the Transition to a Market Economy* (Baltimore: Johns Hopkins University Press, 1991); and Ronald McKinnon, "Financial Control in the Transition from Classical Socialism to a Market Economy," *Journal of Economic Perspectives* 5, no. 4 (Fall 1991).

12. *The Economist*, "A Survey on Business in Eastern Europe," 26 September 1991, 10.

13. Michal Mejstrik and James Burger, "On the Brink: CSFR Privatization Readies for the Start of the First Round," *Privatization Newsletter of Czechoslovakia*, no. 6 (May 1992).

14. An unprofitable (loss-making) enterprise is producing negative value-added output when the enterprise would be *unprofitable* even if it paid *nothing* to the workers. See G. Hughes and P. Hare, "Competitiveness and Industrial Restructuring in Czechoslovakia, Hungary and Poland," *European Economy* (June 1991).

15. In the former Soviet Union, the enterprise debt problem is even more complicated: The *ruble debts* could be owed to banks and enterprises of different republics (now independent nations). The foreign-currency debts of the former Union government have been allocated to various successor states according to a mechanical formula. But the legal condition imposed by the G-7 governments (before the breakup of the Soviet Union) that each republic is "jointly and severally" responsible for all the Union debt to foreigners is still a stumbling block for the governments of former republics desperately seeking an IMF program. At the time of this writing, Russia is the only post-Soviet country that confronts this problem as it engages in seemingly endless negotiations with the IMF to become eligible to receive a $24 billion loan package that was announced with much fanfare in April 1992.

16. *The Economist*, May 1992, 8.

17. "A Survey on Business in Eastern Europe," *The Economist*, 30.

18. For an analysis of how privately owned creditor banks and enterprises display similar behavior, see David Begg and Richard Portes, "Enterprise Debt and Economic Transformation: Financial Restructuring of the State Sector in Central and Eastern Europe," Discussion Paper no. 695, Center for Economic Policy Research, London, June 1992.

19. See, for example, United Nations, "Dilemmas of Macroeconomic Management: Stabilization and Adjustment in Developing Countries," *Supplement to World Economic Survey 1990-1991* (1992); M. Kiguel and N. Liviatan, "Inflationary Rigidities and Orthodox Stabilization Policies: Lessons from Latin America," *World Bank Economic Review* 2, no. 3 (September 1988); and M. Kiguel and N. Liviatan, "Lessons from Heterodox Stabilization," World Bank Working Paper no. 671, 1991.

20. This analysis owes its origin to McKinnon, "Financial Control in the Transition from Classical Socialism to a Market Economy."

21. Dhar, "Enterprise Viability and the Transition to a Market Economy."

22. See Saburo Okita, "Transition to a Market Economy," paper prepared for Part 2, Section 2 of this book; and Yukitsugu Nakagawa, "Reflections on Restoring the Former Soviet Union: Can the Japanese Experience Help?" International Institute for Global Peace Policy Paper 92E, June 1992.

Section 4 · Difficulties in Transforming Economies

Daniel Daianu

New phenomena, such as open inflation and open unemployment, suggest new forms of operating disequilibria in the emerging market economies. They still coexist with substantial hidden unemployment and price controls, making up complex and intricate combinations of imbalances.

Other genres of disequilibria, outside of the realm of conventional economics, can help us to better understand how economies and societies in transition function. I have in mind something that could be called "organizational disequilibrium," meaning the shortage of market-required organizational capital. Another important topic is the gap between people's expectations and what governments can deliver in the short run. This is known as "expectational disequilibrium," or excess expectations. We should also examine the microfoundation of macrodisequilibria, that is, the extent to which Say's principle operates and hard budget constraints are imposed.

Failures in Transition

Recently there has been a flurry of research obsessed with the alarming drop in economic activity in the transforming economies.[1] Why is this fall so dramatic? To give an answer to this question one needs first to define the potential performance of these economies.

I remember in February 1991, R. Portes asked rhetorically during a conference in Luxembourg why we had so greatly overestimated the actual and potential performances of the former centrally planned economies? If we admit to this "performance illusion" (similar to Holzman's "salability illusion"), then part of the fall in output can be seen as a normal depreciation at world market values of production. This "Midas-touch" effect in reverse explains the damage caused to the economy in its performance potential. In other words, institutional rearrangements (turning the system into a market-based economy) would not lead to that increase of performance that might be suggested by the pat flows of inputs (accumulated capital and human stock) and macrostructural changes. Another way of looking at this issue is by exploring missing factors in an extended (multifactor) production function, such as "organizational capital"[2] and critical institutions[3] that cannot be built overnight. Let us not forget that imports are not a solution since the aforementioned factors must be home grown. From this perspective the proper set of property rights appears as a structural constraint affecting potential performance.

What about the corrected (after depreciation) J-curve (or L-curve) effect mirroring aggregate disequilibrium? Taken as outcome, the performance deficit of these economies can be related to structure, policy, and environment.[4]

Structure is not meaningless in explaining performance deficit when its major flaws can be dealt with in a timely fashion, that is, by not inviting criticism that the required changes are developmental in nature and that they take time and should rather be put under the already-used roof of performance depreciation.

The reform of property rights shows that drawing the conceptual dividing line is not an easy task. When private property laws can be quickly enacted and enforced, they actually motivate people and enhance efficiency (land reform and active privatization are examples). But when the texture of property rights is harder to define and the governance issue clouds the sky, one easily trespasses into the territory of developmental matters. Nonetheless, it is clear that policy-related confusion about property rights requires immediate action.

I will give an example from Romania's experience. Law 15 of August 1990 on "Restructuring of State Economic Units" devolves power by creating confusion as to the owners of enterprise assets. In this way collusion phenomena are encouraged, management contracts (to monitor the performance of managers) are easily avoided by managers, and ultimately, the attributes of the state (as the owner of the still unprivatized property) are devoid of substance.

Admittedly, the fuzziness created by this law has been embedded in a climate of "citizens' rebellion" against any kind of authority, but the fact remains and gives much concern to policy makers. Together with "citizens' rebellion," fuzziness about property rights can explain the rise in X-inefficiency and the nonprofit-centered objective function of enterprises, which strive to boost wages and preserve jobs.

My contention is that as long as property rights will not be well defined and enforced, budget constraints will be soft enough to undermine efforts to stabilize the economy. The softness of budget constraints represents the weakest point of stabilization policy.

Privatization Is Not a Panacea

Clamoring in favor of privatization does not help much when the real process is slow and cumbersome. Nevertheless, all available means must be used in order to impose a modicum of financial discipline. Structure can help us understand the difficulty in imposing financial discipline—apart from the general climate in the economy and inadequate property rights—by focusing on the given distribution of resources (assets) in society. Transformation sets in with an initial endowment of resources for a variety of enterprises: negative value added; nonprofitable, but still positive value added; and profitable units. "The power of the weak" (the loss-market enterprises) is the power of the structure over those that can make ends meet financially, but are trapped into the network. Interenterprise arrears are, perhaps, the most relevant embodiment of this *emprise de la structure*;[5] the higher are the discrepancies in real performances and the larger is the share in total output held by giant loss-making units, the more overwhelming is the power. The events that occurred in Romania ("the global compensation" in December 1991), Russia, and other transforming economies properly fit, I think, this description.

An Effective Income-Control Policy

A way out of this mess would be devise a sort of industrial policy that would buttress stabilization policy by means of an effective income-control policy and enterprise reform.

This initial endowment with resources, as a legacy of Communist industrialization, can bring fortune to some and misery to others; it lies at the roots of what can be construed as a distributional struggle within society between potential haves and have-nots. In so heavily monopolized and monopsonized economies inflation is practically unstoppable and a vicious circle can be at work. Because of external and internal shocks, the social pie shrinks, pressure groups ask for and get high wages to keep pace with rising prices, the wage-price spiral is given a further twist, monetary and fiscal policy get tighter, output shrinks further, and the vicious circle continues. The scenario is more plausible the less mobile resources are and the less competitive markets are.

The Macroeconomics of Transition

What would be the theoretical underpinnings of the macroeconomics of transition? A way to proceed is to link stylized theoretical explanations with the two competing visions within the paradigm provided by neoclassical analytics (equilibrium economics). One of them that is best represented by the new classical macroeconomics, rejects any state intervention in the economy, since agents, as rational beings, supposedly optimize using all available information (as opposed to agents' "bounded rationality").[6] This optimization would secure full price flexibility and, therefore, sufficiently fast allocation of resources. According to this vision any rate of unemployment is natural, since it expresses agents' preferences. The other vision starts from the assumption that prices are rigid to an extent that induces adjustments through quantities as well, so that aggregate demand equilibrates aggregate supply below full employment; there is then talk of a non-Walrasian equilibrium, which would invalidate Walras's Law. The two visions look at the functioning of a market economy. If the transforming system is viewed as a pathological form of market economy, wherein structural disfunctionalities and rigidities are extreme, a hypothesis can be submitted; implementation of shock treatments would lead to significant drops in production, at least in a first phase. In this stage of the process of transformation, the entrenched structures are being broken and changed, which means that the quantity of friction inside the system goes up considerably and important energies (resources) are consumed in order to accommodate, adjust, change; a lot boils down to a change of the organizational capital. In this phase of the transition there exists a territory over which both commands and markets—as regulatory mechanism—do not function according to their logic, and at the congenital inefficiency of the old (to a large extent, still existing) system is added the net inefficiency caused by friction. Over this territory "market coordination failures" combine with the "abandoned child" feeling of many enterprises, which are no longer able to rely on central allocation of both suppliers and customers. For these enterprises information and transaction costs skyrocket. This perspective can get interesting insights from Taylor's "structuralist macroeconomics" that can help highlight perverse effects of orthodox policies undertaken during transition.[7]

The Weakness of Market Discipline

What none of the two visions can adequately tackle is the weak microfoundation of macroeconomic policy in a transforming system, wherein budget constraints are still soft and short-term economic rationality of many units and individuals clashes with the need to reallocate resources. Monetary and fiscal policies can hardly be effective when market discipline is weak. The temporary quasimoney represented by arrears, as a symptom of weak market discipline, shows the relative ineffectiveness of tight monetary policy under the circumstances.

A neglected issue has been the "implementation of stabilization policies in free-falling economies." It is clear that much of the decline in output is due to what was named depreciation of potential performance, to structure and external shocks, like the collapse of the Council for Mutual Economic Assistance (CMEA) and foreign competition. The crux of the matter here is not apportioning of the blame for the drop of output,[8] but realizing the impact of stabilization on rapidly falling aggregates.

Another way of looking at the impact of policy on the dynamics of output is to consider the process of market destruction and construction. In this respect, I would use the term "network deconstruction" which connotes delinkages produced in the system because of its functional opening. A command system relies on chain links, whereas a market system is based on parallel connections. The opening of the economy perturbs entrenched relationships and it starts a process of delinking whose outcome is that a growing number of domestic players may be out of the game; this process can be viewed as a short-run market coordination failure that leads to falls in aggregate effective supply and aggregate effective demand. For the delinked parties information and transaction costs are exceedingly high. It can be argued that delinking puts pressure on inefficient units and speeds up restructuring. But this does not necessarily compensate for the undesirable effects on aggregate domestic supply. Within such a framework hysteresis phenomena can and should be dealt with. Let us only think about rising unemployment and the effects of an overly open (too unprotected) economy in a world with imperfect markets and fierce competition.

Dual Economy

The discussion can be broadened and led in terms of a "dual economy," with a healthy and dynamic sector and a retrenching, declining sector. As long as the declining sector has the upper hand, economic aggregates would follow downward shaped curves. The recovering sets in when the growth sector goes down a threshold as to the share of output held in GDP. Four key variables can be thought of as influencing the dynamic of aggregate supply: the shares held initially by the two sectors, the speed of growth and that of decline, and the metamorphosis speed. Recently restructured parts of the declining sector resource reallocation can join the healthy sector. Different situations can be imagined by manipulating the key variables. A situation can involve rapid and brutal downturn, quick recovery, and intense metamorphosis, hopefully brought about by substantial inflows of foreign investments.[9] A J-curve situation means a less brutal decline than in the first case, but still impressive, whereas the upturn is not in immediate sight. An L-curve situation denotes strong imbalance between market destruction and market construction with upturn remote. The intensity of metamorphosis (of resource reallocation) determines the scope of hysteresis phenomena and, broadly speaking, the dynamics of "social equilibrium," the fewer are the losers, the smoother transformation will unfold. Obviously, foreign investment has a major role to play in helping restructuring in general.

The transforming economies have experienced severe expectational shock. People expect governments to deliver the goodies after decades of Communism, and in the Romanian case, after a terrible shock therapy. Expectations are high, whereas output—even if corrected for the increase of variety, quality, and availability of goods—has been going down dramatically. Expectations should be related to moral goods seen as public goods. What also makes the post-Communist transition difficult is a legacy of pervasive moral crisis. It is hard to build new institutions when honesty, trust, and loyalty are very scarce commodities. As K. Arrow said, "They are goods...they have real, practical, economic value; they increase the efficiency of the system, enable you to produce more goods or more of whatever value you hold in high esteem."[10] Two ideas can be put forward in this respect. First, production of intangible goods—understood as moral reconstruction of society—is a must for helping a recovery of the output of material goods and services; the former "crowds in" the latter. Secondly, trust, honesty, and loyalty can partially substitute for tangible goods during a dangerously long depression. In any event, an excess of expectations can easily disrupt fragile social and political equilibria and undermine the stabilization policy.

The Resumption of Growth Through Effective Industrial Policies

It is unclear how quickly overall growth can be resumed. A pessimist would point out that Chile needed over 15 years to embark on sustainable growth, and would doubt that people in Eastern Europe and the Commonwealth of Independent States (CIS) will be so patient.[11] An optimist would, perhaps, stress the comparative advantages of these economies—an abundance of highly trained labor and considerable research and development capabilities—that might trigger a miracle in the not too distant future.

How to stabilize the economy, that is, achieve aggregate equilibrium in the narrow sense and how to stop the fall of output and eventually resume growth are daunting tasks for policy makers in the transforming systems.

In these economies, the policy mix of stabilization cannot use the classical tools only; fiscal and monetary policy, exchange rate policy, trade policy, and income-control policy need to be complemented by an industrial policy that helps tackle the crucial issue of enterprise reform and impose market discipline.

When stabilization policy overshoots and takes the economy outside an assumed optimal state (mix) of disequilibria, at fault is not necessarily the decision maker, but the weaponry available. Policy makers always overshoot or undershoot, as markets do. This means that they can rush things above the natural rate of adjustment[12] of society, or underestimate the potential for change of the social body. Since policy over- and undershooting is practically unavoidable, the problem lies with reducing the deviation as much as possible. Another problem is deciding on which side policy erring is preferred by assuming that the goal of keeping the deviation at a minimum is kept in sight. In my opinion, industrial policy (that means more than enterprise reform) has been neglected. This has crippled economic policy in general and stabilization in particular. Industrial policy can reduce the costs of stabilization, and can help policy makers deal with the three major constraints—the foreign exchange gap, the budget deficit, and the low level of savings—in making choices about the trade off between external disequilibrium and internal disequilibrium. It can also help in dealing with the big trade off,[13] which has come into the open in post-Communist societies: efficiency versus equality.

A complete "hands-off" reform policy on the part of the governments is unjustified not only by the lack of institutional prerequisites for market forces to operate effectively, but also, by the simple fact that these forces alone, would impose unbearable costs on the social body. In Central and Eastern Europe, we deal with markets in their infancy, which need to be nurtured in a world of imperfect information and competition. An industrial policy is needed that would restructure as it is suggested by market signals and protect the main asset of these societies, segments of highly skilled labor and a large pool of scientific and technical intelligentsia. A paradox of these societies is that striking ignorance coexists with tremendous intellectual and labor capabilities; this combination obscures potential progress by a possible across-the-board overdepreciation of the factors of production. Capital and technology inflows as well as the functional opening of the economies could counteract this overdepreciation for certain segments of the economy, but they could also impose undue hardships on it and stall reforms.

Industrial policy must bridge the gap between the effectiveness of controlling demand and that of stimulating supply. When I mention industrial policy I refer to a combination of income-control measures and industrial restructuring (including privatization) initiated by public authorities which process information provided by markets. The goals would put a lid on high inflation, alleviate unemployment (to cope with the hysteresis phenomena), and promote exports. Such a policy is more urgently needed when the social pie is considerably smaller, redistribution effects impact negatively on many people, and safety nets are inadequate. A possible scheme would be to link incomes with the dynamics of saleable output, in the vein of what M. Weitzman proposed in his 1984 book *The Share Economy.* Thus, assuming that market-clearing prices operate (and that optimal size for producing units are observable, or can be estimated), enterprises can be split into the aforementioned categories: negative value-added units; unprofitable, but positive value-added producing units; and profitable enterprises. Negative value-added units should be closed down without any delay; it is less costly to pay workers unemployment benefits and retrain them than to keep these enterprises running. Profitable units do not present any problem since they are in good business. The zone of concern for policy makers is represented by unprofitable enterprises which, under normal conditions (with sufficient flexibility of resources), would have to be done away with. The idea is to resort to a phased in elimination according to a timetable that pursues reducing the costs of adjustment. There are two key variables in the whole scheme: one is the unemployment benefit and the other is the additional income provided by the state to workers so that they have an incentive to continue working in an enterprise instead of preferring to accept unemployment benefits.

Unprofitable enterprises would be phased out gradually, so that unemployment would be attenuated and its cost redistributed over time. At the same time, public authorities would have an easier time securing resources for a safety net and for reallocating labor through training programs. The problem lies in convincing workers about the benefits of this scheme for the economy as a whole and for each and every one of the targeted enterprises. This can be achieved as part of a social compact within the framework of an industrial relations agreement that sees workers as an active voice in the management of transformation. It could be argued that this scheme may slow down restructuring, that is a valid statement if social and political constraints are dismissed. But for the sake of process sustainability there are many reasons for advocating an industrial policy.

Conclusion

Finally, a few words about contrasting the equilibrium approach with the evolutionary approach. It can be argued that transformation is a process with a pronounced social and cultural dimension, that involves overcoming inertia, changing mentalities and psychologies (the creation of a new social ethic for a market economy), a fierce struggle among "coalitions of interests," some of which support change, and others who withstand it. The clash of various interests in society raises the degree of autonomy of the process in the sense of reducing the room to maneuver held by decision makers should they want to force the pace of change. In order to have a fair chance of progressing smoothly, the process needs to be backed by a strong coalition of interests—social basis, and this "reform constituency" cannot be build overnight. Seen in this light, transformation should not be conceived of as a sort of "one-stroke policy," since as a real process, change cannot be but evolutionary and policy would have to be shaped appropriately. Stabilization itself would have to be understood as a process most likely to show a stop-and-go (including setbacks) dynamic.

However a reality can be derived from the different approaches; it is the time pressure exerted by the disintegration of old institutional structures, by the "rebellion of citizens." This pressure induces policy makers, who have to cope with the "freefall syndrome," to be bold and to resort to the presumed effectiveness of the impersonal disciplining power of market forces.

Notes

1. Expression concocted by J. Winiecki several years ago in the German journal *Intereconomics*. Winiecki referred to King Midas of Ancient Greece who turned into gold everything he put his fingers on, including his own food.

2. See P. Murrell, "Evolution in Economics an in the Economic Reform of the Centrally Planned Economies," manuscript, 1991.

3. Rules enjoying wide social acceptability are also to be included.

4. T.C. Koopmans and J.M. Montias, "On the Description and Comparison of Economic Systems," in *Comparison of Economic Systems; Theoretical and Methodological Approaches*, ed., A. Eckstein (Berkeley and Los Angeles: Univ. of California Press, 1971).

5. François Perroux, *Independence de la Nation* (Paris, 1968).

6. H. Simon, "Theories of Decision-Making in Economics and Behavioral Sciences," *American Economic Review* 49, no. 3 (1959): 253-283.

7. See G. A. Calvo and F. Coricelli, "Stagflationary Effects of Stabilization Programs in Reforming Socialist Countries: Enterprise-Side and Household-Side Factors," *World Bank Review* 6, no. 1 (1992): 71-90, where the authors emphasize the similarities between the "enterprise-side view" and the neostructuralist approach.

8. Some of the drop, as shown by J. Winiecki, "The Inevitability of a Fall in Output in the Early Stages of Transition to the Market: Theoretical Underpinnings," *Soviet Studies* no. 4 (1991): 669-676, is beneficial, since it does away with useless production.

9. As happened in the former East Germany.

10. K. Arrow, *The Limits of Organization* (New York: Norton, 1974) 23.

11. See S. Edwards, "Stabilization and Liberalization Policies in Eastern Europe: Lessons from Latin America," manuscript, Department of Economics, University of California, Los Angeles, 1991.

12. The natural rate of adjustment (of accommodating change) of society can be definedas an imagined optimal speed of change that maximizes society's welfare function temporarily; it itself is adjustable because of the learning capacity of society.

13. A. Okun, *The Big Trade-Off: Efficiency vs. Equality* (Washington: Brookings Institution, 1975).

Chapter 2 · Countries in Transition and the World Economy

Section 1 · Changing the International Economic Environment

Christian Ossa

While attempts at deep economic—and in a few cases political—reforms in the East[1] go back to the 1960s, only in the late 1980s, after the ascent to power of Mikhail Gorbachev, did the process gather momentum and become widespread. The improved relations with the West, the promotion of *glasnost* and *perestroika,* the internal pressures for economic and political reform in the East, and the Soviet leadership's refusal to intervene to save existing regimes in other members of the Warsaw Pact have ushered in a period of radical changes whose end is not yet in sight. Such changes have profoundly altered the international political landscape and have left virtually no country in the world unaffected.

Two Aspects of Changes in the External Environment

During this period, the external economic environment faced by the East has not remained static. Two aspects of this change will be examined in this section.

The first will be that this environment itself was changed by the traits and comprehensiveness of the transition, and by changes in perceptions as the transition progressed. If the transition had occurred in a different way, many aspects of the external environment facing the economies in transition (e.g., cooperation policies) would now be different. In the late 1980s, the people of Eastern Europe saw a window of opportunity and took advantage of it. Hopes for change towards freedom and democracy had been frustrated before: in Hungary and Poland in 1956, in Czechoslovakia in 1968, and in Poland in 1981. This time, they were determined that there would be no possibility of a return to the old ways. Thus, while arguments could be made—especially by outsiders—that a more cautious approach would have been better, at the time what appeared most important for the people of the countries now in transition was to achieve a swift change. This in itself profoundly altered external perceptions.

The second aspect of the external environment that will be discussed is that many features of it are different from a few years ago, or even what could have been expected a few years ago. Many of these differences had little to do with actions by the economies in transition, and therefore can hardly be changed by actions on their part. However, the changes that did occur can be expected to complicate rather than facilitate their progress.

Initial Reasons for Optimism

To assess how the external environment, primarily the perceptions of the developed market economies, changed during the course of the transition, it is useful to discuss the environment that a reforming government in Eastern Europe could have expected to be facing in the few years after about 1988-89 with what actually happened.

The country whose government had been in the forefront of economic change among the Eastern countries was Hungary and its reforms had been perceived as justifying strong support from the international financial institutions. For instance, its standby agreement with the IMF in May 1988 was for SDR 265 million ($364 million), which was larger than for any country except Argentina.[2] There was no question but that it and the other Eastern European economies had a more highly trained labor force than many developing countries, which was especially important with the renewed emphasis being placed, especially by multilateral lending agencies, on correct domestic policies, rather than domestic endowments or the external situation, as the key to economic success.[3] It appeared that they would be able to achieve high rates of growth, once the impediments of the distorted economic structure they had been bequeathed by central planning had been removed. For this reason alone, they seemed assured of considerable assistance during the transition.

In 1980, the only centrally planned economy that was a member of the International Monetary and the World Bank was Romania,[4] whose membership was more an expression of its independent foreign policy, which masked to outside observers the oppressive nature of the regime, than of its commitment to market forces. Membership of the General Agreement on Tariffs and Trade (GATT) was confined to Czechoslovakia, Hungary, Poland, and Romania.

Hungary became a member of the International Monetary Fund and the World Bank in May 1982. Poland applied for membership in November 1981, its application being granted in 1986. This application was particularly significant in that Poland had been a founder member of the Fund and Bank but had withdrawn in 1950: its withdrawal, just as the earlier refusal of the Eastern European countries to participate in the Marshall Aid program, was a sign that reliance would be placed on solidarity within the socialist confraternity rather than integration in the Western dominated capitalist economy.[5]

Hungary's membership signalled that socialist economic integration had not so far contributed much to growth and was also an indication of its economic difficulties. It was granted a standby agreement in December 1982. Similarly, Poland's application was another sign of economic difficulties, and of the inability to resolve them within the community of centrally planned states. The implication, which became increasingly apparent in the course of the decade, was that the Soviet Union would not be able to bail out countries in distress and that the way forward for them was towards closer integration in the world economy and increased reliance on domestic impulses. This change in direction was itself a further reason for optimism. It should be stressed that the analysis applied to the central European countries (Czechoslovakia, Hungary, and Poland) and not to the Soviet Union as it was still widely felt that Communism had sufficiently strong roots there to remain the main directing principle for society.

The external environment appeared favorable to these countries precisely because they were centrally planned economies and their being weaned away from this system towards fuller integration in the world economy would be of considerable strategic significance to the developed market economies. Compared to the hundreds of billions of dollars that were being expended annually on containing Soviet expansionism, it was argued that spending even tens of billions of dollars to detach individual Eastern European economies from the Soviet sphere was as a very sound investment.

The Eastern European economies were also particularly advantaged in that they had the right to apply for membership in European institutions, such as the Council of Europe and the European Economic Community,[6] once they had adopted democratic norms. A comparison between the Eastern European countries and Portugal, one of the newest entrants to the Community, was not that unfavorable to the former in that it was estimated, in 1988, that several had higher levels of GNP per head.[7] Also, the difference between their levels of GNP per head and that of Portugal was not as great as that between the latter and the wealthier members of the Community, in particular Germany.

There were also special historic, and indeed moral, reasons to expect that the Western European countries would do their utmost to help the Eastern European economies make the transition to more pluralistic societies, giving at least as much support to them as to Greece, Portugal, and Spain when they had made the transition from dictatorships to democracies. While it is historically questionable whether the Western European countries, by their actions during and after World War II, could have prevented the imposition of Stalinist regimes in Eastern Europe, there is no question but that before the war their conduct had left much to be desired. They had failed to respond to the challenges of fascism in the early years, had bullied democratic Czechoslovakia into ceding its vital defenses to a dictatorship and had given guarantees to Poland but had not mounted a serious challenge to relieve the pressure when aggression began.

It was understood that the Eastern European countries could not expect to join the Community immediately—the demise of the Iberian dictatorships had taken place in 1974 and 1975 and they only entered the Community in January 1986. Therefore, of more immediate concern to them was access to this market. Such access would be even more important if the market were itself expanding rapidly. The portents were good. After a period of flux in the mid-1980s, the Community seemed on its way to regaining its earlier vigor, with the entry into force of the Single European Act in 1987 which, in particular, foresaw the creation of a single barrier-free internal market by the end of 1992.

Just as Western Europe could be expected to be a dynamic market for the East, so could the East for the West. With high quality human capital, low labor costs, a great need for infusions of capital and expertise to satisfy a domestic market with pent-up consumption needs, the Eastern European countries promised to be excellent prospects for foreign investment. Even if this investment were not for the domestic market, the fact that eventually the Eastern European countries would be part of the European Community provided an incentive for third parties to invest in the near future in order to build up a presence for the more distant future. Ireland had proved to be an attractive site for foreign investment for similar reasons—it gave an entree into the European Economic Community (EEC).

Revolution Rather Than Reform

There were certain problems with this optimistic outlook to which some observers drew attention. The first is that the size or strength of the centrally planned economies had been grossly inflated. This has sometimes been attributed to the intelligence agencies of the developed market economies having a vested interest in stressing the magnitude of the political and economic challenge of the Warsaw Pact countries in order to justify continued high levels of military expenditure. Official government publications frequently gave much higher figures for output in the former socialist countries than did the multilateral agencies. However, in the absence of reliable data, such agencies had to make "guesstimates."

It should also be recalled that before *glasnost,* the picture officially presented by the regimes in the economies now in transition was one of continued progress, although, since the late 1970s, with a constant need to "reform." At the governmental level, plans were still being taken seriously, even though more and more plan implementation figures deviated significantly from targets, despite the "unreliability" of official data.[8] The skepticism of the population in the centrally planned economies continued to grow, since they could see with their own eyes the economic disaster around them.

The speed of events took most Western analysts by surprise. In 1985 and 1986, there are had been elections in most of these countries under the traditional rules, except in the case of Hungary. The voting had reaffirmed the position of the leaders of the various levels of government and of the Communist party, under whatever name it functioned, and had endorsed their five-year plans.[9] Hope that reform was on the way could be justified by what was happening in the Soviet Union,[10] in Hungary, and also in Poland as Western creditors kept up pressure on the regime. However what took place was not reform but rather a revolution. Once the Soviet leadership in effect abandoned the Brehznev doctrine in the late 1980s and took the decision not to intervene to keep the existing regimes in power in Eastern Europe, they collapsed with extraordinary rapidity. Some, like Poland's, had been tottering for some time, but others that were thought to be considerably more resilient also collapsed surprisingly quickly. Only in Romania did the regime attempt to preserve itself by resorting to violent repression.

The rapidity of the collapse could perhaps have been foreseen from the experience of Solidarity in 1980 to 1981. The formation of an independent union showed that the basic ideological principle of the regime—that the ruling party represented the working class—was largely false. Such was the intense questioning and review of past events during the brief period of relative freedom that much remaining legitimacy was removed and no hope was placed in an internal reform of the party. This situation was different from the 1968 Prague Spring when society backed the reformist groups in the Czechoslovak Party. Even in the Soviet Union, *glasnost* did not lead in the direction its chief advocate, M.S. Gorbachev expected. He hoped that it would earn him support from the intelligentsia in the campaign to revitalize the country, and would cause popular pressure to be exerted on the party apparatus that was resisting reform.[11] In the event it led to the total discrediting of the one-party system.

It was probably unrealistic to have expected, as many did, that the way forward for Eastern Europe would be a middle way between the market economy and central planning, more similar to the Scandinavian model. However, the system was so discredited that the aim to abandon all vestiges of the old order proved irresistible. The rush to embrace democracy and market mechanisms was, therefore, partly the result of a fervent desire for change, even at the cost of improvisation.

The rapidity of the collapse meant that several potential halfway houses, which might have been of some use in a gradual transition, were abandoned. In particular, transforming the Council for Mutual Economic Assistance into an effective regional organ that contributed to the enhancement of economic integration had ranked highly in the policy of the Soviet Union in the early 1980s.[12] In June 1984, the first economic summit of the Council since 1969 was held. Yet the decision by the Soviet leadership to not only permit but to actually facilitate the end of the Communist regimes in Eastern Europe meant the rapid end of such attempts at cooperation. It can be argued that the Soviet Union for its part wanted to pass the burden of sustaining its allies onto the West and this could most rapidly be done by the installation there of non-Communist governments.[13] The new governments rapidly drew away from close economic relations with each other and with the Soviet Union. In March 1990, senior officials of the Council for Mutual Economic Assistance agreed to remove two of the organization's most important functions: multilateral cooperation and the coordination of economic planning; trade relations would in future be conducted primarily on a bilateral basis. In July 1990, the Soviet Union announced that after 1 January 1991 trade among CMEA members would be concluded in hard currency rather than the transferable ruble and at prices that would reflect world prices. On 28 June 1991, it was decided to formally dissolve the CMEA. Any cooperative mechanism that might have played a role as a customs union or payments facility in easing the transition to the market economy was swept away. As a result, the economies in transition were faced with a very severe contraction in trade amongst themselves.

A little later, in August 1991, after the unsuccessful coup, the activities of the Russian Communist Party were suspended, and the property of the Communist Party of the Soviet Union was confiscated, the Central Committee was dissolved and party cells in the armed forces, the KGB and the police were banned. In December 1991, the formal demise of the Soviet Union took place. There was no longer any possibility that the Eastern European countries might return to the Soviet orbit if domestic conditions did not improve, or that the reforms instituted under Gorbachev would be reversed.

The disintegration of the Soviet Union mirrored a collapse in that country's creditworthiness. In 1989 and 1990, the Soviet Union's creditworthiness was considered high, largely in view of its substantial foreign currency reserves and other assets, especially gold. In 1991, however, economic difficulties resulted in commercial banks pulling away from new lending. In their July 1991 meeting, the G-7 put off requests for relief on Soviet debt, and extended an offer not for membership in but only for "special associate status" with the Bretton Woods institutions, which carried with it the promise of technical but not financial assistance. However, the demise of the Soviet Union, the economic difficulties of the successor republics and their increasing commitment to market economies assured them full membership in these bodies in 1992. In contrast to the previous year, the G-7 meeting in July 1992 endorsed the proposal for the IMF to extend $24 billion to the Russian Federation.

The transformation of the Soviet Union into a number of countries increasingly—in some cases irrevocably—committed to market economies with full membership in, and seeking assistance from, multilateral financial institutions was a development that, while undoubtedly of long term benefit to the other economies, has nevertheless taken away some of the breathing space that might have come from a more gradual transformation and has introduced an important new source of demand for multilateral assistance.

The internal developments in the Soviet Union did not just affect the economies in transition but also the European countries that were not members of NATO. With the disappearance of an ideological divide between East and West, being neutral or nonaligned lost its significance. In the case of Finland, for instance, the Soviet Union took the decision to shift from barter to convertible currency arrangements, forcing the country to seek new markets in Western Europe. Later, in October 1991, the 1948 treaty of friendship between the two countries was abandoned and in 1992 Finland applied for membership in the European Economic Community. The other neutral countries similarly reacted to events throughout Europe by moving closer to the Community. In October 1991, the members of the European Free Trade Association (EFTA)[14] reached an agreement with the Community to form a European Economic Area, removing nearly all obstacles to the free flow of people, goods, money, and services. In 1989 Austria, in 1990 Sweden, and in 1992 Finland applied to join the European Community. The Swiss government also stated in 1992 that it wanted the country to join.

The entry negotiations for these EFTA countries will take place before those for other applicants, including not just the central European applicants, Czechoslovakia and Hungary, which applied in 1992, but also Malta, Cyprus, and Turkey. However, this next round of negotiations could complicate the negotiations for the new applicants from central Europe simply because there are more national interests to reconcile. The association agreements that were drawn up with the three Central European countries—Czechoslovakia, Hungary and Poland—in December 1991 partly reflected this. The Community continued to subject to quotas the two sectors of most export importance to these countries—agriculture and textiles. Moreover, unlike Greece and Turkey, the central European countries obtained no "financial protocols" in their agreements. In general, these agreements struck observers as "deeply ungenerous."[15]

Quasiparalysis in the Developed Market Economies

From the previous review of events, it can be appreciated that the advent of democracy to Eastern Europe and the breakup of the Soviet Union were enormous strategic gains for the developed market economies, removing the chief threat to their security. These developments had come about primarily through domestic forces in Eastern Europe and had not required any military intervention, or even, except in the special case of Germany, a particularly large financial outlay. In the face of a change of quite historic magnitude, the developed market economies seemed to many, especially in the East, to have acted with an extraordinary lack of generosity and imagination.

The policy perceptions of the developed market economies changed from initially rather broad support to the general objectives of the transition process with the promise of considerable Western credits to more sober support, characterized by a string of conditionalities. Yet, this was only partly due to the fact that the number of countries requiring support increased rapidly; first Hungary and Poland, then the rest of Eastern Europe and subsequently the members of the Commonwealth of Independent States. The realization that the economies in the East were in much greater disarray than had been first thought and that a return to Communism was becoming less and less likely can help explain their increasing emphasis on conditionalities. The duration of the economic transition toward "working" market economies will depend mostly on internal efforts and the progress achieved in internal political reform and institutionalization of democracy and some conditions can be seen as providing guidelines along the path.

However, for a full explanation as to why circumstances have changed, the rapid turnaround in the economic conditions in the West after the mid-1980s must be brought up. As previously mentioned, many of these changes had very little to do with what was occurring in Eastern Europe.

The basic premise concerning the external environment remains true: a supportive international environment can considerably ease the difficulties of—and probably shorten—the transition process. However, the economic progress and self-confidence prevailing in most Western industrial countries between 1985 and 1989 have turned sour. At that time, it was felt that the problems of inflation and low and often interrupted growth that had characterized the Organization for Economic Cooperation and Development (OECD) countries in the 1970s had been largely solved and that these economies could look forward to steady economic expansion.[16] Of special importance was the belief that many of their structural rigidities, including those in labor markets, had been successfully tackled in the course of the 1980s.

Yet, as of mid-1993, these economies remain almost stagnant after protracted sluggishness in the previous 36 months. Compounding the problem, there appears to be a political paralysis in key OECD governments despite the perception of being the clear winners in the Cold War. This paralysis, reflected in an inability to take the urgent actions necessary to address the accumulation of social and economic problems in their own countries, is also affecting their external economic relations.

The Lack of Vigor in Industrial Economies

A higher rate of growth is associated with higher import demand—and, therefore, increased exports by trade partners—and it is also associated with improvements in domestic employment and public finances that would lessen the political resistance to extending financial assistance to foreign countries.

Six years ago, and even up to 1989, economic growth in OECD countries was considered quite satisfactory. Not only was growth of output above three percent on average, but the rate of unemployment was declining. Moreover, after the large fall in the value of the dollar starting in 1985, trade imbalances among major countries were starting to narrow. Indeed, in the late 1980s, many envisioned an era of uninterrupted and significantly improved living standards in OECD countries for many years to come. However, output growth decelerated significantly in 1990.

The considerable slowdown of output in 1990 has had at least three consequences: a weakening of import demand, an increase in domestic unemployment, and a widening in budget deficits. Whereas the position improved between 1987 and 1989 in Canada, France, Germany, the United Kingdom, and the United States, there was a considerable worsening in 1990 and 1991. In Germany, the change was almost four percent of GNP, reflecting the heavy commitments after reunification. Italy's deficit fell by one percent of GDP between 1987 and 1991, but remained at the two-digit level that should be contrasted with the 3 percent target required, according to the Maastricht agreement, for membership of the Economic and Monetary Union by the end of the 1990s.

In spite of this economic slowdown, exports from Eastern Europe to the OECD have increased; yet this has not been the result of dynamic import demand from the West. It was largely the result of special efforts by many Western countries to accommodate more exports from Eastern Europe, and also because trade among members of the CMEA declined quite abruptly, as discussed above, and Eastern European countries made additional efforts to find alternative buyers anywhere in the world.

The sluggishness of the OECD economies in the early 1990s has been much more protracted than could have been expected if it had simply been the trough of a normal business cycle. Moreover, key developments that were expected to dynamize the industrial economies have either failed to materialize, such as the Uruguay Round, or have had a reduced positive impact, as in the case of the Single Act of the European Economic Community. These are not extraneous developments. Agreement on the Uruguay Round lies very much in the hands of the developed market economies and, in particular, on their ability to come to a settlement on agriculture. Yet pressures to satisfy domestic agricultural producers in order to win their acceptance of the Maastricht agreement have complicated progress in the Uruguay round.

Another important domestic factor is that rehabilitation of financial institutions, particularly banks, in Japan, the United Kingdom and the United States is taking longer than expected. Much of the difficulties in financial institutions were caused by falling real estate prices, and a reversal has not yet occurred in any of these three countries.

All these factors are helping to delay the recovery, which under present circumstances can only be expected to be weak. The world economy became increasingly more open in the 1980s, with, in particular, restrictions being removed on capital flows. In these circumstances, countries are reluctant to take bold steps to ensure their own domestic growth but that might give rise to fears of inflation and thus to severe capital outflows. It is, then, unrealistic to expect an individual country to go out on a limb to be a "locomotive."

The sluggishness in aggregate demand has reduced inflationary pressures and in most countries the growth in consumer and wholesale prices has slowed down. Short-term interest rates have also fallen considerably from the levels of the late 1980s. In August 1992, the three-month Libor on U.S. dollar deposits was 3.4 percent, about 6 percentage points less than the rate of 9.3 percent in 1989. Long term rates have also fallen, but not so dramatically. But this has been of little benefit to Eastern Europe and the members of the Commonwealth of Independent States (CIS) as today they have virtually no access to private bank credit.[17]

Assistance has been provided by regional and international institutions: the European Community, the European Investment Bank, the International Monetary Fund, the World Bank, and the European Bank for Reconstruction and Development. However, such assistance is affected by the general aid fatigue that has beset many donors and is manifested in the present debate in the United States over commitments to the multilateral financial institutions and in the decline in the rate of growth of ODA (Official Development Assistance) in the course of the 1980s. There is a feeling that, with the Cold War over, resources should be devoted to domestic uses rather than to foreign assistance. This feeling has become all the stronger as the financial position of governments has weakened. Yet there is a deeper reason for aid fatigue—simply that the whole concept of development aid, as opposed to short-term humanitarian or emergency assistance, is being increasingly questioned. After several decades and hundreds of billions of dollars expended on official development assistance to developing countries, the results are deemed meager. Assistance to stave off famine or address a special emergency or even to help a country during the transition to a market economy has found favor, but a long term commitment to rebuild the economies of the East is unlikely. The prevailing sentiment is that if the economies of the East are a sound investment proposition then private banks and international corporations should eventually appreciate this and invest there.

Accordingly, in April 1991, the European Bank for Reconstruction and Development was launched with a mandate was to promote private enterprise in Eastern European. For this reason, its public sector lending was limited to 40 percent of the bank's investments. In the first year, the bank had committed $770 million. The bank is intended to be a catalyst for other investors and so its commitments are expected to be only a fraction of those that it generates.

An additional factor that also altered considerably the external environment was the unexpected invasion of Kuwait by Iraq in August 1990. This led to the imposition of sanctions by the UN Security Council that had important consequences for the world economy. Many developing countries and countries in transition were severely affected. Countries such as Bulgaria, Czechoslovakia, Poland, Romania, the ex-Soviet Union, and Yugoslavia exported heavily to Iraq[18] and some of them purchased Iraq's oil under special, more favorable conditions. Sanctions led to considerable output and foreign exchange losses in these countries (from several hundred million dollars up to a few billion dollars annually) as sales to other countries could not easily be substituted for sales to Iraq. The sanctions are still in place, and therefore the accumulated losses incurred by the economies in transition have grown quite substantially.[19] For some Eastern European countries these problems have been compounded further by the situation in the Balkans and the imposition of sanctions on what is left of Yugoslavia.[20]

Conclusion

In mid-1993, the external economic environment is less supportive and more unpredictable than when the transition started in earnest. There is widespread concern because of the prolonged slowdown in output in the developed market economies and their limited room for policy maneuver. The completion of the Uruguay Round that was expected to provide a major impulse to international trade has not occurred yet. Budget deficits have been on the increase in the 1990s despite lower defense expenditures. The concentration of attention on domestic economic problems and fiscal conditions do not augur well for financial support to other countries. Indeed, assistance policies have fallen quite short of what many analysts and policy makers in the East envisaged when the process gathered momentum in the second half of the 1980s. The points of reference regarding the external environment that policy makers in the East used to assess the potential for trade and private and official capital flows have moved in a way that will make the transition process more difficult and—quite possibly—considerably longer.

However, the endowments that were originally thought to be the most attractive for outside investors—a highly skilled and comparatively disciplined labor force—and, in the case of several countries, eventual entry into the European Community have not changed. These points, which are reasons for optimism, should be stressed. The countries of Eastern Europe and the Soviet Union showed considerable maturity in effecting an historic revolution at very little cost in human lives or, as in the case of Romania, in showing extraordinary courage in confronting violent repression. International goodwill and their chances of attracting foreign investment could be seriously, and perhaps irreparably, damaged if they allowed ethnic strife and social divisions generated by the transition to impede their progress to fully working democracies. While official assistance, bilateral and multilateral, is important at an early stage and for certain tasks, large volumes of capital will only be found in international capital markets: commercial credit, portfolio investments and direct foreign investment. Policy makers in the East are well aware of the need to regain creditworthiness and become hospitable to foreign investment.

The economies of the East have the great advantage, gained by bitter experience, recognizing the deadend streets to development. If they engage fully in international negotiations, arguing for fair treatment and for further liberalization of markets, they could make a major contribution to their own and to world economic growth. The success of the Iberian countries is one of the best signposts on the road ahead.

Notes

1. The East will be used here as comprising all the countries in Eastern Europe and the former Soviet Union.

2. *IMF Survey*, 27 June 1988, 233.

3. For instance, the IMF, in 1986, reported on a study by Helen Hughes, Professor of Economics and Director of the Development Studies Centre at the Australian National University and former Director of the Department of Economic Analysis and Projections at the World Bank, entitled "The Policy Lessons of the Development Experience." The paper concluded that "as countries overcome their human resource constraints, they can adopt high-growth policies by using their existing technologies . . . developing country problems must be tackled at the national level." *IMF Survey*, 17 February 1986, 63.

4. Significantly, Yugoslavia never ceased its membership in the Bretton Woods institutions; however it effected its break from the Soviet orbit in 1948.

5. Czechoslovakia, which withdrew in 1954, was also a founding member of the Bretton Woods institutions.

6. Article 237 of the Treaty of Rome states that "any European state may apply to become a member of the Community."

7. The 1988 update of *The 1987 World Bank Atlas* gave the following as levels of GNP per head in 1986: Germany, Federal Republic, $12,080; Portugal, $2,230; Hungary, $2,010; Poland, $2,070; and Romania, over $1,726.

8. For example, despite comparatively modest levels of growth in planned gross industrial output in the countries of Eastern European and the former Soviet Union for the period 1981-85, none achieved the target. Nevertheless, several of them raised the target for the 1986-1990 plan. See *The World Economic Survey 1987*, 113.

9. In Albania, in April 1985, Ramiz Alia was elected by the Central Committee of the Albanian Party of Labour to succeed Enver Hoxha on his death. In February 1987, elections took place to the People's Assembly and Alia was reelected as Head of State.

In Bulgaria, in April 1986, the 13th Congress of the Bulgarian Communist party reelected Todor Zhivkov as general secretary along with an unchanged politburo and secretariat. The ninth five-year plan (1986-90) was approved, and, in June 1986, parliamentary elections led to the formation of a largely unchanged government.

In Czechoslovakia, the 17th Congress of the Communist party reelected Gustáv Husák general secretary, along with an unchanged presidium, and the eighth five-year plan (1986-90) was approved. In May 1986, general elections were held and a largely unchanged government was sworn into office in June.

In the German Democratic Republic, the 11th Congress of the Socialist Unity party reelected Erich Honecker as general secretary and the directives for the 1986-1990 plan were approved. General elections were held in June 1986 and Honecker was reelected for a further five-year term as Chairman of the Council of State.

In Hungary, the 13th congress of the Hungarian Socialist Workers' party took place in March 1985 and endorsed the economic reform program. János Kádár was reelected secretary-general of the Central Committee. In June 1985, elections took place under a system introduced in 1983 which made it mandatory to have a choice of candidates in parliamentary and local council elections.

In Poland, in November 1985 General Wojciech Jaruzelski resigned as Chairman of the Council of Ministers to be succeeded by Zbigniew Messner. However, he remained first secretary of the Polish United Workers' party, and was in addition elected chairman of the council of state (president). In June 1986, the 10th Congress of the Party was held and the 1986-1990 plan was approved.

In Romania, in November 1984, the 13th Congress of the Romanian Communist party was held. The eighth five-year plan, (1986-1990) and the economic objectives for the year 2000 were accepted. Nicolae Ceausescu was reelected general secretary of the Romanian Communist party.

10. Mikhail Gorbachev became general secretary in March 1985 on the death of Konstantin Chernenko and in February and March 1986, he proposed radical economic and political reforms and "new thinking" in foreign policy at the 27th Congress of the Communist party of the Soviet Union. An indication of how far advanced the Soviet Union was on the path to reform—and also how old age and deaths amongst the senior leadership was a fortuitous assistance to Gorbachev—is that of the 22 full members and candidate members of the Politburo elected at the 26th Congress in 1981, only four full members and four candidate members were reelected at the 27th Congress.

11. Michael Mandelbaum, "The End of the Soviet Union," *Foreign Affairs* 71, no. 1 (1992): 169-170.

12. See *World Economic Survey 1989* for a discussion of the planned revitalization of the CMEA.

13. For instance, the first non-Communist government in the region was formed in Poland in August 1989. This had been assisted by a telephone call from Mikhail Gorbachev to the Polish Communist party leader Miecyslaw Rakowski. The reason for Gorbachev's support for a Solidarity-led government was said to be to shift the burden of sustaining Poland's economy from the Soviet Union to the West. See Michael Howard, "The Springtime of Nations," *Foreign Affairs* 69, no. 1 (1990): 22.

14. Austria, Finland, Iceland, Liechtenstein, Norway, Sweden, and Switzerland.

15. "A Survey of the European Community," *The Economist*, 11 July 1992, 26.

16. See "Some Factors Underlying the Prolonged Expansion of the Major Developed Market Economies" in *World Economic Survey 1990* for an analysis of the reasons for optimism.

17. On the other hand German interest rates have climbed also dragging higher the rates of other European countries which in the past were significant lenders to the East.

18. Exports consisted mostly of semimanufactures and manufactures, including military hardware, and sales of services, such as construction contracts.

19. The longer the time period, the easier it should be to find new buyers. Yet, the end of the war led many to believe that sanctions would be lifted soon and normal commercial relations would return. As of mid-1992, 16 months after the Persian Gulf War, this has not occurred.

20. For many analysts, the former Yugoslavia was not seen as a political part of Eastern Europe. It only had observer status in the CMEA, was not a member of the Warsaw Pact but rather a founder of the nonaligned movement, and belonged throughout to the Bretton Woods institutions. In any event, present developments in the Balkans have consequences for the East that go far beyond sanctions.

Section 2 · Integrating East and West

Salvatore Zecchini

Since the beginning of the economic reforms in the Central and Eastern European countries (CEEC),[1] one of the main policy objectives of all of their governments has been to achieve their rapid integration into the world economy, and particularly, into its most advanced part, the OECD area. The reasons stated by the governments for such a policy orientation are clear and straightforward, but the means necessary to achieve such integration are not equally clear in their plans. Nor, so far, have they adopted adequate measures to speed up the integration process.

A sustained increase in economic growth is possible only when a country gains access to capital and technology inputs from the advanced industrial economies of the world and then applies these inputs in accordance with the rules of effective market competition. This means making the CEECs part and parcel of the world economy by using all the channels of integration to achieve this goal. This section will discuss the integration strategy followed by most of the CEECs, the results of those strategies, the problems encountered, the main issues that stand in the way towards integration in the world economy, and some possible solutions.

The Integration Strategy So Far

Although economic integration is generally considered synonymous with the expansion of trade, the international exchange of goods and services are not the only channel of successful integration. Borrowing abroad, foreign investment, international movement of labor, transfers of technology and know-how, and foreign technical assistance are also important, even if their role and impact can be maximized only through the development and expansion of trade. Broadening the size of the market to which an enterprise can have access, beyond the national boundaries, has proved to be in Western Europe the main engine for triggering the other integration mechanisms. For instance, trade offers to the economy undergoing integration, the most likely opportunity to increase its capacity to borrow the resources that are needed to enhance economic growth, since it allows the economy to gain convertible currencies through exports of goods and services.

The integration strategies followed by the various CEECs are broadly similar to each other and focus on four main directions. First, comes the correction of major macroeconomic imbalances with a view to create conditions of monetary stability and sustainability of a balance-of-payments deficit. Without price and exchange rate stability, decisions on output, trade, and investment would be subject to distortions not less harmful than those that once characterized the old, centrally planned system. Second, prices and external trade were liberalized to a large degree. External tariffs were initially lowered in Czechoslovakia,

Hungary, and Poland to a level comparable to the lowest level applied in the OECD countries, and a gradual reduction of nontariff barriers to trade was started. Third, a measure of external convertibility of the currency was introduced, forcing enterprises to face foreign competition in the domestic marketplace and to price foreign inputs in line with the relative scarcity of foreign exchange. Fourth, foreign direct investment was promoted by granting preferential tax treatment to foreign investors. This strategy was not pursued with the same determination in the four directions, but by and large it was correctly applied at least in the first year of the transition towards a new economic system.

First Results

In 1993, three years after the beginning of the economic transformation the results in terms of degree of integration in the OECD area appear mixed. As to trade, there has been a rapid reorientation of export and import flows of the CEECs from exchanges within the area towards exchanges with the OECD countries, and particularly Western Europe. Between 1990 and 1991 CEEC' exports to the OECD zone rose on yearly average by 17.5 percent with peak percentage increases of more than 26 percent per year for Poland, Bulgaria, and Czechoslovakia. The only exception was Romania whose exports decreased substantially, while the USSR managed to continue increasing its exports in spite of severe disruptions in the production of tradable goods and particularly oil output. In the same period, CEECs' exports within their zone declined sharply. In this respect, it is worth noting the higher import absorption of the European Community countries than those of the United States or Japan. At the same time, the CEECs's imports from the OECD area grew even more than their exports in spite of the convertible currency shortages, thereby evidencing a high potential for trade expansion in both directions.

However, the increase of the share in the OECD market does not seem to reflect a stable gain due to higher penetration capacity or a more competitive product structure, but mirrors mainly the recent trade concessions of OECD countries and the resulting trade creation effect. CEECs' exports are heavily concentrated on food and agriculture products, raw materials, energy, textiles and apparel, iron and steel, and organic chemicals. These sectors are highly protected by OECD governments, particularly through nontariff measures. Therefore, it would have been unlikely that, without trade concessions, the CEECs would have succeeded in expanding their exports.

As far as international capital flows are concerned, the results are less positive than for trade. Since 1989, all the CEECs have been subject to a tight credit rationing by the private financial community due to the perception of high credit risk and low credit worthiness. Credit rationing has been applied to the area as a whole without taking into account differences among CEECs' external debt positions, repayment record, economic conditions and prospects. Now borrowing under syndicated loans has dried up and only marginal new funding has been made available to the Czech and Slovak Republics and Hungary through securities purchase. The burden of providing critical financing for balance of payments deficits has been shifted to the official sector. The share of official credits in total CEECs' debt has risen from 41.3 to 52.2 percent between 1989 and 1991.[2] This disappointing trend has not been offset by foreign investment into equity instruments as has been the case in the integration of the former East Germany's economy. Foreign direct investment (FDI) has risen sharply, but has not yet reached a level sufficient to cover trade deficits or to boost gross domestic product (GDP) growth. Hungary, the only exception, has succeeded in attracting, between 1990 and 1992, about $4 billion of FDI, amounting to almost 7 percent of GDP.

Labor flows have played so far, a minor role in the integration process in spite of the many concerns in the recipient countries of the OECD areas as regards mass immigration. Albeit statistical evidence on migratory flows is sketchy and not fully reliable, emigration from CEECs has not achieved impressive dimensions. Most of the OECD countries have received immigrants from Eastern Europe but these flows have been increasingly subject to tighter controls and regulation. Consequently, prospects for an increasing integration of CEECs labor forces in the OECD markets do not seem encouraging.

As to transfers of technology and technical assistance, their support to the economic integration has been significant and in relative terms appears to be as important as the trade channel. In part, technology transfers are embodied in the goods and services imported from OECD countries. In part, they have occurred in the context of OECD countries' direct investment in an enterprise.

Obstacles to Integration

Overall, the economic policies pursued by the CEECs in the first four years of the transition to a new economic system, have not resulted in a rapid progress towards the assimilation of these economies in the OECD economy. Three main groups of obstacles can explain this outcome: important gaps in the CEECs' strategy, the fact that changes in economic structures require long periods for their implementation, and the permanence of constraints on trade and financial flows on the side of OECD countries. Among them, the most damaging obstacles are clearly on the domestic front and are mostly imputable in inaction or inadequate action on the part of the CEECs' governments.

The strategies implemented so far have not tackled the fundamental weakness of the economy in the enterprise sector and in the institutional legal infrastructures. CEECs' governments have not made headway in restructuring the enterprises they own. Nor have they created adequate incentives to promote such a restructuring. Mindful of the need to preserve social and political support, they have been leaning more towards preserving old inefficiencies than removing them. In the face of such attitudes and public enterprises being still predominant in the CEECs, the response of these economies in general has been lagging behind the new trade opportunities that have been offered by the new economic liberalization.

Another group of obstacles is related to the markets, both markets for goods and markets for factors of production. The infrastructure to operate in a market environment is seriously deficient, if not existent, in these countries. Marketing skills are in very short supply. Ownership rights are not properly defined and protected. Commercial law and accounting standards for enterprises are seriously deficient. As to the factors of production, a large number of restrictions, constraints, and social subsidies limit the flexibility in using and remunerating the labor force. Capital markets are at a very early stage of development and do not meet average efficiency standards both in mobilizing private savings and in allocating financial capital to the most profitable projects. The banking system is in general in a very precarious state, with a good portion of its assets (in some countries about one third) not performing, and a scarcity of properly trained staff.

Furthermore, CEECs' exports are not in a position to compete effectively with exports of other countries, to the OECD area, because they do not have the support of an export credit system and modern promotion techniques. Trade expansion is also hampered by the CEECs' limited capacity to absorb advanced technologies. The CEECs economic fabric is still so tightly tied to outdated technologies that it is not easy to diffuse profitably the advanced technologies of the OECD countries. In addition to these structural factors, an obstacle is represented by the shortage of convertible currencies in the CEECs and the limited, current account convertibility of CEECs' currencies. Trade and capital flows cannot grow if such monetary relationships are subject to restrictions or inappropriate exchange rate policies.

Some hindrances to trade integration are due to trade barriers in the OECD area. In trading with centrally planned economies, OECD countries applied high trade barriers mainly to stem unfair competition of state-subsidized imports. Once the centrally planned system was eliminated and market-based competition was established the OECD countries moved swiftly to eliminate tariff barriers. Most favored nation treatment was extended to the CEECs and later this was complemented by the generalized system of preferences treatment. Consequently, average tariff rate protection was reduced to very low levels ranging from a minimum of 1.7 percent applied by Sweden to a maximum of 7 percent by Austria.[3] However, the impact of these concessions on trade is less beneficial than it might appear for several reasons. Tariff rates in many OECD countries are much higher than average rates in the export sectors that constitute the bulk of CEECs' exports, namely agricultural products, textile and apparel, iron and steel, and chemicals. These sectors constitute between one third and a half of CEECs' total exports to the OECD area. In contrast, the CEECs' exports in these four sectors are relatively small if compared with the corresponding production or consumption of the OECD countries or with the total of OECD imports of the same goods.

Overall, it is clear that market access to the OECD area should be improved if CEECs economic integration has to be fostered and that the measures to be taken should focus on lowering nontariff barriers and limiting discriminatory treatment. At present, there is no strong tendency to proceed in this direction, except in the context of some bilateral agreements limited to few countries.

General Orientation in Integration

In 1993, integration into the OECD area has become a matter of increasing urgency for the CEECs as new conjunctural reasons have emerged in addition to the structural factors that have been highlighted before. After an initial phase aimed at stabilizing domestic demand and liberalizing price and private economic initiative, all the CEECs are faced with a continuing output decline, rising unemployment and large shortfalls in output demand. Currently, the major challenge is to trigger a recovery of economic activity that can be sustained in the following years without giving rise to higher inflation or unbearable external deficits. Such a recovery is hampered by the sluggish growth of domestic demand and a loss of demand from the CEECs area. More rapid integration with the OECD area could offer a way out of this situation to the extent that increasing trade and capital flows could boost overall demand. This is an instrument to diversify geographically and to strengthen qualitatively the demand impulses to growth. Hence, it is necessary that the CEECs face this issue squarely and clarify the model of integration they want to pursue before measures affecting or interfering with channels of are adopted.

As regards the model, some general criteria should be met. First, integration should be based in the market place and on market opportunities, rather than relying on government preferences, public subsidies, public protection from competition, or discriminatory trade arrangements. Two corollaries follow from this criterion. Domestic distortions of market mechanisms and impediments to market competition must be corrected rapidly. Improvements in domestic market structure are needed in order to benefit from the incentives of market competition to higher efficiency and innovation. Furthermore, privatisation of a large share of the enterprise sector and commercialization of remaining public-owned firms should not be delayed any further. If the predominant share of production units continue to be in public hands and with the legacy of old inefficiencies, it is extremely difficult for these economies to reach such a flexibility as to be able (and even willing) to compete in foreign markets or to maximize returns on capital received from abroad.

The second criteria is that the CEECs should abandon the attitude, which was typical of the old system, to aim at self-sufficiency in production and consumption. By pursuing a high degree of external openness, they would spur the economic system to find its proper place or specialization in the international division of labor. This implies relinquishing many sectors and concentrating resources in a reduced number of sectors where economies of scale and efficiencies could be enhanced.

Third, the new pattern of specialization should not be decided by the government or directly promoted through specifically oriented subventions or discriminatory preferences. Authorities have limited knowledge of the market while enterprises are better placed to assess their comparative advantages in trade, besides being responsible for taking the risk of exploiting these advantages. Government intervention must be limited to creating the general conditions under which enterprises can arrive at undistorted decisions on their specialization pattern and can have access to the capital, labor and technology inputs required to carry out their production plans.

It follows that government support to a new specialization pattern should focus, on the one hand, on preserving the relative labor cost advantage and, on the other hand, on promoting a faster pace in absorbing advanced technologies and in innovating the product mix and the production systems. On such a basis, it is possible for the CEECs to exploit the enlarged access to or the higher integration with the OECD economy for the purpose of accelerating their economic growth.

The Main Issues and Approaches

The implementation of the integration strategy raises a number of important issues. First, should gradualism or rapidity be applied in opening up the CEECs economies to external competition? An abrupt liberalization might jeopardize the prospects for survival of the majority of CEECs' enterprises including those undergoing restructuring. However, this is not enough to justify industrial protectionism since it is of overriding importance for these economies to expand the participation of foreign enterprises and technologies in the renovation of the economy. A phased approach towards trade liberalization could be a good compromise, provided it includes the following five steps:

First, to introduce transparency in external trade relations by converting the extensive nontariff barriers used by the old regime into tariffs; to establish a timetable for tariff reduction over a limited number of years and to adhere strictly to this timetable that should be made public; to obtain an asymmetric opening of OECD markets in such a way that their barriers are lowered much more rapidly than in CEECs; and finally, to pursue an exchange rate policy that for any given level of trade liberalization does not lead to a balance of payments crisis.

The second major issue is whether to aim at integration on a regional basis or at a multilateral opening of the economy. Poland, the Czech and Slovak Republics, and Hungary have chosen to integrate themselves in the European Economic Community (EEC). The Common Market is in many respects the natural area of integration for these economies both because of the geographical proximity and in view of the cultural ties and a past tradition of capital flows and migration currents. But should this regional integration be at the expense of a wider integration? CEECs should avoid such an outcome and instead use their participation in the Common Market as a vehicle to accelerate the construction of a production base that can allow them to compete in world markets. Among other measures, this requires CEECs not to offset deductions in trade barriers vis-a-vis the region of integration with new trade obstacles or discriminatory trade measures against other regions. they should instead pursue a liberalization of trade on a worldwide and multilateral basis, in parallel with the European integration.

The third major issue is related to the priority to be assigned to the introduction of external monetary convertibility in the sequence of measures aimed at achieving a rapid integration with the OECD area. Clearly, no integration can take place without a degree of monetary convertibility because its absence makes it extremely difficult for Western and Eastern enterprises to develop trade and financial relationships. However, the CEECs, lack the international reserves that are needed to underpin external convertibility. Between no convertibility and full convertibility there are intermediate degrees of convertibility that currently seem accessible to these reforming economies today. Thus, the move toward full convertibility should be seen as a process rather than an act.

The exchange rate has been used by the CEECs so far in order to fulfill two different functions: to boost export competitiveness and to provide an anchor for monetary stability. The two roles often have been mutually incompatible. For instance, in the period 1990-91 Poland fixed the exchange rate of the zloty for several quarters each period to bolster its disinflationary strategy. However, failure to control inflation led to a loss of competitiveness because of the appreciation of the real exchange rate. To reconcile the two conflicting roles it is advisable that exchange rate policy be geared at maintaining trade competitiveness while other monetary and fiscal instruments be used to stem domestic inflationary pressures. Furthermore, it is essential that the system of foreign exchange allocation be market-based and nondiscriminatory.

The fourth issue concerns the financing of trade integration or trade imbalances. The borrowing capacity of these countries is very limited at present and the shortage of foreign exchange is severe, in spite of the catalytic role of stabilization programs supported by the International Monetary Fund (IMF) and the increase in loan commitments of institutions, such as the World Bank and the European Bank for Reconstruction and Development (EBRD). This difficulty can only be overcome over the long term by restoring normal financial relationships between the CEECs and the private banking community. This requires raising the CEECs's credit worthiness through the implementation of extensive reforms and proper macroeconomic management. In the meantime, the CEECs can gain foreign exchange by favoring foreign direct investment, promoting savings, and strengthening the export sectors.

The fifth issue involves the redefinition of the role of government's intervention in promoting integration. In the CEECs the government still fulfills two conflicting functions; it is at once the owner of the majority of enterprises and the regulator of the economy. The state-owner is not by its nature in a good position to orient enterprises in their decisions about what and how to produce for the foreign markets. This is even more so with the passage to a market-based economy, since the government has limited those parts of its administration that were responsible for managing the enterprise sector. This resulted in a vacuum of decision making by enterprises as they were not able to cope with the uncertainties of market competition and an absent owner. In some cases the result was a de facto appropriation of the enterprise managers and workers who operate it in an undefined context.

The issue that the government confronts is basically what type of industrial policy to develop in the transition to the new economic system. While pulling itself out of direct responsibility for the enterprise sector, the government should develop its functions in two directions: to establish general conditions under which all enterprises can produce, invest and compete effectively and to strengthen the infrastructure of the market economy.

This involves several additional measures. The economy should be deregulated to a large extent so as to free economic initiative from the existing multitude of administrative constraints. Markets, for labor and capital should be developed and made flexible enough to accommodate the production and investment needs of the enterprises. Legal institutions, such as property law and commercial law, should be built rapidly to create a base of certainty in economic relationships and obligations. Transport, means of communication, and the physical infrastructure must be upgraded to allow the new market economy to conduct business in foreign markets. Exports should be supported by the establishment of an export credit system so as to eliminate the disadvantage that enterprises face in competing in world markets with countries that already have such systems.

Measures by OECD Countries

Economic integration should not be seen as a one-sided effort by the CEECs but in order to succeed rapidly, it also needs the cooperation of the OECD partners. Albeit less extensive than the measures required from the CEECs, OECD countries' support should extend over a number of areas. The most important form of support relates to trade and involves a reduction of average tariffs as well as an easing of the nontariff trade barriers that protect some sectors. As to tariff levels, an asymmetric trade liberalization of the type agreed by the EEC could be adopted by other OECD countries. What should be envisaged is a sizable cut of the existing tariffs for a limited period, say five to seven years.

On the financial side, integration has to be backed by large capital flows into the CEECs. The OECD countries have still room to expand official lending and this could be framed within the economic policy supervision exercised by the main international economic organizations over the implementation of reforms. Clearly, this is not enough to relieve financial shortages; and a bigger involvement of private financial institutions is essential and should be promoted. To this end, OECD countries could help improve the level of information on the

CEECs; economic development and prospects. This would contribute to reducing the risk component in lending decisions by OECD area banks.

Furthermore, OECD countries should boost technical assistance for reforming and managing the CEECs' economies. They could promote cooperation between enterprises or between banks and financial institutions of the two areas in view of upgrading the levels of managerial skills, and general know-how. An approach in this direction could be to revive an initiative of the Marshall Plan, by establishing a "productivity agency" along the lines of the old European Productivity Agency. Such an agency would constitute an official framework for promoting transfers of technology and know-how outside the constraints imposed by market competition. As regards migration, transferring people across borders raises many more difficulties than transferring goods, services, or capital. If migration can contribute to integration, it has to be in a regulated framework. Hence, more attention should be paid to the development of bilateral agreements aimed at ensuring and regulating labor flows on a predetermined timetable.

Conclusion

At this stage in the construction of a prosperous market economy in the CEECs, integration with the OECD economy is a matter of necessity, both to force a deep transformation of the economic system, and to fill gaps in aggregate demand that are responsible for the current stagnation in economic activity.

The focus of these measures should, first, be on trade and economic liberalization. Other measures must complement trade and economic liberalization and they must aim at laying the foundations of radical changes of the economic structures. in particular, labor and capital must be allocated on the basis of market mechanisms that are made responsive to the new needs of the enterprises. Moreover, the legal framework of a market economy should be constructed as a matter of urgency, starting from property law. Enterprises still in public hands should be exposed to the competitive and accountability pressures that all the other enterprises have to face in the market place.

The cooperation and support of OECD countries is essential to accelerate the pace of integration. In view of the importance of the channel of integration, OECD countries should focus on reducing trade barriers, particularly the non-tariff ones.

Financial assistance also needs to be expanded and OECD countries could consider some incentives directed to promote a bigger involvement of the private financial community in the financing of economic integration. Equally important is the expansion of technical assistance and transfers of know-how. The launching of a "productivity agency" similar to the European Productivity Agency of the Marshall Plan should be considered by the OECD countries, being an effective instrument to favor collaboration between the enterprise sectors of the two areas.

Notes

1. For the purpose of this paper, the CEECs group of countries refers to all the formerly centrally planned economies of Europe and the former USSR.

2. See *IMF World Economic Outlook*, May 1992, Table A46.

3. OECD W.P. Trade Committee, East-West Trade, "Synthesis Paper on Barriers to Trade with the CEECss," February 1992; and P.A. Messerlin, "Restrictions on OECD Imports from Eastern Europe: An Overview," March 1992.

Section 3 · Transition and Its Particularities

Adrian Nastase

When we speak of transition, we are too often tempted to think of it as a purely Eastern European phenomenon. In fact, this is only partly true. If we think of transition as a passage from dictatorship to democracy, then there had been notable cases of such transition elsewhere well before the fall of Communist structures in Central and Eastern Europe. Chile, Portugal, Spain, and Turkey, are often mentioned in this regard. Their experience is no doubt of great relevance to the current efforts to ensure the successful outcome of the reforms under way in Central and Eastern European countries.

Different Challenges of Transition

There are, however, important differences between transition in Central and Eastern Europe and transition in other parts of the globe. The major difference is the ideological dimension of dictatorships born out of the Communist experiment. They aimed not only at imposing the will of the rulers, but also at controlling their societies through the minds of the people. The type of command economy they shaped brought about a sort of egalitarianism at increasingly lower levels of poverty, while wasting and depleting the resources of their nations.

These characteristics of the old Communist regimes raise particular challenges for the transition processes in Central and Eastern European countries.

The Pace of Transition

One challenge is to speed up the pace of change, which has been relatively slow in comparison with the high hopes of the people who expected instant democratic societies as well as an instant rise in their living standard. This gap between expectations and reality is due in large measure to a lack of new political leaders and managers. In the case of the former, most of these countries resorted to university people and cultural personalities; in the case of the latter, there were extremely limited resources of trained people upon which to draw. This situation has had a dramatic effect on their economies.

Traces of Old Habits

Changing old mentalities and habits is another major challenge of the transition. There is no doubt that fifty years of dictatorial regimes and their corollary—a serious lack of democratic exercise resulting in a certain awkwardness in understanding and practicing the rules of democracy—have left deep wounds on the society. It was relatively easy to establish the institutions of political pluralism and the rule of law in all Central and Eastern European countries, but to make them work properly is a different matter. Healing those wounds will take considerable time. One way to shorten the road to a healthy democratic society would be through educational reform and a sustained effort in training all sections of the society.

Financial Needs

There exists a serious gap between the modest financial resources that transition countries possess and what they need to carry out the economic reforms, together with the limited resources available to them from abroad. To meet this challenge a special effort is needed from Western countries, much greater than has been the case so far, without affecting the traditional programs of assistance to developing countries.

On the one hand, the success of transition to market economies is important to and in the interests of all participating states, and cooperation in the field of economy, science, and technology stands for a major pillar of European construction. Needless to say, a failure in carrying out political and economic reform throughout Central and Eastern Europe would have repercussions, not only within the area but also far beyond it. On the other hand, experience has shown that progress of democratic processes is directly dependent on economic development.

Ethnic Conflicts

Last but not least, societies in transition countries are confronted with the challenge of overcoming interethnic conflicts. The suppression of national aspirations and manipulation of national feelings characteristic of Communist regimes made their societies like boiling pots. When the lids were taken off, ethnic tensions burst out into the open. Although understandable, it is unwise that they be encouraged either willingly or unwittingly. This happens through an excessive focus on them in international fora or by devising all sorts of new concepts and international mechanisms that, despite the appearance of general application, are in fact aimed solely at transition countries.

This is certainly not the way to overcome ethnic tensions and conflicts. Here again, the solution lies in economic development. The current priorities of international efforts aimed at meeting this challenge must be changed. Rather than stimulating national feelings, the international community should concentrate on helping the devastated economies of transition countries.

We should remember Western Europe immediately after World War II, when the Marshall Plan helped Western countries make the breakthrough. Nobody emphasized at that time the ethnic dimensions that had, in fact, been quite acute both prior to and during the war. Let us learn from this effective approach. It is common knowledge that poverty generates nationalism. It has been proved that it is easier to win an electorate through exploitation of nationalist feelings than by convincing it of the rightfulness of a coherent platform of economic reforms.

All these challenges give transition in Central and Eastern European countries an unprecedented character. Solutions cannot be entirely borrowed from earlier transition experiences. Time is needed. These countries are akin to people who have stayed a long time in the darkness and have suddenly come out into the sun and must allow their eyes to adjust. Therefore, solutions to challenges must be worked out in an innovative manner by a thorough study of the particularities, traditions, and potential of each country concerned. Hence the particular importance and significance of initiatives such as this book, *A World Fit for People* and the previous one *Change: Threat or Opportunity?*

Section 4 · Towards a New Era: Market Economy and Democracy

John Brademas

The subject of this book is *A World Fit for People*. The international environment is far different from the time, just nearly two years ago, of the publication of the first set of books in this series, *Change: Threat or Opportunity?*

Positive Developments

The cascade of events since then has been dizzying—the crumbling of the Communist empire, the disintegration of seventy years of totalitarian governments and command economies and the beginnings of reform of the old, inhuman, and ultimately unworkable structures.

Last fall, as President of New York University, I was in Moscow, a city I had as a Member of Congress visited over thirty years ago. I have, therefore, seen with my own eyes something of the extraordinary changes during those three decades. In the summer of 1991, I welcomed to New York University, nine days after his election as the first President of the Russian Republic, Boris Yeltsin, and what Yeltsin said then would have been unthinkable even three years ago. He endorsed human rights, a market economy, freedom for the Baltic states and the teachings of the Gospel!

In the Middle East, ancient enemies are flirting fitfully with the prospect of genuine dialogue about how to find a lasting peace. Authors of the accord that merged the European Community and the European Free Trade Allocation seek economic and other benefits for 380 million people in 19 nations. The North American Free Trade Agreement, signed by Canada, Mexico, and the United States, promises a market of nearly as many consumers, with a combined economic output of $6 trillion.

Negative Trends

Alongside these generally positive developments, however, are the horrendous war in the former Yugoslavia; violent ethnic struggles in some of the new republics of the former Soviet Union, including Romania's neighbor, Moldova; ongoing strife in Kashmir and Cambodia; and continuing Communist dictatorships in China and North Korea.

Standing on the sidelines, as it were, with the bulk of the planet's population and least of its comforts, are the developing countries of Africa, Asia, and Latin America. The terrible tragedy of Somalia is the most dramatic example of how distant humankind is, as we approach the twenty-first century, form a world where thousands of people no longer starve.

Americans, too, face a burgeoning array of problems of our own, from combating crime and drugs to cleaning up the environment, from fighting AIDS to dealing with homelessness, from reinvigorating a listless school system to reigniting a stalled economy. Worse, our ability to finance the immense efforts necessary to address these troubles has progressively deteriorated. This year's deficit in the budget of our federal government has soared to nearly $400 billion, over $1 billion a day, a fact with profoundly crippling consequences for our strength at home and abroad.

U.S. Obligations

Despite our domestic dilemmas, Americans cannot ignore our obligations to the wider world. Indeed, last year, I served on a commission, sponsored by the Carnegie International Endowment for Peace, of twenty-three Americans—Democrats, Republicans, independents—former senators, representatives, secretaries of defense, ambassadors—all of whom had served in government with some responsibility in foreign affairs. Our charge was to articulate a new rationale for U.S. foreign policy following the collapse of Communism.

The Commission's report, *Changing Our Ways: America and the New World,* says the following about the first of the two subjects I wish to discuss:

> "If countries of the former Soviet bloc can establish functioning market economies in this decade, it would be an historic accomplishment at least equal to the reconstruction of Western Europe and Japan in the 1950s. . . .

The Commission strongly endorses a major U.S. commitment to this transition. The United States has taken on such a challenge before and has been the better for it. . . ."

With respect to my second theme, our Commission report declares that Americans must care about democratization elsewhere in the world and that "expanding freedom" must be "one of the central pillars of our foreign policy."

How should the United States pursue these twin objectives of democracy and market economies in the former Communist bloc countries? First, I believe we must forge in the United States, a partnership across several sectors—business and industry, labor, private foundations, colleges and universities, and the federal government. Second, a significant portion of the resources of that partnership must be targeted on the training of managers and on education in market economics. Without knowledgeable practitioners, flourishing economies cannot be successfully developed. Third, some of the resources must be directed to encouraging the building of genuinely democratic political institutions.

Why, the United States working with our European and Japanese colleagues—and competitors!—should create such a partnership must be obvious, At our best, Americans are champions of free peoples and open markets. Again, to cite our Carnegie Commission report, history teaches that democratic societies do not attack one another; that stable democracies are generally better trade and investment partners that repressive regimes; that environmental policies are more advanced in democratic nations because initiated by an informed pubic; that free nations more effectively protect the rights of their citizens.

The Role of the Private Sector

The U.S. contribution need not come only from the government. Nor must our participation always take the form of money. The United States has much else of value to offer. As fundamental to economic development as roads, bridges, tunnels, power, and communications is brainpower—trained minds, skilled managers, educated leaders.

The development of competitive economies in Central and Eastern Europe will depend in large part on how rapidly and well new managers can be trained and new knowledge imparted. However, these countries have some conceptual difficulties on such issues as: What is a free market? How does it work? What are the basic skills required to operate in a market economy? How does one set up a business, calculate profit and loss, perform basic accounting, establish production and marketing goals? All these functions, essential to economic advance in the modern world, require education and training. Certainly, one source of education and training in Central and Eastern Europe will be U.S. business and industry as U.S. firms become actively involved here.

I note, for example, the purchase by Phillip Morris of a controlling interest in the Tabak cigarette maker and the K-Mart acquisition of the Prior & Maj department store, both in Czechoslovakia; the purchase by General Electric of a half-interest in Tungsram of Budapest and, by Sara Lee, of a controlling interest in Compack, third-largest food company in Hungary.

Acquisitions like these, as well as the move to privatize industries in Central and Eastern Europe demand specific financial know-how. But from where does this know-how come? As the *New York Times* reported recently, Czech officials anxious to do business with Western firms realized quickly that they were not equipped for high-finance transactions and so welcomed the arrival of U.S. bankers and investment advisers who both improved the terms of the agreements for the Czechs and provided them some hands-on education in market economics. Clearly, Western and Japanese acquisitions in Central and Eastern Europe can bring with them both an infusion of management skills and experience in a market economy. These capabilities can be imparted either by on-the-job example or in formal training session set up by the companies.

The Role of Universities

Even as each corporation will tailor in-house instruction to fit its own needs, broad-gauged educational programs remain the province of colleges and universities. In the United States there are some 3,500 institutions of higher learning with an enormous diversity of academic strengths. Here I return to the idea of partnership for although many U.S. institutions of higher learning can supply the expertise, most are unable, as non-profit organizations, to subsidize such assistance. Universities must depend for financial support on such sources as private foundations, business, and the SEED program of the federal government. SEED is the acronym for the Support for Eastern European Democracy Act of 1989, a legislative umbrella for a variety of programs directed at stimulating, in Eastern Europe, particularly through the private sector, economic development; and encouraging democratic political institutions. To carry out the purposes of SEED, Congress appropriated $370 million for each of the fiscal years 1991 and 1992.

Although most of the SEED money has gone to Hungary and Poland, SEED projects have also benefited Bulgaria, Czechoslovakia, Yugoslavia, and Romania. This support has provided food, children's relief, orientation for parliamentarians, trade and business advice, water pollution control training, and student exchange. SEED programs in Romania have totaled, in 1991 and 1992, nearly $31 million.

In voting the money for SEED, Congress emphasized several specific uses, among them practical training in business management, which Congress urged be offered in both the United States and Eastern Europe.

The so-called Freedom Support Act, provides $17 million in bilateral aid for humanitarian and technical assistance, for defense conversion and other efforts to encourage free market and democratic reforms. The bill also contains $15 million for a Democracy Corps, to enable private U.S. citizens to promote democratic institutions at the local level in the Commonwealth of Independent States.

Needs Before Support

Although this legislation is commendable, most observers agree that considering the immensity of the stakes, assistance from the United States and the West generally has been too modest and too slow. For the goal is nothing less than to lay the basis for genuine democracy in a vast, once totalitarian land that is still in profound economic trouble where political institutions are by no means assured.

An editorial comment from the *Financial Times* of London "Risks facing Russian reform." 13 August 1992 makes my point in blunt fashion:

> "The fundamental error of the West has been to view reform in the former Soviet Union, particularly in Russia, as just another of those problems of impoverishment that beset it. This attitude explains why assistance was offered too late and probably too little....Reforming Russia is the most important economic challenge since the construction of postwar Western Europe. . . ."

"Things are rotten in the State of Russian reform," warns the *Financial Times*. "Worse, the West's tardy assistance makes it appear as much of the problem as of the solution. If things continue to slide as they have in recent weeks, the question will soon be asked: Who lost Russia?"

During his election campaign, President Clinton delivered an address at the Foreign Policy Association in New York on 1 April 1992 and outlined in specific terms, what ought to be U.S. policy to encourage free political and economic institutions in Russia and the rest of the former Soviet Union. He said:

> . . . From Russia to Central Europe, from Ukraine to the Baltics, the United States and our allies need to speed the transition to democracy and capitalism by keeping our markets open to these countries' products, offering food and technical assistance, helping them privatize key industries, converting military production to civilian uses and employing weapons experts in peaceful pursuits....Our nation's greatest resource is ultimately not our dollars not our technical expertise but our values of pluralism and enterprise and freedom and the rule of law—and our centuries of experience in making those values work. In an era of fledgling democracies, those values can be our proudest export and our most effective tool of foreign policy.

Although Russia is obviously a case to be considered on its own, I believe that what President Clinton said about it represents a perspective applicable in many ways to the formerly Communist countries of Central and Eastern Europe.

What Bill Clinton said in April 1992 in New York is important, because he is now the new President of the United States. His statement of U.S. policy toward the countries of the former Communist world represents the kind of wise, vigorous leadership the world has the right to expect from the United States.

In addition to aid provided by the U.S. government, colleges and universities can play a significant role in promoting market economies with programs of management training. The New York University, through our School of Continuing Education, has already launched a few such programs.

The Building of Free Political Institutions

No one can quarrel with the proposition that to nurture democracy in countries unaccustomed to it is fraught with difficulty. Preparing the most basic voter information materials and recruiting and training volunteer poll watchers for elections are examples of activities that are essential but not easy. Assuring free, fair, and open elections is very hard work.

Of course, even more fundamental—and potentially more difficult—is the recruiting of men and women ready and able to assume political leadership in a fledgling democracy.

There are several ways that the United States and European Community states can assist, through private organizations as well as, where appropriate, governments. From helping to develop political parties and build free labor unions, encouraging independent media, advising local government and stimulating citizen action groups to providing information on campaign and election management and the operation of legislatures, both the U.S. government and private groups can play constructive roles.

Essential to the development of a genuinely democratic society—and of a government to serve it—is tolerance, respect for the ideas and viewpoints of men and women with whom one may not agree. This respect for differences, commitment to pluralism rather than a single ideology or attitude, is indispensable to any nation that pretends to be civilized.

Particularly important in this regard is the treatment of minorities. We need look only to the doctrine of "ethnic cleansing" that has brought such terrible tragedy to what was Yugoslavia.

In any democratic country the majority has a special responsibility to be attentive to the concerns of minorities. As an American of considerable experience in the political life of my own country, I have seen how demagogues have attempted, at times with success, to provoke one group to hate another in the United States.

So I am well aware that no modern democracy is without flaw in assuring tolerance of, if not, respect for, diversity. I do, however, insist that this must be a goal toward which we in the West and more to the point, the peoples of the emerging democracies, must strive. Otherwise there will be more Yugoslavias and more closed societies, of Left and Right.

Conclusion

We all realize that after nearly three generations of command economies and authoritarian governments in Central and Eastern Europe, there are massive obstacles to the establishment of parliamentary democracies and market economies. To achieve these goals will be neither simple nor easy. But to do so is essential.

For building democratic political institutions in the nations of Central and Eastern Europe and transforming their economies are objectives crucial not only to the quality of life of the peoples of this region, but to creating a world where peoples everywhere enjoy the blessings of peace, justice, and freedom.

As an American politician, legislator, and university leader I believe strongly that the nations of the West, particularly the United States, must play a constructive part in encouraging, in the countries of Central and Eastern Europe and the former Soviet Union, the development of democratic political institutions and market-oriented economies.

Section 5 · Transition and Transnational Corporations

David Gold and Persephone Economou

The wave of change that swept through Central and Eastern Europe, including the former Soviet Union, at the end of the 1980s and the beginning of the 1990s has had profound implications not only for the countries involved, but for the world at large. Major economic transformations are taking place, following either a "big bang" or a more gradual approach, aimed at creating full-fledged market economies out of the ruins of centrally planned ones. These transformations are all-encompassing and are not restricted to economic reform. Instead, they seek to change all conditions that affect the functioning of a market-based system, including the institutional arrangements (such as how banks are organized and operated), political and legal infrastructure (including laws regarding the disposition of property), policies concerning taxation and the underutilization of savings, social relations (such as between workers and managers), and even individual behavior as people adjust to the expansion of markets.

The fundamental objective of these transformations is to increase the standard of living of the members of these economies by increasing the productivity of those engaged in producing and distributing goods and services. Creating a market economy involves the transformation, or construction, or a wide range of institutions and relationships. To improve efficiency, prices of goods and services need to closely reflect their real costs of production, which implies that a large portion of these prices need to be determined on markets with a high degree of competition. In addition, decisions with respect to what is produced and how it is produced need to be taken with regard to actual demand and the cost and effectiveness of resources available for use in production. These decisions also need to be placed in the hands of private sector actors or governmental agencies who respond to the incentives implied by market prices.

Action at the Macroeconomic Level

At the macroeconomic level, institutions and incentives to allocate savings among investment projects need to be created to replace much of the work done in this regard by governmental involvement via taxation, borrowing, spending, and administrative allocation. A monetary system to fight both inflation and speculation while maintaining an internationally convertible currency needs to be put in place. And a reasonably open environment for international economic transactions is required in order to stimulate competition and allow these economies to reap benefits from participating in the international division of labor.

The creation of such a market economy is correctly seen as a daunting task. Most of the countries in the region have looked outside of their own borders for help—to scholars for advice, to international organizations such as the International Monetary Fund for financial resources, to the large developed economies for aid and access to markets, and to transnational corporations for capital, technology, and organizational skills. In spite of differences in the nature and speed of transition, all countries in the region regard foreign direct investment as a key contributor to their economic transformation, as evidenced by the liberal legislation enacted by them. In so doing, they aspire to obtain benefits from transnational corporations at a time when there is an expected global shortage of capital and when countries are increasingly competing to attract foreign direct investment.

The Contribution of Transnational Corporations to Economic Growth and Change

According to a recent estimate, there are approximately 35,000 transnational corporations operating worldwide, with over $1.7 trillion invested in countries other than their own, and an even larger amount invested in their home countries.[1] Worldwide foreign direct investment flows grew rapidly in the second half of the 1980s, from $53 billion in 1985 to $225 billion in 1990, although the slow-down in economic activity in the major investing countries in 1990-92 has severely dampened the rate of growth of investment flows. Over the second half of the 1980s, foreign direct investment increased in importance in relation to other macroeconomic variables, such as gross domestic output, international trade, and domestic investment. At the same time, worldwide sales of foreign affiliates—which measure their output in host countries—exceed the value of exports of goods and services, thus indicating the importance of foreign affiliates of transnational corporations in delivering goods and services to markets worldwide.

The growing importance of foreign direct investment, both in absolute and relative terms, is taking place in the context of a world economy characterized by a revival of market forces, a tendency towards the globalization of industries while there is simultaneously a regionalization of markets and the shrinking of economic distance due to improvements in transportation and communications. Transnational corporations are playing a major role in shaping these developments and, therefore, in shaping the economic environment that the countries of Central and Eastern Europe are seeking to enter.

Transnational corporations have helped stimulate economic growth and structural transformation in many developing countries through their contribution to the determinants of growth, especially capital formation, the transfer of technology (including the development of environmentally sound technology), the development of human resources, and the enlargement of trade opportunities. It is not surprising, therefore, that transnational corporations are looked upon as capable of a similar contribution to the transformation of the economies of Central and Eastern Europe.[2]

Transnational corporations may be best seen as bringing an integrated package of attributes to their host companies. In addition to their direct contribution to each of the important determinants of economic growth, the interrelationship among these determinants magnifies the impact of transnational corporations on host countries.[3] An example of the interrelationships among the different channels to growth is the link between capital formation and the transfer of technology. New capital equipment often embodies new technologies that enable host countries to upgrade their technological capabilities in addition to enlarging their capital stock. Trade and the transfer of technology often embodied in imports of capital goods into host countries by the foreign affiliates of transnational corporations is another area where interlinkages and synergies among the factors determining growth are apparent. Trade opportunities and new technology are particularly important in aiding the types of structural transformations that many developing countries are seeking to undertake.

As in the case of developing countries, transnational corporations can contribute to growth and transformation in Central and Eastern Europe either directly (through a single avenue to growth), indirectly through the impact of interlinkages with other avenues), or through restructuring of the domestic economy. Perhaps more than in the case of developing countries, the contribution of transnational corporations to economic transformation in Central and Eastern Europe via all channels to growth can be regarded as equally significant. The crucial point may, therefore, be to identify the channels through which transnational corporations can rapidly transform the domestic economy, since it is widely recognized that the overall long-term impacts of transnational corporations on growth are, on balance, positive.

The Formation of Human and Financial Capital

The development of human resources, while an important factor for growth, seems to be less relevant for most Central and Eastern European countries which already enjoy relatively high levels and standards of education, than it is for most developing countries. Nevertheless, the importance of training a workforce in new production methods and new managerial techniques should not be underestimated. More generally, to the extent transnational corporations can reinforce the skills needed to operate successfully in national and international markets, they can be a source of substantial benefits in these countries.

New capital formation, while an important factor for growth and transformation, is an area where the contribution of transnational corporations is seldom large in absolute terms or in relation to total domestic capital formation. This is not meant to downplay the contribution of transnational corporations to growth and structural transformation via new investment. In many developing countries, transnational corporations contribute a small proportion of gross capital formation, usually less than five percent, more frequently between five and ten percent, and occasionally above ten percent. Yet the contribution of transnational corporations to the most technologically advanced and outward oriented industries is frequently substantially larger. In the Republic of Korea, for example, although foreign direct investment accounted for less than two percent of gross investment in the mid-1980s, foreign firms contributed between 19 and 21 percent of new capital to the electronics and transportation equipment industries.[4]

Most foreign direct investment entering Central and Eastern Europe is in the form of new enterprises, largely joint ventures with domestic partners. Even in the case of acquisitions (a number of which have occurred through privatization), it is likely that, given the present state of many domestic companies, foreign direct investment will result in an increase in quantity and quality of capital through the restructuring of the acquired companies (for example, by bringing in modern machinery and discarding obsolete equipment). Moreover, concerns as to a worldwide scarcity of capital in view of the needs of both developing and Central and Eastern Europe countries, the high level of debt from private sources of some Central and East Europe countries resulting in a reluctance to borrow further in international markets, and competition among the new nations in Central and Eastern Europe for soft loans from multilateral institutions and foreign aid, have added to the desirability of foreign direct investment. Nevertheless, the relatively small value of foreign direct investment flows and stock in Central and Eastern Europe, coupled with a low level of implementation of foreign capital committed in joint ventures with domestic partners make capital formation a channel through which transnational corporations are less likely to have an immediate effect on economic transformation.

The Role of Trade

In a simple growth accounting framework, trade does not enter as a factor determining growth; it is mostly regarded as a means of expanding markets, improving access to foreign produced goods and services, and increasing competition. Trade can be a determinant of growth in so far as it provides access to critical inputs and leads to a more efficient allocation of resources stemming from specialization. This is an area where transnational corporations can make a substantial contribution to economic transformation because of their increasing involvement in international trade. Transnational corporations will ensure that the output of their foreign affiliates will be exported to the location where final processing or assembly takes place—in that sense, the market for the output of foreign affiliates is guaranteed. A host country may itself be the location from where the final product will be exported to other countries within the same region (or to other regions) or sold domestically. Such regionally integrated production strategies of transnational corporations have increasinged in Europe in a number of industries, especially automobiles and electronics.

The Single Market Programme within the European Community and the possible expansion of the EC into a wider European Economic Area gives most of the countries of Central and Eastern Europe a huge market in close geographical proximity. An integration of the Central and Eastern Europe countries into the European Community cluster, already in progress informally, will strengthen the trade performance of these countries. Transnational corporations can stimulate a substantial amount of integration at the production level prior to more formal integration at the political level. Expansion of trade opportunities can provide much needed hard currency (some of which can be used to service debt), boost reserves,[5] and foster "learning from exporting." Transnational corporations can also smooth the transition from export reliance on the former Council for Mutual Economic Assistance (CMEA) countries and help to diversify the destination of exports to European Community countries.

The Transfer of Technology

Technology transfer is another way through which transnational corporations can have a substantial and immediate impact on economic transformation. The low and environmentally hazardous technology that had been used by Central and Eastern European countries is, in many cases, either obsolete or in need of considerable upgrading. Foreign affiliates, in order to produce internationally competitive goods, require a certain minimum of technology that they automatically transfer to the host country by investing and operating there. The acquisition of existing companies by foreign investors, in most cases, results in substantial upgrading of the production equipment and technology utilized. The fact that the majority of investment in Central and Eastern European countries are of joint ownership with domestic producers facilitates the transfer of technology. The existing level of education and skills ensures that the absorptive capacity of the domestic labor force is significant. It seems, therefore, that the transfer of technology by transnational corporations is another area with important and immediate implications for economic restructuring in Central and Eastern Europe.

The transfer of technology may also be related to export-oriented foreign direct investment. The fact that the output of joint ventures is geared to regional or world markets implies that the quality has to satisfy certain minimum requirements, which can be reached only with the use of modern equipment and machinery. As a result, it would be expected that joint ventures result in a surge of imports of capital goods that embody advanced technology and that is then transferred to the host country. In addition to such hard technology, foreign affiliates train the local labor force in the use of the equipment and machinery and transfer business and organizational skills.

Finally, the interlinkages between foreign affiliates and domestic producers is another area where the former can have a considerable impact on industrial restructuring. Such interlinkages may take the form of nonequity relationships (for example, local procurement and sourcing, subcontracting, or informally linking final buyers and domestic producers) and have been shown to be significant for a number of developing countries.[6] Transnational corporations can stimulate growth through backward and forward linkages with the domestic economy, and via spillovers of technology and managerial skills. The existence of such linkages and spillovers facilitates the diffusion of the growth stimuli of transnational corporations to the local economy, thus enhancing the overall impact of transnational corporations. The experience of some Asian countries in this regard is particularly instructive as an example of the acceleration of the process of continuous structural upgrading with the assistance of transnational corporations. A similar linkage between transnational corporations and structural upgrading appears to be underway in Mexico.[7]

Transnational Corporations and the Transition Process

The transition process has been difficult for all Central and Eastern European countries, with living standards falling sharply from an already low base. Industrial output has dropped by as much as 20 percent,[8] unemployment has risen to unforeseen levels and continues to increase, international trade has declined dramatically with the collapse of CMEA and the privatization of state enterprises is proceeding slowly in most countries. At the same time, the surfacing of intense political differences in some countries and weaknesses in governmental structures in others, has contributed to a perception of uncertainty and instability.[9]

Many countries in the region have not been able to attract large amounts of foreign direct investment. As of October 1991, only $9.5 billion had been committed to the region. The total number of foreign affiliates more than doubled between the beginning of 1991 and January 1992, although the number of foreign affiliates that have actually invested in Central and Eastern Europe is considerably less (estimated to be about two thirds of the total). In terms of value, the majority of foreign direct investment is concentrated in manufacturing (over 60 percent in most countries); services account for approximately 25 percent (except in Hungary, where the share of services is 40 percent).[10]

Apart from the amount of foreign direct investment, the activities of foreign affiliates seem to be of considerable importance for Central and Eastern Europe countries. Although the lack of data on such activities make it difficult to generalize, the experience of Hungary may be instructive. Foreign affiliates of transnational corporations play a particularly significant role in exports, accounting for 16 percent of total nonruble exports.[11] (Another source places that share at about 25 percent.)[12] Although that share may not seem high by the standards of some developing countries,[13] it is substantial given the relatively low level of the stock of foreign direct investment in Hungary. Transnational corporations in some industries (for example, automobiles, where they often hold a dominant position) are significant exporters as part of their overall corporate strategy. In terms of other indicators of significance to the host country in the case of Hungary, transnational corporations account for a smaller share of assets and sales, although again that share may be higher in individual industries, with some evidence suggesting that foreign affiliates are dominant in technology-intensive industries.[14]

While foreign affiliates in Central and Eastern Europe may not account for a large share of domestic activity, their importance in triggering structural changes and sustaining economic transformation may be higher than the data suggest. In this respect, foreign direct investment may also be viewed as a mobilizer of domestic savings and as a catalyst for the utilization of domestic resources. The formation of joint ventures with domestic producers, most of which are small or medium enterprises, provides the opportunity to these producers to access technology, managerial skills, foreign markets, capital funds, and other benefits that would, otherwise, be beyond their reach. At the same time, it is those small and medium enterprises that breed the bulk of local entrepreneurs and to which transnational corporations can introduce significant innovations in business practices.[15] As a result, joint ventures between foreign and domestic producers have had a better record in terms of sales, profits, and hard-currency earnings per employee compared to wholly domestically owned firms.[16] Tungsram, the light bulb manufacturer in Hungary, is one such example, where productivity increases have more than compensated for the reduction in employment and have made possible an overall increase in output.

From another perspective, the contribution of foreign affiliates to economic transformation and restructuring in Central and Eastern Europe may be viewed as the result of their corporate strategies. Specifically, the formation of corporate networks within a single region and the linking of discrete outputs produced in different countries and at different points along the value added chain has important implications for the transformation of the host country. Such networks seem to have formed in automobiles, whereby transnational corporations produce components or assemble cars in Central and Eastern European countries which are either exported to the rest of Europe or are sold domestically. Suzuki's joint venture in Hungary for the assembly of cars, for instance, aims to supply the whole of the European market. General Motors also sees its investments in Poland as consistent with its "Pan-European" strategy.[17] These networks can facilitate the integration of host countries into a regional (or global) corporate network that encompasses marketing and distribution facilities which domestic firms would not otherwise be able to access. In addition, host country firms are exposed to international competition and the gains from trade and efficiency that this can bring about. The predominantly export-oriented nature of these corporate strategies provides a growth stimulus and accelerates the process of transformation.

In the long run, the attractiveness of Central and Eastern Europe countries to foreign investors as low-cost, high-skill producers may decrease, as wages may be expected to rise. For example, in the eastern part of Germany, wages have increased by 60 percent since reunification; this in spite of widespread unemployment.[18] However, since labor costs are becoming less important in the production of goods, higher wages may not necessarily have a dampening effect on foreign direct investment. Moreover, the association of Central and Eastern Europe countries with the European Community will continue to give certain advantages to the former in the eyes of foreign investors from third countries.

As with developing countries, the contribution of transnational corporations to growth and restructuring depends on the extent to which the benefits from foreign direct investment and the other activities of transnational corporations can be absorbed by domestic producers through backward and forward linkages. At the same time, the benefits also depend on the amount of transnational corporation activity which in turn will reflect both the economic conditions within host countries and their progress toward reform.

The speed of implementation of market reforms, economic stabilization plans, privatization schemes, and institutional reforms (accounting, banking and capital markets) will enhance the overall attractiveness of Central and Eastern Europe countries to foreign direct investment. For example, the absence of domestic capital markets hampers the valuation of business assets and has contributed to a low level of acquisitions by transnational corporations. However, structural changes also need to take place at the enterprises level for the transformation to be successful and for foreign direct investment to have a greater impact.

The experiences of developing countries suggest that the larger and more central the contribution of the private sector to the economies of Central and Eastern Europe, the greater the potential for transnational corporations to contribute to economic transformation. Privatization is therefore important in enlarging the scope for contribution by transnational corporations; by one account, the private sector is responsible for one half of total production in Poland and nearly as much for Hungary.[19] Land reform, namely, the ability of foreign investors to buy land, is also necessary for greenfield investment.

The extensive involvement of transnational corporations in the economies of Central and Eastern Europe may also produce adverse impacts. In a pattern reminiscent of responses to transnational corporations in developing countries, in Western Europe and, more recently, in the United States, foreign firms have been accused of monopolizing local markets, raising prices, and offering inferior products.[20] Transnational corporations can take steps to mitigate such criticisms, and many foreign firms have adopted policies to source locally as much as possible, engage in charitable activities in the communities in which they operate, train, and promote local employees.

At the same time, it should be recognized that many transnational corporations, by virtue of their size, technological, financial, and managerial resources, and their global linkages, do have the potential to dominate host country markets. To the extent the presence of transnational fosters a noncompetitive environment, the benefits they bring, such as stimulating domestic suppliers and training local manager, could be offset.

Conclusion

There is a high degree of interdependence, and perhaps even a "catch-22," in the relation between foreign direct investment and the process of economic transformation in Central and Eastern Europe. These countries look to foreign direct investment and the activities of transnational corporations to assist in economic restructuring and economic stimulation, yet at the same time, transnational corporations await this growth and restructuring before expanding their investments in the region.

Clearly, governments can do more. The evidence suggests that there are substantial differences among countries in their ability to absorb the benefits from the operations of transnational corporations. Host economies can improve their ability to work with transnational corporations by working rapidly to achieve a stable macroeconomic environment and speeding the process of privatization and the reform of laws and regulations regarding foreign investment. The entire reform process can be more open and visible to both residents and foreigners. However, the evidence also suggests that a more open legal and policy environment, although necessary to attract transnational corporations, is not always sufficient motivaion.[21] Transnational corporations are primarily attracted by the economic conditions existing within host economies and, here, too, more can be done to encourage investment.

For example, infrastructure development needs to be given a high priority, especially with respect to transportation and the modern communications systems necessary to conduct business in finance and trade and to coordinate production networks. Transnational corporations can contribute, as they possess the technology and experience, but the "public goods" nature of such infrastructure makes a large governmental role important. Similar considerations apply to general education and scientific and technical training.

Perhaps the most important thing governments can do it recognize that transnational corporations, although important, cannot do everything. Transnational corporations can make significant contributions to economic growth and structural change, but the stages upon which they act remain dominated by domestic actors.

Notes

1. Unless otherwise noted, all data referred to in this paper are from Transnational Corporations and Management Division (TCMD), *World Investment Report 1992: Transnational Corporations as Engines of Growth*, United Nations Publication, E.92.II.A.19.

2. See TCMD, especially Part II.

3. TCMD, 246.

4. Chung H. Lee and Eric Ramstetter, "Direct Investment and Structural Change in Korean Manufacturing," in *Direct Foreign Investment in Asia's Developing Economies and Structural Change in the Asia-Pacific Region*, ed., Eric Ramstetter (Boulder, Colorado: Westview Press, 1991), 112.

5. The foreign exchange reserves of Hungary have risen from $800 million in 1990 to more than $4 billion in 1992. See Nicholas Denton, "A Kiss of Life from Across the Border," *Financial Times*, 21 April 1992.

6. TCMD, chapter 5.

7. See Terutomo Ozawa, "The Dynamics of Pacific Rim Industrialization: How Mexico Can Join the Asian Flock of Flying Geese," in *Mexico's External Relations in the 1990s*, ed. M. Risadan Roett (Boulder, Colo. and London: Lynne Rienner, 1991) and United Nations Centre on Transnational Corporations, *Foreign Direct Investment and Industrial Restructuring in Mexico*, United Nations Publication, E.92.II.A.9.

8. Barry Wood, "The Eastern Bloc Two Years Later," *Europe*, no. 314 (March 1992): 12-13.

9. For example, according to press reports many transnational corporations have hesitated to undertake investments in Ukraine due to concerns about the pace of privatization and the country's ability to manage its economy. See Anthony Robinson and Chrystia Freeland, "Ukraine: Nation That Is Building the Apparatus from Scratch," *Financial Times*, 3 July 1992.

10. For a detailed Central and Eastern Europe analysis of regional and sectoral trends in inward foreign direct investment, see Transnational Corporations and Management Division and European Commission for Europe, *World Investment Directory: Central and Eastern Europe* (New York: United Nations).

11. Transnational Corporations and Management Division and Economic Commission for Europe, *World Investment Directory: Central and Eastern Europe* (New York: United Nations).

12. Less Talk, More Action Please," *The Economist*, 16 Feburary 1991, 54.

13. In the secondary sector, that share for Singapore was about 87 percent and for Malaysia about 60 percent. See UNCTC, *World Investment Directory*, vol. 1, *Asia and the Pacific*, United Nations Publication, E.92.II.A.11.

14. Denton.»

15. Catherine L. Mann, "Industry Restructuring in East-Central Europe: The Challenge and the Role for Foreign Investment," *American Economic Review*, 81, no. 2 (May 1991).

16. Denton.

17. "Potential New Market of $420 Million," *Financial Times*, 11 September 1991.

18. "Business in Eastern Europe: Survey," *The Economist*, 21 September 1991.

19. "Eastern Europe: Struggling to Stay on the Reform Track," paper submitted to the Subcommittee on Technology and National Security of the Joint Economic Committee, Congress of the United States, 8 June 1992.

20. Such criticisms have recently surfaced in Hungary. See, for example, Christine Keilhauer, "Why Do Hungarians Fear Western Monopolies?" *Business Eastern Europe*, 27 July 1992.

21. UNCTC, *Government Policies and Foreign Direct Investment*, United Nations Publication, E.91.II.A.20.

Section 6 · Regional Cooperation

Yaman Baskut

The recent failures of the Communist system have attracted more attention than the efforts to overcome the legacy of the old order. Such an attitude helped the West to show, once again, the supremacy of its ideology, and helped the East to motivate its people.

Now it is time to consider how the Central and Eastern European countries and the new republics of the former Soviet Union can succeed in their radical reform programs, while an increasing segment of their populations seems to be unsatisfied and demoralized.

The reform programs of these countries generally embrace measures affecting broad political, economic, and human aspects of daily life. Although there are dramatic changes in many fields, most of the reform programs, particularly those related to transforming past economic structures, may not bring changes to present economic conditions.

Mounting Difficulties

While assessing this phenomenon, several considerations should be taken into account. First of all, there is a set of complex issues that are related more or less to the rapid progress achieved in transition to the market economy. Other concerns are due to the consequences of structural problems inherited from the old regime. These difficulties underline once again the need to avoid taking for granted the degree of flexibility and adaptability of each society.

There are also important issues deriving from the collapse of the old, regional system of economic cooperation, the Council for Mutual Economic Assistance (CMEA). All these issues are accompanied by the resurgence of unhealthy tendencies in many of these countries, such as political instability, lack of social consensus, intolerance, racism, and ethnic rivalry.

In all of these countries, success will very much depend on the political and economic conditions prevailing in each country, especially the response to their new policies, their ability to adapt to the changes required, the democratic maturity of their people, their business mindedness, their level of infrastructure, the hard currency earning capacity of their economy, and so on.

The Need for a New Framework

Accordingly, these countries need a framework that will respond to the needs of macroeconomic stability, institutional framework, structural adjustment, social consensus, and regional and international cooperation. In this respect, the international and regional dimensions of the transition issues are of particular importance. Reform programs cannot achieve their goals within the framework of isolated and narrow national markets. In other words, the inherent difficulties of transition cannot be overcome without creating the necessary environment to ensure the integration of these countries into the international economic system, including the promotion of international cooperation at the global, European, and regional levels. These countries urgently need cooperation schemes for the modernization of their infrastructures, new funds to alleviate their balance-of-payments difficulties, and new markets for their exports and imports. All these necessitate policy changes not only in Eastern countries themselves, but also in other countries, particularly in the Western world.

The current global economic environment, however, is not responsive enough to ensure a successful transition. This is particularly true in terms of trade. It is illusory to expect that these countries may create, in the short or medium run, export industries that will be able to compete in the Western markets.

Furthermore, the sharp fall in intraregional trade among former members of the Council for Mutual Economic Assistance (CMEA) has had a severe negative impact on the economy of these countries. CMEA was an ill-conceived trade and payment system. It was conducted on a "government to government" basis, without taking into consideration the links between domestic and foreign prices. This led most of the enterprises far out of line with international standards and removed incentives to upgrade the quality of the production. It is through this system that these countries managed to export their low-quality and often obsolete products to each other, particularly to the former Soviet Union. Also, the prices of energy and raw materials imported under this arrangement were inconsistent with world prices. Accordingly, the collapse of the intra-CMEA trade had a considerable negative impact on them. This collapse pushed these countries to offset their loss by diverting their trade to other countries. The necessity to pay world prices for energy and raw materials was also conducive to this process.

Although this transformation had some positive impact on the capacity of the enterprises of the Eastern and Central European countries, the actual increases in their exports have so far been behind expectations. Consequently, the reforming countries must now move toward greater integration with Western economies, in conjunction with efforts to form new subregional agreements to be built on the ruins of CMEA.

The proposals that have been developed since 1992 to restart trade agreements among former CMEA countries seem to be politically unattractive, since these countries are establishing greater independence from one another. The innovative project of Black Sea Economic Cooperation has sought to overcome present difficulties. The summit declaration, signed in Istanbul on 25 June 1992 by eleven heads of states, constitutes the basic framework for regional cooperation. This initiative responds to the real needs of the countries of the region. Indeed, the member countries, while acknowledging the role of governments in creating favorable parameters of cooperation, recognize that business partners are of primary importance for accelerating the pace of fruitful cooperation.

Consequently, one may speak of two interlinked windows of cooperation. The first concerns "intergovernmental cooperation," in which governments will play the main role in identifying and developing projects, particularly in the areas of transport, telecommunications, statistics, standardization and certification of projects, energy, and the environment. The second window is related to "nongovernmental cooperation," which will be guided by the inner dynamic of the individual and collective initiatives of the enterprises directly concerned. They include measures to improve the business environment, such as the prompt entry and free movement of businesspeople; the expansion of mutual trade in goods and services; more appropriate conditions for capital flows; and different forms of industrial cooperation. Within this framework, the establishment of a Black Sea Foreign Trade and Investment Bank is envisaged to facilitate the whole cooperation scheme.

Some view this cooperation scheme as only a fantasy at a time when there is a growing revival of traditional nationalistic and ethnic tensions in the region. In addition, the potential economic benefits may be limited, as member countries have had great difficulty overcoming the low degree of openness they have displayed in the past.

However, such evaluations are based on a static approach, which only takes into account the old production design and the limited trade volume among the member states. With a dynamic process, the benefits could be substantial. It can improve trade access and increased economic integration to be carried out under the conditions of a market environment.

First, the Black Sea Economic Area, including most of the Balkan countries, potentially enjoys a large market composed of more than 320 million people with changing consumption patterns and strong aspirations for Western living standards. Second, the present endowment with production factors, as well as their possible dynamics in the future, show an important potential for complementary exchanges and corresponding production within the region. Human and material resources of member countries—the comparatively cheap and abundant labor force, the existence of energy and raw materials, and the already-diversified structure of their economies—should be taken into account. Third, the advantages arising from geographical proximity are considerable. Many goods and services which have been produced so far for only internal markets can now be produced for the regional market. This process may lead to economies of scale. Fourth, this multilateral cooperation based on the rule of market economy and accompanied by multilateral guarantees may encourage the supply of external private and official capital throughout the region. At the early phase, infrastructural projects designed for the whole region will probably be found more attractive by investors from abroad.

Finally, the Black Sea Economic Cooperation project can help member countries to realize a higher degree of integration into the world economy. Their economic growth, achieved through improved efficiency and increased flows of trade, capital, and investments, could certainly accelerate interaction with other countries or economic groupings, such as the European Community. The area's strategic location is a further benefit, situated at the crossroads of Europe, Western Asia, the Middle East, and North Africa.

Despite all these advantages, it will not be easy to quickly develop comprehensive cooperation among the countries of the Black Sea area. They still face the daunting tasks of building market institutions and stabilizing their economies. Their success or failure will depend on resource allocation and factor mobility, as well as on the degree to which public opinion can be motivated towards these changes. Accordingly the whole process will take time. That is why the Black Sea Economic Cooperation initiative is based on a "step-by-step" approach. As a first step, priority areas have been determined, such as development of transport and communications networks, cooperation in the financial and banking sectors, as well as in trade, investment, and the environment.

Conclusion

The success of the Black Sea Economic Cooperation initiative depends on a complex interplay of internal and regional efforts to overcome not only economic obstacles, but also political ones. These efforts have to be guided by the maturity and tolerance of the peoples and their willingness to respond to the needs of domestic, regional, and global challenges.

Political will is important to motivate regional economic cooperation. Similarly, the strengthening of economic relations within the region may have considerable impact on solving several existing political differences. Consequently, the present internal and external difficulties should be not considered by the member countries as obstacles hampering the Black Sea Economic Cooperation initiative. The sooner they can realize its application, the better they can overcome their many domestic and intraregional economic and political problems.

Section 7 · The Contribution of Private Citizens

David Bryer

The October Revolution ushered in three quarters of a century of competition between the economic philosophies in the capitalist and Communist worlds. Now we have a broad consensus, globally and in Russia, that Soviet-style economies must give way to some form of market, and that their societies should become civil and plural.

Russia's transition towards these twin objectives, economic and sociopolitical, has made possible a peaceful explosion of nongovernmental life, which remains, like the transition itself, exciting in its rapid progress and difficult to predict in its future pace. OXFAM, United Kingdom and Ireland, has been assessing this nongovernmental activity in Russia, and this section arises from this experience.

Free Responses to Social and Human Needs

Genuinely independent social activity lies at the heart of any civil society, providing the mechanism through which the individual can freely express and put into effect his or her varied responses to social and human needs. This does not just include organizations providing physical services, but trade unions, churches, and any groups advocating the views of differing values and interests. Yet organizations complementing the governmental role in social provision are crucial, since no state in a planned or market economy has so far succeeded in supplying satisfactory provision by itself.

Equally, adequate social provision without the state as direct provider and guarantor of satisfactory private standards is unrealistic. Independent organizations complementing government can provide a moderate model distinct from the more extreme repulsion from any state activity.

This role for the nongovernmental sector is perhaps more necessary than ever in a period of economic transition when significant numbers of people are suffering the traumatic consequences of change before any material benefits arise. For example, Russia's inflation of approximately 150 percent per annum has reduced access to food and other necessities for many vulnerable groups, and future reforms are likely to result in unprecedented unemployment and consequent poverty.

There are not only comparatively short-term humanitarian reasons for acting to relieve this suffering. As the parallels with Weimar Germany, repeatedly referred to in today's Russia, warn us, the twin transitions to a market economy and a plural society could be overturned by poverty feeding a demand for authoritarian nationalist or Communist power. Russia has not necessarily experienced its last revolution of this century.

Local nongovernmental organizations in Russia have a greater role to play in addressing this poverty because of the declining capacity of the state to do so, and the concentration of past and prospective official external support upon the process of economic transition, and not on its human dimensions. Unfortunately, however, the country's independent organizations are still so new that it would be easy to exaggerate their capacity to fill this role. It is one of the ironies of the twin transitions from state socialism that its inheritance has been the need for nongovernmental action without the necessary culture to support it.

The Emergence of Nongovernmental Organizations

With few exceptions, mainly in human rights and the environment, independent organizations have themselves been a response to the "transition" that began in the Soviet Union in the middle 1980s. There is a problem of definition of what did, and in fact still does constitute a nongovernmental organization in a country in transition from a socialist economy, such as in Russia. But the public view is clearly that the host of apparently autonomous funds, committees, and trade unions which essentially existed within the state-party structure were part of the unitary political system.

As genuinely independent groups emerged in the last five years, the state established more social funds. Along with their older counterparts, these have now suffered the end of their funding from state or quasi-state bodies, and are being forced into some form of independence at least from the present state. Some will certainly survive, but the public suspicion of the old Communist bureaucrats means that many will probably fail to find a new nongovernmental role and founder on the rocks of transition.

The earlier period of transition in the late 1980s did however make possible the emergence of genuinely independent groups both by stimulating the social need for them and by allowing them to develop.

The Soviet system had not just been a command economy, but in many ways a command system of both information and power flowing vertically downwards through the state-party structure, and not spreading horizontally outside it. What is called *glasnost* changed that, permitting horizontal information to flow independently, so that news spread first of human needs which had always existed, of people with disabilities for instance, and then of independent initiatives being taken by others. When the seminal group *Miloserdia* (meaning "charity" in English) was founded around the writer Daniel Granin in Leningrad in 1988, the same name was taken up by other groups in different towns.

Glasnost was about a greater tolerance of action as well as a comparative openness of opinion. What was not forbidden became permitted, and though most nongovernmental organizations choose to register with the Ministry of Justice or municipal authorities, others do not.

As the decade drew to a close, the more open information began to expose the new needs that *perestroika*, the first stage of economic transition as it will be seen historically, was ironically creating. Economic decline broke the unwritten social contract that had been agreed between the Soviet state and the individual: that the former would provide, if not very well, and that the latter would work, though with low productivity and high underemployment, and would restrain her or his actions within the state-party structure. Economic decline meant that the state was breaking its side of the contract, and with the greater tolerance the individual was freer to join with others in nongovernmental responses to the increased needs.

1988 was the first year of a significant number of independent groups, and since then all the trends that stimulated and allowed them have accelerated increasingly rapidly.

There are now thousands of nongovernmental organizations within Russia, most of them with missions either born out of the economic transition or with longer-term aims that have been made far more acute by the current economic changes. Groups of people with disabilities, or their parents, appear to be the most common type of mutual assistance group, facing deeply-established official and popular lack of support. Their poverty is now being exacerbated by the falling real value of pensions and the unequal ability to take advantage of the new coping mechanisms to obtain adequate food, such as secondary employment and selling goods on the street.

The developments in the four years since 1988, and the rate of emergence of new groups now, are impressive, but their impact in responding to the immediate relief consequences of transition is inhibited. The coordination of groups delivering supplies of food, medicines, and clothes to vulnerable people is largely poor, a reflection of a broader lack of cooperation, often even contact. Most organizations follow a strategy based upon obtaining and distributing Western privately donated supplies, with some having the ambition of receiving official relief aid as well. Only a small number of groups choose to use locally purchased food, believing it is more cost-effective, more accurately responds to the basic problem of access to available but expensive food, and less obviously dependent on Western donors.

The Role of Values

Without undervaluing what is being done, it is an irony that there appears still to be a lack of sufficient horizontal contact between groups and a priority given to a vertical relationship with Western donors. The threats to nongovernmental action in Russia come from values, and in some cases the interests that they reflect, which remain from the Soviet period. The value system itself is in transition as well, but not as rapidly as the economy, and not fast enough to allow sufficient independent response to the economic changes. There are three main values that are necessary.

The first is pluralism, fundamental to a civil society, but which has developed in Russia far more slowly than the related ideas that there should be commercial and social activity independent of the state, and that there should be "democracy" in the rather limited sense of free elections. This is hardly surprising given that the democratic centralism avowed by the Communist Party of the

Soviet Union (CPSU) maintained at least the image of electoral politics while plural views were suppressed and the pluralism of bourgeois democracy was despised.

Within the nongovernmental sector in Russia, the comparative weakness of the value of pluralism results in some attempts to dominate local independent activity and a considerable amount of distrust between groups fearful of this. Consequent of this is the relative lack of networking among groups, though there seems to be more among organizations concerned with some issues than others. Most noticeably, environmentally-related groups appear to be most closely linked in Russia, though not to the extent that they are in either Ukraine or Belarus where the effect of the 1986 Chernobyl disaster has accelerated the development of comparatively strong national networks, as well as making the environment the most important issue for independent organizations. Though Russia did receive some of the fallout from the disaster, its widespread environmental problems of industrial and agricultural pollution and nuclear safety, are less focused and therefore have not yet energized activity in the same way. Externally to the nongovernmental sector, there remains suspicion of independent action among the old believers in the state's monopolistic competence.

The second value that is developing is independence, which nongovernmental organizations have asserted, by definition, from the state, but not always either internally or from other institutions. Within many groups, there remains a dominant individual or small collection of individuals, and many organizations are structured hierarchically reminiscent of the CPSU. In some cases, these dominant individuals have in fact moved from positions within the Communist Party to these organizations, as they have into private business.

Particularly but not exclusively among people with disabilities, mutual assistance groups have emerged, but most independent organizations operate as philanthropic bodies, reflecting a view of the growing numbers of poor people as dependent on top-down assistance, and in some cases articulated as a suspicion of a poor individual's ability to act collectively rather than selfishly. As the mutual assistance groups show, this suspicion is wrong. It is the more elitist end of the belief that condemns the Soviet period as an ethical disaster which aimed to create a moral *homus sovieticus,* but instead produced the egocentric monster in Bulgakov's *Heart of a Dog.*

It is no coincidence that there is great interest in the research into and emulation of pre-Bolshevik examples of paternalistic philanthropy. It is also unsurprising that much activity is concentrated in the immediate relief of shortages of food, clothes, and medicines, and less on longer-term responses to transition. Dependency is a value which is reflected in both directions, and many such organizations are also those which concentrate upon receiving material donations from private Western donors to act as their distributors, hence acting as the intermediary in a vertical chain, typically of food parcels, from the West to a Russian philanthropic group and onto local beneficiaries.

The belief that the practice of state socialism encouraged a self-seeking individualism is the third value influencing the development of nongovernmental activity. The argument, propounded quite commonly by members of the intelligentsia, asserts that the mechanism of obtaining goods through individual contacts in the party, factory, or farm led people to act as individuals, not as members of groups. Combined with a comparative lack of opportunity to do genuinely voluntary action, this resulted in the supposedly egalitarian social system engineering a lack of concern for others.

This view is used to explain various things: the comparative lack of voluntary activity, though this has often been exaggerated; and the still widespread use of independent social organizations by unscrupulous commercial enterprises. Though this is very different from genuine organizations raising funds through commercial activities, the first has given a bad public image to some of the latter, and popular support for nongovernmental groups has probably declined in the past four years; the interest in them from the Russian media certainly has.

Beyond values, transition itself and the economic decline that precipitated it are providing obstacles as well as demands for nongovernmental activity. State, corporate, and individual wealth has never been donated in substantial quantities to genuinely independent work, but the amounts that were given seem to have declined, reinforcing the conviction among nongovernmental organizations that they must depend upon their own local commercial activity or foreign funding.

As Russia's independent groups struggle with the challenge and difficulties posed by economic transition, their trends and debates reflect wider societal responses to current change. Many organizations combine independent social work with the promotion of entrepreneurial culture, viewing both as the repulsion from Communist dependency upon the state. They share Mr. Gaidar's dependence upon capitalism and, in many cases, Western capital. Some in Russia aspire to a society in which nongovernmental organizations have the dominant role in social provision.

At their most extreme, which is not uncommon, these views express a belief that they have seen the future and it works. That future is North America and Western Europe, and most have seen it on television. It does not often include the homeless of New York or London, which some Russian nongovernmental activists learn of with incredulity.

Conclusion

The transition to a market economy, democracy, and civil society will be more secure if the aspirations are appropriate, and the view of the West is more accurate than a simplified reversal of the previous Soviet propaganda. Many of us, including nongovernmental organizations from the West can play a role in this, as we can in presenting the difficulties, the tensions, as well as the achievements that we experience in our own societies.

In this we can perhaps play a modest part in the development of those values that will lie as a foundation for Russia's civil society. Engagement between nongovernmental organizations in Russia and outside can offer plural models of independent social involvement beyond those of a sanitized view of the West or a nostalgic picture of pre-Communist Russia. We have learnt that the value of nongovernmental life is in its diversity and pluralism.

Engagement can offer experience of how we, as organizations, remain independent, not least in raising our funds. In our own assessment in Russia this year, all these needs have been identified by local organizations; but perhaps the one most often called for is support in exploring fundraising strategies within Russia. One response to this is our contact with groups wishing to sell donated clothes in a way that has helped to fund our own work now for 45 years.

Finally, and crucially, engagement between nongovernmental bodies can show that across the globe poor people themselves have gathered together to solve their poverty. In Russia, that process is still near its beginning. Yet as groups move from idealism to achievement, their pace is still slowed by the values of the past that have failed. The contribution of external organizations can only be limited, but this engagement can provide support as nongovernmental organizations meet the challenges that transition poses.

Chapter 3 · The Learning Curve

Section 1 · Russia's Uncertain Prospects[1]

Oleg T. Bogomolov

Russia has been saddled with extremely difficult economic problems while being mired in bitter debates over the chosen path to a market economy. The population understands the need for market and democratic transformations, but is divided in its opinion of government actions. The president and the cabinet of ministers have demonstrated their resolution in carrying out market reforms, but the results of the measures, such as price liberalization, have so far failed to meet expectations. The public increasingly feels that it is again being subjected to a very risky experiment and that the road taken at the beginning was wrong. Under the pressure of criticism, the government has had to recognize the need of correcting its policies, but it has not analyzed the progress of reforms.

The decline of production and the drop of the standard of living in Russia over the past 25 years will likely surpass the years of the Great Depression of the 1930s. In 1990, the gross domestic product (GDP) of Russia dropped by about 5 percent compared to the previous year. In 1991 it dropped by 10 percent and was anticipated in 1992 to decrease 30 percent.[2]

World Bank experts do not expect any growth of the output of foodstuffs in Russia in 1992-93, although weather conditions will probably be more favorable than in 1991, when the yield of grain dropped by 25 percent. Some government experts anticipated a further decrease of agricultural output by 10-20 percent in 1992.

The national standard of living declines faster than production output decreases. As compared to January 1991, retail trade has decreased in constant prices by nearly a factor of two, and real incomes may have dropped even more. In large cities, the cost of living increased at least 20-25 times while wages increased only 7-8 times.[3]

Usual proportions in incomes of individual population groups have become distorted. Retired persons, students, doctors, teachers, researchers, and culture workers have suffered the greatest decline. Disparity in income levels has increased; many people will face poverty and starvation after their reserves of food and money run out. Today, a rank-and-file citizen cannot afford an apartment, car, refrigerator, television set, or vacation as the threat of mass unemployment becomes quite real. People try to adapt to the new conditions: they save money wherever possible, do market-gardening, and often leave the state enterprises where they were employed for trade and service sector positions where they can earn more money.[4] Theft and economic abuses have reached unprecedented proportions and discipline at state enterprises is falling noticeably.

The Causes of Failures

Questions naturally arise, what are the reasons of such an ominous course of developments and was it inevitable? and Why, despite all the good intentions of Gorbachev and Yeltsin, does the economy remain in its state of free fall? Usually, the following explanations are given.

First of all, Russia has inherited many difficult problems from the totalitarian system. These include the chronic backwardness of agriculture, a lopsided development of the military-industrial complex and heavy industries to the detriment of the consumer sector, technological backwardness of many branches of the economy, its considerable isolation from foreign markets, excessive concentration and nonrational deployment of production, and the underdevelopment of economic infrastructure. Second, during the years of *perestroika* the economy suffered heavy losses due to the Chernobyl disaster, a drop of prices of exported fuel and energy, rapid disintegration of the Soviet Union, and the rupture of the existing contractual links between enterprises. A third reason is that the economy went wrong because hasty destruction of the administrative system went too far and there were no new market mechanisms to serve as buffers. A hesitant attitude toward transition to a market economy is one of the main reproaches leveled at Gorbachev and his policy of *perestroika.*

All of the above reasons are true, but do not sufficiently explain the incipient catastrophe. The economic difficulties that had been accumulating for decades snowballed into a real avalanche as a result of unforgivable mistakes and miscalculations in politics that were made under both Gorbachev and Yeltsin.

An attempt to boost economic growth, the generous increase of government spending for various social needs, the anti-alcohol campaign accompanied by a drop in budget revenues, the debts of collective and state farms that were just written off—all this had weakened the financial system of the Soviet Union. The struggle of Russia and other republics for independence and their refusal to fulfill the financial obligations to central authorities finally undermined it. Having proclaimed the transition to a market economy, Gorbachev, by carrying out his inflationary policy, was methodically destroying the consumer market that had functioned within the administrative system framework.

Price Controls

Hamstrung by price controls, the inflation did not disappear. It instead revealed itself in the empty shelves of shops, which reduced relations between enterprises to barter deals. Financial revenue was no longer an incentive to develop production. By giving in to the pressure of the military-industrial complex and rejecting the idea of the formation of an economic community of the republics with a joint mechanism to regulate money circulation and finances, Gorbachev lost the final chance to save the economy of what was ceasing to be the Soviet Union.

After the failure of a military coup and disintegration of the Soviet Union, the task of stabilizing the economic situation in Russia and other republics became even more complicated. Tough measures were required to prevent a complete collapse. Yeltsin, without a detailed plan of market transformations, decided to go ahead with them without waiting for accords with other republics on policy coordination. From the very beginning, this generated uncertainty in the plans of stabilizing the monetary system, since it was unknown whether the ruble zone would remain unchanged or it would shrink to the territorial limits of Russia. Moreover, financial and credit policies of the other republics—those which would prefer to remain in the ruble zone—were unclear. It was not known if they would accept the austerity policy of rigid restrictions and agree to Russia's control over their monetary and financial policies. The intention of Ukraine, the Baltic states and, probably, of other republics to introduce their own currencies resulted in a massive flow of rubles into Russia and outflow of goods from it. This development affected the choice of priority targets.

Among the standard measures for making the transition from a command economy to a market economy (privatization, demonopolization, liberalization of prices and foreign trade, elimination of the budget deficit, reform of the fiscal system, demilitarization, and restructuring), preference was given to releasing from control (from the beginning of 1992) 95 percent of all prices and wages at enterprises. At the same time, budget spending was significantly curtailed and taxes increased in order to balance the budget within a few months. These steps were to be followed immediately by reforms of the ownership relations and by other necessary transformations. They have been initiated, but their implementation requires years rather than months.

Shock Therapy

The government tried to achieve macroeconomic stabilization by means of "shock therapy." The idea was to ride the crest of popular enthusiasm and hopeful anticipation immediately following the *putsch* in order to undertake measures that would result in a deteriorating standard of living. That is why the first steps of the reform were hasty, and there were no comprehensive discussions of intended measures with experts. The plan was to go ahead with price liberalization reform, and then to make necessary corrections along the way. The result was unstable legal codes that hindered the development of private business.

The government thought that after a once-only price explosion (with prices approximately tripling) an abrupt deceleration of their growth would occur under the influence of a reduced demand, and then prices would start to fall. A relatively rapid (approximately two or three months) restoration of equilibrium at the consumer market and its saturation with goods was expected. A revival of production was forecast which was explained by the emergence of market incentives. It was also assumed that the stabilization of the economy would initially require a reduction of the living standard by not more than 33 percent. It was promised that things would straighten themselves out and people would be better off by the end of the year.

Reality, unfortunately, disproved these calculations, making the country's leadership face new, unforeseen problems. The total price rise turned out to be several times higher than the forecasts, and the prices, with their two-digit monthly growth rates, continue to rise. Their new steep rise is occurring under the influence of gradual liberalization of prices for energy. The living standard has fallen by at least two times, resulting in strikes. The total sum of overdue accounts unpaid by enterprises has surpassed all conceivable limits and continues to grow. As a result, production is paralyzed and declining rapidly. Under the conditions of spiraling inflation and shortages in the money market, investments into new construction and equipment renovation are being phased out. Due to the unfavorable dynamics of relative prices, which are set for agricultural and agriculture-related products, the incentives needed for the development of this sector of the economy are being lost. In May 1992, average monthly wholesale prices rose by 17 times compared to December 1991 and capital investments during the first six months, compared to the corresponding period of previous year, were halved.[5] During the corresponding period, prices for agricultural products went up 5.4 times, while the prices for resources (machinery, fertilizers, fuel) increased 10 times.

A sharp price rise, occuring against the background of a backward banking infrastructure, is accompanied by a slackening of money circulation and a growing shortage of cash. The shortage of paper money continues even though the printing presses are already running at full capacity and the government continues to increase the denomination of bills. Social tensions have resulted from repeated failures to deliver wages and salaries on payday, with delays that last sometimes up to two or three months. By the beginning of the second half of 1992, the total sum of overdue debts of enterprises reached 2,000 billion rubles, and the total sum of unpaid wages, salaries, and pensions amounted to 220 billion rubles.

The weakening of control over foreign trade, which occurs because of the unreasonably low exchange rate for the ruble and a stampede from the depreciating national currency, has resulted in an outflow of raw materials and energy resources, further damaging the Russian economy. A considerable portion of hard currency earnings (about $1 billion per month, according to estimates by Western experts) is concealed and retained abroad, since the monetary and taxation policies of the state make it unprofitable or even impossible to use such earnings for importing many kinds of equipment, materials, pharmaceuticals, and foodstuffs, with the exception of some marginal items such as computers, alcohol, cars, and some items of foodstuffs, clothing, and footwear.

In short, the Russian economy's response to the price and salary liberalization was not a textbook approach to a market economy. The state enterprises showed almost no response to market signals. When there is no competition, such enterprises have no worries; they are concerned neither with cutting their production costs nor increasing the quality of their products. They solve all their problems through price increases, especially since they are free to set their own prices. In spite of the delays in payments for products purchased by their customers and overdue payments for materials and component supplies, such enterprises continue to produce, hoping that ultimately the government will settle the payments crisis that resulted mainly from government policies.

The Impact of Reforms

The authors of reforms appeal to everyone to be patient, and insist that tough measures of taxation, money issuing, and budget policies must continue. They are confident that the market mechanisms of self-adjustment will sooner or later result in an economic revival. But will society be content with the continuing decline of production and standard of living for one or two more years? Will it agree with the principle that the economic collapse we are witnessing now is to be rectified without active interference from the state in the formation of a market infrastructure, creation of incentives to boost production, and support of farmers and private entrepreneurs? Will it acquiesce in the unheard-of redistribution of wealth that is occurring now as a result of poorly planned market experiments?

So far, one can only say that the attempt to apply "shock therapy" in Russia (following Poland's example and recommendations of the International Monetary Fund and some Western experts) was extremely painful. But will it be a healing remedy? According to the evidence obtained from sociological polls conducted among Russian populations, as well as according to the opinions expressed by many experts both in Russia and in the West, doubts prevail even though some hope remains.

Market mechanisms and market psychology are beginning to improve, although in very uncivilized, sometimes even distorted, forms. The sector of private entrepreneurship in trade, banking, services, and to a lesser extent in industry and transport, is steadily growing. Initial steps have been made in privatization, beginning with small-scale and medium-scale enterprises and apartments. A noticeable stratum of energetic and enterprising people has appeared. The number of family farms is also growing and their share of the market has already reached 3-4 percent. However, the land is still not owned by the farmers—it is leased to them (in many cases, it is a life lease with inheritance rights) and many collective and state farms are being gradually transformed into genuine cooperatives. Cuts in military expenditures and state subsidies have forced enterprises to shift their operations to the civilian sector of the economy. Despite restrictions, trade for freely convertible currency within the country is expanding. It is this market, where hard currency is circulating and world prices are used, which serves as a certain point of reference in carrying out reforms. Enterprises with participation of foreign capital or even fully-controlled by foreign owners are being established in the territory of Russia. Even though numerous bureaucratic and tax obstacles to foreign investors have not yet been removed, the changes that are being made are changes in the right direction. The admission of Russia into the IMF and the World Bank, as well as the readiness of the West to offer credits through these institutions can accelerate and facilitate the development of the market economy in Russia.

Domestic threats to the transformations that are now underway are still very serious. These threats result not only from political instability, a continuing decline of production and standard of living, and separatist trends in certain regions, but also from the lack of a clear and comprehensive strategy of transition to the market, which would take into consideration the specific nature of Russian conditions. These conditions include its vast and ethnically inhomogeneous economic space, the militarization and monopolization of its economy, deeply rooted command and administrative habits, a lasting legacy of the collectivization of Russia's agriculture, the popularity of the antiproprietorial, egalitarian psychology, and so on. This is probably why monetaristic prescriptions do not give expected resulted here.

The catastrophic nature of the situation excuses today the use of any corrective measures, including the measures of administrative control to invigorate production, combat inflation, and curb economic crime. Policies to stabilize finances, liberalize prices, and conduct foreign trade without state control should be implemented with a view to creating additional incentives for production, and should not be used as demolition tools. Market regulators should be activated gradually, as the state establishes various market institutions and a competitive environment. These are the main points of criticism leveled at today's "shock" variant of transition to the market.

The Prerequisites for Change

The economy can be revived if the attitude of people towards work is changed. In order to ensure appropriate motivation in their behavior, effective material incentives are needed: decent wages in sound money and the transformation of numerous lumpen classes into owners. The curtailment of the population's consumption has reached a critical level beyond which patience can be exhausted and disturbances may erupt. Money cannot be resuscitated by fiscal measures only. The healing also requires an expanded supply of goods in the market place, and new ways of encouraging entrepreneurial activity. Privatization of state property becomes of primary importance here, but too much time was lost in its implementation. The resistance to privatization by obsolete structures has not been suppressed yet, as evidenced by the parliament's failure to pass land privatization legislature.

State property (land, forests, natural resources, enterprises, buildings, and facilities, among others) assessed at market prices and in hard currency could become an anchor ensuring the stability of the monetary and credit systems, provided, of course, that a considerable portion of this property could become tradable on the market. One of the main drawbacks of the approved privatization program is that not only does it not envisage the mechanism by which the real cost of state property could be determined, but it does not view privatization as a factor conducive to generating economically sound money.

Under Russian conditions, it is only small-scale enterprises that can be privatized by selling. People whose incomes were intentionally kept by the government at such a level as to prevent large savings cannot buy out even a minor portion of state property. The price hike deprived people of even these limited savings. Moreover, the population is puzzled by the offer to buy out property from the state, since this property has always been declared the property of the nation as a whole, with every citizen theoretically its co-owner.

For this reason, in Russia and in some other successor states of the USSR, every citizen is granted a certificate (voucher) credited with a certain amount of money. It is yet unclear what portion of the total cost of state property is to be covered by vouchers; in all probability, it will be a very small portion, less than 10 percent.

Privatization of state property will be carried out not only through buyouts and by granting vouchers, but also in the form of direct free-of-charge property transfer, such as urban apartments and perhaps in the future, arable land. Foreign companies and foreign nations are also gaining extensive rights to buy or lease real estate.

If reasonable and socially equitable methods are used to carry out privatization, then privatization is theoretically capable of strengthening the market and the monetary system by increasing the supply of goods to the market and by transferring property to a large social stratum of owners. Its social function is the formation of a middle class that would be interested in promoting market relations, building up production, and accumulating property.

Unfortunately, however, privatization in formerly totalitarian societies often assumes distorted forms. Former nomenclatura finds it easy to get a piece of the state property pie, feeling that the strength of property is much greater than that of political power; thus former nomenclatura takes property in exchange for that elusive political power which runs away like sand through its fingers. Privatization-by-nomenclatura, if it becomes a large-scale development, can cause social conflicts and slow down the process of democratization.

If a more radical (compared to what has been done so far) reform of agrarian relations is carried out, along with elimination of the feudal system of obligatory deliveries of agricultural produce to the state, then a relatively rapid improvement of the situation in agriculture can be expected. The land given forever to collective and state farms, becoming their eternal property to be used by them free-of-charge, should be returned and should become the property of state authorities, whereafter it could be redeemed or leased to the former or new owners. Artificial barriers in the way of the development of private farms should be removed. The farms should be given support by the state, and the manufacture of the machinery, fertilizers, and materials they need should be organized.

Corrective measures in the policy of reforms are needed to arouse the interest of producers in increasing investment into production, thereby helping the new entrepreneurs. Tough deflationary policies and high taxes deprive producers of incentives, to say nothing about reducing the solvent demand for their products. High taxes put a stranglehold on production, especially on newly created private enterprises. Under the burden of such taxes, the entrepreneurs bypass fiscal obligations to make fast money and quit, rather than develop production efficiency. The only reliable way to increase tax revenues is to create such fiscal conditions under which it would be profitable for producers to increase output and to invest in improving production efficiency and competitiveness. It is in this direction that a revision of government policies can be expected.

Prevention of the further impoverishment of the people has become an urgent task. The government must develop and implement an effective income distribution policy that will suppress dangerous conflicts and protect vulnerable population groups.

Currency and Trade Reforms

Since the chances that the ruble will soon be economically sound are slim and considering that various convertible currencies are more and more extensively used within the country, there is growing support for the idea of having a private credit institution jointly issue a parallel currency with a prestigious Western bank. The currency would from the very beginning have good commodity and hard currency backing and would be convertible. Starting with a limited sphere of circulation, this currency gradually could replace the devalued ruble. Emergence of economically sound money would speed up the establishment of market relations.

The reforms now underway in Russia contribute to overcoming its isolation from the world economy and open up new promising markets for international trade. However, there still remain many bureaucratic obstacles hindering business cooperation with the West. These obstacles are connected with the procedures of obtaining export and import licenses, customs tariffs and regulations, supply of raw materials and components to joint ventures, taxation and banking rules, and deficiencies and instability of the legislation. But the main thing is that in Russia and in other successor states, there is no market environment with a convertible currency. This is the most serious barrier from integration into the world economy.

The government's intention to make the ruble convertible for current transactions already by June 1993 seems too good to be true. It is very difficult to restore confidence in the ruble and to encourage people and enterprises to keep their savings in the national currency and not in hard currencies. Would the government, by way of hard currency interventions, be able to support such an exchange rate of the ruble (taking into account the chronic balance of payments deficit) which would not be as prohibitive as to exclude the import of many needed goods? Would the stabilization fund be sufficient to achieve the desired objectives and on what terms could it be used? It is still difficult to give a positive answer to these questions.

Transnational corporations have become one of the principle motive forces in the process of globalization of economic life. In many respects, the former Soviet Union fenced itself off from participation in world economic affairs by prohibiting both the establishment in its territory of affiliates of Western transnationals and the formation of similar enterprises of its own, which would have capital investments abroad. At present, this mistake in economic strategy is being gradually corrected. Russia sees its future in the active involvement of its economy both in all-European cooperation and in the world community.

Conclusion

The future of Russian economy is still uncertain. However, hope springs from the fact that in Russia there are large numbers of well-educated and enterprising people and influential political forces coming forward in support of a market economy and democratic transformations. There are also abundant natural resources and the enormous industrial potential of the country, and finally, there is the support of the reform policy pledged by the leading Western nations.

Notes

1. Prepared for the conference on "Institutional Economies and the Transition to a Market Economy in Russia," University of Wisconsin at Madison, 8-9 October 1992.

2. According to official statistics, during the first six months of 1992, the national income of Russia dropped by 17 percent compared to the corresponding period of the pervious year. These figures, however, are difficult to trust. Suffice it to recall that in those sectors of the economy where the predominant part of the national income is produced (agriculture, food and light industries, military and industrial complex), the decline, even judged from estimates based on official data, was considerably greater. For example, food production dropped by 23 percent, and similar indicators were registered in the manufacture of footwear, textiles, and clothing. Statistical data for Moscow show a 25 percent decline of industrial output.

3. In large cities, retail prices for bread, milk, butter, sausage, and cheese rose by 50 to 100 times during this period.

4. A sociological population poll, which was conducted in Moscow at the end of July 1992, has indicated that residents of the city try to adapt to the declining level of their incomes and to the high cost of living by cutting down on the number of consumer goods they buy (54 percent of respondents), by saving on foodstuffs the eat (38 percent), and by selling their person property and belongings (6 percent). According to the data published by the State Committee for Statistics of Russia, the total volume of footwear and clothing sold to the population during the first half of 1992 decreased by 2 to 2.5 times compared to the corresponding period of the pervious year.

5. A sociological population poll, which was conducted in Moscow at the end of July 1992, has indicated that residents of the city try to adapt to the declining level of their incomes and to the high cost of living by cutting down on the number of consumer goods they buy (54 percent of respondents), by saving on foodstuffs the eat (38 percent), and by selling their person property and belongings (6 percent). According to the data published by the State Committee for Statistics of Russia, the total volume of footwear and clothing sold to the population during the first half of 1992 decreased by 2 to 2.5 times compared to the corresponding period of the pervious year.

Section 2 · Transition in Ukraine

Anatoli Zlenko

The entire region of Central and Eastern Europe and the independent states of the former Soviet Union are passing through a period of deep and qualitative changes. These transformations have led to a serious rethinking of many political determinations that, until quite recently, seemed to be unshakable. But, unfortunately, the peculiarity of the transitional period is such that it promotes a collision of ideals in the newly imagined model.

Changes in the destinies of many nations during the last decade of this century have not always been simple and painless. As this book provides a comprehensive analysis of ongoing changes and some thoughts on solutions for their success, it may be interesting to consider the following, taking Ukraine as an example.

Market Orientation and Democratization

At present, some politicians and scholars are advising countries, such as Ukraine, which are turning to market economies, to take into account the French, Swiss, U.S., and other models of national economy of the Western developed nations. They believe that Ukraine's experience in carrying out the restructuring process may contribute to the common knowledge in this field.

Parallel to the process of global integration of transition countries, people are expressing their natural aspiration to acquire their own full-fledged statehood, and to live and vote freely in their native land. Having recently celebrated the first anniversary of its survival and victory of democracy over totalitarianism, Ukraine has entered a new era of freedom, democracy, and development.

To consider the speedy disintegration of the USSR as a spontaneous phenomenon would be a mistake. This event was sure to happen regardless of the wishes of some individuals or political parties, because it was connected with the dramatic accumulation of contradictions in the social, economic, cultural, and national heritages of the people who inhabited the former empire. The people of Ukraine have reaped the bitter fruits of seventy years rule of the immoral totalitarian system. Economically, they have inherited a difficult legacy. Ignoring fundamental economic laws, the administrative authoritative system turned Ukraine's economy into a prefabricated appendage, dependent upon the will of the center. Ukraine has inherited a unbalanced economy, outdated technologies, backward infrastructure, critical abuse of the environment, burden of foreign debts, absence of qualified managerial staff, and low living standards. But the most terrible sin was that the long colonial status resulted in an attitude of dependency by the people, a lack of initiative, and a national inferiority complex. Now, with independence and democracy in addition to radical political and economic reforms, the conditions necessary for Ukraine's integration into the world economic, political, and peacemaking processes will have been created. The choice of the market oriented model of economic development is clear-cut. Ukraine rejects senseless military expenditures and wishes to release its intellectual, industrial, and other numerous resource potential for productive purposes to meet the needs of its people.

Economic Transformation

A detailed program for the radical transformation of Ukraine's economy has been approved by the International Monetary Fund. This program strongly supports entrepreneurship and the creation of conditions for the development of foreign economic activities. A strategic task is the elimination of all barriers to foreign trade. In order to give new impetus to its economic development, Ukraine is eager to create favorable conditions for attracting foreign investments, technologies, expertise, including joint ventures and direct investments. The law on foreign investments adopted by the Parliament aims at securing the broadest guarantees for foreign business. At present, Ukraine needs to create an effective national economic security system to carry out an independent economic policy and to provide a reliable social security during the transition to a market economy. Ukraine sees prospects for such an opportunity through it's introduction of a national currency with full convertibility.

Debt Problems

Figuratively speaking, one cannot get loose with the debt looped around one's neck. During 1992, Ukraine had to pay about a billion dollars for debt servicing alone. Due to this heavy burden, she is seeking an extension of previously given credits until some economic stability is attained. Ukraine also needs additional external financing, technological aid, and investments to ensure a successful transition. Ukraine recently became a fully fledged member of the International Monetary Fund and the World Bank, and it is hoped that the problems which she is facing at present will be considered by the international community and creditors clubs with understanding. Unfortunately, Ukraine must admit that the implementation of the laws adopted for reform are progressing very slowly.

That is why, regardless of the continuing crisis in its economy, Ukraine is embarking on an important and pragmatic stage in the application of radical reforms. In carrying out such reforms, Ukraine relies primarily on her own forces, especially on the talent and diligence of her people. We are convinced that Ukrainians will be able to build their own state according to their own principles, and the support given to our efforts by the international community is greatly appreciated. We observe with satisfaction that increasing attention is given by the United Nations system to the process of transition to market economies in the countries of Central and Eastern Europe. The promotion of a more intensive assistance, appears to be the result of a decision adopted by the United Nations Development Programme to grant Ukraine recipient country status. Certainly, the UN/UNDP mission in Ukraine is the first step on the way of intensifying cooperation between Ukraine and UNDP. This is a new initiative and a search for new ways and methods of cooperation with transition countries.

Conclusion

Now, we clearly realize that the process of market oriented transformation has proved to be a good deal more complicated than was originally expected. Frank discussion of the problems encountered by all interested parties will greatly assist in avoiding errors in restructuring processes in the future.

Section 3 · Ukraine Branching Out from the CIS: A Critique

Andreas Gummich

Ukraine, which was among the founding members of the Commonwealth of Independent States (CIS) in December 1991, is branching out economically. It is tackling the transition to a market economy independently of Russia and other CIS states through a reform program of its own. Until recently, the Ukrainian economy had been managed for over 70 years from Moscow. The Ukrainian parliament has now decided to pursue an independent economic reform program.

Although the new program points in the right direction, it also contains some glaring weak points. Given Ukraine's dependence on trade with its neighbors, overhasty separation could lead the country to poverty through self-isolation, instead of to its goal of self-sufficiency.

The Contents of the New Program

The main aim of the program is to map out the country's own route to a market economy, while breaking from the Russian market and the reform program recently introduced there. It contains the main elements of a comprehensive market orientation, such as reform of prices, the financial system and taxes, trade liberalization, the establishment of market institutions, and privatization. The overall goals of the program are for Ukraine to separate its domestic market from the CIS market, and to assume the administration of its own national economy. To this end, individual measures include:

- lowering inflation by limiting the rate of wage increase and exerting strict control over money supply;
- introduction of a Ukrainian national currency;
- creation of attractive conditions for foreign investors (protection of ownership, tax concessions, preferential customs duties), without enabling them to purchase land;
- setting up a clearing agency to settle international transactions in ECU (the EC Commission or the Western European banks have not yet been contacted on this subject);
- privatization (including the auction of arms factories against hard currency); and
- cutting the budget deficit to 2 percent of GDP by the end of 1992 (in 1991 it was 14 percent).

Starting in 1993, most firms in construction, trade, transport, and other service areas are to be privatized, as are large tracts of land used for crop and animal husbandry that have been owned by the state or by cooperatives.

National Currency: A Major Target

Not having an economic policy of its own, Ukraine—like other CIS states—has been obliged more or less to follow Russia's changing stance on price liberalization and other aspects of the economy. An attempt was made in January to oust the ruble as means of payment by introducing coupons (*karbovanez*) as a substitute. But the goal was not achieved first time around. The Ukrainian government has not been put off by this failure. It plans to replace the coupons with a new currency, the *grivna*, which is then to be the only form of legal tender. It remains to be seen whether stability can be instilled into the new money by institutions that have yet to be set up; with the *karbovanez*, money-tending operations started and finished with the printing and issue of the bank notes.

The Protection of the Domestic Market

It is clear that the main motive of Ukrainian government in leaving the ruble zone is to protect its own domestic market. Since the *grivna* is not convertible—at present at any rate—this could, however, block trade with other CIS states and lead to appeals for enormous aid from the West. At the same time, though, it also seems unconscionable to advise Ukraine or other successor states of the USSR to have confidence in the inflation-beleaguered ruble, especially since there are currently no signs of the CIS states agreeing on common fiscal and credit policies.

Some Weak Points

While Ukraine's economic reform basically takes the right path, there are some glaring weak points to the new program:

1. Neither the central bank now being set up nor the commercial banks have experience with a national currency.
2. Other CIS states are unlikely to recognize Ukraine's new currency as a payment instrument between themselves and Ukraine without imposing conditions. Since 85 percent of Ukraine's exports go to the CIS, its trade, which is already precarious, could suffer another heavy blow with corresponding repercussions for Ukrainian industries.
3. The program contains some parameters that will cramp, rather than encourage, market-oriented behavior. Businesspeople from Ukraine's still small private sector are, for example, already horrified at a prohibitive corporation tax of up to 75 percent for private enterprise.
4. The reform program does not include a precise, overall timetable. It is not apparent whether the Ukrainian government favors shock

therapy or a gradualist approach. Where the timing is stipulated, it is questionable whether the deadlines can be met. Apart from the currency question, mentioned above, this also applies to privatization. Small firms were to have been privatized in the second quarter of this year.

Accordingly, praise for the program from the International Monetary Fund (IMF), which has granted its new member a quota of $945 million, has been only lukewarm. There has not yet been any response from the West to Ukraine's wish for the provision of a $1.52 billion stabilization fund to support the convertibility of the *grivna*.

Breaking New Ground in Economic Policy

With its reform plan, Ukraine is breaking new ground in economic policy, especially since the administration of the economy is to be organized within the country itself for the first time. Coping with this additional problem area will almost certainly make the reform process more difficult than in other countries of Eastern and Central Europe. In the past, these states already had their own administrative apparatus for the economic sector and experience of contact with foreign countries.

Like the other CIS republics and the reform countries of Central and Eastern Europe, Ukraine also requires considerable financial aid from the West. Under present circumstances, however, it may receive some help, mainly in the form of technical assistance (consulting, management training, and so on).

Economic Cooperation with Other CIS States

In order to keep the costs of the transformation to a minimum for the population, it would be absolutely essential to maintain existing economic relations with other CIS states, and especially with Russia. After all, Ukraine has up to now exported more than one fifth of its GNP to these markets and has imported goods and services on a similar scale. It depends on other CIS states for crucial products (oil, gas, machinery, and chemical products). Severance of delivery relations, inability to pay for dearer imports from Russia (after the changeover to world market prices), and high costs of subsidizing and/or restructuring the big coal mining and iron industries (almost 40 percent of GNP) could seriously jeopardize the success of Ukraine's reform plans. Precisely those sectors that form the backbone of the Ukrainian economy (grain production, iron, coal, steel) are dogged by problems at the global level because of excess production capacities.

Clearing in freely convertible currencies, which was proposed in the program for intra-CIS trade, contravenes an agreement reached between Ukraine and Russia on 14 February 1992 under which further clearing of their bilateral trade—where Ukraine has a deficit—is to be in rubles. This program, however, contains no special measures whatsoever that could be taken by the Ukrainian government to maintain preferential relations with other republics of the former USSR. It would be extremely difficult to redirect all foreign trade relations towards Western countries at short notices, which until recently had been integrated into a relatively strict system of mutual supply agreements with other Eastern neighbors.

Will Ukraine Secede from the CIS?

Politically, the Ukrainian leaders have so far made the impression that they would like to reduce cooperation with other former Soviet states within the CIS to a minimum, or might even consider departing from the young confederation altogether. To date, the Ukrainian president has not yet signed half of the agreements with the CIS. With regard to the military, for instance, Ukraine's leaders are apparently against any firm commitment other than joint control of nuclear weapons. Instead, they tend to exploit animosity towards Russia on subjects ranging from the Crimea to dividing up army and navy to stir up local populism rather than join forces with their large neighbor to look for compromises acceptable to both. The declarations of intent issued after the latest Ukraine-Russia summit in Dagomys on June 23 could lead to the conclusion that Boris Yeltsin and Leonid Kravchuk were not so much negotiating on increased cooperation as on the most inconspicuous separation possible.

A break between Ukraine, where 11 million Russians live (21 percent of the population), and Russia would by necessity have extremely painful consequences for both sides. It can only be hoped that the national emotions now being whipped up do not win the upper hand. Instead of the self-sufficiency envisioned after restricting relations with the CIS, the present economic experiment could culminate in self-isolation with dangerous repercussions.

Conclusion

The process of change in Ukraine is linked with unpopular steps and high social costs for the nation. Whether the Ukrainian government's reform program can be realized depends on whether or not the necessary political room for maneuver and widespread voter acceptance for the concept can be found and guaranteed over a longer period of time.

Ukraine is indeed relatively rich in natural resources (iron ore, coal) and also stands to gain from its good geographical location, which should help it approach the affluence level of Western industrialized countries in the long run. However, integrating the country into the world economy, developing an entrepreneurial base, and gearing branches of production according to comparative advantages require time and—above all—willingness to cooperate.

Section 4 · Risks in Rapid Transformation

Jozef Pajestka

Although the principal concern of this paper is the process of transformation in Central and Eastern Europe (CEE), it can only be understood if evaluated in the context of the global situation and long-running lines of change. One might easily think that the problems faced by the world today are due to a system that promised Utopia but delivered only failure, and that the obvious answer is the restoration of the sound system known as capitalism. There is some logic in this argument, and it is therefore quite popular, but I consider it to be simplistic, myopic, and unproductive.

It must be taken into account that the incredible change that is now in progress came about suddenly and was certainly unexpected by analysts and politicians even shortly before it happened. The socialist system was economically unsound and it was rumored that reforms were under way, but nobody expected the total collapse that actually happened.

Spontaneity and hazard have played an important role in determining the course of civilization throughout human evolution. They used to work in a way that allowed for a certain continuity and predictability. Nowadays, however, profound changes in the human condition tend to occur so quickly that unpredictability may become the norm. Until recently, we were living in an epoch characterized by the cultural dilemma of socialism versus capitalism. In a day, the world shifted to a new epoch and the old controversies lost their relevance. In countries in transition, there were great expectations for an economic wonder, an optimal systemic model, that would solve all the socioeconomic problems at once. However, history has taught us that the progress of civilization depends particularly on the development of pragmatic thinking. To shift from an extremely dogmatized past to pragmatic rationality is crucial for successful transformation.

The Cost of Transition

The transformation process has brought with it a very deep economic decline that, historically, can be compared to the great depression of the 1930s. This dramatic decline has not been anticipated by anyone, and is still rather ignored and even disregarded by many. Some partisans of systemic change, deeply involved in its ideological and political premises, find it difficult to consider the case with full objectivity. It is worth recalling that the mostly peaceful political process that opened up the way for the present systemic transformation was powered by populist argumentation. The socialist ideology of the past developed strong human expectations for achieving higher living standards and wider social justice. These expectations will not disappear with a change in the political system. They still form an important element of societal reality.

The transition process that has led to a decline in living standards, may create areas of frustration and potential destabilization. It could undermine the process of transformation itself, and further development of the countries concerned.

It may be argued that the present economic decline should be regarded as a necessary cost of transition. However, when living standards are deteriorating so considerably, there are no convincing prospects for a better future. Nor is there any strong evidence to prove that the apparent economic decline is of short duration. Optimistic expectations are based on a general idea that economic growth is a natural process, which will appear once the market system, with accompanying institutions, is fully installed. This argumentation would appear to be weak. In the case of Poland, for example, the economic decline resulted in a major curtailing of capital investment for future development. Expenditures in education, research, culture, etc. have been drastically reduced, and this has weakened the nation's dynamic potential. However, the initial reductions may have been widely beneficial in helping to reduce the excessive bureaucracy and unnecessary state functions. A new dynamic middle class has emerged that has achieved some spectacular results, particularly in the area of trade. Regrettably, most of the workers and peasants have suffered from the present economic decline.

The intellectual elite is extremely divided and far from the societal cohesion needed for a common effort. The bureaucratic apparatus has lost all features of professionalism, and democratic institutions, such as parliament, entangled in ferocious fighting for political power, are unable to stimulate and organize the society for dynamic progress. Migration of talent has reached high dimensions, and the bulk of young people of high school age declare their readiness to leave the country. Those attitudes may, of course, change with an improved economic situation, but they dominate at the present time. If this picture is rather pessimistic, it is because the country is still in a very deep decline. Once the economy is able to show an upward trend, psychological attitudes and real behavior may start to change. The situation in other countries of the CEE region is not much different than that in Poland, although it may be slightly better in Hungary and the Czech Slovak Republics. It is possible that after failed attempts to attain the expected Western standards of living, the region may identify itself with the group of peripheral countries. It is not so much this description that is important, but the lack of internal harmony resulting from failing transformation that may also influence the global arrangement.

The present situation leads us to ask a most pertinent question: Was the deep decline following the transformation process inevitable? This is a tricky question, but it could receive a positive reply from all sides involved. First, conservatives in the CEE countries may use the argument that the such a decline was inevitable. That when governments ventured towards a capitalist market economy, it resulted in sufferings for a wide social strata, and benefits only for capitalists both national and foreign. Second, the political elite, committed to reforms and responsible for their implementation, may use the argument to support their own policy and protect their own position.

From Socialist Dogmatism to Pragmatic Rationality

It is not very difficult to identify what went wrong with the process, and how it went wrong. The literature critically evaluating the process is growing in quantity, but in this paper I am less interested in what went wrong than in why?

I do not think that the actual experience of systemic transformation in the CEE countries has brought any arguments challenging the two main lines of change—towards a market system and towards democratic socioinstitutional order. Let us say that transformation of the centrally planned into a market economy is a kind of cultural shift, going from dogmatism (doctrinaire thinking) to pragmatic rationality. There is no doubt that market economies have developed over a long period during which it was subject to pragmatism. The centrally planned economy, by contrast, was the result of conceptualization, imposed on reality by arguments of "theoretical correctness." With the evident failure of the so-called socialist mutation, one might have expected that the concerned societies would have abandoned all their doctrines in favor of pragmatic thinking and behavior. However, one may claim that the process of transformation tended rather to replace one doctrine with another.

It is my strong belief that the dominance of internal and global doctrinary thinking, while slowly diminishing, is responsible for the deep economic crisis that has come with systemic transformation. To substantiate this assertion, it is important to indicated the four main dogmas responsible for the present deep economic decline

Dogma I: Minimum role for the state and maximum for the invisible hand of the market. This dogma contrasts with the former one, namely, the predominance of the state in economic affairs. It was installed primarily under the theoretical (ideological) influence of neoliberalism. It exercised a critical influence on real policy making, particularly during the first period of transformation (1989-90).

A most important consequence of this approach has been an absolute lack of formulation of industrial policy. The first attempt to draft a vague outline of such policy appeared only at the end of the first half of 1992 and, at the time of writing, is still far from any serious discussion and endorsement. The same is also true of agricultural policy as well as that of science and technology.

Dogma II: Priority of anti-inflation over antidepression policy. It could be argued that the origin of this dogma can be found in the International Monetary Fund (IMF) policy basket. It should be noted, however, that it had certain justification during the first period of the stabilization policy, that is during the first half of 1990. It developed into a real dogma when anti-inflation was strongly contrasted with anti-depression. This resulted from acceptance of the narrow minded monetarist conceptual frame.

Dogma III: The market by itself is a sufficient mechanism for efficiency and socioeconomic development. This dogma was installed as a result of a most simplistic comprehension of the market mechanism. It was particularly and strongly advocated by young, neophytic adherents of the market theory. They were showing ignorance, or total neglect of real historical economic experience, particularly the experience of the underdeveloped countries. Implementation of the dogma has brought the most negative consequences to the economy, and can be considered responsible for great losses in agriculture and for the collapse of a number of industries.

Dogma IV: Systemic transformation demands very fast, radical, and universal change of ownership by privatization. This dogma gained its power in the course of the transformation process, and found strong support from many, through reasons dating back to the nineteenth century's ideological controversies. The basic argument was that the market could not function well unless it was based on private ownership motivations. It seemed evident that since privatization could not be achieved fast and universally, the results of the systemic transformation would also be rather slow. It is in this context that a strong dogmatic stand came into play.

Here again, the question was not whether transformation should embrace privatization, but how to carry out changes in ownership relations.

The belief that privatization could be fast and universal, led to almost total neglect of the necessary systemic improvements of functioning of state enterprises in industry, agriculture, and other fields. Those enterprises, waiting for disappearance in the near future, lost all prospective orientation. Without such orientation, the only criterion of behavior was mere survival. With disruption of the old system of central planning and various strange remnants of previous reforms, they inherited a system in which the management had neither responsibilities nor motivations of efficiency and expansion.

The crippled state sector, representing still the bulk of industrial potential could not continue to sustain the state budget. In addition to drastically curtailed expenditure in public services (education, health, science, culture, etc.) it generally led to a highly decreased public savings ratio that could not have been compensated by growing private savings.

The above presentation of the new dogmatism is perhaps not a well-balanced description of the whole picture of the process of transition. It needs to be complemented also with the positive aspects of the process.

Introduction of the market system has brought a number of very positive benefits. It has changed the external appearance of the country. The shabby world is now disappearing giving place to elegant style. Competition in trade and services brings high satisfaction to the population—a new dimension that does not appear in GNP statistics. The opening of the country and free trade injects increased and new benefits, which also cannot be measured. There is one particular case: a great number of traders coming from abroad are selling commodities at lower prices. This is not counted in statistics, though it improves real incomes of the poorer strata. Wide international contacts spread innumerable small innovations in trading, services, and manufacturing. Their real situation, therefore, is better than shown by the statistics. One could say that the spontaneously operating market in some way compensates for policy errors resulting from dogmatic thinking.

Conclusion

I started this paper with comments on uncertainties, on capabilities to anticipate future challenges. In the case of CEE countries, we have to contend with potential danger to internal and, in consequence, global harmony, and the threat of destabilization. Systemic transformation going on in those countries is intended to meet the encountered challenges. Though the main orientations of the transformation processes are undoubtedly correct, they are unfortunately conducted in a way not guaranteeing, as yet, the eventual full success.

Section 5 · Shock Therapy and Possible Mitigating Measures

John S. Flemming

The argument of this section is more theoretical than empirical but it is nevertheless relevant to the experience of economies in transition to the market from heavily distorting controls. With the breakup of the Council for Mutual Economic Assistance (CMEA), many countries of Eastern Europe have experienced external shocks as they lost product markets or faced high prices for raw materials. Nevertheless the representative reforming country, which dismantles barriers to trade, withdraws subsidies, and makes commodity taxation relatively uniform, experiences no shift in its collective opportunities while sharply changing the relative prices faced by individual enterprises.

Among the enterprises some will gain while others lose. In principle this is not a zero-sum change. There should be scope, possibly limited in the short run, for reallocating resources towards those activities that are more profitable under the new set of less distorted prices. Thus national output (GDP) at world prices should, if anything, rise, and this enlarged output could be traded on world markets so that everyone had at least as much of each good to consume or to invest as before.

Yet in countries pursuing such radical reforms we see falling output, falling investment, falling consumption, and only unemployment rising. Is this entirely due to macroeconomic problems and to external shocks, or might it be inherent in the process of rapid price reform?

The Impact of Price Reform

I wish to argue the latter, especially because there are conditions on technology and social organization that make it very likely that as a direct result of reform real wages will fall sharply while unemployment is likely to rise.

The argument will be developed initially on five assumptions:

1. that there is virtually no scope for employing extra labor on existing machines in different branches of industry;
2. that there is no subsistence agricultural or service sector to set a floor to industrial wages;
3. that labor is homogeneous;
4. that some sectors of industry that were viable at the old distorted prices are actually value-subtracting at the new prices; and
5. that workers, and particularly the unemployed, cannot borrow.

The fourth assumption is strong and may need clarification, but it is also well documented (e.g. by Hare and Hughes) that this was true of some sectors in 1988. That is to say that they were not merely unprofitable at world prices but would have been unprofitable even if they had not had to pay anything to their workers. At world prices the value of the oil and iron, and other material inputs, going into the production of some types of machinery actually exceeded the world market value of the machines produced.

Given this assumption it is clear that when prices are liberalized and trade is freed, the activities in question will cease. If they cannot immediately be replaced by profitable activities, the workers in question will lose their jobs. The first and third assumptions ensure that few if any of them will be absorbed promptly in to other activities.

In the absence of unemployment insurance or another form of income support (remember that borrowing and subsistence agriculture are not by assumption available options), they would accept employment at any wage that covered the cost of their subsistence. Even at this wage, they might not all find employment and more importantly, the third assumption—that labor is homogeneous—means that if the liberalized enterprises pursue profits competitively, wages will fall to the subsistence level throughout the economy.

Thus, on the assumptions listed, a move from distorting controls to undistorted free trade could reduce all workers' real wages to a mere subsistence and would not necessarily ensure employment for them all even at that level. Clearly such an outcome would be politically unacceptable in a democracy. I have already indicated that it should be possible to make everyone better off after the introduction of the reform package.

In the rest of the section I explore two issues: what measures would be necessary to increase the proportion of people who benefit from reforms—ideally to 100 percent; and secondly the sensitivity of the problem to the specific assumptions made.

Benefits from Reforms

The first point to make is that the counterpart to the fall in wages in sectors that continue to operate is a rise in profits. If the enterprises were state owned this profit would accrue to the government. Thus the government would have in hand the resources it needed, both to maintain the incomes of workers and to maintain investment by enterprises. If new private enterprises were not to be discouraged, the maintenance of workers' incomes should be achieved by general fiscal measures rather than the payment of wages in state enterprises in excess of market clearing levels. If, however, enterprises were in private hands, the government would have to resort to fiscal instruments that might not be readily available in a suitable form.

Would it help if wages were required to exceed some statutory minimum level? In this case the fall in wages would be limited, but there would, on the assumptions to date, be a larger number of people who could not find jobs. To prevent them from starving, they would have to be given a subsistence income or its equivalent in kind and this would require the collection of tax revenue from some part of the national income. In the absence of a minimum wage, and on the assumption that most goods could be freely traded internationally, there is a presumption that national income at world prices should be raised by the liberalization. The only problem is that all of the increase goes to profits. The minimum wage, however, may mean that some portion of value added activities become unprofitable and therefore cease, thus reducing GDP, possibly by more than the closure of value subtracting sectors raises it. The combination of a minimum wage, which reduces output, and income for the unemployed, which increases revenue requirements, would aggravate the fiscal problem of the reforming economy that is already likely to be under strain. Moreover, the revenue can only come from profits that might otherwise have been invested.

It should be quite easy to improve on this situation in any one of several ways, such as a temporary general employment subsidy reconciling, like the income transfers possible where enterprises are state owned, a market-clearing real wage with a reasonable income for workers. Such a subsidy would raise employment and reduce the cost of maintaining the unemployed. Under reasonable assumptions less revenue would have to be obtained from profitable sectors; but where unemployment compensation might have been financed by a payroll tax the employment subsidy would have to be financed by a tax falling on profits. Nevertheless output would be likely to rise more than consumption; therefore resources for investment would also rise. Thus a subsidy that averted unemployment in the shrinking sectors would also stimulate the expansion of the others. In practice, an outright employment subsidy would not be necessary as a similar effect could be achieved by reducing the payroll taxes that run at around 50 percent in Eastern Europe. A temporary switch from payroll to profit taxation, if it could be implemented, would therefore be very beneficial in the situation envisaged.

Third, the problem would obviously be diminished if the change in relative prices could somehow be phased in over a number of years. This would be very unattractive if it required price controls to be monitored throughout the transition. It should, however, be possible to estimate and enforce a set of tariffs on imports that would induce a pattern of relative prices, not otherwise controlled, similar to the initial prices distorted by taxes, subsidies, and restrictions on trade that have been abolished. These tariffs could then be phased out over, say, five to ten years. The credibility of such a program could be enormously enhanced by the temporary protection, and its phasing out, being built into international agreements with International Monetary Fund (IMF), General Agreement on Tariffs and Trade (GATT), or European Community (EC). The cost of such protection in distorting trade would be smaller in a large country or if a group of smaller countries with similar initial distortions and embarking on similar reforms were to impose a common transitional tariff structure in a regional free trade area or customs union.

The Impact of Adverse Circumstances

So far I have argued that under a specific set of assumptions rapid liberalization could be very detrimental to real wages and that while some measures that might be proposed as remedies would also have damaging effects, there exist measures that might approximate the realization of the theoretical probability that everyone gains from reform. Now I pursue the question whether the problem arises only if an implausible set of adverse circumstances is present.

There is often some scope for employing more people on a given piece of equipment—although beyond a certain point they may get in each others way. The question is how rapidly the addition to output attributable to each successive person added to the team falls away to zero (or below). There may also initially have been a margin of unused equipment in the sectors benefiting from favorable movements in the relative prices of their inputs and outputs that can be brought back into profitable use.

Partial relaxation of the very strong first assumption does not change the conclusion that the market clearing real wage is likely to fall sharply in response to radical reforms even if real output at world prices rises as a result of increasing the resources used in the now more profitable sectors.

There may well be some labor intense activity, in agricultural or domestic service, which sets a floor below which the real wage cannot fall. If these opportunities were readily available and generated incomes higher than unemployment compensation we should see no unemployment. Unemployment is however now widespread in the region, and growing, so that if this productive floor to the real wage exists it is not in practice operative. In any case this productive floor, though raising further the gain to world price GDP from closing value-subtracting activities, may not establish a politically acceptable real wage level, (remembering that given the homogeneity assumption all wages fall to the floor), and certainly will not suffice to make reform beneficial to by any means the whole population.

Nonhomogeneous labor will tend to induce a relationship between real wages and profitability. Expanding profitable sectors will pay higher wages than contracting unprofitable ones. This does nothing to reduce the problems of those working in the contracting sectors—indeed by reducing the number of acute suffers it may reduce political support for the amelioration of their lot—but it may somewhat reduce opposition to reform.

The existence of sectors with negative value added at world prices was only necessary to dramatize the possibility that there might be no positive floor to the market clearing real wage. We have already seen that subsistence sectors might establish such a floor, so might a positive lower limit to value added per person (at world prices) in industry. What matters is that the impact of reform on relative prices is such as to generate a substantially increased dispersion of value added per employee. Such dispersion ensures that many enterprises cannot afford to pay real wages at previously prevailing norms.

In economies with inadequate financial markets the unemployed are likely to have even less access to credit than in the West where their access is strictly limited. Thus in practice this assumption is not much overstated. Moreover, while borrowing might enable the unemployed to maintain their consumption, it would do nothing to reduce unemployment which, on the arguments advanced here, owes nothing to domestic aggregate demand and everything to the inability, in some sectors, to withstand international competition while paying anything close to conventional real wages.

By reducing the sensitivity of consumption to income, the ability to borrow would reduce the consumption response to the employment effect of an employment subsidy. Thus less of the extra output would be consumed and more would be available to expand profitable activities. Before concluding that there are indeed feasible policies that would mitigate the adverse effects of rapid changes in relative prices arising from price and trade liberalization and make such reforms far more acceptable both as being economically efficient and likely to consolidate political support for reform, there are two final issues to address.

It is of the essence of the argument advanced above that price reform generates winners as well as losers in that some enterprises will find their output prices rising relative to their input prices as well as the opposite—hence the references to growing as well as contracting sectors. Some commentators prefer to think of the Eastern European economies as being divided between old fashioned, state owned, engineering works that will contract, and wholly new private service activities that will expand.

On the assumption that the new private sector cannot arise over night I believe that it is worth considering the short period in which only the old enterprises exist. In that period there should be winners as well as losers among state owned enterprises (SOEs). Only as the new sector grows and thrives will the wage it can afford put pressure on an increasing proposition of the old SOEs (unless they adapt). The view, probably unduly influenced by the special case of Germany's *Neue Länder,* that all of the old capital stock is useless and uncompetitive, cannot be reconciled either with the theory of comparative advantage or with the standard of living achieved in the unreformed centrally planned economies.

The theory of comparative advantage tells us that whatever its endowment of land and capital, a previously closed economy, will be able advantageously to export something to the rest of the world in exchange for imported goods. In the process the margins of the (now) exporting sector(s) will have widened and those producing the goods (now) imported will have narrowed. The former win, the latter lose, and the winners can more than compensate the losers.

Conclusion

Consumption standards have generally fallen in Eastern Europe in the last three years, although the old regime did not attach a high priority to consumption.

Their capital was sufficient to provide a tolerable consumption level despite squandering a lot of resources on the military and on extremely inefficient investment. Freed of some of these handicaps that capital must in total continue to be of some potential value. Even if some elements are now virtually worthless others must be of very considerable value.

An apparently far more damaging criticism is that I have applied market arguments to post reform economies in which the institutions of central planning have not yet been replaced by the organic growth of the institutions of an effective market.

It may well be that much of the general collapse of output and activity is indeed due to the deficiency of market institutions. It is not at all clear, however, that the validity of this proposition undermines the argument I have made for policy measures to mitigate the adverse consequences of rapid micro-economic reform. On the contrary: I have demonstrated that such reforms would call for transitional mitigating policies even if they were introduced into a distorted or closed but otherwise well functioning market economy characterized by a low degree of ex post factor substitutability. Is an economy bereft of market institution more, or less, likely to need such measures if the potential of reform to make everyone better off is to be more nearly realized?

Chapter 4 · Privatization and Trade

Section 1 · A Word in Search of a Denotation

Nicholas Georgescu-Roegen

The word "privatization" is a true newcomer. It is not found in the most often used English language dictionaries—*The Universal Oxford Dictionary, The Random House Dictionary of the English Language, The American Heritage Dictionary of the English Language,* and *The Webster's New Collegiate Dictionary.*

The word is listed for the first time in the second edition of *The Oxford English Dictionary,* with several connotations. The oldest source is from 1959 giving the meaning of a change of ownership of an economic entity from pubic to private. From then until the date of the last reference, 1979, the definition had only slight modifications at intervals of about three years. For example, in 1968 it meant the change of the performance of an event from "public" to "private," in the sense in which we say, for example, that "the wedding was a private affair." The 1968 reference even cited "the privatization of death." As we note in the entry in *The Palgrave New Dictionary of Economics,* the term "has been employed with increasing frequency . . . since 1980" in six branches of economics.

A Process

"Privatization" as a process is the transfer of the ownership of some income-producing commodity from one *social* category of owners to another. That commodity could be, for example, a painting by a socially reputed artist, a bulldozer, a windmill, a piece of arable land, in the main a full enterprise, but *not* a railway ticket or some cubic meters of gas.

The following are some illustrations of *single* privatizations. Following the Law of Commercialization of 1924, which allowed the Romanian government to sell public property, several industrial enterprises owned by that government as payment of reparations after World War I were sold in 1926 to private consortiums. For example, on 3 July 1930 the Romanian Telephone Administration was sold to the Romanian Telephone Company, a subsidiary of the American Company, ITT.

What has not been noted, however, is a transfer in *mass* from public to private ownership, hence *socialization in reverse,* which seems to be the most frequently intended denotation of the term "privatization" today. It is in this respect that we may say the process of privatization is unknown to history and, hence, to economic science.

The Transfer from Communal Land

The emergence of private ownership of land from a communal condition is the oldest of such transfers taking place in great numbers. The question of how this essential change was carried out had long been a controversial issue. Anthropologists finally were able to prove that a piece of *communal* land could become the individual property of whoever had improved it say, by clearing or irrigating it. A reasonable principle such as this—which, it should be noted, relates the origin of private property to the simple provision of useful labor—easily found its way in the Koran: "The land belongs to whomever has vivified it."[1]

Agrarian Reform

Another reversal of properties occurred several times from about 1850 to 1930. These were the "agrarian reforms" that studded that period. The changes were implemented in part by legal rules, which specified who would loose the ownership and who would become the new owners. Overlooking the inherent errors of such extensive operations, it was clear who the parties would be in each case.

The Transfer from Private Ownership

One sort of ownership transfer was made widely known by the Communist political system. Primarily, it required annulment of all private ownership of commodities capable of producing income that is then transferred to the control of a commissar selected by the Party. In this expropriation it was clearer than in the agrarian reforms concerning who would lose ownership, but it was completely arbitrary about who would enjoy the privileges of the commissar.

The Transfer to the Party

There is, finally, a type of ownership transfer to which *horresco referens,* yet it must be referred to for analytical argument. It was practiced by the Nazi party in Germany and by their sympathizers in other countries. Commonly known is the practice of one member of the party receiving authorization to simply take over, without any compensation, a designated firm whose ownership was Jewish. That transfer had no similarity with any already-mentioned transfers and, of course, did not depend on a definite rule about who must be the actual beneficiary of the confiscation, except that the person had to be a favored member of "the Party."

Change of Beneficiary

As conceived by its promoters in various fields, privatization is a plan that purports to achieve a feat identical to the emergence of the individual property.

However, privatization is faced with an insuperable difficulty. All of the transfers effectuated by authority consisted of a "confiscation" in favor of a beneficiary chosen according to *some* criteria, be it, unfortunately, inhuman at times. (e.g., the landless peasant, the faithful member of the political party in power, or the whole party.) Then such transfers, even those of the agrarian reforms, ordinarily resulted in some economic losses, is a well established truth, but it does not bear on the issue under discussion.

The Need of Operational Criteria

Operational criteria are needed for privatization to work to decide who should become the owner of, say, the Galatzi Complex of Iron and Steel in Romania, or, simply, of a certain district's bakery, grocery, etc., the former so-called "Communist cooperatives."

For such small businesses, in some formerly Communist countries, at first small firms were allowed to operate freely by paying a concession fee. The right to earn a "capitalistic" profit was thus paid by the new owners by bearing the risk of losing the savings of a group of, for example, some family relatives. In fact, one condition of the concession was that it could not hire strangers. In any case, since obtaining credit from a bank was impossible, only a group of peers or relatives could provide the necessary capital investment for the venture. That system, if appropriately encouraged and continued by imitating the wondrous evolution from the communal ownership to the present world of free market, could have resulted in an ordinary private economic system.

Yet, this system of concession was quickly discontinued. The patent superiority of concessions over the Communist "cooperatives" could not be stomached. The long lines of patrons at the concessionary restaurants were intolerable, even though prices for the same dish were higher than those of the cooperatives. For the discontinuation of concessions, a high ranking director of National Planning instructed me that some concessionaries' income is stolen income, for according to Marx's indisputable principle: "income belongs only to labor."

A New Overturn

In the aftermath of the overthrow of the Communist regimes in Eastern Europe many governmental leaders with new constitutions and also a substantial number of economists believe that privatization is the only solution for the normalization of their countries economic situations so disrupted by political overturns.

The point seems inarguable: if the "Communist regime" no longer operates, it can be replaced only by a "free enterprise" system. This is followed by the corollary that economics will show us the right way. This is, I submit, the fallacious presumption of the high tide of the privatization solution. Vilfredo Pareto, as economist we may recall, insisted in his *Manuel* that economic theory, like any other theory, can deal only with *repeatable* phenomena. Further, a proper theory may cease to be applicable if a particular kind of its phenomena no longer occur. Rosa Luxenberg argued, with her fine concern for actualities, that at some future time economic theory will become obsolete because world socialist planning will be free of the sort of problems that economic theory is supposed to solve.

From the teaching of Vilfredo Pareto and of Rose Luxenberg, it is clear that economic theory can help us deal with a business crisis, but not in the least tackle the post-Communist crisis, for the simple reason that such crises have not been a repeated phenomenon. The governmental authorities of the countries that have sought advice from the highest international monetary institutions have, therefore, acted on a wrong warrant, but it was the monetary experts who insisted that their prescriptions based on standard monetary theory would work that were truly amiss.

Conclusion

Since the solution of imitating the exceedingly slow evolution begun in the primeval communal system is out of the question, the situation at hand requires persistent activity akin to Xenophon's *Oeconomicus* or Aristotle's *Oeconomica,* in the sense of good housekeeping. The problem that confronts us now may be illustrated by that of how to save and repair the damaged items left after a tornado. Such a destruction needs no theory, only some good household sense, that is, some good administrative sense at the national level coupled with a political leadership worthy of the complete confidence of the masses. Economic knowledge would certainly be helpful, but it cannot prescribe a saving solution for a situation that has never been studied.

A conducive beginning is the resettlement of peasants on previously socialized land and encouragement of the formation of private small and medium sized firms are based on labor and talent rather than on liquid capital. It also stands to reason that for some time the existing large scale enterprises ought to be administered as autonomous institutions of the state. Privatization will then come about, albeit very slowly, a recipe that would not please a world as impatient as the present.

Notes

1. Nicholas Georgescu-Roegen, "The Institutional Aspects of Peasant Communities: An Analytical View," in *Energy and Economic Myths* (1976), chapter 7.

Section 2 · Privatization Process in Countries in Transition[1]

Jozef M. van Brabant

Since mid-1989, the eastern part of Europe has been passing through an unprecedented wave of political and institutional change. This has been particularly noticeable in the case of Eastern Europe.[2] In the former Soviet Union, however, at least until the fall of Communism in August 1991, similar modifications have emphasized more the peculiar nature and perilous evolution of *perestroika* than a steady movement towards economic reconstruction. From the very beginning, the former Yugoslavia has in many ways also been an integral part of this wholesale movement towards economic transformation. Sociopolitical changes have come about more slowly there and, in a number of respects, have gone less far than elsewhere in the East.[3] Of course, the recent declarations of independence of various constituent republics and internal fighting have complicated matters. For its part, Albania has now declared itself bent on pushing for far-reaching changes in society that in many ways parallel the ambitions of the leading reforming countries of Eastern Europe.

To accelerate their transformation into mainstream market economies, not only do these planned[4] economies in transition[5] need to be thoroughly restructured and reorganized, but the very core of their sociopolitical and economic systems will have to be reconstructed almost from the ground up. As distinct from a centrally or administratively planned economy, a planned economy in transition is characterized by pluralistic decision making and the gradual emergence of market mechanisms as the primary vehicle for coordinating the activities of various agents in society, especially as concerns the allocation of resources. Profound changes in ownership and property rights are at the core of this venture into the unknown. This is not a melodramatic claim. The mature market economies matured over at least two centuries. Trying to reproduce this experience in a matter of a few years is indeed a venture into the unknown. This section sets out to provide a backdrop to the debate on and experience with privatization in selected Eastern countries.[6]

Radical Restructuring and the Role of the State

In late 1989 and early 1990, overly optimistic expectations, at times even romantic notions, were aired on how quickly the countries of Eastern Europe could be thoroughly transformed into effective pluralistic societies with functioning market economies. The radical restructuring of the East is proving to be a contentious, protracted, and exceedingly painful process that will probably be stretched out over decades rather than a few years. The tasks ahead encompass virtually all aspects of life itself, not just the Herculean task of restructuring the entire framework of economic decision making. One fundamental issue revolves around the prospective role of the state in the economy and the newly built society following the transition. Eventually, the state will become a central coordinator and orchestrator, rather than a detailed prescriber of production, distribution, and consumption patterns. These tasks should be increasingly devolved upon financially autonomous firms that operate within the guidelines set by the newly emerging institutions and by the framework of macroeconomic policies that aim at coordinating decisions indirectly. However, what precisely the latter entails is still the subject of, at times, acrimonious debate. This debate concerns microeconomic matters as well as the desirable shape of the democratic, market-based[7] institutions and the most appropriate macroeconomic policies, and how the state will have to disengage itself from the legacies of overcentralized decision making and administration. All of these are highly controversial issues.

In pondering the prospective role of the state in these countries, it is instructive to bear in mind that the issue is rarely discussed dispassionately or rigorously. Polemics on the issue are rampant even in the countries that have in principle charted for themselves the fundamental direction in which they would like to move. The range of issues discussed elsewhere, notably in Albania and the former Yugoslavia in recent months and for quite some time in the former Soviet Union, understandably continues to be much wider and less crisp.

This wide diversity of views and passions in the transitional economies is not surprising, especially in view of the key features of a centrally or administratively planned economy that have been jettisoned, but have not yet been fully replaced. These were societies in which public ownership dominated almost completely for over 40 years. From that emanated a power base in the form of an all-powerful bureaucracy, including state-owned enterprises (SOEs), with uncounted tentacles reaching throughout society and even into the innermost life of virtually every citizen. Sovereignty of the individual; autonomy and private property; business, political, and intellectual freedoms; the institutions of democracy; and the rule of law were suppressed for decades. Given this backdrop, it should not be surprising that the recent revolutionary changes in most of the East have included an unrestrained reaffirmation of private property, in some cases in outright opposition even to the principle of nonprivate ownership, let alone state property.

Emotional, ideological, and political considerations are thus inextricably intermingled with the fundamental economic issues of establishing effective markets. One example has been the identification of the virtues of the market mechanism in allocating resources with capitalist ownership. Although a solid, if still controversial, historical argument can be offered in its favor, economic rationality does not necessarily agree with this experience. This reality of the planned economies in transition enormously complicates the task of economic policy making and calls for a good deal of improvisation, pragmatism, and compromise on the economics of privatization. That political philosophy and expediency tend to play a much greater role in these debates than the niceties of economic analysis is unavoidable. Moreover, this is not a feature only of the debate about privatization and the creation of market systems in the East. Yet it is instructive to distinguish between economic rationality and the more emotional, political, and ideological *obiter dicta* that are so pervasive in the literature on transition, if only to sort out the various options from among which policy makers must soon adopt workable variants. Making such distinctions is useful even if in the end privatization must be enacted pragmatically through the compromises of the political process.

As concerns the role of the state in the transition, the various opinions cover a broad spectrum. There is little dispute about having the government concentrate on governance. As far as economics is concerned, there is also a broad consensus in the Eastern economies that the government should create and maintain a stable macroeconomic environment. There is widespread agreement too that the government should promote the institutional framework that is so essential to ensuring an economic order for exchange operations among economic agents that are in conformity with the broad requirements of the market economy. However, all the other functions of the state in the societies under reconstruction, including proscribing environmentally unsound industrialization strategies, regulating economic affairs and redistributing incomes, are matters of vigorous debate.

Perhaps a more fundamental point for discussion is the degree to which the state should get involved in the growth process. There is no doubt that it should be set up, delineate, and maintain a stable and transparent arena for economic agents to pursue their own interests at their own risk. Likewise, there is agreement that the state should extricate itself from the pervasive meddling in economic affairs under central planning. But to become more concrete about what precisely the state's role should be invokes considerable controversy. The very issues of vested interest groups have to be fully taken into account. It is probably hopeless even to try to engineer the big historical turnaround in the East in a smooth manner on the advice of professional economists. Societies that are mutating rapidly cannot be managed in this way.

Yet one of the paradoxes of the present situation is that the transformation to liberal market systems requires strong state involvement. To achieve a properly functioning market, and indeed even to move steadily forward towards that position, central government intervention of the right kind and in the right areas is necessary. Examples of such intervention are safeguarding a competitive framework and taking advantage of the beneficial "crowding in" effects of infrastructural investments.

If the planned economies in transition are to regain a solid growth path in an open environment, pervasive changes in traditional ways of life are inevitable. The decisive break with the past is likely to be agonizing, even traumatic to the point of irrevocably altering much of the historical heritage of these societies. Yet the market economy they envisage cannot take root without forceful political action, which can only come from the state.

Even if decision makers feel they have a mandate to proceed swiftly with the establishment of market systems, progress with the transition will inevitably be influenced by the economic model they have inherited and take the form of incremental changes in strategy, rather than a one-time set of changes. The precise role of the government, especially in providing goods and services, is still very much a subject of debate. This is one of the major reasons for the political discussions about privatization and property rights.

One of the more striking features of the transition process has been the rather casual treatment of the many-sided problem of coordinating economic decisions and what this entails by way of institutional infrastructure and policy instruments. Inasmuch as the transition is by definition a process spread out over time, how to ensure coordination during that fluid phase may not produce the most appropriate answers to how best to design and implement a coherent coordination mechanism once the startup hurdles of the transformation have been overcome. In other words, to being about less government tomorrow, more government today may be just the recipe for proper action.

An inextricable component of the transition is the nature of state-wide economic policy now and in the future. There may be broad agreement about the desirable division of priorities and responsibilities that may have to be enshrined in a new framework for macroeconomic decision making. But this must necessarily emanate from the economic structures, institutions, and policy instruments in place. The role of the government especially in providing goods and services forms part and parcel of the unsettled debate. This is one of the major reasons underlying the political discussions about privatization and property rights.

For the purpose of this section, a property right is a socially enforceable right to select uses of scarce goods. The holder of such a right should be entitled to engage in any mutually agreed contractual arrangement, though not all such agreements need to be validated through government action. That is to say, ownership cannot be satisfactorily defined unless the right of property is the right of dealing with things in the most absolute fashion the law allows. The crucial element, in Roman law, is the *ius utendi, fruendi et abutendi,* that is, the right of use (*usus*), enjoyment of the fruit (*usus fructus*) and disposal of the object of ownership (*abusus*); the latter may comprise the right to change the form and substance, or to transfer one or more, of the rights specified earlier to another party. The divisibility of property rights into separate components is crucial to analyzing the purposes of privatization during the East's transitions. It forms a major element of the central point developed in this section.

Capturing what precisely is meant by privatization is more difficult. The arguments at stake in the debates on privatization are extremely varied, ranging from alternative notions of freedom and democracy to divergent views on the lessons to be derived from past experiences with both public and private enterprises. However, one economic issue, namely the question of the relationship between the efficiency of a firm and its ownership is of paramount importance. It can encompass a wide variety of changes in control over assets; some are concerned with alternative approaches to the supply and financing of services provided by local and central governments. As such, privatization can be described as an umbrella term for a variety of policies that are loosely linked by the way in which they are taken to mean the strengthening of the market at the expense of the state. In this section, privatization means the transfer from the public to the private sector of the entitlement to residual or net profits that accrue from operating an "enterprise."

Market Systems, Property Rights, and Privatization

With the collapse and discrediting of the all-powerful Communist control over Eastern societies, including the bankruptcy of the economic model, the prospects of installing market systems to improve the efficiency and equity of resource allocation in the East are at this juncture quite promising. To establish market-based systems of decision making, the planned economy in transition has to drastically change its economic organization and policy framework; in addition, its leadership must reconceive the very basics of economic decision making almost from the ground up. Economic agents acting in their own interest will now have to make day-to-day decisions on resource allocation, and the rules of the market will have to be assimilated virtually from first principles.

However, the legacies of 40 years of detailed administrative management, including the effects on the expectations of economic agents, as well as the sheer problems of switching regimes, are pervasive. They include lack of familiarity with the operation of markets; the absence of a broad middle class that could take over management from political or administrative decision makers; the absence of a managerial and entrepreneurial culture, expectations of many agents that the reforms would preserve most of the benefits they had taken for granted under Communism; and the absence of the institutions, legal bases and financial infrastructure of a market economy—in sum. Perhaps most troublesome has been the orderly dismantling of the system of central planning.

It is true that the market economies of the West are not the result of the implementation of any complicated blueprint. On the contrary, the strength of the liberal challenge to mercantilism and feudalism was its simplicity. But these market economies, including their regulatory frameworks, have passed through two centuries of gradual adjustment, with some notable economic upheavals. None the less, the Eastern societies want to emulate the existing market economies as soon as possible, and so are not willing to allow gradual evolution to build up the fundamentals of the market economy, as occurred in Western Europe.

The economic model for resource allocation and the behavioral preferences of economic agents in a market environment differ vastly from those typically embraced under central planning. Especially important is the fact that human behavior and attitudes to economic activity will have to change dramatically. Foremost is the fact that society at large will be asked to engage in the ordinary business of bringing together inputs and outputs to generate maximum profits, not just for private benefit. This can occur only within a well-set framework with its own infrastructure, including accountants and accounting standards, lawyers and contract laws, market research and sales people, banking regulations and bankers, clear property rights, brokers, and all kinds of related intermediaries, competition, and regulation of natural monopoly. Furthermore, microeconomic decisions will need to be properly coordinated at the aggregate level in accordance with the social consensus.

Given the prevailing and emerging disequilibria, macroeconomic policy in the planned economies in transition will have to be reformulated as soon as possible to regain stability and guide the transformation. This will take more than simply educating individuals in the finer points of macroeconomics or stabilization policies. It is impossible to intermediate effectively without having a broadly based financial infrastructure. Foremost is the establishment of a strong banking sector, as the foundation stone for the gradual creation of broader-based capital markets.[8] Not at all a small matter is the implantation of operational and well-functioning monetary and fiscal policies in societies that have for so long been dominated by central planning as the presumed omniscient coordinating mechanism.

One of the main elements of the current proposals is privatization. It is usually lumped together with reform of property rights, although the two may be quite distinct, not only in a strict juridical setting. Reform of property rights has several dimensions. One includes questions revolving around the assignment of property rights associated with existing assets. But another aspect is the assignment and guarantee of property rights to assets to be created from gross public and private savings. Reform of property rights is indeed an integral component of the measures to sensitize these societies to market incentives. This has many facets. Not coincidentally, this debate has taken on, with a vengeance, the obverse character of the role played by nationalization at the beginning of the socialization process in these countries. But the focus here is mainly the economic aspects. Privatization of existing assets may or may not be desirable to foster markets and fulfill other objectives of such a policy.

It is almost a tautology to say that a market with basic institutions in the broad sense and subject to adequate competition from other markets is concerned with efficient resource allocation. But the market system as such has little to say about the distribution and possible abuses of ownership. Among the complex conceptual issues associated with the establishment of markets, none has been more controversial than the capital market. Those organizing capital markets should be concerned, at least conceptually, with four core issues: ensuring the efficient allocation of the service streams that come from the existing capital stock as an essential ingredient of reaching the efficient allocation of existing resources; fostering an environment in which capital assets can be traded for holdings in wealth portfolios as one element of intermediating between savers and investors; providing incentives for the most effective creation of new capital, including the provision of liquidity and the transformation of short-term deposits into long-term lending; and setting up the framework for the disposition, through exist and entry, of capital owned by the state or by the private sector and thus to raise capital's net worth through competition.

Under some circumstances, the second and fourth could coincide, but it should prove useful to separate them during the transition process. The first is especially important, for ownership *per se* has little to do with enhancing the techniques of allocating scarce resources. What matters first and foremost is the allocation of user rights to capital through unambiguous contractual relations. This can proceed through effective capital markets, given the level of development of the country in question it could also proceed by internalizing the cost of allocating these services, for example, through private ownership.

Moreover, the complexity of economic activities means that ownership patterns will also be complex. The most efficient owner of a particular attribute of an asset, say ownership *per se,* is not necessarily the most efficient owner of the asset's other attributes (such as utilization of the service stream or the usufruct). It may be advantageous, then, to split the ownership rights of an asset among several economic agents. Because the asset itself as an object of property is not physically unbundled, its owners may find it easy to consume some of each other's unpriced attributes if they are not constrained through the effective enforcement of property rights.

Now that the state has decided in principle to withdraw from exercising direct ownership functions, one of the crucial questions facing the leaders of the planned economies in transition is what to do with publicly owned capital. It is a vexing issue with all kinds of colorations, depending upon the ideological bent of the individual commentator.

The most liberal reformers in the planned economies in transition, advocates the widespread privatization of state assets by selling them off quickly or giving them away, if not all at once, at least swiftly. In some cases, this may be warranted from a strictly economic point of view. If capital services can be allocated at a lower cost by internalizing the coordination of the service stream of assets rather than by going through a formal market process, private property would be the answer, for the ultimate owner then exercises full control. But it does not necessarily follow that divestment should be enacted quickly or below a "fair market value."

The strategy of organizing capital markets can best be tackled by recognizing that neither private nor public ownership of assets by itself guarantees the most efficient exploitation of user rights. One should therefore throw overboard ideological bonds in favor of putting in place an environment for property forms to emerge that is as neutral as possible. By disjoining, at least conceptually, ownership from ownership rights one could start thinking about the proper technical issues at stake.

In that context, it should simply be recognized early on during the transformation process that in a planned economy in transition any kind of property form may prevail. This can be justified in a number of ways, but an economic one would simply be that there will be at least one productive endeavor for which one of the possible property forms will be best suited in the sense that in this way the service stream emanating from the assets can be coordinated at least cost per unit of value-added generated. The potential for disassembling property rights in the case of planned economies in transition is considerable, provided the transition gets off to a robust start and technical issues are considered on their own merits. Furthermore, the exchange of property rights through entry and exit should be ensured, including property rights in exchange for publicly owned funds. That can best be organized through open, competitive bidding.

If there is free exit and entry, subject to regulatory powers to correct market failures, new capital will be formed according to whatever enhances the allocation of resources. However, this cannot be anticipated for the publicly owned capital stock at the outset of the transition. Hence the key questions of privatization and property rights' reform in the case of existing assets should address the allocation of the usufruct of capital assets and how best to guarantee that assets are not misappropriated for "private" gain. This also applies, with minor modifications, to the use of natural resources and intangible assets, most of which cannot be sold. There are, of course, other issues that concern entry, capital formation, innovation, and expansion of existing assets.

Property Rights, Ownership, and Privatization

Privatization as an operational policy category is often poorly defined in countries in transition. This confusion arises because of the real problems and variety of options that have surfaced. In fact, the notion has been used to describe a whole range of activities, including all kinds of deregulation, that may be undertaken with the help of government to improve the functioning of the market economy. It could be seen as a process that takes the state (political bodies as well as government administration, including *nomenklatura*) out of the decision making over the allocation of usufruct, and in some cases even the ownership, of state-owned assets. In that sense, privatization should provide the overriding framework of the East's transformation.

It is important, however, to use one unambiguous definition. "Privatization" here means the transfer to other agents of the right of the state to influence directly the allocation of capital resources to nonstate entities, to whom the residual or net profits of utilizing assets accrue.

When privatization as defined refers to enterprise reforms that alter the legal position of the enterprise from being a state agent into some joint-stock company, the terms "corporatization" is used. Here it, the state remains simply the owner. But the allocation of the usufruct of ownership, which is within the competence of management, will henceforth be monitored by some state asset-management agency. The operations of such an agency, however wide the authority that may be delegated to the agency, should be subject to tight supervision by the emerging democratic process.

The sale of assets in the planned economies in transition is generally separated into so-called "small" (or "petty") and "big" (or "real" or "mass") privatization. This distinction was first introduced by the reform leadership of Czechoslovakia, but it has since gained wider acceptance for two reasons. One is the goal of improving the efficiency of asset use, buttressing private ownership as a key ingredient of strengthening democracy and rewarding the population at large with new forms of assets and risks. The other is that it is now widely recognized that privatization, especially in the case of core industry ("real" privatization), can proceed only over a fairly protracted period of time even if policy makers are bent on divesting assets without having to worry much about proceeds and wealth distribution.

The dividing line between "small" and "big" privatization is not set hard and fast, however. The first is essentially concerned with the sale to the public-at-large (possibly residents, nationals, expatriates, and foreign private and legal persons) of assets that the state should never have arrogated to itself in the first place. These are essentially capital goods (including housing, service shops, retail outlets, catering establishments, small workshops, and similar productive units) for which the process of coordinating the service streams yielded by these capital assets can be ensured at least cost through private ownership. These should be sold quickly through fair allocation mechanisms. The goal of small privatization is, then, to improve the efficiency of asset use, buttress private ownership as a key ingredient of strengthening democracy and reward the population at large with new forms of assets and risks.

On the other hand, "big" privatization refers in particular to the divestment through the sale or the "give-away" of shares in enterprises at present owned by the state. These SOEs tend to be large, organized in conglomerates and highly monopolistic. The objectives of such divestment and the ways of achieving it are therefore considerably more complex than in the case of small privatization.

The Objectives of Privatization

Privatization may be pursued with several different objectives. In market economies, the most commonly cited aims are improving the productive and allocative efficiency of the use of assets, raising government revenues, breaking the back of entrenched interest groups in government-owned property and living up to the libertarian ideology that posits that democracy and freedom can best be served by private ownership.

In the planned economies in transition there are at least four motive for privatization that are largely absent in market economies. One is essentially political in nature; namely retribution for the long years during which private ownership was denied and the state arrogated to itself the entire capital-formation and capital-allocation process. Related to this is the desire of the former planned economies simply to become a liberal market economy.

Another motive derives from the fact that, under central planning, management of SOEs was often entrusted to the Party faithful and their protégés (*nomenklatura*) rather than to individuals who had demonstrated their ability to operate capital assets in the state's best interests and who could accordingly be held responsible and accountable.

The last distinguishing motive of privatization in the planned economies in transition is also largely political. The process of firmly rooting democracy in these societies has some way to go. To buttress it and make it irreversible, a critical minimum of private and other forms of nonstate ownership must be established. A democracy (in the modern sense) without a solid market economy is unthinkable.

In discussing the objectives of privatization, it is necessary to come to grips with the legacies of central planning and the abuses of power under Communist rule. Resorting to the outright divestment of state-owned assets, through sales or free distribution, to break this power structure can be crucial at a time when the move towards democracy has not yet been completed or continues to be rather weak. However, once the new political structures are firmly in place, the abuses of the *nomenklatura* in operating state-owned assets as their own fiefdom should be curtailed and altogether excised through that political process.

Moreover, when discussing the availability of managerial talent in the planned economies in transition, two considerations are important. One is that management under central planning, irrespective of how it came to be appointed, sometimes has a claim to property rights. This was especially the case under administrative planning when management was called upon (at some risk to itself and when the state declined to monitor performance) to allocate resources with the goal of maximizing output. Taking these rights away altogether might well result in their destruction. This might even be unfair as adjudicated by the new democratic values.

The matter of establishing a minimum of private and nonstate ownership, an important consideration is that the ability to raise savings in these countries commensurate with the vast capital required for economic reconstruction is limited. For this reason, it may be desirable to divest quickly some portion of the existing capital stock through imaginative schemes other than outright sales and to foster private-property formation from new savings as rapidly as possible. Among those schemes that are currently being considered, notably in the Czech and Slovak Republics, Poland, and Romania, are the free or nearly free distribution of a certain proportion of shares in SOEs to the public at large, perhaps in the form of a stake in investment or mutual funds yet to be created; allowing workers to buy a stake in their enterprises at a preferential price, something that is especially important in Poland; devolving ownership to local and municipal authorities, which in turn will utilize this stake to finance part of their own expenditures, as pursued to some degree in Hungary and Poland.

Whatever the concrete circumstances surrounding the privatization campaigns, there is rarely a single objective to be served especially regarding the sale of state assets. The desirability of divestment therefore depends not only on the different possible forms of resource allocation, but also on the weights attached to the alternative objectives policy makers pursue. In other words, for each type of divestment a "divestment function" could be specified with, as arguments, revenue generation, improvements in allocative and productive efficiency, contribution to stabilizing democracy, getting even with the Party and its associated bureaucracy, breaking the back of other interest groups, disbursing wealth to society at large to foster private property ownership and so forth.

As the best way to improve the allocation of state assets is a complex matter, it is appropriate to examine the aims of privatization in order to set forth criteria by which its success can be evaluated in terms of the prevailing objectives. For the purposes of this section, six objectives stand out: buttressing democracy and personal freedom; elevating the efficiency of assets currently owned by the state through market discipline, competition, and the elimination of government intervention, which in a number of cases requires outright divestment; raising revenue for the budget and reducing budgetary allocations (such as subsidies), including the administrative burden of the government's administering of state-owned assets, notably SOEs; allowing firms to raise capital in commercial markets; contributing to the widening and deepening of the capital market, possibly to encourage savings (for example, through workers' shareholding or stock-owning incentives); and undercutting entrenched positions of interest groups (such as trade unions, the Communist party, and the *nomenklatura*). As there is a wide diversity in these pragmatic, ideological, economic, and populist objectives, a range of "successful" outcomes can justify privatization.

By its very nature, the key philosophy on privatization in planned economies in transition contrasts markedly with that prevailing in market economies. Indeed, the former's paramount motivation has been twofold. On the one hand, the reaction has been a negative one, namely undercutting the power of the entrenched bureaucracy and getting even for the denial of nonstate property rights for such a long time. On the other hand, many new policy makers of the East hold visions of an economic, political, and social order that is both more free and more prosperous.

As regards the role of private capital formation early on during the transition, it is especially important to encourage new agents into exerting greater domestic competition. Special measures may be required to stimulate this process, possibly by making available most of the cash flow in the state sector for the creation of small and medium-sized private enterprises. The channeling of these funds through commercial banks, which are yet to be created in an effective form, perhaps at favorable, but nondiscriminatory, interest rates, might impart a critical impetus to strengthening the private sector. But other preferential schemes may have to be initiated to overcome the inertia and uncertainty that prevail in the planned economies in transition.

The objectives that decision makers of the planned economy in transition may wish to pursue in the matter of privatization determine to a large degree the methods of divestment to be employed. Thus, if budget revenues must be maximized, assets must be priced at the highest value that can be obtained from those possessing wealth. But if the prime motive is to buttress democracy or advance libertarian values associated with private property, divestment through outright sale of through free distribution of assets should be carried out as rapidly as possible. Whether that should be done by giving each citizen an equal share in social property, as had originally been aimed at by the leadership of Czechoslovakia, or through the creation of the institutions of the emerging capital market (including pension funds, insurance companies, and mutual funds, which are currently being introduced in the Czech and Slovak Republics and Poland), is something to be considered carefully. The broad free distribution of assets, whatever its justification, would result in enormous administrative costs and give rise to formidable monitoring problems, not to mention its adverse wealth effects on capital formation. This is one of the many reasons that persuaded Czech and Slovak policy makers to modify their earlier views on divestment.

There is, however, little doubt that virtually all planned economies in transition have now decided to move forward rapidly with the sale or free distribution of petty assets, while deferring consideration of large privatization because of the many issues involved. In most cases, the drive to divest the state of small assets revolves around the organization of competitive auctions, initially open to resident nationals. There are, however, other important policies, which sometimes act as constraints on the divestment campaign. Thus, in Poland it initiation of the broad divestment effort would have been impossible without the government taking into account the existing property rights of workers' councils. As a result, workers are being offered first choice in divestment efforts and some stakes at a favorable price in the SOEs to be privatized. Likewise in Hungary, policy makers have encouraged "privatization from below," but since the installation of the democratic government this is now being closely supervised by the government, to take advantage of the skills of existing management.

Until the end of 1990, the scale of divestment of petty assets, on the whole, remained very small. In 1991, however, rapid progress was made by Czechoslovakia, the former German Democratic Republic and Poland. Several other countries, including Bulgaria, Romania, and possibly Albania and the former Soviet Union, planned to move forward with it quickly. The process was well under way in the former Yugoslavia too, but has more recently been the victim of ethnic strife and confusion about who is entitled to govern the country and its constituent republics. Without a political settlement, progress with the economic transformation of the former Yugoslavia will remain all but impossible.

Forms of Privatization

Although privatization can take many forms, only four are considered in this paper: spontaneous privatization; gratis transfer of title; leasing and management contracts; and outright sale.

Spontaneous Privatization

Many planned economies in transition have had some experience with this form of divestment. "Spontaneous privatization" means that those entrusted with state assets take possession of them in one way or another. One favored instrument has been the turning of the SOE into a joint-stock company, whose shares can subsequently be sold to private agents, including foreigners. This was the route that Hungary initially chose to take because decision makers did not really wish—or dare—to renationalize assets. Other forms have included the incorporation of state assets, with management signing away property rights to private ventures that it owned wholly. In order to safeguard deals, the rights can be sold to the other owners, which essentially involves the managers trading off the loss in revenue against guarantees for their own jobs. Some of these and other forms of capturing property rights in assets that are ostensibly owned by the state also presented an array of highly contentious issues in the former German Democratic Republic and Poland until the respective non-Communist governments put an end to the most crass abuses. The process is still evolving in one way or another in economies where the debate on the means and ends of transition is still being conducted.

The experience with spontaneous privatization has not been very satisfactory financially, legally, economically, or organizationally. Financially, spontaneous privatization allows former management, and possibly workers, to become owners without paying a fair price and thus deprive the government of revenues needed to offset its liabilities.

From an economic point of view, there is no reason to believe that turning over assets to those who ran these facilities poorly when they were formally under state control will improve resource allocation. Certainly, being entrusted with assets may change the allegiance of management away from the Party to the true asset holders, but for such a change to take place on a scale large enough to make a difference in the process of resource allocation is by no means assured.

Present management was frequently appointed under the *nomenklatura* rules. At the very least, conflict of interest laws should have been used to prevent managers from laundering state assets through the dummy corporations that they created. There is also bound to be a problem of equity. Worker ownership might be fine for those employed in profitable or potentially profitable ventures, but it is not for those in persistent lossmaking operations. Of course, those not employed in SOEs, who none the less involuntarily contributed to asset formation, would be excluded altogether.

Finally, there is an organizational problem with worker management in the sense that those belonging to the former managerial group, who have the experience and know-how to supervise the firms, may be eliminated from the newly formed managerial base.

Gratis Transfer of Title

This form of divestment of state assets has been debated at great length, first in Czechoslovakia, before the cessations, and more recently in Poland. It is, in fact, now being introduced in these two countries; but giving title to assets free of charge in some other form than vouchers or shares in mutual funds has been considered elsewhere too, most notably in Albania and Romania, at least as a conceptually plausible option.

Most common has been worker management of SOEs, which is essentially an extension of the labor-managed firm. This tends to encourage maximization of income per worker rather than the long-run profitability of the firm, unless the organizational form is followed through its internal logic. This bias is exacerbated when there is no capital market to enable workers voluntarily to sell their rights to participate in future profit earnings at a market valuation based on the expected earnings of the enterprise. That is to say, worker management is insufficient to ensure efficiency; clear ownership and a market in which such property can be traded are also required. This market can function well only if individuals with no connections to the firm are allowed to acquire shares; in other words, capitalist ownership must in principle be allowed.

The second form of gratis transfer of title is distributing property to workers on the ground that ownership in state firms should be transferred to those employed, who will be requested to improve the firm's profitability. The key assumption of such transfer is that property owners automatically improve the allocation process and render the firm profitable. Such an assumption is not only fallacious but also inequitable. For one thing, the value of capital per worker in state firms varies a great deal for reasons that have nothing to do with the relative merits of the present labor force. Furthermore, free distribution of assets fails to provide funding for the government to sink some liabilities. It also tends to favor reinvestment in existing activities under present management and continued employment of the present labor force.

Although the labor-managed firm appears to have several drawbacks, some employee share-ownership program is worth considering, especially if it can be coupled with undertakings to limit demands for monetary compensation, to foster productivity, to change work rules, and to embrace other measures that would give workers a material stake in their enterprise. It should be noted that this can be done without outright sale of SOEs. All it requires is that the latter become a joint-stock company: the performance incentives would then include obtaining a share in the firm's capitalized value.

A third form of gratis transfer is the distribution of property to society at large either on an individual basis or by households. There are good reasons to do this, as state assets were accumulated through confiscation or forced savings. However, the merits of an equitable distribution on these grounds are highly debatable. This form of divestment is also advocated in view of the inadequacies of capital markets and the shortage of domestic capital in planned economies in transition. It may also forestall the emergence of proxies for foreign owners, mentioned below.

Although free distribution of shares in SOEs is intuitively appealing, particularly to those who believe in societal rather than state property, there are serious drawbacks to such divestment, apart from wealth effects. First of all, there are potential losers as well as beneficiaries. This may lead to resentment and, eventually, a political backlash. Moreover, the fiscal base of centrally planned economies depends to a significant extent on corporate taxation.[8] In the absence of a personal income tax, the already inadequate revenue-raising ability of the government would be further hampered. Divestment at no cost also deprives the government of future revenues from assets and should ideally be accomplished by the retirement of state obligations and fiscal reform centered on personal income taxation. Clearly, some assets built up over the years can be considered as collateral against the future claims of citizens on disbursements by the state. Most of these claims (such as pension rights, medical and disability benefits, rights to education, and claims on protecting minimal levels of living) will not be voluntarily relinquished during the transition. It would be irresponsible policy making to encumber future generations with fiscal levies of current incomes to meet accumulated past claims for which, at some point, adequate assets were accumulated.

An equitable distribution of shares would, in any case, imply that any household has only a minuscule interest in any single firm, rendering the distinction between the pre-and postreform situation largely nominal. Greater concentration of ownership might come about through the creation of several investment or mutual funds that would each act as core monitors for some sector, yet compete even in supervisory roles with each other. Shares in these funds could be randomly allocated to households. But how to ensure that each household receives portfolios of approximately equal value, given serious asset-valuation problems in the planned economy in transition, is a conundrum yet to be addressed.

Unquestionably the most serious shortcoming of this approach is that divestment does not have beneficial effects on management—normally, the principal aim of privatization. The population at large is unlikely in the near future to consist of sophisticated investors who attend board meetings. Even mutual fund managers will not have the knowledge or incentive to assess managerial performance and promote takeovers when needed. And the question who is to monitor them remains. There is, therefore, a potentially serious principal-agent problem. Numerous alternatives have been considered by, among others, the planned economies in transition themselves.

Leasing and Management Contracts

Taking the state out of enterprise management can be accomplished by distributing user rights, for example, through leasing and management contracts. Custodial rights over the use of social property could in principle be traded in functioning capital markets. Theoretically, the idea of such a market for the usufruct of capital can realistically be entertained and, if it were feasible, it could improve the allocation of scarce resources. What may work in a textbook situation, however, does not necessarily function properly in the real world.

Given the complexity of ensuring such efficient markets even in mature market economies, it is hard to envisage how the planned economy in transition could institute fully functioning capital markets within a comparatively brief period of time at a tolerable transaction cost. The only useful alternative is to enact far-reaching reform of property rights and foster the gradual emergence of capital markets for the bulk of society's capital. Indeed, the internalization of the coordination problem at the outset of the transition may proceed at a lower cost than would be required to ensure coordination through fully fledged capital markets.

Outright Sale of State Assets

The final form of privatization that will be considered entails the outright sale of state assets through auctions or more discretionary channels. How to set prices and for what purposes the proceeds will be earmarked remain difficult questions. Apart from the fact that auctions have to be organized, the sale of state assets runs into the obstacle of the limited volume of private domestic savings. Whether society would be prepared to put even these limited funds into company shares and at what price the auction should be reserved are problematic issues. To mitigate the effects of the lack of funds and to entice individuals into adopting a shareholding culture, one of the more attractive forms of selling off state assets is through debt-financed auctions. Such divestment would essentially consist of putting generous financial resources at the disposal of those willing to acquire state assets. In essence, the state as lender would become a *rentier* while private sectors would end up as debtors and capitalists, hopefully without differential access to foreign capital distorting the process. Of course, how best to ascertain creditworthiness and the potential for successfully managing such assets are pertinent questions that remain unanswered.

Whereas it would in principle be possible to conduct auctions at a fair reservation price, the environment within which this would have to be implemented rules out the imposition of a realistic floor price. That could be set more safely through a divestment program with discrete instruments. The situation could be ameliorated through assistance from outside accounting firms. For most undertakings, there should be some positive price that can realistically be established with some good will on the part of all actors involved.

The Experience with Privatization

It is not easy to specify all of the different privatization mechanisms pursued in the planned economies in transition or to draw a clear picture of where the entire process stands at this juncture. There is little doubt that all Eastern countries have now decided to enact far-reaching reform of property rights and to pursue some form of privatization. New capital formation in new ventures is benefiting from unencumbered property rights, but assignment of rights to existing assets has proved more cumbersome.

Most attention in the privatization campaign has been devoted to bringing manufacturing and service enterprises into the private sector. The latter is the core of the "petty" privatization, while the bulk of the former is the object of the "large" privatization. For some curious reason, the focus of virtually all observers has been on ownership reform in industrial and commercial restructuring. This is a limited perspective: parallel questions are raised in connection with agriculture, public utilities, housing, certain other infrastructure and land, all of which pose difficult problems that derive in part from property rights that cannot be monetized.

There is little doubt that the debate on privatization and the actual enactment of some forms of privatization has proceeded furthest in the Czech and Slovak Republics, Hungary, and Poland. Divestment in the former German Democratic Republic has been a unique experience. The implications of its transformation, in spite of the managers of the transition having to contend with few ideological, political, or philosophical obstacles to divestment, offer some lessons that could usefully be heeded by other countries that still have a range of privatization options to choose from. Its experience also suggests pitfalls that these countries may wisely attempt to avoid. Matters are much less clear in the other countries, including the Baltic republics, but some progress has been made, notably with petty privatization, in virtually all of them. The remaining republics of the former Soviet Union arguably constitute the largest exception. The debate on what to do with state-owned assets there, including agriculture, land, and housing, remains highly divisive and unsettled at this stage.

Throughout the economies in transition large privatization has thus far remained limited. Some SOEs in Hungary and Poland have been divested through open auctions. Others have been sold to domestic managers and workers or to foreigners through more restricted channels. But the task ahead remains daunting. Poland hopes to give away a large stake in SOEs to the population at large through investment funds. The Czechs and Slovaks are now set to do likewise by 1992 through its voucher system. Hungary continues to emphasize sales of SOEs at "fair" market values, even if that slows down the privatization process.

Although there do not appear to be many differences in the situation regarding privatization in other countries, this impression applies mainly to the ultimate goal envisaged. Looking at the actual state of affairs, considerable progress has been made—or promises soon to be made—in Bulgaria, Romania, and Yugoslavia (prior to the current civil strife). The Baltic republics will probably move forward rapidly with privatization in the near term. Albania may follow suit in due course, but matters there are in many respects at least as fluid as they are in the remaining republics of the former Soviet Union. In some, the process continues to be hampered by deeply ingrained ideological and political commitments to state ownership. This obstacle may be weakening, but it will take time to formulate acceptable alternatives to state ownership. The revamped federation and the successor republics, notably the Baltic states, will presumably set a new agenda for property rights and privatization. In any case, because of this reality the entire range of issues pertaining to the best use of existing assets in the remaining republics of the former Soviet Union is a case *sui generis,* as has been true for so many aspects of the transition there.

Much more progress has been made to date with "petty" privatization. This holds true especially for the three Central European countries (as well as the former German Democratic Republic). But even this process has been marred by considerable volatility. In some cases, compensation and restitution claims have been inhibiting the new owners from pursuing their long-term interests. Indeed, uncertainty appears to be one critical component that is hamstringing private economic activities, something that has been most pronounced in the case of capital formation. Elsewhere, progress with "petty" privatization has remained rather uneven and, in some cases, downright spotty.

"Petty" privatization can be undertaken easily through outright sale. In cases where inflation has wiped out savings or available funds are otherwise inadequate, financial incentives can be created. Thus, the government could make available generous credit to those willing and able to run the risk. In the first instance, this refers to small enterprises, chiefly in the service sector. Comparatively small industrial firms can be disposed of through the sale to an individual or a group, preferably through open auctions or at least transparent dealings, or assets can be sold or leased after liquidation of the SOEs for their disposal value (as in the case of "privatization through liquidation" in Poland).

Particularly in the former Czechoslovakia, "petty" privatization has proceeded through open auctions in which resident citizens can participate. The process has on the whole proceeded well, although some lapses have been noted and the process is taking longer than had originally been envisaged. One drawback is that there is a constraint on the number of authorized participants while no questions are asked about the origin of funds. In some cases, this has encouraged the use of domestic proxies for foreign capital. It is said that by means of citizens substantial foreign capital has been channeled into acquiring petty assets, presumably at a favorable price.[9] Similar allegations have been voiced in connection with privatization, notably of housing and land, in Hungary and in some other Eastern countries. These irregularities may lead to popular resentment.

It is perhaps curious that the privatization of small firms has received much less attention than that of the core SOEs. Yet its importance should not be underestimated. For one thing, most of the assets coming under the label of "petty" privatization are for undertakings in which the state itself should never have become embroiled in the first place. From a purely technical point of view, there was no reason to believe the state had any comparative advantage when it came to minimizing the cost of coordinating decisions about the service streams embodied in those assets or even in identifying the potential service streams. Hence, using the criterion for property forms adopted here, ownership of petty assets should not have been restricted to the state.

Future growth in the planned economies in transition is more likely to ensue from small-and medium-sized firms than from the core SOEs, even if they are privatized, restructured, or commercialized. The comparatively rapid pace that can be pursued with the development of firms of this size and with the privatization of existing firms can make a "key contribution to the development of market economies."

When it comes to the core industrial or large commercial SOEs, however, the options are also whether first to corporatize or commercialize by setting the SOEs into a different legal framework and nominating corporate boards. The key issue here is the membership of the boards and control over these enterprises, and how the leadership can avoid reproducing the *nomenklatura* under a different guise. These firms can also be divested by distributing or selling shares. In most Eastern economies, there is now a legal framework for turning SOEs into corporations. Progress with the commercialization of these corporations and with putting them into a more competitive framework has been rather spotty to date, however.

Finally, all planned economies in transition have recognized the need for a transparent framework that recognizes and enforces property rights. Progress with implementing the framework, even in the case of new capital formation, has been quite slow, however. The legacies of administrative planning are formidable. The basic obstacles to taking initiatives and risks in these societies stem from the numerous regulations and special exceptions applicable to privately operated ventures.

Privatization and the Transformation Process

Given the many problems that planned economies in transition face in improving the allocation of capital, the question arises of when and how to privatize. Sequencing could be very useful and could encompass several stages, the time intervals for each essentially depending on concrete circumstances. Thus, when the situation in the country has deteriorated into pervasive paralysis and instability, the intervals between the initial phases would need to be very short indeed. It would probably be pointless to try to manage an orderly privatization campaign in a highly unbalanced socioeconomic environment. It might then be better just to go ahead and do it, and hope that a solid buttress for better governance in both the enterprise and the political spheres will emerge fairly quickly.

Because of the complexity of the divestment and privatization functions outlined earlier, implementation of privatization programs must remain a daunting task. Pragmatism will be the best guide in this case. At the very least, given the East's harsh realities, it needs to be emphasized that if headway is to be made with privatization, it can only be done pragmatically. In the present economic, political, and social situation, policy makers must move ahead comparatively quickly and on a broad front. From the analysis outlined in the present paper, it can be seen that privatization, including divestment, could usefully be carried out in three or four waves, in intervals determined by prevailing circumstances.

Very early on during the transition, the state should unambiguously determine existing property rights, without pulling the economy into the morass of restitution, though compensation may be arranged; recognize in principle the validity of all property forms; and begin to divest itself of assets, such as housing, restaurants, and small retail outlets, that it should never have acquired at all. Pragmatism should be the golden guide, but with a view to preserving as much equity and fairness as possible. For that, a neutral party, in the form of a state asset-management agency, for example, could help in organizing expeditious and equitable auctions open to all. Private property in these instances is the most effective way of coordinating the service flows from them. It is also likely to provide a critical minimum of support for moving towards markets and buttressing democracy.

The second critical part of the transition is the disposal of the remaining assets. As concerns land, a bold move forward with de facto land reform would seem to commend itself. All other state assets used in the economy, especially SOEs (except perhaps those concerned with certain strategic goods and public utilities), should be turned into joint-stock companies placed under the supervision of an impartial, professional body whose main task should be to enforce commercial behavior on the part of management of SOEs. It might also consider leases or managerial contracts. The trustees should monitor such transfers very carefully.

Commercialization of SOEs is critical because divestment of large assets by its nature will take a long time. If for social and political reasons (perhaps also to mitigate the impact on budget outlays) unemployment and wholesale bankruptcy of the economy must be avoided, clear cut rules on wage subsidies must be set. A credible framework for phasing them out is essential. Management that cannot abide by such a "transition impact" must be replaced as soon as feasible. This can be done by exploring alternatives, such as leasing, management contracts, employee or management buyouts and other avenues that can prepare SOEs for eventual privatization. The objective of privatization should be to divest the state of assets and liabilities, and to ensure that private initiative aims at fostering efficiency. Certainly, it will not be easy to commercialize SOEs. But to dismiss such possibilities out of hand begs the question of what to do in the interim with SOEs (and indeed with those that will remain in state hands) and how to ensure that assets that are divested will be managed more effectively.

Finally, once a sufficiently competitive and regulatory environment in a moderately stable economic arena is in place, state-owned assets should gradually be offered for sale to the public at large. Little by little, such assets should be opened up for competitive bidding for leases or management contracts, the supervisory authority being charged with maximizing the return on assets, while protecting their integrity against abuses ("asset stripping" through "insider information"). This should take the form of feeding the budding domestic stock market or opening the bidding process to domestic and foreign capitalists.

Conclusion

This section was deliberately intended to inject some element of skepticism into the undifferentiated advocacy of fast and widespread divestment of state-owned assets in the planned economies in transition. Under most conditions, there will be a better payoff for society if the government focuses its attention on other policies first, including policies for regaining domestic economic stability, formulating balanced macroeconomic policies, fostering domestic and foreign competition, and adequately regulating aberrations from the market environment, and, perhaps most important, if it focuses attention on the structure and governance of industry, which has not been given adequate consideration in the debate on transition, or privatization for that matter.

In addition to the arguments that have been cited in the literature against quick privatization in market economies, skepticism in the case of the planned economies in transition is heightened by the need to come to grips with the legacies of state planning and the Communist system. This includes the massive hold that the Party and government bureaucracy held over economic affairs, as well as the highly monopolized industrial structure, both of which need to be broken as quickly as possible. But there are alternative ways of exerting control over SOEs.

On the basis of these propositions, this section suggests that undertaking a massive program of ill-prepared privatization in a hurry for ideological, political, or sentimental reasons may lead to "casino capitalism." This would be an unjustified way for the state to divest itself of assets that it holds in trust for the nation, however badly these resources may have been utilized in the past and even if the new state in the East aims at substantially slimming down its economic role. Under no circumstances can privatization be viewed as offering a panacea for raising economic efficiency. That depends critically on the creation of the most essential elements of a competitive environment, including effective control mechanisms, and the recognition in principle of the validity of all alternative property rights.

Being fully aware of this is not quite the same as giving up on privatization altogether. Certainly, rapid headway with privatization should be the aim, but preferably the approach should be structured and within the capacity of the new state to manage the transition. If the sociopolitical consensus does not exist for the government or a competent civil service to patiently guide the transition, it may well be wise to dash forward with rapid divestment of some part of state assets as soon as possible after the political revolution.

Notes

1. This section is an abbreviated version of the study "The Economics of Property Rights and Privatization in Transitional Economies" by the same author, published as a part of *The Supplement to World Economy Survey 1991-92*, United Nations Publication, E.9211.C2. It has been edited by Üner Kirdar for the purpose of this book.

2. In what follows, Eastern Europe denotes Bulgaria, the Czech and Slovak Republics, the former German Democratic Republic, Hungary, Poland, and Romania. References to Eastern Europe as a distinct geopolitical entity after 2 October 1991, omit the former German Democratic Republic. Nonetheless, much of this paper applies to that part of the new Germany also. Some of the lessons emanating from the incorporation of the eastern parts into the new Germany will be touched upon when relevant to the transformation of other countries.

3. Because of the recent changes in Albania and the vacillations of reforms in the former Yugoslavia, their cases need to be considered too. "East" refers to Eastern Europe as defined plus Albania, the former Soviet Union, and Yugoslavia.

4. In many ways, the former Yugoslavia has already jettisoned crucial elements of the planning environment in the 1960s. Nonetheless, by the late 1980s, the country on balance still exhibited more features of a modified planned economy than of a market economy.

5. There is at present a wide variety of names for these countries. These include: post-Communist or postsocialist, historically planned, previously centrally planned, Central and East European, newly-emerging market, former Soviet and socialist economies, reforming socialist economies, as well as economies in transition.

6. As such, it is essentially a companion to the earlier published studies of the author.

7. A market economy need not be based on some variant of pluralistic democracy. However, the mutations in the East are currently directed towards emulating the type of political democracy typical of Western Europe.

8. The new East has been much preoccupied with the creation of all-encompassing capital markets. However, it is frequently overlooked that there are only a few efficiently organized fully fledged capital markets in the world and that they have emerged only after protracted evolution. Furthermore, the best way for a new firm to finance itself initially is not through a public issue of stock, but rather through other financial channels for which a strong banking sector is a critical intermediary between savers and investors. This has historically been the case, certainly at the beginning of the process of private capital accumulation.

9. The widespread claim of the loss-making status of the vast bulk of SOEs in the East is, of course, groundless in a number of respects. The key issue is not a profit or loss as such, but rather whether it reflects underlying economic realities.

10. The widespread claim of the loss-making status of the vast bulk of SOEs in the East is, of course, groundless in a number of respects. The key issue is not a profit or loss as such, but rather whether it reflects underlying economic realities.

Section 3 · Trade and Payments after the Soviet Collapse[1]

John Williamson

The successor states of the Soviet Union are seeking what are surely the most dramatic social transformations attempted in human history. Almost all of them are aiming to build functioning democracies in an area with no democratic traditions. All have declared their intention of moving to a market economy, despite there being even less memory of the market than in their neighbors in Central Europe. As if that were not enough, they are trying to build new independent states on the rubble of the last of the world's great multinational empires.

This section concerns the interactions between the second and third of these ambitions: between the aim to transform their economies to a market basis and the replacement of a centralized empire by a series of nation-states. Will market-determined trade between independent states continue with the same intensity, and in the same direction, as that inherited from the Soviet Union? Is there a danger of this trade collapsing, and how severe would the consequences of such a collapse be? What policy measures might avert the danger of a collapse in trade, while helping to shift it to a market basis? How much interest do the new states have in maintaining cooperative relationships among themselves, and what institutional forms might cooperation take?

The Inheritance

Six years of *perestroika* had destroyed not just the traditional command economy of the Soviet Union, but also the "bargaining economy" that some analysts argued had replaced the command economy as the center progressively lost its power to dictate to the enterprises. The damage was done primarily by the fiscal deficit, which increased from an easily-financeable 2.4 percent of GDP in 1985 to close to 10 percent in 1987-90 and more than 20 percent in 1991. In an economy with no mechanism for financing budget deficits other than the printing press, this led to a monetary explosion. The combination of monetary explosion and universal price controls generated excess demand, massive payments deficits, a large monetary overhang, and a progressive disappearance of goods from the shelves at official prices.

The Gorbachev years did achieve progress in some dimensions. Most of these were political: *glasnost,* elections, respect for human rights, and the ending of the Cold War, were massive achievements by any standards. Even in the economic realm some of the seeds of reform were sown: enterprises did achieve independence from the planners (although they had still not started to make much constructive use of it), the beginnings of a private sector emerged in the cooperative movement, and a two-tier banking system was established (though not adequately regulated or capitalized).

The situation of the Soviet economy in its final months was indeed bleak. Inflation was largely repressed by price controls, to the point where almost nothing except a few spices was freely available at the official prices in Moscow, yet prices were still rising by several percent each month. A dollar was valued at 1.6 rubles according to the "commercial" exchange rate at which enterprises were supposed to surrender most of their foreign exchange earnings[2] while a foreigner could buy around 100 rubles for a dollar on the parallel market—an exchange rate that valued Russian labor at under $10 per month. Public services were progressively deteriorating. Corruption was rampant and confidence was virtually nonexistent.

When the Soviet Union vanished in December 1991 and its former republics declared themselves independent nations, none except Russia—which was able to take over most of the Soviet institutions—had the basic institutional infrastructure needed to run a modern state. They all had branches of the former ministries that they proceeded to convert into full-fledged ministries. In some cases, as with the branches of Gosplan and the industry ministries, the well-wishers of a market economy might have desired that these institutions be less able to continue functioning autonomously, but in the key economic ministries like Finance there were acute problems of inexperience and a shortage of trained personnel. For example, Kyrghyzstan is reported to have a ministry of finance with a staff of a dozen. The same was true of the branches of Gosbank, which became republic central banks, but without any of the traditions of central banking or employees familiar with such subjects as how to print money, let alone how to conduct a monetary policy.

There were also problems of dividing the assets and, more importantly, the liabilities of the old Soviet Union among the new states. The G-7 insisted that the foreign debt be divided among the states, but also guaranteed by them "jointly and severally." In other words, each of them was legally responsible for the entire debt. Since it is ridiculous to think that Armenia could in any meaningful sense be held responsible for a Russian failure to service its portion of the debt, this guarantee was presumably intended either to be a formula for getting Russia to assume responsibility for the whole debt or a formula designed to bolster Russian hegemony. Ukraine and Uzbekistan seem to have adopted the latter interpretation, for it was these two republics, rather than Russia, which balked at the formula.

Difficult as these economic questions were, they were dwarfed by the political disputes revealed by Soviet disintegration. The overblown armed forces had to be divided up, without increasing the number of nuclear powers in the world, while satisfying the desire of all the states that had inherited nuclear weapons to keep some element of control over their use. Borders had in many cases been drawn quite casually, as when Khrushchev gave the Crimea to Ukraine as a present in the 1950s, on the assumption that these borders really did not matter much since the whole empire was administered from the center. Partly as a result there are large ethnic minorities, including some 25 million Russians living outside

Russia and a comparable number of non-Russians living within Russia. Considering the potential for disaster and some of the historical precedents of decolonization, it is right to recognize that the dismemberment of the Russian empire has so far been accomplished in a relatively civilized way. The crucial question to be discussed in this section is whether it can also be achieved without causing an economic catastrophe.

The Problems Posed by Disintegration

Despite its formal federal structure, the Soviet Union operated as a highly centralized state. It is therefore not surprising to find that the collapse of the old union has confronted the successor states with severe problems. The present section outlines the nature of six critical problems that will need to be resolved in designing arrangements for trade and payments of, and among, the former republics in a pòst-Soviet world.

The Need for New Trade Patterns

Soviet planners had a very clear idea of the sort of trade pattern that they wished to effect. The Soviet Union, or at least the Council for Mutual Economic Assistance (CMEA) area, should be self-sufficient, but each of its component parts should act as a branch of a giant factory. Hence the pattern noted above of very low levels of exports to the outside world, even including exports to the other former members of CMEA, combined with extraordinarily high levels of trade among the republics.

This "socialist division of labor" was pushed to an extreme. One of the unfortunate legacies of this policy was the extraordinarily high degree of monopoly in the former Soviet republics. Since the planners regarded competition as a social waste rather than as the stimulus that makes an economy efficient and motivates innovation, they were not disturbed by the prevalence of monopoly. Indeed, since they also had an exaggerated faith in the prevalence of economies of scale and underpriced transportation, they tended to regard public monopolies as rational and beneficent institutions.

The absolute level of trade of the former Soviet republics may decline in the long run. That is, market forces can be expected to motivate efficient net import substitution, so that goods currently produced in only a few locations in the former Soviet Union and then sold to the other states will be produced in a larger number of states.

The Need for New Trade Mechanisms

A shift to the market economy will require a fundamental change in the way in which trade is conducted, away from the sort of interstate barter agreements that were negotiated in 1991 and toward direct interenterprise contracts.

As the republics gained more and more power in the course of 1990-91, they began to sign what were called barter agreements in an attempt to prevent a breakdown of interrepublic trade. The government of one republic would commit itself to supplying a long list of goods to another republic, in return for which it was promised another long list of goods. Payment is made in rubles.

The classic disadvantage of barter—the fact that it precludes efficient triangular trade and instead relies on a double coincidence of wants—is the least of the disadvantages of this arrangement. A more important drawback, which became apparent very quickly, is that it contained inadequate incentives for the sellers to fulfill the terms of the agreements. Where goods were in short supply at the controlled prices that prevailed, it made more sense for republics to keep goods at home than to ship them off in fulfillment of a barter agreement, in the knowledge that all they would receive in exchange might be rubles (which could be obtained much more cheaply at home by the republic central bank creating more credit). This led not just to a growth of export restrictions, but also to failures to fulfill the terms of the barter agreements that republics had signed.

A second problem with the barter agreements is that they are poorly specified. In some cases obligations are designated in physical terms, for example as so many tons of oil or so many kilowatt-hours of electricity to be supplied in the course of a year, but even then a failure to specify the date deliveries are due or the time of day when the electricity is to be transmitted creates endless opportunities for disagreement and/or unintended disruption of supply in the importing state. In other cases the obligation is specified as the duty of shipping a given ruble value of some good (like furs), which in an environment of near-hyperinflation obviously invites delay in shipping goods.

The most fundamental difficulty with these barter agreements is, however, that they require the state to do what it is supposedly in the process of renouncing doing: issuing state orders so as to procure the goods that can then be supplied to the other republic in fulfillment of the obligation enshrined in the barter agreement. This difficulty cannot be finessed by raising prices to market-clearing levels or by more careful drafting. If the members of the Commonwealth of Independent States (CIS) are serious about creating a market economy, they must abandon interstate barter agreements formally, and move to enterprise-to-enterprise trade.

The Threat of a Trade Collapse

It is one thing to argue that in the long-term intratrade should decrease. It is quite another to view with equanimity a precipitate collapse of that trade. The very intensive trade among the republics that had been deliberately fostered by the central planners has to be maintained in the short run if the economy is not to be reduced to chaos. That trade can sensibly be run down only as new investment makes possible the redeployment of factors into alternative uses and the satisfaction of needs from alternative sources.

History shows all too clearly the cost of disrupting existing trade channels. Perhaps the two clearest examples are the breakup of Austria-Hungary after World War I and the delayed recovery of Western Europe after World War II. Prior to World War I, Austria-Hungary had been the fourth fastest-growing economy in Europe. After the war, the successor states blocked trade with one another; and only Czechoslovakia among the six successor states was able to reestablish prosperity before World War II intervened. Three of the successor states actually succumbed to hyperinflation. In the other case, Marshall aid is widely credited with having accelerated European recovery after World War II. Yet in fact U.S. aid was no greater after Marshall aid started to flow than it was before; the crucial difference was in the conditionality attached to the aid, which required Europeans to help themselves by dismantling the restrictions that had been blocking their mutual trade.

Monetary Control

One of the first and most disruptive consequences of the erosion of central authority in the Soviet Union was the progressive loss of monetary control that resulted. Under the *ancien régime* it did not matter very much that the central bank automatically monetized the deficits of the republic governments as well as the union government, because the union government kept its own deficit down and it made sure that the republic governments did too. But the practice of automatic monetary emission was carried over to a situation where the union government let its own finances deteriorate and the republic governments gained a large measure of autonomy in their fiscal policy. Since most of the costs of monetary emission by any one republic spill over to the others under a common monetary system, while the benefits of the deficit spending accrue exclusively to the republic that runs a deficit, the system gave each individual republic an incentive to run a deficit even though the collective consequence was most undesirable.[3] In fact the situation was even worse in 1991, inasmuch as the largest republic, which had the clearest incentive not to act as a free rider, wielded its monetary power with a view to destabilizing the union government. The Soviet Union ended up with a budget deficit of around 20 percent of GDP in its final year of existence.

This problem was quickly recognized by the Russian economic team headed by Yegor Gaidar. By November 1991 they asserted unilateral Russian control of the emission of cash rubles, indicating that other republics would be entitled to obtain ruble banknotes on a proportionate scale. Some of the other republics complained strongly. Moreover, they objected that Russia has not in fact been doing what it promised, since it failed to deliver rubles on the same scale as had been issued in Russia itself. An additional grievance was that Russia had been charging interest (admittedly only at a strongly negative real rate, since the nominal interest rate is only 22 percent per year) on the credit represented by "lending" the ruble banknotes to the other republics. In other words, Russia was refusing to share the seigniorage in ruble creation.

Ruble banknotes were not, however, the only problem. Even though the governments of the other republics were constrained in their ability to finance budget deficits with the public by the lack of ruble banknotes, their central banks could still extend credit to their enterprises. The enterprises could use that credit inter alia to buy goods from Russia, implying that excess monetary emission in the other republics could still occur and might undermine Russia's stabilization program. It was to counter this danger that Russia imposed the system of channeling interrepublic payments through correspondent banks in January 1992.

Apart from the question of seigniorage, the heart of the economic case for separate currencies in the states that have now achieved their political independence is based on the desirability of making the monetary domain coincide with the fiscal domain, so that the consequences of monetary emission are borne by the same political jurisdiction that determines the fiscal deficit. However, the economic case is not what is driving the determination of a number of the republics—at least the Baltics, Moldova, and Ukraine—to introduce their own currencies. A separate money is viewed as an attribute of national sovereignty, and it is desired on that score rather than because of any economic arguments.

But even if it is taken as given that separate monies are coming, there is a critical and disputed question of timing about their introduction as to whether it is sensible for republics to introduce their own currencies before stabilization is possible. One may argue that it would be desirable for all the states that plan to introduce their own currencies to do so simultaneously. The counterargument is that stabilization will not have a chance to get off the ground until the republics can free themselves from monetary dependence on Russia and Russia can free itself from the free-rider problem. If one thinks that Russia's nationalization of the ruble has already resolved the latter problem, albeit in a manner that one cannot expect the other republics to applaud, it would seem sensible for them to delay the introduction of their own currencies until they are in a position to make a serious attempt at stabilization. Whether they are in the political mood to listen to such economic advice is another matter.

Fiscal Transfers

Before turning to the political dimension alluded to above, it is convenient to examine a final economic consequence of Soviet disintegration. This is the termination of the extensive fiscal transfers that had developed, primarily to benefit the states of Central Asia.

The withdrawal of these transfers is seen as the central implication of Soviet disintegration in that region. In recent years consumption has exceeded net domestic material product in three of the four republics,[4] leaving the whole of government spending on goods and services, and investment, to be financed by the transfers from the union. These transfers were suspended on the breakup of the union at the end of 1991. Budget deficits without transfers would be around 50 percent of total government expenditures in the absence of adjustments to either revenue or expenditure.

However, it is believed that the Central Asian states do not stand to lose more from the shift to world prices in valuing intratrade. According to Soviet estimates cited in the joint study of the International Monetary Fund (IMF), World Bank, Organization for Economic Cooperation and Development (OECD), and Eropean Bank for Reconstruction and Development (EBRD), three of the four states would gain from the shift to world prices. Turkmenistan was estimated to gain 6.3 percent of NMP, Tajikistan to gain 1.3 percent, and Kyrghyzstan to gain 2.2 percent, while Uzbekistan stood to lose 3.2 percent. Even the latter is trivial compared to estimated costs of (for example) 16 percent of NMP in Belarus and 24 percent in Lithuania. The reason is that the Central Asian states are also exporters of primary products (notably cotton) that had been vastly and systematically underpriced in the Soviet Union, so that the move to world prices was expected to bring them gains that would more or less offset the costs of increased prices for their energy imports.

Even if the loss of transfers is not further aggravated by worsened terms of trade as a result of moving to world prices, it will still be a crippling blow to the region. The Central Asian states will have no alternative but to adjust in the longer run, even if the West adds them to the list of long-term aid recipients, for Western aid programs as a percentage of the recipient's GNP (other than that from western Germany to eastern Germany) never approach the size of the transfers that the union government was making to Central Asia. It seems that this is well understood in Central Asia, and the occasional newspaper report[5] suggests that at least some of the leaders see independence as an opportunity to break away from the role of hewers of wood and drawers of water assigned to them by the socialist division of labor.

Russian Dominance

The Soviet Union was essentially a perpetuation of the Russian Empire. Yet when Boris Yeltsin achieved power he dismantled that empire with none of the vacillation shown by many of the other colonial powers (despite the encouragement he was getting from the West to follow Gorbachev's example in struggling to keep the union together). So far, at least, decolonization has been achieved without any bloodshed that begins to compare with that which accompanied the British withdrawal from India, or the French exodus from Algeria, or the Portuguese pullout from their former empire, not to mention the savage civil war in the former Yugoslavia. The Russians surely deserve credit for their speedy recognition that empires belong with authoritarianism and socialism in the junkyard of history.

Russia nonetheless remains the dominant power in the region. Both the population of Russia and the number of Russians amounted to just over 50 percent of the Soviet total, and the economic weight of Russia was rather larger than that. The Russian government seems to be committed to economic reform and unwilling to be held back by the hesitations of what it sees as the only partly reconstructed former Communists still in office in many of the other new states—states that are showing great reluctance to pick up their share of the burdens inherited from the past, such as paying the army and cleaning up after Chernobyl. Russia too has its grievances against its partners, and it feels itself both big enough and with enough at stake to lay down the law.

It is also unsurprising that the other new states resent what they see as high-handed Russian arrogance: not just about specific actions (like the failure to supply enough ruble banknotes, or the interest charges being levied on the banknotes that are supplied), but also about the inability to negotiate with Moscow. Several states, notably Belarus and Kazakhstan, would clearly prefer to maintain close ties with Moscow, including a common currency, but feel they are being forced toward monetary independence by Russian intransigence.

This is not the sort of problem for which one can anticipate any easy or quick solution. Greater understanding is bound to take time to develop under the best of circumstances. It will have to be nurtured, by discussions and conferences in which the West can surely play an intermediating role, as well as by direct negotiations.

Alternative Payments Systems

The major policy question posed by Soviet disintegration is the nature of the payments mechanism that will be used to conduct the intratrade of the area. This is not to dismiss the crucial importance of moving to interenterprise trade, but rather to assert that there are no controversial policy issues posed by making that transition, except those involved in developing a satisfactory payments mechanism. Nor is it to disregard the need to provide at least transitional help to the Central Asian states in order to mitigate the costs of the big adjustments that they need to undertake, but rather to suggest that that topic does not raise particularly novel economic issues.

What the assertion of the primacy of the payments issue is intended to imply is that this is far more crucial in limiting the collapse of intratrade than a set of trade rules would be. A commitment to free trade within the area of the former Soviet Union, or at least within the CIS, remains highly desirable.[6]

It would be quite wrong, however, to suggest that the issue of organizing payments is exclusively one that relates to interrepublic trade. On the contrary, the payments mechanism within Russia—and doubtless within the other states as well—is in a state of near-collapse. It is reported that on average the banking system takes between four and eight weeks to settle transactions. This is one reason why so much trade takes place on a barter basis, and why hard currency is also being used on a limited scale to settle transactions even within Russia.

The delays in settling payments are also one reason for the reported growth in interenterprise credit. These delays prevent enterprises being able to find out which of their customers are unwilling or unable to pay, or at least to find out quickly enough for the information to be of much use. This is bound to deter the authorities from doing much to harden budget constraints, for fear that the wrong enterprises might be driven into bankruptcy as a result of payments not being received promptly.

The Central Bank of Russia (and the other central banks) should surely make the restoration of a system of rapid and efficient interbank clearing one of its priorities, perhaps even its number one priority. If Western technical assistance can be of help in this regard, it should be made available as a matter of the utmost urgency. Clearly interrepublic payments are unlikely to work satisfactorily until intrarepublic payments are functioning efficiently. Once that condition has been satisfied, there would seem to be four options for the financing of intratrade that are worth discussing: a ruble zone, a Ruble Area, dollar payments, and a payments union.

Ruble Zone

By a "ruble zone" I mean an area that continues to use the ruble as a common currency. It is quite clear that not all of the former Soviet republics are willing to contemplate this solution: at least the Baltics and Ukraine plan to establish their own currencies. But there are some states that would like to continue using the ruble, if they can reach a satisfactory agreement with Russia about the conduct of monetary policy. A major benefit of other states continuing to use the ruble is that they would be able to trade freely among themselves, and with Russia, by transferring rubles.

Or would they? At the moment they all use the ruble, yet there are limits—set by Russia's willingness to allow them to run up debts on the books of their correspondent accounts in Moscow—on the extent to which they can actually pay one another in rubles. If those limits are maintained, then sooner or later some states will presumably run out of credit, and find themselves unable to continue paying their suppliers. One may think it is not much of a common money that cannot be freely used to settle debts, and that is right: since the Russian decision to require interrepublic trade to be settled through correspondent accounts, the ruble has really ceased to be a common currency. (*Cash* rubles are still common, but the bank deposit rubles used to settle trade contracts are distinct, as argued previously.) The prevailing system is in fact already de facto what is below described as a "Ruble Area."

To restore a ruble zone, it would be necessary for the rubles held in any one state to be usable without limit in settling debts in another state. Unless Russia's determination to try and stabilize evaporates, that would be conceivable only if the other states renounce the right to independent policies on monetary emission. Either they must do as Russia says, which hardly seems likely, or else it will be necessary to found a federal central bank that will give the other states some say in the determination of the common monetary policy of the ruble zone. There is no sign that Russia is currently willing to contemplate such an arrangement, which means that the prospects for revival of even a limited ruble zone cannot be considered bright.

Ruble Area

The terms "ruble zone" and "ruble area" have often been used interchangeably, but they here they mean two very different things. As explained above, the term ruble zone is used to refer to a group of countries that continue to use the ruble as a common currency. In contrast, the term ruble area will be used to suggest an analogy with the "sterling area" in its heyday: a group of countries with *separate* currencies that continue to use the currency of the former "colonial" power for *international* purposes, even after establishing monetary independence.

A major attraction of a ruble area is that in essence it already exists (or at least it will do once the reform of the payments mechanism set in train by Russia is complete). The non-Russian states will all have correspondent accounts in Moscow, which they can use in order to receive and make payments, not just with Russia, but also with one another and presumably with the outside world as well. There is no reason why they should not continue to maintain those accounts and use them in exactly the same way even if they establish their own currencies de jure.

The major objection to membership in a ruble zone, which was voiced in a number of the conference papers, has been that it means handing over control of monetary and fiscal policy to Moscow. This objection does not apply to membership of a ruble area. The members could set their own monetary and fiscal policies, and if these turn out to give very different rates of inflation to that in Russia, the balance of payments consequences could be avoided by devaluing against the ruble (if their policies are more expansionary than those in Russia) or revaluing against the ruble (if they succeed in mastering inflation better). Republics could also, of course, choose to devalue or revalue not just to offset differential inflation, but also to facilitate real adjustment, which may be particularly important in some of the states that have suffered a loss of transfer income or that will be particularly hit hard by the forthcoming energy price increases.

There seem to be two possible objections to maintaining a ruble area in order to finance the trade, including the intratrade, of the former Soviet republics. One is that this still gives a privileged place to Russia. So it does, at least in the sense that it gives a special place to the ruble. But it does not give Russia any special ability to dictate the stance of macroeconomic policy to the other states, which is surely what they have a legitimate interest in avoiding. Nor is it clear that it is likely to give Russia the "exorbitant privilege" of having its payments deficits financed by the other countries, in the way that General Charles de Gaulle used to resent vis-a-vis the dollar, for the very basic reason that it is Russia rather than the others that is expected to run the structural surplus in the region once the price of energy has been raised. Rather, Russia is likely to suffer the burden of providing sufficient credit to make the system work. This is the sort of burden that countries with aspirations to remaining global powers can sometimes be persuaded to accept; it would seem an expensive nationalistic gesture of the other states to reject a Russian offer to assume the burden if one is forthcoming.

The other objection to a ruble area is that traditionally only stable currencies have succeeded in fulfilling the role that is here proposed for the ruble. Despite the vigor with which stabilization policies have been pursued by Gaidar and his team, it is still far from clear that Russia is likely to achieve a reasonable degree of price stability in the near future. Is it conceivable that a ruble area might emerge despite such a failure? The answer is not clear. We have usually thought that the reason countries have always been reluctant to use an unstable currency as their vehicle currency and reserve currency was that they anticipated holding net balances in that currency, and since real interest rates are typically negative under high and unstable inflation, they risked suffering partial expropriation. But the situation is in this instance very different: the other states are likely to have net debit positions with Russia, which means that they will *benefit* financially from rapid Russian inflation that erodes the real value of their liabilities. Despite this factor, intuition suggests that it is unlikely that the other states would be willing to remain in a ruble area if the ruble were suffering such rapid inflation as to undermine its acceptability as money within Russia. A reasonable approximation to price stability will surely be needed.

Dollar Settlement

If there is insufficient trust among the former Soviet republics to permit continued use of the ruble to settle interrepublic trade, even in the rather undemanding form of a ruble area, then the natural inclination after the establishment of separate currencies will be to settle trade by the use of dollars (or another hard currency). Indeed, this is apparently already happening to some extent, especially with trade contracted through the commercial exchanges. It is also what happened to trade among the former CMEA members after that organization was abolished.

The problem with dollar settlement is that it requires substantial reserves of hard currency. The sums involved are not as large as they would be if the dollar were adopted as the local currency ("dollarization"), something that tends to happen spontaneously when inflation gets out of hand, and has indeed been happening at the margin in the former Soviet Union already. Nor are they as large as is required by a currency board, which essentially requires as many dollars as dollarization does, although it is much less expensive in flow terms because the dollars are held as interest-earning assets by the central bank rather than a large part of them being held in the form of noninterest-earning dollar bills by the general public.

How many dollars would be required if the economies of the former Soviet republics were completely dollarized (or if all the republics established currency boards)? On the basis of purchasing power parity, Soviet GNP was probably of the order of $500 billion before the collapse started. The currency in circulation was of 133 billion rubles at the end of 1990, a year in which GNP was a trillion rubles, plus other monetary assets of 614 billion rubles. If those other assets required a 10 percent reserve in external dollars, the total dollar requirement would be approximately $100 billion, which is an awful lot of money for a bankrupt group of states that cannot even service their external debt.

Even though the Soviet Union went bankrupt at the end of 1991 and its successor states have not built up much in the way of reserves since, there may actually be a non-negligible stock of dollars available to finance trade. It was the Institute of International Finance (1992) that first drew attention to the evidence of massive capital flight from the Soviet Union. Most observers felt that their estimate of some $14 billion being held abroad was exaggerated, but the IMF estimate that the Soviet Union had an overall surplus of almost $5 billion in convertible currencies in 1991 (in a year when it suffered a heavy loss of reserves) confirms that capital flight must have been substantial. Since that flight overwhelmingly takes the form of enterprises building up hard currency holdings in Western bank accounts rather than remitting all their earnings, the money is in a form that would be readily available to finance trade.

Even allowing for the ability to mobilize flight capital, however, the former Soviet republics would fall far short of the amount of hard currency needed to assure them of reserve ease. Hence the consequence of resorting to dollar settlement would probably be restrictions of "unessential" imports designed to save scarce foreign exchange, even if the victims of the restrictions are other republics that are just as short of hard currency. That is exactly the sort of paralysis of trade from which Western Europe suffered in the early postwar years, before Marshall Plan conditionality and the European Payments Union (EPU) induced intra-European liberalization.

Clearing or Payments Union

The EPU precedent naturally raises the question as to whether a similar arrangement might not be worthwhile in the former Soviet Union today. Could it combine the advantages of denominating trade and debts in a hard currency, and the discipline of knowing that ultimate settlement would be in hard currency, with a saving in foreign exchange that would avoid the danger of republics restricting their imports from one another?

A clearing union is an arrangement in which the member countries agree to accept one another's currencies in payment for exports, deposit their earnings from those exports with the agent of the union, allow the claims to be consolidated and periodically netted out on a multilateral basis, and then settle the remaining imbalances centrally with the union in hard currency. This achieves major economies in the need for hard-currency reserves because it is only net imbalances that have to be settled in hard currency, rather than each individual transaction. A payments union has the additional feature of providing that the resulting imbalances be settled in a mixture of credit and hard currencies, thus further economizing on the need for hard-currency reserves.

It is often said that a clearing or payments union would be redundant if the republics had all established current account convertibility. This view is mistaken. In order to establish convertibility without a payments union, it would be necessary to have reserves approaching five times as high as would be needed with a payments union, given that about 80 percent of trade is intratrade. In fact, a payments union is still a sensible arrangement among countries that have established current account convertibility with the rest of the world, if they trade intensively among themselves and have a shortage of hard currency. It can in fact enable them to establish current account convertibility with the rest of the world more rapidly than would otherwise be feasible, and/or avoid as sharp a depreciation as would otherwise be necessary.

There is no technical difficulty in combining payment through a payments union for one group of countries with payment in dollars to another, as long as exchange controls still exist so that an importer has to demonstrate a foreign purchase before he is entitled to buy dollars. If the importer's purchase is from a supplier within the region covered by the payments union, he is channeled through that mechanism rather than allowed access to dollars. The feasibility of this arrangement is demonstrated by the fact that it was operated by Switzerland, which had current account convertibility with the dollar area, during the days of the EPU.

Another question that is sometimes raised is the scope of membership, notably whether former CMEA members in Central and Eastern Europe, and Mongolia, should be invited to participate. Their inclusion would seem to offer a chance of reversing the drastic decline in trade that followed the move to hard-currency financing at the start of 1991. Now that the geopolitical fear of continued Soviet domination that underlay their refusal to contemplate such arrangements when they were first proposed in 1990 has vanished, and the countries of Central Europe have experienced the hardship caused by the disappearance of Soviet orders, one might have expected the idea to be welcomed in the non-Soviet former CMEA members. In fact there seems no weakening in their hostility to the idea.

Policy Recommendations

It has been argued above that, even though the total trade of the ex-Soviet republics will and should diminish in the long run, and even though the share of intratrade in that diminished total will and should decline in the long run, an excessive and precipitate fall could give a further vicious twist to the downward spiral in which the region is currently trapped. This is not only a theoretical possibility, it is something that the fragmentary evidence available indicates is actually happening. Historical precedents suggest that it would be worth trying to arrest and reverse this development, and that outside influence could be of strategic importance in doing so.

Hence it is appropriate to turn to a discussion of what it would be sensible for the governments of the former Soviet republics to do, and of the extent to which the West should try and push them to act on that advice. The discussion starts by considering the central issue of the payments system, and goes on to consider two other topics—transfers and aid, and stabilization—the resolution of which is also critical to relations among the republics.

The Payments System

Of the four options for settling interrepublic transactions discussed above, a ruble zone will certainly not be acceptable to all the new states, because some of them have made a firm political commitment to introducing their own monies. The rump of a ruble zone may survive if the Russians can bring themselves to give the other participants a genuine share in monetary decision making, but it will not solve the main problem because its membership will be too restricted.

That leaves two options, a ruble area and a payments union. Either of these could support multilateral interenterprise trade without requiring vast sums of hard currency that the republics do not have and without requiring them to forego or share monetary sovereignty. The West does not have a strong interest in seeing one of those solutions adopted rather than the other, but it surely does have a crucial interest in seeing one or the other implemented. It should therefore be prepared to give such financial support as may be needed to get one or other off the ground, and it might reasonably hesitate to put in a lot of money unless the ex-Soviets can get their act together to the point of agreeing on one or the other.

The ex-Soviet republics might, however, find difficulty in reaching agreement on this issue even if they were told it was necessary to be eligible for Western aid. Russia would almost certainly favor a ruble area, and the other republics might decline to go along. Should the West then refuse to help any of them, irrespective of the merits of their case? Surely not. This is a topic where the primary responsibility for deciding which system to adopt should be that of the non-Russian republics. If Russia can persuade them that it is in their interests to remain within a ruble area (and Russia does have some weapons that it can deploy for that purpose, such as the amount of credit it would be prepared to advance and the extent to which it might credit the correspondent accounts of the republics for ruble banknotes withdrawn from circulation), well and good. But Russia should not be allowed to force other republics into a ruble area by refusing to join a payments union.

The form of the financial support would be very different depending on which solution was adopted. To make a ruble area work, the key need—despite the argument that indebted republics might not mind too much if their ruble liabilities were eroded by inflation—is to stabilize the ruble. The possible role of a Stabilization Fund in achieving that objective is discussed below. With a payments union solution, in contrast, ruble stabilization would be a matter of national interest to Russia rather than of systemic interest to all the new states. The key systemic need would instead be for a capital fund that would permit the payments union to extend rather more credit to those states in cumulative deficit than it would need to obtain from those in cumulative surplus.

It turns out that such a fund set up on the same relative scale as that which catalyzed the EPU would require the surprisingly modest sum of $1.3 billion if it were restricted to the former Soviet republics, or $2.5 billion in the unlikely event that it was extended to include the other former members of CMEA.

The purpose of a payments union is to provide swing credits to finance the bulk of the short-term variations in net balances inherent in reasonably free trade. A payments union cannot finance structural imbalances, and any attempt to rely on it for that purpose would simply guarantee an early crisis as the structural deficit countries exhausted their credit limits. This does not mean that structural deficit countries cannot participate in a payments union, but simply that the size of the structural deficit that they will be allowed to run must be determined *ex ante* and then financed from outside sources. Each year they would then receive a credit in the accounts of the payments union equal to the finance provided from outside, and a deficit on the books of the payments union would arise only if their total deficit exceeded the size of that credit.

Transfers and Aid

Obviously a crucial question is to whom such credits might be made available and from where the finance might come. Note that this issue is not specific to a payments union, but would arise also with a ruble area. If structural deficit states fail to get finance, then in that system too they will be faced with a need to adjust when they reach the credit limit that Russia is willing to permit. A difference would arise only insofar as Russia might be willing to be less (or more) generous in allowing credit within a ruble area than in financing structural deficits in association with a payments union. The usual argument has been that the leavening of outside credit in a payments union can help to persuade the structural surplus countries to extend more credit through a payments union than they would otherwise be willing to sanction, but it could be that the reverse would be true in the present instance; a ruble area might appeal to Russian pride.

Two groups of countries seem all too likely to emerge as structural deficit countries for the next few years. The first consists of the Central Asian republics that had become large recipients of transfers from the union government. As already argued, there is no way that these states are going to continue receiving aid on the scale of recent transfers in the long run. Presumably the West will add them to the list of developing countries eligible to receive aid, but that will replace no more than a fraction of what they had been getting from the union government. Instead of the 25 percent of GDP, or more, that they have been receiving, they will be lucky to get 5 percent on a continuing basis. The balance will have to be adjusted. But there is a limit to the speed with which adjustment can be effected if it is to take the efficient form of developing new tradable goods industries rather than the wasteful form of repressing demand, and adjustment of that efficient form is feasible only if there is finance for the deficit that will persist in the interim while the structure of productive capacity is being changed.

Even if this basic argument for providing finance for temporary structural deficits on the part of the Central Asian states is accepted, two issues remain. One is the size and duration of the aid. Presumably it should start out at some substantial fraction of the level of the former transfers whose withdrawal has caused the problem, and should then progressively decrease over a normal planning horizon (five years?).

The other issue is the source of the aid. It can be argued that Russia should be a major contributory, since Russia will get a windfall benefit from energy price increases. On the other hand, Russia itself is a candidate for substantial aid in the short term. Might it not make sense for the West to give a part of that aid, not directly to Russia, but in the form of grants to the Central Asians that they can use to finance structural deficits with Russia? This would allow Russia to earn a substantial part of its dollars through trade, reducing the risk that it might become aid-dependent.

The second group of countries that may emerge as structural deficit countries in the next few years consists of those that will be adversely impacted by the energy price increases. According to the joint study, these are Belarus (with an adverse impact of 16 percent of NMP expected from the switch to world prices), Moldova (20 percent), the Baltics (adverse impacts of 15 percent to 24 percent), and the Caucasians (with costs estimated as varying between a surprisingly modest 5 percent of NMP in Armenia to 15 percent in Azerbaijan).

The case for providing interim finance to these states is similar to, although not as compelling as, that developed above for helping the Central Asians to soften the brutality of the adjustment process. It is less compelling for two reasons: because the economies are more diversified, and should therefore be better placed to adjust reasonably quickly, and because living standards are not as low (except in Azerbaijan). In view of these differences, it might make sense to help these countries by increasing the credit provided through a payments union (or by a deal whereby Russia would enlarge their credit limits in a ruble area in return for additional aid), rather than assuming that they are predestined to be structural deficit countries.

That leaves three of the new states that are not affected by adverse shocks emanating from the dissolution of the Soviet Union. They happen to be the three largest republics in economic terms: Russia, Ukraine, and Kazakhstan. Of course, all three are heavily affected by the shocks that have resulted from the collapse of the Communist system. The West has already theoretically accepted the case for helping them make the transition to a market economy by giving substantial financial help: for example, Michel Camdessus, the Managing Director of the IMF, has spoken of a financing requirement for Russia alone of $20 billion to $25 billion in 1992, plus another $20 billion or so for the other republics. However, in practice the case has been different. At the recent summit meeting if G-7 in Tokyo July 1993. The seven major industrialized nations agrreed to provide only $3 billion in aid to Russia in the form of loans, grants, and export credits. Most of this amount was not new money, but a reallocation of funds previously committed and not yet disbursed.

What Russia needs really is something like a Marshall Plan: a substantial but relatively brief injection of external funds, on condition that it get together with its neighbors to create conditions that will permit efficient intratrade to flourish. One way of doing that is to give the Central Asian states the funds they will need in the short run to allow an efficient adjustment program, and then allow Russia to earn hard currency from them by selling its oil. Drawing the analogy with the Marshall Plan should do something to limit the assault on Russian pride implied by accepting aid.

Central Asia is at the other extreme. It is likely to need a continuing aid program for many years, but the amounts involved are not excessive. A "typical" aid level of around 5 percent of the recipients' GDP would cost under $2 billion per year. Even an additional adjustment program that started off at $4 billion per year would not be unmanageably large.

The other republics are likely to require intermediate treatment. They do not have the natural resources that will permit a rapid balance of payments turnaround, but neither are they so backward as to justify a long-term continuing aid program. A reasonable objective might be to restore self-reliance within a decade.

A part of any aid program will take the form of debt restructuring. The G-7's record on this topic has so far been abysmal: it spent the autumn of 1991, when all the new republics should have been concentrating on the strategic design of their programs for moving to a market economy, in bullying the former Soviet republics to sign on to the formula—for which there is no historical precedent—that they will be "jointly and severally" responsible for the debt of the former Soviet Union. The G-7 did ultimately, if grudgingly, concede the reality that repayment of a year's debt principal would have to be deferred, but it insisted on continued payment of interest, arguing that suspending such payments would make the republics ineligible to receive new credits. Since it is only their own rules that prevent new credits being granted to a country in arrears on interest payments, this is lame.

The situation demands a much bolder initiative, though not in the form of generalized debt relief. On the contrary, the level of debt—something like $68 billion—remains modest in comparison with the size of the economy. But there is a chronic liquidity problem, it is not going to disappear quickly, and attempts to extract debt service in the next few years are just going to divert effort from more urgent subjects. The right solution is to abandon the "jointly and severally" formula, restructure the debt of each republic to give 10 years grace and 10 years of interest capitalization, and then come back in a decade's time to see which republics are in a position to accept their obligations and which will have to be granted debt reduction. Given the fundamental strengths in Russia's position, one would expect Russia to be able to accept its obligations.

Stabilization

The fact that a successful ruble area is unlikely to develop without a successful stabilization of the ruble makes it appropriate to add a few words on that topic.

Russia has already taken strong action this year to bring the budget deficit under control. It is unlikely that the deficit will come down as far as was originally targeted (one percent of GDP), but, given the increased energy prices as well, the fiscal accounts should be in an acceptable state provided that the government succeeds in appropriating a reasonable part of the rents from energy production.

The other central elements of a stabilization program remain to be addressed. In the first place, monetary control has still not been achieved. It is currently impeded by several factors. One is the ambiguous commitment to the cause of the governor of the central bank, who reports to parliament rather than to the economic team in the government and who makes use of his or her independence to reduce the threat that hard budget constraints will drive enterprises to bankruptcy. Another factor is the lack of an efficient interbank settlements system, which leads to unreasonable delays in payments and thus contributes to the explosion in interenterprise credit. That is reinforced by the incentive to exploit interenterprise credit that arises from the fact that it is interest free. The least that needs to be done is to modernize the interbank settlement system and to index the nominal value of these interenterprise credits to the price level (so that the real interest rate would rise at least to zero).

A second problem is the lack of any sort of incomes policy, despite the acute need for one caused by the absence of any countervailing power with an interest in resisting wage demands. One can understand that the Russian authorities were reluctant to introduce an incomes policy that they would have been unable to enforce, and one can also accept that wage anomalies had become so enormous that any simple wage formula would have been unthinkable. But it is also true that inflation is unlikely to come down to a reasonable level without a recession far worse than anything seen so far unless some sort of incomes policy can be agreed.

A third problem is the lack of a stable exchange rate at a level supportive of price stability. At present there are still several exchange rates, with all of them—including the most important, the one that most enterprises use to pay for their imports—sharply undervaluing the ruble. At the beginning of the year, the main ruble rate was around 100 rubles to the dollar, at a time when the average wage was just under 1,000 rubles per month. Russian labor may be worth as little as $100 per month until the economy begins to get back on its feet, but it is certainly worth more than $10 per month! In other words, the exchange rate was perhaps ten times the rate that would have made sense.

It would be wrong to dismiss these pressures just because the Soviet economy was relatively closed. The OECD statistics suggested that Soviet nonenergy exports had almost doubled in 1991, implying that at least some of the enterprises are already capable of responding to price incentives coming from the exchange rate. The experience of rising prices stimulates wage demands, nurtures inflationary expectations, and encourages the development of other sources of inflationary momentum such as indexation. At the same time, the price increases reduce real demand: through squeezing real wages, through creating paper profits on inventory appreciation that are then taxed at a high rate given the structure of enterprise taxes, through reducing the real value of the money supply (the real balance effect), and doubtless through hurting confidence as well. Thus the macroeconomic effect of an acutely undervalued currency is highly stagflationary.

Let it be repeated once more that this is not a hypothetical danger, but rather the major mistake in the design of the transition that has so far been identified. Yet it looks as though Russia may be going to repeat the blunder. It is currently suggested that the various exchange rates will be unified, and access of the typical Russian enterprise to foreign exchange will be eased, to the point where current account convertibility can be said to be establishe. That is a bold and sensible proposal, but it will not support macroeconomic stability unless the unified exchange rate is at a level consistent with the fundamentals.

Conclusion

It remains to summarize the answers that were suggested above to the set of questions laid out at the beginning of this section.

The first of those questions was: Will market-determined trade between independent states continue with the same intensity, and in the same direction, as that inherited from the Soviet Union? The answer suggested was that the total volume of trade is likely to decline, and that there will be a dramatic shift in the composition of trade, with much less intratrade among the former Soviet republics and much more trade between each of them and the West.

The second question was: Is there a danger of their intratrade collapsing, and how severe would the consequences of such a collapse be? The evidence that a collapse is in process is still somewhat fragmentary, but it is nonetheless sufficiently widespread to demand a prompt response. Similarly, the evidence that this collapse will further intensify the downward spiral in economic activity is a little on the casual side, but so many fears were expressed on this score that it would be the height of irresponsibility to dismiss concern until the consequences can be more conclusively documented. In particular, it is wrong to argue that, because intratrade will decline in the course of a move to the market economy,

the sooner the decline comes the better we should be pleased. However inefficient current practices may be, it is better that any activity that produces positive
value-added continue functioning until it is possible to make the investments that
will permit the factors it employs to be redeployed into new activities.

The third question was: What policy measures might avert the danger of a
collapse in trade, while helping to shift it to a market basis? It was argued that
the current interstate barter agreements need to be phased out quickly, and that
support needs to be given to allowing enterprises to trade directly with one
another. The primary issue on which that focuses attention is the system for
effecting payments between republics. The first priority in this connection
should be to improve the intrarepublic interbank system of settlement, which is
currently subject to extreme delay (settlement takes between four and eight
weeks). The second issue is to choose a mechanism for effecting interrepublic
payments. It was urged that the IMF and G-7 abandon their hankering after a
ruble zone, which has already de facto broken down as a result of Russia's decision to channel interrepublic payments through a set of correspondent accounts
in Moscow. It was also argued that any resort to hard currency to settle trade
would be likely to induce strong restrictive pressures as republics attempted to
compensate for their reserve shortages.

The two more promising ways to finance trade would involve either a ruble
area, modelled on the old Sterling Area (and thus permitting each of the republics whatever degree of monetary independence it chooses), or a payments
union. The West has a strong interest in ensuring that one or other of those
arrangements should be implemented, but it has no legitimate interest in which
of them is chosen. It was also argued that the choice between the two is
primarily one for the non-Russian republics to make, but that it would be quite
legitimate for Russia to offer them inducements (like generous credit limits or
credits for ruble banknotes when these are withdrawn from circulation and
returned to the Central Bank of Russia) to stay in a ruble area.

If a ruble area is chosen, then a successful early Russian stabilization
acquires a systemic as well as a national importance. This justifies the stabilization fund that has been proposed for Russia—but this should be made available
before the ruble exchange rate is fixed, so that the fund can be used to induce an
appreciation of the ruble to a level that does not carry the same threat of stagfla-
tion as would a rate in the vicinity of that currently prevailing.[7] Achieving such
an appreciation will also require that Russia scrap most of its current deterrents
to exporting and to inward direct investment.

If a payments union were chosen, then the West should be prepared to endow
it with a capital fund of several billion dollars. This endowment, which would
be proportionately larger than that which the United States gave to start the
European Payments Union, would be justified as a way for the West to help the
heavy net energy-importing republics while they adjust to the increased price of
their energy imports.

Neither a ruble area nor a payments union will suffice to ease the adjustment
problem facing the states of Central Asia as a result of the withdrawal of their

past fiscal transfers. This is another burden that the West should pick up, though with a level of aid that declines over five years or so. Since Russia would earn most of that hard currency as a result of its energy exports, it would reduce the need for direct aid to Russia.

The final question posed in the introduction was: How much interest do the new states have in maintaining cooperative relationships among themselves, and what institutional forms might cooperation take? Continued cooperation is important, especially in the short run until production and trade can adapt to the requirements of a market economy and integration into the wider world, but there is clearly a danger of tensions over Russia's role jeopardizing that cooperation. In the short run, the most important form of cooperation is to institute an interrepublic payments mechanism that allows multilateral and interenterprise trade without requiring excessive quantities of hard currency. Once that mechanism is functioning satisfactorily, it will make sense to start thinking of creating an economic community that will allow intratrade to develop on a more liberal basis.

It will then be time to think about the appropriate institutional form of longer-term cooperative arrangements. Russia and its neighbors have to learn to interact in a forum that provides a judicious combination of nominal equality with a realistic acceptance of actual differences in power. This arrangement must embody an agreed-on set of principles that define the ends being sought and that generates strong pressures to reach agreement.

This forum will have to combine the roles filled in the West after World War II by the IMF and the Organization for European Economic Cooperation. Both of these institutions provided a civilized and principled way for the United States to exert its power, while paying adequate attention to the interests and concerns of its smaller partners. It also, however, pressured the Western Europeans to act together in their common interest. One of the first tasks of such an institution established for the republics of the former Soviet Union should be to create an economic community that will allow intratrade to develop on a liberal basis. If the CIS cannot be adapted to play this role, it should be disbanded and replaced.

The euphoria that followed the defeat of the attempted coup last August has long since dissipated. No one now imagines that the massive social transformations being sought in what used to be the Soviet Union will be easy, quick, or painless. But nothing that has happened in the past year suggests them to be either impossible or undesirable. They remain perhaps the greatest challenge to our age.

Notes

1. "Trade and Payments after Soviet Disintegration," by John Williamson (Washington: Institute for International Economics, 1992). Copyright 1992 by the Institute for International Economics. All rights reserved. Reprinted by permission.

2. There was also an even more ludicrously overvalued "official" exchange rate of 0.6 rubles to the dollar, but no transactions took place at that rate.

3. See the discussion in Oleh Havrylyshyn and John Williamson, *From Soviet dis-Union to Eastern Economic Community?* (Washington: Institute of International Economics, 1991), 30-31.

4. The exception is Turkmenistan, where consumption was some 89 percent of "produced national income" (net domestic material product) in 1989, the last year for which data are available.

5. See, for example, Leyla Boulton, "Painful and Protracted Birth of a Nation," *Financial Times*, 8 May 1992.

6. Suggestions regarding the desirable content of a commitment to free intra-trade were presented in Havrylyshyn and Williamson, 24. The topic is also discussed by Nuti and Pisani-Ferry, "Post-Soviet Issues: Stabilization, Trade, and Money," paper presented at a conference on "Economic Consequences of the East," Frankfurt, April 1992. They give a brief account of a conference on the topic in Brussels convened by the Centre for European Policy Studies and the Soros Foundation in February 1992.

7. Obviously it is also of critical importance that any stabilized exchange rate for the ruble should be a highly competitive rate, which will stimulate the growth of Russian exports and investment in new export industries. The latter requirement indicates the desirability of the Russian government making an early commitment to a crawling peg that would prevent future inflation leading to overvaluation. Establishing a competitive exchange rate is not, however, the immediate policy problem.

Acknowledgment

The UNDP Development Study Programme acknowledges with appreciation the contribution of the Finnish International Development Agency (FINNIDA) to the financing of the publication of this book. The Agency is, however, not responsible for the views presented in it.

The contents of the book similarly do not necessarily reflect the views of the United Nations or the United Nations Development Programme, or any other organizations with which the authors are connected.

About the Editors

Üner Kırdar is a Senior Adviser to the UNDP Administrator and Director of the UNDP Development Study Programme.

Born in Turkey on 1 January 1933, he graduated from the Faculty of Law, Istanbul, undertook postgraduate studies at the London School of Economics, and received his Ph.D. from Jesus College, University of Cambridge, England.

Dr. Kırdar has served the United Nations system in various capacities, including Secretary of the Preparatory Committee and United Nations Conference on Human Settlements (1974-76), Secretary of the Group of Experts on the Structure of the United Nations System (1975), and a Senior Officer for Inter-Agency Affairs in the Office of the United Nations Secretary-General (1972-77). He was the Director of the Division of External Relations and Secretary to the Governing Council Secretariat of UNDP from 1980 to 1991.

He has been the main architect of the UNDP Development Study Programme and has organized several seminars, round-table meetings, lectures, and discussion groups attended by high-level national and international policy makers.

He has also held senior positions in the Ministry of Foreign Affairs of Turkey, including Director for International Economic Organizations and Deputy Permanent Representative of Turkey to the United Nations Office at Geneva.

Dr. Kırdar is the author of the book *Structure of UN Economic Aid to Underdeveloped Countries* (1966; 1968). He is a coeditor and contributor to other books, including *Human Development: The Neglected Dimension* (1986); *Human Development, Adjustment and Growth* (1987); *Managing Human Development* (1988); *Development and People* (1989); *Equality of Opportunity Within and Among Nations* (1977); "Human Resources Development: Challenge for the '80s," *Crisis of the '80s* (1983); "Impact of IMF Conditionality on Human Conditions," *Adjustment with Growth* (1984); *The Lingering Debt Crisis* (1985); *Change: Threat or Opportunity?* (five volumes, 1991). He has also contributed numerous articles to professional books and journals.

Leonard Silk is currently Senior Research Fellow of the Ralph Bunche Institute on the United Nations at the Graduate School of the City University of New York and Distinguished Professor of Economics at Pace University. From 1970 to 1992, he was the Economics Columnist of *The New York Times* and has served as a member of the Editorial Board of that newspaper.

Prior to joining *The New York Times*, Dr. Silk was a Senior Fellow at the Brookings Institute and Chairman of the Editorial Board of *Business Week* magazine.

Born in Philadelphia on 15 May 1918, he graduated from the University of Wisconsin at Madison, was a Fellow of the American-Scandinavian Foundation in Stockholm, and received his Ph.D. in economics from Duke University in Durham, North Carolina.

Dr. Silk served in the United States Army Air Forces from 1942 through 1945. For the United States Army, he covered the founding conference of the United Nations in San Francisco. He was Director of Research at the Housing and Home Finance Agency in Washington (1949-50) and Assistant Commissioner of the United States Mission to the North Atlantic Treaty Organization and other regional organizations in Paris (1951-55). He has been a member of Presidential commissions of Labor-Management Relations and Budget Concepts, of the President's Task Force on the War Against Poverty, and of the Research Advisory Board of the Committee for Economic Development.

Dr. Silk has been Ford Distinguished Research Professor at the Graduate School of Industrial Administration of Carnegie-Mellon University, Marsh Professor at the University of Michigan, and Poynter Fellow of Yale University. He has received honorary degrees from the University of Wisconsin, Duke University, Southern Methodist University, Haverford College, and several other institutions.

Dr. Silk is the author of *Sweden Plans for Better Housing, The Research Revolution, Forecasting Business Trends, Contemporary Economics, The Economists, Ethics and Profits, The American Establishment, Economics in Plain English, Economics in the Real World*, and other books. He is currently conducting a study on the future of capitalism for The Twentieth Century Fund.